D0138711

Case Studies in Financial Decision Making

Second Edition

Diana R. Harrington

Darden Graduate School of Business Administration
University of Virginia

The Dryden Press
Chicago New York San Francisco Philadelphia
Montreal Toronto London Sydney Tokyo

For Will
for his wit, support, patience, and perspective . . . again.

Acquisitions Editor: Ann Heath
Developmental Editor: Penny Gaffney
Project Editor: Cate Rzasa
Design Supervisor: Rebecca Lemna
Production Manager: Barb Bahnsen
Permissions Editor: Cindy Lombardo
Director of Editing, Design, and Production: Jane Perkins

Cover Designer: Anna Post
Copy Editor: David Talley
Compositor: Weimer Typesetting Co., Inc.
Text Type: 10/12 Palatino

Library of Congress Cataloging-in-Publication Data

Harrington, Diana R., 1940–
    Case studies in financial decision making.

    1. Corporations—Finance—Case studies. I. Title.
II. Financial decision making.
HG4015.5.H37 1989   658.1′5   88-6952
ISBN 0-03-022033-5

Printed in the United States of America
890-016-9876545321
Copyright © 1989, 1985 by The Dryden Press, a division of Holt, Rinehart and Winston, Inc.

All rights reserved. No part of this publication may be reproduced or transmitted in any form or by any means, electronic or mechanical, including photocopy, recording, or any information storage and retrieval system, without permission in writing from the publisher.

Requests for permission to make copies of any part of the work should be mailed to: Permissions, Holt, Rinehart and Winston, Inc., Orlando, Florida 32887.

Address orders:
The Dryden Press
Orlando, FL 32887

Address editorial correspondence:
The Dryden Press
908 N. Elm Street
Hinsdale, IL 60521

The Dryden Press
Holt, Rinehart and Winston
Saunders College Publishing

Foreword

Case Studies in Financial Decision Making is an important, sustained contribution to the field of financial management education. The second edition represents a significant and continuing investment of time and effort by Professor Diana Harrington in an area of scholarship often ignored or taken for granted by academicians—course development. Without such investment, however, the vitality and relevance of business schools' curricula would soon wane.

The critical factors in an effective case-method course are innovative, up-to-date teaching material and a creative, dedicated classroom instructor. Professor Harrington has provided both ingredients in developing her well-received corporate finance courses for MBAs and executives. Her material has been adopted in whole or in part by a number of faculty in other leading graduate business schools.

Working with a series of research assistants, Professor Harrington has devoted eight years of field research to investigating the financial management problems faced by senior corporate executives in the United States and overseas, to describing these situations in carefully written case studies, and then to field-testing her work with MBA candidates and executives in the classroom. The result of this process is innovative material in corporate finance.

The case studies here are all original, field-based research. Each is structured to allow students and teachers to explore the latest theory of finance in a current, real-world context. Insights gained from teaching these cases are reflected in the sequence of the topics and cases in the book as well as in the detailed and thoughtful teaching notes for each case and for the course as a whole.

It is particularly satisfying for me to note that the second edition of *Case Studies in Financial Decision Making* is only one of a number of new case books and course modules written by the Darden School's faculty as part of our continuing program of applied research. Sponsored by leading corporations, this research reflects a continuing commitment by the Darden School to provide students and colleagues here and at other schools with the best materials that integrate current theory with the problems that confront business practitioners.

John W. Rosenblum
Dean
Darden Graduate School of Business Administration
University of Virginia

Preface

More than ever, students and practitioners of finance face complex situations in an increasingly integrated and changing world. New problems and changed environments challenge us all. Clear thinking, born of good skills and broad knowledge, is needed. The cases in this book attempt to provide students with an opportunity to learn and hone their skills on real problems that have confronted managers over the last decade. Cases from a variety of economic environments inside and outside the United States allow students to analyze and make decisions that require an analysis of both the micro and macro environments. Computerized case data allow students the opportunity to bring all the tools at their command to the analysis. The second edition of *Case Studies in Financial Decision Making* attempts to broaden the scope of the case issues addressed in the first edition and to provide students with cases that introduce issues on which to learn as well as practice skills.

THE CASE METHOD

Although many in the past have mistakenly believed that cases were useful only to teach practical skills, suggest tools, and present institutional information, cases have also proved to be a good method for teaching the understanding and use of theory. Cases can and do include problems that some might label theoretical or abstract but that are in fact drawn from actual situations. By studying the factual descriptions of problems that have been faced and dealt with by managers, students can learn about the application of theory as well as gain practice in using tools and skills in realistic situations. In short, cases deal with real-world problems and managers; they contain more than simple problems involving a test of a single skill or concept. Students should find them interesting to use today and useful as they grow as financial managers or analysts.

For some students the case method is new and perhaps somewhat frightening. The fear comes from the fact that there is rarely a right and verifiable answer in a case. That is not to suggest that any approach is acceptable. Clearly, certain kinds of analysis are more appropriate in certain situations, and certain courses of action show more insight, skill of analysis, and probability of success than others. The challenge of cases is to combine the appropriate skills and tools with judgment and creativity to solve problems that are as realistic as the written word can make them. Apprehension is the last thing that the case method should engender.

INTENDED MARKET

While the basic skills and tools of financial analysis can and will be used in analyzing these cases, the situations also offer advanced or more complex problems. To gain full value from these cases, the student using this book should already have had an introductory finance course and should thus have learned the basic tools and concepts of finance. Each student should have and use a favorite basic finance book as a reference during the course featuring these cases.

FEATURES OF THE BOOK

Value Creation.   The concept of value creation is the thread that connects the cases in this book, just as identifying, choosing, and implementing value-creating opportunities is the problem facing managers. Because value is in the eye, and hand, of the shareholder, the manager or student must be concerned with the share price and the effect that the investment and financing decisions will have on the price of the shares. Thus the cases in this book provide more data about the capital markets, and especially the market for the subject company's stock, than cases in the past. In addition, a note at the end of the book, "The Business Environment: A Retrospective, 1929–1987," gives a brief overview of the business environment to emphasize the link between the macroeconomic conditions for business, corporate profitability, cash flow, and changes in shareholders' value. The link can be a difficult one to make, but since the corporate objective is to create value, every student and manager must make it. Understanding that link comes only with practice. These cases should give the current and future manager some of that practice.

International Focus.   Some of these cases are set in corporations outside the United States for two reasons. First, some of the simple insights and methods we use in solving problems in U.S. domestic situations do not work elsewhere in the world. The problem of determining an appropriate capital structure provides an example. Capital structure theory based on interest-tax deductibility is a useful concept, but only in a situation where the taxing authorities allow such deductions. A student or manager who believes this theory is applicable in all situations could well decide on an improper course of action. Second, the integrated nature of worldwide business means that most students who are in school today will, at some point in their careers, work for or with a non-U.S.-based corporation. It would be a disservice to concentrate cases in only one of the many environments in which managers may find themselves.

Technical Notes.   Five technical notes provide background for understanding the issues in the cases and/or the environments in which they are set. These notes cover such topics as the evolution of the cash tender offer markets and managing foreign exchange risk. The final technical note is a comprehensive retrospective on the U.S. business environment from 1929 to 1987.

NEW TO THIS EDITION

Additional Issues for Analysis.   In this edition, a number of new cases have been added that emphasize basic tools and concepts of analysis. Learning how to analyze and interpret historical data is featured in Financial Footprints and the General Motors series. The latter encourages the students to compare a company across time [General Motors (A)], with its domestic competitors [General Motors (B)], and with its international competitors [General Motors (C)]. Following this section are cases that teach forecasting and test students' abilities to forecast the future. United Telesis Corporation is a simple case for teaching basic tools and concepts of forecasting; it provides the opportunity to understand a new company in a newly unregulated market. Fantastic Manufacturing, Inc. adds an international flavor to the forecasting problem, as students concern themselves with the working-capital needs of a small, fast-growing company. Polymold Division presses students to understand the division of a larger corporation and how changes in technology can affect its future. Finally, in Mushrooms Division (A) and (B), students must determine what a change in strategy will do to the working-capital and overall capital requirements first for the division, and then for the whole corporation.

The cases in the first two sections rely on the basic tools of historical analysis and forecasting. Although more sophisticated analysis is possible with many of the cases, these cases provide the less sophisticated student with some short, basic experiences in learning, using, and interpreting analysis.

New Topics.   This edition expands the link between theory and practice, between sophisticated analysis and usable interpretation. Several new topics have been introduced. For example, National Industrial Bridge introduces the problem of defeasing high-yield debt, and Green Mountain Power involves the subject of leasing. In addition, Fantastic Manufacturing, Inc. focuses on international trade financing and the impact of exchange-rate changes on the costs of imported parts. Working-capital problems are featured parts of Mushrooms Division (A) and (B) and Fantastic Manufacturing, Inc.

New Introductory Cases.   Each part of this edition now includes basic cases that introduce a topic and allow students to learn the tools and concepts necessary to address the problems faced by management. These cases are shorter and less demanding in the tools, concepts, and skills needed to analyze them than are the cases that follow. The basic cases add flexibility, as they can be used either as refreshers with more sophisticated students or introductions for those relatively new to finance.

Computer Assistance.   Exhibit data in each case that students may choose to manipulate are contained on the disk that adopters can obtain from The Dryden Press. Thus, students familiar with spreadsheet modeling can do more analysis in a shorter time: they do not need to enter the desired data manually. The data are in *Lotus 1-2-3* format. In addition, a computer disk containing four basic *Lotus 1-2-3* templates can facilitate historical analysis, forecasting, capital budgeting, and choosing among financing alternatives. These programs may be shared with students at the instructor's discretion. Also on this disk are the template-compatible historical financial statements for all the relevant cases. The disk is available to instructors upon request.

ORGANIZATION OF THE BOOK

Analyzing Corporate Performance.   The cases in this part highlight the tools needed to analyze the historical performance of a company. In Financial Footprints, the differences in how a variety of companies in different industries operate and their resulting performance at the end of 1987 can be seen. General Motors (A), (B), and (C) provide data on the U.S. and international auto manufacturers for several years. These cases feature the performance over time of the significant players in one important worldwide industry.

Forecasting Future Corporate Performance.   After students have mastered evaluation of historical performance and ratio analysis, which are necessary to understand the strategies and success of a variety of companies, we turn to the future. The cases in the second part of the text require a forward-looking analysis of performance. Forecasting financial statements for an entre-preneurial venture in the midst of entering a new market provides the challenge in the United Telesis Corporation case. In Fantastic Manufacturing, Inc., a rap-idly expanding company that obtains much of its materials from Asia has rapid growth that requires careful management control and good forecasts. Manage-ment of Polymold, a division of a much larger company, considers alternative strategies for its markets and must deal with uncertain forecasts. Mushrooms Division (A) and (B) describe the division of a company, and its parent, as the division expands into a new product. Coordinating marketing plans with finan-cial requirements and resources is the challenge in this two-case series.

Valuation: Capital Budgeting—Forecasting.   To decide whether an investment or strategy should be pursued, one must decide whether it creates value for the firm's shareholders. To create value, the strategy's returns must exceed its costs. Deciding which costs and benefits are relevant in investing capital is the focus of the cases in this part. Metalcrafters, Inc. is a straightfor-ward look at the process of making such investment decisions. The Federal Reserve Bank of Richmond (A) and Zukowski Meats, Incorporated feature the investment decision itself—one at a public corporation, the other at a small private company. In Massalin Particulares, the investment decision is taken to an international setting.

Valuation: Capital Budgeting—Analyzing Risk.   More than in the previous cases, risk is a special feature in The Jacobs Division, Eastern Airlines, and the Interchemical Consumer Products series. Capital-investment forecasts must accommodate uncertainties in the product markets. Alaska Interstate (A) and (B) both deal with the nature of risk and how it should be measured and incorporated in investment decision making. The final case in the part, The Becker Corporation, provides a link between the capital-investment process, a company's cost of capital, and use of that concept in making value-creating investment decisions.

Valuation: Cost of Capital.   Following the discussion of the capital-budgeting process and how risk should be included in it, the Star Appliance and American Telephone & Telegraph series directly address the best way of estimating a company's required rate of return—its cost of capital. The Federal Reserve Bank of Richmond (B) addresses the same question in a public-sector corporation.

Financing Capital Investments.   After management has decided to make a new investment in property, plant, and equipment or in inventory or accounts receivable, a company must find the capital to fund the project. The cases in this part deal with the financing of a corporation. New Hampshire Savings Bank Corporation focuses on whether a company is better off paying dividends or retaining the funds for future investment. Hop-In Food Stores examines issuing new equity. Kelly Services, Inc., and Marriott Corporation deal directly with the relative value of debt. Bearings, Inc., and Van Deusen Air, Inc. look at the costs and relative value of equity and debt of various types. Moving into the international capital markets is the decision that faces management in Philip Morris, Incorporated: Swiss Franc Financing. Other financing alternatives, leasing, refinancing, and high-yield debt are dealt with in the cases that remain—Green Mountain Power Corporation and National Industrial Bridge, Inc.

Strategic Investment and Financing Decisions.   The cases in the final part call on most of the tools, skills, and concepts learned and exercised in the preceding sections. Valuing a company, both historical analysis and valuation, is the problem facing management in Omni Services, Incorporated and Philip Morris: Seven-Up Acquisition—one a closely held company, the other a widely known consumer-products giant. In Diamond Shamrock Corporation and Piedmont Transmission Co., the concern is the divestiture of a division and its effect on the company. In Cities Service Company and Norris Industries, the challenge is valuing unused operating and financial capacity.

Technical Notes.   Five technical notes provide a richer background for understanding the issues in the cases and/or environments in which they are set. The technical notes cover such topics as managing foreign exchange risks and the evolution of the cash tender offer markets. The final note is a comprehensive retrospective on the U.S. business environment from 1929 to 1987.

ANCILLARY PACKAGE

Instructor's Manual.   Each set of case notes includes the objective of the case, a teaching plan, extensive case analysis focusing on key issues, and references to chapters in widely used textbooks and relevant journal articles that might be used in conjunction with the cases. Each teaching note is based on the author's classroom experience with the case.

    To enhance the range of topics available for class use, the *Instructor's Manual* also contains five additional cases and accompanying teaching notes.

Computer Disk.   The Dryden Press will make available to adopters upon request an accompanying disk for IBM PC or IBM-compatible microcomputers. The disk contains data for the cases and template models that will aid in case analysis. The templates are designed for use as overlays on *Lotus 1-2-3* or workalike programs. The disk may be obtained by completing the request card in the *Instructor's Manual*.

ACKNOWLEDGMENTS

Students at a number of business schools have used and found these cases challenging and exciting. I am indebted to these students for their enthusiasm and skill in analyzing the cases. They have not only been lively subjects on which to test this material, but have contributed in no minor way to the excitement of teaching and learning with the case method.

In the gathering of the case studies, numerous managers contributed by providing material about and insight into their problems. Without willing subjects, the case method would not be possible. The corporations, in the main, are not disguised; where possible, the managers who faced the problems are identified by name. Special thanks must go to Alaska Interstate's (now ENSTAR) Treasurer David Ross; to John Segal, Executive Vice President at AT&T; and to Juan Munro, Chairman of the Board and President of Massalin Particulares. These managers supported this research in tangible and intangible ways.

The following colleagues gathered materials for, wrote, or supervised the writing of cases: Brent D. Wilson of Nexus Consulting Group; Bill Sihler, Director of the Center for International Banking Studies and a professor at the Darden School; the late Robert Vandell, Richard Brownlee, Leslie Grayson, Robert F. Bruner, William Rotch, and C. Ray Smith, professors at the Darden School; and J. Peter Williamson of the Amos Tuck Graduate School of Business at Dartmouth College. In addition to contributing case study material and their case-writing talents, these persons provided their helpful comments as the revision proceeded.

Numerous research assistants helped me and the other case contributors to gather, organize, and write the cases. Primary among them was Debra Lalor, a Darden graduate, who researched and wrote cases with skill and character. Sharon Graham, now on the faculty of the University of Central Florida, helped to develop teaching notes and cases. Guy Brossy, Kathy Ford-Carr, Paul Frankel, John Guertler, John MacFarlane, III, Mary McCall, Emmett McClean, Bill Miller, Emily Morgan, Casey Opitz, Louis Sarkes, Richard Swasey, Jr., and David Wellborn—most of whom are now Darden graduates—played major parts in the development of specific cases. To each of them I am most indebted.

For funding and supporting the case writing in other ways, I am in the debt of John Rosenblum, Dean of the Darden School, and the Darden School, Sponsors.

Finally, there are a number of tireless and priceless people who made the production of this book easier than it otherwise would have been. Ginny Fisher managed the process of producing the manuscript. Her skills in typing, organizing, and supporting are without peer. Bette Collins, Darden's fine editor, did her job with skill and humor. The professionals at The Dryden Press provided good suggestions and skilled support. My academic colleagues and reviewers— Thomas Berry, DePaul University; Nahum Biger, Northwestern University; Neil

G. Cohen, The George Washington University; Kenneth Eades, University of Michigan; M. Andrew Fields, University of Delaware; Charles Haley, University of Washington; John Lewis, Salisbury State University; Susan Moeller, Northeastern University; Timothy Nantell, University of Minnesota; John O'Donnell, Michigan State University; Dennis Officer, Arizona State University; Nikhil Varaiya, Southern Methodist University; and Ralph A. Walkling, The Ohio State University—provided comments and suggestions that were thoughtful and useful. Lastly, I am grateful to my husband, who showed more humor and support than I had a right to expect. In many ways he made this edition possible.

Diana R. Harrington
Crozet, Virginia
October 1988

About the Author

Diana R. Harrington (D.B.A. University of Virginia, M.S.B.A. Boston University) is Professor of Business Administration at the Darden Graduate School of Business Administration in Charlottesville, Virginia. She has also taught at Iowa State University and the University of Northern Iowa after being in industry for 15 years. She has taught in executive programs and has served as a consultant to industry. Professor Harrington has authored or co-authored other books and articles and is president of Eastern Finance Association and on the board of directors of the Southern Finance Association.

Contents

Part 3A

Valuation: Capital Budgeting—Forecasting   95

Part 3B

Valuation: Capital Budgeting—Analyzing Risk   155

Part 3C
Valuation: Cost of Capital   259

Part 4
Financing Capital Investments   337

Part 5

Strategic Investment and Financing Decisions 485

Part 6

Technical Notes 629

Alphabetical List of Cases

The Dryden Press Series in Finance

Berry and Young
Managing Investments: A Case Approach

Brigham
Fundamentals of Financial Management
Fifth Edition

Brigham, Aberwald, and Ball
Finance with Lotus 1-2-3: Text, Cases, and Models

Brigham and Gapenski
Financial Management: Theory and Practice
Fifth Edition

Brigham and Gapenski
Intermediate Financial Management
Second Edition

Campsey and Brigham
Introduction to Financial Management
Second Edition

Chance
An Introduction to Options and Futures

Clayton and Spivey
The Time Value of Money

Cooley and Roden
Business Financial Management

Crum and Brigham
Cases in Managerial Finance
Sixth Edition with 1986 Tax Law Changes

Fama and Miller
The Theory of Finance

Gardner and Mills
**Managing Financial Institutions:
An Asset/Liability Approach**

Gitman and Joehnk
Personal Financial Planning
Fourth Edition

Goldstein Software, Inc.
Joe Spreadsheet

Harrington
Case Studies in Financial Decision Making
Second Edition

Johnson
Issues and Readings in Managerial Finance
Third Edition

Johnson and Johnson
Commercial Bank Management

Kidwell and Peterson
Financial Institutions, Markets, and Money
Third Edition

Koch
Bank Management

Martin, Cox, and MacMinn
The Theory of Finance: Evidence and Applications

Mayo
Finance: An Introduction
Third Edition

Mayo
Investments: An Introduction
Second Edition

Myers
Modern Developments in Financial Management

Pettijohn
PROFIT+

Reilly
Investment Analysis and Portfolio Management
Third Edition

Reilly
Investments
Second Edition

Smith and Weston
PC Self-Study Manual for Finance

Tallman and Neal
Financial Analysis and Planning Package

Turnbull
Option Valuation

Weston and Brigham
Essentials of Managerial Finance
Eighth Edition

Weston and Copeland
Managerial Finance
Eighth Edition

Introduction

Welcome to the case method. To analyze a case successfully, you must do two things—put yourself in the position of the manager making the decision, and make the decision.

Within each case you must assume the role of the manager whose job it is to analyze alternatives for his or her company. In most instances it will be an easy task to determine who is the decision-maker, since he or she will be identified by name in the case and his or her position and role will be described. In the few instances where the decision-maker is not identified by name, your point of view will be that of the company's top management.

Once you have identified the person or group of persons whose role you will assume, you need to gather the information that you, as the manager described in the case, would naturally have. Managers, even young analysts, have considerable knowledge about their company, the industry in which it competes, and the economic environment in which it operates. Since, as a manager, you would have that information, as the case analyst assuming the manager's role, you must acquire it.

Once you have the background necessary for your role, your task is the same one that the manager in the situation would have—to identify, understand, and analyze the problems the company faces. As would the manager, you will define the problems and the available courses of action, and you will gather the information needed to determine which is the appropriate course. The steps you will take in assuming the manager's role and in confronting and solving problems are listed below.

I. *Assume the manager's role*

    1. Understand the environment in which the company operates:
        The worldwide socioeconomic and political environment
        The domestic environment
        The industry situation

    2. Know the company's history, current condition, and future prospects

II. *Solve the problem facing the company*

    1. Identify the problem

    2. Define the alternatives

    3. Gather information about the alternatives

    4. Analyze the risks and returns of the options

    5. Make a decision and develop a plan of action

ASSUME THE MANAGER'S ROLE

As you develop as a case analyst, you will refine your own approach and develop a sense of the depth and breadth of analysis appropriate for the particular situation described in a case. Depending upon the situation, one or more of the areas discussed below could receive more attention than the others.

Understand the Environment in Which the Company Operates.

Perhaps the best way to begin to understand the milieu in which the company operates is to investigate the general economic environment. Frequently the case analyst looks only at the domestic environment; however, with the increased integration of the world's economy, the *worldwide environment* cannot be ignored. Certainly some decisions described in this book are less affected than others by worldwide socioeconomic and political events. However, the isolation of countries and industries from events in the rest of the world has greatly diminished, and, as U.S. managers found after the oil price rises in the 1970s and early 1980s, to ignore events outside the local economy can be dangerous. Since most of the cases in this book are set in the 1970s and 1980s—a period when events profoundly changed the nature of the environment in which all countries, industries, and companies operated—worldwide considerations are particularly relevant.

Because different factors are important at different times and to different companies, the manager, and thus you as the case analyst, should be aware of the relative robustness of the worldwide economy at the time of a particular case, and should sense what concerns for and predictions about the future might have prevailed at that time.

In cases where the company or the decision is, or can be, directly affected by worldwide events, the cases will provide information that you as the manager would have had. However, because of the necessary brevity of the cases, some of the data you might like to have, or believe the manager would have had, may not be included. You must decide on the basis of the information you have. Some basic data about international events are contained in the last section of "The Business Environment: A Retrospective, 1929–1988."

Some case analysts prefer to direct their efforts to analysis of the domestic environment, believing such an analysis is adequate. Indeed, for some of the decisions faced by managers in the cases in this book, the worldwide environment needs only brief attention. For others, it is of prime importance.

The strength and nature of the *domestic economy* are certainly of more obvious concern, and this is an area in which managers often have more personal and professional experience. Although certain factors and events in the economy will affect some companies more than others, nevertheless there are universal touchstones of concern. The analyst should consider such things as (1) the robustness of the economy and its expansion or contraction because it can affect the company's sales, profits, and cost and availability of funds; (2) the level of unemployment because it affects the potential for strikes as well as the sales of certain products; (3) cyclical upturns because they can increase the sales of products such as consumer durables while increasing the potential for strikes; and (4) cyclical downturns because they can decrease the need for productive capacity and the likelihood of protracted strikes in many industries, and because they hurt firms whose sales depend upon the level of consumers' disposable income.

Most cases contain a brief description of the environment in which the firm operates. For more information about the U.S. environment—the setting for the majority of the cases in this book—a background note, "The Business Environment: A Retrospective, 1929–1988," is presented in the last section of this book. The information in this note can be used in analyzing many of the cases.

While the analyst will want to understand the current state of the domestic economy and the future directions it might take, of particular interest is the effect changes in the economy have had and will have on the particular *industry* and company featured in the case. Just as some economies are more sensitive than others to worldwide events, some industries and companies are influenced more than others by domestic events.

Many industries seem relatively immune to ongoing economic changes, while others are so sensitive that managers spend much of their time and effort developing ways to forecast and insulate their firms from probable changes. The relationship of companies to suppliers, customers, and other companies in the industry, as well as the nature of the industry's products, seems to influence how strong an impact outside economic events have on a given industry. The sources of return and the factors that affect the predictability of that return are quite different in each industry.

Know the Company's History, Current Condition, and Future Prospects.

Interestingly, most of the tools and techniques of financial analysis concentrate on the company—its past, present, and future. Moreover, this is the form of analysis with which most students of finance have some experience, and with which many case analysts start and finish their work. Clearly, it is very important; the history and current situation of the firm are of considerable interest to the practicing manager as well as the case analyst. These subjects will occupy the greatest part of the case analyst's time and skill. Keeping in mind the possible effects of changes in the environment, both domestic and worldwide, the analyst will want to review the success of the firm's past investment and financing strategies by analyzing financial statements, market share and competitive product market information, and stock and bond market results.

Typically, the analyst will look first to the way the company has managed its assets, and is likely to be able to manage them, by asking such questions as:

1. Is the company capital-intensive? Does its productive capacity come from plant and equipment, people, and/or a franchise in the market bought with product reputation and/or advertising? How expensive is it to add capacity or enhance a product's reputation? What is the lead time needed to increase or modify any factor of production? If the company is capital-intensive, how old is the equipment, and for how long will it continue to be useful? If it is not capital-intensive, what is the source of the company's productivity, and how readily available are additional resources?

2. To what degree are company assets subject to obsolescence or migration? In a capital-intensive business, do technological innovations change processes slowly or rapidly? If it is not capital-intensive, how firm a grip does the company have on its source of productive capacity? For example, genetic engineering companies with large investments in the expertise of their research staffs can suffer if those research staffs are likely to move from firm to firm.

3. How much of the firm's assets are long term and difficult to redeploy, and how much can be changed rapidly? Firms with significant investments in short-term assets often have much more flexibility in dealing with rapid changes in the economic environment and/or the industry. How well has the firm coped with changes in the recent past—has it managed to maintain control of its assets in both good and bad times—and how likely is it to be able to maintain control in the foreseeable future?

4. What opportunities for new products and processes are on the horizon? Is the company in a position to identify and take advantage of these opportunities?

Second, the analyst will consider where and how the firm has financed itself and how it will be able to finance itself in the future by asking such questions as:

1. How much of the firm's investments have been financed from profits, and how stable are its profits (do they fluctuate widely from year to year, or are they relatively steady)? Companies that have relatively stable profitability are better insulated from the vagaries of the capital markets.

2. Do the shareholders have a call on some portion of the current profits? How important is the dividend level to the stock price, how close is the firm's current dividend policy to what is common in the industry, and how secure are dividends from fluctuations in profits (does the company raise funds to maintain its capital investment program and/or dividend payments)?

3. How much of the funds used, and those likely to be used, have been and will be raised from outside sources?

4. Are the firm's liabilities short or long term? How secure are the sources of capital? Do lenders place any restrictions on the firm by virtue of their position? Are the restrictions by custom or by contract? Is the firm able to deal easily with the restrictions and the costs of its debt?

5. Is the company's equity capital closely held or is the stock publicly traded in the capital markets? If the stock is closely held, what are the objectives and needs of the owners? If it is publicly held, are any large blocks held by individuals or groups, and what is their interest in the firm? What is the degree of institutional interest in the stock? What is the stock price, the relative level of the stock market, and the interest in trading equities in general, both in this industry and in this company? How easy would it be to sell new equity and at what price could it be sold?

Finally, the analyst will want to determine the company's unique strengths and weaknesses.

The above questions are not meant to be exhaustive, nor would the case analyst seek to answer each question or set of questions in depth for every case. They are meant solely as an indication of the form analysis may take, and as a guide to the areas in which the analyst should have an interest and in which he or she should acquire at least cursory information.

Once the company's history, current situation, strength in the industry, and current corporate goals and strategies are coupled with an analysis of the industry and the economy, the case analyst is ready to assume the role of the decision-maker—the manager.

SOLVE THE PROBLEM FACING
THE COMPANY

Identify the Problem.   Obviously, the first task is to understand the situation and to identify the problem or problems facing the manager. Many cases present more than one problem, and some of the problems will be more important than others. As with any real situation, there are times when real problems are obfuscated by concerns of the company or manager that are not critical to the firm and its success. It is up to the analyst to sort through the issues described in the case and to determine which are actually important.

The decisions managers face fall into one or both of two categories. The problem may require (1) investing assets to replace old products or processes, to increase sales, or to decrease costs, and/or (2) securing funds to support the growth of the firm or to replace old processes and products.

For funding the firm, the manager has only three choices. Funds can be raised by (1) increasing the liabilities of the firm—with either short-term obligations such as accounts payable or one of a variety of long-term debt instruments; (2) increasing the equity in the firm by increasing the amount of common stock or retained earnings; or (3) increasing the firm's profits or decreasing the dividends paid to its shareholders.

On the basis of the traditional accounting definition of the firm, the following diagram shows where decisions that change the firm can be made.

Assets = Liabilities + Equity
$$\Leftrightarrow$$
Equity = Common Stock + Retained Earnings
$$\Leftrightarrow$$
Retained Earnings = Profits − Dividends

Another way to look at the same problem is to use the sustainable growth rate framework.

$$
\begin{aligned}
\text{Sustainable Growth Rate} &= \text{Return on Sales} \times \text{Total Asset Turnover} \times \text{Leverage} \times \text{Profit Retention} \\
&= \frac{\text{Profit}}{\text{Sales}} \times \frac{\text{Sales}}{\text{Assets}} \times \frac{\text{Assets}}{\text{Equity}} \times \left(1 - \frac{\text{Dividends}}{\text{Net Income}}\right)
\end{aligned}
$$

If changes are made in one factor, changes need to be made in at least one other factor to keep the formula in balance. Thus, for example, the firm cannot increase its assets without augmenting its profits to sustain the increase or acquiring additional outside funds.

Identifying the most important problem(s) is often easier if the analyst has determined the objectives and goals of the corporation (or division or subsidiary, if that is the level at which the decision is being made) and of the manager. There are instances where the personal position and goals of the manager may conflict with the objectives held by the firm on behalf of its owners. The importance attached to the problems and the decisions that will be made often reflect the goals of the strongest participant rather than those of the owners. Since these conflicts arise in almost every situation, the analyst must recognize them and make decisions on the basis of that recognition.

Define the Alternatives.   Once the problem(s) have been identified, the next task the vicarious manager must undertake is to define the options—the alternative courses of action for dealing with the problem. Many of the cases in this book define some or all of the options or describe the situation so that the alternatives can be identified. In some instances the analyst may want to identify options that are not available in the particular case—options that would have been available to other managers and companies or at different times. These options, alternatives for which there is little or no information, are hard to evaluate. These courses of action often have to be relegated to the realm of "strategies that should be explored" as the case analyst proceeds with consideration of the options that *are* available for analysis.

Developing options is often the most important step in the process of making the decision about the problem the manager and company face. Untried and unidentified options often turn out, in retrospect, to be the plans that might have spelled success. Industry and corporate custom can constrain the creativity of managers in determining possible solutions and, as a result, can limit the company's potential for success. Analysis and understanding of the current situation and future direction of the economic and industry environments can open avenues that were never available when traditional paths were followed almost without thought. Unlike textbook problems where there are few alternatives, the real world provides many alternatives, and so do case descriptions of it.

Gather Information about the Alternatives.   Here the case analyst has an advantage over the manager described in the case. The case usually provides a summary of the information the manager and his or her staff gathered to analyze their options. Much of that data is summarized in the exhibits at the end of each case. One of a manager's frustrations, and one that case analysts feel as well, is the lack of certain information that would be useful in deciding on the appropriate plan. Rarely would that information be omitted from the case unless it was unavailable when the manager sought it or was deemed unnecessary by the manager in making the decision. In either case the manager, and thus you as the vicarious manager, would have to make the decision based on the information available.

Analyze the Risks and Returns of the Options.   This is the heart of the problem facing the case analyst and manager. All the information about the economic environment, the industry, the company, and the problem has to be utilized to estimate the potential risks and returns of alternative solutions to the problem. The task is to find the strategy that will create the most value for the firm's owners over the long term.

Value depends upon three things: (1) the *size* of the returns expected, (2) the *time* it takes before the returns are expected to be received, and (3) the *risk* taken to obtain the expected returns. We know that investors, and thus corporate owners and managers, prefer larger returns received sooner and with less risk. The question is what trade-offs must be made in the size, timing, and riskiness of the expected returns for each alternative course of action. Those trade-offs are presented graphically on the following page.

Value is created when the returns from a given strategy more than offset the risk being taken, that is, when the net present value of the option is positive. Value–creating investments and strategies are difficult to find. When real eco-

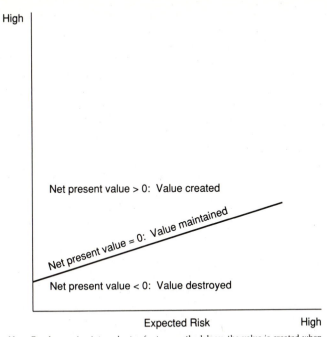

High

Net present value > 0: Value created

Net present value = 0: Value maintained

Net present value < 0: Value destroyed

Expected Risk   High

Note: For those using internal-rate-of-return methodology, the value is created when
the IRR exceeds the hurdle rate, maintained when the IRR equals the hurdle rate, and
destroyed when it falls short of the hurdle rate.

nomic value is available (for instance, when a company has a new product, process, or product source), competitors usually follow rather rapidly and drive out excess profits—unless the firm has some franchise or barrier that keeps competitors at bay. Managers forecast unusual and sustained excess profits (unusual returns) for one of three reasons: the returns really are likely to occur because of some special circumstance, the manager has ignored competitive realities, or the manager is overenthusiastic in his or her forecasts. As the manager, the case analyst should examine any forecasts to make sure that when value is expected to be created, it is because the manager, and the analyst acting on his or her behalf, has exercised skill in finding or creating opportunities for the company and not because of unwarranted optimism.

Value is maintained (the net present value is zero) when the expected returns are just sufficient to compensate the investor for taking the risk inherent in the project. Typically, most investment and financing strategies provide the prospect of a fair return—a return with which the shareholder would be satisfied—that would keep the stock at its current price.

Value is destroyed when the company pays too much, gets too little, or takes too much risk relative to the returns. These are the things that the manager would like to avoid at all cost—they are investments or financing schemes for which the net present value is negative.

As hard as value-creating options are to find, suffice it to say that most managers think they can be found; they do not believe that the product markets (and perhaps capital markets) are fully efficient. Thus managers usually believe they can find real sources of value for the firm's shareholders—investment and financing plans that will increase the price of the common stock.

Make a Decision and Develop a Plan of Action.   Just as the manager must weigh all the information available and come to a decision, so must a case analyst. While it is often difficult to decide between alternative courses of action, the analyst, taking the information developed from the analysis or provided in the case, must weigh the evidence before reaching a conclusion. It is helpful if the analyst has developed the assumptions upon which the analysis rested and detailed the conditions under which the decision would be appropriate. The consistency and reality of the assumptions are critical to making a good decision.

After the decision has been made, the analyst should follow with a plan of action to implement it. The plan is usually sequential in nature and describes what must be done, by whom, and when.

The goals, concepts, and theories of finance will help you, in the manager's role, to guide and focus the analysis. Using the framework of value creation to appraise the options presented in the cases in this book will help you as the case analyst to decide which is the appropriate course of action, given the firm, its strengths and weaknesses, its industry, and the environment in which it is likely to operate.

1

ANALYZING

CORPORATE

PERFORMANCE

Financial Footprints

(1987)

The investment, financial, and profitability characteristics of different industries vary, often significantly. For example, some industries require substantial investments in property, plant, and equipment, while in others a larger proportion is invested in liquid assets such as cash and accounts receivable. Differences also frequently exist in the means of financing assets. One industry may have to rely extensively on long-term debt, while in another trade credit is readily available. Also, certain measures of profitability and asset utilization will reveal significantly different results in industry comparisons. Financial statements and the ratios computed from them reflect these and other differences among industries.

Exhibits 1 and 2 present balance-sheet percentages and selected ratios for one company chosen from each of the 16 industries listed below. The company's fiscal year is also indicated. Study this information and associate each set of figures in the exhibits with a particular industry. Be prepared to explain the basis for your selections.

		Fiscal Year End
1.	Electric utility	12/87
2.	Commercial bank	12/87
3.	Genetic engineering company	12/87
4.	Steel manufacturer	12/87
5.	Retail jewelry chain	8/87
6.	Supermarket chain	12/87
7.	Automobile manufacturer	12/87
8.	Secretarial services company	12/87
9.	Regional airline	12/87
10.	Drug store chain	8/87
11.	Computer manufacturer	12/87
12.	Textile manufacturer	9/87
13.	Hospital-management company	8/87
14.	Meat packer	10/87
15.	Department store chain	8/87
16.	Standard & Poor's 400 average	N. Ap.

N. Ap. = not applicable.

This case was prepared as a basis for class discussion rather than to illustrate either effective or ineffective handling of an administrative situation. Copyright © 1986 by the Darden Graduate Business School Sponsors, University of Virginia, Charlottesville, Virginia.

Financial Footprints (1987)

EXHIBIT 1
■
Balance Sheet (in percentage of assets)

	A	B	C	D	E	F
Cash and securities	1.0%	4.4%	31.5%	12.7%	5.4%	3.3%
Receivables	28.2	23.4	6.8	6.2	25.8	5.2
Inventories	50.9	15.0	8.5	0.6	11.0	55.3
Other current assets	3.1	1.3	1.3	1.0	7.3	1.8
Plant, property, and equipment (net)	16.9	56.0	51.8	79.4	50.4	34.3
Total assets	100.0%	100.0%	100.0%	100.0%	100.0%	100.0%
Notes payable	29.2%	3.5%	0.3%	1.0%	4.9%	1.9%
Accounts payable	12.3	8.0	2.7	2.0	9.6	19.4
Other current liabilities	4.2	16.0	4.1	7.0	19.8	15.8
Long-term debt and leases	2.7	20.2	31.3	36.1	21.5	13.3
Preferred stock	0.0	0.0	0.0	0.0	0.3	0.0
Owner's equity	51.6	52.3	61.7	53.9	43.9	49.6
Total liabilities and equity	100.0%	100.0%	100.0%	100.0%	100.0%	100.0%

Financial Footprints (1987)

EXHIBIT 2
■
Selected Ratios

	A	B	C	D	E	F
Current ratio	182.0%	159.5%	681.1%	206.7%	144.8%	176.9%
Acid test	70.6%	105.1%	560.4%	200.4%	112.5%	27.8%
Inventory method	LIFO	FIFO	FIFO	AvCost	LIFO	LIFO
Inventory turnover (as reported)	180%	747%	450%	12,500%	560%	620%
AR collection period (days)	114	66	64	28	28	5
Net sales/Total assets	89.2%	127.4%	38.0%	78.8%	145.8%	341.3%
Net profit/Total assets (return on assets)	1.5%	2.6%	7.3%	1.8%	5.1%	8.3%
Net profit/Net sales (return on sales)	1.6%	2.0%	19.3%	2.3%	3.5%	2.4%
Net profit/Net worth (return on equity)	2.8%	5.0%	11.9%	3.4%	11.5%	16.6%
Dividends/Net income (payout ratio)	85.2%	82.8%	0.0%	23.6%	50.0%	32.1%
Total assets/Net worth	193.7%	191.3%	162.2%	185.5%	225.7%	201.6%
Notes payable and long-term debt/ Total assets	31.9%	23.7%	31.6%	37.1%	26.3%	15.2%
Long-term debt/Net worth	5.3%	38.6%	50.7%	67.0%	48.4%	26.8%
Market price/Book value	65.3%	79.5%	917.6%	85.4%	63.0%	286.6%
Dividends/Market price	3.7%	5.0%	0.0%	0.9%	7.9%	1.9%
Price/Earnings ratio	23.0	16.7	78.0	25.5	6.3	17.3
Beta	1.1	1.0	1.4	1.2	1.0	1.2

N. Av. = not available.
N.Ap. = not applicable.

G	H	I	J	K	L	M	N	O	P
10.4%	15.0%	1.4%	16.5%	0.5%	6.5%	31.1%	10.9%	43.0%	7.4%
66.5	12.5	4.0	2.5	30.2	13.7	53.7	17.6	30.8	18.1
0.0	6.8	2.8	19.3	25.9	16.8	0.0	25.9	17.2	0.0
7.3	3.2	0.2	1.1	2.9	−1.3	3.1	1.2	8.4	5.1
15.8	62.5	91.6	60.6	40.4	64.2	12.0	44.3	0.6	69.5
100.0%	100.0%	100.0%	100.0%	100.0%	100.0%	100.0%	100.0%	100.0%	100.0%
73.0%	5.6%	0.5%	0.9%	10.3%	8.0%	0.0%	2.4%	0.0%	2.1%
0.0	7.7	1.8	17.1	9.6	9.9	4.4	9.1	15.7	3.0
19.1	19.4	2.7	8.2	16.2	24.7	27.6	14.7	20.7	16.5
3.3	32.4	33.5	29.0	40.7	17.2	0.0	15.7	0.0	43.1
0.4	6.5	8.4	0.0	0.0	1.0	0.0	0.0	0.0	0.0
4.2	28.4	53.2	44.8	23.2	39.3	68.0	58.1	63.6	35.2
100.0%	100.0%	100.0%	100.0%	100.0%	100.0%	100.0%	100.0%	100.0%	100.0%

G	H	I	J	K	L	M	N	O	P
91.8%	114.8%	170.8%	150.4%	165.2%	84.1%	274.5%	212.9%	273.1%	141.0%
91.8%	93.9%	113.2%	76.6%	93.3%	44.6%	274.5%	113.9%	225.9%	141.0%
—	LIFO	LIFO	LIFO	LIFO	N.Av.	N.Ap.	FIFO	FIFO	LIFO
—	1960%	1209%	1680%	650%	485%	N.Ap.	1320%	1180%	N.Ap.
9073	34	34	3	68	43	43	19	55	66
2.6%	133.7%	41.3%	350.0%	161.0%	114.1%	446.6%	341.8%	202.3%	98.6%
0.5%	1.4%	5.7%	9.3%	1.8%	4.3%	18.6%	6.3%	16.5%	6.4%
17.6%	1.1%	13.8%	2.7%	1.1%	3.8%	4.2%	1.8%	8.2%	6.5%
9.3%	4.0%	9.2%	20.8%	7.9%	10.8%	27.4%	10.8%	26.0%	18.3%
59.0%	0.0%	65.3%	26.9%	55.0%	52.3%	25.5%	28.6%	7.3%	41.4%
2001.6%	286.0%	162.3%	223.3%	430.3%	248.1%	147.1%	172.0%	157.2%	283.7%
75.9%	38.0%	33.9%	29.9%	50.9%	25.1%	0.0%	18.1%	0.0%	45.2%
66.2%	92.5%	54.3%	64.8%	175.0%	42.6%	0.0%	27.0%	0.0%	122.3%
81.0%	111.5%	148.5%	261.6%	66.7%	141.6%	557.8%	207.3%	603.3%	202.7%
6.6%	0.0%	5.9%	2.1%	6.1%	4.1%	1.2%	1.5%	0.3%	3.7%
9.0	36.2	11.1	12.7	9.0	12.8	20.5	19.0	24.2	11.3
1.0	1.5	0.7	0.9	0.9	1.0	0.9	0.9	1.4	1.2

General Motors Corporation:

Macroeconomics

and Competition (A)

Rebecca Shepherd began working for General Motors Corporation as a writer in the corporate finance division in June 1984. Although she had taken a couple of accounting and economics courses during her freshman and sophomore years at college, Ms. Shepherd had been hired for her communications skills, not her analytical abilities. Both she and her boss, Isaac Weaver, knew, however, that she would be of little value to the firm until she brushed some of the rust off her business skills and understood at least the rudiments of GM's position in the marketplace and how the firm was affected by the economy and competition. With this in mind, Mr. Weaver sat down with Ms. Shepherd early one morning during her first week to explain the information that he had gathered for her to study.

Mr. Weaver said he wanted her to spend some time that morning analyzing GM's financial statements for the previous four years, as shown in Exhibits 1, 2, and 3. He thought the early 1980s made a particularly good period for her to study, since the U.S. economy had reached the depths of a severe recession in 1982 and had begun to recover in 1983. Given that bit of information, he wanted her to study the way the company earned, spent, and invested its money. He asked Ms. Shepherd to see if she could detect any changes in the statements that may have come about due either to external influences or to internal changes such as management decisions. He said they would discuss what she found over lunch.

This case was prepared as a basis for class discussion rather than to illustrate either effective or ineffective handling of an administrative situation. Copyright © 1986 by the Darden Graduate Business School Sponsors, University of Virginia, Charlottesville, Virginia.

General Motors Corporation (A)

EXHIBIT 1
■

Statement of Consolidated Income for the Years Ended December 31
(in millions except per share amounts)

	1980	1981	1982	1983
Net sales	$57,728.5	$62,698.5	$60,025.6	$74,581.6
Cost of sales and other operating charges, exclusive of items listed below	52,099.8	55,185.2	51,548.3	60,718.8
Selling, general, and administrative expenses	2,636.7	2,715.0	2,964.9	3,234.0
Depreciation of real estate, plants, and equipment	1,458.1	1,837.3	2,403.0	2,569.7
Amortization of special tools	2,719.6	2,568.9	2,147.5	2,549.9
Amortization of intangible assets	0.0	0.0	0.0	0.8
Total costs and expenses	58,914.2	62,306.4	59,063.7	69,073.2
Operating income	(1,185.7)	392.1	961.9	5,508.4
Other income less income deductions (net)	348.7	367.7	476.3	815.8
Interest expense	(531.9)	(897.9)	(1,415.4)	(1,352.7)
Income (loss) before income taxes	(1,368.9)	(138.1)	22.8	4,971.5
United States, foreign, and other income taxes (credit)	(385.3)	(123.1)	(252.2)	2,223.8
Income (loss) after income taxes	(983.6)	(15.0)	275.0	2,747.7
Equity in earnings of nonconsolidated subsidiaries and associates	221.1	348.4	687.7	982.5
Net income (loss)	$ (762.5)	$ 333.4	$ 962.7	$ 3,730.2
Dividends paid on preferred stock	12.9	12.9	12.9	12.9
Earnings (loss) on common stock	$ (775.4)	$ 320.5	$ 949.8	$ 3,717.3
Market price				
High	65	58	50.1	75
Low	49	43.9	34	56
Close	52	44	48	75
Price/earnings (end of year)				
Number of shares	298.1	304.8	312.4	317.7
Earnings per share	$(2.60)	$1.05	$3.04	$11.70
Dividends per share	2.93	2.40	2.40	2.80
Beta	0.95	0.85	0.90	1.00

Source: Annual Reports 1980–1983, and Value Line *Stock Guide*, various years.

General Motors Corporation (A)

EXHIBIT 2
∎
Consolidated Balance Sheet December 31, 1980–1983
(in millions except per share amounts)

	1980	1981	1982	1983
Assets				
Cash	$ 157.2	$ 204.1	$ 279.6	$ 369.5
United States government and other marketable securities and time deposits, at cost	3,558.0	1,116.6	2,846.6	5,847.4
Total cash and marketable securities	3,715.2	1,320.7	3,126.2	6,216.9
Accounts and notes receivable (less allowances)	3,768.4	3,645.5	2,864.5	6,964.2
Inventories (less allowances)	7,295.0	7,222.7	6,184.2	6,621.5
Prepaid expenses	706.5	1,527.2	1,868.2	997.2
Total current assets	15,485.1	13,716.1	14,043.1	20,799.8
Equity in net assets of nonconsolidated subsidiaries and associates (principally GMAC and its subsidiaries)	2,899.8	3,379.4	4,231.1	4,450.8
Other investments and miscellaneous assets, at cost (less allowances)	1,147.3	1,783.5	1,550.0	1,222.5
Common stock held for the GM incentive program	125.8	71.5	35.2	56.3
Real estate, plants, and equipment, at cost	29,202.7	34,811.5	37,687.2	37,777.8
Less accumulated depreciation	15,217.1	16,317.4	18,148.9	20,116.8
Net real estate, plants, and equipment	13,985.6	18,494.1	19,538.3	17,661.0
Special tools, at cost (less amortization)	937.4	1,546.6	2,000.1	1,504.1
Total property	14,923.0	20,040.7	21,538.4	19,165.1
Total assets	$34,581.0	$38,991.2	$41,397.8	$45,694.5
Liabilities and Stockholders' Equity				
Accounts payable (principally trade)	$ 3,967.7	$ 3,699.7	$ 3,600.7	$ 4,642.3
Loans payable	1,676.5	1,727.8	1,182.5	1,255.2
Accrued liabilities, deferred income taxes, and income taxes payable	6,628.8	7,127.6	7,601.8	9,011.5
Total current liabilities	12,273.0	12,555.1	12,385.0	14,909.0
Long-term debt	1,886.0	3,801.1	4,452.0	3,137.2
Capitalized leases	172.3	242.8	293.1	384.6
Other liabilities (including GMAC and its subsidiaries of $300.0 in 1983, $876.0 in 1982, and $424.0 in 1981)	1,482.5	3,215.1	4,259.8	4,698.2
Deferred credits (including investment tax credits)	952.6	1,456.0	1,720.8	1,798.9
Stockholders' equity				
Preferred stock	283.6	283.6	283.6	283.6
Common stock: $1⅔ par value common	496.7	508.0	520.6	526.2
Capital surplus (principally additional paid-in capital)	1,297.2	1,589.5	1,930.4	2,136.8
Net income retained for use in the business	15,737.1	15,340.0	15,552.5	18,390.5
Accumulated foreign currency translation and other adjustments	—	—	—	(570.5)
Total stockholders' equity	17,814.6	17,721.1	18,287.1	20,766.6
Total liabilities and stockholders' equity	$34,581.0	$38,991.2	$41,397.8	$45,694.5
Common stock outstanding (thousands of shares)	298,054	304,804	312,364	317,711

General Motors Corporation (A)

EXHIBIT 3
■
Cash Flow Statement (dollars in millions)

	1980	1981	1982	1983
Sources of Funds				
Net income	$ (762.5)	$ 333.4	$ 962.7	$ 3,270.2
Depreciation of real estate, plants, and equipment	1,458.1	1,837.3	2,403.0	2,569.7
Amortization of special tools	2,719.6	2,568.9	2,147.5	2,549.9
Net deferred income taxes, undistributed earnings of nonconsolidated subsidiaries and associates, etc.	311.5	68.0	75.8	645.5
Total funds provided by current operations	3,726.7	4,807.6	5,589.0	9,495.3
Increase in long-term debt	1,305.1	2,172.7	2,497.4	3,177.1
Proceeds from sale of newly issued common stock	271.9	303.6	353.5	212.0
Other, net	95.2	1,703.3	1,459.2	772.8
Total funds supplied	$ 5,398.9	$ 8,987.2	$ 9,899.1	$13,657.2
Uses of Funds				
Dividends paid to stockholders	$ 874.1	$ 730.5	$ 750.2	$ 892.2
Decrease in long-term debt	299.1	257.6	1,846.5	4,491.9
Expenditures for real estate, plants, and equipment	5,160.5	6,563.3	3,611.1	1,923.0
Expenditures for special tools	2,600.0	3,178.1	2,601.0	2,083.7
Increase (decrease) in other working capital items	(4,267.7)	341.2	(1,306.2)	1,142.0
Investments in nonconsolidated subsidiaries and associates	4.1	311.0	591.0	33.7
Total use of funds	$ 4 ,670.1	$11,381.7	$ 8,093.6	$10,566.5
Increase (decrease) in cash and marketable securities	728.8	(2,394.5)	1,805.5	3,090.7
Cash and marketable securities at beginning of year	2,986.4	3,715.2	1,320.7	3,126.2
Cash and marketable securities at end of year	$ 3,715.2	$ 1,320.7	$ 3,126.2	$ 6,216.9
Increase (Decrease) in Other Working Capital Items				
Accounts and notes receivable	$(1,262.0)	$ (125.1)	$ (778.8)	$ 4,099.7
Inventories	(844.1)	(72.3)	(1,038.5)	437.3
Prepaid expenses and deferred income taxes	243.1	820.6	341.1	(871.0)
Accounts payable	(586.4)	268.0	99.0	(1,041.6)
Loans payable	(752.4)	(51.3)	545.3	(72.7)
Accrued liabilities	(1,065.9)	(498.7)	(474.3)	(1,409.7)
Increase (decrease) in other working capital items	$(4,267.7)	$ 341.2	$(1,306.2)	$ 1,142.0

General Motors Corporation:

Macroeconomics

and Competition (B)

Rebecca Shepherd, a new employee in General Motors Corporation's corporate finance division, had spent a couple of hours one morning analyzing the company's financial statements in order to get a feel for the structure of the firm. Isaac Weaver, her boss, wanted her to devote the rest of the day to comparing GM's financial statements against those of its major U.S. competitors, Ford and Chrysler, taking into account the impact of changes in the economy. He had organized the 1982 and 1983 financial statements of the three firms, as shown in Exhibits 1 through 5. Ms. Shepherd was to compare and contrast the financial statements to see how each company operated in that period and to see if she could detect any corporate strengths or weaknesses reflected in the statements. He thought that this was a particularly good period to study the three companies, for the U.S. economy had been in the depths of a severe recession in 1982 and had begun to recover in 1983.

THE U.S. ECONOMY

The auto industry reacted with great volatility to changes in the economy. Gross national product (GNP) growth, unemployment, interest rates, and fuel prices affected automobile sales. As shown in Exhibit 6, all of these economic variables played important roles in the early 1980s; real GNP declined in 1980 and 1982, the unemployment rate reached 9.5 percent in 1982, and the prime lending rate soared to an average of almost 19 percent in 1981. In addition, crude fuel prices (mostly oil) increased by about 20 percent each year. To compound these problems, the inflation rate was over 10 percent for three straight years. In 1983, the economy began to recover. Unemployment remained high, but fuel–price increases, inflation, and interest rates all dropped as GNP rebounded.

This case was prepared as a basis for class discussion rather than to illustrate either effective or ineffective handling of an administrative situation. Copyright © 1986 by the Darden Graduate Business School Sponsors, University of Virginia, Charlottesville, Virginia.

THE COMPETITION

U.S. automobile production fell from 12.9 million cars in 1978 to 7.0 million in 1982; in 1983, production rebounded to 9.2 million cars. All three auto companies had manufacturing facilities in Canada, and Exhibit 7 shows that about one-eighth of the three firms' total auto production took place there.

General Motors, the largest automobile company in the world, traditionally manufactured a wide variety of cars, but focused its energies on family–sized and luxury models, that is, on higher–priced cars with larger profit margins. The company was founded in 1908 by William C. Durant when Buick Manufacturing Company of Flint, Michigan; Olds Motor Works of Lansing, Michigan; Cadillac Motor Company of Detroit, Michigan; and Oakland (Pontiac) Motor Company of Pontiac, Michigan merged. In the company's first year, it manufactured 165,000 cars and 6,000 trucks. Chevrolet Motor Company of Detroit was founded in 1911 and was bought by GM in 1918.

Ford management had always pictured its company, the second largest in the industry, as being in direct competition with GM, but its niche was in the production of smaller cars such as the Mustang and Pinto. Although it made some larger cars, the company offered little competition for GM's Buick, Oldsmobile, and Pontiac models. The company was founded in Detroit in 1903 by Henry Ford. The Model A was introduced the same year. The Model T, the better known of Ford's early models, was introduced in 1908, the same year the maverick entrepreneur Fold told GM that his company would act alone rather than merge. In 1922, the firm bought Lincoln Motor Company, which had been founded in 1917. Through this company Ford competed in the luxury car market. Henry Ford II succeeded his grandfather as president of the company in 1945, and still held the office of chairman of the board in 1970 when Lee Iacocca, vice president and general manager of the company, took over as president. Since that time, both men have stepped down.

Chrysler Corporation was founded in 1925 in Detroit. The company introduced its lower-priced Plymouth line in 1928 to compete with Chevrolet and Ford, and it bought Dodge in 1935. The recent past had been difficult for Chrysler, however; as demand for small cars grew in the late 1960s, Chrysler introduced several full-sized models. To stave off losses, the company arranged to sell small, Japanese-made Mitsubishi models as it slowly introduced its own mid-size cars. Larger cars came back into demand in the early 1970s, but as Chrysler began to respond to the change, the 1973 oil embargo was announced. Chrysler's costs from retooling its factories rose as its sales fell.

In 1978, Lee Iacocca left his position at Ford to become president of the financially ailing Chrysler Corporation. In 1980, the company was threatened with bankruptcy, but was granted a $1.5-billion loan guaranteed by the U.S. and Canadian governments. Before Walter Chrysler founded the corporation, he had worked for Buick and had saved two smaller automobile companies from bankruptcy. By 1983, Lee Iacocca was trying to do the same thing for Chrysler with innovative marketing techniques and his own charismatic public image. He was also trying to find a niche for the company in the small-car market.

Mr. Weaver asked Ms. Shepherd to compare the three companies' financial statements for similarities and differences, then he wanted her to analyze the statements for possible reflections of relative corporate strengths and weaknesses. Mr. Weaver looked forward to talking with her the next morning to find out how strong her analytical skills were.

EXHIBIT 1

U.S. Auto Manufacturers—Comparative Income Statements
(millions of dollars, except common stock data)

	General Motors		Ford		Chrysler	
	1982	1983	1982	1983	1982	1983
Net sales	$60,025.6	$74,581.6	$37,067.2	$44,454.6	$10,044.9	$13,240.4
Costs and expenses						
Cost of goods sold	51,548.3	60,718.8	32,462.8	37,316.3	8,585.1	10,854.2
Selling and administrative	2,964.9	3,234.8	2,300.4	2,399.7	669.8	775.6
Depreciation	2,403.0	2,569.7	1,200.8	1,262.8	195.9	183.3
Amortization	2,147.5	2,549.9	955.6	1,029.3	236.7	273.9
Interest (income)	1,415.4	1,352.7	182.8	(2.0)	158.0	82.1
Other	0.0	0.0	631.2	642.8	271.7	254.7
Total costs	60,479.1	70,425.9	37,733.6	42,648.9	10,117.2	12,423.8
Operating income (loss)	(453.5)	4,155.7	(666.4)	1,805.7	(72.3)	816.6
Other income (loss)	476.3	815.8	0.0	0.0	182.2	19.8
Other expense	0.0	0.0	(6.7)	29.2	0.0	223.9
Income (loss) before taxes	22.8	4,971.5	(659.7)	1,776.5	109.9	612.5
Income taxes (credit)	(252.2)	2,223.8	256.6	270.2	0.9	401.6
Net income (loss) before extraordinary items and nonconsolidated subsidiaries	275.0	2,747.7	(916.3)	1,506.3	109.0	210.9
Extraordinary items	0.0	0.0	0.0	0.0	66.9	399.0
Nonconsolidated subsidiaries	687.7	982.5	258.5	360.6	(5.8)	90.8
Net income (loss)	$ 962.7	$ 3,730.2	$ (657.8)	$ 1,866.9	$ 170.1	$ 700.7
Preferred dividends	$ 12.9	$ 12.9	0.0	0.0	0.0	0.0
Average shares outstanding (millions)	307.4	313.9	180.6	181.4	77.7	117.8
Earnings (loss) per share of common stock	$ 3.09	$ 11.84	$ (3.64)	$ 10.29	$ 2.19	$ 5.94
Average annual stock price	$ 46.04	$ 68.67	$ 16.85	$ 34.99	$ 7.95	$ 24.72
Dividends per share	2.40	2.80	0.0	0.50	0.0	0.0
Automobile production (thousands)	3,507.8	4,513.9	1,387.1	1,832.2	749.9	1,010.1
Employees (thousands)	657.0	N.Av.	379.2	N.Av.	73.7	N.Av.

N. Av. = not available.

EXHIBIT 2
∎
U.S. Auto Manufacturers—Comparative Balance Sheets
(millions of dollars)

	General Motors		Ford		Chrysler	
	1982	1983	1982	1983	1982	1983
Assets						
Cash	$ 279.6	$ 369.5	$ 943.7	$ 2,185.4	$ 109.7	$ 111.6
Marketable securities	2,846.6	5,847.4	611.7	966.7	787.5	957.8
Accounts receivable	2,864.5	6,964.2	2,376.5	2,767.6	247.9	291.2
Inventories	6,184.2	6,621.5	4,123.3	4,111.7	1,133.0	1,301.4
Other	1,868.2	997.2	743.7	787.7	91.0	91.8
Total current assets	14,043.1	20,799.8	8,798.9	10,819.1	2,369.1	2,753.8
Property, plant, and equipment	39,687.3	39,281.9	19,683.2	19,920.9	4,728.9	5,389.0
Less depreciation	18,148.9	20,116.8	9,546.9	10,119.0	2,255.2	2,334.0
Net property, plant, and equipment	21,538.4	19,165.1	10,136.3	9,801.9	2,473.7	3,055.0
Investments in associated companies	4,231.1	4,450.8	2,413.4	2,582.7	352.4	128.5
Other assets	1,585.2	1,278.8	613.1	665.2	1,068.3	835.0
Total assets	$41,397.8	$45,694.5	$21,961.7	$23,868.9	$6,263.5	$6,772.3
Liabilities and Equity						
Accounts payable	$ 3,600.7	$ 4,642.3	$ 4,119.6	$ 5,247.1	$ 897.8	$1,628.7
Short-term debt	1,182.5	1,255.2	2,265.0	942.0	100.4	416.8
Income taxes	0.0	0.0	383.0	362.1	0.0	0.0
Other	7,601.8	9,011.5	3,656.4	3,764.7	1,114.4	1,408.4
Total current liabilities	12,385.0	14,909.0	10,424.0	10,315.9	2,112.6	3,453.9
Long–term debt	4,745.1	3,521.8	2,353.3	2,712.9	2,189.0	1,104.0
Deferred credits	1,720.8	1,798.9	1,054.1	1,103.2	0.0	0.0
Other liabilities	4,259.8	4,698.2	2,052.8	2,191.6	970.8	849.1
Stockholders' equity						
Preferred stock	283.6	283.6	0.0	0.0	1,320.9	222.2
Common stock and additional paid-in capital	520.6	526.2	241.2	366.0	501.4	121.8
Retained earnings	17,482.9	19,956.8	5,836.3	7,179.3	(831.2)	1,021.3
Total equity	18,287.1	20,766.6	6,077.5	7,545.3	991.1	1,365.3
Total liabilities and equity	$41,397.8	$45,694.5	$21,961.7	$23,868.9	$6,263.5	$6,772.3
Common shares outstanding (millions)	312.4	317.7	180.61	183.00	119.21	182.72

General Motors Corporation (B)

EXHIBIT 3
■

General Motors Corporation
Cash Flow Statement
(in millions)

	1982	1983
Sources of Funds		
Net income	$ 962.7	$ 3,730.2
Depreciation of real estate, plants, and equipment	2,403.0	2,569.7
Amortization of special tools	2,147.5	2,549.9
Deferred income taxes, undistributed earnings of nonconsolidated subsidiaries and associates, etc., net	75.8	645.5
Total funds provided by current operations	5,589.0	9,495.3
Increase in long-term debt	2,497.4	3,177.1
Other	1,459.2	772.8
Proceeds from sale of newly issued common stock	353.5	212.0
Total sources	$ 9,899.1	$ 13,657.2
Uses of Funds		
Dividends paid to stockholders	$ 750.2	$ 892.2
Decrease in long-term debt	1,846.5	4,491.9
Expenditures for real estate, plants, and equipment	3,611.1	1,923.9
Expenditures for special tools	2,601.0	2,083.7
Increase (decrease) in other working capital items	(1,306.2)	1,142.0
Investments in nonconsolidated subsidiaries and associates	591.0	33.7
Total uses	$ 8,093.6	$ 10,566.5
Increase (decrease) in cash and marketable securities	1,805.5	3,090.7
Cash and marketable securities at beginning of year	1,320.7	3,126.2
Cash and marketable securities at end of year	$ 3,126.2	$ 6,216.9
Increase (Decrease) in Other Working Capital Items		
Accounts and notes receivable	$ (778.8)	$ 4,099.7
Inventories	(1,038.5)	437.3
Prepaid expenses and deferred income taxes	341.1	(871.0)
Accounts payable	99.0	(1,041.6)
Loans payable	545.3	(72.7)
Accrued liabilities	(474.3)	(1,409.7)
Increase (decrease) in other working capital items	$(1,306.2)	$ 1,142.0

General Motors Corporation (B)

EXHIBIT 4

■

Ford Motor Company
Cash Flow Statement
(in millions)

	1982	*1983*
Cash, cash items, and marketable securities at Jan. 1	$ 2,100.0	$ 1,555.4
Funds Provided (Used) by Operations		
Net income (loss)	(657.8)	1,866.9
Items included in net income (loss) not requiring (providing) funds		
Depreciation and amortization	2,156.4	2,292.1
Deferred income taxes	91.3	49.1
Other liabilities, noncurrent	68.0	55.3
Earnings of unconsolidated subsidiaries and affiliates in excess of dividends remitted	(184.3)	(111.6)
Other	(77.1)	58.3
Changes in Working Capital That Provided (Used) Funds		
Receivables	240.8	(391.1)
Inventories	497.5	11.6
Other current assets	89.8	(44.0)
Accounts payable and accrued liabilities	233.3	1,235.8
Current payable income taxes	174.1	(20.9)
Funds provided by operations	2,632.0	5,001.5
Funds Provided by (Paid to) Outside Sources		
Addition of long-term debt	797.4	1,162.7
Reduction of long-term debt	(966.6)	(1,009.8)
Decrease in short-term debt	(99.9)	(1,116.3)
Cash dividends	0.0	(90.9)
Other	97.3	0.0
Funds provided by (paid to) outside sources	(171.8)	(1,054.3)
Other Sources (Uses) of Funds		
Net additions to property	(2,649.2)	(1,932.8)
Other	132.0	(41.7)
Total other uses of funds	(2,517.2)	(1,974.5)
Effect of changes in foreign-currency exchange rates	(487.6)	(376.0)
Net increase (decrease) in funds	(544.6)	1,596.7
Cash, cash items, and marketable securities at December 31	$ 1,555.4	$ 3,152.1

General Motors Corporation (B)

EXHIBIT 5
■

Chrysler Corporation
Cash Flow Statement
(in millions)

	1982	1983
Funds Provided by (Used in) Operations		
From continuing operations:		
Earnings (loss)	$ (68.9)	$ 301.9
Depreciation and amortization	432.6	457.2
Contribution to employee stock ownership plan	40.6	40.6
Equity in (earnings) loss of unconsolidated subsidiaries	5.8	(90.8)
Other, including write-down of investment in Peugeot S. A.	(19.2)	241.5
Total funds from continuing operations	$ 390.9	$ 950.4
Changes in working capital affecting operations:		
(Increase) decrease in accounts receivable and inventories	$ 415.8	$ (211.7)
Increase (decrease) in accounts payable and accrued expenses	45.3	1,024.1
Total changes in working capital	$ 461.1	$ 812.4
Extraordinary item—utilization of tax loss carryforwards	66.9	399.0
Net change in noncurrent assets and liabilities	(47.2)	(40.8)
Funds provided by continuing operations	$ 871.7	$ 2,121.0
Funds Provided by (Used in) Investment Activities		
Decrease (increase) in investments and advances	$(184.9)	$ 243.0
Sale and purchase of subsidiaries, net	202.5	0.0
Sale of property, plant, and equipment	62.3	9.2
Expenditures for property, plant, and equipment	(146.8)	(642.5)
Expenditures for special tools	(227.0)	(414.5)
Other	(2.3)	(12.0)
Funds used in investment activities	$(296.2)	$ (816.8)
Funds Provided by (Used in) Financing Activities		
$311 million for purchase of warrants in 1983	$ (24.4)	$ 281.7
Proceeds from long-term borrowing	11.0	220.2
Payments on long-term borrowing	(69.9)	(1,269.4)
Purchase of U.S. government–held warrants, including related expenses	0.0	(313.9)
Proceeds from sale of common stock (exercise of public warrants)	0.0	63.1
Other changes in common stock	0.6	3.2
Funds provided by (used in) financing activities	(82.7)	(1,015.1)
Cash dividends paid on preferred stock	0.0	(116.9)
Funds Flow		
Increase during year	492.8	172.2
Cash, time deposits, and marketable securities at beginning of year	404.4	897.2
Cash, time deposits, and marketable securities at end of year	$ 897.2	$ 1,069.4

General Motors Corporation (B)

EXHIBIT 6

■

The U.S. Economy—Selected Data

	Gross National Product		Average Prime Lending Rate	Consumer Prices		Crude Fuel Prices	
	Billions of 1982 Dollars	Percentage Change		Index	Percentage Change	Index	Percentage Change
1979	$3,192.4	2.5 %	12.67%	100.0	11.3%	100.0	18.9%
1980	3,187.1	(0.2)	15.27	113.5	13.5	121.2	21.2
1981	3,248.8	1.9	18.87	125.3	10.4	148.0	22.1
1982	3,166.0	(2.6)	14.86	132.9	6.1	174.6	18.0
1983	3,277.7	3.5	10.79	137.2	3.2	183.5	5.1

	Unemployment Rate	Disposable Income (billions of 1982 dollars)	U.S. Auto Sales (billions of 1982 dollars)	U.S. Auto Production (thousands of units)	Percentage Sold in United States	Auto Imports into United States (thousands of units)
1979	5.8%	$2,092.7	$129.0	11,480	90.8	3,006
1980	7.0	2,104.9	97.9	8,010	91.2	3,248
1981	7.5	2,162.0	104.3	7,943	91.4	2,999
1982	9.5	2,180.5	97.0	6,986	92.7	3,067
1983	9.5	2,257.2	122.9	9,205	91.9	3,667

Sources: *Economic Report of the President,* February 1986; and *Motor Vehicle Facts and Figures,* Motor Vehicle Manufacturers Association of the United States, Inc., 1984, p. 29.

General Motors Corporation (B)

EXHIBIT 7
■

General Motors, Ford, and Chrysler:
U.S. and Canadian Auto Production
(units in thousands)

	United States		Canada		Total	
	1982	1983	1982	1983	1982	1983
Passenger Cars						
Chrysler	601	904	149	106	750	1,010
Ford	1,104	1,547	283	285	1,387	1,832
GM	3,173	3,975	335	539	3,508	4,514
Trucks and Buses						
Chrysler	122	148	96	141	218	289
Ford	712	925	114	134	826	1,059
GM	890	1,125	232	263	1,122	1,388

Source: *Motor Vehicle Facts and Figures,* Motor Vehicle Manufacturers Association, Inc., 1984, pp. 8–9.

General Motors Corporation:

Macroeconomics

and Competition (C)

Rebecca Shepherd, a new employee in General Motors' corporate finance division, had spent a day in June 1984 analyzing GM's financial statements and then comparing them to those of Ford and Chrysler. She was now ready to move on to the more complex analysis that Isaac Weaver, her boss, had prepared for her: a comparison of GM's financial condition and operations against those of nine worldwide competitors over three years, in light of the world economy.

American cars of the 1950s and 1960s reflected and typified, at least in part, the American auto industry of the time; they were large, solid, somewhat ponderous, occasionally glorified, and fairly inefficient. With few exceptions, European imports were either funny looking, very expensive, or exotic, and Japanese imports were derided as cheap little rattletraps. "But then," said Mr. Weaver, "two events conspired against the U.S. auto industry. The OPEC countries discovered that they could make a bundle by hiking up the price of oil, and at the same time the Japanese work ethic and their goal of zero-defects began to pay off. Suddenly, Japanese cars began to look like good alternatives to the big, gas-guzzling American models," and the young, affluent buyer was attracted to the luxurious European "sport sedans."

THE ECONOMY

Due to its size and importance, the U.S. economy strongly influenced the state of the world economy. Exhibit 1 provides some details on the U.S. economy between 1970 and 1983. Crude fuel (primarily oil) prices had almost doubled between 1973 and 1976, and had tripled by 1979. OPEC's initial price increases hastened and deepened the worldwide recession of the mid-1970s and caused consumer prices to rise sharply. U.S. gross national product declined and unemployment rose in 1974 and 1975. Prices rose by more than 20 percent over the same period. A modest recovery in the late 1970s did not last long, and by 1982, GNP had fallen almost 1 percent from its 1979 level, unemployment had risen to almost double-digit levels, and prices had risen by an average of over 10 percent per year for four years. Finally in 1983, although unemployment remained high,

This case was prepared as a basis for class discussion rather than to illustrate either effective or ineffective handling of an administrative situation. Copyright © 1986 by the Darden Graduate Business School Sponsors, University of Virginia, Charlottesville, Virginia.

GNP improved by 3.5 percent, the consumer price index rose only 3.2 percent (its smallest increase in over 10 years), and lending rates began to fall. The effect of the recession on the economies of Europe and Japan can be seen in Exhibit 2, which provides production, inflation, and employment data for Japan, Germany, Sweden, the United Kingdom, and France.

The auto industry reacted with great volatility to the state of the economy. Exhibits 3, 4, and 5 provide information on world auto production and exports and U.S. imports and exports.

Mr. Weaver asked Ms. Shepherd to compare GM's balance sheets and operating ratios with those of nine competitors from the United States, Japan, and Europe to determine similarities and differences, strengths and weaknesses. Exhibits 6, 7, and 8 show the financial information he had gathered for Ms. Shepherd's analysis. It presented financial data from 1980 to 1982 for three U.S., two Japanese, and five European auto manufacturers. (Complete 1983 data were not yet available.) Before leaving, Mr. Weaver also gave her a verbal sketch of each foreign company grouped by country.

THE INDUSTRY

Japan.   Nissan (Datsun) was the world's fifth largest and Japan's second largest automobile company, having produced 2.4 million cars in 1979. The company first entered the U.S. market in 1965 and began to flourish in the 1970s when consumers began to demand the company's smaller, less expensive, well-built cars. The company was also well known for its sports car, the Datsun 280Z.

Honda was the world's 12th largest auto manufacturer in terms of output. In 1979, it produced 802,000 cars; in addition, motorcycles accounted for 25 percent of the company's dollar sales and parts for 15 percent. Honda entered the U.S. market in 1970 with a tiny car called the Civic. Since that time, the company had broadened its offerings to include luxury compacts in addition to its small, less ostentatious models.

Germany.   In the 1930s, Adolph Hitler commissioned the development of a "Peoples' Car," in German a *"Volkswagen,"* that was to be inexpensive enough to be widely affordable. The plan survived World War II and two Volkswagen Beetles were imported to the United States in 1948. By 1960, 160,000 were being imported each year and it went on to become the biggest-selling car of all time. The Beetle resembled the Model T Ford of 1908 to 1927 in that it was inexpensive and its style did not change from year to year. The company halted production of the Beetle in the mid-1970s, and by 1978, Volkswagen was manufacturing the successful Rabbit model in both the United States and Europe. More recently, it had introduced several luxury and sports cars to fill out and complement the higher-priced line of cars manufactured by its Audi subsidiary.

Daimler–Benz had always manufactured high-priced luxury and sports cars. A Mercedes Benz was a status symbol and usually cost more than any of the standard American-made cars. The origins of the company dated back to 1886, when Gottlieb Daimler and Karl Benz developed their first self-propelled road vehicle. By 1888, the company held U.S. patents and by 1890, U.S. distributors of the car had been appointed.

Sweden.   Volvo was founded in 1927. Its cars became increasingly popular in the United States throughout the late 1960s and early 1970s due to the company's reputation for quality. The company used an unusual manufacturing technique, in that each car was built by a team of workers, rather than on an assembly line. By 1979, Volvo was the world's 18th largest auto company, manufacturing 352,000 cars a year. The auto company was part of a conglomerate; 40 percent of Volvo's dollar sales came from cars, 44 percent from energy sales, and the rest from miscellaneous operations.

Great Britain.   British Leyland manufactured a variety of cars from the small, practical Mini and Metro, and the MG, Lotus, and Triumph sports cars, to the Jaguar luxury cars. The corporation formed over a period of years after World War II. In 1952, the Austin and Morris auto companies merged to form British Motor Corporation (BMC); in 1966, BMC merged with Jaguar to form British Motor Holdings (BMH); in 1968, BMH merged with Leyland to form British Leyland.

The oil price increases of the 1970s caused demand within the United Kingdom to drop; in addition, government export policies had undermined the company's ability to sell overseas. In 1974, when the company was on the verge of bankruptcy, it was purchased by the British government. Production fell from 587,000 units in 1980 to 525,000 in 1981 and 519,000 in 1982. Over the same period, the total number of employees fell from 160,000 to 111,000.

France.   Peugeot, the world's sixth largest auto company, manufactured 2.3 million cars in 1979. The firm was best known for its small, economical touring cars. The company had begun as a bicycle manufacturer and made its first car in 1890. Peugeot had made diesel powered cars as early as the 1950s and sales of its diesel models soared in the 1970s when fuel prices rose, due to their 25-percent greater fuel efficiency. Soon, Nissan, Volkswagen, Oldsmobile, and others followed suit. Peugeot bought Chrysler's European subsidiaries in 1978.

CONCLUSION

Mr. Weaver expected that, by the time Ms. Shepherd finished analyzing the financial statements and operating results of the ten auto makers, she would have a strong feeling for GM's relative financial strengths and weaknesses. "The best way to understand how well a company works is to see how it looks compared to its competition. Each similarity or difference in their financial statements may reflect corporate strategies or the effects of the economy or competition. I'll talk to you tomorrow morning about what you find."

General Motors Corporation (C)

EXHIBIT 1
■
U.S. Economy—Selected Data

	Gross National Product (billions of 1982 dollars)	Percentage Change	Average Prime Lending Rate	Consumer Prices		Crude Fuel Prices		Unemployment Rate
				Index	Percentage Change	Index	Percentage Change	
1970	$2,416.2	(0.2)%	7.91%	116.3	5.9%	122.6	15.0%	4.8%
1971	2,484.8	2.8	5.72	121.3	4.3	139.0	13.4	5.8
1972	2,608.5	5.0	5.25	125.3	3.3	148.7	7.0	5.5
1973	2,744.0	5.2	8.03	133.1	6.2	164.5	10.6	4.8
1974	2,729.4	(0.5)	10.81	147.7	11.0	219.4	33.4	5.5
1975	2,695.0	(1.2)	7.86	161.2	9.1	271.5	23.7	8.3
1976	2,826.7	4.9	6.84	170.5	5.8	305.3	12.4	7.6
1977	2,958.6	4.7	6.83	181.5	6.5	372.1	21.9	6.9
1978	3,115.2	5.3	9.06	195.4	7.7	426.8	14.7	6.0
1979	3,192.4	2.5	12.67	217.4	11.3	507.6	18.9	5.8
1980	3,187.1	(0.2)	15.27	246.8	13.5	615.0	21.2	7.0
1981	3,248.8	1.9	18.87	272.4	10.4	751.2	22.1	7.5
1982	3,166.0	(2.6)	14.86	289.1	6.1	886.1	18.0	9.5
1983	3,277.7	3.5	10.79	298.4	3.2	931.5	5.1	9.5

Source: *Economic Report of the President,* February 1986.

General Motors Corporation (C)

EXHIBIT 2
■

European and Japanese Economic Data

	Gross Domestic Product		Consumer Prices		
	Local 1980 Currency (billions)	Percentage Change	Index	Percentage Change	Unemployment Rate
Japan					
1979	¥225,085	5.2%	92.6	3.6%	2.1%
1980	235,834	4.8	100.0	8.0	2.0
1981	245,371	4.0	104.9	4.9	2.2
1982	253,569	3.3	107.7	2.7	2.4
1983	262,073	3.4	109.6	1.8	2.7
Germany					
1979	DM1,458	4.0%	94.9	4.2%	3.8%
1980	1,486	1.9	100.0	5.4	3.8
1981	1,483	(0.2)	106.3	6.3	5.5
1982	1,468	(1.0)	111.9	5.3	7.5
1983	1,487	1.3	115.6	3.3	9.1
Sweden					
1979	K516	3.8%	87.9	7.2%	2.1%
1980	525	1.7	100.0	13.8	2.0
1981	524	(0.2)	112.1	12.1	2.5
1982	528	0.8	121.7	8.6	3.2
1983	541	2.5	132.6	9.0	3.5
United Kingdom					
1979	£235	2.1%	84.8	13.5%	5.1%
1980	230	2.2	100.0	17.9	6.4
1981	227	(1.3)	111.9	11.9	10.0
1982	231	1.7	121.5	8.6	11.7
1983	238	3.0	127.1	4.6	12.4
					Unemployment (thousands)
France					
1979	FF2,741	3.3%	87.9	10.7%	1,350
1980	2,769	1.0	100.0	13.8	1,451
1981	2,782	0.5	113.4	13.4	1,773
1982	2,832	1.8	126.8	11.8	2,008
1983	2,853	0.7	139.0	9.6	2,042

Sources: *International Financial Statistics,* International Monetary Fund; unemployment data from *Main Economic Indicators, 1964–1983,* Organization for Economic Cooperation and Development, 1984.

EXHIBIT 3
■
World Motor Vehicle Production (units in thousands)

	United States	Canada	United States and Canada Total	Europe	Japan	Other	World Total	United States Percentage of World Total
1983	9,205	1,524	10,729	15,813	11,112	2,053	39,727	23.2%
1982	6,986	1,276	8,262	14,929	10,732	2,190	36,113	19.3
1981	7,943	1,323	9,266	14,561	11,180	2,223	37,230	21.3
1980	8,010	1,374	9,384	15,530	11,043	2,538	38,495	20.8
1979	11,480	1,632	13,112	16,389	9,636	2,387	41,524	27.7
1978	12,899	1,818	14,717	16,205	9,269	2,108	42,299	30.5
1977	12,703	1,775	14,478	15,979	8,515	1,977	40,949	31.0
1976	11,498	1,640	13,138	15,316	7,841	2,046	38,346	30.0
1975	8,987	1,424	10,411	13,590	6,942	2,056	32,998	27.2
1974	10,071	1,525	11,596	14,513	6,552	2,073	34,733	29.0
1973	12,682	1,575	14,256	15,700	7,083	1,878	38,918	32.6
1972	11,311	1,430	12,741	14,836	6,294	1,674	35,545	31.8
1971	10,672	1,347	12,018	13,956	5,810	1,640	33,424	31.9
1970	8,284	1,187	9,471	13,154	5,289	1,352	29,267	28.3
1969	10,205	1,326	11,532	12,367	4,675	1,236	29,810	34.2
1968	10,820	1,150	11,971	11,241	4,085	1,058	28,356	38.2
1967	9,204	940	9,943	9,969	3,146	965	24,023	37.6
1965	11,138	847	11,984	9,549	1,876	858	24,267	45.9
1960	7,905	398	8,303	6,824	482	879	16,488	47.9
1955	9,204	452	9,656	3,742	68	162	13,628	67.5
1950	8,006	391	8,397	2,128	32	20	10,577	76.2
1973/1983 Percentage Change	(27.4)	(3.2)	(24.7)	0.9	56.9	9.3	2.1	N.Ap.

N. Ap. = not applicable.
Source: *Motor Vehicle Facts and Figures,* Motor Vehicle Manufacturers Association of the United States, Inc., 1984, p. 31.

EXHIBIT 4
■
World Motor Vehicle Exports
(in thousands)

	World Total[a]	*Percentage of World Motor Vehicle Exports from*								
		Japan	Belgium	France	Germany	Italy	Sweden	United Kingdom	Canada[b]	United States[b]
1982	14,595.2	38.3	6.5	12.8	16.4	3.6	1.5	2.8	7.6	3.5
1981	14,537.5	41.6	5.9	12.8	14.8	3.5	1.4	2.9	6.2	4.9
1980	15,161.7	39.4	5.8	14.6	13.7	3.9	1.3	3.2	6.2	5.3
1979	14,570.5	31.3	7.1	16.7	14.9	5.0	1.6	3.7	7.2	7.2
1978	14,598.8	31.5	7.1	15.7	14.2	4.8	1.4	4.2	9.0	6.5
1977	13,895.3	31.3	7.4	16.3	15.3	5.1	1.2	4.8	9.5	6.5
1975	10,807.2	24.8	7.3	18.0	15.3	6.6	1.8	6.4	9.3	8.0
1970	8,660.5	12.5	8.5	17.6	24.3	7.8	2.4	10.0	10.7	4.4

[a]World total includes countries with a small number of vehicle exports not shown separately. In 1982, vehicle exports from these countries totaled 1,024,200 units, 7.0 percent of world vehicle exports.
[b]Includes intercompany shipments between the United States and Canada.
Source: *Motor Vehicle Facts and Figures,* Motor Vehicle Manufacturers Association of the United States, Inc., 1984, p. 32.

General Motors Corporation (C)

EXHIBIT 5
∎

U.S. Automobile Trade: U.S. Imports of New, Assembled Passenger Cars by Country of Origin

	Belgium	Canada	France	Germany	Italy	Japan	Sweden	United Kingdom	Others	Total Imports
1983	5,230	836,756	212,858	330,263	5,347	2,112,011	109,494	53,284	1,780	3,667,023
1982	825	703,530	90,142	337,628	9,307	1,823,111	89,231	13,023	1,195	3,066,992
1981	66	563,943	42,477	376,327	21,635	1,911,525	68,042	12,728	1,818	2,998,561
1980	40	594,771	47,386	470,528	46,899	1,991,502	61,496	32,517	3,127	3,248,266
1979	85	677,008	27,887	495,565	72,456	1,617,328	65,907	46,911	2,376	3,005,523
1978	1,530	833,061	28,502	416,231	69,689	1,563,048	56,140	54,478	2,303	3,024,982
1975	38,176	733,766	15,647	370,012	102,344	695,573	51,993	67,106	36	2,074,653
1970	50,602	692,783	37,114	674,945	42,523	381,338	57,844	76,257	14	2,013,420
1965	332	29,135	24,941	376,950	9,509	25,538	26,010	66,565	450	559,430

1983 U.S. New Passenger Car Exports by
Country of Destination, Engine Size

	Six Cylinders or Less		More than Six Cylinders	
Country	Units	Value (thousands)	Units	Value (thousands)
Arab Emirates	69	$ 688	590	$ 7,698
Belgium	371	4,083	97	1,607
Canada	438,102	2,840,622	93,936	1,013,410
Colombia	288	2,410	125	1,961
Ecuador	67	488	78	1,315
Germany, West	2,171	20,389	507	7,172
Japan	866	8,797	1,349	21,226
Kuwait	172	1,630	2,071	27,647
Mexico	60	347	206	3,007
Peru	288	2,583	150	1,858
Qatar	52	500	304	4,123
Saudi Arabia	974	8,169	9,009	119,475
Switzerland	130	1,346	412	5,544
Taiwan	166	1,504	105	1,566
Venezuela	116	1,084	79	993
Others	2,977	25,760	2,378	35,905
Total	436,869	$2,920,400	11,396	$1,254,507

Source: *Motor Vehicle Facts and Figures,* Motor Vehicle Manufacturers Association of the United States, Inc., 1984, p. 31.

General Motors Corporation (C)

EXHIBIT 6
■
Automobile Industry Comparative Data, 1980

	GM	Ford	Chrysler
Balance Sheet Percentages (percentage of assets, except as noted)			
Cash and marketable securities	10.79%	10.63%	4.50%
Receivables	10.94	12.32	7.20
Inventories	21.17	21.07	28.95
Other current assets	2.05	3.47	2.59
Plant and equipment (net)	43.31	41.18	38.08
Other assets	11.74	11.35	18.68
Total assets	100.00	100.00	100.00
Accounts and notes payable	16.38	19.39	40.80
Other current liabilities	19.24	26.09	4.98
Long-term debts and leases	3.11	8.46	37.52
Other liabilities	7.60	10.32	9.76
Capital stock and surplus	5.66	3.71	25.30
Retained earnings	48.01	32.03	(18.36)
Total liabilities and stockholders' equity	100.00	100.00	100.00
Total sales (millions 1982 dollars)	$52,699	$33,851	$8,421
Total assets	31,450	22,224	6,041
Selected Ratios (percentage, except as noted)			
Current ratio	126.17%	104.40%	94.45%
Acid test	60.98	50.45	25.53
Inventory turnover	751	673	487
Accounts and notes receivable collection (days)	48	47	62
Net sales/Total assets	167.55	152.32	139.40
Cost of goods sold/Sales	97.49	98.88	105.14
Selling, general, and administrative/Sales	4.59	7.26	6.08
Net profit/Net sales	(1.32)	(4.16)	(13.17)
Net profit/Total assets	(2.21)	(6.34)	(18.36)
Total assets/Net worth	186.32	284.17	14.41
Net profit/Net worth	(4.12)	(18.01)	(264.59)
Total debt/Total assets	3.11	18.34	42.31
Long-term debt/Total capital	5.79	24.04	540.63
Employees (thousands)	746.0	426.7	92.6

N. Av. = not available.

Nissan	Honda	Volkswagen	Daimler–Benz	Volvo	British Leyland	Peugeot
11.37%	10.04%	19.94%	21.64%	2.18%	0.83%	3.08%
21.93	12.22	5.89	14.41	33.33	19.08	23.38
16.42	35.29	24.26	25.59	37.99	41.62	31.77
4.85	5.57	12.35	12.54	0.00	0.00	0.00
26.68	29.59	33.36	23.58	24.49	37.90	36.49
18.75	7.29	4.20	2.24	2.01	0.57	5.28
100.00	100.00	100.00	100.00	100.00	100.00	100.00
15.26	23.68	11.55	10.67	14.11	44.11	16.81
36.65	32.57	25.61	16.93	28.01	9.50	36.89
6.20	8.47	6.69	2.39	14.97	14.49	18.46
5.40	0.73	30.89	37.10	30.64	3.41	4.91
7.97	11.16	4.80	7.77	9.55	51.83	5.85
28.52	23.39	20.46	25.14	2.72	23.34	17.08
100.00	100.00	100.00	100.00	100.00	100.00	100.00
$15,104	$6,936	$13,444	$12,542	$4,291	$4,291	$11,943
10,237	4,040	10,079	7,059	4,167	4,208	8,889
105.13%	112.22%	168.01%	268.70%	174.51%	106.58%	108.43%
64.14	39.58	69.49	130.56	84.31	34.48	49.27
951	529	638	784	285	290	432
25	53	51	51	12	24	22
147.54	171.70	133.39	177.66	102.96	126.57	134.34
77.19	65.18	N. Av.	N. Av.	N. Av.	N. Av.	N. Av.
18.04	24.41	N. Av.	N. Av.	N. Av.	N. Av.	N. Av.
2.92	5.52	0.97	1.55	0.16	(26.57)	(2.12)
4.31	9.49	1.30	2.75	0.17	(23.56)	(2.84)
274.05	289.44	395.72	303.86	813.67	351.00	436.30
11.82	65.25	5.14	8.36	1.36	(161.40)	(12.40)
25.94	26.70	25.89	8.75	28.55	25.41	43.78
16.99	52.76	26.47	7.26	121.80	49.88	80.54
N. Av.	N. Av.	N. Av.	N. Av.	N. Av.	160.2	245.0

General Motors Corporation (C)

EXHIBIT 7
■
Automobile Industry Comparative Data, 1981

	GM	Ford	Chrysler
Balance Sheet Percentages (percentage of assets, except as noted)			
Cash and marketable securities	3.39	9.12	6.45
Receivables	9.37	11.28	6.85
Inventories	18.56	20.17	25.52
Other current assets	3.92	3.64	2.66
Plant and equipment (net)	51.49	42.77	39.03
Other assets	13.27	13.02	19.49
Total assets	100.00	100.00	100.00
Accounts and notes payable	13.95	16.90	34.89
Other current liabilities	18.31	26.27	3.68
Long-term debt and leases	4.34	11.77	32.84
Other liabilities	18.05	13.07	16.14
Capital stock and surplus	6.11	3.34	39.42
Retained earnings	39.24	28.65	(26.99)
Total liabilities and stockholders' equity	100.00	100.00	100.00
Total sales (millions 1982 dollars)	$60,744	$37,054	$6,074
Total assets	37,706	22,303	9,661
Selected Ratios (percentage, except as noted)			
Current ratio	109.25%	102.38%	107.54%
Acid test	39.56	47.24	34.48
Inventory turnover	864	783	567
Accounts and notes receivable collection (days)	62	50	80
Net sales/Total assets	161.10	166.13	159.03
Cost of goods sold/Sales	95.04	96.23	93.93
Selling, general, and administrative/Sales	4.33	7.05	8.88
Net profit/Net sales	0.53	(2.77)	(4.77)
Net profit/Total assets	0.86	(4.60)	(7.59)
Total assets/Net worth	220.51	312.70	803.86
Net profit/Net worth	1.89	(14.40)	(60.99)
Total debt/Total assets	4.34	21.23	36.68
Long–term debt/Total capital	9.57	36.81	266.00
Employees (thousands)	746.0	404.8	46.0

N. Av. = not available.

Nissan	Honda	Volkswagen	Daimler–Benz	Volvo	British Leyland	Peugeot
11.83	8.24	14.89	20.29	2.14	1.04	3.82
19.43	13.68	6.80	14.73	36.12	16.03	24.64
17.19	36.29	23.54	23.58	31.60	40.95	28.25
5.52	5.50	11.79	12.90	0.00	0.00	0.00
27.04	29.57	40.22	26.48	22.88	41.47	37.46
18.99	6.72	2.76	2.03	7.26	0.51	5.84
100.00	100.00	100.00	100.00	100.00	100.00	100.00
13.83	24.16	12.68	10.29	15.77	33.69	16.08
37.45	31.20	23.82	17.74	31.68	19.97	41.72
8.19	11.42	7.03	2.66	17.58	13.29	20.40
4.64	(0.66)	30.89	37.40	24.56	1.77	3.99
9.31	9.43	4.73	7.48	7.59	79.83	5.44
26.58	24.45	20.85	24.43	2.82	(48.55)	12.37
100.00	100.00	100.00	100.00	100.00	100.00	100.00
$15,176	$7,325	$15,122	$14,636	$7,404	$4,865	$10,670
11,499	4,560	10,130	8,155	5,651	3,607	8,376
105.26%	115.11%	156.18%	255.11%	147.24%	108.13%	101.25%
60.97	39.61	59.41	124.94	80.64	31.82	42.64
853	489	630	789	472	316	327
26	49	87	48	17	27	18
131.98	160.64	149.29	179.47	131.03	134.86	127.38
75.94	67.83	N. Av.	N. Av.	N. Av.	N. Av.	75.61
17.60	23.93	N. Av.	N. Av.	N. Av.	N. Av.	21.83
2.61	3.49	0.36	0.83	0.94	(17.32)	(2.75)
3.44	5.60	0.54	1.49	1.24	(23.37)	(3.51)
278.55	295.16	390.93	313.29	960.61	319.69	558.35
9.58	16.54	2.10	4.66	11.88	(74.70)	(19.58)
29.10	30.42	23.92	7.42	34.10	32.15	45.48
22.81	33.71	27.48	8.33	168.88	42.49	113.90
N. Av.	N. Av.	246.9	188.0	76.1	130.2	231.5

General Motors Corporation (C)

EXHIBIT 8
∎
Automobile Industry Comparative Data, 1982

	GM	Ford	Chrysler
Balance Sheet Percentages (percentage of assets, except as noted)			
Cash and marketable securities	7.56%	7.09%	14.32%
Receivables	6.93	10.82	3.96
Inventories	14.95	18.77	18.09
Other current assets	4.52	3.39	1.45
Plant and equipment (net)	52.07	46.15	39.49
Other assets	13.97	13.78	22.69
Total assets	100.00	100.00	100.00
Accounts and notes payable	11.56	18.76	14.33
Other current liabilities	18.38	28.70	19.39
Long-term debt and leases	4.77	10.72	34.95
Other liabilities	21.16	14.14	15.50
Capital stock and surplus	6.61	3.48	40.16
Retained earnings	37.52	24.20	(24.33)
Total liabilities and stockholders' equity	100.00	100.00	100.00
Total sales (millions 1982 dollars)	$60,026	$37,067	$10,045
Total assets	41,360	21,962	6,264
Selected Ratios (percentage, except as noted)			
Current ratio	113.39%	84.41%	112.14%
Acid test	48.37	37.72	54.20
Inventory turnover	895	846	735
Accounts and notes receivable collection (days)	67	54	108
Net sales/Total assets	145.12	168.78	160.37
Cost of goods sold/Sales	93.46	93.40	89.77
Selling, general, and administrative/Sales	4.94	7.91	9.37
Net profit/Net sales	1.60	(1.77)	1.69
Net profit/Total assets	2.33	(3.00)	2.72
Total assets/Net worth	226.60	361.40	632.11
Net profit/Net worth	5.27	(10.82)	17.16
Total debt/Total assets	4.77	21.03	36.47
Long-term debt/Total capital	10.81	38.74	220.92
Employees (thousands)	657.0	379.2	73.7

N. Av. = not available.

Nissan	Honda	Volkswagen	Daimler–Benz	Volvo	British Leyland	Peugeot
11.94%	6.01%	11.87%	20.13%	2.25%	1.92%	2.30%
16.69	15.08	6.12	15.31	36.17	18.74	19.91
12.73	32.06	21.79	21.96	30.99	37.49	28.83
5.41	6.14	12.91	12.18	0.00	0.00	0.00
32.22	33.56	44.25	28.04	20.49	41.54	38.99
21.01	7.15	3.06	2.39	10.10	0.31	9.97
100.00	100.00	100.00	100.00	100.00	100.00	100.00
12.17	22.30	13.58	9.77	14.70	35.64	17.18
35.39	28.35	24.23	17.73	31.73	12.13	40.95
12.49	12.17	5.59	3.51	18.73	23.09	23.43
4.36	0.83	33.23	37.61	23.37	1.82	4.55
8.81	10.64	4.63	6.66	8.55	84.94	5.26
26.78	25.71	18.74	24.72	2.92	(57.62)	8.63
100.00	100.00	100.00	100.00	100.00	100.00	100.00
$16,345	$8,953	$15,425	$16,031	$12,035	$5,377	$11,450
12,897	5,308	10,684	9,459	7,365	4,035	8,952
98.32%	117.07%	139.35%	253.10%	149.50%	121.75%	95.36%
60.18	41.64	47.58	128.92	52.75	43.26	35.03
888	525	644	789	583	354	315
27	45	83	44	18	29	17
126.73	168.68	144.37	169.49	163.42	133.26	127.91
75.93	66.82	N. Av.	N. Av.	N. Av.	N. Av.	84.07
18.71	24.55	N. Av.	N. Av.	N. Av.	N. Av.	16.45
2.57	3.24	(0.80)	0.90	0.66	(9.53)	(2.85)
3.25	5.46	(1.16)	1.52	1.07	(12.71)	(3.65)
280.98	275.10	427.90	318.47	871.84	366.03	722.02
9.14	15.03	(4.89)	4.85	9.34	(46.51)	(26.36)
33.96	29.71	23.36	8.38	35.75	33.55	46.90
35.09	33.48	23.92	11.18	163.30	84.51	169.39
N. Av.	N. Av.	243.0	186.8	75.6	111.0	213.0

2

FORECASTING FUTURE

CORPORATE PERFORMANCE

United Telesis Corporation

In early March 1985, John Cunningham, executive vice president of the San Diego–based United Telesis Corporation (UT), was debating whether to proceed with a new venture in the business of vending (owning, operating, and servicing) private coin-operated telephones. Since the divestiture of AT&T, the Federal Communications Commission (FCC) had ruled that pay telephones could be owned and operated by firms other than the regional telephone companies. The Public Utilities Commissions (PUCs) in nine states had approved the operation of such companies and had established appropriate tariff structures for access to local telephone lines. United Telesis, through a subsidiary acquired early in the industry's existence, was already gaining valuable operating experience vending pay phones in high-tariff Minnesota, and had received publicity as the "largest private coin-operated telephone (COT) operator in the country." Using Minnesota as a proving ground for its operations, UT hoped to capitalize on its industry-leading reputation by expanding services into Florida, Texas, New York, and California—all prime COT states on the verge of establishing tariffs.

The California PUC had made it illegal for a company like UT to install telephones until a tariff structure had been established. Industry analysts had advised Mr. Cunningham that they expected a tariff would be established in the near future. Originally the California PUC had been scheduled to deliver the long-awaited tariff in early February 1985, but almost on the eve of the tariff's release, it was delayed in the courts. Having believed the February date to be accurate, Mr. Cunningham had just spent $50,000 on a 45-day marketing blitz in San Diego and had obtained 1,000 phone contracts in prime locations. Because the contracts contained a clause requiring installation of the phones by June 30, 1985, Mr. Cunningham faced a difficult question: Should he go ahead and illegally install his company's phones in anticipation of the tariff, risking an unknown fate in the courts, or should he wait for the PUC to act and risk losing his signed contracts because of the installation deadline? In either case, the tariff terms could be set too high for companies like UT to operate COTs profitably in California.

Mr. Cunningham faced another question as well, one that depended in part on his current actions and their success. If he proceeded, how much external financing would UT need over the next several years?

This case was prepared as a basis for class discussion rather than to illustrate either effective or ineffective handling of an administrative situation. Copyright © 1987 by the Darden Graduate Business School Sponsors, University of Virginia, Charlottesville, Virginia.

THE COT INDUSTRY

Private ownership of COTs was first permitted by the FCC on June 14, 1984. State jurisdiction called for each PUC to establish the amount a private company could charge callers and a tariff for the connection of private COT service to local lines. PUCs in most states were expected to permit private phone companies to charge 25¢ for a local phone call. Because the local (Bell) phone companies were still under the regulatory eyes of their PUCs, each company had to file a proposed tariff and price schedule for the state agencies to review and either accept or reject.

Currently, local phone companies, called regional Bell operating companies (RBOCs), installed pay phones and vended the service; they owned the equipment, installed and maintained it, and, if the phone produced over $75 revenue per month, paid the location account a commission, which averaged 3 to 6 percent of the phone's gross revenue. If the phone did not meet the minimum revenue level, the location account was charged between $28 and $50 per month per phone.

The pay phone business represented a small portion of the local phone companies' total revenues. Many of them viewed their COT business as a public service that did not have to be profitable. Those RBOCs that were interested in profitability could not be sure their operations were breaking even, however, because of the awkward way most of them allocated overhead. As a result, now that the business was deregulated, a few were considering abandoning the COT business altogether.

The COT industry generated revenues of $1.6 to $1.8 billion in 1983. It was estimated that 62 percent of these revenues were generated by 20 percent of the COTs. The COT market had three distinct but related segments:

1. High coin/low credit card revenue: Only 6 to 25 percent of all COTs generated coin revenues over $250 a month. These COTs were generally in high-traffic locations with a large percentage of local calls such as busy bars and restaurants, gas stations at intersections, or shopping malls.

2. Medium coin/medium credit card revenue: 75 percent of the coin market consisted of COTs with coin revenues between $50 and $250 a month. Owners of most of these locations received little commission from the phones. Included in this segment were "semi-public" phones, typically low-revenue phones for which location accounts paid the $28 to $50 a month per phone to have this service available to their employees and customers.

3. High credit card/low coin revenue: The credit card COT market generated annual revenues in excess of $2 billion. AT&T, MCI, Sprint, and other long-distance carriers were competing for a share of this growing market, mostly by focusing on the large transportation centers (e.g., airports and hotels). Technological advances in equipment were expected soon to allow conversion of strictly coin phones into combination coin and credit card units.

Presently, private COT companies like UT were only able to pay locations a commission on cash revenues because long-distance carriers like MCI and AT&T did not pay commissions to private COT companies for providing access through their phones. Mr. Cunningham believed, however, that as UT expanded the size of its operation, long-distance carriers would begin to bid for access through UT's phones, which would enable UT to receive revenue and pay commissions on all business, coin and card.

THE COMPANY

United Telesis Corporation was founded in 1984 by two Santa Clara University classmates, John Cunningham and Ed Benkman. They had become interested in the pay-phone industry through their involvement in a small vending company called Vidcom. At the height of operations, Vidcom had placed video games and pinball machines in over two thousand locations in 12 states. By early 1985, however, decline in public interest in video games had shrunk the business to one thousand sites in four states (California, Ohio, New York, and Arizona). Vidcom owned 45 percent of UT's stock, current UT management and insiders owned another 35 percent, and the rest was held by the public. UT was a Nevada corporation that had been "blue-skied" in 42 states. Its stock was traded over the counter (the "pink sheets") and was currently selling at about $1 per share.

Mr. Cunningham, 28, a 1983 MBA graduate of the Darden School at the University of Virginia, had previously been an account executive and trader with Dean Witter Reynolds in Menlo Park, California. He joined UT in 1984 after a year in real estate investment banking in Seattle. Friends from school believed "John's personality, personal resources, and his ability to cultivate, develop, and utilize contacts to be perhaps his company's biggest asset."

Mr. Benkman, also 28, president of Vidcom and UT, was a 1979 graduate of the University of Santa Clara. He was a classic entrepreneur, who had only once in his life ever worked for someone other than himself (managing a hotel his first summer after school). In his first venture in the vending business, he had invented an electronic monitoring device for video games called the "Nighthawk" that remotely counted the number of coins deposited into a vending machine. He had also obtained contracts with all the Circle-K and 7–11 stores in southern California, Arizona, and Nevada. Mr. Benkman was detail-oriented, operations-minded, and a proven financier. By age 28, he had formed several different companies. Both he and Mr. Cunningham had high expectations for their new venture.

UT had until now been heavily financed by a group of foreign investors who had pledged $1.65 million to purchase stock in the young company. An initial 650,000 had been funded, with the remaining $1 million due in the next several months. These funds were expected to get the company set up in California, where the success of one operation could generate follow-up capital from such sources as limited partnerships, leasing companies, and private placements of stock.

THE CALIFORNIA COT MARKET

United Telesis was particularly interested in the California market for a number of reasons. First, the company's home office was in San Diego, a city in the southern part of the state known for its beaches and year-round perfect climate. Second, California was the second-largest COT market (189,000 phones in place) in the country, and over two-thirds of the COTs in California were located in the southern part of the state. Third, because weather conditions permitted less–

expensive protection for outdoor phones, initial capital investment levels in California were as much as 20 percent lower than in, for example, Minnesota, where all outdoor phones required some sort of enclosure. UT was interested in Texas (129,000 COTs) and Florida (89,000) COTs for the same reasons. Fourth, the southwest portion of the United States, known as the "sunbelt," was expected to be the fastest-growing area of the country during the next 25 years, and the company wanted to take part in this growth.

UT's mode of operation was similar to that of Vidcom, the video game company. Locations such as gas stations, bars, restaurants, shopping malls, and convenience stores would be solicited to contract with UT to have phones installed. The company sought to convert current locations that were proven revenue producers to its equipment, so that once a phone was installed, it would immediately begin producing positive cash flow. In addition, installation costs were much lower at those sites because RBOC wall mountings were already in place.

In southern California, UT obtained locations by promising the prospective account 20 percent of the COT's gross margin (total cash in the box, less local phone company charges). As a result, net income to the various customers' accounts was expected to be twice that of the area's RBOC (Pacific Bell), all with no investment on the part of the accounts. After obtaining a contract at a location, UT planned to instruct Pac Bell to remove its existing equipment, and then install its own. UT would collect the money from the phones and provide monthly preventive maintenance. It also guaranteed seven-day, 24-hour service, and would pay the account its commission by the 20th of each month.

The key to obtaining accounts was reaching the decision-maker at a particular location. At a local bar with one or two phones, this person was probably the owner. A sale to a restaurant or convenience store chain with 50 to 100 phones at sites all over the state meant contacting the regional office. Obviously, UT was interested in obtaining corporate accounts, where one visit could produce a contract for hundreds of phones, but these sales often took months, sometimes years, to close, because the accounts were not as interested in higher commissions as in continued high-quality equipment and service. Thus UT was equally interested in the small, independent locations. Choice sites could be hand-picked, often for far lower commissions than the chain accounts demanded, and the decision-making process was much faster.

COT EQUIPMENT

Mr. Cunningham wanted to establish routes, each with a minimum of three thousand pay phones, in the California, Florida, and Texas markets. Each route would have a district office, and a two-person service/collection team for every 500 phones. At this point, UT had purchased one thousand phones manufactured by Seiscor, a division of Raytheon. Distributed by Cointel Corporation of Los Angeles, this phone model was considered attractive because it had several months of field testing behind it. Although the number of new COTs on the market was increasing and their prices were falling, none of the new phones had any performance history.

The new, privately owned COTs were termed "smart phones"; their intelligence was contained on a microchip within the phone. The intelligence included a rate table that would determine for the user exactly how much a call would cost without the assistance of an operator. Existing COTs were termed "dumb phones," because they relied on a central switching location and directory assistance for the rate information. Most smart phones also had an LCD display that indicated the number dialed, the cost of the call, the amount deposited, the time remaining at that cost, and any additional charges.

UT was already using the Cointel phone in its Minnesota test market, with mixed results. All the RBOCs in the states where United Telesis intended to compete operated "pre-pay" COTs, meaning the user picked up the hand set, deposited the coins, dialed the number, and if the party answered, could immediately begin speaking. If no one answered, the coins were returned. Over 99 percent of the COTs in the United States were pre-pay phones.

Because the answer-supervision technology required for a pre-pay system was still very expensive, the Cointel phone, like all the new phones then on the market, was a "post-pay" phone, meaning that the user picked up the hand set, dialed the number, deposited the coins, and, if the call was answered, pushed a button in order to speak; pushing the button signaled the phone to take the coins. If the party did not answer and the button was not pushed, the coins were returned. Any coins that had been inserted before the number was dialed were not returned.

Though instructions were printed clearly on the phones, this different mode of operation caused many users to have difficulty with the new phones. Most of the complaints came during the first 60 days after installation, however, and the company expected this natural resistance to change to diminish. Answer supervision, the highly desired feature that would allow the COTs to operate in a more traditional way, was expected to be available in the next generation of phones due to be released during the next year, perhaps within 3 to 6 months. All current manufacturers' phones, including Cointel's, had other potential problems such as vulnerability to vandalism.

All the COT manufacturers were anxious for a significant industry member like UT to make a large purchase of their phones, so they could capitalize on the publicity. Mr. Cunningham felt that, for the price ($1,395 per phone for one thousand phones), the Cointel phone presented the best value, despite its shortcomings. As new phones with more advanced features were produced, he intended to replace the Cointel phones in the best locations with newer models and rotate the older phones to less profitable locations. His main concern now, however, was to sign up the best locations and install the phones.

COMPETITION

Although few firms like UT currently served the California market, heavier competition was expected in the wake of the upcoming PUC decision. Mr. Cunningham expected the strongest competition in the near term to come from established vending companies such as ARA ($4 billion sales) and Canteen (owned by Trans World Corp., TWA's parent company), neither of which had yet entered the market. He expected later competition from smaller operators, from both the vending industry and new entrants. This competition was expected to reduce profit margins, forcing many of the marginal firms to go out of business or to consolidate their operations with those of other firms. Initial capital requirements were the greatest barrier to entry: one thousand phones required an investment upwards of $1.8 million.

Mr. Cunningham also believed that Pacific Bell, despite its claim that it wanted to get out of the pay phone business, would inevitably become UT's key competitor. After all, its phones and operations were already in place; all Pac Bell needed to do was double its current commissions of between 3 and 6 percent of gross revenue (coin and card) to be competitive. He felt sure that once Pac Bell began to examine the cost of getting out of the business, it would choose to stay.

Historically, state PUCs and established local phone companies, while sometimes adversarial, had worked very closely together. Their relationships generally offered an opportunity to structure tariffs and privately owned COT regulations in favor of the phone companies. What these relationships did not give them, lobbying power did. Regardless of how you looked at it, the RBOC–PUC combination was a powerful competitor for new companies like UT. Nevertheless, Mr. Cunningham felt UT would not only be the leader among the new entrants, it could compete against giants like Pac Bell because of its low-cost operation.

UT PROJECTIONS

Before establishing a pay-phone operation in California, Mr. Cunningham had examined the economies of the business. In order to determine the company's breakeven point of operation (in terms of number of phones), he assumed the average monthly revenue of a phone would be $220. He expected that the PUC's tariff would include a $30 per month line charge, plus per-call charges of $0.08, all to be paid to Pac Bell. Tariffs ranged from $10 per month and $0.045 in Illinois to Minnesota's $57.50 per month for 200 calls, $0.10 per call for the next 200 calls, $0.08 for the next 200 calls, and $0.05 per call thereafter. Commissions at each location were projected to cost 20 percent of the phone's gross margin (total cash revenue less line charges and per-call charges).

To calculate the monthly debt service for each COT, Mr. Cunningham used an interest rate of 16 percent, a 48-month time frame, and a purchase price of $1,800 (including both phone and booth). Sales commissions would be $25 per phone to secure a location contract and installation costs were expected to average $100 per phone. For maintenance and service, Mr. Cunningham projected costs of $20/month/COT. For projection purposes, depreciation was handled on a straight-line basis, although the ACRS depreciation schedule shown in Exhibit 1 would apply for tax purposes. An investment tax credit of 8 percent could be taken on the total cost per phone, including installation. (See Exhibit 2 for a calculation of revenues, costs, and profits per phone.) Other costs expected to be incurred by the company, including a personnel budget large enough for 3,000 phones, are shown in Table 1.

Mr. Cunningham wanted to target accounts with locations that would provide at least break-even levels of gross cash revenues. This information was to be obtained after each particular account signed a preliminary contract. With the agreement of the account, UT would submit a request to Pac Bell for the account's pay-phone revenue history, which was available under the Freedom of Information Act. If the phone revenue was high enough, a UT officer would sign the contract to activate the terms.

UT planned to operate a total of 3 thousand COTs by the end of 1985, 7 thousand by the end of 1986, 12 thousand by 1987, and 17 thousand and 22

United Telesis Corporation

TABLE 1
■
UT Projected Monthly Fixed Corporate Overhead

Operational salaries	$ 8,000
Administrative salaries	15,000
Rent and utilities	3,000
Postage	750
Travel and entertainment	2,000
Telephone	1,500
Auto	3,000
Advertising	2,000
Contingency	5,000
Total projected fixed overhead	$40,250

thousand by the end of 1988 and 1989, respectively. Three-minute local calls were expected to constitute 85 percent of the total number of calls on the phones, while long-distance calls would make up the remaining 15 percent. From this information, Mr. Cunningham felt that he could generate UT's projected income statement.

Mr. Cunningham also wanted to determine his internal funding and external capital needs over the next several years. Because this industry was new and exciting, a warm investor reception was expected, but, since both Mr. Cunningham and Mr. Benkman received much of their compensation in the form of stock and stock options, he naturally wanted to avoid substantial equity dilution if possible.

United Telesis Corporation

EXHIBIT 1
■
Tax Depreciation Schedule
for Telephone Equipment (as of 1985)

Year of Service	Percent of Purchase Price Depreciated
1	15%
2	22
3	21
4	21
5	21

United Telesis Corporation

EXHIBIT 2
■
Average Margin per Phone per Month

Revenue	$220.00
Telephone charges	(92.40)
Gross margin	127.60
Location commission	(25.52)
Gross profit	102.08
Service and maintenance	(20.00)
Overhead	(13.42)
Depreciation[a]	(30.00)
Profit before debt service and income taxes	$ 38.66

[a]Depreciation calculation:

Installation and equipment	
COT cost	$1,400.00
Installation	100.00
Booth/enclosure	300.00
Total cost per COT	$1,800.00
Depreciable life	5 years
Annual depreciation	$ 360.00

Fantastic Manufacturing, Inc.

In late October 1980, David Rose and Pierce Turner, principals of Fantastic Manufacturing, Inc., were preparing forecasts for their rapidly growing business assembling and marketing ceiling fans. A product many had thought of as a fad, ceiling fans had instead been accepted by consumers as energy conservers, and new-home builders and homeowners were installing them in record numbers.

Fantastic Manufacturing was incorporated in late 1976 by Mr. Rose and Mr. Turner in Charleston, South Carolina. Mr. Rose had his own manufacturers' representative, Rose Sales, Inc., with annual sales of approximately $40 million to accounts around the world. He specialized in sales of building materials to mass-merchandisers.

In 1976, Mr. Rose had found many of his accounts interested in ceiling fans, and at the end of that year he approached Mr. Turner, a tax attorney by training and head of his own manufacturing company, to discuss the possibility of importing and assembling ceiling fans. Agreeing with the idea, Mr. Turner accompanied Mr. Rose to Taiwan and Hong Kong to find parts suppliers for a new, low-priced, assemble-it-yourself fan. The men took their specifications to all the fan factories they could find in Taiwan and Hong Kong and selected exclusive suppliers.

Fantastic's first order for fans was placed in September 1977 and arrived in late November. After assembly, the fans were shipped to customers in December. By the end of the first fiscal year, which ended January 31, 1978, total sales were approximately $230,000.

Fantastic had begun operations by emphasizing sales of low-priced fans to the do-it-yourself market, selling largely through small stores. Initially, Mr. Rose and Mr. Turner had viewed the product as appealing to nostalgia, and they expected limited growth potential. The initial objective of the business was to get the product on the shelf, and the company encouraged retailers to advertise heavily. Many stores used the product initially as a faddish draw.

Studies had shown, however, that ceiling fans were economically beneficial, reducing both cooling costs in summer and heating costs in winter. As consumers began viewing ceiling fans as energy-saving devices, the growth prospects for the industry improved. Much of this improvement was expected to come from the upper end of the market, for which Fantastic Manufacturing

This case was prepared as a basis for class discussion rather than to illustrate either effective or ineffective handling of an administrative situation. Copyright © 1980 by the Darden Graduate Business School Sponsors, University of Virginia, Charlottesville, Virginia.

had positioned its recently introduced Cotillion line. Their major premium-line competition came from two domestic lines, Hunter and Casablanca, both produced by Emerson Electric. Emerson had done little to promote its products.

Not much public information was available about fan sales in general, so Mr. Rose and Mr. Turner had little to go on in estimating the potential for competition. They did know that Fantastic held a cost advantage because of its overseas sourcing. Customers were pleased with Fantastic's products and had commented positively on the high level of service and timeliness of delivery. The company's 7-year warranty on the fans had also encouraged consumer acceptance.

Fantastic's revenues increased rapidly from the beginning. In fiscal 1979 and 1980, the first two full years of operations, Fantastic had sales of $3.1 million and $9.9 million, respectively. Net profits in those years were $72,000 and $109,000, as shown in Exhibit 1. Although 1980 revenues had increased 213 percent from the prior year, net income rose only 48 percent because of substantially higher costs. Increased rent, advertising, bad debts, and interest costs had caused selling, general, and administrative costs to increase over 250 percent.

Fan sales were seasonal, with over 65 percent of revenues coming between April and September, as shown in Exhibit 2. Sales were made by salespeople working exclusively on commission. Commissions were paid in the same month the sales were made. The company served more than 100 customers, including many small accounts as well as mass-merchandisers and home center stores such as Kmart, J. C. Penney, Zayre, Ace Hardware, Best Products, and 84 Lumber. Two customers, however, had accounted for approximately 40 percent of total sales in 1980.

Salespeople wrote and confirmed the orders with no penalty for cancellation. Customers typically paid between 60 and 90 days after Fantastic shipped the merchandise. Accounts receivable were of good quality, although the bad debts/sales ratio was 2.1 percent in 1980 because of unpaid accounts from some small stores. Balance sheets for the period are shown in Exhibit 3.

The lead time for Fantastic's orders was 60 days—30 days for their suppliers to manufacture the fan parts once the order had been received and 30 days for shipping. Because the manufacturers had limited capacity, they could not supply highly variable quantities on short notice. As a result, Fantastic management had decided to place regular fan component orders, assemble the fans, and hold them in inventory until they were sold.

To finance the parts orders, their suppliers in Taiwan and Hong Kong required that letters of credit (L/C) be issued at the time the merchandise was ordered. A typical L/C was for 30 days, the time required to manufacture the goods and prepare them for shipment. The L/Cs were submitted for payment by the supplier when the merchandise was shipped. Because growth had been rapid, Fantastic did not keep cash available to pay for the goods when the L/C documents arrived at the bank. Thus, the company typically drew a 60-day draft on the bank in the amount of the needed funds. The bank would accept the draft under an arrangement already established with Fantastic and extend the loan for a discounted amount of the draft. All Fantastic's current financing arrangements are summarized in Exhibit 4, along with representative short-term borrowing costs for 1978 to 1980.

The cost of the fans delivered at the Charleston plant had averaged 63 percent of Fantastic's final selling price. This cost varied with exchange rates shown in Exhibit 5. So far about half of the fans had been sourced from Hong

Kong and half from Taiwan. Mr. Rose and Mr. Turner were satisfied with their suppliers and expected the relationships to continue.

The company's warehouse was located near Charleston in a building that had been purchased in July 1979 by a partnership owned by Mr. Rose and Mr. Turner and subsequently leased back to Fantastic. The term of the lease was 15 years, with annual payments of $185,000. The 116,000-square-foot facility was sufficient to support a sales volume of approximately $100 million. Most of the operations were simple; the company used the facility for unloading, inspecting, processing, repacking, and shipping the imported goods. The trickiest part of the operation was weighing and balancing the fan blades.

For the first half of fiscal 1981, sales were $15.8 million and profits $1 million. By year-end, Mr. Rose and Mr. Turner expected sales to reach $30 million. Mr. Rose believed sales for 1982 would be over $71 million. He knew that this represented substantial growth in demand that far outstripped forecasts,[1] but with Fantastic's $40-million order backlog, the forecast seemed reasonable. Furthermore, he believed that a return on sales of 9.8 percent was likely.

Up to now Fantastic had grown more rapidly than had been expected and planning had been lacking. Orders to suppliers had been based on forecasts of sales with a lead time of two months, and Fantastic's creditors had been willing to satisfy the growing company's capital needs on demand. Mr. Rose and Mr. Turner believed that, to continue good relations with these two critical groups, longer range forecasts would be useful. As sales grew, suppliers would have to arrange for ways to produce more, and Fantastic would have increasing needs for funds.

Mr. Rose and Mr. Turner looked at the company's brief history, considered their forecasts for the expected demand for ceiling fans, and decided their first decision would be for how long to forecast. So far demand had grown so rapidly that forecasts for even a few months would be rapidly outdated. On the other hand, some order needed to be brought to their relationships with their parts and capital suppliers. Good forecasts would help.

---

[1]The U.S. Department of Commerce had forecast little growth in retail sales of home appliances through mid-1982 and a slight decline in sales in the second half of that year.

Fantastic Manufacturing, Inc.

EXHIBIT 1
■
Income Statements (in thousands)

	Year Ending		Three Months Ending April 31, 1980	Six Months Ending July 31, 1980
	January 31, 1979	January 31, 1980		
Net revenues	$3,155	$9,860	$6,693	$15,818
Cost of goods sold	2,263	7,306	4,543	10,310
Gross profit	892	2,554	2,150	5,508
Salaries and payroll taxes	252	308		
Commissions	149	487		
Freight	19	62		
Rent	0	128		
Bad debts	24	209		
Interest[a]	78	496		
Other selling, general, and administrative	278	709		
Total operating expenses	800	2,399	1,615	3,428
Income before taxes	92	155	535	2,080
Taxes	19	47	239	998
Net income before extraordinary item	73	108	296	1,082
Extraordinary item (net of income tax credit)	0	0	0	(94)
Net income	$ 73	$ 108	$ 296	$ 988

[a]Includes line-of-credit charges.

Fantastic Manufacturing, Inc.

EXHIBIT 2
■
Monthly Pattern of Sales, 1979 and 1980

	Proportion of Annual Sales
January	2.8%
February	5.9
March	7.8
April	9.8
May	10.8
June	11.2
July	11.7
August	12.7
September	9.8
October	7.8
November	5.8
December	3.9
	100.0%

Fantastic Manufacturing, Inc.

EXHIBIT 3

■

Balance Sheet[a]

	January 31, 1979	January 31, 1980	April 30, 1980	July 31, 1980
Assets				
Cash	$ 3	$ 1	$ 1	$ 1
Accounts receivable	387	2,045	3,898	4,568
Due from affiliates	0	160	70	317
Collateral on letters of credit	97	83	171	249
Inventory	928	2,092	2,761	1,536
Inventory in transit	478	2,690	1,414	1,864
Prepaid expenses	26	78	155	112
Insurance claims receivable	0	0	0	756
Income tax refund receivable	0	0	0	134
Note receivable	0	0	0	53
Total current assets	1,919	7,149	8,470	9,590
Net property and equipment	384	241	402	614
Deposits	0	57	65	61
Total assets	$ 2,303	$ 7,447	$ 8,937	$ 10,265
Liabilities and Shareholders' Equity				
Accounts payable	$ 294	$ 613	$ 774	$ 628
Bank overdraft		312	445	51
Due to banks:				
Receivable financing	252	2,046	2,682	4,493
Inventory financing	1,127	3,531	3,518	1,716
Other	0	100	100	0
Current portion of long-term debt	22	31	44	74
Due to affiliates and shareholders	43	533	719	1,161
Taxes payable	8	23	85	891
Total current liabilities	1,746	7,189	8,367	9,014
Long-term debt	360	36	53	43
Notes payable, shareholders	85	0	0	0
Total liabilities	2,191	7,225	8,420	9,057
Shareholders' equity[b]	1	1	1	1
Retained earnings	111	221	516	1,207
Net worth	112	222	517	1,208
Total liabilities and shareholders' equity	$ 2,303	$ 7,447	$ 8,937	$ 10,265
Net of allowance for doubtful accounts	$23,126	$121,821	$300,000	$336,447

[a]In thousands of dollars.
[b]Common stock, $5 par; authorized, issued, and outstanding, 100 shares.

Fantastic Manufacturing, Inc.

EXHIBIT 4
■

Summary of Financing Arrangements

Lender	Amount	Use	Rate	Collateral
Congress Financial Corp.	Varied	Direct loan on eligible accounts receivable	Prime + 6%	All accounts receivable Personal guarantees Deposits by stockholders
Standard Chartered	$6 million	Letters of credit Banker's acceptances ($4.5 million limit)	Prime + 1½% Banker's acceptances + 2%	All inventory and personal guarantees Deposits by stockholders Partial guarantee by Congress Financial 10% deposit on L/Cs
Capital Bank	$1 million	Letters of credit	Prime + 1½%	Unsecured

Recent Prime and Banker's Acceptance Rates

Year/ Quarter	Average Prime Rate	Banker's Acceptance, Annual Average Rate (90 days)
1978		
1	8.0%	6.8%
2	8.5	7.3
3	9.5	8.2
4	10.5	10.1
1979		
1	11.0	10.1
2	11.5	9.9
3	12.6	10.1
4	14.9	13.4
1980		
1	17.6	14.9
2	16.0	11.8
3	11.8	9.9

Fantastic Manufacturing, Inc.

EXHIBIT 5
■
Recent Exchange Rates

Hong Kong Dollars (HK$)
per U.S. Dollar (US$)

March 31, 1978	4.6202	February 6, 1980	4.8616
June 30	4.6505	February 13	4.8668
July 31	4.6396	February 20	4.9221
August 30	4.7102	February 27	4.9421
December 29	4.7869	March 26	5.0751
March 30, 1979	4.9927	March 30	4.9059
June 29	5.0690	May 28	4.8898
July 26	5.1814	June 9	4.9179
September 28	4.9784	June 30	4.9300
October 17	4.9468	July 30	4.9564
December 31	4.9516	August 27	4.9481
January 30, 1980	4.8011	September 29	4.9916

New Taiwan Dollars (NT$)
per U.S. Dollar (US$)[a]

June 18, 1980	36.1312	September 3, 1980	35.8680
July 2	35.9703	September 17	36.0711
July 16	36.0590	October 1	35.9891
July 30	35.5765	October 8	36.0685
August 6	35.5158	October 13	36.0000

[a]In July 1978, the NT$ was allowed to float around its fixed exchange rate of NT$38 = US$1.

Source: National Westminster Bank.

Polymold Division

The Polymold Division of Congeries Corporation was planning to purchase a computerized manufacturing and designing system known as "CAD/CAM" in January 1984. In September 1983, the manager of the Polymold Division, Joel Martin, curious to know how the CAD/CAM investment would affect Polymold's financial condition, was preparing to forecast the division's financial statements for the following five years.

THE COMPANY

Congeries Corporation was a conglomerate, divisions of which manufactured a wide variety of low- and medium-technology products ranging from small construction parts such as hinges and doorknobs to plastic injection molds. As shown in Exhibit 1, Congeries had been affected by the recent recession; in 1982 the firm lost over $1 million after posting a net income of $8.3 million in 1981. Given a $5-million loss in the first quarter, corporate management was not yet sure whether 1983 would be a profitable year.

Congeries' Polymold Division was one of the largest manufacturers of precision injection molds in the country. Exhibit 2 presents the division's financial statements from 1976 through 1982. Earnings and return on assets ranged from a high of $1.5 million and 29.9 percent, respectively, in 1980 to $679,000 and 13.2 percent in 1982. This precipitous decline was, as far as management could tell, simply the effect of the business cycle. Mr. Martin believed, however, that sales would continue to decline: if Polymold did not invest in the new computer-aided designing and manufacturing system, it would lose market share on its remaining products to its more technologically advanced competitors.

THE MARKET

The basis of Mr. Martin's fear was a change in the marketplace. Polymold manufactured high-quality precision molds with interchangeable parts. The company's larger clients produced all sorts of small plastic items, such as plastic

This case was prepared as a basis for class discussion rather than to illustrate either effective or ineffective handling of an administrative situation. Copyright © 1985 by the Darden Graduate Business School Sponsors, University of Virginia, Charlottesville, Virginia.

bottles and caps, razor handles, various computer parts, and cosmetic, camera, video, and cassette cases. More customers' needs were met with multi-cavity molds (molds with more than four cavities) or single-complex molds (molds with four or fewer cavities that were more difficult to design and manufacture). Multi-molds (several molds of a single type) were also common; there was one remaining category, single-simple molds.

Polymold's 1983 sales by mold type were expected to be as follows:

Multi-mold	$ 2.5 million
Multi-cavity	2.5
Single–complex	2.8
Single–simple	1.0
Repairs and spares	2.0
Total sales	$10.8 million

This $10.8 million represented a 5.1 percent market share. Mr. Martin was worried about Polymold's ability to retain this share for several reasons:

1. The injection-mold manufacturing industry was highly segmented and regional, but it was believed that the greater the degree of manufacturing precision a company could attain, the more national its potential market was.

2. Some of Polymold's large competitors already had highly computerized operations that made them more efficient than Polymold.

3. Others had become vertically integrated to provide customers not only the molds, but also large presses and peripheral equipment. This integration was attractive to customers, because they could purchase more of their equipment from one source, sometimes as packages. The integrated firms had already lured customers away from small competitors.

4. Still other mold manufacturers were being bought out by large plastics companies and turned into exclusively in-house suppliers.

5. Several new competitor mold shops had been established by former Polymold employees, who knew the company's organization and clients.

Mr. Martin deduced from a variety of economic projections (shown in Exhibit 3) and his knowledge of the industry that the market for injection molds would grow from a total of $210 million in 1983 to $278 million by 1987. Demand and growth were expected to be greatest for multi-cavity and single–complex molds. Exhibit 4 breaks down forecasts for total demand by type of end-user. The packaging industry, with its demand for bottles and caps, was expected to continue as the largest customer, although it required less precise molding capabilities than Polymold provided. It was followed by the commercial products, home entertainment, consumer products, and medical products industries.

Polymold already had a strong presence in the consumer and home entertainment segments, as shown in Exhibit 5, and Mr. Martin had been discussing new marketing efforts to attract more buyers from the commercial and medical markets. The commercial products segment, made up of the data storage, computer, office products, and telecommunications industries, was expected to grow 70 percent over the next six years.

Polymold's business by industry segment in 1983 was expected to break down as follows:

Segment	Polymold Sales
Consumer	$ 3.7 million
Medical	0.8
Commercial	3.8
Home entertainment	1.5
Packaging	0.3
Miscellaneous	0.7
Total sales	$10.8 million

The consumer products segment had dominated Polymold's sales for the previous 15 years, for 5 years in conjunction with the commercial products segment. These two markets continued to be the most important, but Mr. Martin expected the medical and home entertainment sectors to grow.

Polymold's customers consisted of a small number of large nationally and internationally known firms. This dependency contributed to the cyclical nature of the demand for the company's products. Should even a small number of firms demand fewer molds, Polymold's sales would greatly diminish.

Despite the new marketing plans, without the use of the computer design and manufacturing, Mr. Martin considered a further loss of market share in all segments to be likely. He had supplemented his own judgment with data from a consultant's study,[1] which pointed out, as shown in Exhibits 6 through 11, that even though Polymold's market share had increased during the recessionary period of declining sales, the company was not keeping pace with its closest competitors. Furthermore, although Polymold's productivity remained higher than that of similar companies and the company was becoming increasingly capital intensive, real productivity per employee was stagnant. The study also indicated that the quality of Polymold's products, although high, was slipping dramatically when compared with its closest competitors'.

MANUFACTURING TECHNOLOGY

During the 1970s, most of Polymold's major competitors upgraded their production processes by installing numerically controlled (NC) machines. Numerically controlled equipment had been available for about 20 years, but had basically been ignored by the industry until the machines had become computerized and until the demand levels and the needs of plastics manufacturers justified the investment. Computerized NC machines, which referred to machines that were both computerized and numerically controlled, raised the capital intensity of

---

[1]The consultants carried out a PIMS, or Profit Impact of Marketing Strategy, study. PIMS was a service of the Strategic Planning Institute, Cambridge, Massachusetts, which combined a company's answers to a strategy–and–marketing questionnaire with a data base outlining the characteristics and experiences of a large sample of other companies. The resulting data were used to derive a complete report on the potential impact of a strategic move.

the manufacturing process and permitted greater precision and efficiency than previously possible. The equipment carried out many functions by itself, so that less staff was required and errors were minimized.

The CAD/CAM system was the industry's latest technological advance. With the aid of CAD/CAM, injection molds could be designed and drawn on the computer rather than at the drafting table, the flow and cooling of the plastic in the mold could be analyzed, and the mold-manufacturing NC equipment could be controlled. In addition, CAD/CAM could be used to inspect the machined parts, to order materials, and to estimate the costs of production more accurately than previously possible. Using the system in both design and manufacture almost eliminated human error.

Mr. Martin saw CAD/CAM first as a time-saver, because it could remove design errors. Furthermore, the system would enhance the company's ability to expand its product line into rubber and powdered metal molds, which demanded more precision than plastics. Perhaps most importantly, because many customers designed their own molds, CAD/CAM could improve communications between the designer and the builder, especially if the customer also owned the system for its own design purposes. If both companies used CAD/CAM, designs and ideas could be readily transferred. The firms with CAD/CAM clearly would control the precision mold market.

In 1981, recognizing that it had begun to fall behind its competition technologically, Polymold had invested in two pieces of NC equipment and two programmable inspection stations. Recently the division had also leased a small, single-station CAD/CAM unit with limited computing power, so that it could assess the equipment's benefits, train operators, and determine whether to purchase a full, four-station CAD/CAM system.

FINANCIAL ANALYSIS

To determine the effect of CAD/CAM, Mr. Martin projected the financial positions of the division with and without the device. Specifically, he wanted to project the financial condition of the division through 1988, first assuming the CAD/CAM was not purchased, and then assuming it was purchased in January 1984 for $750,000 ($190,000 of which was the price of the software). Mr. Martin also considered the possibility of leasing the full CAD/CAM system at an average cost of $184,000 per year for five years. Regardless of whether CAD/CAM was leased or purchased, other capital investments would have to be made in the future. All would be depreciated using ACRS depreciation guidelines over five years. In addition, except for depreciation, Polymold would bear all the expenses for the CAD/CAM operation whether leased or purchased. He used the economic and market projections given in Exhibit 3 as the basis for his forecasts.

Without CAD/CAM.   With the division's marketing strategy, but without CAD/CAM, Mr. Martin projected a slow decrease in Polymold's market share from 5.1 percent of the total in 1983 to 4.2 percent in 1988.

Total cost of goods sold (COGS) was expected to be about 73 percent of sales in 1983, rising by slightly more than four percentage points by 1988. The 4-percent increase would come from a combination of factors affecting the various components of the cost of goods sold: labor, 34 percent of sales in 1982, was expected to rise slowly to 37 percent or more; raw materials were also expected to rise from their current level of 11 percent to 13.5 percent; plant administration, a component of cost of goods sold that currently consumed 2.4 percent of sales, would double by 1988, largely because of its labor component; overhead, the second largest COGS expense, was expected to decline slightly; the costs of electricity, heat, water, and maintenance were expected to change little, since no new plants would be added and there would be no major change in operations without the addition of CAD/CAM. Polymold's accountants noted that they had not included in their COGS forecasts the savings expected from a special cost-reduction program recently instituted by management. For 1983 the savings were expected to be only $37,000, but they would rise rapidly to $210,000 in 1984 reaching $391,000 by 1988.

Mr. Martin believed that the salespeople would have a hard job trying to maintain Polymold's decreasing market share without CAD/CAM. That factor, coupled with increases in other general and administrative expenses, would increase selling, general, and administrative costs by an average of two percentage points to 12.5 percent by 1988. This figure did not include research and engineering, usually buried in that category, which would stay at about $130,000 per year.

Depreciation, capital expenditures, and interest expense were expected to be as shown in Exhibit 12, which also shows tax credits that Polymold currently had available. Because Polymold was a division, it also paid a corporate expense assessment that rose each year. The amount would be the same regardless of whether CAD/CAM was purchased or not. The corporate accountants had told Mr. Martin that in 1983 this expense would be $168,000; in 1984, $176,000; and in 1985, $185,000. It had not yet been projected beyond 1985.

Even with the drop in market share, Polymold would need more working capital. Although that need had declined in the recent past, Mr. Martin believed that small increases each year would create a total increase in net working capital of $125,000 by 1988. For convenience Mr. Martin always used a 50-percent tax rate for his projections.

With CAD/CAM.   With the new system, Mr. Martin projected an increase in Polymold's market share from 5.1 percent in 1983 to 7.3 percent in 1988, although he believed that by 1988 the division's market share could be as little as 6.3 percent or as much as 7.7 percent.

Mr. Martin estimated that, once CAD/CAM was in full operation, overall cost of goods sold would remain at about 72 percent of sales even though materials costs would increase from 11 to 13.5 percent of sales. Cost of goods sold would be affected by the same forces with or without CAD/CAM, with overhead providing a compensating decline. However, overhead and labor were hard to forecast for a new process; the overhead forecast could be off by as much as 10 percent, and labor could be 5 percentage points higher than forecast.

In dollars, plant administration would be the same with or without CAD/CAM, but the savings from the new cost-efficiency program were expected to increase to $445,000 in 1984 and $802,000 by 1988. However, Polymold's accountants were less certain in making these savings forecasts than those for savings without CAD/CAM. They had given Mr. Martin a range, as shown in Exhibit 13, and had suggested that an outbreak of inflation like that recently experienced could wipe out about half of any savings.

Mr. Martin expected research and development costs with CAD/CAM to be double what they would have been without CAD/CAM; the system, when in place, would simply require more development and engineering time. While selling this new process would initially require considerable new effort, selling, general, and administrative expenses were expected to decline relative to sales, by 1988 declining to as much as two percentage points below the level expected without CAD/CAM. Mr. Martin had been reminded by the accountants that, if sales were lower than forecast, selling, general, and administrative costs would not decline as much, and could reach a level three percentage points higher than originally forecast.

The forecast predicted that working capital would certainly decrease with the acquisition of CAD/CAM. In 1984, if things went as expected, working capital would drop by $317,000. By 1988, working capital would be no higher than 12.8 percent of sales. The precise figure would depend on sales: if sales were lower than forecast, Mr. Martin believed that both inventory and accounts receivable would be higher, and working capital would probably be at a level equal to the current level. If sales were better than expected, however, inventory would move faster and accounts receivable would be lower, because Polymold could concentrate on the faster-paying accounts.

The purchase of the new system would require further capital expenditures as old processes and machines were updated to complement it. Forecasts for capital expenditures (including CAD/CAM), interest, and depreciation are shown in Exhibit 12.

On Polymold's books, CAD/CAM would be depreciated over a 5-year period on a straight-line basis. The ACRS depreciation schedule would be used for tax purposes (at 15 percent the first year, 22 percent the second, and 21 percent each of the following three years). In addition to full depreciation, an 8-percent investment tax credit was available for this investment. No terminal value was expected, because changes in technology could rapidly make the equipment obsolete.

Mr. Martin planned to calculate the division's cost of capital, basing his estimate of the company's systematic risk, beta, on that of similar companies, which, along with industry financial information, are given in Exhibit 14. He believed that Polymold's capital structure would have reflected the industry average if the division had been a public company. The division's investment base was projected to be $4.06 million in 1983.

EXHIBIT 1

■

Congeries Corporation Consolidated Financial Statements
(in thousands, except per share data)

Balance Sheet

	1982
Assets	
Cash	$ 3,945
Securities	2,649
Receivables	46,808
Inventories	39,706
Other current assets	10,649
Total current assets	103,757
Property, plant, and equipment	59,805
Other assets	18,546
Total assets	$182,108
Liabilities and Shareholders' Equity	
Current portion of long-term debt	$ 2,960
Accounts payable	23,533
Other current liabilities	1,298
Total current liabilities	27,791
Long–term debt	42,574
Other liabilities	6,418
Total liabilities	76,783
Preferred stock	8,169
Common stock	13,430
Additional paid-in capital	18,249
Retained earnings	88,461
Translation adjustment	(4,689)
Less treasury stock	(18,295)
Stockholders' equity	105,325
Liabilities and shareholders' equity	$182,108

Income Statements

	1979	1980	1981	1982
Net sales	$280,148	$274,737	$281,886	$247,502
Operating income	34,268	28,753	29,814	12,880
Corporate expense	8,850	5,711	6,472	7,489
Interest expense	3,097	3,323	779	2,237
Earnings before taxes	22,321	19,719	22,563	3,154
Earnings of foreign affiliates	739	896	1,043	897
Provision for income tax	(9,995)	(8,642)	(9,811)	(913)
After-tax earnings	13,065	11,973	13,795	3,138
After-tax loss, discontinued operations	(658)	(1,876)	(5,457)	(4,196)
Net after-tax earnings	$ 12,407	$ 10,097	$ 8,338	$ (1,058)
Earnings per share, common	$4.55	$3.51	$2.77	($0.89)

Polymold Division

EXHIBIT 2
■

Financial Statements (in thousands)

| | For the Years Ended December 31 | | | |
	1979	1980	1981	1982
Income Statement				
Net sales	$11,697	$13,280	$11,494	$10,763
Cost of products sold	7,838	9,064	7,805	7,713
Selling, general, and administrative	837	990	1,214	1,287
Depreciation	264	311	365	415
Other expense	0	0	0	37
Total costs and expenses	8,939	10,365	9,384	9,452
Pretax earnings	2,758	2,915	2,110	1,311
Tax	1,379	1,457	1,038	632
Net earnings	$ 1,379	$ 1,458	$ 1,072	$ 679
Proceeds to parent	$ 1,252	$ 2,539	$ 655	$ 790
Balance Sheet				
Receivables, net	$ 3,630	$ 2,660	$ 2,804	$ 2,306
Inventories, net	235	97	130	110
Prepaid expenses	95	89	64	53
Total current assets	3,960	2,846	2,998	2,469
Fixed assets	4,206	4,225	4,918	5,433
Less accumulated depreciation	(2,058)	(2,189)	(2,379)	(2,750)
Fixed assets, net	2,148	2,036	2,539	2,683
Total assets	6,108	4,882	5,537	5,152
Accounts payable	219	194	186	64
Other current liabilities	635	515	761	609
Total current liabilities	854	709	947	673
Net worth	5,254	4,173	4,590	4,479
Total liabilities and net worth	$ 6,108	$ 4,882	$ 5,537	$ 5,152

EXHIBIT 3

■

Economic Trends and Polymold Sales Projections with CAD/CAM

	1980	1981	1982	1983	1984	1985	1986	1987	Average Growth Rate 1984–1987
						Forecast			
U.S. GNP nominal (billions of dollars)	$2,633	$2,937	$3,059	$3,283	$3,605	$3,992	$4,430	$4,889	10.5%
U.S. GNP (billions of 1980 dollars)	$2,633	$2,691	$2,645	$2,713	$2,813	$2,948	$3,080	$3,187	4.1
Inflation rate	13.5%	10.4%	6.1%	3.2%	6.1%	5.9%	6.5%	6.9%	N.Ap.
Correction factor for inflation	1.0	0.906	0.854	0.813	0.775	0.737	0.699	0.664	N.Ap.
Index for rubber and plastic products (1980 = 100)	100.0	107.0	99.5	106.6	114.8	123.8	168.0	141.8	8.9
Index for fabricated metal products (1980 = 100)	100.0	101.7	85.6	93.2	102.9	114.1	122.3	129.8	8.6
Injection mold market (millions of current dollars)	N.Av.	N.Av.	N.Av.	$210.0	$229.0	$253.9	$267.0	$278.0	7.3
Polymold actual and forecast sales with CAD/CAM (millions of dollars)	$13.3	$11.5	$10.8	$10.8	$12.8	$15.8	$17.4	$19.1	15.5
Polymold actual and forecast sales with CAD/CAM (millions of 1980 dollars)	$13.3	$10.4	$9.2	$8.8	$9.9	$11.7	$12.2	$12.6	9.6

N.Av. = not available; N.Ap. = not applicable.

Polymold Division

EXHIBIT 4
■

Forecasted End-User Injection Mold Market
(in millions)

	1983	1984	1985	1986	1987	1988
Consumer	$ 20	$ 25	$ 28	$ 30	$ 31	$ 30
Medical/pharmaceutical	23	26	28	29	29	29
Commercial	25	28	32	35	37	37
Home entertainment	26	26	28	30	33	34
Packaging	44	46	50	52	54	55
Miscellaneous	23	25	29	31	32	32
Subtotal	161	176	195	207	216	217
All single–simple mold products	49	53	58	60	62	63
Total	$210	$229	$253	$267	$278	$280

Polymold Division

EXHIBIT 5
■

Involvement in Polymold's Markets by Competitors A–D

	Heavy	Medium	Light	No Involvement
Consumer products	Polymold C	A	D B	
Medical/pharmaceutical products		D	Polymold C A B	
Commercial products		Polymold	A B C	D
Home entertainment products	Polymold A C		B	D
Packaging	B A	Polymold	D C	
Interdivisional sales	B A		Polymold	D C
Miscellaneous	D	Polymold C	B	A

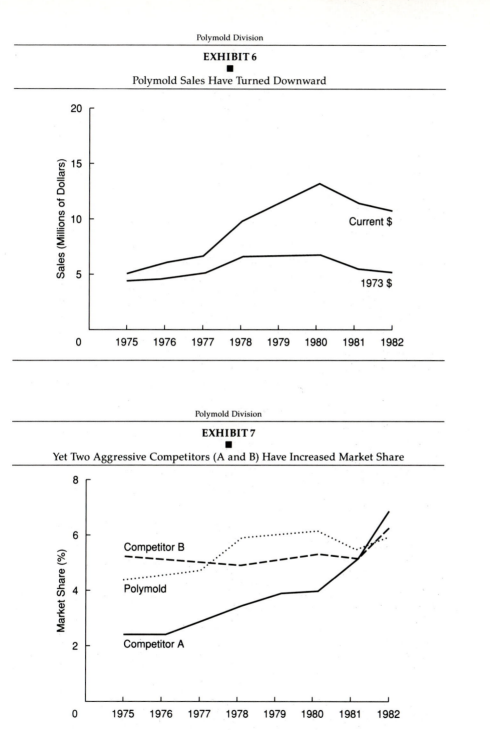

Polymold Division

EXHIBIT 6

■

Polymold Sales Have Turned Downward

Polymold Division

EXHIBIT 7

■

Yet Two Aggressive Competitors (A and B) Have Increased Market Share

Polymold Division

EXHIBIT 8

■

Productivity Has Been Consistently Better Than Expected

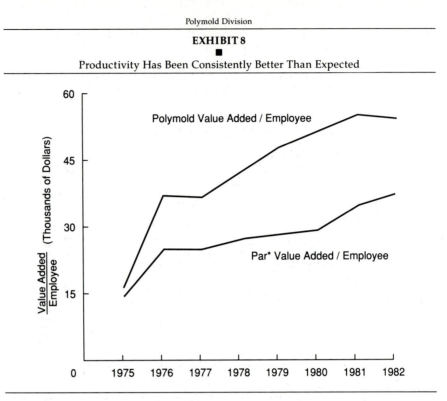

* Par indicates universe of competitors.

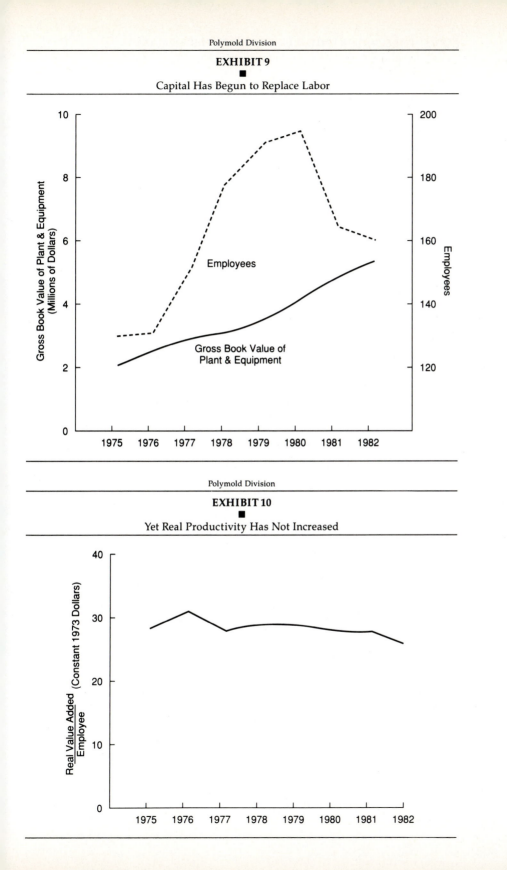

EXHIBIT 9

■

Capital Has Begun to Replace Labor

Employees

Gross Book Value of
Plant & Equipment

EXHIBIT 10

■

Yet Real Productivity Has Not Increased

Polymold Division

EXHIBIT 11
■

Polymold ROI, Relative Product Quality, and Productivity

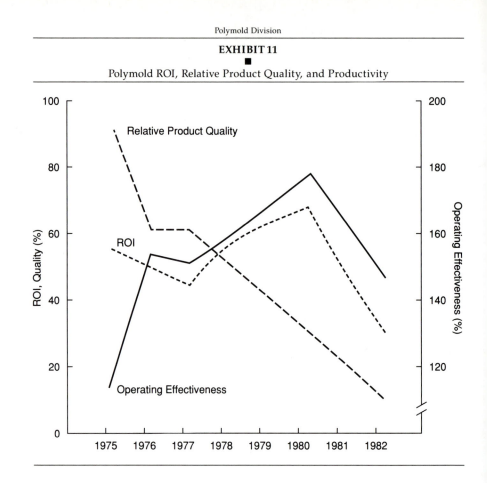

Polymold Division

EXHIBIT 12
■

Depreciation, Interest, and Capital Expenditure Forecasts
without and with CAD/CAM
(in thousands)

	1983	1984	1985	1986	1987	1988
Without CAD/CAM						
Depreciation	$420	$ 416	$436	$449	$446	$465
Interest expense	144	136	129	112	112	101
Capital expenditures	287	458	534	362	381	541
Tax credits	38	81	117	124	146	155
With CAD/CAM						
Depreciation	420	509	622	671	714	764
Interest expense	144	136	129	112	112	101
Capital expenditures	287	1,106	831	652	870	954
Tax credits	38	141	148	164	224	250

Polymold Division

EXHIBIT 13
■
Efficiency-Program Savings Estimates with CAD/CAM

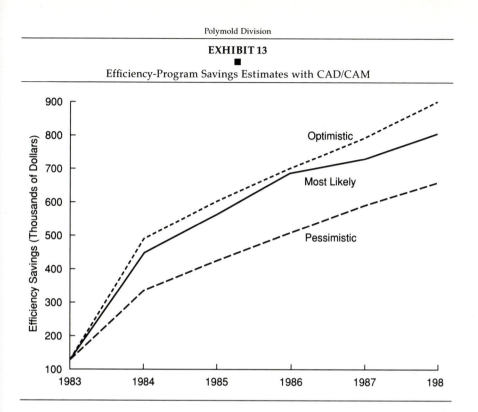

Polymold Division

EXHIBIT 14
■

Tooling Industry Financial Information
(dollars in millions)

Company	Sales 1981	Sales 1982	Net Income/Sales 1981	Net Income/Sales 1982	Return on Assets 1981	Return on Assets 1982	Return on Equity 1981	Return on Equity 1982
Acme–Cleveland	$ 400.7	$ 327.0	2.7%	3.6%	4.8%	4.6%	9.0%	9.3%
Brown & Sharpe	205.4	143.8	2.9	−0.1	0.3	−7.0	6.8	−18.0
Cincinnati Milacron	934.4	759.7	6.5	1.6	8.7	3.5	17.4	6.7
Ex-Cell-O	1,124.6	1,027.1	5.1	4.7	8.1	7.6	13.8	13.3
Gleason Works	239.9	179.7	3.7	−0.1	4.9	5.2	8.0	−9.6
Monarch Machine	140.1	95.2	13.6	7.3	21.3	7.6	27.1	9.5
Norton	1,334.6	1,264.1	7.1	1.5	9.4	3.6	17.5	6.7
Snap-on Tools	441.5	430.5	9.1	8.7	11.8	11.9	18.8	16.0
Stanley Works	1,009.5	962.8	5.5	3.9	8.3	5.9	14.4	9.6
Starrett	122.5	112.7	11.3	10.0	14.1	11.9	19.1	14.6
Vermont American	203.9	181.9	6.2	3.6	8.6	4.5	15.8	7.8

[a]As of September 1983.
N.Av. = not available.
N.Ap. = not applicable.
Sources: *Value Line Investment Survey* and Standard & Poor's *Bond Guide.*

Debt/Total Assets		Working Capital/Sales		Market/Book Value		Price/Earnings Ratio		S&P Debt Rating[a]	Beta[a]
1981	1982	1981	1982	1981	1982	1981	1982		
23.4	14.3	24.4	22.8	0.78	0.66	10.5	7.8	N.Av.	0.90
25.0	23.5	36.4	38.5	0.65	0.54	12.1	N.Ap.	N.Av.	0.95
15.0	13.6	28.6	30.1	1.70	1.75	12.3	24.6	N.Av.	1.10
8.6	6.8	21.8	24.5	0.82	0.89	7.4	6.2	N.Av.	1.10
10.7	17.8	18.3	23.6	0.55	0.58	9.3	N.Ap.	N.Av.	1.05
0.0	0.0	38.4	54.4	1.01	0.96	4.1	9.1	N.Av.	1.05
17.7	18.2	26.1	23.6	1.31	0.99	8.5	14.9	A	0.95
8.1	8.0	37.2	43.1	2.00	2.35	11.2	12.1	N.Av.	1.00
12.8	14.1	24.6	25.0	1.21	1.69	8.6	12.4	A+	0.95
0.0	0.0	45.0	52.0	1.38	1.34	6.7	8.3	N.Av.	0.70
23.2	21.7	26.7	32.4	1.46	1.08	7.1	11.0	N.Av.	0.80

Mushrooms Division (A)

INTRODUCTION

Dick Burrell, Vice President—Finance of R. G. Barry Corporation, looked at the memo he had received that morning from Barry's president, Gordon Zacks, asking for revised projections reflecting the new plan for the Mushrooms line. The day before at the executive committee meeting Mr. Burrell, Mr. Zacks, and the other committee members had been presented with test-market results for their new Mushrooms brand of women's shoes. Barry had recently changed its marketing strategy for Mushrooms in several markets to emphasize saturation television advertising. The television campaigns had been more successful than expected, and revised sales estimates (shown in Exhibit 1), called for doubling 1978 sales from the previous plan. The marketing manager of Mushrooms and his staff were quite confident the new strategy would succeed. The Mushrooms division manager supported the proposed changes.

Before actually accepting the new strategy, Mr. Zacks wanted to look at revised, detailed financial forecasts for the division. He had asked Mr. Burrell to make forecasts for Mushrooms.

THE FOOTWEAR INDUSTRY

R. G. Barry was a producer of comfort footwear products, including slippers, sandals, moccasins, and after-ski boots. The company was a part of the $11.6 billion (1976 retail sales) footwear business in the United States. Although sales of the major footwear manufacturers had grown steadily over the years, profits were cyclical, as shown in Table 1.

The variation in profitability of footwear manufacturers was caused in part by the industry's basic cost structure. The major factor was the price of leather hides, the industry's principal raw material. Hide prices fluctuated widely, depending primarily upon the rate of domestic cattle slaughter. Since leather typically accounted for approximately 40 percent of the industry's production costs, price changes caused significant changes in profit. In addition, the industry was labor-intensive, and footwear manufacturers found it difficult at times to pass on their full labor cost increases to consumers.

This case was prepared as a basis for class discussion rather than to illustrate either effective or ineffective handling of an administrative situation. Copyright © 1980 by the Darden Graduate Business School Sponsors, University of Virginia, Charlottesville, Virginia.

TABLE 1
■

Sales and Profits of Major Footwear Manufacturers
(millions of dollars)

	1968	1969	1970	1971	1972	1973	1974	1975	1976
Sales	$2,381	$2,263	$2,908	$3,224	$3,724	$4,149	$4,509	$5,052	$5,975
Net income	97.1	98.0	106.9	115.6	132.2	97.8	142.8	187.6	250.1
Net income/sales	4.1%	4.3%	3.7%	3.6%	3.6%	2.4%	3.2%	3.7%	4.2%

The industry was fashion-oriented, and the vagaries of such business heightened profit variability. Individual manufacturers experienced significant inventory markdowns when they failed correctly to anticipate changing fashion trends.

In the late 1960s, changes had begun to occur in the domestic footwear industry. Several of the leading manufacturers, in order to offset the effects of the footwear industry's cyclicality, had begun to integrate vertically into footwear retailing and to diversify into nonfootwear businesses.

Still, by the early 1970s, the industry's domestic cost structure had put it at a competitive disadvantage to foreign manufacturers. Imported footwear products had increased their share of the U.S. market from less than 25 percent of unit sales to over 45 percent. The principal beneficiaries of increased import sales were manufacturers in Taiwan, South Korea, and Spain, all lower labor–cost producers. Some of the pressure had been reduced in mid-1977, when Taiwan and South Korea signed an orderly marketing agreement to limit their exports of footwear to the United States for the four years ending June 30, 1981. This agreement was coupled with a U.S.-government program designed to increase the mechanization of domestic manufacturers. It was expected that the import-limitation agreement would principally aid domestic manufacturers of low- and moderately priced footwear, that segment previously supplied by Taiwanese and South Korean manufacturers.

By 1976 domestic production and distribution were fragmented and highly competitive. The largest domestic footwear manufacturers were:

	Total Company Sales, 1976 (in millions)	Major Brands
Interco	$1,500	Florsheim
Melville	1,200	Thom McAn
Brown Group	843	Buster Brown
U.S. Shoe	607	Red Cross, Joyce, Pappagallo, and Cobbies

In addition to these manufacturers and foreign imports, there were many other smaller domestic producers of specialty footwear products. Barry was classified in this diverse group.

Barry's principal competition for its primary product, washable slippers, came from unbranded merchandise produced by a number of different manufacturers. In addition to competition from unbranded products, Daniel Green, Inc., a small, publicly held corporation with 1975 sales of $10.4 million, marketed a high-priced line of branded slippers sold primarily in shoe departments of better department stores.

R. G. BARRY CORPORATION

R. G. Barry Corporation was established in 1945. The company's first product was Shold-a-Shams, removable shoulder pads used to achieve the square–shouldered look in women's fashions. In 1947 Barry introduced Angel Treads, its first line of foam-soled slippers. During the next two decades Barry added other brands to its line of soft, washable slippers (Dear Foams, Snug Treds, Pim Poms) and began to produce terry cloth bath wraps and to manufacture pillows from the slipper operation's scrap.

Until the mid-1960s, Barry management had sought opportunities in whatever businesses seemed to have some profit potential. As a result, Barry's 1966 sales of $12.7 million came from an odd collection of profitable and unprofitable products sold in diverse markets. In the late 1960s, after an evaluation of the business, management redefined the firm's primary objective: to be a leader in every market served or entered. Strategically, Barry would innovate in the design, manufacture, and marketing of leisure footwear, selling most of its products under its own brand names. As a result of this new strategy, management wanted to identify niches in the footwear market neither served by larger manufacturers nor especially attractive to them.

Barry management began to implement this new long-range strategy with a series of acquisitions and divestitures. The pillow business, a user of scrap, was sold, and bath-wrap manufacture was suspended. The space used by those operations was easily converted for use by the still-growing slipper business. Employees were transferred to the other operations with little disturbance, and most continued to work at similar jobs at the same location. This employee reassignment procedure was important to Barry management, which was very concerned with employee satisfaction. An operation would not be sold or suspended without a great deal of thought if such a move involved firing or laying off workers.

R. G. Barry acquired the leading producer of lingerie-matched glamour slippers, Madye's Inc., in 1967. Additional acquisitions to implement the new strategy included Bernardo sandals, a maker of women's high-fashion sandals, in 1969, and Quoddy, a producer of moccasins and outdoor footwear, in 1971. As distribution channels for these products were more fully developed, Barry added manufacturing capacity for its increasing sales. By 1976, Barry sales had grown to $58 million. Profits had grown at a rate of greater than 10 percent for the 10 years ending in 1976.

MUSHROOMS DIVISION

In the early 1970s, Gordon Zacks had identified another segment of the footwear market he believed was not being adequately served by larger manufacturers. This market segment was defined as women who valued foot comfort above style, and Mushrooms were designed for their needs. Mr. Zacks believed the key to producing a really comfortable shoe was creating a soft, flexible sole. Barry staff, as well as outside consultants, had looked at materials already in use by other manufacturers and had rejected them. The materials were too heavy to provide real comfort, so inflexible that they restricted walking, or too quickly worn out. A new product was needed.

Barry management looked at a variety of different materials and processes with which to create a new sole. Eventually, polyurethane was chosen because it produced a light, soft, and flexible sole while still providing the desired durability. The sole was finally developed by an outside subcontractor, and in 1974 Barry purchased its first 100,000 pairs of polyurethane soles.

In addition to creating the sole, Barry designed the complete shoe to be comfortable yet fashionable. Low- and high-heeled sandals, clogs, and closed shoes were designed for both the spring and fall seasons. In creating the uppers, management had encouraged designers to avoid using leather and to concentrate on designs that might stay in the line for several years rather than being faddish, single-year products. The uppers were attached to the soles by a subcontractor. The first shoes were sold in test markets to selected department-store accounts under the Mushrooms brand name.

Product design and test marketing continued through 1974 and 1975, and the number of Mushrooms test-market areas was gradually increased. During this time, the subcontractor that had developed and supplied the Mushrooms sole discontinued its plastics operations. Since the proprietary sole was Mushrooms' principal product advantage, Barry decided to purchase the subcontractor's sole-making equipment and produce the soles itself. The machinery was installed in a small, unused portion of one of the Barry slipper plants. Production and attachment of the uppers was still to be subcontracted.

Sales of the Mushrooms brand in 1976 were $2.38 million.

MARKET TEST

Since Barry did not offer a full line of women's shoes, and because its slipper lines were sold primarily in the notions and hosiery departments of department stores, Barry had experienced some difficulty in securing the desired distribution outlets in large department-store shoe departments. Barry's advertising agency therefore suggested a saturation campaign, and in late 1976, Barry decided to evaluate the effect that television advertising would have on Mushrooms sales. In part, the television campaign was intended to create product demand among consumers so the shoe-department buyers would be encouraged to stock Mushrooms. Barry decided to test the new campaign in two markets, Denver and Miami.

The results of the two advertising campaigns were better than had been expected. The results supported the advertising agency's conclusion that Mushrooms could achieve a 6- to 8-percent share of the market for moderately priced women's footwear during the first year of an intensive advertising campaign since no one had a product to compete with Mushrooms. Based upon these test-market results, the revised sales estimates appearing in Exhibit 1 had been prepared. These estimates reflected both the larger sales from increased advertising and market-share growth over time.

At the same time the advertising campaigns were underway and the results were being evaluated, Barry management had changed the way Mushrooms were produced. Barry had subcontracted production during the product-development stage to avoid brick–and–mortar investments. Problems with subcontractors, coupled with the change in expected demand confirmed by the test-market results, encouraged management to assume total responsibility for manufacturing the shoe. This move would ensure both product quality and availability. One additional change was made: the line was expanded to include Mushrooms with leather uppers.

Although present capacity was adequate for current needs, Barry's sole-manufacturing capabilities would not service the anticipated demand. The company would need an additional sole-manufacturing plant and a shoe-assembly plant. By mid-1977, management was investigating possible plant sites and anticipated securing, equipping, and renovating two separate facilities. The estimated cost of the plants was $2.5 million. The two plants were to be leased or purchased using industrial revenue bonds issued by the county where they would be located. The facilities would be depreciated over approximately 20 years on a straight–line basis.

PROJECTIONS

Working with his staff, as well as with people from the Mushrooms marketing and operations group, Mr. Burrell had revised estimated operating costs and profits. Cost of goods sold were expected to be 63 percent of gross sales in 1977. As Barry's own production facilities began operations in 1978, cost of goods sold was expected to decline, perhaps to 58 percent. The Mushrooms product line was expected to have larger sales adjustments and inventory markdowns than other Barry product lines. The adjustment for defective Mushrooms was expected to exceed 10 percent of sales in 1977 and 7½ percent thereafter.

Because Mushrooms were sold to different department-store buyers than other Barry products, a separate sales force was needed. That cost, coupled with the cost of the saturation television advertising campaigns, meant that projected selling expenses would be high—19 percent of 1977 gross sales and 15 percent from then on. General and administrative expenses would decline from 15 percent of gross sales the first year to the company average of 10 percent. All these figures were estimates based on the company's past experience in its other businesses.

Sales would follow the pattern shown in Exhibit 2, and accounts receivable balances were expected to fluctuate as a function of sales. On average, management expected that sales outstanding in accounts receivable would exceed the net-30 credit terms by 30 days. Accounts payable and accruals, current liabilities, would be about 20 days of average annual sales.[1] Barry's work in progress usually averaged 25 days of average annual sales, and the Mushrooms experience was not expected to be very different. Finished goods inventory would, of course, rise and fall during the year because of the level production schedule, a feature of Barry's strong commitment to steady employment for its workers. Once Barry's production facilities began operation in 1978, year-end finished goods inventory was expected to be about 82 days of average annual sales, up from the 40 days of average annual sales projected for December 1977.

---

[1]Barry management used average annual sales in forecasting many of their current asset and liability accounts, even though the business was seasonal.

In addition to the Mushrooms sales and profit projections, Mr. Burrell had made forecasts for funds needs. Mushrooms' planned plant expansion would require $2.35 million in 1978 and $150,000 more in 1979. As he forecasted for Mushrooms, Mr. Burrell wanted to include in his analysis a consideration of what might happen if sales actually grew faster than what had been forecast. What if the projections were wrong—how would that affect R. G. Barry?

Mushrooms Division (A)

EXHIBIT 1

■

Sales Projections (in millions)

	1977	1978	1979	1980	1981
Original dollar volume	$4.0	$ 6.0	$ 8.0	$10.0	$12.0
Revised dollar volume	5.0	12.6	19.95	28.9	42.5
Units	0.6	1.2	1.8	2.5	3.5

Mushrooms Division (A)

EXHIBIT 2

■

Projected Monthly Percentage of
Total Annual Sales

	Monthly Percentage
January	7.5%
February	7.5
March	15.0
April	7.5
May	2.5
June	20.0
July	10.0
August	7.5
September	5.0
October	5.0
November	7.5
December	5.0
	100.0%

Mushrooms Division (B)

Dick Burrell, Vice President—Finance for R. G. Barry Corporation, looked once again at the memo he had received from Gordy Zachs, Barry's president. The memo, reproduced in Exhibit 1, had become familiar to him and his staff over the previous few days as they had made financial forecasts for the Mushrooms Division. They had not yet concerned themselves with the last part of Zachs' request to determine the effect of Mushrooms on R. G. Barry's financial needs over the next 5 years. Mr. Burrell also wanted to look at what effect, if any, doubling the sales in the Mushrooms Division would have on the future funds requirements for Barry as a whole. Since Mr. Burrell's job was to assure adequate financing, he was the logical person to make the projections, to present them, and to lay out a course of action for securing whatever funds were required.

THE FOOTWEAR INDUSTRY

R. G. Barry was a producer of comfort footwear products, including slippers, sandals, moccasins, and after-ski boots. The company was a part of the $11.6 billion (1976 retail sales) footwear business in the United States.

   Although sales of the major footwear manufacturers had grown steadily over the years, profits were cyclical. The impact on Barry's financial statements can be seen in Exhibits 2 and 3. In addition to the cyclicality of the footwear industry as a whole, which affected Barry to a degree, Barry's own sales were seasonal, as shown in Exhibit 4. As a consequence of this seasonality, Dick Burrell had secured seasonal financing for the company.

CURRENT SITUATION

Barry's $6-million line of credit, spread evenly among three banks, was intended to finance the company's seasonal working-capital needs. Seasonal needs had been quite predictable. In terms of average annual sales, a shorthand measure

---

This case was prepared as a basis for class discussion rather than to illustrate either effective or ineffective handling of an administrative situation. Copyright © 1980 by the Darden Graduate Business School Sponsors, University of Virginia, Charlottesville, Virginia.

Barry's staff used to track seasonal needs,[1] Barry's peak need came in October, as seen in Exhibit 5. That was, of course, without the new Mushrooms venture.

While Barry's business had grown rather slowly, it had needed capital. During March 1977, Barry had obtained additional permanent financing from its principal lender, a major insurance company. This insurance company loaned Barry an additional $4 million at 9⅜ percent. While the insurance company had formerly required short–term borrowings to be repaid for 60 days each year, the new covenants shown in Exhibit 6 no longer had this "clean-up" requirement. Barry also expected to pay off $900,000 of notes during 1977 and to lease some $750,000 of computer equipment.

For the $6-million line of credit, the banks charged the prime rate with compensating balances to equal 10 percent of the credit line extended. Presently, the banks did not require those loans to be repaid for any portion of the year. These covenants could, of course, be changed any time Barry sought additional financing.

Exhibit 7 shows the projected funds needed for investments and debt repayments planned by Barry management for the company, not including Mushrooms. The financing arrangements, together with the expected balances for plant and equipment, receivables, and inventory, were used to project the December 31, 1977 balance sheet. As Exhibit 8 shows, Barry expected to end 1977 with a comfortable cash position. In addition, the company's projected 1977 peak seasonal borrowing requirement (determined with assumptions shown in Exhibits 4 and 5) was not expected to exceed $3 million, or half of the existing credit line. Of course, more would be needed as sales grew. Exhibit 9 provides forecasted income statements through 1981.

When the additional $4 million in notes had been sold to the insurance company in early 1977, Mr. Burrell had stated that Barry would require no additional permanent financing for the next three years. Now, only a few months after that transaction had been completed, he was not so sure. Barry had already decided to acquire two new production plants, and sales growth for Mushrooms was projected to skyrocket. If the plants were financed by industrial revenue bonds, not considered part of long-term financing by the lenders, Mr. Burrell believed Barry might be able to avoid renegotiating the covenants.

CONCLUSION

As he began to evaluate Barry's financing needs, Mr. Burrell wanted to be prepared to answer several questions about Barry's future with and without the Mushrooms Division.

1.   Was the present line-of-credit arrangement adequate to finance peak seasonal working-capital requirements through fiscal 1979? If not, how much should the line be increased?

---

[1]Balances in working-capital accounts were tracked by Barry management in average annual sales. They did not reflect the seasonal average day's sales. For example, in Exhibit 5, accounts receivable for October are 100 days of average annual sales of $58 million in 1976. If expressed in days of average September sales (which are 13 percent of the annual sales), it would only be 64 days.

2. Were the present long-term financing arrangements adequate to support projected growth over the next few years? If not, how much additional permanent financing would be required, and when?

3. If funds were needed, should they be raised through long-term debt or equity?

4. What if the present Mushrooms sales projections were wrong? Phenomenal sales growth was anticipated over the coming 5 years. What if sales actually grew at an even faster rate? Mr. Burrell wondered if his plans should include some sort of reserve financing arrangements to meet such a contingency.

Mr. Burrell was sure these questions would be raised at the meeting on the 25th. It was his job to be ready with the answers.

Mushrooms Division (B)

EXHIBIT 1
■
Memo Requesting a Presentation of Mushrooms Projection

OFFICE OF THE PRESIDENT

TO: Dick Burrell

FROM: Gordy Zacks

DATE: May 15, 1977

RE: May 25, 1977 meeting

Please bring your revised Mushrooms projections to the meeting on the 25th. After presenting them you should be ready to discuss the effect the changes will have on Barry's financial needs over the next 5 years.

EXHIBIT 2

∎

Income Statements and Selected Financial Statement Data
(in thousands, except as noted)

	1967	1968	1969[a]	1970	1971	1972	1973	1974[b]	1975[a]	1976
Ten-Year Comparative Summary of Operations										
Net sales	$15,938	$19,404	$24,667	$28,164	$34,123	$39,162	$43,162	$49,615	$52,260	$58,008
Cost of sales	10,642	12,514	16,237	18,222	21,919	25,667	28,621	33,233	34,586	37,666
Gross profit	5,296	6,890	8,430	9,942	12,204	13,495	14,541	16,382	17,674	20,342
Selling, general, and administrative	3,887	5,104	6,672	7,481	9,264	10,012	10,784	12,429	13,735	16,117
Interest expense, net	171	142	337	282	395	549	599	723	639	789
Earnings before income taxes	1,238	1,644	1,421	2,179	2,545	2,934	3,158	3,230	3,300	3,436
Income taxes	522	831	721	1,094	1,271	1,484	1,523	1,589	1,617	1,629
Net earnings	$ 686	$ 813	$ 700	$ 1,085	$ 1,274	$ 1,450	$ 1,635	$ 1,641	$ 1,683	$ 1,807
Financial Summary										
Current assets	$ 5,192	$ 7,200	$10,004	$10,945	$12,810	$16,409	$18,312	$19,495	$19,759	$21,245
Current liabilities	1,922	2,652	5,716	3,652	3,061	3,218	3,909	4,228	3,746	3,790
Net working capital	3,270	4,548	4,288	7,293	9,749	13,191	14,403	15,267	16,013	17,455
Long-term debt	1,616	1,495	1,936	2,179	5,095	7,285	6,970	8,513	8,129	8,640
Stockholders' equity	3,208	4,743	5,356	8,074	9,403	10,865	12,462	13,957	15,634	17,093

Net property, plant, and equipment	1,317	1,466	1,771	1,682	3,343	3,372	3,500	5,743	6,069	6,661
Total assets	6,804	8,950	13,070	13,983	17,654	21,484	23,485	26,842	27,653	29,668
Capital expenditures, net	329	421	639	262	2,043	468	589	2,749	866	1,249
Depreciation and amortization	228	272	334	351	382	439	461	507	540	657
Additional Data										
Earnings per share	$ 0.41	$ 0.46	$ 0.38	$ 0.53	$ 0.61	$ 0.69	$ 0.78	$ 0.79	$ 0.81	$ 0.88
Market price per share, high	3.00	6.60	8.30	5.50	7.00	8.70	6.30	3.60	3.00	5.90
Market price per share, low	1.30	2.70	4.20	1.90	3.50	5.20	2.10	2.10	2.10	2.60
Book value per share	1.91	2.58	2.91	3.90	4.49	5.18	5.95	6.75	7.54	8.36
Annual change in net sales (percentage)	25.6%	21.1%	27.1%	14.2%	21.2%	14.8%	10.2%	15.0%	5.3%	11.0%
Annual change in net earnings (percentage)	47.5%	18.5%	(13.9%)	55.0%	17.4%	13.8%	12.8%	0.4%	2.6%	7.4%
Net earnings/Average stockholders' equity	23.9%	20.5%	13.9%	16.2%	14.6%	14.3%	14.0%	12.4%	11.4%	11.0%
Average number of shares outstanding (in thousands)	1,675	1,785	1,839	2,049	2,087	2,096	2,099	2,078	2,069	2,054
Dividends and distributions:										
Cash	$ 0.02	0.03	0.04	0	0	0	0	0	0	0.09
Stock	10% and 5 for 4 split	5 for 4 split	5 for 4 split	10%	10%	3 for 2 split	5%	5%	5%	0

aFiscal year includes 53 weeks.
bEffective in 1974, the company changed its method of valuing a substantial portion of inventory to the last-in, first-out (LIFO) method.

Mushrooms Division (B)

EXHIBIT 3
■
Consolidated Balance Sheets (in thousands)

	December 31, 1975	December 31, 1976
Assets		
Cash and marketable securities	$ 3,031	$ 1,698
Accounts receivable	6,461	7,372
Inventories	9,742	11,822
Other	525	353
Total current assets	19,759	21,245
Property, plant, and equipment	10,029	10,705
Less: Accumulated depreciation	(3,960)	(4,044)
Net property, plant, and equipment	6,069	6,661
Other assets	1,825	1,762
Total assets	$27,653	$29,668
Liabilities and Stockholders' Equity		
Accounts payable	$2,235	$1,947
Accrued expenses	1,039	1,176
Income taxes	88	278
Current installments of long-term debt	384	389
Total current liabilities	3,746	3,790
Long-term debt	5,289	5,885
Capitalized lease obligations	2,840	2,755
Other	144	145
Total liabilities	12,019	12,575
Stockholders' equity		
Common stock ($1 par value)	2,072	2,043
Paid-in capital in excess of par	6,506	6,506
Retained earnings	7,056	8,544
Total stockholders' equity	15,634	17,093
Total liabilities and stockholders' equity	$27,653	$29,668

Mushrooms Division (B)

EXHIBIT 4
■

Projected Monthly Percentage
of Total Annual Sales, R. G. Barry
without Mushrooms, 1978–1981

	Monthly Percentage
January	6%
February	6
March	6
April	6
May	6
June	6
July	6
August	10
September	13
October	18
November	11
December	6
	100%

Mushrooms Division (B)

EXHIBIT 5
■

Projected 1978 Monthly Working-Capital Requirements
for R. G. Barry without Mushrooms in Days of Average Annual Sales
(all divisions *except* Mushrooms)

	Jan.	Feb.	March	April	May	June	July	Aug.	Sept.	Oct.	Nov.	Dec.
Accounts receivable	38	38	38	38	38	38	35	53	74	100	88	52
Inventory												
Finished goods	49	55	61	67	73	78	84	82	71	49	44	49
Work–in–progress	25	25	25	25	25	25	25	25	25	25	25	25
Accounts payable	20	20	20	20	20	20	20	20	20	20	20	20

Mushrooms Division (B)

EXHIBIT 6
■

March 1977 Loan Repayment Schedule and Summary of Loan Covenants

The $4-million loan made in March 1977 was payable in annual installments of $225,000 from 1981 through 1986, $440,000 from 1987 through 1991, and $450,000 in 1992. The most restrictive covenants agreed to by Barry in connection with this loan included the following:

1. Consolidated net tangible assets (defined as current assets plus net property, plant, and equipment less capital lease obligations) must exceed 300 percent of senior long-term debt. Industrial revenue bonds (IRBs) would not be considered part of long-term debt for purposes of this covenant. IRB payments were considered property rental payments. Debt service payments for IRBs could not exceed 2½ percent of consolidated net income.

2. Consolidated net tangible assets must exceed 200 percent of total long-term debt (senior long-term debt plus subordinated debentures).

3. Current assets must exceed 175 percent of current liabilities.

4. Payment of dividends, repurchase of Barry common shares, and other specified transactions must be limited to $1 million plus net income.

5. For at least one consecutive 60-day period during the year, the amount of borrowings made under short-term line-of-credit arrangements must be convertible into long-term debt and still satisfy the covenant described in (1) above.

Mushrooms Division (B)

EXHIBIT 7
■

Projected Capital Expenditures and Other Funds Uses,
All R. G. Barry Divisions Except Mushrooms
(thousands of dollars)

	1977	1978	1979	1980	1981
Capital investment	$1,460	$810	$1,110	$900	$1,000
Long-term debt repayments	415	690	700	705	710

Mushrooms Division (B)

EXHIBIT 8
∎

Projected Balance Sheet as of December 31, 1977[a]
for R. G. Barry without Mushrooms
(in thousands)

Current Assets		Current Liabilities	
Cash	$ 2,605	Accounts payable and accrued expenses	$ 3,820
Accounts receivable	9,850		
Finished-goods inventory	9,250	Accrued taxes	750
Work-in-progress and raw-material inventory	4,570	Total current liabilities[b]	4,570
		Other	145
Prepaids, etc.	500	Long-term debt[c]	8,570
Total current assets	26,775	Long-term lease obligations	3,505
		Total long-term debt	12,075
Property, plant, and equipment	12,165		
Less: Accrued depreciation	(4,775)	Common stock	2,050
Net property, plant, and equipment	7,390	Paid-in capital	6,500
		Retained earnings	10,600
Other	1,775	Total stockholders' equity	19,150
Total assets	$35,940	Total liabilities and stockholders' equity	$35,940

[a]Includes Mushrooms' performance through 12/31/76. Mushrooms' performance (and projected performance) for 1977 is not included.
[b]Excludes debt due within 1 year.
[c]Includes $2.5 million of subordinated debentures.

Mushrooms Division (B)

EXHIBIT 9
∎

Five-Year Profit and Loss Projections Excluding Mushrooms Division

	1977	1978	1979	1980	1981
Sales	$64,737	$73,152	$81,920	$91,697	$104,617
Cost of goods sold	41,290	46,958	52,650	59,015	67,330
Gross profit	23,447	26,194	29,270	32,682	37,287
Selling expense	6,855	7,659	8,585	9,617	10,972
General and administrative expense	7,237	8,176	9,141	10,214	11,653
Divisional profit before corporate expenses	9,355	10,359	11,544	12,851	14,662
Corporate expense[a]	3,665	3,937	4,274	4,577	4,902
Interest expense	862	957	921	896	871
Inventory adjustments	300	350	425	500	575
Other	125	150	175	200	225
Profit before tax	4,403	4,965	5,749	6,678	8,089
Income taxes	2,166	2,443	2,829	3,285	3,979
Net income	$ 2,237	$ 2,522	$ 2,920	$ 3,393	$ 4,110
[a]Includes depreciation of	$695	$755	$860	$950	$1,055

3A

VALUATION:

CAPITAL BUDGETING—FORECASTING

Metalcrafters, Inc.

In September 1985, Mark Chen, a new financial analyst at Metalcrafters, Inc. was preparing the analysis of four investments and two contracts that Metalcrafters' budget committee would review at the end of the week. This analysis was the first real assignment he had received from his boss, Dena Brownowski, chief financial officer at Metalcrafters, and he wanted to make a good impression.

THE COMPANY

Metalcrafters was founded in the early 1960s by two Korean War buddies who had returned home to Detroit, Michigan after the war and gone to work in the automobile industry. They had seen an opportunity to go into business producing specialized polished and anodized[1] aluminum hardware and molding parts for the auto industry, and Metalcrafters was the result. The plant was located just outside Detroit.

In the late 1960s, the company diversified in an attempt to insulate itself from the cyclicality of the auto industry. By 1985, Metalcrafters was producing parts for aluminum windows, ladders, and industrial lighting fixtures, as well as some consumer products. Of the 800 different parts produced in 1985, over half were for customers outside the auto business, accounting for about 40 percent of total revenues.

Metalcrafters management was known for its conservativism. The company expanded slowly, and large investments were carefully considered. For instance, all capital-investment proposals exceeding $5,000 were submitted to the company's budget committee. The proposal for each investment had to include a description and justification of the investment as well as detailed forecasts for costs and revenues. Ms. Brownowski and her staff had the job of reviewing the proposals and preparing a detailed financial analysis for each. The budget committee, consisting of the company's four top officers—the president, CFO, and directors of marketing and operations—relied on these analyses in making their decisions.

This case was prepared as a basis for class discussion rather than to illustrate either effective or ineffective handling of an administrative situation. Copyright © 1987 by the Darden Graduate Business School Sponsors, University of Virginia, Charlottesville, Virginia.

[1]Anodizing is a process that treats parts electromagnetically to make them corrosion resistant.

In September 1985, several requests were on Mr. Chen's desk. Two were for investments in new equipment—replacement of a stamping press and the purchase of an extrusion press. In addition, Ms. Brownowski had asked Mr. Chen to look at two orders for extruded parts to see whether capital-budgeting techniques could be adapted for use in deciding between them. Ordinarily the company would fill both orders, but because it currently lacked the capacity to do so, and new equipment could not be installed in time to meet the contract provisions, the company would have to choose between the orders.

THE STAMPING PRESS

Because of rapidly rising repair costs of the old machine and the greatly im-proved efficiency of new presses, management had decided that it was time to replace an old stamping press. The two options that had been proposed differed primarily in expected life and cost. Both machines could be purchased from the same company. The first, called the SX-65, would cost $65,000 installed and would last 5 years. At the end of its 5-year life, management believed it could be sold for about $5,000. Annual savings of $28,000 were expected from its operation.

The second press, the MD-40, was more durable. It cost $90,000, but would last 10 years. Annual savings were also expected to be $28,000 and, at the end of its life the press could be sold for an estimated $5,000. Regardless of which press management decided to purchase, the old, fully depreciated press could be sold for $1,000.

THE EXTRUSION PRESS

Metalcrafters' management had been forced to turn down several contracts re-cently because the company lacked sufficient extrusion capacity. Management had considered two extrusion presses and engaged in considerable debate over the choice. One had a much larger capacity, and a price to match.

A small press was available for $650,000 installed. The press could handle aluminum billets up to 4 inches in diameter and it would allow Metalcrafters to fill most of the orders it currently turned away. The press was expected to produce annual sales of $750,000 for its 10-year life. Of the revenues, 65 percent would cover labor and materials. An additional 5 percent would be needed to cover marketing and administrative costs, which were typical of extrusion-press operations and would not be incurred if the sales did not materialize. At the end of 10 years, management believed that it could sell the small press for $20,000.

With the larger press, Metalcrafters could accept all the orders that it could not now take and, because the press could accept 8-inch billets, the company could consider expanding by producing larger parts used in consumer products. This press costs $1 million, would also last 10 years, and was expected to result in annual sales of $1.075 million. At the end of its life, management forecast that it could be sold for $45,000.

Some of the sales that were forecast for each of the two new extrusion presses would come from parts that would otherwise have been produced on Metalcrafters' present presses. Management estimated that about $100,000 of sales per year would have been produced without a new press. The old presses were expected to be used for only 7 more years before being scrapped.

THE NEW PARTS ORDERS

Because the company had limited extrusion–press capacity, management had to choose between orders from the Sawmasters and Eades companies. Once a new extrusion press was in place, they would not be confronted with the same problem, particularly if they chose the larger press. However, both Sawmasters and Eades had written in their contracts that capacity had to be in place at the time the contract was accepted. Mr. Chen was not sure that a capital-budgeting approach was the way to choose between these two projects. Neither required new capital.

Eades Electric was one of Metalcrafters' oldest and largest customers, but it had been switching from aluminum to plastic for many of its components. The result had been a decline of 15 percent in orders from Eades during the last 2 years. Eades urgently needed a new part that Metalcrafters could easily produce. The contract would generate sales of $50,000 each year for 3 years.

Sawmasters' order was for a special chainsaw part. Sawmasters had never ordered from Metalcrafters before, although it was a customer that Metalcrafters had long courted. The contract would add sales of $30,000 in the first year, $36,000 in the second, and $99,000 in the third and final contract year.

To set up the equipment and train staff to produce the parts for either order would cost $8,000. Cost of materials and labor averaged 65 percent of sales for parts of this type. New expenses associated with administering either of the projects would be 5 percent of sales.

CAPITAL BUDGETING

As Mr. Chen prepared to do his analysis, he recalled Ms. Brownowski's comments about the criteria used by the budget committee. Two of the committee members preferred payback, the other two, net present value. The committee was using a 15-percent required rate of return for all projects.

Mr. Chen had failed to ask Ms. Brownowski how to handle taxes. Currently the marginal tax rate was 48 percent, and depreciation was calculated according to ACRS (accelerated cost recovery system) rules passed by the U.S. Congress as part of the Economic Recovery Tax Act of 1981. Metalcrafters could take an investment tax credit of 8 percent on the presses and still depreciate the full purchase price. The four presses were classified as 5-year ACRS property and could be depreciated as follows:

ACRS Depreciation Schedule,
5-Year-Life Equipment

Year	Proportion Depreciated
1	15%
2	22
3	21
4	21
5	21

There was, however, ongoing and serious consideration of a change in the tax code by the president and Congress. The new tax code would reduce the tax rate (most companies would pay 34 percent), eliminate the investment tax credit, extend depreciable lives, and use an accelerated method of depreciation called double-declining balance.[2] Mr. Chen talked with old classmates from his MBA days who worked for Big Eight accounting firms, and they said that the stamping presses would probably still be depreciated over 5 years, but the extrusion presses' depreciable lives would be 7 years.

Ms. Brownowski was on vacation until Friday, the budget committee's meeting day. Mr. Chen was to be ready on her return to brief her on his analysis and recommend which, if any, of the projects should be approved.

---

[2]To calculate double-declining balance, take double the straight-line depreciation rate for the same project life and apply it to the undepreciated value of the investment. When it is advantageous, a switch can be made to straight-line depreciation.

Federal Reserve Bank of Richmond (A)

As manager of planning at the Federal Reserve Bank of Richmond (FRBR), Reid Carter had been asked to find a way to reduce costs of savings bond processing. During late 1977, he had been working with the director of the fiscal agency department at the bank, who supervised savings bond processing, as well as with people from the bank's computer services group, to develop the three options that now lay before him. Opinions of FRBR's managers as to which of the three should be implemented differed widely. What Reid Carter needed to do now was evaluate the costs and benefits, as well as the less tangible pros and cons of each option, and make a firm recommendation that his boss, Roy Fauber, could pass on to the Federal Reserve Board of Governors for approval.

BACKGROUND

The Federal Reserve System, supervised by its Board of Governors, was established in 1913 by the Federal Reserve Act. That act, plus subsequent legislation (e.g., the Banking Act of 1934), placed the Federal Reserve System in the position of responsibility for:

1. Monetary Policy. The Federal Reserve Board attempted to control the availability and cost of money and credit through its control over the reserves held by the banking system. Reserves could be influenced by:

a. The Federal Reserve System Open Market Committee's trading of government securities. To expand credit, securities were purchased, bank reserves rose over the required limit, and the banks' funds were freed for loans. To tighten credit, securities were sold, reserves were reduced, and previously loanable funds were reduced.

b. The rediscount rate. The Board of Governors loaned money to its member banks at a rate it controlled.

c. The level of reserves held by member banks. All national banks were required to be members of the Federal Reserve System. State banks were allowed

---

This case was prepared as a basis for class discussion rather than to illustrate either effective or ineffective handling of an administrative situation. Copyright © 1979 by the Darden Graduate Business School Sponsors, University of Virginia, Charlottesville, Virginia.

but not required to become members. The membership was required to maintain a percentage of their deposits in reserve.[1] A change in the level of reserves changed the percentage of deposits loanable by the bank.

2. Supervision and Regulation. The Federal Reserve Board set maximum interest rates on time and savings deposits, examined state-chartered member banks, regulated offshore activities of U.S. banks, regulated bank holding companies, established rules for credit and repayment terms disclosure, voted on the establishment of state member branch banks, and approved bank mergers.

3. U.S. Government Bank. The board acted as the fiscal agent for the federal government. U.S. government securities were issued, delivered, and handled by them.

4. Bank Services for Member Banks. Activities such as collecting and cashing checks, wiring money, making loans, and holding securities for commercial banks were provided. Between 75 and 80 percent of the expenses of each of the 12 district banks resulted from executing these services.

All federal reserve activities in the Fifth District were under the jurisdiction of the Richmond Federal Reserve Bank.

Most of the services provided by the district banks were to benefit federal reserve member and nonmember banks. In general, these services were provided without charge; the reserve balances that the banks maintained with the district banks were viewed as compensation for the services provided throughout the Federal Reserve System. A district bank could, however, determine the level of the particular service it wished to provide. For instance, all district banks processed commercial bank checks, but the conditions under which credit was granted were under the district's control.

Operating decisions made by the district banks had little effect on their income, which came from the interest on U.S. government securities held as a result of monetary policy. In order to meet the system-wide goal of maximizing the surplus returned to the U.S. Treasury, the FRBR had to minimize costs rather than maximize revenue. That is why savings bond automation looked promising.

CAPITAL ALLOCATION PROCESS

The process of making capital investments had recently become more formal at the FRBR. Based on the size of the expected expenditure, proposals were divided into three categories. Department managers could authorize expenditures of up to $5,000. For investments between $5,000 and $100,000, approval had to come from top management of the district bank, and for anything in excess of $100,000, from the Board of Governors of the Federal Reserve System in Washington, D.C.

In general, proposals that exceeded $5,000 were of two varieties. The first were investments to maintain a required level of service (e.g., to replace worn-out equipment), and little economic justification was required for their approval.

---

[1]Membership also required the purchase of stock in the Federal Reserve District Bank serving the area. The amount of stock purchased was based on the size of the national bank's capital and surplus accounts.

The second were cost-reduction projects, and those were expected to meet certain minimum standards based on present value analysis. Controversy over those projects centered around what the minimum standard, the discount rate, should be.

THE SAVINGS BOND AUTOMATION PROJECT

During his tenure as chairman of the Federal Reserve Board, Arthur Burns had put intense pressure on the 12 federal reserve banks to reduce their internal costs. Budgets at the FRBR had risen less than 5.5 percent annually over the past four or five years in spite of increased volume and the effects of inflation. The Richmond bank had been effective in cost cutting, but in 1977, management believed that several areas still remained where more could be done. Savings bond processing under the fiscal agency department was one of those areas. The unit costs for the process had been higher at the FRBR than those for the same function performed at other federal reserve banks. In fact, they were higher than the system-wide average by a significant margin. (See Exhibit 1.) Since the banks competed to have the lowest costs, the FRBR had an incentive to find a way to reduce the costs.

Because little of the current savings bond processing at the FRBR was automated, it remained one of the most labor-intensive operations at the bank. Even so, the rate of cost increase could have been contained if the U.S. Treasury had not been planning tighter reporting requirements, which, together with increasing volume, led to only one thing—hiring more people and higher unit costs. The vice president, Roy Fauber, and his planning staff had therefore become involved in the problem. Mr. Fauber asked Reid Carter to work with the director of fiscal agency, Harold Lipscomb, in solving the problem.

The savings bond group issued, processed, and redeemed bonds for individuals, issuing agents, and payroll accounts. Currently, the main use of the computer in the savings bond function was at the Richmond office for keeping records related to consignment accounts held by the district's issuing agents (that is, the banks), the initiation of reserve accounts, and the automated printing of savings bonds for several payroll accounts. In the first 6 months of 1977, charges for computer operations in savings bonds had been $15,057. The savings bond function had also been charged $5,570 for data system support in the first 6 months. Everything else was done manually. The reissue activity alone required 18 separate steps, all done manually. The kind of work done in the section obviously lent itself to computerization, which preliminary estimates suggested might eliminate up to 50 percent of the current staff (Exhibit 2).

A variety of alternatives for reducing the cost of handling savings bonds had been explored, and three had been considered in detail. All the suggestions involved further automating the process. Two of the proposals relied on using the excess capacity of the computer equipment already owned by the FRBR; the other required the purchase of a minicomputer system similar to that used by the New York Federal Reserve Bank.

1. Four Phase Mini-System.

As a result of a discussion with a Federal Reserve System bank-examining team, Mr. Carter and Mr. Lipscomb had learned about a new system in use at the New York district bank. The FRBNY had employed an outside consultant to install a minicomputer and provide software specifically designed for their savings bond process. Such a system would do just what the Richmond team believed was needed: it would automate the routine bookkeeping, clerical, and reporting activities; it would centralize much of the work now being done at the Charlotte and Baltimore branch banks; and it could be ready 6 months from the time the consultant was notified. Mr. Carter, Mr. Lipscomb, and the consultant had worked out some preliminary estimates of the costs involved in bringing the Four Phase system to FRBR. The hardware itself was expected to cost $285,245, although a discount might be offered. The FRBNY consultant said the software could not be directly transferred to the new FRBR system and, therefore, estimated further software development costs of $28,000, modifications costing $35,000, and conversion costs running no more than $15,000. The FRBR would provide a part-time staff member to coordinate the project, which would take between one-quarter and one-third of the person's time; a cost of $7,500 was estimated.

In addition to those start-up costs, continuing annual hardware and software maintenance would require $11,556 and $18,000, respectively. The current main computer charge for the operation was about $41,000 per year.

The real benefit of this system would come from the smaller staff needed to perform the same tasks. It appeared that, with this system, seven fewer people would be needed for savings bond processing (Exhibit 3). Intrabank transfers and normal attrition would make the effect on the people involved negligible.

2. IBM 370s.   After a description of the Four Phase system had been circulated at the FRBR, the computer services and planning department responded by supplying the following information. They had the staff necessary to create similar software. The in-house computer system (dual IBM 370s) was operating at about 30 percent of capacity, and even if the back-up time required for the wire transfer of funds was added, the system was committed for only 50 percent of its time. Putting the savings bond processing onto the IBM 370s would reduce the unit costs to all other users at FRBR. Furthermore, the use of the IBM 370s would meet the computer-utilization plan filed by the FRBR with the Systems Committee of the Board of Governors.

The department believed, however, that the time to create the software necessary to satisfy the savings bond needs could take up to two years (Exhibit 4). Allocation for programmers' time would be as high as $285,896 (Exhibit 5). Continuing software maintenance could cost $3,000 per year. A total of eight staff positions could be eliminated.

The Board of Governors' Systems Committee, in charge of the planning and the utilization of system-wide computer resources, had strongly suggested that everything be loaded on a district's main system. The district banks at San Francisco, Dallas, and St. Louis were involved in projects to do just that. If the FRBR waited, the committee felt sure that software adaptable for the savings bond activity would become available within the Federal Reserve System in two or three years.

3. IBM 370s with Consultant Software.   The third option was to use the IBM 370 capacity, but hire the firm that had created the FRBNY mini-system to provide the software. Although language differences existed between the two systems, the consultants were familiar with the needs of the savings bond process, and their New York system had received the necessary approval of the

U.S. Treasury. The consultant had estimated it would take up to 14 months to have this system ready for use.

Costs for this system included software ($250,000), its conversion ($15,000), and the in-bank coordinator ($7,500). Yearly software maintenance was estimated at $18,000. This system would also reduce the processing staff by eight people.

Each of the systems reduced the labor intensity of the operation and provided identifiable benefits. The pros and cons for the three options had been well summarized by one of the systems analysts (Exhibit 6).

CONCLUSION

As Mr. Carter and Mr. Lipscomb prepared to make cost and benefit estimates for each of the alternatives, Mr. Carter had several concerns: in making the estimates, they expected to treat real dollars and in-house allocations in the same way. For instance, if the FRBR chose the mini-system, they would be obligated to pay up to $285,245 for the Four Phase hardware. If, however, they used the IBM 370s, the computer charges would be allocated as in-house costs that must be borne by someone regardless of the system chosen for this project. They planned to treat both costs in the same way for in-house programming help versus the hiring of the outside consultant for development of the software. Mr. Carter wondered if all these costs and allocations should, in fact, be treated similarly. Furthermore, the payments for the Four Phase hardware and the consultant's charges would be contractual, while the in-house costs and benefits were merely estimates. Should that, he wondered, be taken into account?

Capacity provided another nagging question. The IBM 370s were not fully utilized, but in the past, whenever there had been time available, the capacity seemed to be used eventually. Right now the computer people estimated that the capacity of the 370s probably would be adequate for about three more years. The Four Phase, on the other hand, brought excess capacity with it.

The Systems Committee had encouraged the use of main systems and the system-wide standardization of software. The FRBR's computer-utilization plan, which had been filed with the committee, had covered the use of the main systems alone. Thus, there was some doubt that a proposal for mini-system investment would be welcomed by the Board of Governors.

Finally, Mr. Carter was not sure whether any of the projects should be recommended. Would they solve the savings bond processing problems at economically justifiable costs? Putting the costs and benefits together was Mr. Carter's first step.

EXHIBIT 1

■

Fifth District Performance Measures, Fourth Quarter, 1978

The following chart illustrates the District-wide Performance Indexes for the fourth quarter of 1978. The First Level Aggregates compare the direct, support, and allocated overhead costs associated with an activity to the system average for the same activity. Two or more activities are combined to derive the Second Level Aggregates, and all Second Level Aggregates are combined to form the Overall District Aggregate Index. The performance measures indexes cover 85 percent of the district's expenses. Major excluded functions are Monetary and Economic Policy, Supervision and Regulation, Bank and Public Relations, and several smaller functions. These performance indexes are based upon a system average index of 100. Variations above 100 indicate that unit cost is greater than the system average, and those below 100 indicate that unit cost is below system average.

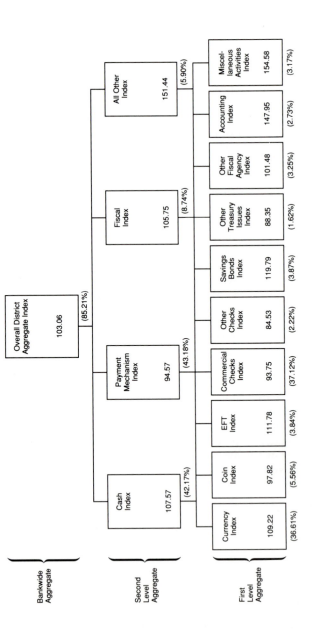

The following graphs illustrate the variations of the Performance Measures Indexes, by quarter between the first quarter 1977 and the fourth quarter 1980. The first graph illustrates the comparison of the district activity unit cost index and the system average unit cost index (100). The second graph for a given activity illustrates both the unit cost index and the aggregate volume index over time and compares the activity against a base index using 1977 as a base of 100.

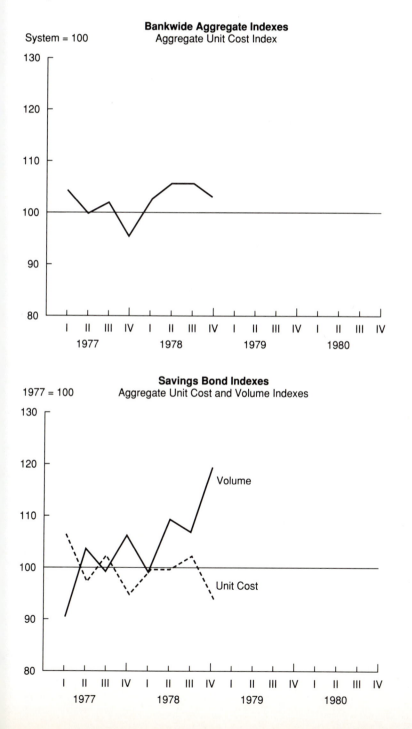

continued

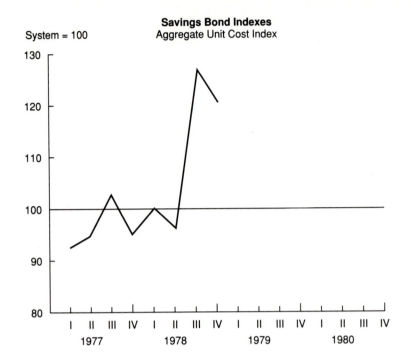

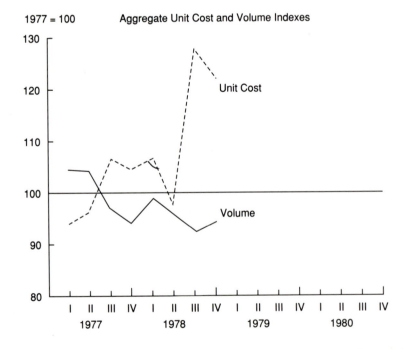

continued

Current Savings Bond Processing Costs,
1977 Aggregate Unit Cost Calculation

Activity	Cost	Volume
Original issue	$178,207	1,048,351
Accounting for stock	424,610	126,667
Reissues and replacements	147,167	404,809
Direct redemptions	168,980	207,270
Processing retired bonds	180,885	325,039
	$1,099,849	2,112,136

Aggregate unit cost: $0.52

Federal Reserve Bank of Richmond (A)

EXHIBIT 2
■
Project Title: Savings Bond System

Description

The Savings Bond Section plans to implement a comprehensive Automated Savings Bond System that will provide computer support in the following areas:

1. Consignment accounting
2. Vault custody
3. Original issue
4. Reissue
5. Book entry
6. Paid bonds
7. Direct redemption
8. Administration.

Benefits

The primary benefit from the system results from the elimination and/or simplification of many tasks in the savings bond area. The major areas of improvement are listed below:

1. Elimination of reissue activities at Baltimore and Charlotte. (These activities will be moved to Richmond.)

2. Elimination of original issue activities at Baltimore and Charlotte. (These activities will be moved to Richmond.)

continued

3. Elimination of direct redemption activities.

4. Elimination of the manual recording of bond serial numbers.

5. Elimination of manually kept accounting records by fiscal agency bookkeeper.

6. Elimination of addressographing bond registrations and dating of bonds.

7. Elimination of manual preparation of checks for direct redemption.

8. Simplification of settlement procedures.

9. Simplification of mail procedures and elimination of typing of labels and mail manifests.

10. Reduction of work caused by errors.

11. Elimination of manual preparation of certain letters to issuing agents.

12. Elimination of sorting reserve and certain account entries by office.

13. Manual accumulation of certain statistics and preparation of reports.

14. Elimination of the need to enter reserve account entries into the IBM 370.

15. Specific audit trails would be produced and response to issuing agents would improve.

In addition, the system will result in the following benefits not directly related to a reduction in manual work:

1. Improved accuracy in handling of data should lead to fewer errors and their resulting complications.

2. Simplified work flow should lead to improved control of work and valuables.

3. Broader and more timely management information will contribute to the department management.

4. Future enhancements or new applications could improve operations; benefits to other fiscal agency activities could result.

Federal Reserve Bank of Richmond (A)

EXHIBIT 3
∎
Automation of the Savings Bond Function

Personnel Requirements and Savings

	Current System	Four Phase System	Savings
Richmond			
Original issue	5.8	2.5	−3.3
Accounting for stock	5.8	3.0	−2.8
Reissue	3.4	2.5	−0.9
Data entry	N.Ap.	3.0	+3.0
Total personnel	15.0	11.0	−4.0
Baltimore: See note below.			−2.0
Charlotte: See note below.			−1.0
Total district personnel			−7.0

N.Ap. = not applicable.
Note: The personnel savings at the Baltimore and Charlotte branches represent the minimum number of personnel involved with the savings bond activity who could be eliminated after automation and centralization of the activity at Richmond. The personnel savings are the same under the IBM 370 alternative with the exception that one additional individual could be eliminated in the data entry area: i.e., the Four Phase system requires an individual to control the operation of the computer system, whereas in the IBM 370 system this function would remain in the data processing department.

Annual Cost Savings

	Personnel	Average Wages and Benefits	Total Annual Savings
Richmond	4	$9,858	$39,432
Baltimore	2	11,172	22,344
Charlotte	1	9,858	9,858
Total			$71,634

Federal Reserve Bank of Richmond (A)

EXHIBIT 4
∎
Implementation Schedule

IBM 370, In-House Software	
Consignment and vault custody	10.0 months
Original issue	6.0 months
Reissue	3.0 months
Paid bonds	1.5 months
Book entry	3.0 months
Total implementation time	23.5 months
IBM 370, Consultant Software	14 months
Consultant Software on Four Phase	4–6 months

Federal Reserve Bank of Richmond (A)

EXHIBIT 5
■

Savings Bond System Detailed—IBM Alternative Costs

I. *Development and Implementation Costs (IBM 370)*
In-House Software

	Man Weeks		Hrs./Wk.		Rate	Cost
Analyst (1)	95	×	30	×	$32.35	$ 91,913
Programmers (3)	240	×	30	×	23.00	165,600
Operations specialist (1)	40	×	30	×	23.00	27,600
Transfer time[a]						783
Total	375					$285,896

[a]Transfer time is that time spent by computer services production support to become familiar with the system in general

II. *Computer Operations Charges (IBM 370)*

	Unit/Mo.		Rate	Cost
Print lines	924,766	×	$.0007	$ 647
Characters	2,500,000	×	.00063	1,575
CPU time/Sec.	10,800	×	.17	1,836
Hardware (CRT)	2	×	70	140
Total/Month				$ 4,198
Total/Year				$ 50,376
Total/6 Years				$302,256

Federal Reserve Bank of Richmond (A)

EXHIBIT 6
■

Savings Bond System Options—Intangible
Pros and Cons Unique to Alternatives Investigated

Alternative 1.   Purchase Four Phase computer and pay consultant to install New York savings bond software.

Pro

■ Four Phase equipment is rated favorably by users. In *Datapro* (a trade publication), users rated the equipment 3.2 on a scale of 4 for overall satisfaction.

■ Provided no unique changes must be made to the New York software for New York, Boston, or this bank, the cost advantage of software resource-sharing may be realized by these banks.

■ The hardware and software have run successfully at the New York Federal Reserve Bank for over a year and a half.

■ The New York system has been endorsed by the Subcommittee on Computers and Related Resources, and the reports have been endorsed by the U.S. Treasury.

■ By acquiring the Four Phase hardware, excess computer capacity will be available. This excess could be used by the fiscal agency department for new applications.

■ Work turnaround may be faster on a dedicated computer.

continued

Con

- Unless a Four Phase high-speed printer is leased, potential operational and hardware interface problems may be incurred because of the requirement to use another vendor's printers (IBM or Burroughs) for high-volume reports.
- Out-of-pocket expenses will be required by the district if this alternative is chosen.
- A minicomputer creates the opportunity to add other applications to the system. However, additional problems for management arise if applications are added because the district would be less flexible in considering long-term hardware changes.
- Hardware maintenance support in the Richmond area is currently dependent upon two maintenance persons. The acquisition of replacement parts, if not stocked here in the city, may be time consuming.
- Due to the limited number of Four Phase users in the city (six at this time), off-site equipment backup may be difficult to find.
- This alternative will introduce a new device and computer vendor into the district and is in conflict with the direction of the district's approved automation plan.
- The Four Phase minicomputer uses two programming languages that are new to computer services personnel and are not widely used in the industry. They are Four Phase COBOL (Basic) and Four Phase Assembler. Training of personnel will be required. The possibility exists that, unless the personnel use the languages frequently, time will be lost in relearning the language each time software maintenance is required.
- Because the system was not developed in-house, computer services personnel may have to spend more time in learning the software. Therefore, maintenance may be more time consuming than it would be if computer services had developed the system themselves. This disadvantage is shared with Alternative 2.
- Detailed program documentation is poor. This may hinder the production support (maintenance) by increasing learning time.
- Problems with the New York consultant's support of the system:

  Distance. The consultant's office is in New York City.

  Control. The consultant will not be an employee of the Federal Reserve Bank but just another service vendor.

  Availability. The consultant's availability may be limited and will only be controlled by a detailed maintenance contract; e.g., the consultant could not give us a detailed estimate on Alternative 2 because he was leaving for Europe.

  Inflexibility. The consultant should only make changes to the system when these changes have been approved by all federal reserve banks who use the system. If we make our own permanent changes to the software, the consultant would not support us.

Alternative 2. Consultant rewrites software to be processed on Richmond's IBM 370 computer.

Pro

- The system architecture has proved successful at the New York Federal Reserve Bank for over a year and a half.
- The New York system's reports have been endorsed by the U.S. Treasury and will be available under this alternative.
- IBM hardware support is readily available.
- Trained programmers and computer operators are already employed; this is an advantage over Alternative 1.
- The consultant, who knows the New York savings bond system well, will do the conversion. Therefore, no program logic should be lost or misinterpreted in the translation.

continued

Con

■ Production turnaround on the IBM computer(s) may be slower than on a dedicated Four Phase computer; this is a disadvantage shared with Alternative 3.

■ Out-of-pocket expenses will be required by the district if this alternative is chosen.

■ The New York savings bond system was not originally designed to be processed on an IBM computer. Because of the code conversion, some additional inconvenience to the user and data processing may be expected during system implementation.

■ The system will not be developed in-house; therefore, computer services personnel may have to spend more time in learning the software. Program maintenance may be more time consuming than it would be if computer services personnel had developed the system themselves. This disadvantage is shared with Alternative 1.

Alternative 3.   Develop the software in-house to be processed on Richmond's IBM 370.

Pro

■ The system architecture has proved successful at the New York Federal Reserve Bank for over a year and a half. This software will be the basis of the new system design.

■ The New York system's reports have been endorsed by the U.S. Treasury and will be available as output from this system.

■ IBM hardware support is readily available.

■ Trained computer operators are already employed; this is an advantage over Alternative 1.

■ A full understanding of the software is guaranteed because the programs will be written by computer services personnel. Therefore, product support (maintenance) will be more timely.

■ No out-of-pocket funds would be expended due to the allocation of existing resources.

■ Personnel could be made available to begin this alternative in a short amount of time, whereas Four Phase approval (Alternative 1) may be time consuming.

■ Programs may be written to meet specific needs of the Fifth District without approval from the New York or Boston Federal Reserve Banks.

Con

■ Because of the extensive development and implementation effort required, it would be 28 months before *full* project benefits can be realized, assuming one analyst and four to five programmers are committed to the project.

■ Production turnaround on the IBM computer may be slower than on a dedicated Four Phase computer; this is a disadvantage shared with Alternative 2.

Zukowski Meats, Incorporated

Stanley Zukowski, president of Zukowski Meats, Inc., was confused. Sales of the company's Polish meats, kielbasa and ham, which had increased steadily over the previous years, had declined during 1987. Stanley's son, Donald, a recent business-school graduate, suggested that his father change the credit terms on these sales to reestablish the family's market position. Mr. Zukowski thought that the idea warranted serious consideration and wanted to make the decision before the onset of the Christmas season in November, three weeks away. However, he was unsure of exactly how to analyze his son's proposal.

COMPANY BACKGROUND

The Zukowski family had been manufacturing and selling various types of German and Polish meats in the Greenpoint section of Brooklyn, New York, for over 30 years. The family had met with considerable success: their products were excellent and appealed to a wide range of consumers. Sales in 1986 were $20 million on assets of $12 million, as shown in Exhibit 1. The Zukowskis sold their meats through the numerous neighborhood butcher shops in the New York metropolitan area as well as through certain supermarkets. Over the years their products had found a ready market in Brooklyn among the successive waves of eastern European immigrants who made Greenpoint their first stop in America, as well as the wider markets in Manhattan and Queens. The Zukowskis' products and their levels of profitability in 1986 are shown in Table 1.

Between 1981 and 1986, the company's sales had increased steadily. However, preliminary results for 1987 showed a considerable decline in the growth rates in sales of the company's Polish sausage and hams. Mr. Zukowski believed the major problem was an increase in the supply of these specialty meats. Substantial growth in the Polish population in the metropolitan area, particularly in Greenpoint, had increased the demand for the products enough to encourage new producers to enter the market. Furthermore, these producers were themselves recent immigrants who were able to match the authentic quality of the Zukowski company's meat products. Mr. Zukowski realized that he would have

This case was prepared as a basis for class discussion rather than to illustrate effective or ineffective handling of an administrative decision. Copyright © 1984 by the Darden Graduate Business School Sponsors, University of Virginia, Charlottesville, Virginia.

TABLE 1

■

Product Line Sales and Profits, 1986 (in thousands)

	Net Sales	Profit before Tax[a]
German Meats		
Knockwurst	$3,700.0	$111.0
Bratwurst	3,000.0	84.0
Polish Meats		
Kielbasa	9,500.0	332.5
Polish ham	3,800.0	133.0
Total	$20,000.0	$660.5

[a]Tax rate of 34 percent expected under the 1986 Tax Reform Act.

to so something to reclaim his former market share and reestablish the company's dominant position in the market for Polish meats. Little competition had arisen in the market for German sausages, sales of which were relatively stable. Consequently, Mr. Zukowski did not believe that the new credit terms needed to be extended for those products.

DONALD ZUKOWSKI'S PROPOSAL

Historically, the Zukowski company and its competitors had offered credit terms of net 30 days. While many Polish sausage manufacturers required their accounts to pay on delivery, Zukowski primarily sold to larger commercial accounts, for which credit was arranged. A few accounts were required to pay on delivery. An increase to net 45 days on all sales of kielbasa and Polish hams might therefore provide a significant competitive edge for the company. Donald had made several points to support his proposal. First, he argued, sales would increase as existing and new customers were attracted by the relaxed credit terms. Second, the change would improve the Zukowski family's competitive position by making the larger competitors realize that the Zukowskis intended to maintain their dominant market position in Polish meat products, while possibly even forcing some of the smaller competitors out of business. And all of this was at no cost and with no risk, Donald pointed out. The company had excess capacity available to meet the anticipated increase in sales. Thus, even if the competition did match the new credit terms, the Zukowskis would at least maintain their current market share with no additional investment. Donald was confident that this strategy would allow the family to recoup the estimated $500,000 in sales lost so far in 1987 and to increase the products' growth rate to 4 percent per year, the rate at which the whole market was growing.

They made some preliminary cost estimates, shown in Table 2, for increased sales of their Polish meats. With increased sales, the profits were sure to rise.

Stanley Zukowski pondered his son's arguments. Although he respected Donald's ability as an "idea man," he knew his son often did not consider all of the ramifications. For instance, the Zukowskis had experienced almost no bad-debt losses with their existing clientele. However, Mr. Zukowski thought that

TABLE 2

∎

Polish Meats—Cost Estimates

Sales (in millions)	Variable Costs/Sales	Fixed Costs/Sales	Profit before Taxes/Sales
$12.0–12.9	70.20%	27.10%	2.70%
$13.0–13.9	70.20	26.80	3.20
$14.0–14.9	70.20	26.55	3.25
$15.0–15.9	70.20	26.20	3.60
$16.0–16.9	70.20	26.00	3.80

the proposed relaxation in credit might attract customers who were a little shakier financially. Bad-debt losses might reach 1 percent of the new sales, he thought. Mr. Zukowski knew also that, for each additional sales dollar generated by the relaxed credit terms, he would have to maintain cash and inventory balances 10 cents greater than the credit he could get from his suppliers. That was in addition to the expected increase in accounts receivable resulting from the credit he would be offering his clients.

These funds would have to come out of the company's planned capital budget, Mr. Zukowski knew, because his lenders were not eager to invest more in the company at this time. The company might therefore have to postpone purchases necessary for its planned entry into the lunch meat market. Mr. Zukowski had planned to make capital expenditures of about $1.5 million per year over the next five years. Roughly one-third of this amount was earmarked for annual routine machinery replacements. The remainder was to have been invested in 1988 in lunch meat processing and packaging machines. These investments had already undergone financial analysis and had met the company's 12 percent after-tax hurdle rate. Mr. Zukowski thought it only reasonable to argue that any other use to which these funds might be put should also meet that same criterion.

Furthermore, Mr. Zukowski wasn't sure he agreed with Donald that there was no cost associated with using the excess plant capacity. For example, it seemed to him that some cost should be incorporated into the analysis to reflect the fact that increased use of the machinery would speed the need both to replace existing equipment and to expand the plant's capacity over the next five years.

CONCLUSION

Although he had managed to keep the company growing since his father's death, Mr. Zukowski knew that his strength lay in production and marketing rather than in the financial end of the business. He decided to seek the advice of his friend Peter Zelig, a retired accountant. Mr. Zukowski gathered up all the papers he thought he and Mr. Zelig would need, stuffed a kielbasa under his arm as a gift for his friend, and left the office.

Zukowski Meats, Incorporated

EXHIBIT 1

■

Balance Sheet (in thousands)

	1986
Cash	$ 1,840
Marketable securities	780
Net accounts receivable	1,600
Inventory	1,000
Other	260
Total current assets	5,480
Net property, plant, and equipment	6,000
Other	520
Total assets	$12,000
Short-term debt	$ 1,100
Accounts payable	1,800
Accruals	450
Other	250
Total current liabilities	3,600
Long-term debt	3,800
Common stock	2,000
Retained earnings	2,600
Total liabilities and owners' equity	$12,000

Austin, Ltd.

Since the 1960s Austin, Ltd. had assumed a hands-off cash management posture. In the 1980s however, economic factors and the increasing competition from specialty and discount retailers had caused Austin management to begin looking at its internal operations to cut costs and to boost profits and sales. The company hoped to increase sales by renovating existing stores and to control costs by reducing operating expenses and inventory levels. A part of this internal review had been to reevaluate the entire company's cash management philosophy and structure. To this end, Austin, Ltd. had asked its lead credit bank's cash management specialist to review the company's practices and to suggest any changes deemed appropriate.

In February 1984, the president, Kate Austin, was reviewing the proposal prepared by the company's cash management consultant. The proposal reviewed current cash management practices at Austin and recommended changes in the receipt, disbursement, and information systems, via cash management services offered by various bankers. As a result, Ms. Austin was considering once again centralizing the treasury function at the headquarters in order to gain more control over cash inflows and outflows.

BACKGROUND

Austin, Ltd. was a group of general merchandise stores dealing primarily in clothing for men and women with 100 locations in 20 states. Austin, Ltd. began as a small operation in the 1930s started by Robert Austin, Sr. Under his astute but conservative guidance, the company had grown over the years into a $1-billion business (see Exhibit 1 for financial statements for 1980 to 1982). For the first 30 years, the entire organization was controlled from the headquarters, but in the early 1960s, the company was reorganized into a decentralized structure to allow for more regional focus. Retail operations were divided into six divisions: New England, Mid-Atlantic, South Central, Midwest, Southwest, and Northwest, each under the supervision of a divisional president. While Robert Austin, Sr., remained at the helm as chairman of the board, his daughter Kate

This case was prepared as a basis for class discussion rather than to illustrate either effective or ineffective handling of an administrative situation. Copyright © 1984 by the Darden Graduate Business School Sponsors, University of Virginia, Charlottesville, Virginia.

had recently been named president and managed most of the activities of the company.

The late 1970s and early 1980s were characterized by high interest rates and inflation and a decline in consumer spending for durable goods. Directly affected by these factors, the retailing industry experienced sluggish sales, slow growth, and eventually, price cutting among department stores and general merchandise companies. Austin's suppliers had helped the company through the difficult period.

Historically, Austin, Ltd. had a good relationship with its merchandise and clothing suppliers. While dealing directly with large suppliers for about 60 percent of its merchandise, Austin employed resident buyers, or intermediaries, to purchase 40 percent of its goods from smaller merchandise and garment dealers. Austin had remained loyal to several of its largest suppliers over the years and, as a result, had been shown some favoritism by the dealers—it usually received prompt delivery of goods and quality merchandise. In fact, Austin's loyalty had paid off in the 1970s: when the company was feeling the impact of the slowing economy, its main suppliers had allowed Austin to slow payments for goods shipped with no penalty to the company.

The late 1970s and early 1980s also saw strong growth in specialty and off-price stores. Specialty stores posed a threat to department stores because of their depth of merchandise, while off-price stores posed a threat because they competed for the same consumer at price differentials from 20 to 60 percent of retail levels. In an effort to reverse the slow growth trend seen in 1981 and 1982, most department stores concentrated on building market share by improving productivity at their existing profitable locations and by closing the less productive and profitable stores. By early 1983, however, things improved as inflation and interest rates declined, and a "consumer led" recovery took place. The outlook for retail sales was brighter because of the trend toward higher spending.

TREASURY FUNCTION AT AUSTIN

When the reorganization occurred in the 1960s, a regional treasury office (RTO) was created at each of the six divisions. These RTOs had authority over all revenue locations within their boundaries, and the headquarters treasury (HQT) allowed the RTOs full autonomy over the collections and disbursements in each geographic location. The RTOs were encouraged to forward to the HQT as much excess cash as possible, but the practice had not been monitored closely, which allowed balances to accumulate in the RTO bank accounts. Only when the HQT ran short for a large tax payment or other major expenditure did it canvass the RTOs for excess funds.

The retailing industry was seasonal, and there was a period from late spring to shortly after the Christmas holidays when the company was low in cash because of the buildup of inventories and credit charges by customers. Then, during the early part of the year, cash was replenished as customers' payments for purchases were received. For this reason, Austin, Ltd. was a net borrower of funds throughout most of the year, and only on occasion was it a net investor in the marketplace.

Austin's banking relationships included 20 local banks used by the 100 stores, six regional banks used by the RTOs, and five large banks used by the HQT. Credit lines of $3 million each were established at three of the regional banks, and lines of $8 million each were established at the five headquarters banks. To reduce some of Austin's need for funds, the analyst had recommended changes in its banking relationships.

The cash management consultant had recommended changes to Austin's cash management structure in the following areas:

1. *Collection System:* Reduce and consolidate the number of lockboxes used to gather receipts.

2. *Concentration System:* Upstream funds daily to the HQT through the use of depository transit checks.

3. *Information System:* Monitor bank balances and transactions daily through an automated balance-reporting system.

4. *Disbursement System:* Consolidate all disbursements through one checking account located at a remote bank location.

The following sections outline the current structure of Austin's cash management activities and the proposed changes in greater detail. (See Exhibit 2 for a summary of the costs of cash management services.)

CASH MANAGEMENT

Collection Practices.   Approximately 30 percent of retail sales were made on Austin's own in-house credit card. All sales made were registered on point-of-sales terminals in the stores, which were on-line to a central processor in the regional operations departments. Bills were sent to customers each month, and payments were directed back to one of several collection points, or lockboxes, in various cities. These lockboxes were special post office boxes established by Austin to speed collections of funds to the RTOs. The checks received were opened, recorded, and endorsed, and then were deposited into Austin's account at each of the lockbox banks. Currently Austin had 20 lockbox banks which processed approximately 15,000 checks per month at each location.

The proposal prepared for Austin by its lead bank suggested a revision of its lockbox system. The bank had prepared a study to identify, by means of a computer-based optimization model, the optimal number and locations for a lockbox system for Austin, Ltd. By using actual data on the points from which Austin's remittances were mailed, the model was able to determine that eight of the present 20 lockboxes could collect all remittances and would allow for the least amount of time in transit (mail float) possible. By shrinking the number of lockboxes, Austin would be able to reduce the number of banks it used for collections, thereby freeing balances previously held to cover the costs of these lockbox services. The average cost for each of Austin's lockboxes was $200 per month plus $.50 per check processed. In consolidating the lockboxes, it was assumed that Austin could receive a volume discount from the remaining lockbox banks and that the average costs would decline to $200 per lockbox per month plus $.45 per check processed. The consultant suggested that in order to maintain relationships with the 12 banks no longer having Austin lockbox arrangements, the payroll and petty cash accounts should continue to be handled by the RTOs, and account balances should be maintained at those banks to cover the costs of those services.

Concentration Practices.   Because each RTO retained responsibility for its own cash, there was no structured concentration of funds at the HQT. Usually, funds received through lockboxes and cash deposits were wired from the local stores' banks to the RTO banks three times a week. Wire transfers were also used to move money from the RTOs to HQT once a week.

As a part of the effort to centralize the treasury function at Austin, the cash management consultant proposed that funds be concentrated at the headquarters rather than at the RTOs. The consultant suggested that a deposit concentration system be implemented that would allow funds to be moved each day from the lockbox banks to a main "concentration" bank used by Austin HQT. The funds would be moved daily to headquarters via depository transfer checks (DTCs), non-negotiable, unsigned checks drawn on Austin's account at the lockbox banks and deposited into Austin's account at the concentration bank. The funds would then be available to the HQT for its funding needs. The concentration bank would charge $50 per month for the account, plus $1 per DTC created to move funds from each lockbox bank each day. By using such a system, the wire transfers from the local stores to the RTOs and from the RTOs to the HQT would be eliminated at a cost of $15 each. In this way, cash and control would be centralized.

Information Practices.   Almost no structured daily-bank-balance reporting was used at Austin. Some local stores and RTOs monitored balances in banks using historical information, past monthly bank statements, and balance analyses. Others called their banks several times a week for balance information. Compensating-balance requirements for monthly bank services rendered were then adjusted after the fact. (See Exhibit 3 for an explanation about how bank service costs were translated into equivalent compensating balances.) Using information supplied from the various operating departments, the clerical staff at Austin manually tracked the headquarters' accounts in the five banks that the company employed.

The consultant recommended that Austin, in order to receive more timely information on its bank balances, use the automated account-reporting services available from its various banks. Through the use of a computer terminal or telex machine, Austin could receive daily reports of its accounts' activities from the banks. The monthly cost of such a service averaged $75 per account for summary balance information and $150 per account for detailed transaction information. In this way, Austin would be able to monitor the daily opening and closing balances in each of its eight regional lockbox banks, as well as the detailed transaction activities of the HQT concentration account.

Disbursement Practices.   Currently the RTOs made disbursements from accounts at six regional banks that were located near each of the six RTOs. Most of the disbursement accounts were funded in one of two ways, depending on the time of year. For the most part, RTOs funded their accounts as checks were written, leaving substantial balances in the accounts until the checks were presented to the banks for payment. However, in financially tight periods during the year, some of the more sophisticated RTOs attempted to forecast the dollar volume of the checks that would be presented for payment. Funds would be transferred into the accounts the day before they expected the checks to clear. In both cases, balance levels at most of the RTO banks were high. Currently, the "free" balances held at the six RTO banks approximated $200,000 per bank. Free

balances were those above and beyond any balances held for service or credit-line compensation. In general, a company would choose to leave free balances, on which it would earn no interest, in its banks only as a way to show appreciation and maintain good relationships. In Austin's case, there had been no decision to have such large balances. They had resulted from a lack of control over funds flows and an inadequate tracking of daily bank balances.

The bank proposed that the disbursement function should also be centralized. While some disbursement needs would continue to require same-day responses and would be accomplished using wire transfers, the consultant proposed that Austin eliminate the six RTO-level bank accounts and establish a controlled disbursement account with one of its banks. A controlled disbursement account allowed a company to write checks on a bank account that had a zero balance. After processing all checks presented to it by the Federal Reserve, the bank offering the service notified the company via telephone or transmission by 10:00 a.m. daily the exact dollar amount that would be clearing through the account that day. The company would then provide the necessary funds by the end of the day. In most cases, the bank offering the service was located some distance from the Federal Reserve office through which the checks would be processed, thus allowing for additional float on the checks written.

Currently, Austin's disbursements were handled by the six RTOs, all located in major cities. Total disbursements to creditors and suppliers were usually about 3,000 checks per month averaging $40,000 per check. To determine the best location from which to centralize the disbursements, the bank performed a disbursement study. The study was designed to measure and quantify the float generated by Austin's disbursement system. From a list of potential disbursing locations, a computer-based optimization program selected the optimal disbursement location and quantified the float of the optimal location. From the current disbursement input given by Austin, it was determined that by disbursing from a selected remote location in Delaware, Austin could expect to gain almost an extra day of float on each item. The dollar amount of the extra day of float could be determined as follows:

(Total checks disbursed per month x Average dollars per check)/22 Days per month = Average clearings per day.

These extra funds could then be translated into either an overnight investment or a one-day reduction of borrowings. See Exhibit 3 for investment and borrowing rates.

Through the use of a controlled disbursement service, the HQT would take calls each day reporting the total for that day's clearings and would set an exact position accordingly. The rest of the funds gathered over the day would then be available to satisfy other obligations. Through the use of this service, cash forecasting, prefunding, and/or estimating the disbursements would be eliminated, as well as the occasional risk of overdrafts. The cost for a controlled disbursement service averaged $400 per month plus $.20 per check paid, processed, and reconciled.

While Austin had established $3-million credit lines with three of the six RTO banks, it was assumed, even with all the changes, that the lines would remain in place because of the positive economic climate and Austin's possible need for access to credit to fuel its growth. Austin would continue to maintain balances at the three banks to cover credit-line facility obligations, as it had done in the past.

After reading the proposal, Ms. Austin concluded that the changes rec-ommended by the bank would indeed enhance Austin's cash management struc-ture and capabilities. From a monetary standpoint, the costs to use such services would no doubt be far offset by the use of the balances freed throughout the system. However, Ms. Austin remembered the consultant pointing out in a recent meeting that, while these services provided quantifiable advantages over the present structure, other, nonmonetary factors had to be considered as well, before making the changes.

POLICY ISSUES

Since its origination, controlled disbursement had been subject to some scrutiny. Although it was promoted as a control service, the Federal Reserve still frowned on its use because of the float it created in the check clearing system. In fact, as the consultant informed Ms. Austin, the Fed was seriously considering changing its cash letter presentment practices in order to reduce the float in the system. If this happened, banks might not be able to notify their customers as to daily clearings until 11:00 or 12:00 a.m., thereby impeding the customer's ability to know its cash position and obtain acceptable rates in the debt and/or investment markets. Thus, the benefits of such a system would decline.

The consultant reminded Ms. Austin of another consideration: the impact on those being paid by a controlled disbursement check. Obviously, if Austin gained float on the checks written, the recipients would lose a few days of availability on those items. Whereas the checks had been drawn on city banks and had received good availability when deposited, checks now drawn on a remote bank might not receive the same availability, and recipients might be forced to wait for the funds. For this reason, Ms. Austin thought that the con-trolled disbursement account should not be used for payments to individuals, such as employee payrolls or reimbursement checks. Instead, Austin would only be using the account to pay its merchandise suppliers and dealers. Given the long-standing relationships with some of the company's dealers, Ms. Austin wondered if a delay of several days on a check deposited by a supplier might prove detrimental to Austin. The company's reputation in the marketplace and the favoritism for prompt delivery and quality goods shown by some of the dealers could be threatened by the changes in the payment practices. In addition, terms of trade might have to be renegotiated (usually 2/10 net 30 or 60). Further-more, recent economic conditions had tested the merchandise dealers' loyalty to Austin, Ltd. Ms. Austin certainly did not want suppliers to think that she was beginning to delay payments again. Because competition in the retail clothing market was becoming stiffer, she wanted to maintain the corporate image and reputation she and her father had developed over the years.

Finally, Ms. Austin wondered what effect these proposed changes would have on Austin's various banking relationships. By removing the major portion of operating business from 12 of the 20 lockbox banks and by removing the disbursing function from the six RTO banks, Austin would no longer have strong ties to these banks. While credit-line facilities were still in place at three of the six regional banks, only payroll and petty cash accounts remained at the rest. Ms. Austin was aware that in times of financial need, like those recently expe-rienced, banks were most generous to those companies with whom they had credit-line facilities or operating business. By closing or reducing the Austin accounts, she knew that the access to funds might be more difficult in the future.

Overall, Kate Austin was impressed by the collection and information-system changes proposed by the consultant. If the savings were significant, she was prepared to make the changes. She was less certain about the disbursement recommendations. Given the company's history of a conservative approach to money matters, as well as Austin's satisfactory relationships with its merchandise suppliers and banks, she was not so sure she wanted to change these practices. It was a balance between bank relationships and the opportunity to free balances for more productive uses.

Austin, Ltd.

EXHIBIT 1
∎
Austin's Financial Statements (dollars in thousands)

	Fiscal Year Ending		
	2/2/80	1/31/81	1/29/82
Income Statement			
Net sales	$866,372	$969,143	$1,065,395
Cost of goods sold	640,062	691,251	744,924
Selling and general expenses	139,480	167,919	185,272
Depreciation	11,342	15,965	18,857
Operating profit	75,488	94,008	116,342
Interest expense	996	6,949	13,744
Other expenses	26,900	32,400	32,601
Earnings from continuous operations	47,592	54,659	69,997
Income taxes	21,305	24,324	32,814
Net earnings from continuous operations	26,287	30,335	37,183
Net earnings from discontinued operations	1,609	2,629	1,598
Net income	$ 27,894	$ 32,964	$ 38,781
Balance Sheet			
Assets			
Cash and short-term investments	$ 5,392	$ 5,398	$ 8,395
Accounts receivable, net	105,719	126,381	157,402
Merchandise inventories	103,322	125,984	149,140
Current assets of discontinued operations	(169)	407	(147)
Other current assets	2,436	9,643	2,822
Total current assets	$216,700	$267,813	$ 317,612
Investments and other assets	1,058	1,411	1,723
Noncurrent assets of discontinued operations	6,953	2,384	1,870
Property, plant, and equipment	220,388	263,061	309,112
Less: accumulated depreciation	(54,671)	(67,032)	(81,930)
Leased property	19,067	17,845	18,602
Total assets	$409,495	$485,482	$ 566,989
Liabilities and Equity			
Notes payable	5,412	18,730	—
Accounts payable	71,096	74,477	85,414
Accrued liabilities	34,111	38,399	49,050
Income taxes payable	12,694	16,186	17,567
Deferred income taxes	18,357	21,239	27,239
Current portion of long-term debt	2,590	2,090	1,856
Total current liabilities	$144,260	$171,121	$ 181,126
Long-term debt	60,256	81,334	119,938
Deferred credits	2,370	6,417	9,659
Common stock	4,579	9,150	9,168
Additional paid-in capital	12,061	8,342	9,145
Retained earnings	185,969	209,118	237,953
Total liabilities and equity	$409,495	$485,482	$ 566,989

Austin, Ltd.

EXHIBIT 2
∎
Cash Management Services Price List

	Cost
I. *Lockbox*	
Monthly maintenance per lockbox	$200.00/month
Checks processed through each lockbox:	
0–10,000 items	0.53/check
10,000–20,000	0.50
20,000–50,000	0.45
50,000 and over	0.40
II. *Wire Transfers*	$15.00/transfer
III. *Deposit Concentration System*	
Monthly maintenance	50.00/month
DTC creation and processing	1.00/DTC
IV. *Balance Reporting*	
Summary level information	75.00/month
Detailed transaction information	200.00/month
V. *Controlled Disbursement System*	
Monthly maintenance	400.00/month
Checks processed and reconciled	0.20/check

Austin, Ltd.

EXHIBIT 3
∎
Compensating Balance Calculation

To translate the cost of any bank service into a compensating balance, the following formula was used:

$$\text{Annual compensating balance} = \frac{BSC}{ECR} \times 12.$$

ECR was a bank's earning rate on any balances held by corporations to cover the cost of bank services (e.g., deposit concentration system). For instance, the rate used might be the rolling average yield on three-month Treasury bills. The following were 1982 rates quoted by Austin's lead bank, including the ECR:

Average short-term rate at which Austin could borrow: 14.85 percent

Average short-term rate at which Austin could lend: 11.08 percent

Average 1982 money market (lending) rate: 11.08 percent

Average bank earnings credit rate: 10.53 percent

BSC was the cost of providing bank services (for instance, a deposit concentration system).

Massalin Particulares

Massalin Particulares' overcrowded manufacturing facilities in Buenos Aires definitely contributed to the company's position as the high-cost producer in the competitive Argentine cigarette market. Massalin Particulares (M.P.) management believed a potential solution might be found in their yet-to-be-developed Merlo plant, but changes to the Merlo property would be required if they were to proceed. Those changes would require investments well beyond those already approved for the initial purchase of the plant. To begin the process of adapting the Merlo plant, Massalin Particulares President Juan Munro and his staff would need to convince the board of directors to invest an additional US$ 59 million in the cigarette business in Argentina.

HISTORY OF MASSALIN PARTICULARES[1]

Massalin Particulares, S.A., was born of the 1980 merger of three separate cigarette companies: Massalin y Celasco, Particulares, and Imparciales. Massalin y Celasco had been an affiliate of Philip Morris (effectively a wholly owned subsidiary) and produced a number of international (Philip Morris) brands as well as a local cigarette named Colorado. Imparciales and Particulares produced, in addition to Kent, domestic brands of blond, black, and mixed tobacco cigarettes. Both firms had been owned, in the main, by the German firm Reemstma prior to the merger that made M.P. one of the ten largest companies in Argentina. Massalin Particulares' board of directors consisted of those representing both Philip Morris and Reemstma, although Philip Morris had equity control (51 percent) and a 62.5 percent share in the earnings.

At the time of the merger, each of the firms purchased and processed tobacco and produced and packaged cigarettes. Manufacturing consisted of three

This case was prepared as a basis for class discussion rather than to illustrate either effective or ineffective handling of an administrative situation. Copyright © 1982 by the Darden Graduate Business School Sponsors, University of Virginia, Charlottesville, Virginia.

[1]Background on the socioeconomic and political history of Argentina is in the appendix to this case.

steps. The purchased tobacco was sorted and graded and the stems separated from the leaf in a stemmery. The tobacco was then processed. The leaf portions were cut to size and mixed with the stems, tobacco types, and flavorings to the brand specifications in an operation housed in the primary. The processed tobacco was then used in the manufacture of cigarettes. This process was known as a *make-pack* or *secondary operation.*

The firm's tobacco purchasing and stemming operations were carried on in one of the two main tobacco-growing regions of Argentina. Massalin and Imparciales had operations in and around Salta and Jujuy, two provinces in the foothills of the Andes near the Chilean and Bolivian borders in the northwestern part of Argentina. This area was known for its fine Virginia tobaccos grown on large farms by sophisticated producers. Burley was purchased in the province of Tucuman. Particulares' primary tobacco purchasing and processing operations were concentrated in Goya in the northeastern province of Corrientes, a large area situated between two broad rivers, the Parana and Uruguay. This area typically had small farms and sharecropper farmers who were more dependent upon the success of their tobacco crop than farmers running large operations.

The cigarette-manufacturing operations of Particulares and Massalin in Buenos Aires were within ten blocks of each other. Massalin also produced cigarettes in Salta, and Imparciales in Goya. (See Exhibit 1 for a map of the location of the operations of the three firms.) The plants, while clean, were old, and at least half the equipment was antiquated. It was clear that these old facilities were not designed to accommodate the higher speed equipment needed to produce the quantity or quality of cigarettes M.P. management believed the consumer of international brands demanded. Exhibit 2 further describes the facilities.

CIGARETTE MARKET

Cigarettes, generally a slow-growth product, had sales growth of 6 percent per year from 1972 to 1976 in Argentina because of government-imposed price controls: price controls, in an economy experiencing high inflation, effectively decreased the real price. Once price controls were lifted, prices rose, in some cases more than 100 percent overnight, and demand dropped. Demand from 1978 to 1981 grew about 3 percent, and management expected growth in demand to dwindle to near zero over the next decade. The infant antismoking movement had not yet had a significant impact on consumption in Argentina. Actual and forecast growth in the Argentine population and in the cigarette market and market share by cigarette type are shown in Exhibit 3.

In 1976 five companies were producing cigarettes for the Argentine market. By early 1980 mergers and acquisitions had reduced the number to two: Nobleza-Piccardo, a British–American Tobacco affiliate, and Massalin Particulares. The market was dominated by Jockey Club, a blond, filtered, Nobleza product. The many versions of Jockey Club accounted for 60 percent of Nobleza's sales and 25 percent of the total Argentine cigarette market, excepting the hard to define roll-your-own segment. Nobleza had other brands, but none with the stunning and enduring success of Jockey Club. Currently Nobleza had 59 percent of the market volume but, because M.P.'s brands commanded a higher price, only 55 percent of market sales. In 1981 M.P.'s market position by segment was:

Massalin Particulares Estimated
Market Position by Segment 1981

Cigarette Type	Market Share
Blond	45.3%
Light	20.5
Black	46.1
Imports	69.0
Total market share	41.0

M.P. had a total of 52 brands, none of which held more than a 6-percent market share. Marlboro, one of M.P.'s leading brands, had gained 3.4 share points in 1981.

M.P. management did not intend to remain number two in a two-competitor market. With the larger resource of brands from Philip Morris, and the strong position in the black cigarette market they had acquired in the recent merger, management believed they could own 52 percent of the market volume by 1984. Their plan for achieving that target is outlined below.

Massalin Particulares Market
Position by Segment, 1981–1984 Forecast

Current Types	1981	1984(est.)	Market Growth 1981–1984
Blond filters	45.3%	53.9%	0.2%
Light filters	20.5	40.3	14.3
Black cigarettes	46.1	53.0	0.4
New brands as percentage of total M.P. volume	10.0	24.0	N. Ap.
Total market share	41.0	52.0	N. Ap.

N. Ap. = not applicable.

This plan could be achieved only if M.P. could upgrade the quality of their cigarettes to maintain and expand the sales of international brands, increase their capacity to meet the current and projected peak-season demand, and continue mounting successful marketing campaigns. The Merlo plant might be the answer.

In part, the interest in the Merlo plant had been sparked by Nobleza's purchase of a large General Motors plant. Nobleza bought the plant just outside the Buenos Aires Federal District for several reasons. First, in 1978 the government required that all manufacturing be moved outside the capital of Buenos Aires. The move had to be made before a firm's license to manufacture expired (the mid-1980s for M.P.). While a firm could seek a variance in order to continue manufacturing within the capital,[2] M.P. management believed there were other, more compelling, reasons behind Nobleza's intended move. M.P. expected that Nobleza would concentrate on improving both the quality of their product and the efficiency of their operation. Being a low-cost producer was critical in the highly competitive environment, and high quality was critical to the success of international brands.

The General Motors plant purchase by Nobleza portended increasing difficulties for M.P. Capacity had been desperately needed even before the merger; in fact, in December, the peak of the summer selling season, M.P. could not meet demand for their most popular brands and had to institute an unpopular quota system. As for quality, there were obvious and continuing problems. There was no doubt that M.P. needed to improve both quantity and quality, even without a new, aggressive marketing plan. A revision to the plan for Merlo gave M.P. management the opportunity to do both.

HISTORY OF THE MERLO PLANT

The Olivetti plant in the Merlo barrio of Buenos Aires had originally been bought by Massalin y Celasco in early 1980 for US$ 20.6 million. The building, although considered modern, was actually more than ten years old. Fully air conditioned, it had been used by Olivetti to produce mechanical typewriters and calculators until 1976. By 1976 the military government, which had replaced the Peronists, had begun reducing the tariff barriers that had protected local industry, and the overvalued peso made imported goods more attractive to the Argentine consumer. The dated Olivetti line expired in a market filled with electronic alternatives. For a plant of 40,000 sq. meters (461,000 sq. ft.) on 15 hectares (38 acres), including a nearby park for employees, management believed the US$ 20.6 million had been very reasonable. Only because local industry was experiencing some slowing of business from competition with foreign-made goods, and because the size of the plant was larger than average, was the price so attractive.

The original plan had been to consolidate all Massalin y Celasco operations, except tobacco purchasing, at Merlo. Now, with the merger, another plan had been developed: to continue operations at the Goya and Salta plants, moving all other primary and cigarette-manufacturing operations to Merlo. The Salta plant would continue operations and be reevaluated after the move to Merlo.[3] Another change in the original plan for Merlo had been made: the equipment that was to have been moved from the discontinued operations in Buenos Aires was reevaluated and found unlikely to survive the move. Management thus believed it was better to invest in new equipment for the Merlo operation.

While some intermediate adjustments would be made, by 1985 the following would constitute M.P.'s operations:

---

[2]Greater Buenos Aires surrounded the Federal District of Buenos Aires. The system of government and the delivery of services resembled that of many U.S. states where independent cities operated surrounded by a county, both delivering services to their residents.

[3]By law the company paid excise taxes on cigarettes manufactured in tobacco-growing regions like Salta and Goya 36 days after shipment from the factory. From all other plants, taxes were due within 15 days after shipment. Excise taxes constituted 70 percent of the average retail price in 1981.

Projected Cigarette Production Facilities, 1985

	Goya/Corrientes	Perico/Jujuy	Merlo	Rosario/Salta	Total
Stemmery	Black	Blond	—	Blond	3
Primary	Black/Mixed[a]	—	Blond	—	2
Secondary	Black/Mixed[a]	—	Blond	Blond[b]	3

[a]Black and mixed cigarette manufacture would be centralized at Goya, with blond tobacco coming from the Perico and Rosario Stemmeries, and black from the Goya Stemmery.
[b]Blond-tobacco cigarette manufacture would be centralized primarily at Merlo with tobacco coming from the Perico and/or the Rosario de Lerma Stemmeries.

The changes that would be made to the original plans for Merlo were expected to raise the total investment from US$ 20.6 million to a total of almost US$ 80 million. The majority of the funds would go into new primary and make-pack equipment—equipment designed to replace the outmoded and unmovable equipment currently being used at the two old Buenos Aires plants. While the original plan had no investment for moving old equipment or purchasing new equipment, the additional US$ 59 million would be used as follows:[4]

Stemmery improvements	$ 1.4
Merlo primary	11.1
Merlo building improvements	11.7
Make-pack equipment	20.5
Other and contingency	14.3
Total	$59.0

The cost of the Merlo plant, the equipment, and ancillary costs are detailed in Exhibit 4. Operating the primary for one shift and make-pack for two, the volume would be 15.2 thousand million cigarettes in 1982 and would reach 18.5 by 1985. Included were some modifications to other plants that were necessary to keep them running and to increase the quality of the tobacco that would be used at Merlo.

While the Merlo plant would add appreciably to M.P.'s fixed expenses, by using Merlo the firm could solve its quantity and quality problems. The projected cash flows without and with Merlo are found in Exhibit 5.

While any number of items could change as the plan progressed, two variables seemed to be most important to the success of this project:

1. The willingness of the employees at Donato Alvarez and Belaustegui to move to the Merlo plant. Manufacturing personnel and office and support staff (all unionized), many of whom lived in the residential neighborhoods surrounding

---

[4]All figures are expressed in constant US$. As of the exhibit date, the exchange rate used to translate pesos into dollars was 3,953 to US$ 1.00. Because of the rate of inflation, and the fact that the majority of M.P.'s directors represented a U.S.-based corporation's interest in Massalin, all financial transactions were kept or projected in both Argentine pesos and US$s.

the plants, might choose to avoid the additional hour of commuting across the busy back streets of Buenos Aires. The contingency funds included some temporary transportation assistance to encourage employees to make the move, but the final cost was not known.[5]

2. Much of the equipment would be imported from the United States, Great Britain, and Germany. Thus, as the value of the peso changed, so would the cost of equipment.

CONCLUSION

The merger had been more successful than management had expected. While the financial results had been good, market share was up, operating losses continued but were smaller, and profits from investing the excise tax float were significant, more than covering operating losses, it had been in merging the two diverse organizations that Juan Munro believed they had been most successful. Much of the management of Imparciales and Particulares had left, but what remained was a young, strong, aggressive management team.

Furthermore, Argentina itself was increasingly attractive for business investment. Politically stable, the military government had taken steps to increase imports (forcing local business efficiency), to control the money supply (bringing inflation down to 60 percent in 1981 from a 1976 high of 500 percent), and to continue energy self-sufficiency. All profits that were less than 12 percent of capital could be repatriated without added taxes. While the peso was 30 to 50 percent overvalued, management believed there were no government policies that would deter foreign investment.

To convince the members of the parent company's board of directors, Mr. Munro and his staff would have to put together a persuasive case for Merlo, substantiating the return they expected and detailing the risks of this new, more capital-intensive plant producing cigarettes in the rapidly changing world of Argentina. In early 1980 they began to do so.

---

[5]Moving a manufacturing operation had costs peculiar to Argentina. Employees could claim, by virtue of the new commuting distance, that the move essentially eliminated their jobs. In the case of such claimed terminations, the employee was entitled to a form of severance pay equal to 1 to 2 months' pay for every year of employment by the firm. This was true for all employees in all industries in Argentina.

Massalin Particulares

EXHIBIT 1
■
Map of Massalin's Operations in Argentina

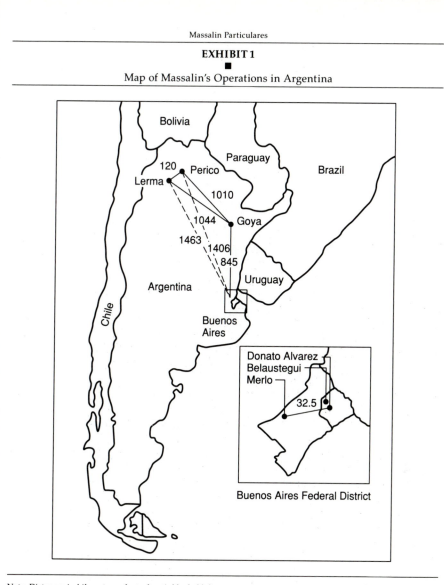

Note: Distances in kilometers; plants denoted by bold dots.

Massalin Particulares

EXHIBIT 2
■
Present Facilities of the Merged Companies

Buenos Aires

■ Donato Alvarez: A Massalin y Celasco plant that produced blond cigarettes. The plant was old and operated well beyond its designed capacity. Most of the international brands were produced here.

■ Belaustegui: An underutilized tobacco-preparation and -manufacturing plant producing black cigarettes and supplying black tobacco to the Goya cigarette-manufacturing plant. Originally owned by Particulares, this black-tobacco operation could not be used for blond-tobacco production, but could be used with limited success for the production of mixed tobacco.

Interior

■ Goya, Corrientes: An Imparciales plant that produced black, blond, and mixed cigarettes. The layout was poor and the plant small, forcing some operations into adjacent buildings. An underutilized primary was also located there.

■ Rosario de Lerma, Salta: A blond-tobacco primary and cigarette-manufacturing facility. The operations were inefficient, and the primary produced tobacco that could not be used in the higher quality international brands. A Massalin y Celasco plant.

■ Perico, Jujuy: An Imparciales stemmery.

Stemmeries

	Contributed to Merger by	Capacity in Tons (Green Weight) per Season		Total Leaf Processed 1979–1980 Season (tons)	Kg/Hr.
		Virginia/Burley	Black		
Rosario de Lerma	M&C	8,750	—	8,584	5,000
Perico	Imparciales	8,750	—	6,943	5,000
Goya	Particulares	—	5,400	4,513	2,500

Cigarette-Production Facilities

	Contributed to Merger by	Production Type		Yearly Primary Capacity[a] (millions of cigarettes)
		Primary	Make-Pack	
Donato Alvarez	M&C	Blond	Blond	8,800
Belaustegui	Particulares	Black	Black	4,200
			Blond	
Goya	Imparciales	Blond	Black	7,000
			Blond	
			Mixed	
Rosario de Lerma	M&C	Blond	Blond	1,900

[a] Operated with two shifts.

Massalin Particulares

EXHIBIT 3
■
Cigarette Market Profile

	Actual						Projected				Growth from 1981
	1976	1977	1978	1979	1980	1981	1982	1983	1984	1985	
1. Total population (millions)	25.2	25.6	26.2	25.6	26.5	27.3	27.7	28.1	28.5	28.9	1.4%
2. Total industry unit sales (billions)	37.0	36.9	36.9	38.2	38.7	39.3	40.2	41.0	41.5	41.8	1.6
3. Year per capita consumption	1,470	1,440	1,410	1,440	1,440	1,440	1,451	1,459	1,456	1,446	0.1
Annual growth rate percentage	—	—	—	—	—	—	0.8	0.6	(0.2)	(0.7)	—
4. Filter segment (share of market)	98.7	98.6	98.6	98.6	99.5	99.7	100.0	100.0	100.0	100.0	0.1
5. Market segmentation (share of market)											
a. Black filters	21.7	22.2	24.0	24.8	24.0	23.5	23.5	23.2	22.8	22.5	(1.1)
b. Blond/light filters	75.7	75.0	73.2	72.4	74.1	74.9	75.1	75.4	75.8	76.1	
Blond	—	—	—	—	—	67.1	67.2	65.0	64.4	63.6	(1.3)
Light	—	—	—	—	—	7.8	7.9	10.4	11.4	12.5	12.5
c. Nonfilters	1.3	1.4	1.4	1.4	0.5	0.3	—	—	—	—	—
d. Nonfilters	1.3	1.4	1.4	1.4	1.4	1.4	1.4	1.4	1.4	1.4	—

Massalin Particulares

EXHIBIT 4

■

Projected Costs and Benefits of Merlo Renovation
Capital Expenditure Program (US$ in thousands)

	Previously Authorized 1979/1980	This Request					
		1980/1981	1981/1982	1982/1983	1983/1984	1984/1985	Total
Stemmeries	—	$ 1,413	—	—	—	—	$ 1,413
Merlo plant purchase	$20,621	—	—	—	—	—	—
Make-pack equipment	—	9,631	$4,037	$4,860	$1,476	$ 514	20,518
Other machinery and equipment	—	3,170	2,320	1,320	1,190	930	8,930
Merlo building improvement	—	10,220	1,500	—	—	—	11,720
Merlo primary	—	10,560	500	—	—	—	11,060
Subtotal	—	34,994	8,357	6,180	2,666	1,444	53,641
10 percent contingency	—	3,499	836	618	267	144	5,364
Grand total	$20,621	$38,493	$9,193	$6,798	$2,933	$1,588	$59,005

Philip Morris International Appropriation Request
Supplemental Information
Detail of Cost Estimate
(in thousands)

Description	Previous Authorization	This Request	Total
Merlo plant purchase	$20,621	—	$20,621
Merlo plant building improvement	—	$11,720	11,720
Merlo primary	—	11,060	11,060
Stemmeries modifications	—	1,413	1,413
Make-pack equipment	—	20,518	20,518
Other production and misc. equipment	—	8,930	8,930
10 percent contingency	—	5,364	5,364
	$20,621	$59,005	$79,626
Ultimate Distribution of Expenditure			
Land	696	—	696
Land improvements	—	—	—
Buildings	14,882	5,703	20,585
Building equipment	5,043	8,512	13,555
Machinery and equipment	—	39,406	39,406
Data processing equipment	—	—	—
Furniture and fixtures	—	20	20
Transportation equipment	—	—	—
Leasehold improvements	—	—	—
Other: 10-percent contingency	—	5,364	5,364
Total	20,621	59,005	79,626
Other expense	1,300	295	1,595
Total estimated expenditure	$21,921	$59,300	$81,221

EXHIBIT 4 *continued*

Philip Morris International Appropriation Request
Supplemental Information
Detail of Cost Estimate
(in thousands)

Description	Previous Authorization	This Request	Total
Merlo Facility			
Plant purchase	$20,621	—	$20,621
Building improvement	—	$11,720	11,720
Primary	—	11,060	11,060
Total	$20,621	$22,780	$43,401
Ultimate Distribution of Expenditure			
Land	696		696
Land improvements			
Buildings	14,882	4,058	18,940
Building equipment	5,043	7,662	12,705
Machinery and equipment			
Data processing equipment			
Furniture and fixtures			
Transportation equipment			
Leasehold improvements	1,300[a]		1,300[a]
Other: Primary		11,060	11,060
Total	$20,621	$22,780	$43,401

[a]Moving expense item not included in capital appropriation total.

Massalin Particulares

EXHIBIT 5
■

Net Earnings Projections without Proposed Investments
(in thousands of constant US$)

	1981	1982	1983	1984	1985
Volume (millions of units)	16,307.7	15,530.3	17,144.5	17,854.5	17,985.2
Net sales	$1,170,090	$1,260,263	$1,242,573	$1,240,984	$1,192,141
Standard variable cost of sales	72,628	93,180	96,590	97,487	98,143
Federal and federal excise taxes	948,303	1,021,384	1,007,147	1,005,759	966,174
Shipping	5,776	5,063	4,976	4,940	4,728
Marginal contribution	143,383	140,636	133,860	132,798	123,096
Leaf usage	26,123	22,074	16,757	11,395	6,710
Fixed manufacturing expenses	33,671	40,199	36,138	35,655	35,218
Depreciation	8,463	6,576	6,721	7,174	7,672
Total cost of sales	68,257	68,849	59,616	54,224	49,600
Available profit	75,126	71,787	74,244	78,574	73,496
Advertising	19,944	20,553	22,103	23,096	23,273
Sales expenses	6,929	7,122	6,797	6,948	6,555
Promotion	3,017	3,117	3,645	3,252	3,158
Affiliate royalties	3,693	3,452	3,622	3,831	3,892
Total marketing	33,583	34,244	36,167	37,127	36,878
General and administrative	28,207	26,735	25,213	23,938	22,549
Total expenses	61,790	60,979	61,380	61,065	59,427
Operating profit	13,336	10,808	12,864	17,509	14,069
Interest expenses	8,834	9,841	9,076	6,227	3,117
Currency translation gain	12,878	10,484	8,853	7,330	5,634
Earnings before income taxes	17,372	11,451	12,641	18,612	16,986
Federal income taxes	3,596	3,778	4,172	6,142	5,605
Net earnings	$ 13,776	$ 7,673	$ 8,469	$ 12,470	$ 11,381

EXHIBIT 5 *continued*

	1981	1982	1983	1984	1985
Volume (millions of units)	17,310.7	18,232.3	19,781.5	21,152.6	21,843.2
Net sales	$1,242,056	$1,381,665	$1,433,694	$1,470,212	$1,447,862
Standard variable cost of sales	76,030	99,762	108,836	112,788	116,402
Federal and federal excise taxes	1,006,628	1,119,775	1,161,941	1,191,538	1,171,280
Shipping	6,131	5,551	5,741	5,583	5,763
Marginal contribution	153,267	156,577	157,176	160,033	154,417
Leaf usage current to historical	27,346	23,830	18,972	13,183	7,976
Fixed manufacturing expenses	33,085	39,454	35,353	34,519	33,776
Depreciation	12,734	11,602	12,284	12,517	12,677
Total cost of sales	73,165	74,886	66,427	60,219	54,429
Available profit	80,102	81,691	90,749	99,814	99,988
Advertising	21,476	23,043	26,268	28,148	29,075
Sales expenses	6,929	7,122	6,797	6,948	6,555
Promotion	3,017	3,117	3,645	3,252	3,158
Affiliate royalties	3,920	3,758	4,179	4,539	4,727
Total marketing	35,342	37,040	40,889	42,887	43,515
General and administrative	28,208	28,385	27,460	24,978	23,548
Total expenses	63,550	65,425	68,349	67,865	67,063
Operating profit	16,552	16,266	22,400	31,949	32,925
Interest expenses	8,857	10,274	9,346	6,199	2,282
Currency translation gain	13,662	11,494	10,215	8,684	6,843
Federal income taxes	5,074	4,702	7,756	11,478	12,370
Net earnings	$ 16,283	$ 12,784	$ 15,513	$ 22,956	$ 25,116

continued

EXHIBIT 5 *continued*

Cash Flows Proposed with and without Investment
(in thousands of constant US$)

	80/81	81/82	82/83	83/84	84/85
With Proposed Investment					
(A) Net earnings	16,283	12,784	15,513	22,956	25,116
(B) Depreciation	12,734	11,602	12,284	12,517	12,677
(C) Interest due investment plan	6,694	8,306	8,580	8,154	7,527
(D) Income tax due to (C) (33 percent)	(2,231)	(2,768)	(2,860)	(2,718)	(2,509)
(E) Operating cash flow	33,480	29,924	33,517	40,909	42,811
(F) Fixed assets investment	(59,914)	(9,193)	(6,798)	(2,933)	(1,588)
(G) Expenses net of tax	(1,069)	—	—	—	—
(H) Working capital increase	(13,452)	(21,729)	(16,922)	(16,225)	(6,047)
(I) Net cash flow	(40,955)	(998)	9,797	21,751	35,176
Without Proposed Investment					
(J) Net earnings	13,776	7,673	8,469	12,470	11,381
(K) Depreciation	8,463	6,576	6,721	7,174	7,672
(L) Interest due investment plan	852	1,145	1,624	1,800	2,021
(M) Income tax due to (L) (33 percent)	(281)	(378)	(536)	(594)	(667)
(N) Operating cash flow	22,810	15,016	16,278	20,850	20,407
(O) Fixed assets investment	(4,867)	(1,681)	(3,504)	(2,080)	(2,490)
(P) Working capital increase	(7,405)	(5,288)	(8,109)	(10,693)	(1,790)
(Q) Net cash flow	10,538	8,047	4,665	8,077	16,127
(R) Differential cash flow (I − Q)	(51,493)	(9,045)	5,132	13,674	19,049

ROI 20.01 percent, payback 5.1 years

EXHIBIT 5 *continued*

85/86	86/87	87/88	88/89	89/90	90/91	91/92	92/93	93/94	94/95
25,116	25,116	25,116	25,116	25,116	25,116	25,116	25,116	25,116	25,116
—	—	—	—	—	—	—	—	—	—
7,527	7,527	7,527	7,527	7,527	7,527	7,527	7,527	7,527	7,527
(2,509)	(2,509)	(2,509)	(2,509)	(2,509)	(2,509)	(2,509)	(2,509)	(2,509)	(2,509)
30,134	30,134	30,134	30,134	30,134	30,134	30,134	30,134	30,134	30,134
—	—	—	—	—	—	—	—	—	—
—	—	—	—	—	—	—	—	—	—
—	—	—	—	—	—	—	—	—	74,375
30,134	30,134	30,134	30,134	30,134	30,134	30,134	30,134	30,134	104,509
11,381	11,381	11,381	11,381	11.381	11,381	11,381	11,381	11,381	11,381
—	—	—	—	—	—	—	—	—	—
2,021	2,021	2,021	2,021	2,021	2,021	2,021	2,021	2,021	2,021
(667)	(667)	(667)	(667)	(667)	(667)	(667)	(667)	(667)	(667)
12,735	12,735	12,735	12,735	12,735	12,735	12,735	12,735	12,735	12,735
—	—	—	—	—	—	—	—	—	—
—	—	—	—	—	—	—	—	—	33,285
12,735	12,735	12,735	12,735	12,735	12,735	12,735	12,735	12,735	46,020
17,399	17,399	17,399	17,399	17,399	17,399	17,399	17,399	17,399	58,489

continued

EXHIBIT 5 *continued*

Detail of Financial Assumptions, 1981–1985

	1981	*1982*	*1983*	*1984*	*1985*
Inflation rate (wholesalers' prices, annual percent)	82	65	53	43	34
Inflation rate US$ (annual percent)	10	10	10	10	10
Devaluation rate (annual percent)	79	73	61	51	40
US$ interest rate (annual percent)	17.5	17.5	17.5	17.5	17.5
Total market increase (over previous year, percent)	—	2.2	2.2	1.1	0.8
Salaries total increase (annual percent)	106	82	55	45	36
Selling price increase (annual percent)	82	65	53	43	34
Raw material purchasing price increase (annual percent)	73	59	49	40	33
Dividends ($ 000)	7,000	4,000	4,000	4,000	4,000
Royalties ($ 000)					
With proposed investments	3,920	3,785	4,179	4,539	4,727
Philip Morris International	3,402	3,662	4,053	4,410	4,589
Others	518	123	126	129	138
Without proposed investments	3,963	3,452	3,662	3,831	3,892
Philip Morris International	3,175	3,329	3,496	3,702	3,754
Others	518	123	126	129	138

Other assumptions

Nominal excise-tax rate: 70.0 percent

Tobacco fund rate: 5.85 percent

Leaf inventory duration (months at
the beginning of each crop):   Virginia   12
                                 Burley   12
                                 Criollo Correntino   14

New office building not included.

Disposal of Belaustegui and Donato buildings not considered.

Income tax, corporate rate: 33 percent

Project Financial Review

Cash Flow Analysis The return on investment was calculated on the incremental cash flow derived from an aggressive "invest and grow" business plan. This planned investment is projected to provide an after-tax return of 20 percent with a payback period of 5.3 years. This return is attributable to increased volume, more favorable product mix, and cost-efficient machinery.

In examining the analysis, the following should be noted:

■ The Merlo Project was previously approved.

■ Expenditure request of US$ 20.6 million is included in the cash flow in order to reflect a total project approach.

■ Interest expense related to the investments is added back so as to not confuse the investment and financing decisions.

The cash flow analysis includes the following assumptions:

1.   All new investment is depreciated over a 10-year life.

2.   The project is analyzed over a 15-year period.

3.   All results after 1985 except for depreciation and investment are assumed to remain at the 1985 level.

4.   Additional investment requirements after 1985 are assumed to be equal to depreciation.

5.   A peso devaluation rate which would equal the U.S.–Argentina inflation differential by 1985.

6.   Financing is assumed for the full investment at the US$ interest rate of 17.5 percent.

7.   Payroll costs are increased faster than inflation. It is assumed that the government will advocate an economic policy with an objective to increase wage earners' living standards.

8.   Cigarette selling prices and tobacco costs are increased in line with inflation.

9.   Annual royalty payments are projected.

10.   No funds for a new central office building are included. This project is being reviewed and will be submitted separately.

11.   Increased volume and operating efficiencies will provide cost savings on a per-thousand basis in direct cost of sales, fixed manufacturing expense, sales expense, and administrative expense.

12.   In the net earnings projections, the leaf usage current to historical and currency translation gain numbers are included in the cash flows to approximate further the economic reality of a hyperinflationary economy within the constraints of U.S. accounting principles. If they were excluded, the return would be higher.

Massalin Particulares

■

APPENDIX
Argentina, 1979

Argentines are making their money work in an economy that defies all conventional definition. A recent visitor described the general population as being savvy about financial matters. He told of middle-class housewives moving their money from one source to another as often as necessary (sometimes daily) to get the best return. Long-term investments? One month. Other visitors believe Argentine businessmen may actually thrive on the gamesmanship of managing money under such adverse circumstances.

To the outsider doing business in Argentina, the country has the atmosphere of a busy casino because of the volatile economy and trading environment. Without money one does not play, but if one has money, then it is solely a matter of using it in the most lucrative way.

And what is the outstanding feature of this economy? Inflation. Inflation is at such high levels that, to the outsider, coping seems impossible. In fact, many believe the years of hyperinflation should have, by now, brought all economic activity to a complete standstill. So difficult is the situation to comprehend that foreign companies and investors have in the recent past written off their Argentine interests as losses, only to be tantalized, once again, by apparent opportunities for financial gain.

Referring to Argentina as a model developing country is unfair in both political and social terms. Nevertheless, the economy has become an interesting study for world organizations attempting to balance the needs of have and have-not countries. The effects of various economic policies on different sectors of the economy, and ultimately on investors, consumers, and businessmen, could prove to be instructive to other young countries attempting to stabilize in a tumultuous world.

Argentina is endowed with rich natural resources. Most of the country lies in the southern hemisphere's temperate zone. The country boasts a 90-percent literacy rate, a skilled labor force, and a relatively low birth rate. With these things in mind, it is hard for the outsider, and perhaps even the Argentine, to find logic and reason in the current state of affairs.

At the turn of this century, between 1880 and 1920, Argentina was considered one of the ten strongest economic powers in the world. Politically, the people supported fair elections and a democratic process. Culturally, the sophisticated Argentines invited and received renowned world artists as visitors and performers in their country.

To understand what has happened since then, as well as to consider Argentina's possibilities for the future, one must be familiar with the country's traditions. Many have concluded that Argentina's future rests solely on the shoulders of her population. The Argentine people's ability to demonstrate discipline, patience, and perserverance is as important as their demonstrated financial savvy in their unique economy.

Argentina is a country of immigrants: 40 percent are Italian and 30 percent are Spanish, the rest being English, Irish, and German, with a smattering of Syrians, Greeks, Turks, Poles, and Russian Jews. Most groups have immigrated within the last 120 years. The native Indian population and the blacks brought as slaves have almost disappeared because of miscegenation and extermination during the Indian wars.

Since the 1500s, Argentina has been a land of promise. The vast expanses of resources awaiting exploitation have provided people with grand dreams, if not grandeur, for generations. The early settlers came primarily from the western part of South America, with a small part of the population coming directly from Europe to the Argentine coast. This dichotomy between the coast and interior established the roots for several Argentine traditions.

For three centuries the country developed unevenly with the interior gaining economic predominance over the coast. The interior maintained a strict loyalty to Spain; its settlers retained Spanish attitudes and lifestyles and remained closely allied with the Catholic Church. They provided the mother country with the raw materials she needed. Cottage industries for the development of basic goods developed under the protection of Spain.

In the meantime, the coastal settlers developed trading as their leading industry, even though most of it was conducted against the wishes of Spain. The region's location, combined with the type of business conducted, gave the coastal population a bolder character than that of the interior.

With independence from Spain in 1816, the coastal interests assumed leadership, leaving the interior to stagnate. Protection of cottage industries was lost and their products were no match for lower-priced, higher-quality imported goods. On the coast, free trade (in a sense, a free-market economy) was in vogue. When the two interests attempted to form a national government, the result was division and even opposition in political goals. Although the first national constitution was written in 1853, it wasn't until 1880 that the entire country accepted the new governmental structure.

Throughout the 19th century, the interests of the wealthy guided the development of the country. The wealthy landowners ruled their territories and assumed positions of leadership as their capabilities were demonstrated. The *caudillo*, or local strongman, usually a wealthy landowner with a cavalry of men in his employ, emerged to create the common form of leadership and local government. He provided a sense of security to those in his territory, allowing the people to pursue their own interests. The *caudillos* did not necessarily trust each other, but they shared one goal—financial gain.

During this time the central region of the country, known as the *Pampas*, developed its potential as fertile land for livestock and agriculture. Europe, and particularly Britain, were ready markets for Argentine livestock products, and in turn viewed Argentina as an opportunity for profitable investment.

In many respects, Britain was a prime force in building Argentina. British capital helped to finance the struggle for independence, and British capital and technical skill built the railroads. At one time Britain owned Argentina's public utilities. Trade agreements between the two countries heavily favored Britain and kept Argentina in the position of an unofficial colony.

As the economy rapidly developed through trade, immigrants from Europe poured into the country. Argentina, a country of 1,800,000 inhabitants in 1869, received 2,500,000 immigrants in less than 50 years. By 1910 three out of every four adults in the city of Buenos Aires had been born in Europe. Upon arrival in Buenos Aires, some would make their way to the interior to work the land, but the great majority gravitated to the city's neighborhoods. There they found others from their homelands, surrounded themselves with what was familiar, and effectively separated themselves from the "New World."

Most of these people were not forced into making the transatlantic voyage for religious or political reasons. Word had traveled that there was money to be made, land to own, and opportunities to be had in this New World. For a great many, the promises of Argentina were realized.

But for how long and for how many people could the Argentine economy support this rapid and profitable growth? When the world economy took a downturn in the 1920s, Argentina's ties with Great Britain weakened, and new markets had to be sought.

The constitution formulated in 1853 provided for a political system much like that in the United States. In keeping with the strong leadership tradition, it permitted broad intervening powers for the president. While the concepts of democracy were appealing, in practice democracy in Argentina lacked the support of the total population. So long as opportunity for financial gain and social mobility existed, the majority supported the government in power. When these opportunities diminished, the seeds of discontent took root; the first publicly sanctioned coup occurred early in the 20th century. Since 1930 Argentina has been ruled by a series of military juntas, provisional governments, and dictators.

In 1949, Juan Peron came to power, and under the Peronist Constitution, the president's powers were enlarged at the expense of the provisional governments, legislature, and judiciary. Peron's support came from the labor unions, because his economic policy promoted the redistribution of wealth to the working class. Economic difficulties eventually led to a military coup in 1956, but leaders from 1955 to 1973 were unsuccessful in dealing with the political and economic problems. After 17 years of exile in Spain, Peron regained power in 1973. After his death his widow, Isabel, who succeeded him, was ousted in a military coup in 1976 following months of political and economic turmoil. The political terrorism that started in the early 1970s became pervasive throughout the country by the mid-1970s. The fear was so widespread that the general population was willing to support almost any measures that would return a sense of stability and security to the country. A junta of army, navy, and air force commanders took control, and General Jorge Videla was sworn in as president. The presidency was to be rotated every five years to establish a government as the collective responsibility of the armed forces rather than as an office for personal power. The new regime had the responsibility of ending what appeared to be terrorism on the verge of civil war and of stimulating an economy headed for ruin.

Peron's regime had advocated state participation in many areas of the economy, particularly in the oil, natural gas, coal, steel, railway, electric, and banking industries. The government also influenced economic activity through export and industrial incentives, import controls, tariffs, price controls, subsidies, support prices, and minimum wage legislation. The government's excessive size led to deficits financed by printing money. Business cycles usually consisted of economic spurts followed by recession, inflation, balance-of-payments problems, budget deficits, and substantial foreign debt.

Early in 1976, after Videla assumed the presidency, the economy was facing three major interrelated problems: impending hyperinflation, severe domestic recession, and possible external payments default. General Videla's first step was to select a new minister of the economy, Jose Martinez de Hoz. Sr. de Hoz was a member of one of the richest families in Argentina and was former chairman of Acindar, the country's largest private steel company. His strategy was to keep the state out of everything that private enterprise could do. He developed a massive economic reorganization program that advocated increased grain and beef exports to generate foreign exchange and new foreign investment to finance industry. Interest-rate ceilings and price controls were lifted.

By 1977 inflation had been brought from a 1976 level of over 300 percent to just over 150 percent, and the exchange rate went from 140 pesos per U.S. dollar to 408 pesos per U.S. dollar. Throughout 1978 improvements continued, creating a favorable environment for business, attracting foreign investment, and satisfying the immediate needs of the general public.

In 1979 the military had been in power for about three years, and the worst of the antiguerrilla war seemed to be over. Because the economic situation was showing signs of improvement and the gross domestic product was predicted to increase by fully 8.5 percent, the politicians were fairly quiescent. There had been an improvement in the real level of wages and salaries, inflation was at last showing signs of flagging, and unemployment was also on the decline. The strong peso–dollar relationship had Argentines traveling extensively and made imported goods very attractive. The balance of payments, as measured by the variation in gross revenues, was positive by about US$ 4.5 billion, with the total reserves position reaching almost US$ 11 billion by year's end. All told, the situation and the prospects looked distinctly rosy, and both President Videla and Sr. de Hoz basked in the glow of national and international approval.

Argentina, 1979

■

30-Day Borrowing Interest Rates (Domestic
Deposit Interest Rates) (percentage per month)

	January		February		March		April		May		June	
1977	N.Av.	N.Av.	N.Av.	N.Av.	N.Av.	N.Av.	4.49	N.Av.	4.49	N.Av.	7.43	(6.14)
1978	13.42	(10.24)	11.14	(8.19)	9.30	(7.03)	8.34	(6.73)	8.17	(6.89)	8.30	(7.17)
1979	7.59	(6.68)	7.06	(6.36)	7.03	(6.36)	7.06	(6.42)	7.14	(6.52)	7.26	(6.68)

	July		August		September		October		November		December	
1977	7.17	(6.63)	8.20	(7.34)	9.17	(8.01)	12.23	(9.45)	13.66	(10.28)	13.58	(10.52)
1978	8.02	(6.52)	7.79	(6.70)	7.35	(6.16)	7.38	(6.40)	7.58	(6.74)	7.87	(7.00)
1979	7.60	(6.99)	8.10	(7.31)	8.10	(7.35)	8.00	(7.21)	7.00	(6.18)	6.90	(5.93)

N.Av. = not available.

Source: Roque B. Fernandez, "Argentina: Macroanalytic Description (1976–1981)," Preliminary Draft, World Bank, Washington, D.C., January 1983, Tables 21 and 22.

Argentina, 1979

■
Economic Data on Argentina

	1974	1975	1976	1977	1978	1979
Resources and Expenditures at Current Market Prices (billions of US$)						
GNP at market prices	101.5	100.7	99.9	108.2	102.2	109.6
Net foreign investment from abroad	−0.7	−0.8	−0.9	−1.0	−1.0	−1.2
Gross domestic product at market prices	102.2	101.5	100.8	107.2	103.2	110.8
Imports of goods and NFS[a]	8.5	9.1	6.7	8.7	7.8	11.9
Exports of goods and NFS	8.3	7.4	9.7	12.3	13.2	12.9
Total resources	102.4	103.2	97.8	103.6	97.8	109.8
Private consumption	69.3	69.0	64.9	67.0	62.9	72.6
General government consumption	13.0	13.8	11.5	11.0	12.7	12.8
Gross domestic investment	20.1	20.4	21.4	25.6	22.2	24.4
Domestic Price Indexes						
Retail/consumer price index	426.5	1,204.8	6,542.2	18,072.2	49,771.0	129,168.7
Percentage change from previous year	123.3%	282.5%	543.0%	276.2%	275.4%	259.5%
Wholesale price index	444.2	1,298.7	7,779.2	19,415.6	47,766.2	119,077.9
Percentage change from previous year	120.0%	292.4%	599.0%	249.6%	246.0%	249.3%
Implicit GDP deflator	477.9	1,430.2	7,485.9	19,440.1	50,191.8	125,547.1
Export price index	544.6	1,525.7	9,677.3	22,183.7	46,207.6	97,514.7
Import price index	481.2	1,276.9	9,049.9	23,865.5	51,960.3	102,900.0
Terms of trade	113.2	119.5	106.9	93.0	88.9	94.8
Marginal domestic savings	16.8	28.4	32.9	29.9	27.6	21.7

[a]NFS = Nonfactor services.
Source: World Bank, *EPD Data Bank Country Report*, World Bank, Washington, D.C., January 25, 1983.

Argentina, 1979

■

Argentina Balance of Payments (millions of U.S. dollars)[a]

	1974	1975	1976	1977	1978	1979
Current Account						
Merchandise exports FOB	3,985	2,961	3,918	5,651	6,401	7,810
Merchandise imports FOB	−3,216	−3,510	−2,765	−3,798	−3,488	−6,028
Other goods and services and income credit[b]	784	625	773	1,807	1,435	2,106
Other goods and services and income debt	−1,381	−1,368	−1,293	−1,844	−2,560	−4,458
Balance of trade	172	−1,292	633	1,816	1,788	−570
Private unrequited transfers	N.Av.	6	24	32	48	35
Official unrequited transfers	N.Av.	−1	−6	−1	20	22
Current account balance	172	−1,287	651	1,847	1,856	−513
Capital Account[c]						
Net direct investments	10	N.Av.	N.Av.	145	273	265
Portfolio investment, net	−119	−56	−66	−1	101	222
Other long-term capital, net	107	−114	912	330	1,144	2,667
Other short-term capital, net	−66	373	−359	109	−1,251	1,276
Capital account balance	−68	203	487	583	267	4,430
Errors and Omissions, Net	26	4	−219	136	12	243

N. Av. = Not available.

[a]Minus sign indicates debit.

[b]Other goods and services and income include: transportation; investment earnings, abroad and domestic; other direct investment income; labor income; property income; other goods and services and income.

[c]Capital account:

Direct investment accounts for investment abroad and in the reporting economy and includes equity capital; reinvestment of earnings; other long-term capital; and short-term capital.

Portfolio investment accounts for public-sector bonds; other bonds, and corporate equities; and includes assets; liabilities constituting foreign authorities reserves; and other liabilities.

Other long-term capital accounts for the residential official sector; deposit money banks, and other sectors, all of which include drawings on loans extended; repayments on loans extended; other assets; liabilities constituting foreign authorities reserves; drawings on other loans received; repayments on other loans received; other liabilities.

Other short-term capital accounts for (a) residential official sector, including loans extended, other assets, liabilities constituting foreign authorities reserves, other loans received, and other liabilities; (b) the deposit money banks, including assets, liabilities constituting foreign authorities reserves, and other liabilities; and (c) the other short-term capital of other sectors, including loans extended, other assets, liabilities constituting foreign authorities reserves, other loans received, and other liabilities.

Source: Foreign Exchange Rate 1974–1979, World Bank, EPD Data Bank Country Report, World Bank, Washington, D.C. All other data, International Monetary Fund, *International Financial Statistics*, February 1976: October 1979, March 1983, International Monetary Fund, Washington, D.C.

	1974	1975	1976	1977	1978	1979
Official Reserves Account						
Counterpart to monetization/ demonetization of gold	N.Av.	N.Av.	N.Av.	N.Av.	N.Av.	N.Av.
Counterpart to Special Drawing Rights allocation	− 20	N.Av.	N.Av.	N.Av.	N.Av.	72
Counterpart to valuation change	90	N.Av.	2	− 18	96	128
Liabilities constituting foreign authorities reserves	N.Av.	N.Av.	N.Av.	N.Av.	4	65
Total Changes in Reserves	− 76	1,081	− 921	− 1,828	− 2,235	− 4,425
Foreign Exchange Rate—Annual Average Peso/Dollar	36.57	139.57	139.98	407.63	795.75	1,317.0

N. Av. = not available.

3B

VALUATION:

CAPITAL BUDGETING—ANALYZING RISK

The Jacobs Division

Richard Soderberg, financial analyst for the Jacobs Division of MacFadden Chemical Company, was reviewing several complex issues relating to possible investment in a new product for the following year, 1984. The product, a specialty coating material, qualified for investment according to company guidelines. However, Mr. Reynolds, the Jacobs Division manager, was fearful that it might be too risky. While regarding the project as an attractive opportunity, Mr. Soderberg believed that the only practical way to sell the product in the short run would place it in a weak competitive position over the long run. He was also concerned that the estimates used in the probability analysis were little better than educated guesses.

COMPANY BACKGROUND

MacFadden Chemical Company was one of the ten largest in the world, with sales in excess of $1 billion. Its volume had grown steadily at the rate of 10 percent per year throughout the 1960s until 1973; sales and earnings had grown more rapidly. Beginning in 1973, the chemical industry began to experience overcapacity, particularly in basic materials, which led to price cutting. Also, more funds had to be spent in marketing and research for firms to remain competitive. As a consequence of the industry problems, MacFadden achieved only a modest growth of 4 percent in sales in the 1970s and an overall decline in profits. Certain shortages began developing in the economy in 1982, however, and by 1983, sales had risen 60 percent and profits over 100 percent as the result of price increases and near-capacity operations. Most observers believed that the "shortage boom" would be only a short respite from the intensely competitive conditions of the last decade.

The 11 operating divisions of MacFadden were organized into three groups. Most divisions had a number of products centered around one chemical, such as fluoride, sulphur, or petroleum. The Jacobs Division was an exception. It was the newest and, with sales of $30 million, the smallest division. Its products were specialty industrial products with various chemical bases, such as

This case was prepared as a basis for class discussion rather than to illustrate either effective or ineffective handling of an administrative situation. Copyright © 1983 by the Darden Graduate Business School Sponsors, University of Virginia, Charlottesville, Virginia.

dyes, adhesives, and finishes, which were sold in relatively small lots to diverse industrial customers. No single product had sales over $5 million, and many had only $100,000. There were 150 basic products in the division, each with several minor variations. Jacobs was one of MacFadden's more rapidly growing divisions—12 percent per year prior to 1983—with a 13 percent return on total net assets.

CAPITAL BUDGETING FOR NEW PROJECTS

Corporatewide guidelines were used for analyzing new investment opportunities: return criteria were 8 percent for cost-reduction projects, 12 percent for expansion of facilities, and 16 percent for new products or processes. Returns were measured in terms of discounted cash flows after taxes. Mr. Soderberg believed that these rates and methods were typical of those used throughout the chemical industry.

Mr. Reynolds tended, however, to demand higher returns for projects in his division, even though its earnings growth stability in the past marked it as one of MacFadden's more reliable operations. Mr. Reynolds had three reasons for wanting better returns than corporate requirements. First, one of the key variables used in appraising management performance at MacFadden was the growth of residual income, although such aspects as market share and profit margins were also considered.[1] Mr. Reynolds did not like the idea of investing in projects that were close to the target rate of earnings imbedded in the residual-income calculation.

Second, many new projects had high start-up costs. Even though they might achieve attractive returns over the long run, such projects hurt earnings performance in the short run. "Don't tell me what a project's discount rate of return is; tell me whether we're going to improve our return on total net assets within three years," Mr. Reynolds would say. Third, Mr. Reynolds was skeptical of estimates. "I don't know what's going to happen here on this project, but I'll bet we overstate returns by 2 to 5 percent on average," was a typical comment. He therefore tended to look for at least 4 percent more than the company standard before becoming enthusiastic about a project. "You've got to be hard-nosed about taking risk," he said. "By demanding a decent return for riskier opportunities, we have a better chance to grow and prosper."

Mr. Soderberg knew that Mr. Reynolds's view were reflected in decisions throughout the division. Projects that did not have promising returns according to Mr. Reynolds's standards were often dropped or shelved early in the decision process. Mr. Soderberg guessed that at Jacobs almost as many projects with returns meeting the company hurdle rates were abandoned as were ultimately approved. In fact, the projects that were finally submitted to Mr. Reynolds were usually so promising that he rarely rejected them. Capital projects from his division were accepted virtually unchanged, unless top management happened to be unusually pessimistic about prospects for business and financing in general.

---

[1]Residual income was the division's profit after allocated taxes minus a 10 percent capital charge on total assets after depreciation.

THE SILICONE-X PROJECT

A new product was often under study for several years after research had developed a "test tube" idea. The product had to be evaluated relative to market needs and competition. The large number of possible applications of any product complicated this analysis. At the same time, technological studies were undertaken to examine such factors as material sources, plant location, manufacturing process alternatives, and economies of scale. While myriad feasible alternatives existed, only a few could be actively explored, and they often required outlays of several hundred thousand dollars before the potential of the project could be ascertained. "For every dollar of new capital approved, I bet we spend $.30 on the analysis of opportunities," observed Mr. Soderberg, "and that doesn't count the money we spend on research."

The project that concerned Mr. Soderberg at the moment was called Silicone-X, a special-purpose coating that added slipperiness to a surface. The coating could be used on a variety of products to reduce friction, particularly where other lubricants might imperfectly eliminate friction between moving parts. Its uniqueness lay in its hardness, adhesiveness to the applied surface, and durability. The product was likely to have a large number of buyers, but most of them could use only small quantities: only a few firms were likely to buy amounts greater than 5,000 pounds per year.

Test-tube batches of Silicone-X had been tested both inside and outside the Jacobs Division. Comments were universally favorable, although $2.00 per pound seemed to be the maximum price that would be acceptable. Lower prices were considered unlikely to produce larger volume. For planning purposes, a price of $1.90 per pound had been used.

Demand was difficult to estimate because of the variety of possible applications. The division's market research group had estimated a first-year demand of 1 to 2 million pounds with 1.2 million cited as most likely. Mr. Soderberg commented, "They could spend another year studying it and be more confident, but we wouldn't find them more believable. The estimates are educated guesses by smart people. However, they are also pretty wild stabs in the dark. They won't rule out the possibility of demand as low as 500,000 pounds, and 2 million pounds is not the ceiling." Mr. Soderberg empathized with the problem facing the market research group. They tried to do a systematic job of looking at the most probable applications, but the data were not good.

The market researchers believed that, once the product became established, demand would probably grow at a healthy rate, perhaps 10 percent per year. However, the industries served were likely to be cyclical with volume requirements swinging 20 percent depending on market conditions. The market researchers concluded, "We think demand should level off after eight to ten years, but the odds are very much against someone developing a cheaper or markedly superior substitute."

On the other hand, there was no patent protection on Silicone-X, and the technological know-how involved in the manufacturing process could be duplicated by others in perhaps as little as 12 months. "This product is essentially a commodity, and someone is certainly going to get interested in it when sales volume reaches $3 million," observed Mr. Soderberg.

The cost estimates looked solid. Mr. Soderberg continued, "Basic chemicals, of course, fluctuate in purchase price, but we have a captive source with stable manufacturing costs. We can probably negotiate a long-term transfer price with Wilson [another MacFadden Division], although this is not the time to do so."

PROJECT ANALYSIS

In his preliminary analysis, Mr. Soderberg used a discount rate of 20 percent and a project life of 15 years, since most equipment for the project was likely to wear out and need replacement during that time frame.

"We also work with most likely estimates. Until we get down to the bitter end, there are too many alternatives to consider, and we can't afford probabilistic measures or fancy simulations. A conservative definition of most likely values is good enough for most of the subsidiary analyses. We've probably made over 200 present value calculations using our computer programs just to get to this decision point, and heaven knows how many quick-and-dirty paybacks," observed Mr. Soderberg. "We've made a raft of important decisions that affect the attractiveness of this project. Some of them are bound to be wrong—I hope not critically so. In any case, these decisions are behind us. They're buried so deep in the assumptions, no one can find them, and top management wouldn't have time to look at them anyway."

With Silicone-X, Mr. Soderberg was down to a labor-intensive, limited-capacity approach and a capital-intensive method. "The analyses all point in one direction," he said, "but I have the feeling it's going to be the worst one for the long run."

The labor-intensive method involved an initial plant and equipment outlay of $900,000. It could produce 1.5 million pounds per year. "Even if the project bombs out, we won't lose much. The equipment is very adaptable. We could find uses for about half of it. We could probably sell the balance for $200,000, and let our tax write-offs cover most of the rest. We should salvage the working capital part without any trouble. The start-up costs and losses are our real risks," summarized Mr. Soderberg. "We'll spend $50,000 debugging the process, and we'll be lucky to satisfy half the possible demand. However, I believe we can get this project on stream in one year's time."

Exhibit 1 shows Mr. Soderberg's analysis of the labor-intensive alternative. His calculations showed a small net present value when discounted at 20 percent and a sizable net present value at 8 percent. When the positive present values were compared to the negative present values, the project looked particularly attractive.

The capital-intensive method involved a much larger outlay for plant and equipment: $3,300,000. Manufacturing costs would, however, be reduced by $.35 per unit and fixed costs by $100,000, excluding depreciation. The capital-intensive plant was designed to handle 2.0 million pounds, the lowest volume for which appropriate equipment could be acquired. Since the equipment was more specialized, only $400,000 of this machinery could be used in other company activities. The balance probably had a salvage value of $800,000. It would take two years to get the plant on stream, and the first year's operating volume was likely to be low—perhaps 700,000 pounds at the most. Debugging costs were estimated to be $100,000.

Exhibit 2 presents Mr. Soderberg's analysis of the capital-intensive method. At a 20-percent discount rate, the capital-intensive project had a large negative present value and thus appeared much worse than the labor-intensive alternative. However, at an 8-percent discount rate, it looked significantly better than the labor-intensive alternative.

PROBLEMS IN THE ANALYSIS

Several things concerned Mr. Soderberg about the analysis. Mr. Reynolds would only look at the total return. Thus, the capital-intensive project would not be acceptable. Yet, on the basis of the break-even analysis, the capital-intensive alternative seemed the safest way to start. It needed sales of just 325,900 pounds to break even, while the labor-intensive method required 540,000 pounds (see Exhibit 3).

Mr. Soderberg was concerned that future competition might result in price cutting. If the price per pound fell by $.20, the labor-intensive method would not break even unless 900,000 pounds were sold. Competitors could, once the market was established, build a capital-intensive plant that would put them in a good position to cut prices by $.20 or more. In short, there was a risk, given the labor-intensive solution, that Silicone-X might not remain competitive. The better the demand proved to be, the more serious this risk would become. Of course, once the market was established, Jacobs could build a capital-intensive facility, but almost none of the labor-intensive equipment would be useful in such a new plant. The new plant would still cost $3,300,000, and Jacobs would have to write off losses on the labor-intensive facility.

The labor-intensive facility would be difficult to expand economically. It would cost $50,000 for each 100,000 pounds of additional capacity (only practical in 250,000-pound increments). In contrast, an additional 100,000 pounds of capacity in the capital-intensive unit could be added for $25,000.

The need to expand, however, would depend on sales. If demand remained low, the project would probably return a higher rate under the labor-intensive method. If demand developed, the capital-intensive method would clearly be superior. This analysis led Mr. Soderberg to believe that his break-even calculations were somehow wrong.

Pricing strategy was another important element in the analysis. At $1.90 per pound, Jacobs could be inviting competition. Competitors would be satisfied with a low rate of return, perhaps 12 percent, in an established market. At a price lower than $1.90, Jacobs might discourage competition. Even the labor-intensive alternative would not provide a rate of return of 20 percent at any lower price. It began to appear to Mr. Soderberg that using a high discount rate was forcing the company to make a riskier decision than would a lower rate and was increasing the chance of realizing a lower rate of return than had been forecast.

Mr. Soderberg was not sure how to incorporate pricing into his analysis. He knew he could determine what level of demand would be necessary to encourage a competitor, expecting a 50-percent share and needing a 12-percent return on a capital-intensive investment, to enter the market at a price of $1.70, or $1.90, but this analysis did not seem to be enough.

Finally, Mr. Soderberg was concerned about the demand estimates on which he had based the analysis. Even though he could not justify his estimates on the basis of demand analysis, as could the market research department, he prepared a second set of estimates that he thought were a little less optimistic.

Exhibit 4 shows his estimates for achieving various levels of demand in the first year.

Mr. Soderberg's job was to analyze the alternatives fully and recommend one of them to Mr. Reynolds. On the most simple analysis, the labor-intensive approach seemed best. Even at 20 percent, its present value was positive. That analysis, however, did not take other factors into consideration.

The Jacobs Division

EXHIBIT 1

■

Analysis of Labor-Intensive Alternative for Silicone-X (dollars in thousands)

				Year		
	0	1	2	3	4	5–15
Investments						
Plant and equipment	$ 900					
Working capital		$ 140	$ 14	$ 15	$ 17	$ 20
Demand (000s pounds)		1,200	1,320	1,452	1,597	N.Av.
Capacity (000s pounds)		600	1,500	1,500	1,500	1,500
Sales (000s pounds)		600	1,320	1,452	1,500	1,500
Sales price/unit		$ 1.90	$ 1.90	$ 1.90	$ 1.90	$ 1.90
Variable costs/unit						
Manufacturing		1.30	1.30	1.30	1.30	1.30
Marketing		0.10	0.10	0.10	0.10	0.10
Total variable costs/unit		1.40	1.40	1.40	1.40	1.40
Contribution/unit		0.50	0.50	0.50	0.50	0.50
Contribution in dollars		300	660	726	750	750
Fixed costs						
Overhead		210	210	210	210	210
Depreciation		60	60	60	60	60
Start-up costs		50	0	0	0	0
Total fixed costs		320	270	270	270	270
Profit before tax		(20)	390	456	480	480
Profit after tax (taxes = 50%)		(10)	195	228	240	240
Cash flow from operations (PAT + depreciation)		50	255	288	300	300
Total cash flow	$(900)	$ (90)	$ 241	$ 273	$ 283	$ 280
Terminal value (year 15)						$ 381

N.Av. = not available.

The Jacobs Division

EXHIBIT 2

■

Analysis of Capital-Intensive Alternative
for Silicone-X (dollars in thousands)

					Year			
	0	*1*	*2*	*3*	*4*	*5*	*6*	*7–15*
Investments								
Plant and equipment	$ 1,900	$ 1,400						
Working capital			$ 160	$ 11	$ 17	$ 20	$ 24	$ 30
Demand (000s pounds)			1,320	1,452	1,597	1,757	1,933	2,125
Capacity (000s pounds)			700	2,000	2,000	2,000	2,000	2,000
Sales (000s pounds)			700	1,452	1,597	1,757	1,933	2,000
Sales price/unit			$ 1.90	$ 1.90	$ 1.90	$ 1.90	$ 1.90	$ 1.90
Variable costs/unit								
Manufacturing			0.95	0.95	0.95	0.95	0.95	0.95
Selling			0.10	0.10	0.10	0.10	0.10	0.10
Total variable costs/unit			1.05	1.05	1.05	1.05	1.05	1.05
Contribution/unit			0.85	0.85	0.85	0.85	0.85	0.85
Contribution in dollars			595	1,234	1,358	1,494	1,643	1,700
Fixed costs								
Overhead			110	110	110	110	110	110
Depreciation			167	167	167	167	167	167
Start-up costs			100	0	0	0	0	0
Total fixed costs			377	277	277	277	277	277
Profit before tax			218	957	1,081	1,217	1,366	1,423
Profit after tax (taxes = 50%)			109	479	540	608	683	712
Cash flow from operations								
(PAT + depreciation)			276	646	707	775	850	879
Total cash flow	$(1,900)	$(1,400)	$ 116	$ 635	$ 690	755	$ 826	849
Terminal value (year 15)								$1,384

The Jacobs Division

EXHIBIT 3
■

Break-Even Analysis for Silicone-X

	Labor-Intensive	Capital-Intensive
Normal ($1.90 price)		
Fixed costs		
Operations	$210,000	$110,000
Depreciation	60,000	167,000
Total	$270,000	$277,000
Contribution per unit	$ .50	$ .85
Units to break even	540,000	325,900
Price Competitive ($1.70 price)		
Contribution per unit	$ .30	$ .65
Units to break even	900,000	426,200

The Jacobs Division

EXHIBIT 4
■

Probability Estimates of 1985 Demand for Silicone-X

Demand Range (thousands of pounds)	Market Research Department Probabilities	Market Research Department Expected Value	Mr. Soderberg's Probabilities	Mr. Soderberg's Expected Value
400– 600	.02	10	.03	15
600– 800	.03	21	.06	42
800–1,000	.12	100	.15	135
1,000–1,200	.32	352	.40	440
1,200–1,400	.31	403	.22	286
1,400–1,600	.12	180	.08	120
1,600–1,800	.03	51	.02	34
1,800–2,000	.02	38	.01	19
2,000–2,200	.01	21	.01	21
2,200–2,400	.01	23	.01	23
2,400–2,600	.01	25	.01	25
Expected value		1,224		1,160

Eastern Airlines: Fleet Planning

Daniel Klein, director of strategic planning for Eastern Airlines, was about to make a presentation to management regarding the possible addition of a large number of new jets to Eastern's fleet. It was early October 1978, and the idea of developing and purchasing a new type of fuel-efficient jet had infiltrated the thoughts of the fleet planning and management group so thoroughly over the previous two years that most of the employees were already speaking in terms of when, not whether, it would happen. Mr. Klein recognized that he had not been immune to this tide of optimism and excitement, so he had asked Gary Purvis, manager of fleet planning, to join him in reconstructing the chain of events of the previous two years. He hoped that, between the two of them, they could discuss the financial implications and the future of the aircraft without being swept up in the excitement of the plan.

THE PURCHASE OPTIONS

Eastern had always been considered one of the more forward-thinking airlines in every respect. It had been the first to eliminate the old DC-8s, the first generation of jets, and throughout the late 1960s, the airline had expanded its fleet considerably with the newly introduced Boeing 727. As of October 1978, the airline had a total of 257 jets, 125 of which were some version of the 727. (Exhibit 1 shows the types and numbers of jets that Eastern then owned or leased.) The economic lives of both jets and jet engines were being extended for two reasons: improved technology and higher replacement costs. By 1978, however, Eastern's fleet of 727s was growing old, and the airline was faced with some choices: refurbish the jets, purchase new 727s or other aircraft of various models already available, or become involved in a plan to develop a larger, more fuel-efficient, technologically advanced airplane that could replace 727s and readily serve transcontinental flights.

Eastern management preferred to phase out old jets gradually. It knew that, if it waited too long, it would have to retire most of its 727s together. Many of Eastern's 727s had been purchased over the short span of a few years in the

---

This case was prepared as a basis for class discussion rather than to illustrate either effective or ineffective handling of an administrative situation. Copyright © 1985 by the Darden Graduate Business School Sponsors, University of Virginia, Charlottesville, Virginia.

TABLE 1

■

Number of Eastern's 727s and DC-9s
Reaching 20 Years in Service

	1984	1985	1986	1987	1988	1989
Aircraft	24	18	20	33	57	16

1960s, and they were not immortal; 16 to 20 years was the standard projected life of a fuselage for industry forecasting purposes. Eastern's fleet of 257 planes included 209 727s and DC-9s, and of that total, as shown in Table 1, 168 would reach 20 years old between 1984 and 1989. Therefore, management believed that it needed to make a decision as soon as possible.

In addition, Eastern management felt the need to expand its fleet. General experience in the airline industry told management that in fleet and service cutbacks, revenues always contracted faster than expenses, while expansion allowed costs to be spread over a larger base. The conventional wisdom within Eastern was summed up in the phrase, "expand or die."

Eastern was currently implementing plans to increase flights to the Midwest and West Coast, while continuing to grow steadily on the East Coast, its primary domain where it held a dominant position in the industry. Of course, airline deregulation could affect the plan. The first stages of deregulation were just beginning to take effect, and there was some concern about how it might change Eastern's scheduling and equipment needs. Other airlines were expected to drop unprofitable routes and scramble for more desirable ones, many of which Eastern already served. As more airlines scheduled flights on the more profitable routes, revenues could be squeezed as the number of passengers per flight declined.

Since 1976, Eastern management had discussed with Boeing the possibility of developing a fuel-efficient, 174-passenger, narrow-bodied jet that could fly a distance like that between Atlanta, Georgia and Portland, Oregon. By mid-1978, having designed the 197-passenger 767, Boeing management believed that the company was capable of designing the aircraft Eastern management described and that it could be available beginning in 1983. It was now up to Eastern to decide whether it wanted to sponsor the development program jointly with British Airways, which also was interested in such an aircraft.

There were advantages and disadvantages to sponsoring the development of a new aircraft. On the positive side, sponsors were able to incorporate their own design ideas, take first delivery, and receive concessions on the price. On the other hand, sponsors also took the risk of spending hundreds of millions of dollars on a project that could fail or prove to be unsuitable for the airline's needs.

The advanced narrow-body aircraft was especially attractive to Eastern management for four reasons: fuel efficiency, size, noise levels, and new technology. As shown in Exhibit 2, no plane presently existed to fill the gap between the 137-seat 727-200 and the 240-seat A300. Eastern was considering purchasing the new 197-seat 767 wide-body, but even if it were ordered now, it was not expected to be available much earlier than the new narrow-bodied aircraft. Exhibit 3 displays the options available to Eastern. The airline could develop and order the new narrow-bodied aircraft; order the 767 or A310, both of which would be available at about the same time; or purchase 727-200s or A300s for delivery within 2 years.

At first, Eastern had hoped to retrofit the new Rolls-Royce engines that would be the source of much of the proposed plane's fuel-efficiency onto old 727s, but found it was technically impossible. Eastern also considered stretching some 727s—cutting the plane near the mid-section and welding in a new section—and using the new engines on them, but that was expected to cost as much as the new narrow-body jet.

Exhibit 4 provides information on Eastern's proposed schedule for the acquisition of new aircraft. If Eastern sponsored the advanced narrow-body aircraft program, the plane would begin in 1983 to replace some of the 727-100s and -200s. These planes would, in turn, replace older 727QCs and DC-9-30s. These older aircraft would be sold, and were expected to bring $3 to $4 million.[1]

THE ALTERNATIVE COSTS

Boeing expected the new narrow-bodied aircraft, including two Rolls-Royce jet engines per plane, to cost $17.8 million, or $102,241 per seat. The prices and seating capacities of the various alternative jets are shown in Table 2.

Management considered the operating cost per average seat-mile to be the most important cost determinant when considering the purchase of a new aircraft. In 1978, jet fuel cost an average of 38 cents per gallon, but the price could rise well beyond that level, especially because of the potential at the time for an OPEC price increase. As can be seen in Table 3, the price of jet fuel had been increasing more quickly than the price of crude oil. Table 4 shows the fuel consumption for the alternative aircraft, including that expected for the 767 and the advanced narrow-body, over an average flight length of 500 miles.

Mr. Klein assumed that the new narrow-body and the 767 would require a three-person flight crew, but Boeing management suggested that new technology properly incorporated into the cockpit design could reduce the crew to only two people. If so (and if the pilots' union allowed the two-person cockpit), the flight crew expense for these two jets could be decreased by between 20 and 25 percent. Mr. Klein derived the operating figures shown in Table 5 on the basis of a three-member crew for the new jets and a 500-mile flight.

To cover the added costs of using the new narrow-bodied aircraft to replace some of the smaller 727-200s, Eastern would have to increase the passenger loads on these flights. Mr. Klein did not know how regularly the additional 37 seats could be filled, so he used historical information to try to determine whether the replacement would be cost-effective from an operational standpoint. Information on load factors for individual flights was not available, but the data in Exhibit 5 indicate that, between 1970 and 1977, on average, the 727-200s flew at between 48 and 60 percent of capacity; the growth in the number of aircraft miles was erratic. Mr. Klein was concerned not only with the ability to cover and exceed the cost differences between the 727-200s and the new narrow-bodies, but with the ability to fill the extra space in each 727 bumped down to replace

---

[1]For accounting purposes, straight-line depreciation was used for all jets, providing a 5- to 15-percent residual at the end of 16 to 20 years. For tax purposes, the Asset Depreciation Range (ADR) of 9.5 to 14.5 years was applied to the double-declining balance method; a 10-percent residual was assumed.

TABLE 2
■
Prices of Alternative Aircraft (dollars in millions)

	Aircraft					
	A-300-B4	A-310	767	New Craft	DC-9	727-200
Price	$25.10	$25.00	$23.99	$17.79	$12.40	$9.68
Seats	240	193	197	174	133	137

TABLE 3
■
Jet Fuel and Crude Oil Prices and Indexes (1973 = 100)

	1973	1974	1975	1976	1977	1978
Jet fuel						
Cents per gallon	12.0	22.1	27.9	29.6	36.0	38.0
Price index	100.0	184.2	232.5	246.7	300.0	316.7
Crude oil price index	100.0	168.1	195.0	201.2	217.6	238.2

TABLE 4
■
Fuel Consumption of Alternative Aircraft, Average 500-Mile Flight

	Aircraft					
	A-300-B4	A-310	767	New Craft	DC-9	727-200
Gallons/mile	5.21	4.27	4.10[a]	3.37[a]	2.94	3.91

[a]Estimated.

TABLE 5
■
Operating Costs per Average Flight of 500 Miles

	A-300-B4	A-310	767[a]	New Craft[a]	DC-9	727-200
Flight crew	$ 669	$ 652	$ 645	$ 600	$ 498	$ 488
Maintenance	518	456	471	413	260	266
Attendants	343	294	294	239	193	189
Landing	195	173	164	129	85	100
Station costs	727	623	623	554	450	450
Depreciation	724	688	688	513	366	276
Total	$3,176	$2,886	$2,885	$2,448	$1,852	$1,769

[a]Estimated.

TABLE 6
■
Revenue per Passenger Mile (cents)

	1970	1971	1972	1973	1974	1975	1976	1977
Passenger-mile yield	5.95	6.29	6.34	6.68	7.72	8.00	8.42	8.87

smaller, older aircraft. Specifically, he was concerned whether Eastern would at least recover the added operating expense of replacing 727QCs and DC-9s with old 727-100 and -200 models.

As indicated in Table 6, between 1970 and 1977, the airline's average passenger-mile yield—its revenue per passenger per mile—increased in nominal terms from 5.95 cents to 8.87 cents. Mr. Klein used this information to determine how many of the additional seats in each plane would have to be filled on average to break even between the operating expenses and revenues of the new narrow-bodies and the 727s they would replace, and between the 727s and the older planes that they would, in turn, replace.

Mr. Klein had a good idea of what the payment schedule for the narrow-bodied jets would be, and he knew that Eastern's management was at least tentatively interested in having 11 delivered in 1983 and 10 in 1984, the first 2 years that Boeing management believed they would be available. At the signing of the agreement, probably late in 1978, 5 percent of the total price would be due. Another 5 percent would be payable 2 years prior to delivery, and 6.66 percent would be due every 6 months for the remaining 18 months. The final 70 percent of the price of each plane would be paid on delivery. Essentially, the same sort of payment schedule applied to any of the alternative jets, in that all would be paid for in installments prior to delivery. The 767 and the A310 would be available about 6 months earlier than the narrow-bodies; any of the other jets could be delivered about 2 years after an order was placed.

In June, management had contracted for the purchase of 16 A300-B4s to be delivered over the next 2 years, and in September, the airline ordered 10 727-200s for delivery in late 1979. These planes would not fill Eastern's total expected needs, however.

EASTERN'S FINANCIAL CONDITION

The years 1976 and 1977 had been good; the airline made record profits of $45 million and $28 million and grew to $1.7 billion in assets and $331 million in equity. But the earlier years had been, in Eastern management's own assessment, "rocky." A $20-million profit in one year turned into a $51-million loss the next, and a $10-million profit into an $89-million loss. Exhibits 6 and 7 provide Eastern's financial statements from 1970 to 1977.

The company's debt was of particular concern. Between 1970 and 1977, Eastern's long-term debt ranged between 1.5 and 3.0 times equity and between 44 and 61 percent of assets; in 1977 one-half of the long-term debt consisted of leases. In 1978, however, Eastern had already agreed to purchase a large number of planes, none of which were suited to the niche that the new narrow-body could best fill.

Eastern Airlines: Fleet Planning

EXHIBIT 1
■

Current and On-Order Aircraft, October 1978

Aircraft	Current Fleet			On Order	Scheduled Deliveries				On Option
	Owned	Leased	Total		1979	1980	1981	1982	
Four-Engine Jets									
DC-8-61		5	5						
Three-Engine Jets									
L-1011	21	11	32						13
L-1011 (Seasonal)		2	2						
B-727-225	32	23	55	10	10				31
B-727-100	46		46						
B-727-QC	21	3	24						
Two-Engine Jets									
A310									25
A310-B4	3	4	7	16	4	4	4	4	9
DC-9-51	4	13	17						
DC-9-31	33	25	58						
DC-9-14		9	9						
Subtotal: Jets	160	95	255	26	14	4	4	4	78
Electra	2		2						
Total	162	95	257	26	14	4	4	4	78

Eastern Airlines: Fleet Planning

EXHIBIT 2
■

Size Gap in Airline Planes: Capacity Gap without the New Aircraft

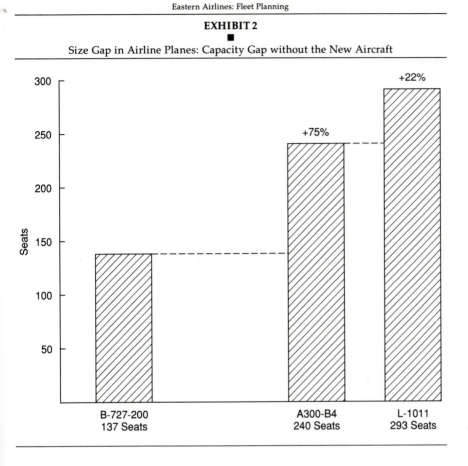

Eastern Airlines: Fleet Planning

EXHIBIT 3
■
Specifications of Candidate Aircraft

	B-727-200	New Aircraft	B-767-200	A-310	A-300-B4
Aisles	1	1	2	2	2
Seats abreast	6	6	7	8	8
Passengers	137	174	197	193	240
Range (statute miles)	2,000	2,600	2,500	3,000	2,700
Engines	3	2	2	2	2

Eastern Airlines: Fleet Planning

EXHIBIT 4
■
Aircraft Acquisition/(Retirements)

	1977	1978	1979	1980	1981	1982	1983	1984	1985	1986	1987	1988	1989	1990
L-188	(14)													
DC-9-14				(4)	(5)									
DC-9-30	(3)	(5)	(5)	(5)	(5)	(8)	(7)	(10)	(10)	(7)	(7)			
B-727-QC		(5)	(5)	(5)	(5)	(2)	(3)							
B-727-100										(8)	(6)	(6)	(13)	(13)
DC-9-50	9	6		12	14									
B-727-200	3	3	10	5	5	5								
A-300 or 767			4	4	4	4		3	8	10	9	7	7	6
L-1011	2	3		3	2					2	4	6	8	9
Net	(3)	2	4	10	10	(1)	(10)	(7)	(10)	(1)	0	0	2	15
Total units	255	257	261	271	281	280	270	263	253	252	252	252	254	269

Eastern Airlines: Fleet Planning

EXHIBIT 5
■
Seat-Miles and Occupancy, 1970–1977 (millions)

	727-225		727-QC		DC-9		Eastern Total	
	Available	Occupied	Available	Occupied	Available	Occupied	Available	Occupied
1970	2,512	1,278	2,762	1,483	6,498	3,731	28,245	15,493
1971	4,358	2,107	2,771	1,503	6,576	3,748	29,156	15,502
1972	4,829	2,659	2,680	1,670	6,992	4,323	29,128	17,023
1973	6,913	3,782	2,620	1,526	7,301	3,372	31,441	17,458
1974	6,754	4,049	3,004	1,826	6,387	4,164	29,912	17,860
1975	6,726	3,889	N.Ap.	N.Ap.	6,777	4,124	32,511	18,294
1976	6,978	3,919	N.Ap.	N.Ap.	7,171	4,430	34,766	19,520
1977	8,512	4,863	N.Ap.	N.Ap.	7,001	4,262	36,783	20,657

N.Ap. = not applicable.

EXHIBIT 6

Statements of Income, Years Ended December 31, 1970–1977
(in thousands)

	1970	1971	1972	1973	1974	1975	1976	1977[g]
Operating Revenues								
Passenger								
First class	$ 158,545	$ 143,963	$ 164,219	$ 152,098	$ 186,617	$ 181,851	$ 190,365	$ 191,152
Coach	738,166	803,520	888,182	978,178	1,162,170	1,264,295	1,451,635	1,638,103
Military airlift command	12,105	2,887	2,769	4,712	3,942	3,679	1,459	595
Other	3,451	3,806	3,903	3,691	9,401[a]	10,235	12,325	13,460
Commercial charter	8,820	20,114	20,686	18,356	12,089	4,627	1,116	1,825
Security charges	—	—	—	9,256	13,823	8,615	—	—
Mail	12,207	13,895	15,467	17,955	15,717	17,449	21,578	31,430[h]
Express	3,341	3,170	3,426	3,678	3,713	2,319	—	—
Freight	39,523	45,038	49,260	56,009	53,827	60,143	67,545	77,064
Excess baggage	1,742	1,824	1,551	1,863	2,899	2,956	3,487	3,457
Incidental revenue	40,402	47,850	45,354	57,290	66,090	68,225	75,965	78,807
Total operating revenue	$1,018,302	$1,086,067	$1,194,817	$1,303,086	$1,530,288	$1,624,394	$1,825,475	$2,035,893
Operating Expenses								
Flying operations	$ 270,766	$ 324,849	$ 327,688	$ 377,349	$ 445,325	$ 532,392	$ 570,852	$ 641,516
Maintenance								
Direct maintenance	88,423	91,977	97,133	106,713	129,392	142,127	160,019	158,207
Maintenance burden	61,141	66,483	77,072	93,401	97,050	101,907	113,557	130,181
Total maintenance	149,564	158,460	174,205	200,114	226,442	244,034	273,576	288,388
Passenger service	91,642	97,563	114,636	127,501	128,196	140,685	159,761	187,779
Aircraft servicing	77,655	86,937	96,325	102,760	103,226	94,036	110,848	113,483
Traffic servicing	72,081	80,121	96,177	131,698	147,491	169,913	194,089	213,495
Servicing administration	13,772	14,770	15,876	19,373	17,332	18,168	22,609	23,118
Reservations and sales	94,788	98,742	117,665	132,184	146,957	162,639	186,355	208,155
Advertising and publicity	28,949	27,915	28,646	31,419	28,115	29,238	34,444	43,089
General and administrative	44,611	49,198	57,213	63,174	62,266	65,558	69,235	60,860
Depreciation and amortization	83,336	79,372	79,351	93,829	97,582	67,078	103,144	147,173
Cost of incidental revenue	47,252	32,310	33,898	43,198	56,621	98,248	54,234	52,005
Total operating expenses	$ 974,416	$1,050,237	$1,141,680	$1,322,599	$1,459,553	$1,621,989	$1,779,147[f]	$1,979,061
Operating profit (loss)	43,886	35,830	53,137	(19,513)	70,735	2,405	46,328	56,832

Nonoperating Income (Expense)

Interest income	3,699	2,333	2,241	3,827	10,261	6,598	5,740	6,133
Interest expense	(37,613)	(33,505)	(27,411)	(45,366)	(65,821)	(50,881)	(43,718)	(70,048)
Profit (loss) on disposal of equipment	(1,714)	2,432	3,422	4,979	4,843	3,956	(620)	21,996
Other, net	(185)	549	(646)	(253)	(2,401)	4,991[c]	5,536[c]	11,711
Total nonoperating income	(35,813)	(28,191)	(22,394)	(36,813)	(53,118)	(35,336)	(33,062)	(30,208)
Income (loss) before special program, income taxes, and extraordinary item, airline operations	8,073	7,639	30,743	(56,326)	17,617	(32,931)	13,266	26,624
Cumulative effect of accounting change	—	—	—	—	—	(35,000)[d]	—	—
Equity in operations of nontransport subsidiaries	(735)	(161)	(366)	(7,708)	(7,222)	(20,783)	—	—
Income (loss) before special wage programs, income taxes, and extraordinary item	7,338	7,478	30,377	(64,034)	10,395	(88,714)	13,266	26,624
Net effect of special wage programs	—	—	—	—	—	—	31,973	1,253
Income (loss) after special wage programs, and before income taxes and extraordinary item	7,338	7,478	30,377	(64,034)	10,395	(88,714)	45,239	27,877
Provision for (reduction in) income taxes	1,877	1,788	7,364	(12,765)	2,495	—	10,857	—
Income (loss) before extraordinary item	5,461	5,690	23,013	(51,269)	7,900	(88,714)	34,382	27,877
Extraordinary item (expense)	—	—	(3,253)	—	2,495[b]	—	10,857[b]	—
Net income (loss)	$ 5,461	$ 5,690	$ 19,760	$ (51,269)	$ 10,395	$ (88,714)	$ 45,239	$ 27,877

[a]Reflects industry discount travel on a forward basis only.
[b]Utilization of tax loss carry-forward.
[c]1976 reflects a gain of $4.8 million relating to the translation of foreign currency indebtedness and the devaluation of the Mexican peso. 1975 reflects a gain of $4.6 million on translation of foreign currency indebtedness; years prior to 1975 are immaterial.
[d]Reflects $35.0-million accrued vacation liability for prior years.
[e]Security charges included in passenger revenue.
[f]Operating expenses for 1976 do not reflect the impact of the wage freeze reduction.
[g]Data for 1977 reflect the adoption of FASB No. 13 (capitalization of leases).
[h]Includes $7.2 million retroactive mail settlement in 1977 and $0.3 million in 1978.

EXHIBIT 7

■

Balance Sheets, December 31, 1970–1977
(in thousands)

	1970	1971	1972	1973	1974	1975	1976	1977[i]
Assets								
Current Assets								
Cash	$ 45,255	$ 38,404	$ 37,935	$ 60,486	$ 55,083	$ 45,930	$ 41,971	$ 31,342
Short-term investments	15,451	28,812	16,902	29,615	90,475	45,074	93,186	46,091
Accounts receivable								
U.S. government receivables	5,561	6,374	6,062	8,719	6,679	6,005	7,467	17,327
Traffic receivables	60,934	65,951	93,394	96,824	109,892	117,275	118,820	137,084
All other receivables	24,369	18,552	22,212	20,849	21,775	18,236	19,671	16,567
Subtotal accounts receivable	90,864	90,877	121,668	126,392	138,346	141,516	145,958	170,978
Materials and supplies, net	59,028	50,053	49,457	67,774	68,352	78,065	81,040	81,233
Prepaid expenses and other current assets	11,617	12,570	11,703	14,047	11,285	12,481	12,211	9,030
Total current assets	222,215	220,716	237,665	298,314	363,541	323,066	374,366	338,674
Investments and Advances								
Real estate held for sale	25,964	27,388	28,794	32,304[a]	28,017	8,000[b]	4,418[g]	3,983
Other	12,224	8,488	11,575	14,998[a]	9,417	11,120	8,438	17,902
Total investments and advances	38,188	35,876	40,369	47,302	37,434	19,120	12,856	21,885
Property and Equipment								
Flight equipment	956,534	909,186	1,040,231	1,233,395	1,207,330	1,217,279	1,252,525	1,260,901
Less: accumulated depreciation	309,494	336,568	362,162	354,837	413,017	463,196	525,554	563,307
	647,040	572,618	678,069	878,558	794,313	754,083	726,971	697,594
Other property and equipment	178,163	194,287	210,632	230,104	241,930	249,879	244,226	256,047
Less: accumulated depreciation	78,418	92,625	104,644	119,832	136,485	153,050	150,280	159,745
Total net property and equipment	99,745	101,662	105,988	110,272	105,445	96,829	93,946	96,302

Leased property	—	—	—	—	—	—	—	654,850
Less accumulated amortization	—	—	—	—	—	—	—	220,331
								434,519
Advance payments for new equipment	746,785	674,280	784,057	988,830	899,758	850,912	820,917	1,228,415
Property and equipment, net	99,422	120,512	164,347	58,144	74,337	65,227	67,698	52,875
Total property and equipment from advances	846,207	794,792	948,404	1,046,974	974,095	916,139	888,615	1,281,290
Deferred Charges								
Preoperating costs	13,690	9,889	12,630	15,350	12,989	10,316	7,210	6,379
Route acquisition and development costs	—	—	—	11,029[b]	9,470	8,178	5,470	4,612
Unamortized debt expense	—	—	—	—	—	—	6,290	7,702
Equalization reserve	—	—	—	—	—	—	—	—
All other	8,259	11,415	14,944	13,654[b]	13,188	13,033	5,861	3,420
Total deferred charges	21,949	21,304	27,574	40,033	35,647	31,527	24,831	22,113
Total assets	$1,128,559	$1,072,688	$1,254,012	$1,432,623	$1,410,717	$1,289,852	$1,300,668	$1,663,962
Liabilities and Stockholders' Equity								
Current Liabilities								
Notes payable within 1 year	$ 61,466	$ 57,127	$ 88,876	$ 92,869	$ 98,949	$ 108,557[c]	$ 120,012[h]	$ 71,271
Current obligations—capital lease	—	—	—	—	—	—	—	41,162
Accounts payable and accrued liabilities	56,757	58,523	90,017	117,451	147,887	139,628	132,515	134,272
Air travel plan deposits	4,953	4,810	4,714	4,583	4,385	4,231	4,106	3,978
Collections as agent	17,565	18,753	21,549	17,290	29,313	34,774	33,223	39,423
Salary and wage accruals	17,855	15,422	24,774	17,239	20,510	17,968	25,404	28,149
Accrued vacation liability	—	—	—	—	—	39,000	40,000	45,000
Dividends payable—preferred	—	—	—	—	—	—	—	—
Unearned transportation revenue	34,077	32,189	26,262	41,748	43,291	53,694	68,902	80,123
Total current liabilities	192,673	186,824	256,192	291,180	344,355	397,492	424,162	443,378
Long-Term Debt								
Bank and insurance company notes	393,250	344,265	378,884	584,581	527,536	470,479	421,892	259,746
Installment purchase obligations	69,053	57,139	43,112	37,895	25,171	10,798	9,101	6,016
Convertible subordinated debentures	207,427	125,000	125,000	125,000	125,000	125,000	125,000	165,650
Manufacturers' subordinated notes	24,192	22,192	33,515	37,035	22,518	16,284	10,049	4,415
Noncurrent obligations—capital lease	—	—	—	—	—	—	—	444,911
Total long-term debt	693,922	548,596	580,511	784,511	700,225	622,561	566,042	880,738

continued

EXHIBIT 7 *continued*

	1970	1971	1972	1973	1974	1975	1976	1977[i]
Deferred Credits and Other Long-Term Liabilities								
Reserve for aircraft overhaul	—	—	—	—	—	—	—	—
Deferred federal income taxes	4,639	6,427	—	—	—	—	—	—
Long-term liabilities	—	16,037	12,765	17,486[c]	17,630	12,377	4,468	4,146
Other	7,752	16,037	19,645	6,425[c]	5,111	6,138	7,382	4,598
Total deferred credits and other	12,391	22,464	32,410	23,911	22,741	18,515	11,850	8,744
Stockholders' Equity								
Preferred stock, $1 par value 1965–1969, 1977–1979	21,674	21,674	21,674	21,674	21,674	21,674	—	2,000
Paid-in capital in excess of par	—	—	—	—	—	—	—	45,349
Common stock, $1 par value	11,922	17,041	19,043	19,043	19,043	19,043	19,843	19,843
Capital in excess of par value	148,379	223,614	272,760	272,760	272,760	272,760	295,725	298,531
Earnings (deficit) retained at close of previous fiscal year	42,950	47,598	52,475	71,423	19,544	(8,479)[f]	(62,193)	(62,497)
Amortization of excess of redemption value over carrying value	—	—	—	—	—	—	—	—
Income (loss) fiscal-year-to-date	5,461	5,690	19,760	(51,269)	10,395	(53,714)	45,239	28,877
Cash dividends—preferred	(813)	(813)	(813)	(610)	—	—	—	—
	229,573	314,804	384,899	333,021	343,416	251,284	298,614	331,102
Total liabilities and stockholders' equity	$1,128,559	$1,072,688	$1,254,012	$1,432,623	$1,410,717	$1,289,852	$1,300,668	$1,663,962

[a] Hotel properties includes advances (formerly in Other) on a forward basis only.

[b] Route acquisition and development costs (formerly in Other) separated in December 1978 on a forward basis only.

[c] Long-term liabilities and Other were separated in December 1973 on a forward basis only.

[d] Hotel properties reflect the cumulative effect of $2.8 million as the result of FASB Statement No. 7 and a $16.8 million impairment in investment.

[e] Liability data for 1975 are restated to reflect accrued vacation liability.

[f] Earnings retained reflect a $3.4-million decrease resulting from the impact of FASB Statement No. 7 on a forward basis only.

[g] Real estate held for sale 1976 forward—Hotel properties—through 1975.

[h] Liability data for 1976 reflect the cumulative effect of changing method of recording vacation liability.

[i] Data for 1977 reflect the adoption of FASB No. 13 (capitalization of leases).

Interchemical Consumer
Products Division

In late May 1977, Mr. Bismark, vice president of Interchemical Consumer Products Division, was considering the introduction of a new furniture polish in the Italian market. The management of Interchemical–Torino (Interchemical's Italian subsidiary) had recommended to appropriate members of the headquarters corporate planning group that the product be launched and had received tentative approval. Mr. Bismark was aware that top management at Interchemical was only half sold on the appropriateness of a venturesome growth program in the consumer products business, and he wanted to be sure that the new division's first investment had an excellent chance for success.

COMPANY BACKGROUND

Interchemical Ltd., a major international chemical and pharmaceutical complex based in The Hague, the Netherlands, had a significant worldwide market position in fibers, industrial chemicals, pharmaceuticals, agricultural chemicals, and certain consumer goods. Annual sales in 1978 were projected to be approximately 1,966 million florins, of which almost 90 percent originated outside the Netherlands. Approximately 583 million fls. of the goods sold were manufactured in the Netherlands, excluding the output from German facilities located nearby.

Interchemical had grown at a very rapid rate. In 1963, it had total sales of 327 million fls. with fibers accounting for 50 percent of the firm's volume. Forecasts of sales for 1977 indicated that the year-to-year increase would almost equal the 1963 level of volume. Sales had increased tenfold in the past 20 years and had more than doubled during the last five years. Sales trends since 1969 are shown in Exhibit 1. Management was striving to maintain or improve upon this growth.

This case was prepared as a basis for class discussion rather than to illustrate either effective or ineffective handling of an administrative situation. Copyright © 1983 by the Darden Graduate Business School Sponsors, University of Virginia, Charlottesville, Virginia.

THE CONSUMER
PRODUCTS DIVISION

The attention focused on the Consumer Products (CP) division by the top managers of Interchemical was partly the result of a recent consultant's study. Analysis of the company's strategy and structure led management to establish and build the CP division as one of the five main business units. Although Interchemical already had a limited range of consumer product ventures—primarily garden products housed as a group under Agricultural Chemicals—sales of this group, largely concentrated in France and Italy, represented just 4 percent of the total corporate volume.

Interchemical's earlier CP efforts had been scattered throughout the four remaining business units of the corporation. Top management had given Mr. Bismark the task of consolidating all Interchemical's CP activities and developing smooth working relationships with the corporate executives responsible for these products.

Expansion of the CP business was particularly attractive to Interchemical management because they believed consumer products were likely to achieve both high sales and profits with a reasonable degree of stability. In addition, these products did not have short patent lives or the problem of market control by a few key customers like the products in other parts of Interchemical's business.

Management expected the following major trends in the CP field:

- Growth at a rate faster than that of disposable income.
- Concentration of demand in a limited number of key countries.
- Continued shift from selective to mass-distribution channels.
- Mergers and acquisitions to increase concentration, strengthen competitors.
- More aggressive competition led by the big soap/detergent and oil companies
- Increased importance of mass merchandising and promotion efforts.
- Increased numbers of private labels.

When it was formally established in January 1977, the CP division was given the task of safeguarding existing market positions while providing supplementary consumer markets for traditional Interchemical product strengths. Furthermore, it was to develop products and build markets in (1) household products, (2) prescription-free medicinals marketed directly to consumers, and (3) toiletries and cosmetics. The division would first concentrate in these areas, which had been selected after careful study of the market trends, competitive conditions, and internal resources of the various industries.

Sales of the CP division were expected to be approximately 65.3 million fls. in 1977 (66 percent were in France, 21 percent in Italy, with the balance in Latin America). In only two products, garden products and room deodorizers, and in one country, France, could Interchemical's CP division be said to be in a commanding market position. The business had grown at 8 percent per year in the past, and management had set an earnings growth target of 13 percent for the next two years.

By mid-1977, Mr. Bismark had already begun the task of assembling a consumer products team and establishing priorities for expansion. One of his highest priorities, developing a cooperative working relationship with the research laboratories of other Interchemical businesses that had prior experience in the CP business, was particularly important if the new division was to maintain a consistent flow of new consumer products.

Top management thought that new product introductions had strategic importance. Limited numbers of products increased the division's vulnerability to competition and made adequate levels of diversification nearly impossible. Although headquarters wanted to strengthen the CP division's competitive position substantially within three to five years, investments to achieve these goals needed sound economic justification, compatibility with the divisional strategy, and levels of risk that correlated satisfactorily with their return on investment.

INTERCHEMICAL–TORINO

Interchemical management had set forth the following financial objectives for Italy:

1. 10-percent growth in sales in 1978 (excluding furniture polish), and 15-percent growth from 1979 to 1982.

2. Total net sales volume of 16.2 million fls. in 1978 and 19.1 million fls. in 1979, moving up to 29.9 million fls. in 1982.

3. Total profit before taxes (from all products except furniture polish) of 1 million fls. in 1978.

4. Average annual profit increase before taxes of 15 percent in 1979 through 1980 in all products except furniture polish.

5. Start-up losses in new product introductions limited to a level below the Interchemical–Torino profit forecast for 1978.

6. Controllable costs at 41 percent of sales in 1978 and 40 percent of sales in 1979, moving toward a 1982 goal of 34 percent.

7. Sales and profit targets should be met for all furniture-care products.

Interchemical–Torino's success had been mainly based upon garden products (87.6 percent of revenues in 1976) which accounted for only 12 to 13 percent of the total Italian market and which had been losing ground. A new household garden-product line had recently been introduced to arrest this decline. Furniture polish accounted for 5.3 percent of revenues, and room deodorizers were just 4.1 percent with the balance in a minor item.

While a new program had been developed to strengthen the ebbing garden-product market share, the volume was not yet large enough to warrant an in-house sales force. Furthermore, continued dependence upon independent sales agents had not provided a reliable means of assuring comprehensive distribution to the outlets where sales were likely. Garden-product sales were both seasonal and modest, and many agents represented other products to assure themselves adequate, steady incomes. The Interchemical product was not considered a large income source by these individuals when compared with their other products. In short, Interchemical did not have a strong distribution system to support the new marketing program for garden products.

Consequently, management sought to develop products that could be distributed through the same channels. With other products in the line, Interchemical–Torino could command better attention from its agents, secure better agents, and ultimately build its own sales force. A new product would further provide the division with the opportunity to build the marketing staff necessary for subsequent efforts to expand the sales base in the Italian market.

Several types of products were considered, but attention increasingly focused on the furniture-polish market, one in which management had some experience. In 1967, Interchemical–Torino had introduced an aerosol furniture polish in the Italian market under the brand name "Moderne." This product had never been particularly successful and currently had less than 1 percent of the market.

While Moderne was the first, and initially the only, aerosol on the market, the product itself was not superior and the novelty of a spray application never caught on. The cost of the can, valve, and propellant made its price more than the customer seemed ready to pay. Management concluded that they needed a different product—one better supported by advertising, promotion, and eventually, by an in-house sales force—in order to succeed in the market.

MODERNE LIMONE

Interchemical had already developed a furniture polish with special ingredients that was particularly effective on the old furniture typically found in most Italian homes. This product was as good as any currently on the market and better than some. While it had no unique polishing or cleaning properties, it did have one distinguishing feature: a lemon ingredient that many consumers associated with superior polishing characteristics. To accent this feature, the new product was named "Moderne Limone." Management believed the consumer would find greater satisfaction from polishing with a wax that would nourish heirloom furniture and had a pleasant aroma. The product could and would be sold at a competitive price.

In recent years, furniture wax products with additional features had taken over an increasing share of the Italian market:

Competitor	Special Ingredient	1969 Market Share[a]	1977 Market Share[a]
Fodora	No	28%	3%
Ultra	Yes	15	23
Brown (English)	Yes	4	19
Lutricia	Yes	5	13

[a]A large number of smaller firms accounted for the balance.

Ultra, Brown, and Lutricia advertised their products aggressively and pushed them with promotions. Brown, in particular, used promotional inducements to gain 5-year placement contracts. The three main competitors all had good sales organizations capable of supporting the distribution of the product. Despite this competition, Torino management believed that it would be possible to carve out a 10-percent share of the attractive 10-billion-lire market.

Distribution in Italy was complicated by the predominance of small retail shops (there were approximately 40,000 potential outlets for this product) and Interchemical's past efforts had not been effective in building substantial shelf space. Most shops made purchases based on anticipated market acceptance, margins, special promotions, and relationships with sales agents; Interchemical's agents had divided loyalties. Of the 80 agents, about one-third handled Interchemical lines exclusively, another one-third thought Interchemical lines were important, and the last one-third thought that Interchemical products were less important than other lines.

To push the new product, Torino management was prepared to advertise and promote it aggressively. They believed that an initial budget of 120 million lire would provide a good campaign. Total industry advertising outlays were running at ten times this sum in 1977, and management hoped that this stepped-up campaign would lead to a 5-percent market share in the first year. By sustaining or increasing this relatively heavy outlay for several years, a 10-percent market share seemed an ambitious but attainable objective. About two-thirds of the funds would go to advertising in various types of media, and the balance to coupons, discounts, and "stock-in" deals.

Advertising had grown quite rapidly in recent years in Italy, and it was sometimes difficult to place the media budget in prime television spots. Often, the advertiser had to accept a package that included television and radio from available spots in the network's schedule. In addition, newspaper space with little advertising value, theater spots, and miscellaneous other media would be included as part of a total deal. Because of this practice, planning an effective media campaign was extremely difficult.

The message of the initial advertising campaign would be:

Moderne Limone is an ultra-brilliant furniture polish. Moderne Limone's unique lemon ingredients nourish your heirloom furniture; it is easy to use; apply it with a cloth, let the lemon sink in and enrich the wood, then polish the surfaces gently. A beautiful shine develops that is more than surface deep when you use Modern Limone. The enriching qualities of Modern Limone are due to its special properties. . . .

Although the Torino management was fully prepared to launch Moderne Limone, the product's economic potential had not been determined. Mr. Bismark believed that a simulation modeling technique could be of tremendous assistance to him and his staff in making this product introduction decision.

TECHNIQUE FOR ANALYSIS: THE RISK ANALYSIS MODEL

On the basis of a consultant's report, top management had encouraged Mr. Bismark to evaluate new product introductions using a risk analysis model like that described by David Hertz in his January–February 1964 *Harvard Business Review* article, "Risk Analysis in Capital Investments." Since Mr. Bismark was interested in minimizing the chances for error, particularly during the early phases of his division's history, the concept underlying the model appealed to him.

A model would not only measure the potential return on investment of a project but could also give an indication of its risk. Rather than measuring the various elements of an investment analysis by single estimates, a probability distribution was developed for such critical components as market size, market growth rate, market share, selling price, operating costs, fixed costs, level of investment, useful life, and residual value of the investment. In some instances (for example, market share), management could choose to estimate different probability distributions for each year. Other elements known with greater certainty, such as depreciation and taxes, could be treated as constants.

A model like that described by David Hertz could use all of management's probabilistic estimates in a computer simulation. A value for each variable in each year was randomly chosen for each sample run. The various elements were combined systematically to determine the annual cash flows and then analyzed over the useful life of the project to determine the internal rate of return, discounted cash flow, or another measure of return that management might choose. A large number of runs were made, each using a new set of randomly determined estimates. The computer would calculate the average return, expected value, and probability distribution of the returns. These data would provide Mr. Bismark with key information necessary to evaluate risk/return trade-offs and reach a decision.

This model could also be used to test alternative strategies. For example, if the sales price assumptions were changed (which could also require adjustments to other variables such as market share and market size), the model could be useful in determining the impact such a decision would have on the project's return.

This model still required astute judgments on the likelihood of outcomes for each of its elements. The probability distributions that might be determined for each element could be defined in several ways. Hertz, for example, suggested starting with the high, medium, and low estimates of the outcome for an element. A probability distribution could be ascribed to these measures by the computer before the sample runs.

The variables that were considered to have the greatest effect on the project's return were identified. For each of these factors, probabilities were assigned to various outcomes, and these would become the input data for the simulation runs. In order to arrive at these assessments, historical data along with inputs based on experience were reviewed jointly by management at Interchemical–Torino and Mr. Bismark's staff, and the probabilities and outcomes were determined on the basis of their collective wisdom.

MODEL ESTIMATES

The forecasts of the parameters that Mr. Bismark and his staff believed necessary to build and use a simulation model of the Moderne Limone decision were as follows:

1. Market Size–1976. Management had no data on the actual size of the market, and a Nielsen survey of the Italian furniture-polish market was considered too expensive. To estimate 1976 market size, management relied on published information, discussions with trade sources, and experience. Volume in units

Chart 1
∎

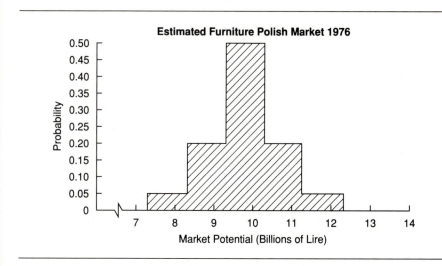

Estimated Furniture Polish Market 1976

was difficult to determine separately; thus the market potential was defined in terms of wholesale shipments in lire.[1] Their assessments are shown in Chart 1.

2.   Market Growth. Historic market growth rates were calculated and then interpreted in light of population trends, purchasing power, growth rates, furniture-care requirements in new households (more plastic surfaces), and other factors. Chart 2 contains this estimate.

3.   Price. Management believed market size depended on the initial size of the market, its growth, and the level of furniture-polish prices. For instance, management believed that if prices rose, the total market size in lire would equally increase. Since prices were not expected to remain stable, management tried to estimate the effect of price changes on the size of the market. Their estimates for possible changes in price are shown in Chart 3.

4.   Market Share. Market share was believed to be a function of the quantity and quality of investment in the product's advertising, promotion, and distribution. The probability of success for Interchemical's marketing program was impossible to forecast accurately. Because the advertising program created the greatest uncertainty, its two possible outcomes were consequently explored: (1) favorable market share if the advertising program proved very effective, and (2) unfavorable market share if the advertising program proved less effective. Annual probability distributions (from 1978 to 1982), shown in Chart 4, were developed for each of these two outcomes. Uncertainties were expected to increase as competitors had more time to react to the program.

5.   Cost of Goods Sold. Real manufacturing costs were based on experience. However, the cost of goods sold was expected to increase over time as the result of inflation. To account for these changes, the inflated costs were tied to sales

---

[1]florin = 172 lire = US$ 0.278.

Chart 2
■

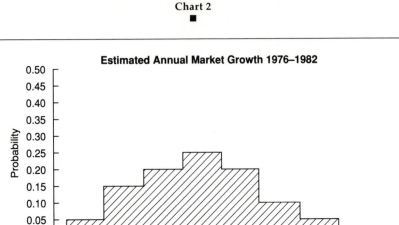

Estimated Annual Market Growth 1976–1982

Chart 3
■

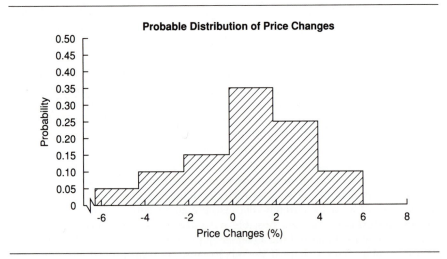

Probable Distribution of Price Changes

volume (in lire) assuming initial prices held constant. Results are shown in Chart 5.

6. Variable Sales and Distribution Expenses. Three factors were considered: cost of transportation, commissions to agents, and interest on working capital employed. Furthermore, the cost for gradually replacing agents with an internal sales force (initially more costly, but a more effective distribution system) was built into the calculations. Costs were then expressed as a percentage of sales and shown in Chart 6.

Chart 4

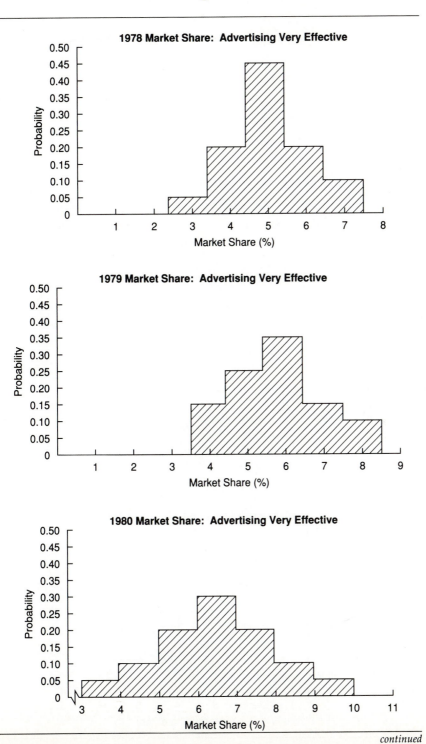

continued

Chart 4 *continued*
∎

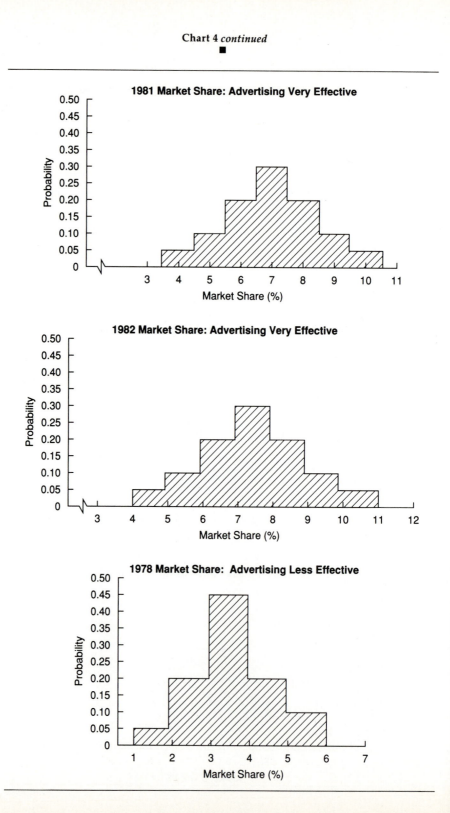

Chart 4 *continued*

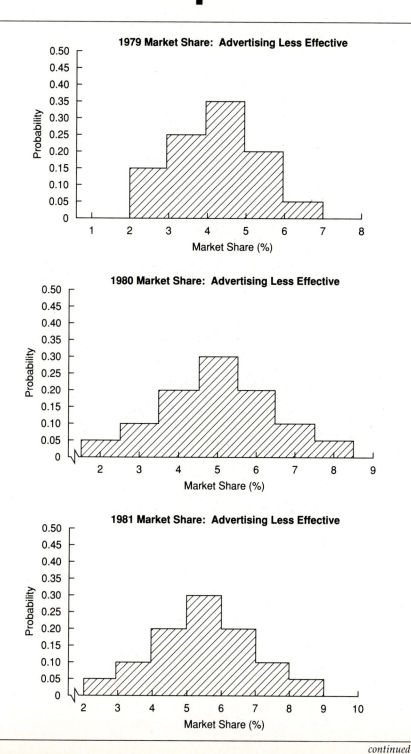

continued

Chart 4 *continued*

■

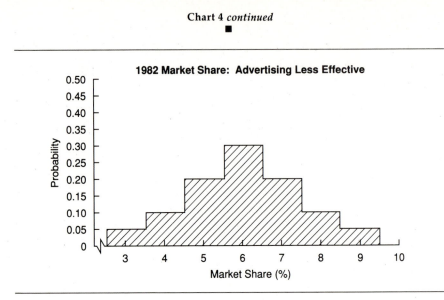

7.   Advertising and Promotion Expense. Management considered two advertising and promotion strategies. The first required a fixed outlay of 120 million lire per year throughout the period. The second assumed advertising and promotion expenses would be set equal to 10 percent of the industry total. In 1976, the industry had spent 650 million lire on television advertising and an estimated 320 million lire on various other media. When other promotional forms were included, total industry outlays were estimated to be 1.2 billion lire. Thus, under the second strategy, Interchemical–Torino expected to spend 120 million lire in the first year. The expenditure thereafter would be 10 percent of the industry

Chart 5

■

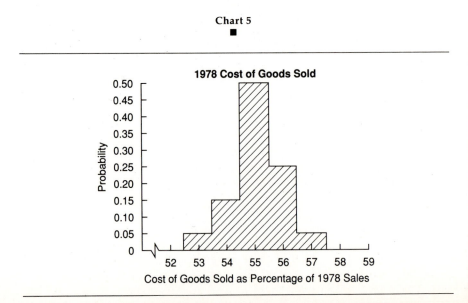

Chart 5 *continued*
■

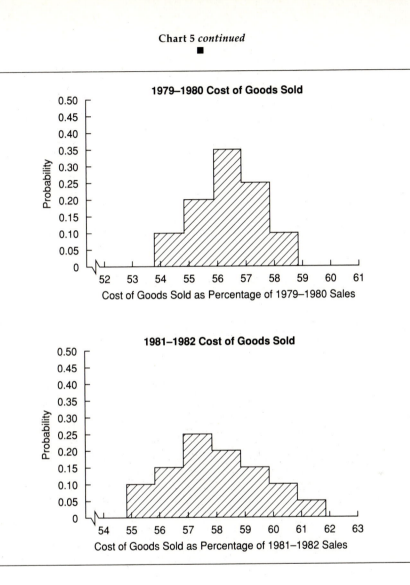

total. Because this figure was uncertain, management supplied as good an estimate as possible for 1977, shown in Chart 7.

8.   Industry Advertising and Promotion Expenditures. Costs of advertising had risen rapidly in Italy and were expected to continue to increase in the future. Since the second advertising strategy was tied to industry outlays, another estimate of future costs had to be made. After reviewing historic trends in media costs, an estimated growth rate shown in Chart 8 would be applied to the 1977 advertising expense, determined from the distribution in Chart 7.

9.   Other Incremental Costs. These costs, which included personnel, market research, storage space, and finance costs, were expected to average 28 million lire in 1978 and 10 million lire higher in 1980. The related uncertainties are illustrated in Chart 9.

Chart 6
■

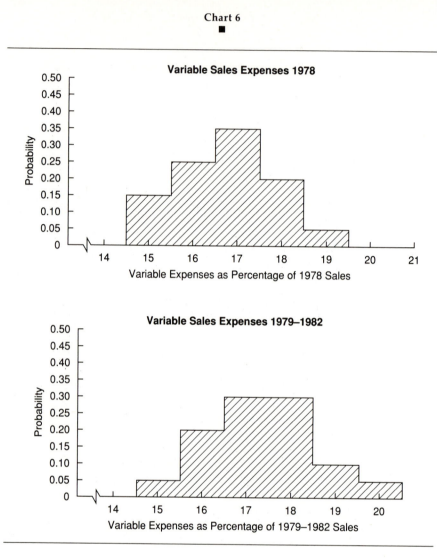

10.   Local Taxes. Taxes in Italy were determined by negotiation. Reported profits were viewed skeptically by the authorities, and often taxes were calculated in relation to sales. Since the incremental tax effects were very unpredictable, taxes would be omitted from the model.

11.   Investment. No capital was required for plant and equipment since this work would be subcontracted. However, there would be initial operating losses until the level of sales offset introductory marketing costs. These were considered investments in the model. While costs for working capital and warehouse space were not treated as investments, they were included as part of the other incremental costs.

12.   Depreciation and Terminal Values. None were considered.

Chart 7
■

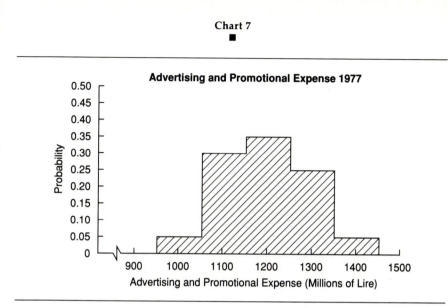

Chart 8
■

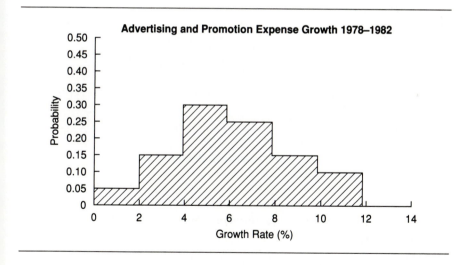

13. Life of Investment. Although a successful product introduction would tend to indicate a long product life, Mr. Bismark wanted the analysis to be conservative. He therefore considered cash flows for just the first five years.

Mr. Bismark recognized that the simulation model was primarily a financial and not a marketing model, but he was attracted by its ability to measure risk as well as return, especially in evaluating unusually risky investments, such

Chart 9

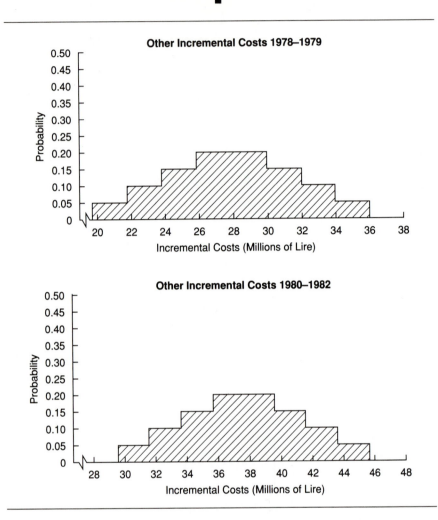

as new product introductions. Furthermore, the model could be adapted and improved as experience warranted.

CONCLUSION

As he reviewed the data that had been collected, Mr. Bismark pondered his next step. He was inexperienced in using simulation. Consequently, his first temptation was to perform the analysis manually. While he believed that as a tool the simulation could be of tremendous assistance, he wondered whether the members of the corporate planning staff would approve of his use of such a sophisticated tool for this project, or whether they would even believe its results. However, the first problem facing him was the task of building a suitable model.

Interchemical Consumer Products Division

EXHIBIT 1
■
Sales and Profits of Interchemical Ltd., 1969–1976 (millions of florins)

	Sales	Profits after Taxes
1969	648	110
1970	758	109
1971	857	92
1972	1,010	149
1973	1,138	136
1974	1,379	244
1975	1,558	177
1976	1,749	192

Alaska Interstate (A)

Bill Camp, assistant vice president for planning and budgeting at Alaska Interstate Corp. (AKI), was preparing the staff report for the 1978 annual corporate planning meeting. At that meeting the top executives would decide on AKI's long-range strategy and plan the firm's capital investments. These plans would then be presented to the board of directors for their approval.

Everything used to be so simple. In the good old days, a couple of people made the decisions. Now the firm was staffed and managed by 22 people trained at some of the best business schools in the country. They wanted to understand the real returns and risks of their business as well as those inherent in the major capital investments proposed by the subsidiaries and contemplated for Alaska Interstate itself.

Of immediate concern to Mr. Camp was the capital allocation portion of the corporate strategy. The problem was, how should management decide which of AKI's subsidiaries to invest in? Mr. Camp had data on the historical performance of and forecasts for the future of each subsidiary and for AKI itself. In the past, management had analyzed the historical data and, using a discounted cash flow technique, had converted the forecasts into expected returns for each division. It was these data that management used in choosing among the various proposed investments. Management now questioned whether the discounted cash flow method adequately dealt with risk. There was no doubt that management had considered the riskiness of each project, but it had not necessarily done so in a systematic or objective way. Was there a method of evaluating risk that could provide more and better information for use in making these capital decisions?

This question had been discussed by AKI management for some time. In fact, Mr. Camp had a copy of a recent study written by Bob Santoski, a Carnegie–Mellon graduate and a new addition to the AKI staff, and David Ross, the AKI treasurer. In that paper they discussed several methods for directly evaluating risk. Among the methods analyzed were AKI's current approach (what Mr. Santoski and Mr. Ross called the *subjective approach*) and a method for evaluating the subsidiary manager's accuracy in making budgets.

Mr. Camp wondered how to use the information in the study in his presentation. One problem was that some of the methods relied on advanced

This case was prepared as a basis for class discussion rather than to illustrate either effective or ineffective handling of an administrative situation. Copyright © 1982 by the Darden Graduate Business School Sponsors, University of Virginia, Charlottesville, Virginia.

statistical techniques. While the AKI board of directors comprised some very sophisticated people, perhaps not all of them were completely up-to-date on these techniques. Whatever was presented to the directors had to be clear and to make good business sense.

Mr. Camp's second problem was that he wondered if each of the approaches used by Mr. Santoski and Mr. Ross measured the same thing. He wasn't sure whether more than one approach should be used or, if not, which of the methods was best for describing the AKI situation. Were there flaws in any of the methods to which he should be alerted before presenting this material to management and the board? How could this information be used in forming AKI's strategy and capital expenditure plans? Could any or all of these methods be used to set hurdle rates for evaluating proposals? He decided to begin by applying the approaches to two of the subsidiaries, Alaska Gas and Service Co. and Lockwood. He believed that if he could draft clear evaluations of the current and potential risks and returns for these subsidiaries, evaluating the others would be easy.

THE COMPANY

Alaska Interstate began as a joint venture in 1966. The corporation was formed by combining Alaska Gas and Service Co., a natural gas transmission company; the Anlin Companies, sulphur-recovery operations in New Jersey and Illinois; Baldwin Properties, primarily a real estate developer; and Rone Associated, Inc., a real estate management firm. The 1966 sales were $8.6 million with net earnings of $825,000.

In 1967, the original AKI group was joined by three other companies: Kran Company, a crane manufacturer in Houston; Gulfstream, whose major product was PT boats; and Vicon, a producer of hearing aids. Sales in that year reached $41.6 million for the combined corporation. In 1968 Alaska Interstate listed its shares on the American Stock Exchange. It also added Sauder Tank Company to the corporate portfolio in 1968, National Aircraft and Burgess Construction Company in 1969, and Lockwood Corporation in 1970. AKI stock was listed on the New York Stock Exchange in 1970. Further acquisition activity ceased until 1977, and some earlier acquisitions—Vicon, Gulfstream, and Burgess—were divested during this period. In 1974, the first president and chief executive officer stepped down to be replaced by Charles Honig, a co-founder of AKI.

Over the past year the AKI portfolio of firms had undergone quite a change. In January 1977, McAlester Fuel, a domestic oil and gas exploration company, had been acquired for cash and notes. In February, the portion of the AKI sulphur-recovery business that had not been sold in 1976—the Anlin Company of New Jersey, wholly owned by AKI—was sold to Chevron for over $14 million.

In July 1977, AKI merged with Virginia International Company, a member of a six-principal joint venture that was conducting oil and gas exploration and development in two areas of Indonesia. AKI had previously owned less than 20 percent of Virginia International, although it indirectly owned another piece of the Indonesian joint venture through its ownership of 37.15 percent of Roy M. Huffington, Inc. Thus, AKI's stake in the venture was significantly increased by the merger.

During 1977, management proposed that a new subsidiary be formed, Alaska Petrochemical Company (Alpetco), to contract with the state of Alaska for the purchase and refining of Prudhoe Bay oil paid in royalty to the state of Alaska. Alpetco was one of the finalists in the competition for the contract, and AKI management expected Alpetco to be chosen. If it received the contract, Alpetco would have to obtain sales contracts for 70 percent of the refinery output as well as financing commitments for at least $1.5 billion, all within 18 months. Alpetco would become a very large investment compared to AKI's current portfolio of firms.

PLANNING AND THE SUBSIDIARIES

AKI divided its subsidiaries, called *profit and investment centers,* into two groups, energy and manufacturing. The eight subsidiaries (not including Alpetco) were evenly split between the two groups, although four of AKI's subsidiaries represented 80 percent of the total AKI investment. Three of these centers were in the energy group.

AKI management had evaluated each subsidiary to identify the business segments in which it operated (see Exhibit 1) and had gone into some detail in developing the information from the subsidiaries on which to base long-range corporate strategy and capital allocations. The planning and budgeting group, along with each subsidiary's president, completed what they called a *planning grid.* They believed that by answering a series of questions related to the subsidiary's current and future business and its competition, they were simply "verbalizing what is known or that which can logically be deduced from available data." In preparing the report, they considered:

1. The market environment (e.g., stage in the product life cycle and market growth rate)
2. Competitive position (e.g., relative product quality, market share, and costs of production)
3. Use of resources (e.g., fixed capital employed and value added per employee)
4. Financial returns (e.g., return on capital employed and free cash flow)
5. Other risk factors (e.g., nature of demand, management depth)
6. The current strategy and a projection of future strategy.

In some cases, the subsidiary would be asked to repeat the process, answering the questions as if it were its major competitor. The final result was a thumbnail sketch of its current position, near-term opportunities and problems, and future potential of the business. Summaries for two of the subsidiaries, the Alaska Gas and Service Company and Lockwood, are reproduced in Exhibit 2. All this information was used by the planning group to help in formulating AKI's intermediate and long-range strategy and for making the necessary capital allocation plans. This summary of strategy and tactics was also used in establishing performance targets for evaluating and compensating subsidiary managers.

From the basic financial data shown in Exhibits 3 to 5, Mr. Camp developed a visual representation of the changing corporate position (Exhibit 6) vis-à-vis capital employed and return on sales. Exhibits 7 and 8 are plots of the actual and projected positions for the energy group and the manufacturing subsidiaries. The size of each circle on the graph represents the total relative capital employed by the particular subsidiary. Mr. Camp also plotted the Alpetco data (Exhibit 9) to enhance management's and the board's perspective on the decision to form that subsidiary.

Although these planning steps were helpful in identifying the sources of risk, the quantifying of risk presented a major problem. Nevertheless, management believed they needed to examine risk explicitly to be able to compare projects with different degrees of risk when making capital-constrained decisions.

THE SANTOSKI–ROSS STUDY

Subjective Risk Analysis.   The study identified the firm's current method of risk analysis as *subjective risk analysis.* Some time ago, the treasurer, David Ross, had asked seven other members of the AKI management team to express their personal opinions regarding the risk of each product line. A worksheet (see Exhibit 10 for a sample) was provided to each person for use as a framework for assessment. All seven managers had seen the results of the subsidiaries' planning grid exercises, and all were quite familiar with the subsidiaries. The results of the assessment process for 1976 and 1977 and the managers' forecasts are shown in Exhibits 11 and 12. Mr. Camp thought that the graphs demonstrated well the return/risk relationship for each subsidiary.

Budget Accuracy and Risk.   The Santoski–Ross report suggested that the definition of risk as "the inaccuracy of predictions" offered a more objective approach to quantifying risk than AKI's current system. Management planning and control was done with budgets, they said. Since a budget was similar to an investor's prediction of the future financial performance of the firm, "the total risk of the business might therefore be measured by analyzing the accuracy of budgets as predictors of financial performance." AKI management maintained constantly updated financial data for AKI Consolidated as well as for each of its subsidiaries. The budget-to-actual variances had been evaluated by Mr. Camp for each line item. If consistent forecasting errors occurred, AKI management could add a compensating factor. Only unpredictable errors were considered to be risk (as measured by standard deviation). The result of Mr. Camp's study of the subsidiaries' forecast variances is shown in Exhibits 13 and 14.

These forecast variances were used for one task in addition to planning: The subsidiary presidents and other top managers in each subsidiary were evaluated and were compensated according to how close to their budget they performed. Although other objectives such as market share growth or cost minimization could also be set for any subsidiary, forecast accuracy was of first importance.

Mr. Camp wanted to be sure he understood the budget-to-actual variance analysis in case anyone in the planning meetings questioned him about it. He therefore read again the part of the Santoski–Ross report that dealt with their estimation of budget prediction risk:

In examining budget prediction errors, we have considered seven separate businesses over a 48-month period. The 48 months of data were grouped into 24 two-month periods [on the basis of the] trade-off between information content and apparent random fluctuations. Means and standard deviations were calculated for each 24-data-piece set. Occasional outliers were observed, which would usually be associated with a controllable extraordinary event, such as an acquisition. To eliminate these from consideration, all points exceeding 3.0 standard deviations on either side of the mean were excluded. (There was less than 1 chance in 1,000 that these were true members of the set.) Means and standard deviations were then recomputed for the remaining set, and again outliers were excluded. The process was continued until no outliers were found. In addition, all data items with base values of less than $50,000 were excluded, since such small items might give rise to large spurious percentage variances. The resulting data sets generally included 20 to 24 pieces of data. The following two graphs indicate the percentage of net earnings variances for two different businesses.

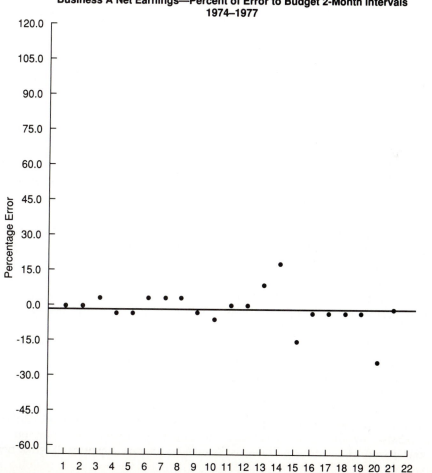

Business A Net Earnings—Percent of Error to Budget 2-Month Intervals 1974–1977

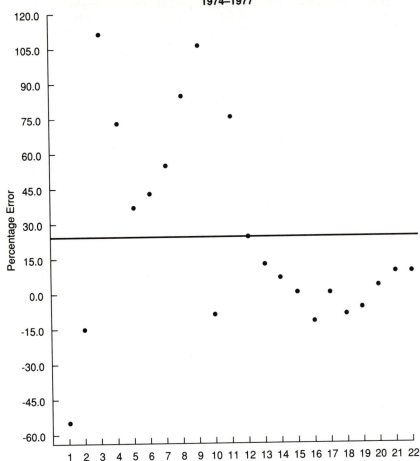

Besides offering a way to compare capital investments with different degrees of risk, Mr. Santoski and Mr. Ross had listed in their report a number of other reasons for developing methods of measuring and evaluating risk:

1.   To quantify and manage a level of risk that is "acceptable to management." The level of risk may be easily tailored through increases and decreases in leverage.

2.   To understand the nature of the risk in its various operations, enabling the company to diversify away a portion of its unsystematic risk. This understanding is of value to management, employees, customers, and undiversified shareholders.

3.   To identify and analyze the sources of risk, perhaps making it possible to reduce some of them. It is likely that the company is experiencing risks that are avoidable. By identifying these items, management can focus its attention on high-payoff, risk-reducing strategies. Knowledge of the company's marginal risk

attributable to a given item should help determine a rational maximum level of cost that should be incurred to reduce the risk.

4. To aid in setting performance goals for internal control. Management expects higher returns from higher risk operations, but the question of the appropriate quantitative trade-off between risk and return can be handled only if an acceptable measure of risk is available.

5. To aid in forming a rational policy for communicating with shareholders. Discussing risks with shareholders and explaining management's attempt to cope with them should provide the shareholder who is not well-diversified with additional useful information and should reduce his or her uncertainty (and risk) in purchasing the company's shares.

6. Above all, to help improve management's decision making. A specific quantitative assessment of risk establishes a mind-set and common risk/return vocabulary.

Even though Mr. Camp agreed that quantitative risk information would be very useful, he was not sure which of the methods that Mr. Santoski and Mr. Ross described was best. Moreover, he thought that the managers' planning process might provide better information than the methods of risk quantification.

Alaska Interstate (A)

EXHIBIT 1
■
Breakdown of the Businesses in the AKI Portfolio

Alaska Gas and Service Company/Alaska Pipeline Company
Natural gas transmission and distribution

McAlester Fuel Company
Oil and gas exploration and production for Rocky Mountain and Gulf Coast regions
Coal reserve ownership and coal sale
Shortline Railroad operation
Other natural resources investments

Delta Engineering Corporation
For each geographic region—Gulf Coast, Western Canada, Alaska, North Sea, Middle East:
  Design and construction of natural gas processing facilities
  Design and construction of oil production facilities
  Design and construction of oil and gas transportation facilities
  Design and construction of petrochemical facilities
  Design, construction, and operation of enhanced hydrocarbon recovery facilities

Kranco, Inc.
High-technology cranes for each Houston and Cleveland gantry
Service

---

continued

EXHIBIT 1 *continued*

Low-technology cranes for each Houston and Cleveland tred
  UHG
  USH Service
Polar Cranes—nationally

Lockwood Corporation
Center pivot irrigation system manufacture and sale
Irrigation coupler manufacture and sale
Manufacture and sale of potato harvesters and planters
Beet equipment manufacture and sale
Bean equipment manufacture and sale
Other field equipment manufacture and sale
Orchard equipment manufacture and sale
Bulkbox manufacture and sale
Agricultural replacement parts manufacture and sale
Foreign agricultural project management

National Aircraft Service, Inc.
Jet engine (JT8 series) overhaul
Piston engine (1830 and 3300 series) overhaul
Aircraft engine parts remanufacture and sale
Commercial metal plating

Sauder Industries, Inc.
Medium wall (1½"–4") vessel manufacture and sale
Industrial furnace manufacture and sale
Ceramic fiber furnace lining manufacture and sale
Standpipe vessel manufacture and sale

Stardust Cruiser Manufacturing Company
Houseboat manufacture and sale
Special-use boat manufacture and sale
Marina/resort and operation

Mineral and Chemical Resources Company
Oil production
Contractual research and development related to chemical industry
VICO
Direct interest in Indonesian oil and gas exploration and development

Huffington (37-percent owned)
Indirect interest in Indonesian oil and gas exploration and development

Other Businesses
Properties/assets held for sale

Alaska Interstate (A)

EXHIBIT 2
■

Alaska Gas and Service Company and Lockwood Key Strategy Points

Alaska Gas and Service Company

Basic Business Position	*Near-Term Opportunities, Problems*

Market

Anchorage area population growth is expected to continue in the 4-percent range over the near future; that's about 7,500 people per year (or about 2,000 additional gas customers per year). Although that number of additional customers per year is in line with historical new customer hookups, the increase as a percentage of base customers is declining, thus growth rate is slowing considerably. With prices controlled by the APUC,[a] we can expect that the beneficial effects of operational scale and efficiency will be passed on to the consumer not to the shareholder. Gas is clearly the most practical, efficient, and one of the cheapest fuels available to the community.

Production

We have an efficient, well-managed pipeline and utility operation with a superior supply of gas on long-term contract.

The forecast assumes normal weather based on 30-year moving average annual degree days. The weather recently has been warmer than that average, but we know of no better available practical method. Continuation of the warm weather pattern would adversely affect performance.

Our present approach with the APUC is hard line. Hard lining is often accompanied by unpredictable responses.

Weather, earthquakes, or major equipment failure are the only significant operational exposures. Administratively, the regulatory process with the APUC is our largest exposure.

[a]Alaska Public Utilities Commission.

Lockwood

Basic Business Position	*Near-Term Opportunities, Problems*

Irrigation

The market is in early maturity phase, with say 6-percent real growth. In the short run (from 1978 to 1979), unit volume will likely decline due to the long-term decline in units used for barren land conversion. Low crop prices (corn in particular) makes dry land and/or irrigated land conversion less attractive. Lockwood is presently third in the market.

Potato Equipment

The market is mature. We are the leading competitor and have the best distribution system and product.

Other Field Lines

Markets are generally mature, regionally fragmented, and tend to be heavily dependent on local agriculture market conditions.

Irrigation

Our irrigation network favors new market growth, provided we can hold it during present downturn period.

There is considerable product innovation going on in the industry. The success of these innovations is uncertain.

Potato Equipment

Although potato prices have been more resilient than grain prices, poor farm income psychology has adversely affected equipment buying. Inventory on dealers' floors will hurt short-run performance at the manufacturing level.

Other Field Lines

Competitive barriers to entry are few. Demand is often unpredictable. Competitors are largely regional, operate nonunion shops, and are generally entrepreneurial.

Alaska Interstate (A)

EXHIBIT 3
■

AKI Consolidated Income Statements and Balance Sheets, 1970–1977
(dollars in thousands)

	1970	1971	1972	1973	1974	1975	1976	1977
Income Statements								
Operating revenue	101,491	105,164	146,662	163,414	189,293	163,416	174,853	189,464
Operating cost	77,292	80,878	117,052	142,898	157,025	124,619	132,239	144,709
Gross operating profit	24,199	24,286	29,610	20,516	32,268	38,797	42,614	44,755
Percentage of operating revenue	23.8%	23.1%	20.2%	12.6%	17.0%	23.7%	24.4%	23.6%
Operating expense	12,092	14,151	18,493	22,287	22,862	24,165	27,271	30,378
Operating earnings	12,107	10,135	11,117	−1,771	9,406	14,632	15,343	14,377
Percentage of operating revenue	11.9%	9.6%	7.6%	−1.1%	5.0%	9.0%	8.8%	7.6%
Interest income	278	434	476	355	683	1,196	905	754
Interest expense	−3,723	−3,114	−3,867	−4,899	−8,435	−7,722	−6,197	−10,011
Intracompany interest income (expense)	0	0	0	0	0	0	0	0
Gain on sale of asset	150	300	379	594	2,000	28	2,823	3,978
Miscellaneous income (expense)	692	27	63	−264	−526	1,213	1,381	−492
Earnings before taxes and management fee	9,504	7,782	8,168	−5,985	3,128	9,347	14,255	8,606
Percentage of operating revenue	9.4%	7.4%	5.6%	−3.7%	1.7%	5.7%	8.2%	4.5%
Management fee	0	0	0	0	0	0	0	0
Earnings before taxes	9,504	7,782	8,168	−5,985	3,128	9,347	14,255	8,606
Percentage of operating revenue	9.4%	7.4%	5.6%	−3.7%	1.7%	5.7%	8.2%	4.5%
Provision for taxes	5,429	3,617	2,953	−4,196	−577	1,815	6,461	4,409
Tax rate (percent)	57.1%	46.5%	36.2%	70.1%	18.4%	19.4%	45.3%	51.2%
Less: minority earnings	0	0	0	0	0	0	0	−92
Net earnings	4,075	4,165	5,215	−1,789	3,705	7,532	7,794	4,289
Percentage of operating revenue	4.0%	4.0%	3.6%	−1.1%	2.0%	4.6%	4.5%	2.3%
Balance Sheets								
Current assets								
Cash—local	7,603	11,041	7,823	6,682	7,570	5,822	3,637	7,569
Cash—central	0	0	0	0	0	0	0	0
Total receivables	16,706	20,934	27,582	29,707	29,026	23,927	26,373	38,125
Total inventories	15,956	18,803	23,866	28,655	32,042	36,243	35,203	36,636
Other current assets	1,107	1,019	1,263	743	4,203	598	974	1,856
Total current assets	41,372	51,797	60,534	65,787	72,895	66,590	66,187	84,186
Long-term notes and accounts receivable	0	0	0	0	0	0	0	0
Gross fixed assets	56,416	61,913	77,751	93,060	101,871	115,342	108,163	189,872

EXHIBIT 3 continued

	1970	1971	1972	1973	1974	1975	1976	1977
Accumulated depreciation	15,625	18,339	21,770	25,664	25,889	25,089	26,185	32,592
Net fixed assets	40,791	43,574	55,981	67,396	75,982	90,253	81,978	157,280
Investment subsidiary equity	0	0	0	0	0	0	0	0
Intangible assets	12,669	13,441	13,803	14,164	14,269	15,202	15,283	14,479
Other long-term assets	3,843	5,041	11,226	15,628	31,987	33,254	25,490	15,158
Total assets	98,675	113,853	141,544	162,975	195,133	205,299	188,938	271,103
Current liabilities								
Short-term debt Bank and other	19,156	2,443	0	6,440	28	17	3,002	1,000
Intracompany financing	0	0	0	0	0	0	0	0
Current maturities of long-term debt Bank	193	3	0	0	4,746	738	3,700	0
Other	4,460	2,794	3,230	3,979	2,232	3,195	3,597	7,324
Accounts payable: Trade	6,433	7,153	13,997	20,372	18,296	15,565	11,244	10,405
Accrued liabilities: Interest	1,153	815	1,200	1,611	1,836	1,808	1,639	3,068
Current/deferred taxes payable	3,844	1,086	435	−4,516	−1,386	514	4,708	−494
Other current liabilities	2,834	6,275	7,098	7,352	10,374	10,816	8,950	13,626
Total current liabilities	38,073	20,569	25,960	35,238	36,126	32,653	36,840	34,929
Long-term debt Bank	13	11,555	9,100	22,050	41,181	48,670	28,489	42,500
Other	21,581	31,925	46,628	46,838	53,989	53,143	48,320	85,543
Deferred taxes payable	798	1,173	1,528	2,242	3,156	2,335	4,332	5,610
Other long-term liability	1,173	1,046	1,051	853	1,472	1,580	745	1,430
Stock and additional paid-in capital	24,074	30,577	34,933	35,196	35,217	35,394	32,790	62,031
Prior-year retained earnings	8,888	12,964	17,129	22,347	20,287	23,992	31,524	37,422
Current year to date	4,075	4,165	5,215	−1,789	3,705	7,532	7,794	4,289
Less dividends	0	0	0	0	0	0	1,896	2,633
Less treasury stock	0	121	0	0	0	0	0	0
Total equity	37,037	47,585	57,277	55,754	59,209	66,918	70,212	101,091
Total liabilities and equity	98,675	113,853	141,544	162,975	195,133	205,299	188,938	271,103
Discrepancy	0	1	0	3	271	0	0	0

Alaska Interstate (A)

EXHIBIT 4

■

Alaska Gas and Service Co. Income Statements and Balance Sheets, 1970–1982
(thousands of dollars)

	Actual									Forecast			
	1970	1971	1972	1973	1974	1975	1976	1977	1978	1979	1980	1981	1982
Income Statements													
Operating revenue	4,300	5,254	5,840	6,325	6,818	8,958	10,297	10,604	12,145	13,198	13,734	13,557	13,855
Operating cost	2,052	2,376	2,845	3,177	3,401	4,915	6,332	6,702	7,854	8,233	8,500	8,437	8,675
Gross operating profit	2,248	2,878	2,995	3,148	3,417	4,043	3,965	3,902	4,291	4,965	5,234	5,120	5,180
Percentage of operating revenue	52.3	54.8	51.3	49.8	50.1	45.1	38.5	36.8	35.3	37.6	38.1	37.8	37.4
Operating expense	531	679	747	784	748	962	1,088	1,152	1,345	1,403	1,465	1,537	1,620
Operating earnings	1,717	2,199	2,248	2,364	2,669	3,081	2,877	2,750	2,946	3,562	3,769	3,583	3,560
Percentage of operating revenue	39.9	41.9	38.5	37.4	39.1	34.4	27.9	25.9	24.3	27.0	27.4	26.4	25.7
Interest income	7	4	4	19	7	4	4	21	0	0	0	0	0
Interest expense	374	338	394	464	487	624	779	910	998	1,104	1,140	1,168	1,187
Intracompany interest income (expense)	0	0	0	0	32	0	0	31	0	0	0	0	0
Gain on sale of asset	0	0	0	0	0	0	0	0	0	0	0	0	0
Miscellaneous income (expense)	27	–39	12	32	32	26	41	45	35	35	35	36	36
Earnings before taxes and management fee	1,377	1,826	1,870	1,951	2,253	2,487	2,143	1,937	1,983	2,493	2,664	2,451	2,409
Percentage of operating revenue	32.0	34.8	32.0	30.8	33.0	27.8	20.8	18.3	16.3	18.9	19.4	18.1	17.4
Management fee	78	91	97	97	97	97	97	156	156	182	197	206	203
Earnings before taxes	1,299	1,735	1,773	1,854	2,156	2,390	2,046	1,781	1,827	2,311	2,467	2,245	2,206
Percentage of operating revenue	30.2	33.0	30.4	29.3	31.6	26.7	19.9	16.8	15.0	17.5	18.0	16.6	15.9
Provision for taxes	691	834	889	948	979	1,095	934	709	623	985	1,145	1,019	983
Tax rate (percent)	53.0	48.0	50.1	51.0	45.3	45.8	45.6	39.8	33.9	42.5	46.3	45.3	44.4
Net earnings	608	901	884	906	1,177	1,295	1,112	1,072	1,204	1,326	1,322	1,226	1,223
Percentage of operating revenue	14.1	17.1	15.1	14.3	17.3	14.5	10.8	10.1	9.9	10.0	9.6	9.0	8.8

Balance Sheets

Current assets													
Cash—local	326	299	546	355	355	15	224	73	184	221	221	221	221
Cash—central	1	0	0	0	16	0	0	0	0	0	0	0	0
Total receivables	769	725	792	807	932	1,252	1,345	1,888	1,443	1,384	1,440	1,421	1,451
Total inventories	157	180	176	278	436	517	501	495	627	553	553	553	553
Other current assets	40	32	49	48	38	60	214	492	125	129	129	129	129
Total current assets	1,293	1,236	1,563	1,488	1,777	1,844	2,284	2,948	2,379	2,287	2,343	2,324	2,354
Long-term notes and accounts receivable	0	0	0	0	0	0	0	0	0	0	0	0	0
Gross fixed assets	11,237	12,419	13,179	13,846	17,456	19,717	21,373	23,378	27,406	28,864	30,481	32,113	33,975
Accumulated depreciation	2,386	2,720	3,044	3,376	3,835	4,402	5,139	5,620	6,506	7,336	8,198	9,135	10,130
Net fixed assets	8,851	9,699	10,135	10,470	13,621	15,315	16,234	17,758	20,900	21,528	22,283	22,978	23,845
Investment subsidiary equity	0	0	0	0	0	0	0	0	0	0	0	0	0
Intangible assets	1,139	1,214	1,209	1,359	1,349	1,539	1,596	1,565	1,527	1,508	1,508	1,508	1,508
Other long-term assets	162	37	392	290	222	0	0	0	0	0	0	0	0
Total assets	11,445	12,186	13,299	13,607	16,969	18,698	20,114	22,271	24,806	25,323	26,134	26,810	27,707
Current Liabilities													
Short-term debt: Bank and other	0	886	0	517	0	0	1,107	369	471	65	65	65	65
Intracompany financing	0	1	0	0	15	0	6	0	0	0	0	0	0
Current maturities													
Long-term debt													
Bank	0	0	0	0	0	0	0	0	0	0	0	0	0
Other	487	487	487	487	498	691	692	821	821	922	715	656	656

continued

EXHIBIT 4 *continued*

	Actual									Forecast			
	1970	1971	1972	1973	1974	1975	1976	1977	1978	1979	1980	1981	1982
Accounts payable: Trade	268	262	374	296	636	910	658	883	590	775	812	867	886
Accrued liabilities interest	313	151	148	94	271	275	355	394	287	369	387	406	424
Current/deferred taxes payable	636	151	32	4	-116	-34	61	28	18	332	369	249	443
Other current liabilities	185	235	156	254	268	375	796	1,014	185	62	94	94	163
Total current liabilities	1,889	2,173	1,197	1,652	1,572	2,217	3,675	3,509	2,372	2,525	2,442	2,337	2,639
Long-term debt													
Bank	0	0	0	0	923	0	0	0	0	0	0	0	0
Other	5,332	4,784	6,143	5,656	7,159	8,318	7,626	9,400	12,261	12,082	12,355	12,613	12,686
Deferred taxes payable	77	114	228	475	716	983	1,174	1,425	1,558	1,514	1,551	1,587	1,624
Other long-term liabilities	218	365	375	304	457	496	209	255	184	184	184	184	184
Stock and additional paid-in capital	2,112	2,112	2,112	2,112	2,112	2,112	2,112	2,112	2,112	2,112	2,112	2,112	2,112
Prior-year retained earnings	1,293	1,817	2,635	3,240	3,406	4,029	4,571	5,314	5,481	6,317	6,905	7,488	7,976
Current year to date	608	901	884	906	1,177	1,295	1,112	1,072	1,204	1,326	1,322	1,226	1,223
Less dividends	83	83	279	740	553	754	369	819	369	738	738	738	738
Less treasury stock	0	0	0	0	0	0	0	0	0	0	0	0	0
Total equity	3,930	4,747	5,352	5,518	6,142	6,682	7,426	7,679	8,428	9,017	9,601	10,088	10,573
Total liabilities and equity	11,446	12,183	13,295	13,605	16,969	18,696	20,110	22,268	24,803	25,322	26,133	26,809	27,702
Discrepancy	1	3	4	2	0	2	4	3	3	1	1	1	5

Alaska Interstate (A)

EXHIBIT 5

∎

Lockwood Corp. Income Statements and Balance Sheets, 1970–1982
(thousands of dollars)

	Actual									Forecast			
	1970	1971	1972	1973	1974	1975	1976	1977	1978	1979	1980	1981	1982
Income Statements													
Operating revenue	5,335	6,668	8,814	12,534	19,709	18,703	22,947	19,121	17,690	20,766	23,793	27,219	27,219
Operating cost	3,353	4,161	5,833	10,186	14,115	13,197	16,574	14,385	13,241	15,224	16,868	19,264	19,264
Gross operating profit	1,982	2,507	2,981	2,348	5,594	5,506	6,373	4,736	4,449	5,542	6,925	7,955	7,955
Percentage of operating revenue	37.2	37.6	33.8	18.7	28.4	29.4	27.8	24.8	25.1	26.7	29.1	29.2	29.2
Operating expense	984	1,485	1,788	2,384	2,581	3,166	4,053	4,051	3,472	3,766	4,136	4,579	4,579
Operating earnings	998	1,022	1,193	−36	3,013	2,340	2,320	685	977	1,776	2,789	3,376	3,376
Percentage of operating revenue	18.7	15.3	13.5	−0.3	15.3	12.5	10.1	3.6	5.5	8.6	11.7	12.4	12.4
Interest income	12	17	17	16	37	29	69	81	88	88	88	88	88
Interest expense	182	180	43	46	62	71	70	85	261	257	252	248	248
Intracompany interest income (expense)	0	(18)	(176)	(413)	(545)	(559)	(533)	(646)	(927)	(867)	(840)	(775)	(775)
Gain on sale of asset	0	−4	−5	2	7	9	−12	5	0	0	0	0	0
Miscellaneous income (expense)	14	7	72	45	43	79	(11)	(756)	0	0	0	0	0
Earnings before taxes and management fee	842	844	1,058	−432	2,493	1,827	1,763	−716	−123	740	1,785	2,441	2,441
Percentage of operating revenue	15.8	12.7	12.0	−3.4	12.6	9.8	7.7	−3.7	−0.7	3.6	7.5	9.0	9.0
Management fee	129	176	202	202	204	203	203	392	392	392	392	392	392
Earnings before taxes	713	668	856	−634	2,289	1,624	1,560	−1,108	−515	348	1,393	2,049	2,049
Percentage of operating revenue	13.4	10.0	9.7	−5.1	11.6	8.7	6.8	−5.8	−2.9	1.7	5.9	7.5	7.5
Provision for taxes	366	330	393	−312	1,095	737	709	−586	−298	176	700	1,029	1,029
Tax rate (percent)	51.1	48.8	45.4	49.1	47.8	45.3	45.3	53.0	57.9	49.7	50.1	50.2	50.2
Net earnings	347	338	463	−322	1,194	887	851	−522	−217	172	693	1,020	1,020
Percentage of operating revenue	6.5	5.1	5.3	−2.6	6.1	4.7	3.7	−2.7	−1.2	0.8	2.9	3.7	3.7

continued

EXHIBIT 5 continued

	Actual								Forecast				
	1970	1971	1972	1973	1974	1975	1976	1977	1978	1979	1980	1981	1982
Balance Sheets													
Current assets													
Cash—local	697	804	262	47	68	99	120	67	110	110	110	110	110
Cash—central	0	0	0	42	126	245	426	426	620	620	620	620	620
Total receivables	1,497	1,962	2,268	2,487	3,127	2,713	4,430	4,148	4,122	4,431	5,356	5,945	5,945
Total inventories	2,525	3,106	4,122	5,317	6,466	7,924	7,991	7,890	7,349	7,401	7,441	7,582	7,420
Other current assets	29	50	61	47	385	54	21	25	22	22	22	22	22
Total current assets	4,748	5,922	6,713	7,940	10,172	11,035	12,988	12,554	12,223	12,584	13,549	14,279	14,117
Long-term intracompany notes and accounts receivable	0	0	0	0	0	0	0	0	0	0	0	0	0
Gross fixed assets	1,589	1,783	2,390	2,788	3,381	3,751	6,017	6,096	6,808	7,153	7,523	7,966	8,409
Accumulated depreciation	466	554	712	914	1,140	1,357	1,652	1,940	2,320	2,689	3,059	3,465	3,771
Net fixed assets	1,123	1,229	1,678	1,874	2,241	2,394	4,365	4,156	4,488	4,464	4,464	4,501	4,438
Investment subsidiary equity	0	0	0	0	0	0	0	0	0	0	0	0	0
Intangible assets	0	24	20	18	16	109	173	42	38	39	39	39	39
Other long-term assets	116	90	295	337	294	155	149	144	155	143	143	143	143
Total assets	5,987	7,266	8,706	10,169	12,723	13,693	17,675	16,898	16,904	17,230	18,195	18,962	18,740
Current liabilities													
Short-term debt: Bank and other	1,110	0	0	14	10	6	0	0	0	0	0	0	0
Intracompany financing	316	2,781	2,668	3,695	4,232	5,194	6,717	8,207	8,359	8,235	7,940	6,929	6,275
Current maturity													
Long-term debt													
Bank	71	0	0	0	0	0	0	0	0	0	0	0	0
Other	46	186	73	109	89	113	175	107	152	152	152	152	152

Accounts payable: Trade	605	321	1,113	2,214	1,677	1,291	1,790	610	745	627	590	553	553
Accrued liabilities interest	11	2	7	20	6	3	3	1	3	3	3	3	3
Current/deferred taxes payable	224	9	247	−196	780	109	−106	570	−1,155	−923	−225	803	347
Other current liabilities	210	342	474	464	710	1,048	940	1,251	1,517	1,716	1,657	1,458	1,458
Total current liabilities	2,593	3,641	4,582	6,326	7,504	7,764	9,519	9,606	9,621	9,810	10,117	9,898	8,873
Long-term debt Bank	0	0	0	0	0	0	0	0	0	0	0	0	0
Other	681	573	612	659	768	708	2,012	1,919	1,898	1,863	1,828	1,793	1,758
Deferred taxes payable	0	0	0	0	8	0	67	−181	22	22	22	22	22
Other long-term liabilities	0	0	0	0	57	24	27	26	22	22	22	22	22
Stock and additional paid-in capital	1,874	1,874	1,874	1,874	1,874	1,799	1,799	1,799	1,799	1,799	1,799	1,799	1,799
Prior-year retained earnings	488	836	1,175	1,638	1,316	2,510	3,397	4,249	3,756	3,538	3,711	4,404	5,242
Current year to date	347	338	463	−322	1,194	887	851	−522	−217	172	693	1,020	1,020
Less dividends	0	0	0	0	0	0	0	0	0	0	0	0	0
Less treasury stock	0	0	0	0	0	0	0	0	0	0	0	0	0
Total equity	2,709	3,048	3,512	3,190	4,384	5,196	6,047	5,526	5,338	5,509	6,203	7,223	8,061
Total liabilities and equity	5,983	7,262	8,706	10,172	12,721	13,692	17,672	16,896	16,901	17,236	18,192	18,958	18,736
Discrepancy	4	4	0	3	2	1	3	2	3	6	3	4	4

Alaska Interstate (A)

EXHIBIT 6

■

Return on Capital Employed by Components[a]

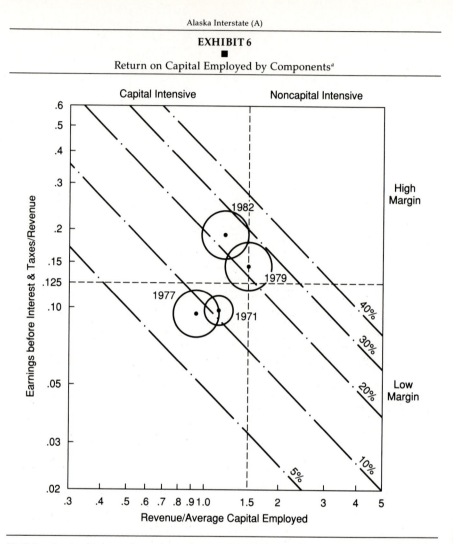

[a]Capital employed = Total assets less noninterest-bearing current liabilities. Return on capital employed = Earnings before interest, taxes, and management fee of this business expressed as a percentage of the average capital employed during the year.

$$\frac{\text{Sales}}{\text{Capital employed}} \times \frac{\text{EBIT and management fee}}{\text{Sales}} =$$

Actual return on capital employed or, equivalently, $\dfrac{\text{EBIT and management fee}}{\text{Capital employed}}$

Alaska Interstate (A)

EXHIBIT 7
■

Return on Capital Employed—Energy Subsidiaries, 1971

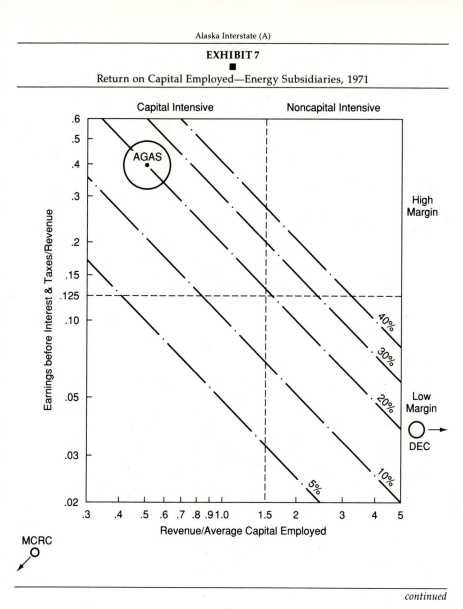

continued

EXHIBIT 7 *continued*

EXHIBIT 7 *continued*

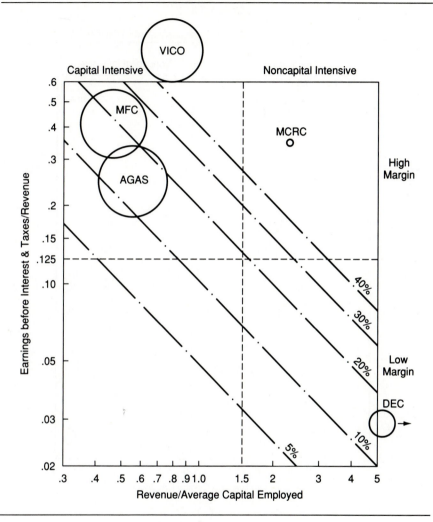

Alaska Interstate (A)

EXHIBIT 8
∎
Return on Capital Employed—Manufacturing Subsidiaries, 1971

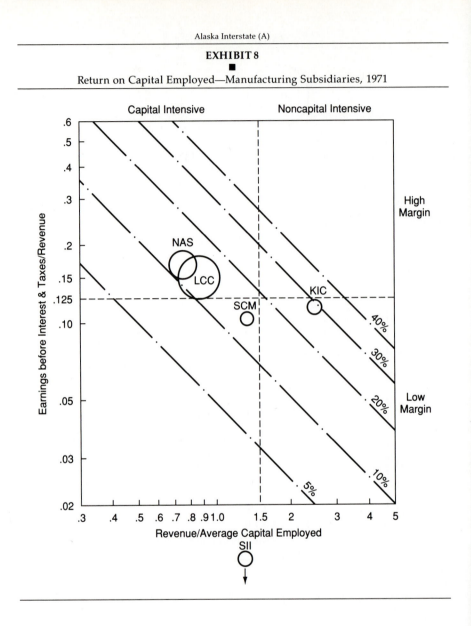

EXHIBIT 8 *continued*

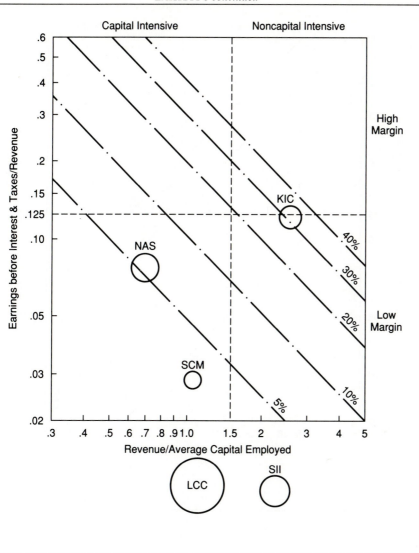

continued

EXHIBIT 8 *continued*

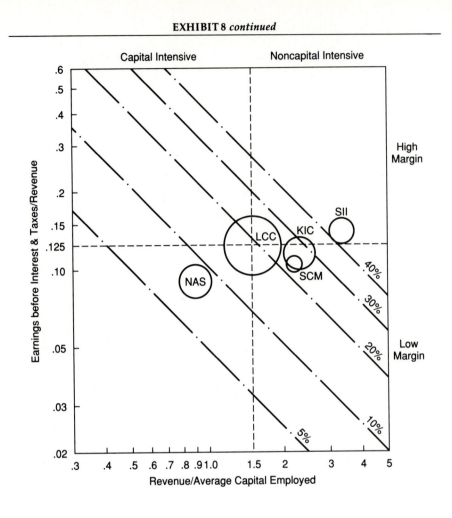

Alaska Interstate (A)

EXHIBIT 9

■

Return on Capital Employed—Alpetco at Start-up

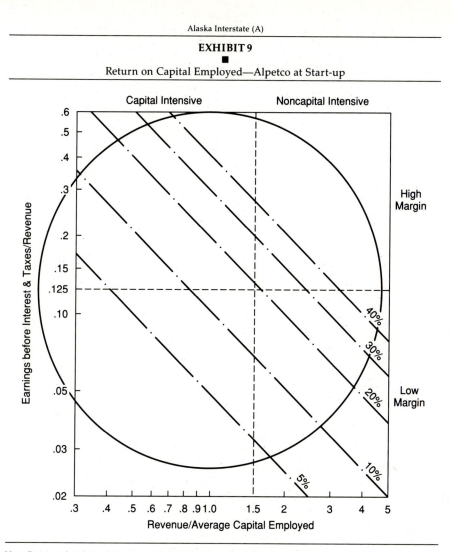

Note: Position of circle is arbitrary since the ROCE had not been estimated at that time.

continued

EXHIBIT 9 *continued*

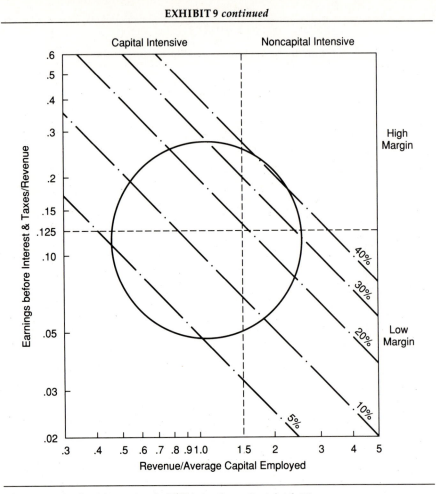

Note: Position of circle is arbitrary since the ROCE had not been estimated at that time.

Alaska Interstate (A)

EXHIBIT 10

■

Subjective Risk Assessment Worksheet

Subsidiary: _____

Product line: _____

Rater: _____

Date: _____

Consideration	*A* Weight[a]	*B* Score[b]	*A* × *B*
1. Predictability			
2. Depth and quality of management			
3. Marketability of assets			
4. Attractiveness of industry			
5. Competitive position within the industry			
6. Political considerations			
7. Other: _____			
Total	(x)		(z)

Risk index = (z)/(x) =

Comments:

---

[a]Weights of 0 (low) to 10 (high) should be assigned according to the relative importance of the consideration to the rater.

[b]Scale: $\begin{array}{cc} 0 & 10 \\ \text{(no risk)} & \to & \text{(most risk)} \end{array}$

Alaska Interstate (A)

EXHIBIT 11
■
Managers' Subjective Risk Assessments as of 12/77

| | Managers | | | | | | | | Average | | | |
	1	2	3	4	5	6	7	8	Mean	Standard Deviation	Percent CE[a] as of 11/30/77	Weighted Average
Domestic oil and gas	4.0	5.5	7.0	6.1	4.0	8.0	5.0	6.0	5.7	1.4	17.6	1.0
Foreign oil and gas: VICO	7.0	7.5	8.0	7.1	8.0	10.0	5.0	4.0	7.1	1.9	20.1	1.4
Huffington	8.0	8.0	8.0	7.2	9.0	10.0	6.5	8.0	8.1	1.1	4.4	0.4
Gas transportation and distribution	3.0	3.0	4.9	2.3	2.0	2.0	2.0	2.0	2.7	1.0	22.0	0.6
Gas processing and construction	7.0	6.5	6.2	7.5	5.0	9.0	7.0	8.0	7.0	1.2	1.4	0.1
Capital good manufacturing	6.0	5.0	4.5	4.9	4.0	5.0	4.5	3.0	4.6	0.9	5.6	0.3
Houseboats	9.0	4.0	6.8	8.5	4.0	8.0	7.0	8.0	6.9	1.9	1.7	0.1
Shortline agricultural equipment	5.1	8.0	4.2	6.6	8.0	4.0	5.0	4.0	5.6	1.7	16.2	0.9
Irrigation equipment	6.9	6.5	6.1	8.1	8.0	7.0	6.0	7.0	7.0	0.8	3.9	0.3
Aircraft engine overhaul	9.0	6.0	7.5	7.2	8.0	8.0	—	8.0	7.5	0.9	4.9	0.4
Mineral and Chemical Resource Co.	6.0	2.0	—	4.0	5.0	2.0	—	3.0	3.2	1.6	0.1	0.4
Average	6.5	5.6	6.3	6.3	5.9	6.6	5.3	5.6			97.9	5.9

[a]Percent CE = average total capital employed by the business. It can be calculated in two ways:
    1. Fixed capital + Working capital
    2. Equity + Long-term debt + Other long-term liabilities + Interest-bearing liabilities.

Alaska Interstate (A)

EXHIBIT 12
■
Business Risk and Return on the Components of the AKI Portfolio

Business	Subsidiary/Investment
1. Gas transmission and distribution	APC/AGAS
2. Shortline agricultural equipment	Lockwood
3. Irrigation equipment	Lockwood

Note: Circle sizes are proportional to average budgeted 1978 capital employed.

EXHIBIT 12 *continued*

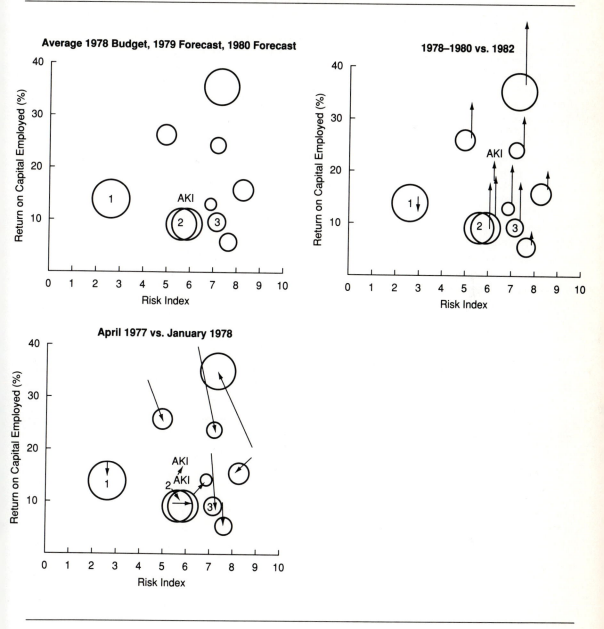

Alaska Interstate (A)

EXHIBIT 13
■

Selected Financial Items Analysis: Standard Deviation
of Percentages of Budget Forecast Errors (two-month intervals)

Accounts	Consolidated	A[a]	B	C	D[b]	E	F	G	Other
Revenue	12.5	13.4	17.8	29.7	18.6	48.3	29.2	24.4	62.4
Operating cost + operating expenses − depreciation	12.3	9.7	18.2	25.5	15.6	42.3	29.7	24.6	51.9
Revenues − (operating cost + expenses + depreciation)	0.6	2.6	11.4	61.1	4.3	63.8	40.7	29.3	73.5
Pretax cash from operations	220.5	46.4	131.5	185.2	97.1	60.7	827.3	278.6	522.0
Net financial flows	113.1	162.8	26.7	107.1	127.8	30.9	195.7	551.3	164.0
Net returns to capital	2.6	43.5	38.3	69.7	4.0	NMF[c]	217.6	94.2	339.9
Other cash flows (taxes)	57.4	33.1	65.6	114.0	15.3	35.0	462.5	147.5	11.7
Preborrowing cash charge	8.5	23.3	182.3	222.4	6.2	65.6	46.6	277.7	5.1
Earnings before interest, taxes, and management fee	1.5	4.5	14.9	101.0	7.5	81.9	78.5	22.7	397.3
Net operating profit after tax	2.7	6.0	28.3	227.9	26.8	62.4	190.8	48.4	348.7
Change in capital employed	4.3	168.4	164.5	126.2	2.4	79.2	98.4	293.3	17.7
Free cash flow	2.9	11.0	286.2	106.6	4.6	75.2	44.3	323.2	17.3
Net earnings	8.5	8.1	43.2	83.8	25.1	79.6	206.6	122.4	91.5

[a]Alaska Gas and Service Co.
[b]Lockwood.
[c]No meaningful figure.

Alaska Interstate (A)

EXHIBIT 14

■

Rank-Ordered Standard Deviations of
Percentages of Budget Forecast Errors

Accounts	A^a	B	C	D^b	E	F	G
Revenue	1	2	6	3	7	5	4
Operating cost + operating expenses − depreciation	1	3	5	2	7	6	4
Revenues − (operating cost + operating expenses − depreciation)	1	3	6	2	7	5	4
Pretax cash from operations	1	4	5	3	2	7	6
Net financial flows	5	1	3	4	2	6	7
Net returns to capital	—	—	—	—	NMF^c	—	—
Other cash flows (taxes)	2	4	5	1	3	7	6
Preborrowing cash charge	2	5	6	1	4	3	7
Earnings before interest, taxes, and management fee	1	3	7	2	6	5	4
Net operating profit after tax	1	3	7	2	5	6	4
Change in capital employed	6	5	4	1	2	3	7
Free cash flow	2	6	5	1	4	3	7
Net earnings	1	3	5	2	4	7	6

Note: Data items falling outside 3.1 standard deviations from the mean or having an absolute dollar deviation less than $50,000 were omitted.

[a]Alaska Gas and Service Co.

[b]Lockwood.

[c]No meaningful figure.

Alaska Interstate (B)

The Santoski–Ross report [see Alaska Interstate (A)] that Bill Camp was contemplating had discussed a third method of analyzing risk. This method, the capital asset pricing model, was based on modern portfolio theory, a set of concepts about risk and return in portfolio investing that had been developed and refined by a number of academics. It seemed to Mr. Camp that the Santoski–Ross report made a good case for using this theory to analyze holding companies such as AKI, because holding companies, the Santoski–Ross report suggested, were just like investment portfolios.

MARKET RISK

Modern portfolio theory (MPT) defined risk as the sensitivity of an asset's returns to changes in general economic conditions. Most often those using this theory compared a stock's returns to the returns on a stock market index, like Standard & Poor's 500. A risky stock was one whose total returns (price changes plus dividends) were more volatile than the average total returns of all stocks in the index. The measure of risk, variability compared to the chosen index, was called beta or systematic risk. All other risk, unsystematic risk, could be eliminated by diversification and was thus irrelevant. In describing modern portfolio theory, the Santoski–Ross report stated:

> This theory assumes the firm's objective is to maximize shareholder wealth. To a well-diversified investor it is the sensitivity of its price to changes in general economic conditions . . ., as reflected in broad stock market indices. The well-diversified investor is not exposed to company-specific risks, i.e., competitive moves, technological changes, shifts in demand, strikes, organizational efficiency, etc. These risks have been diversified away by the rational investor, and he can safely ignore them. Total company risk has two components: 1) uncertainty in predicting overall economic conditions and the company's response (systematic risk); and 2) uncertainty in predict-

---

This case was prepared as a basis for class discussion rather than to illustrate either effective or ineffective handling of an administrative situation. Copyright © 1982 by the Darden Graduate Business School Sponsors, University of Virginia, Charlottesville, Virginia.

ing changes in the company's immediate environment, both internal and external (unsystematic risk). Only systematic risk is critical to the shareholder.

Appendix A to this case describes the capital asset pricing model (CAPM), which is the specific model from modern portfolio theory that Mr. Ross and Mr. Santoski used.

By analyzing changes in the firm's stock prices over the past 4½ years, Mr. Santoski and Mr. Ross had developed a measure of AKI's overall riskiness. The betas they calculated from 1973 to 1978 are graphed in Exhibit 1. Mr. Santoski and Mr. Ross noted on the graph the events that they believed had affected AKI's beta. AKI's stock prices from 1976 to 1978 are shown in Exhibit 2. Mr. Santoski and Mr. Ross observed that both AKI's beta and stock price had dropped since mid-1977.

The betas for AKI's subsidiaries could not be calculated using the same method that had been used to estimate the AKI beta, since market price information was not available for the subsidiaries. Instead, Mr. Santoski and Mr. Ross had used a technique for developing a surrogate beta for each subsidiary. Their technique assumed that businesses in the same industry were subject to the same economic influences and therefore were subject to a similar degree of systematic risk. Thus, betas of similar firms could be used as proxies for the subsidiaries' unknown betas.

Mr. Ross and Mr. Santoski had gone one further step in developing their proxies. Systematic risk, they said, was in part determined by financial leverage. Firms with high debt ratios experienced more volatile changes in price than those with little debt. Therefore, the surrogate beta they calculated was "de-levered." Their process is described at the bottom of Exhibit 3. Exhibits 3 and 4 summarize the surrogate betas for Lockwood and Alaska Gas and Service Co.'s distribution and transmission companies. The analysis for Alaska Gas and Service Co. resulted in a beta of 0.89 and for Lockwood, a re-levered beta of 1.71 at a 50-percent debt/equity ratio. Exhibit 5 provides the summary for all the subsidiaries and AKI.

Mr. Camp knew that Mr. Santoski and Mr. Ross believed this approach was "objective, derived from easily accessible capital market data, and based on a sound financial and statistical foundation." Further, the CAPM did seem to fit the need for quantitative risk information better than any method so far.

However, Mr. Camp had talked with Mr. Ross about some of the problems with using the method. Mr. Ross had explored some of the statistical problems that linear regression presented when used to derive a beta from historical data and he had talked about the choice of a risk-free rate and risk premium. In addition, he had brought up other things that seemed important for Mr. Camp to consider.

The CAPM assumed that the firm's (and its management's) objective was to maximize value to a well-diversified shareholder. This assumption raised questions management believed it should consider:

1.   Are our shareholders well-diversified?

2.   What are the implications for using portfolio theory if AKI's shares are one of two or three assets in most of our shareholders' portfolios?

3.   Should maximizing value to the shareholder be our only portfolio objective? Or are there others who have stakes that must be considered? Should we worry, for instance, about the needs and expectations of our customers, employees, management, the Internal Revenue Service, and other government agencies? How do we, or should we, involve their interests in these decisions? If they are critical elements in building a corporate portfolio, how do we go about considering them?

Mr. Camp knew he had to decide whether to include the information about betas and surrogate betas in his presentation. It was a method Mr. Santoski and Mr. Ross had proposed and favored. Yet if CAPM measured the same things as the other methods, presenting it alone or with the other methods might make the presentation confusing.

Alaska Interstate (B)

EXHIBIT 1
■
AKI Systematic Risk[a] (Beta), 1970–1978

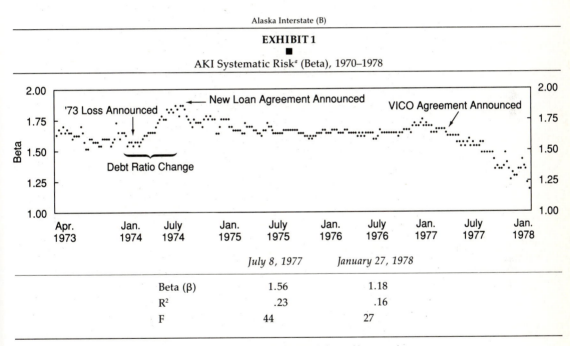

	July 8, 1977	*January 27, 1978*
Beta (β)	1.56	1.18
R^2	.23	.16
F	44	27

[a]Computed using simple linear regression on AKI stock returns and the S&P 500 Index weekly returns for the most recent 2½ years.

$$[R_j = \alpha_j + \beta_j(R_m) + E_j].$$

Alaska Interstate (B)

EXHIBIT 2

■

AKI Weekly Stock Prices, November 5, 1976 to January 27, 1978

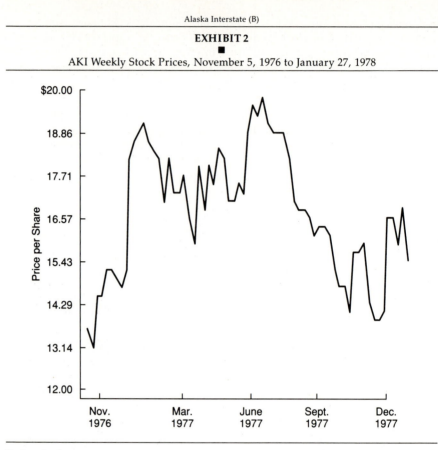

Stock market data:
Average beta = 1.0
Average P/E = 9.7

Alaska Interstate (B)

EXHIBIT 3
■
Surrogate Beta Analysis for Lockwood

Company Name	Debt/Equity (D/E)	Levered Beta	Unlevered Beta
Valmont	0.36	1.67	1.24
Dekaulb	0.16	1.27	1.10
Gifford	0.73	1.05	0.61
Thiokol	0.33	1.02	0.77
Hesston	0.59	0.97	0.62

Average unlevered beta for industry: 0.867058
Average unlevered beta for S&P 500:   0.70
Average levered beta assuming AKI D/D + E of 70%:   2.83528
                                               50%:   1.70811

To determine the unlevered beta, the following process was used:

1. Surrogates were chosen on the basis of product line homogeneity with the subsidiary; betas were taken from *Security Risk Evaluation,* published by Merrill Lynch in June 1976; betas were calculated based on 5 years of monthly returns when available.

2. Computation of the unlevered beta (S&P 500 = 0.70) was based on the following formula:[a]

$$\beta_L = \beta_U \left(1 + \frac{D\,(1 - tR_F)}{S\,(1 + R_F)} \right),$$

where:

β_L = Company's levered beta
β_U = Company's unlevered beta
D = Market value of company's debt
S = Market value of company's equity
R_F = Risk-free rate
t = Tax rate.

[a]Alaska Interstate management used their variation of Mr. Hamada's formula, which is described in "The Effect of Leverage on Beta" in Appendix B to this case.

Alaska Interstate (B)

EXHIBIT 4
■

Surrogate Beta Analysis for APC—Transmission

Company Name	Debt/Equity (D/E)	Levered Beta	Unlevered Beta
Floridagas	1.21	0.96	0.44
Houstonnat	0.23	1.26	1.03
Northwest	1.49	0.62	0.25
Panhandle	0.99	1.00	0.51
Southern	0.82	0.79	0.44
Texaseastern	0.88	1.00	0.54
Texasgas	0.85	0.86	0.47
Transco	1.59	0.98	0.38
Westcoast	0.95	0.79	0.41

Average unlevered beta for industry: 0.496952
Average unlevered beta for S&P 500: 0.70
Average levered beta assuming AKI D/D + E of 70%: 1.62503
                                              50%: 0.97899

Surrogate Beta Analysis for APC—Distribution

Company Name	Debt/Equity (D/E)	Levered Beta	Unlevered Beta
Alabamagas	1.33	0.77	0.34
Amernatres	1.33	0.68	0.30
Arkanlagas	0.67	0.79	0.48
Atlgaslight	1.09	0.94	0.46
Brookunion	1.05	0.75	0.37
Cascade	1.80	0.86	0.31
Columbia	1.27	0.81	0.36
Consolidated	0.77	0.61	0.35
Entex	0.68	1.12	0.67
Gasservice	1.36	0.98	0.42
Indianagas	1.27	0.99	0.44
Laclede	1.22	0.80	0.37

Average unlevered beta for industry: 0.404976
Average unlevered beta for S&P 500: 0.70
Average levered beta assuming AKI D/D + E of 70%: 1.32427
                                              50%: 0.79780

Alaska Interstate (B)

EXHIBIT 5
■
Risk Breakdown by Subsidiary

	Capital Employed	Percent	Surrogate Beta	Weighted Average
Subs. A	$ 18,998	7.9%	N.Av.	N.Av.
Alaska Pipeline Co.	51,886	21.7	0.89	0.193
Subs. B	47,426	19.8	N.Av.	N.Av.
Subs. C	41,955	17.5	1.90	0.333
Subs. D	1,772	0.7	2.53	0.018
Subs. E	7,188	3.0	1.45	0.044
Lockwood Corp.	49,056	20.5	1.72	0.352
Subs. F	11,679	4.9	1.37	0.067
Subs. G	5,563	2.3	1.86	0.043
Subs. H	3,852	1.6	1.78	0.028
Total	$239,375			
Weighted average		100.0%		1.08[a]

N.Av. = Not available.

[a] To arrive at the most recently computed beta of 1.18, the beta of subsidiaries A and B must be about 0.4.

■

APPENDIX A

A Brief Description of the Capital Asset Pricing Model

The CAPM used by Mr. Ross and Mr. Santoski was a simplified version of the first portfolio model called *modern portfolio theory* (MPT) proposed by Harry Markowitz (1958).[1] Developers of the CAPM had taken Mr. Markowitz's idea— assuming the risk of every asset's returns in relation to the risk of other assets in the portfolio (its covariance)—and reduced the number of relationships (covariances) that had to be calculated. In the early Markowitz model, MPT, as the number of assets increased, the number of relationships (covariances) rapidly increased: two assets meant two relationships, three assets meant six relationships, and so on. Using the concepts of MPT could therefore become quite cumbersome. The CAPM had reduced the interrelationships by comparing the return of each asset to an index of the returns of all assets (often an index like the S&P 500). Because each asset's returns were compared only to the index, the number of covariances that must be estimated was equal to the number of assets being evaluated, a number of covariances much smaller than required when using MPT. The measure of this variability was called *beta* (β). The asset's beta was used with a basic risk premium model to estimate the return. The particular risk premium model was:

$$\tilde{R}_j = \tilde{R}_f + \tilde{\beta}_j (\tilde{R}_m - \tilde{R}_f),$$

where:

R_j = Return on the asset j
R_f = The minimum required return; the risk-free rate
R_m = The returns on the market
β_j = The asset's risk factor
$\sim$ = Expected returns or expected betas.

---

[1] Harry Markowitz, "Portfolio Selection," *Journal of Finance* XII (March 1952): 77–91.

The CAPM rested on several assumptions about investors and the world in which they operated:

1.   Asset markets are informationally efficient.

2.   All investors have homogeneous expectations, seek to maximize single-period expected utility of terminal wealth, and choose among alternative portfolios on the basis of mean and variance (or standard deviation) of returns.

3.   Markets are liquid, and all investors can borrow or lend an unlimited amount at an exogenously given risk-free rate of interest. There are no taxes, transaction costs, new issue repurchases, or restrictions on short sales.

Alaska Interstate (B)

■

APPENDIX B
The Effect of Leverage on Beta

Academics continue to debate whether there is an optimal capital structure for a company. The argument hinges on what effect different capital structures have on the equity holders' risk and, thus, on their risk premium—the cost of equity. This note provides an overview of what we know about the relationship between leverage and one measure of equity risk, beta.

BACKGROUND

Briefly, there are two schools of thought regarding capital structure: the traditional view, which holds that an optimal capital structure does exist, and thus differences in capital structure can affect a company's value; and the view of Modigliani and Miller (M&M)[1] who concluded that, excepting the tax deductibility of interest payments on debt, differences in capital structure do not affect the value of the firm. M&M assumed that a firm's weighted-average cost of capital must remain constant across all debt/equity ratios and thus the firm's value remains unchanged as leverage increases or decreases. Since debt is cheaper than equity, M&M argued that to keep the cost of capital constant, the cost of equity for a firm must be a linearly increasing function of the debt/equity ratio: as debt increases, so does the shareholders' risk and thus their cost of equity.

Traditionalists argue that increases in leverage do not result in linearly increasing equity costs. They argue that since the judicious use of debt reduces the weighted-average cost of capital, an optimal capital structure for a firm does exist, and the firm's value is a nonlinear function of the debt/equity ratio. The optimal capital structure is one where the cost of capital is the lowest: the cost of equity has not risen to offset the decreased capital costs accruing from cheaper debt, and the firm's value thus is at its highest.

---

[1]Franco Modigliani and Merton Miller, "The Cost of Capital, Corporation Finance and the Theory of Investment," *American Economic Review* 48 (June 1958): 261–297; "The Cost of Capital, Corporation Finance and the Theory of Investment: A Correction," *American Economic Review* 48 (September 1958): 655–669.

In practice, we assume that a firm has an optimal debt/equity ratio. This ratio, the relative proportions of debt and equity, is used, along with estimates of the costs of debt and equity, to calculate the weighted-average cost of capital (WACC). The value of any firm or investment is determined by discounting the after-tax cash flows (excluding financing costs such as interest) by the weighted-average cost of capital. Since this assumes that the firm is at its optimal capital structure, the true value of an investment is obtained only if all the estimates, including the cost of equity, are appropriate. We focus on the difficult-to-determine cost of equity in this note.

In estimating an investment's value, the discount rate (the WACC) plays a major role. To demonstrate the discount rate's importance, suppose Rangeware were considering the acquisition of SEH Industries, a closely held manufacturer of small electrical household appliances. To value the acquisition, Rangeware would need a forecast of SEH's future cash flows and a rate at which to discount those cash flows. SEH's after-tax cash flows are expected to remain relatively constant at $17.1 million per year. Table 1 illustrates that, depending upon the discount rate chosen, the value of SEH can vary dramatically—from $114 to $77.7 million. The appropriate rate, the cost of capital,[2] at which to discount the cash flows depends upon SEH's operating risk and its financial leverage.

Since SEH is privately held, we cannot use any of the traditional approaches for estimating its cost of capital. A particular problem for the analyst in this situation is the cost of equity. To focus on the cost of equity, the subject of this note, let us presume that Rangeware has determined the amount of debt it will use to finance SEH. Since SEH already borrows, its reputation is known by lenders, and thus its cost of debt would be easy to determine.

All that remains is the cost of equity. The capital asset pricing model (CAPM)[3] can aid in this analysis. The CAPM is:

$$\tilde{R}_j = \tilde{R}_f + \tilde{\beta}_j\,(\tilde{R}_m - \tilde{R}_f),$$

where:

R_j = Security's rate of return
R_f = Risk-free rate of return
β_j = Risk measure
R_m = Market rate of return
$\sim$ = Expected.

To use the CAPM, Rangeware's analyst needs a beta that is appropriate for SEH.[4] Since SEH is not publicly traded, an estimate of its beta from the historic activity of its stock and the market is not readily available. In this situation, the typical analyst will turn to a group of publicly traded firms to deduce an estimate of the beta.

---

[2]In this note, we assume that the analyst will use the cost of capital as a discount rate.
[3]The theory behind the CAPM is beyond the scope of this note. For further information about it, see Diana R. Harrington, *Modern Portfolio Theory and the Capital Asset Pricing Model: A User's Guide* (Englewood Cliffs, N.J.: Prentice-Hall, 1983).
[4]The risk-free and market rates of return do not vary from company to company and thus will not be discussed in this note.

TABLE 1
∎
Value of SEH Industries (January 1981)

Cash Flow (millions of dollars)	Discount Rate (percent)	Value[a] (millions of dollars)
$17.1	15%	$114.0
17.1	16	106.8
17.1	17	100.6
17.1	18	95.0
17.1	19	90.0
17.1	20	85.5
17.1	21	81.4
17.1	22	77.7

[a]For the purpose of this example, the terminal value was determined assuming the annual cash flow was a constant in perpetuity. Thus, the terminal value for the 15-percent discount rate would be:

$$\frac{\text{Cash flow}}{\text{Discount rate}} = \frac{\$17.1}{0.15} = \$114.0.$$

TABLE 2
∎
Home Appliance Manufacturers, January 1981
(dollars in millions)

Company	Sales	Debt/ Total Capital[a]	Percentage of Total Capital	Equity/ Total Capital[a]	Percentage of Total Capital	Tax Rate	Market Beta
Hobart Corp.	$ 750	$ 65	21%	$250	79%	44.5%	0.75
Hoover Co.	900	14	5	280	95	47.0	0.90
Magic Chef	680	131	53	117	47	45.0	0.80
Maytag	390	0	0	184	100	45.5	0.80
National Presto	120	0.2	0	122	100	50.0	1.00
Sunbeam	1,650	165	27	450	73	47.5	1.10
Whirlpool	2,400	60	7	750	93	43.0	0.85
White Consolidated	2,350	353	43	467	57	45.5	0.95
Average			20%		80%	46.0%	0.89

Source: *Value Line.*

[a]For the purposes of this example, book values of the debt (including preferred stock) and equity are reported. If 1981 market values were used, the proportion of debt in the total capital of these firms might have been lower because of the effects of inflation.

Table 2 provides information about a group of publicly traded firms in SEH's industry that an analyst might use.

Even though these companies are in the same industry, their betas are quite different. Many ascribe part of that difference to the differences in leverage among the firms.

Hamada[5] was among the first to describe the effect of leverage on a firm's equity/beta. By assuming Modigliani and Miller's[6] theory of the cost of capital was accurate, he provided the following formula to describe the relationship between beta and leverage:

$$\beta_L = \beta_u \left(1 + \left[\frac{D}{S} (1 - t) \right] \right)$$

where:

β_L = Levered or equity beta
β_u = Unlevered or asset beta
D = Market value of debt
S = Market value of equity
t = Corporate tax rate.

Using Hamada's formula, an analyst could test the effect that changes in leverage would have on the beta of any firm. Hamada's approach is particularly useful in estimating the beta for a firm, division, or subsidiary that does not have publicly traded common stock. Since similar publicly traded firms often have quite different financial leverage, Hamada contended that neither the equity beta of any of a group of similar firms nor a simple average of the equity betas for the industry would provide a useful proxy for beta for a nonpublicly traded company or division.

Using the information from Table 2 and Hamada's formula, the unleveraged (or unlevered) beta for Magic Chef would be

$$0.80 = \beta_u \left(1 + \left[\frac{131}{117} (1 - 0.45) \right] \right),$$
$$\beta_u = 0.50.$$

And the relevered betas for Magic Chef at different levels of debt are shown in Table 3.

The unlevered betas for our sample of appliance manufacturers are reported in Table 4.

Mechanically straightforward, the technique's simplicity comes from the following underlying assumptions: in a group of similar firms, the only difference in systematic risk is from differences in leverage; changes in leverage are reflected in the beta and thus in the cost of equity. In other words, M&M's view of leverage's effect is true.

EVIDENCE

Research into these questions has produced mixed results. Hamada,[7] the first to test his own model, compared the standard deviations associated with estimates

---

[5]Robert S. Hamada, "The Effect of the Firm's Capital Structure on the Systematic Risk of Common Stocks," *Journal of Finance* (March 1969): 435–452.
[6]See footnote 1.
[7]Hamada, "The Effect of the Firm's Capital Structure on the Systematic Risk of Common Stocks."

TABLE 3

■

Magic Chef Relevered Asset Beta

Debt/Equity	Unlevered Beta	Equity Beta[a]
0%	0.50	0.50
20	0.50	0.55
40	0.50	0.61
60	0.50	0.67
80	0.50	1.72
100	0.50	0.78
120	0.50	0.83

N.Ap. = not applicable.
[a]Tax rate of 45 percent.

TABLE 4

■

Home Appliance Manufacturers'
Equity and Unlevered Betas, January 1981

	Equity Beta	Unlevered Beta
Hobart Corp.	0.75	0.66
Hoover Co.	0.90	0.88
Magic Chef	0.80	0.50
Maytag	0.80	0.80
National Presto	1.00	1.00
Sunbeam	1.10	0.92
Whirlpool	0.85	0.81
White Consolidated	0.95	0.67
Average	0.89	0.80

of observed levered betas to unlevered betas derived using his formula.[8] He concluded that, within the same risk class (defined as the same SIC code), unlevered betas were less diverse than levered betas, a finding that seemed to support M&M. He was unable, however, to verify the existence of a linear leverage effect on beta.

Jones and Joy[9] criticized Hamada for using SIC code groups to determine equivalent-risk classes. They believed that such firms might not have equivalent operating risks. Thus, to assume that differences in the total risk (operating plus financial risk) were solely attributable to financial risks would lead to a wrong

---

[8]Hamada assumed that Modigliani and Miller were correct and, therefore, firms within the same risk class should have the same unleveraged costs of equity and, hence, the same unleveraged betas.
[9]Maurice Joy and Charles P. Jones, "Leverage and the Valuation of Risky Assets," *Quarterly Review of Economics and Business* (Winter 1975): 81–92.

estimation of the leverage effect. Jones and Joy grouped firms according to their total risk (standard deviation of returns) and, on the basis of two separate tests, concluded that their results "supported the M&M leverage hypothesis: holding total risk constant, there was no systematic relationship between financial leverage and required rate of return on equity."[10] Their test was criticized later by Chance,[11] however, who concluded, "It is not clear that a satisfactory test can be designed, since appropriate risk classes must first be identified, and if that can be done, there remains the question of how significant must the relationship between leverage and equity return be before M&M is supported."[12] Chance also tested the Hamada formula, but was unable to "infer any conclusions about the validity of the theory."[13]

Fuller and Kerr,[14] using a technique similar to the proxy method used in deriving Table 2, tried to determine whether the sum of divisional betas derived by a proxy method was equal to the equity beta of their publicly traded parent. They tested three proxy betas: (1) an average of the proxy firms' equity betas, (2) the proxy firms' unlevered and relevered betas that resulted from using capital structure at book value, and (3) the unlevered and relevered proxy betas derived by using the market value of capital structure. They found that:

1. The parent's beta approximated the average of the divisional betas derived from the proxy betas. Hence, analogy served as a reasonable technique for estimating divisional betas.

2. The simple average of the proxy firms' betas provided a better estimate of the parent's beta than either of the betas adjusted for differences in leverage.

Fuller and Kerr hypothesized that financial synergies accounted for the unexplained difference between the parent's beta and the larger average beta derived from the proxy betas adjusted for leverage.

CONCLUSION

The question of how capital structure affects the cost of equity is far from resolved. Supporters of M&M argue that there is no optimal capital structure, and, except for the tax effect, a firm's value is independent of its capital structure. This hypothesis about the irrelevancy of capital structure, along with the existence of the CAPM, permits one to leverage and unleverage betas using Hamada's formula. Traditionalists still believe that the leverage effect is not linear and that the judicious use of debt can and does increase the value of the firm to its maximum. Since the traditional model does not provide for a simple relationship between the equity costs for a leveraged and an unleveraged firm, this model

---

[10]Ibid., 89.

[11]Don M. Chance, "Leverage and the Valuation of Risky Assets: A Comment," *Quarterly Review of Economics and Statistics* (Spring 1981): 125–127.

[12]Ibid., 127.

[13]Don M. Chance, "Evidence on a Simplified Model of Systematic Risk," *Financial Management* (Autumn 1982): 53–63.

[14]Russell J. Fuller and Halbert S. Kerr, "Estimating the Divisional Cost of Capital: An Analysis of the Pure Play Technique," *Journal of Finance* (December 1981): 997–1009.

does not yield a formula for adjusting betas for leverage. Whether one chooses to adjust betas for differences in leverage depends exclusively upon the analyst's view of the relationship between leverage and capital costs and value.

ADDITIONAL READINGS

Thomas E. Conine, Jr. "Debt Capacity and the Capital Budgeting Decision: A Comment." *Financial Management* (Spring 1980): 20–22.

James M. Gahlon and James A. Gentry. "On the Relationship between Systematic Risk and the Degrees of Operating and Financial Leverage." *Financial Management* (Summer 1982): 15–23.

Ned C. Hill and Bernell K. Stone. "Accounting Betas, Systematic Operating Risk, and Financial Leverage: A Risk-Composition Approach to the Determinants of Systematic Risk." *Journal of Financial and Quantitative Analysis* (September 1980): 595–637.

Joe Yagill. "On Valuation, Beta and the Cost of Equity Capital: A Note." *Journal of Financial and Quantitative Analysis* (September 1982): 441–49.

The Becker Corporation

In May 1987, Dave Zalinsky of Becker Corporation's project-appraisal group was trying to decide what course of action to recommend on a capital-expenditure proposal submitted by the company's Rubber Division. The proposal called for the construction of a barge dock and storage facility, estimated to cost $810,000, at the division's New Orleans plant.

The Rubber Division managers agreed with Mr. Zalinsky that the estimated annual savings did not meet the Becker Corporation's minimum return requirements, but they argued that the proposed project should not be judged by the normal criteria. In their presentation, the Rubber Division managers had raised two issues concerning the projected return on the dock investment—"committed" savings and Becker's absolute standard for judging projects.

The first issue was the company's requirement for "commitment of savings." Savings were said to be committed when those responsible for managing the proposed project and achieving the projected savings were willing to put themselves on the line by having their future performance measured against those savings. For the dock project, although the Rubber Division managers thought that additional savings were possible, even probable, they had committed to only the portion of the potential savings of which they were certain. The result was that the projected return on investment was below Becker's minimum.

The second issue concerned the nature of the dock project itself, in comparison with other projects. If the company did not build its own dock, the division would have to continue using the public terminal. The projected savings if the dock were built would be the commercial loading and unloading rates for the raw materials and finished goods expected to be handled. The actual volume of goods and the rates charged were unlikely to fluctuate much from the projections. Because the savings were almost certain, the division management dubbed the project a "banker's risk."

Unlike the dock project, many of Becker's capital-budgeting projects were for manufacturing facilities to produce new products or expand the production of existing ones. For such projects, the return on investment depended to a great extent on prices of the products. In the rubber business, product prices had fluctuated considerably and had been on a generally downward trend for many years. Thus, managers of the Rubber Division argued, returns for production

This case was prepared as a basis for class discussion rather than to illustrate either effective or ineffective handling of an administrative situation. Copyright © 1987 by the Darden Graduate Business School Sponsors, University of Virginia, Charlottesville, Virginia.

projects were much less certain that those for the dock project, and the dock project should meet different, lower standards that were commensurate with its risk.

COMPANY BACKGROUND

The Becker Corporation was a diversified company with headquarters in Houston, Texas. It was organized into operating divisions responsible for manufacturing and marketing chemicals and related products as assigned by headquarters. The company had grown, both internally and by acquisition, to sales of $376 million in 1987.

Becker's capital budgeting was controlled by a group at corporate headquarters, but administered by the operating divisions. Each division requested funds annually for specific projects. Financing acceptable projects had not been a serious problem for Becker, because although the total amount of funds available for capital expenditures was something of a limiting factor, the company had been able to supplement internally generated cash with public offerings of its securities. For instance, the company's favorable credit standing had recently helped to secure it long-term debt at 10 percent.

Each division's capital-spending forecasts were presented in two reports prepared annually:

1. Two-year forecasts of capital expenditures gave detailed lists of proposed projects, their returns on investment, and the capital required for each. Although the projects listed had not been formally reviewed by the corporate project-appraisal group, the total of the funds was taken as the division's estimated need for the next year.

2. Longer term forecasts of divisional activity described the types of activity that each division's management planned for the future. The report was general and listed specific projects only when major expenditures would be required.

Division management could use its own approach in evaluating capital investments unless the gross fixed investment exceeded $100,000. For those investments, the approval of the company's Administrative Committee was needed. Any project over $1 million required approval by the board of directors.

When Administrative Committee approval was required, the project-appraisal group reviewed the division's request on the basis of such criteria as its financial acceptability and its fit with the company's long-range plans. Because the group was also responsible for making recommendations on changing financial requirements, it had to consider the Rubber Division's request for different standards for projects of different risk.

For a project requiring review by the project-appraisal group and approval by the Administrative Committee, the division prepared a lengthy, formal report, the Capital Spending Request. The purposes of the request were:

1. to explain and justify the project as a good investment
2. to establish a basis for later performance review

The request had four sections:

1. a summary of the project highlights

2. data showing return on investment, payout, and the effect of the project on corporate income

3. a description of the assumptions underlying calculations of return on investment and payout

4. information about the project and any effect it might have on the division and the company

The report went to the project-appraisal group, which made a recommendation to the Administrative Committee. Although this recommendation did not represent approval or rejection, it was usually a major factor in the committee's decision.

The two financial standards used at Becker Corporation were as follows:

1. Return on investment. Annual profit, after straight-line depreciation based on the useful life of the facilities, operating expenses, and federal income taxes, had to exceed 7.5 percent of the gross investment.

2. Payback. The time required to return the cash investment to the company could not exceed 5 years.

In 1987 these standards were used for all divisions of the company and for all types of projects.

REVIEW OF THE DOCK PROJECT

The project-appraisal group's review of the New Orleans dock project began on April 27, 1987. After this first review, the group did not recommend acceptance to the Administrative Committee because the return did not meet the company's minimum guidelines. One of the members of the review group commented about the request,

> We felt that the project had some potential. The main problem was that the Rubber Division would not commit itself to an acceptable return and payout. What we suggested was that they redraft the request and include the other potential savings they mentioned. But, as written, the return was not acceptable in my mind.

After the initial comments about the project, the division revised its request. This time it described, but did not commit to, savings from other products being shipped through the new dock. The request said,

> We appreciate your comments on the initial draft, and several changes have been made based on them. We have, however, left the project as a "banker's risk."

During the period in which the members of the project-appraisal group discussed the project, conflicting opinions were expressed:

1. "I'm not sure Becker should be in this business. There are a lot of places where we could use our staff and money to better advantage. We're not a shipping firm."

2. "I know the dock seems like a good project. The savings committed still don't meet our standards, though. I know the division says the facility will pay for itself in time and yield a good return. But if they won't commit to the additional savings, I wonder just how sure they are of getting them. I don't go for this low-risk-business stuff. If the profit isn't there, we shouldn't go into it."

3. "I think that the low-risk aspect should be considered. After all, these savings are a sure thing. I think we should use a different standard to judge a low-risk project like this. There aren't any prices involved except the loading and unloading rates. They have been very steady. The savings really only depend on our projected volumes, and the division seems very sure of them."

At the request of the other members of the project-appraisal group, Mr. Zalinsky met with William Sams from the Rubber Division. Mr. Sams had been deeply involved in the dock project from the beginning. "The history of this project goes back a long way," he said. "Years ago, management began to realize the economic advantage of water transportation. We have known for some time that one of the major advantages of the New Orleans Plant was its location near water deep enough for barge traffic."

"I understand that the master plant site showed a dock, Bill. Why wasn't it built before now?" asked Mr. Zalinsky.

"We haven't needed it. We were buying our main raw materials from Billingsley's plant just down the river and using trucks for the short haul involved. Now that situation has changed. We are now shipping by barge to the New Orleans Plant from another plant of ours. We have been unloading at a terminal near there. We're also shipping one of our products produced in that plant by barge from the terminal."

"But Bill, what prompted the capital-spending request at this time? Was it the savings?"

"That was a major factor," said Mr. Sams. "We pay that terminal a lot of money every year."

"Now about the savings?"

"They are outlined here on this paper along with the other data." Mr. Sams referred Mr. Zalinsky to the information shown in Exhibit 1. "It's really a problem, though. These are only the committed savings—the ones we are sure of. A few years ago, the division asked me to justify a dock at another plant. I talked with all kinds of people in the plant. All of them felt it was a good idea—the purchasing agent, in particular. She said she could save money on raw materials and shipping costs when she bought in barge-load quantities. But when I asked how much she could save, she said that it was impossible to tell. The prices for materials varied considerably and she could not commit herself for any savings. I talked to the shipping personnel and got the same answer—no commitment. It was really difficult to firm up the savings that the dock would give us.

"To make a long story short, a request was submitted, and finally approved by the Administrative Committee. We paid for that dock in less than a year. We got savings from buying in bulk and from freight costs. This is why we are not sure just how much the dock will save. In this case, for example, there are a few other products that we might be able to ship into New Orleans, but we're just not sure."

"Just what do committed savings mean to you?" asked Mr. Zalinsky.

"Well, as you know, these projects are reviewed periodically to determine management performance. When a manager commits savings to a project, he or she is held responsible for them on that performance appraisal. I've always thought it was sort of a control procedure to ensure reasonable estimates."

"Now, Bill, how about explaining these figures for the new dock," asked Mr. Zalinsky.

"Well, the savings shown, $170,000, is our forecast of billings from the terminal if we do not install the dock. Raw materials account for $86,000 and finished goods for $84,000. The $65,000 is our cost of operating the facility. Maintenance was estimated on a fixed percentage of the investment."

"How much risk is there that these savings will not be realized?" Mr. Zalinsky asked.

"Assuming normal conditions in the economy, there is very little risk. If anything, the savings may be low. That plant has been doing very well and some of our costs, maintenance for example, may not be that high," replied Mr. Sams.

"You know that the project-appraisal group rejected the proposal as written the first time?"

"Yes. I guess you felt it was a good project, but you wanted more savings committed to the return and payout. Our revised request did give more potential savings, $200,000 worth, but these were not committed. We sent it on without including them," said Mr. Sams.

"Bill, what about joint use with another company?" asked Mr. Zalinsky. "I noticed it was mentioned as a possibility in the request."

"Yes, but we haven't done anything about that. One company that expressed interest was a customer. But we really cannot commit ourselves to another company until after the dock is installed."

"How long will a dock like this last?" asked Mr. Zalinsky.

"It's difficult to say, Dave. We used 20 years in the depreciation schedules and income-tax calculations, but we feel sure it will last much longer than that."

"Thanks, Bill, I appreciate your coming to talk about the dock project. Let me pull my thoughts together. I really need to take your dock request back to the capital-spending group along with my thoughts about our committed-savings requirement and our two absolute standards."

As Mr. Zalinsky prepared to take the project back to the project-appraisal group he collected the information found in Exhibits 1 through 8.

The Becker Corporation

EXHIBIT 1

■

New Orleans Dock Project (in thousands)

Initial Costs

Dredging	$230
Dock	270
Machinery	310
	$810
Initial start-up costs (to be expensed for tax purposes)	6
Total costs	$816

Annual Operating Expenses

Steam	$ 10
Electricity	2
Labor	10
Maintenance	43
Total annual expenses	$ 65

Annual Savings

Raw materials	$ 86
Finished goods	84
Total savings	$170

Supplementary Data

1. Straight-line depreciation over 20 years with no salvage value for income-reporting purposes.

2. Sum-of-the-years'-digits depreciation over 20 years for tax reporting.

3. Historic marginal rate of 48 percent.

4. Federal income taxes are paid on July 31.

The Becker Corporation

EXHIBIT 2
■
Sum-of-the-Years'-Digits Depreciation Schedule (in thousands)

Year	Annual Depreciation	Cumulative Depreciation	Year	Annual Depreciation	Cumulative Depreciation
1	$77,142.90	$ 77,142.90	11	$38,571.40	$636,429.00
2	73,285.70	150,429.00	12	34,714.30	671,143.00
3	69,428.60	219,857.00	13	30,857.10	702,000.00
4	65,571.40	285,429.00	14	27,000.00	729,000.00
5	61,714.30	347,143.00	15	33,142.90	752,143.00
6	57,857.10	405,000.00	16	19,285.70	771,429.00
7	54,000.00	459,000.00	17	15,428.60	786,857.00
8	50,142.90	509,143.00	18	11,571.40	798,429.00
9	46,285.70	555,429.00	19	7,714.29	806,143.00
10	42,428.60	597,857.00	20	3,857.14	810,000.00

The Becker Corporation

EXHIBIT 3
■
Yearly Profits and Cash Flows—
Committed Savings Only (in thousands)

Year	Terminal Billing Savings	Operating Expenses	Depreciation	Before-Tax Profits	After-Tax Profits	Net Cash Flow
1	$170	$65	$77	$ 28	$14.5	$91.5
2	170	65	73	32	16.6	89.6
3	170	65	69	36	18.7	87.7
4	170	65	65	40	21.8	86.8
5	170	65	62	43	22.3	84.3
6	170	65	58	47	24.5	82.5
7	170	65	54	51	26.5	80.5
8	170	65	50	55	28.6	78.6
9	170	65	46	59	30.7	76.7
10	170	65	42	63	32.8	74.8
11	170	65	38	67	34.8	72.8
12	170	65	35	70	36.4	71.4
13	170	65	31	74	38.5	69.5
14	170	65	27	78	40.6	67.6
15	170	65	23	82	42.6	65.6
16	170	65	19	86	44.6	63.6
17	170	65	15	90	46.7	61.7
18	170	65	12	93	48.4	60.4
19	170	65	8	97	50.4	58.4
20	170	65	4	101	52.5	56.5

The Becker Corporation

EXHIBIT 4

■

Financial Results from the
Project's Committed Savings (in thousands)

Standard 1: Annual Profit/Gross Investment

Average yearly savings		$ 170.0
Costs		
Operating expenses	$ 65.0	
Depreciation (straight-line)	40.5	
	$105.5	(105.5)
Profit before taxes		64.5
Taxes (48 percent)		31.0
Profit after taxes		$ 33.5

Gross investment = $810

Yearly profit/gross investment = $33.5/810 = .0414
  or 4.14 percent

*Standard 2: Payback (the point where cumulative yearly cash
flows are zero)*

Year	Annual Cash Flow	Cumultive Cash Flow
0	(772.0)	(772.0)
1	91.5	(680.5)
2	89.6	(590.9)
3	87.7	(503.2)
4	86.8	(416.4)
5	84.3	(332.2)
6	82.5	(249.6)
7	80.5	(169.1)
8	78.6	(90.5)
9	76.7	(13.8)
10	74.8	61.0

Payback = 9.2 years

The Becker Corporation

EXHIBIT 5

■

Sensitivity of Standards to Additional Savings (dollars in thousands)

| | Increment of Uncommitted Savings Realized | | | | | | | | | | |
	0%	10%	20%	30%	40%	50%	60%	70%	80%	90%	100%
Average yearly income	$33.5	$43.9	$54.3	$64.7	$75.1	$85.5	$95.9	$106.0	$116.7	$127.1	$137.5
Percentage of gross investment[a]	4.1%	5.4%	6.7%	8.0%	9.3%	10.5%	11.7%	13.1%	14.4%	15.7%	17.0%
Payout (years)[b]	9.2	8.1	7.2	6.6	6.0	5.5	5.1	4.8	4.5	4.2	4.0
Discounted cash flow return[c]	8.0%	9.9%	11.7%	13.4%	15.0%	16.6%	18.1%	19.7%	21.2%	22.6%	24.1%
Net present value @ 7.5 percent[d]	$62	$167	$272	$377	$482	$587	$692	$797	$902	$1,007	$1,112

[a] A 10-percent increment of uncommitted savings is $20,000 before taxes or $10,400 after taxes (assuming 48-percent tax rate). Each increment thus adds $10,400 to the average yearly income and 1.29 percent to the percentage return.

[b] The increment of $10,400 after taxes can be added to the net cash flow for each year for each increment. Payout is then found in the same way as for Exhibit 4.

[c] The same cash flows used to find payout are used to calculate a discounted cash flow return.

[d] The yearly 10-percent savings increment of $10,400 for 20 years has a net present value of $105,000 at a discount rate of 7.5 percent. Each 10-percent increment thus adds $105,000 to the net present value of the project.

The Becker Corporation

EXHIBIT 6
■
Financial Data 1975–1978 (millions, except per share data)

	1974	1975	1976	1977	1978
Assets					
Cash	$ 10	$ 21	$ 26	$ 17	$ 18
Receivables	31	36	41	49	55
Inventories	32	35	39	44	53
Net property, plant, and equipment[a]	140	158	160	180	213
Other	21	22	24	25	27
Total assets	$234	$272	$290	$315	$366
Liabilities and Equity					
Payables and accruals	$ 22	$ 26	$ 25	$ 32	$ 40
Income taxes payable	10	8	14	15	12
Long-term debt[b]	57	76	74	73	98
Deferred income taxes	6	7	9	10	11
Other liabilities	5	8	7	6	8
Total liabilities	100	125	129	136	169
Common stock	78	81	85	87	89
Retained earnings	56	66	76	92	108
Total liabilities and equity	$234	$272	$290	$315	$366
Sales		$293	$320	$354	$376
Cost of goods sold		181	199	218	238
Selling, general, and administrative		83	88	92	97
Federal income tax		13	16	20	16
Total expenses		277	303	330	351
Net income		16	17	24	25
Dividends		6	7	8	9
Change in retained earnings		$10	$10	$16	$16
Earnings per share		$1.59	$1.55	$2.15	$2.06
Dividends per share		0.60	0.65	0.70	0.75
Stock market price high/low		23/25	25/30	26/30	28/32

[a]Depreciation is $24 million for 1978, $21 million for 1977, $20 million for 1976, and $18 million for 1975.
[b]Cost is between 9 and 10 percent.

The Becker Corporation

EXHIBIT 7
■
Capitalization (dollars in millions)

| | Balance-Sheet Date | | | | |
	12/31/74	12/31/75	12/31/76	12/31/77	12/31/78
Total long-term debt	$ 57	$ 76	$ 74	$ 73	$ 98
Total equity	134	147	161	179	197
Total capitalization	$191	$223	$235	$252	$295
Debt proportion	29.8%	34.1%	31.5%	29.0%	33.2%
Equity proportion	70.2	65.9	68.5	71.0	66.8

One cycle[a]

$$\text{Average percent debt} = \frac{34.1 + 31.5 + 29.0 \text{ percent}}{3} = 31.5 \text{ percent}$$

Average percent equity = 100 percent − 31.5 percent
= 68.5 percent

[a]Because major debt issues occurred in 1976 and 1978, the debt proportion was determined as an average of 3 years' data.

The Becker Corporation

EXHIBIT 8
■
Cost of Equity—Dividend-Growth Model

	1975	1976	1977	1978
Dividend Yield				
Average market price/share	$24.00	$27.50	$28.00	$30.00
Dividend per share	0.60	0.65	0.70	0.75
Dividend yield (percent)	2.50%	2.36%	2.50%	2.54%

$$\text{Average yield} = \frac{2.50 + 2.36 + 2.50 + 2.54}{4}$$
= 2.48 percent

Growth
Market-price appreciation for ten years at 6.3 percent (1978 price of $16.25, 1987 price of $30.00)

After-Tax Cost of Capital

	After-Tax Cost	Proportion	Weighted Value
Debt	4.68%	31.5%	1.47
Equity	8.83	68.5	6.05
Weighted-average cost of capital			7.52%

3C

VALUATION:

COST OF CAPITAL

Star Appliance Company (A)

Arthur Foster, the financial vice president of Star Appliance Company, thought that the opportunity had finally presented itself. Since joining the company in early 1978, he had been concerned about the hurdle rate used in the capital allocation process. He had not wanted to create a controversy immediately after accepting his position, but now in early October 1979, with the company considering a move into new products, he thought that the time had come for discussing the company's cost of capital.

HISTORY OF STAR APPLIANCE COMPANY

Star Appliance had been founded in 1922 by Ken McDonald to manufacture electric stoves and ovens. During the prosperous 1920s, the demand for electric stoves and ovens as replacements for wood- and-coal-burning stoves increased, and Star became a respected brand name and the market leader. Capitalizing on this success and the burgeoning equity market during the 1920s, Mr. McDonald financed the rapid growth of the company through the sale of common stock. This move proved to be farsighted. The company was able to enter the Depression with a debt-free balance sheet. Many firms, plagued with dwindling sales and poor or nonexistent profits, had defaulted on their debts: they were forced into bankruptcy and eventually out of business. Star suffered severely during the Depression, but was able to survive by significantly reducing its operations and concentrating its sales efforts on the least affected part of the market, the premium end. As a result, Star remained alive and viable, emerging at the end of World War II with a smaller base of operations, a strong balance sheet, and a well-established reputation in the marketplace.

In the ensuing three decades, the company grew and prospered. Star continued to concentrate on the premium market and over the years expanded its product line. Continuing its focus on kitchen appliances, Star first added gas ranges to its products, followed by a line of refrigerators. Microwave ovens were the company's newest product. The company's marketing program emphasized the sale of new appliances as replacements for older models, rather than target-

This case was prepared as a basis for class discussion rather than to illustrate either effective or ineffective handling of an administrative situation. Copyright © 1979 by the Darden Graduate Business School Sponsors, University of Virginia, Charlottesville, Virginia.

ing the market for installations in newly constructed dwellings. This strategy provided some protection from the vicissitudes of the highly cyclical housing industry.

As for financing, Mr. McDonald believed he had learned a valuable lesson from the Depression and had continued to keep debt financing to a minimum. Although he retired from active management in 1963, his philosophy concerning the capital structure had become well-ingrained. Through its period of growth, the company had relied solely on equity to finance itself. In fact, Star's premium image had allowed it to price its products to command a higher margin than could its competition; as a result, all of Star's equity financing had come from its profits—additions to retained earnings.

Furthermore, Star maintained a liquidity reserve of cash and marketable securities. During seasonal and cyclical slumps, the company had been able to draw on this reserve, eliminating the need to borrow. In part because of this solvency, Star had been able to maintain a stable work force, which management believed contributed to its superior labor productivity. On the few occasions when the growth of the company had been limited by the lack of internal funds, Star had temporarily reduced its liquid reserve to provide the necessary financing. Only three times since the end of World War II had this reserve not been large enough, and Star had sold new equity. These marketing and financial strategies had created a strong company whose stock in 1978 was widely held by the investing public. The most recent financial statements for Star are shown in Exhibits 1 and 2.

Despite Star's previous growth, management believed that growth in the current product lines had slowed. Exhibit 3 provides 5-year forecasts for Star's earnings, assuming no significant changes in the current product lines. However, Star's president, Chris Weeks, who had originally joined the company in 1955 as a sales representative, believed real growth would come only with the addition of new products. Mr. Weeks believed that if Star were to capitalize on its market reputation and brand-name recognition, any new products should be kitchen-oriented.

EVALUATING PRODUCT EXPANSION

The desire to expand the product line was also a response to a general industry slump. Despite Star's continued growth in sales and profits during a period when its competitors' sales and margins declined, Star's stock price had fallen. Management believed the company's stock price had been adversely affected by the industry's problems. It was thought that the introduction of new products might provide an impetus to the stock market, thus increasing the company's price/earnings ratio back to its normal levels.

Three new product lines had been proposed—a dishwasher, a food disposer to be installed in kitchen sinks, and a trash compactor. The marketing department believed that each of these products had good sales potential and would fit with the company image of high-quality, premium-priced kitchen products.

Each of the three projects had been analyzed following the requirements of Star's capital allocation process. Like most projects at Star, these had originated in either the marketing or manufacturing departments. For each, the costs, benefits, expected lives, and terminal values had been determined. The results of the analysis for each project are shown in Exhibit 4. Using Star's marginal tax rate, the after-tax cash flows were used to calculate the internal rate of return (IRR) for each project. Following Star's usual procedures, the IRR would then be compared to the company's 10-percent hurdle rate. Star's management would accept projects whose IRR exceeded the hurdle rate as long as funds were available. In years when capital was short, projects with the highest IRRs were implemented, and lower return projects were postponed until funds became available.

Several parts of this process troubled Mr. Foster. First, he was concerned about the appropriateness of the 10-percent hurdle rate. When he joined the company, he had asked about the source of the rate, but no one seemed to be able to give a precise reason for it. The best he could determine was that the return on equity seemed to have been about 10 percent during the period when the capital budgeting system was being established, and since that time the 10-percent rate had been used.

Mr. Foster was convinced that the hurdle rate was too low. The interest rate on various U.S. Treasury securities is shown in Exhibit 5. Treasury bills had recently exceeded 11 percent, and one study[1] showed that common stock historically had a return of about 8.5 percent above the average return on Treasury bills and 6 percent above longer-term Treasury securities. He was certain that Star's projects were more risky than Treasury bills, and thus the projects should have a higher expected return if they were to be accepted. How high he was not sure.

At the manufacturing company where Mr. Foster had worked before joining Star, a dividend growth model had been used in calculating the cost of equity. This model ($D_1/P_0 + g = K_e$) described the return expected by the shareholders (K_e) from investing in the company's common stock as a combination of the next dividend (D_1), current market price (P_0) [the dividend yield (D_1/P_0)], and the forecasted growth in dividends (g). Star's current stock price was $22.50, and the company's management and board of directors intended to continue its policy of maintaining or slightly increasing dividends. Information about Star's historic dividends, along with other information about Star's stock and the stock market, can be found in Exhibit 6.

Since Star had only short-term debt, Mr. Foster did not believe he should consider the cost of debt in calculating the cost of capital. However, there was one thing that perplexed him. If an all-equity financed firm was less risky in economic downturns, why would its cost of capital be higher? It was obvious that debt cost less than equity, especially after taking taxes into account.

In reviewing the hurdle rate and cost of capital, several other questions occurred to Mr. Foster. First, was inflation adequately accounted for in Star's present system or in a system that used a current cost of capital for the hurdle rate? Mr. Foster believed that the rates on U.S. Treasury securities (Exhibits 5 and 6) included a return to offset expected inflation, but was that enough?

Second, Mr. Foster wondered whether Star management should accept projects that just met the hurdle rate, or only those that exceeded it by a margin of safety. Some of the forecasts had, in the past, exceeded the results. Perhaps the hurdle rate should be raised to compensate for poor forecasts. Furthermore,

---

[1]Roger G. Ibbotson and Rex A. Sinquefield, *Stocks, Bonds, Bills and Inflation: Historical Returns (1926–1978)* (Charlottesville, Va.: The Financial Analysts Research Foundation, 1979).

Star, like other U.S. companies, had increased its investment in safety and environmental projects to satisfy the U.S. government's increased requirements. Like most companies, Star categorized these as nonproductive investments, investments with no return. The hurdle rate, Mr. Foster believed, should certainly be increased to cover those investments, for failing to do so would guarantee that Star would earn less than its hurdle rate, and shareholders would be hurt.

Finally, the staff making the forecasts for the three projects believed that two of the projects were riskier than the other one, because they required new plant and equipment that would add appreciably to fixed costs. In downturns, or if the projects proved unsuccessful, they could cost Star more. Some of the staff thought that the hurdle rate should be increased to compensate for risk. Others argued that the more risky projects should be evaluated on the basis of their strategic importance and that the hurdle rate was irrelevant—the company should accept the sound strategy. One young analyst contended that if different rates were used for different projects, the company would be mixing the financing and investment decisions—something that should not be done.

CONCLUSION

As Mr. Foster began to investigate Star's cost of capital in developing a new hurdle rate, one contingency troubled him. Although Star had recently built up its liquid reserves in the expectation of launching some new products, whether all three of the products could be financed internally was questionable. He expected that depreciation would need to be reinvested to maintain Star's current production facilities. According to the marketing department's sales projections, he would have about $12 million from operations in 1979. He thought that he could safely reduce the cash and marketable securities by $15 to $20 million. If all three projects were approved, he would need about $30 million in external financing. Even if management decided to approve only the new dishwasher project, Star would require $3 million in new funds. Because of the strong financial position of the company, Mr. Foster was certain that he would be able to sell a reasonable amount of new equity to net, after issue costs, about 95 percent of the current market price. He was not certain how or whether the issue costs should be included in his evaluation of the cost of capital.

EXHIBIT 1
■

Statements of Consolidated Income
(thousands of dollars, except per share data)

	Year Ended December 31, 1977	Year Ended December 31, 1978
Income		
Net sales	$248,505	$269,787
Interest	2,065	3,126
Miscellaneous	242	265
Total income	250,812	273,178
Costs and Expenses		
Cost of products sold	160,021	173,338
Selling, administrative, and general expenses	36,533	41,079
Total costs and expenses	196,554	214,417
Income before income taxes	54,258	58,761
Federal and state income taxes	25,655	28,303
Net income	$ 28,603	$ 30,458
Net income per share of common stock	$ 2.13	$ 2.27
Dividends per share of common stock	$ 1.45	$ 1.52

Star Appliance Company (A)

EXHIBIT 2
■

Statements of Consolidated Financial Condition (thousands of dollars)

	December 31, 1977	December 31, 1978
Assets		
Cash	$ 2,122	$ 2,430
Marketable securities, including certificates of deposit—at cost (approximately market)	27,209	37,759
Trade accounts receivable, less allowance ($100,000)	15,577	17,333
Inventories		
Finished appliances	11,323	11,302
Work in process	13,527	13,100
Materials and supplies	8,309	6,930
Total inventories	33,159	31,332
Deferred federal taxes on income	1,536	1,747
Total current assets	79,603	90,601
Other assets	495	818
Property, plant, and equipment		
Land	713	713
Buildings and improvements	36,024	36,185
Machinery and equipment	76,879	79,411
Construction in progress	1,372	5,430
Less allowances for depreciation	(58,699)	(62,610)
Net property, plant, and equipment	56,289	59,129
Total assets	$136,387	$150,548
Liabilities and Shareowners' Equity		
Trade accounts payable	$ 2,860	$ 3,287
Compensation to employees	4,040	4,473
Miscellaneous accounts payable	2,122	1,778
Accrued local taxes	1,515	1,699
Accrued liabilities	2,742	2,961
Federal and state taxes on income	5,634	7,117
Total current liabilities	18,913	21,315
Deferred federal taxes on income	4,349	5,666
Shareowners' equity		
Common stock (13,414,268 shares issued, including shares in treasury)	27,835	27,835
Retained earnings	86,343	96,298
Less cost of shares of common stock in treasury	(1,053)	(566)
Total equity	113,125	123,567
Total liabilities and shareowners' equity	$136,387	$150,548

Star Appliance Company (A)

EXHIBIT 3
■
Forecast of Earnings, Sales, and Dividends from Continuing Operations

	Sales (thousands of dollars)	Profit after Tax (thousands of dollars)	Dividends per Share
1979	$297,734	$34,375	$1.64
1980	307,000	35,500	1.70
1981	317,000	36,500	1.75
1982	326,000	37,300	1.80
1983	334,000	38,000	1.85

Star Appliance Company (A)

EXHIBIT 4
■
Projected Cash Flows (thousands of dollars)

Costs	Dishwasher	Food Waste Disposal	Trash Compactor
Addition to plant	$ 7,000	$ 0	$ 3,000
Production equipment	21,500	13,600	10,000
Installation of equipment	1,500	400	1,000
Initial promotion expenditures	5,000	1,000	8,000
Total costs	$35,000	$15,000	$22,000
Expected project life[a]	15 years	15 years	15 years
Expected net cash flow after tax			
Year 1	$ 1,000	$ 100	$ 400
Year 2	4,000	500	1,300
Year 3	8,000	1,000	3,000
Year 4	11,000	1,650	4,500
Year 5 and subsequent years	11,000	3,000	5,500
Terminal value[a]	0	0	0
Internal rate of return	20.8%	10.6%	15.2%

[a]Actually, the marketing department projected sales beyond 15 years; however, the engineering staff predicted that, at best, the equipment would last 15 years before it would need to be completely replaced. Thus, to be conservative, the projections had included no terminal value.

Star Appliance Company (A)

EXHIBIT 5

■

U.S. Treasury Security Yields,
October 25, 1979

Term	Yield
3 months	13.04%
6 months	13.54
1 year	13.35
2 years	12.53
3 years	11.97
5 years	11.31
7 years	11.15
10 years	10.97
20 years	10.43
30 years	10.28

EXHIBIT 6

∎

Historical Company and Stock Market Data

	Stock Market Price Index[a] 1943=10	Stock Market Return[b] (percent)	Annualized Treasury Bill Yield[a] (percent)	Annualized AA Corporate Industrial Bond Yield[a] (percent)	Annual Consumer Price Inflation Rate[b] (percent)	Star Appliance Company			
						EPS	P/E Ratio	Dividends per Share	Dividend Yield (percent)
1964	83.96	16.48%	3.856%	4.31%	1.19%	$1.01	16.1	$0.79	4.9%
1965	91.73	12.45	4.362	4.72	1.92	0.95	17.3	0.79	4.8
1966	81.33	(10.06)	5.007	5.38	3.35	1.00	13.3	0.81	6.1
1967	95.30	23.98	5.012	6.23	3.04	1.06	14.0	0.83	5.6
1968	106.50	11.06	5.916	6.56	4.72	1.30	14.8	0.94	4.9
1969	91.11	(8.50)	7.720	7.62	6.11	1.34	16.6	1.04	4.7
1970	90.05	4.01	4.860	7.36	5.49	1.41	16.0	1.08	4.8
1971	99.17	14.31	4.023	7.14	3.36	0.75	41.1	1.08	3.5
1972	117.50	18.98	5.061	7.08	3.41	1.73	19.3	1.12	3.4
1973	94.78	(14.66)	7.364	7.64	8.80	1.83	14.0	1.25	4.9
1974	67.07	(26.47)	7.179	8.63	12.20	1.35	14.0	1.16	6.1
1975	88.70	37.20	5.504	8.68	7.01	1.61	14.5	1.16	5.0
1976	98.20	(23.84)	4.354	8.24	4.81	2.05	13.9	1.37	4.8
1977	95.10	(7.18)	6.152	8.92	6.77	2.13	11.9	1.45	5.7
1978	96.11	6.56	9.336	9.28	9.03	2.27	9.5	1.52	7.0

[a]As of last business day in the year.
[b]Annual return of the S&P Composite Index based on capital appreciation and dividend income. Source: Roger G. Ibbotson and Rex A. Sinquefield, *Stocks, Bonds, Bills, and Inflation: Historical Returns (1926–1978)* (Charlottesville, Va.: The Financial Analysts Research Foundation, 1979).

Star Appliance Company (B):

January 1985

In 1982 Star Appliance expanded its business by purchasing a company that made machines to clean fruits, grains, and vegetables for market.[1] The firm, Rhinescour Company, was located near Star's headquarters in Nebraska and had been managed into mediocrity. The quality of its management, along with the state of the U.S. farming economy, made the price very low. Star management considered its purchase a good investment and, because Rhinescour's continuation ensured jobs in the area, a local community service. To make the purchase, Star contracted long-term debt—for the first time in the company's history—$17.8 million.

In January 1985, Arthur Foster, Star's treasurer, realized that he had not reevaluated Star's cost of capital since taking on the debt. He wondered what changes the debt had caused. Mr. Foster found that the company was considered more risky since he had begun to deal with lenders, a new experience for him.

The more he worked to develop a new corporate hurdle rate, the more concerned Mr. Foster became about Star Appliance's cost of capital. When he had been in business school 25 years earlier, there had been only two methods for estimating the cost of equity: the price/earnings ratio (the implicit cost of capital) and the dividend discount model. Many of Star's recently hired MBAs said the best method to use was a capital market equilibrium approach called the capital asset pricing model (CAPM). Mr. Foster was determined to explore all the alternatives before settling on one method to use in future hurdle-rate revisions.

Two issues were being discussed among the staff and needed to be resolved. Some of the younger staff members, along with Mr. Foster, questioned whether the company's present hurdle rate accurately reflected capital costs, given the debt picture. Some also wondered whether one hurdle rate should apply to all projects. Several suggested that different hurdle rates should be used with different kinds of investments. The point had come up in connection with a discussion of whether to develop a market for new crop dryers or increase plant space for the production of refrigerators.

---

[1]Background about Star Appliance Company is found in Star Appliance Company (A).

This case was prepared as a basis for class discussion rather than to illustrate either effective or ineffective handling of an administrative situation. Copyright © 1985 by the Darden Graduate Business School Sponsors, University of Virginia, Charlottesville, Virginia.

COST OF EQUITY

Debbie Schofield, assistant to the corporate treasurer, was one of the more vocal advocates of multiple hurdle rates and using the CAPM for determining the cost of equity for various projects. "The projected return of the project," she said, "should be set off against its risk to determine value, and the CAPM does that and does it well. We've had lots of experience calculating betas, and the risk-free and market rates of return. That makes the CAPM easy—anyone can use it."

As its measure of risk, the CAPM used beta (β), the relative volatility of a security's return in relation to all other assets. A security's beta represented expected risk, but was often determined by fitting a least squares regression, also called the market model, to a series of returns for the total market and for an individual stock over the most recent 5 years. If a security's returns moved less than those of the market as a whole, its risk would be lower than average and its beta would be less than 1.0; if its movement was greater, its beta would be greater than 1.0. Using a beta, the return expected for the market, and that expected for a risk-free asset, one could estimate a security's expected return from the CAPM equation:

$$(R_j) = R_f + \beta_j(R_m - R_f)$$

where:

R_j = the expected total rate of return for a security (j)

R_f = the risk-free rate of return, for which analysts often used a U.S. Treasury security rate

β_j = the variability of total returns for a security (j) relative to those of the market, called the security's beta

R_m = the expected total rate of return for the market. Analysts often used a broad market index, such as Standard & Poor's 500 Index, as a proxy

Exhibit 1 provides the betas, profitability ratios, and other pertinent data for firms in the home-appliance and agricultural-machinery industries. Exhibit 2 provides information on Star's stock performance and that of the S&P 500 Index.

To use this model, Mr. Foster would need estimates of expected market returns. He sought help from Star's bankers. Sam Ralfson, his primary contact at Kennelworth Bank and Trust, sent the letter shown in Appendix A in response to Mr. Foster's inquiry. This letter provided some direction in determining what rate to use for the market's expected return (R_m). As for the risk-free rate (R_f), the consensus among Mr. Foster's staff seemed to be that they would use the yield on a Treasury security (see Exhibit 3), but there was little agreement on which security offered the best proxy. Mr. Foster believed that the decision boiled down to choosing the security with the least risk (very short-term) but one that incorporated the inflation expected over the investors' horizon.

Mr. Foster wanted to compare the CAPM estimate with those made from the implicit and dividend discount models. He also wanted to understand how increased debt affected the cost of equity using each of the models.

Once he had determined Star's cost of capital, Mr. Foster knew he would need to deal with the issue of multiple hurdle rates which Ms. Schofield had originated. Her initial arguments for multiple rates seemed overwhelming. She said, "It is obvious that different degrees of risk should be accounted for in the expected returns of the projects, just as riskier stocks and bonds typically yield higher returns." She questioned whether it was rational for Star to expect the same 10-percent rate of return from both a relatively risk-free project and a riskier one. By applying the same hurdle rate to both types of projects, the riskier one, which typically would have the higher expected rate of return, would appear disproportionately attractive.

The arguments against the use of multiple hurdle rates, presented by Jude Weathers, another member of the finance staff, were also compelling, however. Mr. Weathers said, "To me it is obvious that, given the fundibility of capital, the company should seek to invest where the expected returns are best. Less profitable projects should receive less funding. That was the reason behind establishing a single hurdle rate in the first place. The corporation is financed as a whole, not by product lines, divisions, or projects."

Ms. Schofield had disagreed, stating her belief that a properly applied multiple-hurdle-rate system would help ensure that Star remained conservative by "scientifically allocating funds to projects with various degrees of risk." As a result of this conservatism, if the company were to decide at some point to contract more long-term debt, lenders would be willing to supply funds at better rates. Similarly, she said, stockholders would be more willing to pay more for shares. The P/E ratio might fall farther than at present, she warned, if riskier projects were accepted with too little consideration for their relative rates of return.

Mr. Foster was concerned about how risk and discount rates were related. He believed his staff had already accounted for risk, in an intuitive sense, by adjusting the cash flows on the returns of riskier projects, but he appreciated Ms. Schofield's approach, which he believed made the analysis systematic.

Ms. Schofield suggested that the same conclusion could be reached from a different angle. The company was historically conservative, in that it had until recently been entirely equity financed. Even now, the ratio of debt to total capital of 9.5 percent was below the industry average. "Maybe Star was too conservative in using costly equity on relatively risk-free, low-return projects," she said. A multiple-hurdle-rate system that used modern portfolio theory techniques like the CAPM to determine the cost of capital for various divisions or projects might allocate those costlier funds more scientifically. "Perhaps," she suggested, "we could use a method like the one used by Kennelworth Bank. They combine the CAPM, or at least the beta, and the dividend discount model to determine whether a stock is fairly valued. Maybe we could do something similar in ranking our projects."

In discussing Ms. Schofield's proposal, the staff had raised several questions. If Star were to use different discount rates for each division or project, how would the costs of capital be estimated? How would the cost of equity be estimated for divisions of companies and projects that are not publicly traded? If beta were used to determine the equity cost or in a method similar to Kennelworth Bank's, how could a beta be determined for a division or project? What was to be done about weighting debt and equity? The debt question was especially important at Star, because all financing was done at the corporate level; divisions had no long-term debt.

Mr. Weathers strongly disagreed with Ms. Schofield's total approach. He said, "Risk should be accounted for by presenting best- and worst-case scenarios for all projects and, as we already do, by making conservative cash-flow forecasts. The use of divisional or project hurdle rates would be redundant at best, and at worst, could prematurely discourage consideration of riskier projects." While several staff members supported his approach, one said, "In my opinion, we should forecast a number of different scenarios and discount each at an appropriate hurdle rate. Use a different rate for each scenario."

THE DECISION

As Mr. Foster thought about the diverse opinions expressed by his staff, he knew he had to deal with three issues. First, what effect did debt have on Star's cost of capital and how should that effect be determined? Second, should the CAPM be used to evaluate Star's cost of equity? Third, should Star use multiple hurdle rates for future capital-budgeting decisions, and if so, how should the rates be determined and used?

Mr. Foster analyzed Star's position and the arguments for and against the CAPM and multiple hurdle rates in light of two strategic moves Star management was contemplating: increasing plant capacity to produce more refrigerators in an attempt to increase market share, and expanding the operations of Star's 1982 acquisition into a new product, grain dryers. A net present value of zero was expected at 14.5 percent for the refrigerator project, and Rhinescour Division's vice president said he expected a zero net present value at 17.2 percent on the dryer project. To Mr. Foster, however, the returns on this latter project would clearly be highly influenced by the state of the economy and farm prices. Intuitively, he felt that the first option was less risky than the second, but the potential rewards of the second were enticing.

Mr. Foster weighed the advantages and disadvantages of the CAPM and then, using the company's financial data provided in Exhibits 4 and 5, studied the effects of the company's long-term debt on its cost of capital. (The current long-term debt consisted of a promissory note with a variable interest rate, on which the company was currently paying 12.20 percent. Rates on various forms of public debt are shown in Exhibit 6.) Mr. Foster wanted to determine Star's cost of capital at its current ratio of debt to capital, and if the company were to borrow up to the industry average of 19 percent.

Mr. Foster then attempted to apply his findings to the issue of multiple hurdle rates. As he did so, several questions arose:

1.   Once a base rate was calculated for the least risky projects, could higher rates be scientifically determined for consistent use on other projects, or should rates be varied for strategic reasons?

2.   Considering the controls already in place, would the use of multiple rates overcompensate for risk? Should multiple rates replace those controls?

3.   Would multiple hurdle rates lend a greater sense of conservatism to the company?

4.   Would the use of multiple hurdle rates mix the investment decision with the financing decision?

EXHIBIT 1

∎

Selected Data for the Home-Appliance and Agricultural-Machinery Industries

	Debt/Equity	Debt/Capital	ROE	ROA	ROS	Beta[a]	Average Market Price	Average P/E	Payout Ratio	Dividend Yield
Home Appliances										
Magic Chef	35%	26%	22.2%	10.6%	5.2%	1.35	$44	6.2%	16%	2.6%
Maytag	11	10	27.6	20.7	9.8	0.90	29	10.0	60	6.1
National Presto	4	4	10.1	8.7	17.6	0.90	28	11.9	45	3.8
Ranco	39	28	14.6	7.3	4.5	0.80	19	9.4	44	4.7
Robertshaw	19	16	17.5	11.0	5.8	0.95	35	7.5	26	3.4
Toro	49	33	11.1	5.1	3.0	0.65	16	8.1	18	2.2
Whirlpool	5	5	17.2	12.4	6.0	1.00	46	9.7	42	4.3
White Consolidated	40	29	9.5	5.1	2.5	1.05	30	13.5	68	5.0
Unweighted averages	25%	19%	16.2%	10.1%	6.8%	0.95	$31	9.5%	40%	4.0%
Agricultural Machinery										
Deere & Co.	43%	30%	3.1%	1.3%	1.6%	1.05	$29	6.4%	220%	3.4%
Hesston Corp.	73	42	(10.5)	(3.5)	(2.4)	0.90	8	NMF	NMF	NMF
Massey-Ferguson	205	67	2.3	0.5	0.5	0.75	4	NMF	NMF	NMF
Steiger Tractor	20	16	4.2	2.4	1.6	0.80	9	NMF	NMF	NMF
Selected unweighted averages	85%	39%	(2.3)%	(1.8)%	0.3%	0.88	$13	NMF	NMF	NMF

NMF = no meaningful figure.

[a]Calculated using 2.5 years of weekly total returns, adjusted for known problems.

Source: Value Line *Investment Survey*.

Star Appliance Company (B)

EXHIBIT 2
■
Historical Company and Stock Market Data

		Stock Market Price Index[a] 1943 = 10	Star			
Year/Month			Market Price Changes[b]	EPS	Average P/E Ratio	Average Dividend Yield
1979	1	99.93	2.1%			
	2	96.28	1.4			
	3	101.59	1.1			
	4	101.76	8.4			
	5	99.08	(8.2)			
	6	102.91	9.2			
	7	103.81	(1.0)			
	8	109.32	2.8			
	9	109.32	6.5			
	10	101.82	(7.3)			
	11	106.16	(5.0)			
	12	107.94	(9.2)	$2.58	9.2	6.7%
1980	1	114.16	2.9			
	2	113.66	(4.6)			
	3	102.09	(4.8)			
	4	106.29	2.6			
	5	111.24	7.8			
	6	114.24	8.3			
	7	121.67	0.6			
	8	122.38	(5.7)			
	9	125.46	2.3			
	10	127.47	2.3			
	11	140.52	(5.8)			
	12	135.76	(1.7)	2.02	11.0	7.2
1981	1	129.55	(0.2)			
	2	131.27	4.5			
	3	136.00	13.5			
	4	132.81	(1.1)			
	5	132.59	(3.3)			
	6	131.21	4.0			
	7	130.92	(2.9)			
	8	122.79	(1.9)			
	9	116.18	(6.3)			
	10	121.89	1.4			
	11	126.35	14.4			
	12	122.55	(10.2)	2.18	11.2	7.1

Year/Month		Stock Market Price Index[a] 1943 = 10	Star			
			Market Price Changes[b]	EPS	Average P/E Ratio	Average Dividend Yield
1982	1	120.40	(4.7)			
	2	113.11	(2.2)			
	3	111.96	7.3			
	4	116.44	4.3			
	5	111.88	5.4			
	6	109.61	9.7			
	7	107.09	3.6			
	8	119.51	19.1			
	9	120 .42	(2.0)			
	10	133.71	10.3			
	11	138.54	3.7			
	12	140.64	1.6	2.06	14.9	5.4
1983	1	145.30	8.3			
	2	148.06	16.0			
	3	152.96	1.3			
	4	164.42	18.1			
	5	162.39	(3.1)			
	6	168.11	(7.0)			
	7	162.56	9.7			
	8	164.40	(17.5)			
	9	166.07	3.0			
	10	163.55	(44.8)			
	11	166.40	5.8			
	12	164.93	(3.3)	3.38	14.1	4.4
1984	1	163.41	81.6			
	2	157.06	(6.7)			
	3	159.18	1.4			
	4	160.05	(4.3)			
	5	150.55	(11.6)			
	6	153.18	3.0			
	7	150.66	2.0			
	8	166.68	11.3			
	9	166.10	9.6			
	10	167.42	(1.6)			
	11	163.58	1.6			
	12	167.24	(4.0)	3.51	14.0	4.6

[a]Standard & Poor's 500 Index as of last trading day of each month.
[b]Stock price at end of 1984 was $63.29.

Star Appliance Company (B)

EXHIBIT 3
■
U.S. Treasury Security Yields (end of quarter)

Year/ Quarter		3-Month Bill	6-Month Bill	5-Year Note	7-Year Note	10-Year Bond
1982	1	13.04%	14.12%	14.11%	14.07%	13.99%
	2	11.97	12.52	13.78	13.81	13.69
	3	8.66	10.20	12.72	12.86	12.77
	4	8.51	9.00	10.47	10.77	10.69
Monthly average		11.09	12.00	13.11	13.22	13.18
1983	1	8.15	8.38	9.92	10.14	10.24
	2	8.91	9.23	10.49	10.77	10.79
	3	9.56	10.10	11.71	11.88	11.92
	4	9.17	9.56	11.40	11.51	11.58
Monthly average		8.83	9.18	10.79	10.94	11.01
1984	1	9.47	9.89	11.80	11.99	12.04
	2	10.08	11.25	13.65	13.73	13.78
	3	11.01	11.44	12.74	12.82	12.76
	4	8.68	9.14	11.25	11.53	11.50
Monthly average		9.89	10.44	12.28	12.45	12.45

Source: *Analytical Record of Yields and Yield Spreads* (New York: Salomon Brothers, 1985).

Star Appliance Company (B)

EXHIBIT 4
∎
Statement of Consolidated Income (dollars in thousands, except per share data)

	1979	1980	1981	1982	1983	1984
Income						
Net sales	$302,670	$286,346	$339,169	$352,647	$477,590	$514,048
Interest	5,516	6,549	10,153	7,603	6,505	6,207
Miscellaneous	140	457	737	755	1,039	1,167
Total income	308,326	293,352	350,059	361,005	485,134	521,422
Cost of products sold	195,207	189,704	233,854	237,053	309,002	337,413
Operating profit	113,119	103,648	116,205	123,952	176,132	184,009
Selling and administrative	44,744	50,415	59,383	66,988	81,802	87,598
Interest expense	0	0	0	1,682	3,538	3,136
Income before taxes	68,375	53,233	56,822	55,282	90,792	93,295
Federal and state taxes	31,250	24,108	25,481	25,600	42,240	42,800
Net income	$ 37,125	$ 29,125	$ 31,341	$ 29,682	$ 48,552	$ 50,495
Net income per average share	$ 2.58	$ 2.02	$ 2.18	$ 2.06	$ 3.38	$ 3.51
Dividends	$ 23,002	$ 22,926	$ 25,110	$ 23,802	$ 29,991	$ 32,697
Average dividend yield	6.7%	7.1%	7.1%	5.4%	4.4%	4.6%

Star Appliance Company (B)

EXHIBIT 5
■

Consolidated Statement of Financial Condition (dollars in thousands)

	1979	1980	1981	1982	1983	1984
Assets						
Current assets						
Cash	$ 2,653	$ 3,303	$ 3,259	$ 3,413	$ 5,262	$ 4,870
Short-term investments	47,036	47,625	45,587	37,191	47,315	35,482
Prepaid pension	2,460	6,150	9,180	9,600	6,800	2,000
Accounts receivable, net	18,967	20,977	16,754	30,892	38,313	37,630
Inventories	31,941	41,397	40,819	50,504	60,518	62,147
Deferred taxes	1,620	—	—	—	—	1,913
Total current assets	104,677	119,452	115,599	131,600	158,208	144,042
Other assets						
Marketable securities	0	0	0	0	0	9,758
Prepaid pension	0	0	1,079	4,000	12,000	16,800
Miscellaneous	728	1,685	1,113	1,770	2,200	3,854
Total other assets	728	1,685	2,192	5,770	14,200	30,412
Property, plant, and equipment						
Land	708	1,241	1,018	1,686	2,078	2,224
Buildings and improvements	41,511	44,782	43,462	46,631	48,794	51,398
Machinery and equipment	83,737	93,678	101,860	113,048	122,674	133,772
	125,956	139,701	146,340	161,365	173,546	187,394
Less depreciation	65,242	67,899	74,709	79,344	88,274	98,120
Total property, plant, and equipment	60,714	71,802	71,631	82,021	85,272	89,274
Total assets	$166,119	$192,939	$189,422	$219,391	$257,680	$263,728
Liabilities and Shareholders' Equity						
Current liabilities						
Accounts payable	$ 7,173	$ 9,193	$ 6,553	$ 10,076	$ 16,106	$ 13,066
Compensation to employees	5,600	6,171	6,871	8,301	9,238	10,077
Accrued liabilities	5,127	6,188	6,078	8,155	11,243	12,765
Federal and state taxes	7,523	3,954	1,315	2,609	6,317	5,539
Deferred taxes	0	0	2,322	2,079	1,418	0
Total current liabilities	25,423	25,506	23,139	31,220	44,322	41,447
Deferred taxes	6,784	8,029	10,867	8,385	13,011	16,493
Long-term debt	0	0	0	17,797	19,351	19,417
Shareholders' equity						
Common stock						
Authorized—20,000,000 shares						
Issued—14,382,518 shares	26,540	28,765	28,765	28,765	28,765	28,765
Additional paid-in capital	0	17,368	17,579	17,078	17,084	17,070
Retained earnings	109,154	115,353	121,584	127,464	146,025	163,823
	135,994	161,486	167,928	173,307	191,874	209,658
Less treasury stock	2,082	2,082	12,512	11,318	10,878	23,287
	133,912	159,404	155,416	161,989	$180,996	$186,371
Total liabilities and shareholders' equity	$166,119	$192,939	$189,422	$219,391	$257,680	$263,728

Star Appliance Company (B)

EXHIBIT 6

■

Interest Rates on Debt of Different Qualities

Year/Quarter		Corporate Bonds		Prime Lending Rate	90-Day Treasury Bills	7-Year Treasury Notes
		Aaa	Baa			
1982	1	14.58%	16.82%	16.50%	13.04	14.07
	2	14.81	16.92	16.50	11.97	13.81
	3	12.94	15.63	13.50	8.66	12.86
	4	11.83	14.14	11.50	8.51	10.77
1983	1	11.73	13.61	10.50	8.15	10.14
	2	11.74	13.37	10.50	8.91	10.77
	3	12.37	13.55	11.00	9.55	11.88
	4	12.57	13.75	11.00	9.17	11.51
1984	1	12.57	13.99	11.21	9.47	11.99
	2	13.55	12.66	12.60	10.08	13.73
	3	12.66	14.35	12.97	11.01	12.82
	4	12.13	13.40	11.06	8.68	11.53

Source: *Federal Reserve Bulletin*, 1985.

Star Appliance Company (B)

■

APPENDIX

To: Mr. Arthur Foster
         Financial Vice President, Star Appliance Company

From: Sam Ralfson
         Kennelworth Bank and Trust

Date: January 3, 1985

You asked us to provide you with an estimate of the return expected for the market. Unfortunately there is no single estimate (or even definition of the market), but rather, various estimates made by various groups. On *Wall Street Week*'s year-end program, one analyst was predicting that the Dow Industrial would go from its level of about 1,200 at the end of 1984 to 1,500. Another believed the U.S. deficit would take it 100 points below its current level by year's end.

Over history, the market has yielded from −26.5 percent to 54.0 percent, but the geometric average was 9.5 percent from 1926 to 1984. As shown in Exhibit A-1, the realized market returns have been quite variable. However, some of our analysts find the long-term average a reasonable estimate since, they believe, time averages out the extremes.

The analysts in our Investment Analysis and Advisory Group prefer another method. They use a combination of the dividend discount model and a measure of risk called beta to forecast and evaluate expected returns from almost 500 common stocks.

Their first step is to forecast the dividends they anticipate from each company for at least 15 years. I have attached a chart (Exhibit A-2) they used to explain their method to me. They go about forecasting dividends by looking first at the basic sources of the company's earnings—its markets, products, and competitors—as well as its costs. Using their earnings forecasts and estimates of dividend payout ratios, they determine each company's dividend payments over three periods: for the next few years (usually 5) in detail; for a time of earnings and dividend growth (the analyst determines how long this period will be); and when the company is mature, with a final, low rate of growth in earnings and a higher payout ratio.

As you can see, this is just a more detailed version of the dividend discount model you told me Star has used to estimate its cost of equity. The model assumes that as companies mature they have more cash available than they need and can thus increase dividends.

Once the dividends have been forecast, they are compared to the stocks' current market prices, and rates of return (sometimes called internal rates of return) are calculated. The analysts then compare the expected return (the internal rate of return) with the beta for each stock.

By the way, the analysts tell me they buy their beta estimates from what they call a "beta service." These betas, they say, are calculated over 5 years of history and are adjusted for some statistical problems, but are quite similar to a simple regression historic beta. The expected returns and betas for each stock are plotted on a graph like that shown in Exhibit A-3. A line of best fit is drawn, or calculated using a regression package like that provided with most computer spreadsheet models such as *Lotus 1-2-3*, and the market's expected return is derived by looking at the return expected for a stock or portfolio with a beta of 1.0.

Star Appliance Company (B)

EXHIBIT A-1
∎
Basic Series: Total Annual Returns, 1926–1984

Series	Geometric Mean	Arithmetic Mean	Standard Deviation	Distribution
Common Stocks	9.5%	11.7%	21.2%	
Small Stocks	12.4	18.2	36.3	
Long-Term Corporate Bonds	4.4	4.6	7.6	
Long-Term Government Bonds	3.7	3.9	7.5	
U. S. Treasury Bills	3.3	3.4	3.3	
Inflation	3.0	3.2	4.9	

-90x   0x   +90x

Source: *Stocks, Bonds, Bills, & Inflation 1985 Yearbook* (Chicago: Ibbotson Associates, 1985).

Star Appliance Company (B)

EXHIBIT A-2
■
Data for Present Value Calculation

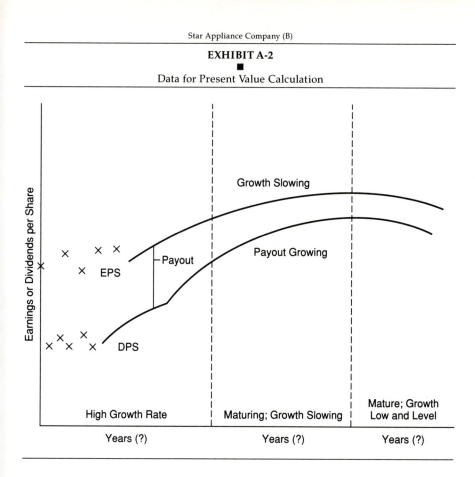

Star Appliance Company (B)

EXHIBIT A-3
■
Expected Value

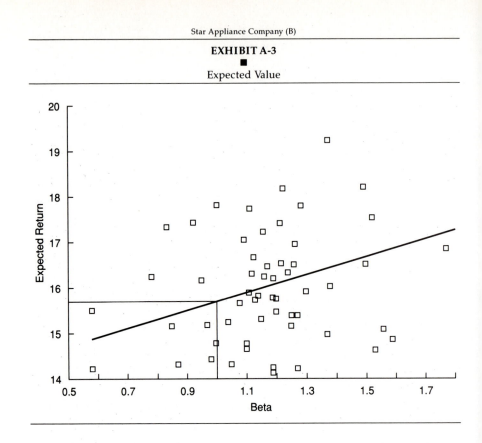

Federal Reserve Bank of Richmond (B)

"I'd rather try skydiving than put this savings bond automation proposal to-gether," Roy Fauber thought. He glanced once again at the reports his staff at the Federal Reserve Bank of Richmond (FRBR) had put together. Since up to 3 months might be required just to get the project approved, he knew he couldn't delay much longer. Also, depending on the system chosen, the layout of the savings bond processing area might need modification. Since the FRBR was in the process of building new offices, any necessary changes would be much easier, and cheaper, if made soon.

Each of the three options before him proposed greater computerization of the FRBR savings bond processing system. Analyzing them had been difficult because the questions they raised were complex: allocated costs versus cash outlays, decentralized versus centralized computer hardware, and differences in start-up dates. Even so, his staff had prepared estimates, and their cost/benefit analyses lay before him now (Exhibit 1). What had not been done was to choose a discount rate for use in the present value analysis. That Mr. Fauber had to do, and the choice was troublesome.

The discount rate question had been a problem in the federal government for years. By 1965 many agencies and departments had adopted cost/benefit analysis, but the discount rates they used varied both between and within the agencies. For instance, the Department of Defense evaluated weapons systems using rates ranging from 5 percent to 10 percent. The rate depended on the type of system being evaluated.

The problem had become especially vexing at the FRBR since the imple-mentation of a new planning system that required the use of present value analysis, and thus a discount rate, for the evaluation of larger projects. Even though the concept of present value analysis had been introduced to the Federal Reserve districts, the discount rate issue had not been resolved. In order to gain approval for any one of the proposals before him, however, Mr. Fauber had to choose a discount rate.

The new planning system posed another problem: FRBR approval for the project was not enough by itself; investments in excess of $100,000 required approval by the Board of Governors of the Federal Reserve System. The three

---

This case was prepared as a basis for class discussion rather than to illustrate either effective or ineffective handling of an administrative situation. Copyright © 1984 by the Darden Graduate Business School Sponsors, University of Virginia, Charlottesville, Virginia.

proposals Mr. Fauber was considering each exceeded $100,000. Since this would be the first proposal using present value analysis that the FRBR would send to the Board of Governors, it could set a precedent for later projects.

THE FRBR DISCOUNT RATE

The methodology for the Federal Reserve System present value analysis was widely used in business. For a corporation competing for funds in the capital markets, the discount rate or standard would be the firm's cost of capital (the market-determined trade-off between present and future consumption). Any investment in which benefits would equal or exceed the total cost, including costs of capital for implementing the project, would be beneficial for the shareholders of that firm and should be accepted. Because it was difficult to estimate the cost of capital, the concept was not quite as easy for corporations to put into practice as it appeared. When it was used in a government agency, the problems multiplied.

Since the Federal Reserve did not compete for its funds in the traditional capital markets, the notion of a cost of capital was complicated for the FRBR. The Federal Reserve System created money when it drew a check on itself; thus, under no circumstances would it ever be short of credit. As an example, when the FRBR wrote a $70-million check for its office building under construction on the banks of the James River, the contractor took the check to his commercial bank, the bank presented the check to the Federal Reserve for payment, and the FRBR credited the member bank's reserve account—money was created. Thus it was unclear whether the FRBR even had a capital cost.

The capital budgeting system at the FRBR clearly required that the discount rate satisfy one of the following objectives, whose terms are explained in the appendix to this case:

a. Equal the FRBR's explicit cost of capital stock

b. Allow the FRBR to operate at minimum cost to the Treasury

c. Satisfy the FRBR's own opportunity costs, or

d. Allow the FRBR to invest at an optimal social rate.

Often several rates would satisfy an objective, and supportable arguments for each of the rates surfaced every time the question was raised. The staff had summarized the cost of capital arguments for Mr. Fauber to consider in making his decision. Those arguments are presented in the appendix to this case.

CONCLUSION

One statement that Mr. Fauber could make with certainty about the decision confronting him was that there was no shortage of possibilities. The fate of an investment could hinge on the discount rate chosen, and the range of discount rates being considered was very wide. What rate should be used and which, if any, of the alternatives should be recommended was now up to him.

Federal Reserve Bank of Richmond (B)

EXHIBIT 1
■

Analysis of Options

I. Cost/Benefits of Four-Phase System

	Year 1	Year 2	Year 3	Year 4	Year 5
Development					
Hardware	$(285,245)				
Software					
Development	(28,000)				
Modification	(35,000)				
Conversion	(15,000)				
In-bank coordinator	(7,500)				
Operations					
Hardware maintenance	(11,556)	$(15,408)	$(15,408)	$(15,408)	$(15,408)
Software maintenance	(18,000)	(18,000)	(18,000)	(18,000)	(18,000)
Net costs	(400,301)	33,408	33,408	33,408	33,408
Personnel savings	71,634	73,932	80,488	85,317	90,435
Computer charge savings	41,000	41,000	41,000	41,000	41,000
Net benefits	$(287,667)	$ 81,524	$ 88,080	$ 92,909	$ 98,027

II. Cost/Benefits of IBM 370 In-House Software

	Year 1	Year 2	Year 3	Year 4	Year 5
Development					
Software	$(151,756)	$(134,140)			
Operations					
Software maintenance	(3,000)	(3,000)	$ (3,000)	$ (3,000)	$(3,000)
Personnel benefits		43,191	91,564	97,058	102,882
Net benefits	$(154,756)	$ (93,949)	$ 88,564	$ 94,058	$ 99,882

III. Cost/Benefits of IBM 370 Outside Consultant Software

	Year 1	Year 2	Year 3	Year 4	Year 5
Development					
Software	$(250,000)				
Software conversion	(15,000)				
In-bank coordinator	(7,500)				
Operations					
Software maintenance		$(13,000)	$(18,000)	$(18,000)	$(18,000)
Personnel benefits		60,286	91,564	97,058	102,882
Net benefits	$(272,500)	$(47,786)	$ 73,564	$ 79,058	$ 84,882

Federal Reserve Bank of Richmond (B)

■

APPENDIX
Office Correspondence

TO: R. Fauber

FROM: Computer Services and Planning Department

RE: Discount Rates and Federal Government Agencies

There has been a continuing discussion regarding the proper discount rate to use for public sector investment analysis. The following summarizes the main arguments and provides recent data for estimating each rate.

Explicit Cost of Capital Stock

The only external capital used by the Federal Reserve Bank of Richmond with an explicit cost is the stock held by Fifth District member banks. The return paid by the FRBR on that stock is 6 percent.

Minimum Cost to the Treasury

Any investment made by the Federal Reserve Bank of Richmond represents funds taken from the Treasury to be returned at some point in the future. Since one of the objectives of FRBR is to return the maximum profit to the Treasury, the discount rate should, it is argued, represent the time value of money to the Treasury. That rate could be the Treasury's marginal borrowing cost. (See Exhibit A–1.)

FRBR Opportunity Costs

Federal Reserve Banks invest funds in a variety of assets. Many believe that the rate on one of these earning assets, or an average of the rate on all of them, represents an opportunity cost. Whatever discount rate is chosen should reflect the cost of forgone opportunities. Several choices for an opportunity cost have been suggested:

1. Rediscount Rate. The rate at which member banks borrow from the FRB (Exhibit A–2).

2. The Rate on Agency Securities. These are rates on obligations of federal agencies (e.g., Federal Land Bank, Federal National Mortgage Association) owned by the FRB (Exhibit A–3).

3. Treasury Securities. The opportunity cost of investing in government securities; the rate on Treasury securities (Exhibit A–4).

All these rates have the advantage of being observable, market-determined rates. However, that does not mean that any one is the best choice for evaluating the economic potential of FRBR investments. Some suggest other, less observable choices are preferable.

Optimal Social Rate

Many argue that the discount rate should be based on circumstances beyond the Federal Reserve System alone. Since the system operates in the public sector, drawing resources away from the private sector, a rate should be used that will result in socially beneficial investment decisions. Yet very little agreement is found on the subject of what the optimal social rate actually should be. However, the discussion centers between two extremes.

The first group suggests there is a rate at which the public, in aggregate, would be willing to forgo income today for certain income at some time in the future. This rate, the *public's time preference of money,* is the optimal social discount rate. Since the public is willing to purchase long-term government bonds, and the return is default-risk free, this rate would be an adequate proxy.

The other extreme holds that public expenditures take resources from the private sector. Thus investments must earn a rate of return equivalent to what would be earned in the private sector—the *opportunity cost in the corporate sector* (Exhibit A–5).

In a society where there are no taxes and in which all investment returns are certain, corporations would be required to earn the investors' rate of time preference. However, in the real world, risk and taxes cloud the issue. If, for example, the rate of time preference is 6 percent, investors in the securities of a private corporation would demand a premium for risk. If the corporate income tax rate is 50 percent and the risk premium is 2 percent, the firm would earn 16 percent before tax on its capital expenditures if it provided an 8 percent required after-tax rate of return. All this assumes the firm had issued no debt. The proponents of this view argue that if the average corporation is required to earn 16 percent on its investments, the public sector should use this rate to ensure socially beneficial decisions. (Tax information is summarized in Exhibit A–6.)

These rates represent very different estimates of the social rate. Disagreement over these and other possible choices hinges on one's view of the riskiness of government versus corporate investments, the source of funds used for such investments, and how unestimated social benefits should be treated.

1. Risk.   The rate of individual or corporate time preference suggests there is no risk to government expenditures. Although returns from individual projects could vary, the public investment portfolio is so large that aggregate returns would vary only slightly from what is expected. In essence, there is no risk.

The use of the cost of corporate investments, on the other hand, suggests public investments of the same risk as corporate investments be discounted at the same rate. From the point of view of society, no single public or private investment carries any risk. However, the public sector is still responsible for meeting the opportunity cost established when an individual investor requires a risk premium from an individual firm.

2. Fund Source.
The use of either the rate of time preference or the corporate opportunity cost suggests resources are drawn from either the corporate sector or forgone individual consumption. However, noncorporate businesses (e.g., partnerships) also exist. Tax rates among these sectors vary significantly, and thus the pretax required return varies, as well. Whether one rate or a combination of effective rates from these sectors is appropriate is the source of some debate (Exhibit A-6).

3. Social Benefits.
Finally, many argue that the use of a market rate of interest would result in general underinvestment. Investments have nonquantified social benefits that are ignored in their economic evaluation. A new plant, for instance, may appear to break even, but the analysis ignores the benefits from the 200 new jobs the plant provides. The firm may have no economic return, yet society benefits. Thus a lower discount rate is justified when there are such benefits.

Federal Reserve Bank of Richmond (B)

EXHIBIT A–1
∎
Yields on New Treasury Issues in 1978[a]

	Bills		Notes						Bonds	
	3-Mo.	6-Mo.	1-Yr.	2-Yr.	3-Yr.	4-Yr.	5-Yr.	7-Yr.	10-Yr.	15-Yr. +
January (35)[b]	6.64	7.01	7.03	7.55						
February (36)	6.65	7.07	7.29	7.69	7.53	7.89		7.88		8.23
March (35)	6.51	6.98	7.34	7.56						
April (36)	6.50	7.01	7.55	7.80			7.94			
May (37)	6.64	7.37	7.95	8.09		8.27			8.29	8.47
June (37)	6.92	7.56	8.24	8.32						8.63
July (37)	7.30	7.91	8.39	8.61						
August (39)	7.28	7.72	8.48	8.38	8.46	8.41		8.36		8.43
September (39)	8.11	8.37	8.57	8.65						8.64

[a]Three- and six-month T-bill rates are the average for all issues in the month.
[b]Numbers in parentheses under each month represent the average maturity of all Treasury debt in months.

Federal Reserve Bank of Richmond (B)

EXHIBIT A–2
■
Federal Reserve Bank of New York Rediscount Rate[a]

	Rate (percent)		Rate (percent)
1961	3%	1973	4.5–7.5%
1962	3	1974	7.5–8
1963	3–3.5	1975	6–7.75
1964	3.5–4	1976	5.25–6
1965	4–4.5	1977	5.25–6
1966	4.5	1/1/78	6
1967	4–4.5	1/9/78	6.5
1968	4.5–5.5	5/11/78	7
1969	5.5–6	7/3/78	7.25
1970	5.5–6	8/21/78	7.75
1971	4.5–5.5	9/22/78	8
1972	4.5		

[a]The rediscount rate at the FRBR and all other district banks followed the New York rate very closely.

Federal Reserve Bank of Richmond (B)

EXHIBIT A–3
■
Average Yields on Agency Issues during 1978

	6-Mo.	1-Yr.	2-Yr.	5-Yr.	15-Yr.
3/7/78	6.99%	7.25%	7.55%	7.96%	8.15%
6/1/78	7.65	7.98	8.15	8.30	8.53
9/6/78	8.20	8.34	8.40	8.36	8.51

Federal Reserve Bank of Richmond (B)

EXHIBIT A–4
■
Average Yields of Long-Term Bonds

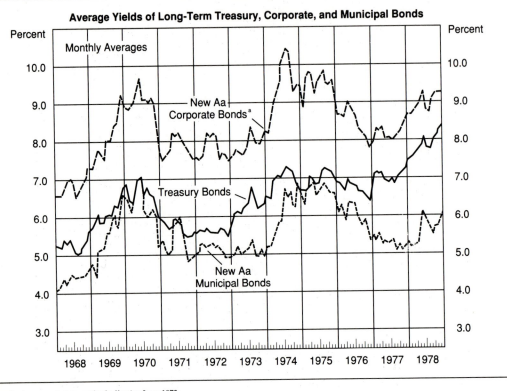

Average Yields of Long-Term Treasury, Corporate, and Municipal Bonds

[a]Change in Aa computation method effective June 1973.
Source: *Treasury Bulletin,* January 1979.

Federal Reserve Bank of Richmond (B)

EXHIBIT A–5
■
Estimating Cost of Equity in the Corporate Sector

Data for Dividend Yield Plus Growth and Earnings Price Models

	1974	1975	1976	1977
Dividend/Price ratios[a]	4.47%	4.31%	3.77%	4.62%
Earnings/Price ratios[b]	11.59%	9.04%	8.90%	10.30%

Five-Year Compounded Growth Rates[c] for the Period Ending

	1974	1975	1976	1977	1978
Sales	10.9%	11.6%	11.8%	12.4%	12.9%
EPS	5.2	6.5	9.4	10.1	12.6
Stock price	−10.0	−3.3	−2.3	−2.2	4.2

[a]Average of Standard & Poor's 500.
[b]From *Economic Report of the President*, 1978.
[c]Taken from *Forbes Annual Reports on American Industry.* Survey includes approximately 1,000 corporations.

*Annual Compounded Returns
Actually Realized from
Common Stock Investments[a]*

1926–1964	10.4%
1965–1969	5.0
1970–1974	−2.4
1975	37.2
1976	23.8
1977	−7.2

[a]Standard & Poor's 500 (returns include dividends).
Source: Roger G. Ibbotson and Rex A. Sinquefield, *Stocks, Bonds, Bills and Inflation: Historical Returns (1926–1978)*, (Charlottesville, Va.: The Financial Analysts Research Foundation, 1978).

Federal Reserve Bank of Richmond (B)

EXHIBIT A–6
■
Federal, State, and Local Tax Information (billions of dollars)

	1975	1976	1977[a]
Federal Government Receipts			
Individual income tax	$ 125.6	$ 147.3	$ 170.7
Corporate income tax	43.1	55.9	59.5
Social insurance revenue	94.2	105.7	118.9
Other	24	23.4	24.8
Total	$ 286.9	$ 332.3	$ 373.9
State and Local Government Receipts			
Personal income tax	$ 43.4	$ 49.6	$ 56.8
Corporate taxes	7.1	8.9	9.7
Indirect business taxes and nontax accruals	114.7	127.1	140.3
Social insurance receipts	15.9	18.1	20.1
Other	54.6	61.0	67.6
Total	$ 235.7	$ 264.7	$ 294.5
Gross national product	1,528.8	1,706.5	1,890.4
Personal consumption	980.4	1,094.0	1,210.1
Corporate profits (pretax)	99.3	128.1	140.3

[a]Preliminary.
Source: *Economic Report of the President,* January 1978.

American Telephone & Telegraph (A)

In early summer 1983, American Telephone & Telegraph (AT&T) was in the midst of what many observers called the most ambitious corporate transformation ever attempted. Measured by its $150 billion in assets, AT&T was the world's largest corporation. Its massive capital investment program represented 4 percent of the total new capital invested by U.S. businesses in 1983. With over 900 million common shares outstanding, AT&T was easily the most widely held security listed on any exchange; over 3 million investors owned telephone common stock for its high dividend yield and low risk, exemplified by its highly regarded Aaa debt rating. Since the January 1982 agreement with the Department of Justice to divest the corporation of the assets and liabilities related to local telephone service (and the Yellow Pages), enormous uncertainty had come to surround the AT&T breakup scheduled for January 1, 1984, and the entry of the "new" AT&T into the highly competitive telecommunications industry. AT&T no longer would be the classic "widows and orphans" investment. Its very nature would change.

As the divestiture approached, uncertainty about AT&T and its future increased. The consequences of divestiture for AT&T and its rapidly multiplying competitors were certainly affecting both corporate and industry risk. As a result, the task of estimating a cost of capital for AT&T had become far more difficult than it had been in the past. In determining capital costs, AT&T's financial analysts had to keep both the corporation's history and its future in perspective. However, the future was less certain than it had ever been.

In the past, AT&T's cost of capital[1] had been used for setting telephone rates, but as the divestiture approached, the corporation's cost of capital had taken on another meaning. It had also become a measure of the return required by the corporation in allocating its capital and it would be used in analyzing new investments. What was AT&T's cost of capital, early in the summer of 1983?

This case was prepared as a basis for class discussion rather than to illustrate either effective or ineffective handling of an administrative situation. Copyright © 1983 by the Darden Graduate Business School Sponsors, University of Virginia, Charlottesville, Virginia.

[1]In setting telephone rates the cost of capital, based in part on imbedded costs, was used. In analyzing new investments a marginal cost of capital would be used.

BACKGROUND

As the world's largest regulated monopoly, AT&T had maintained its commitment to provide nationwide phone service to its customers for almost a century. In addition to its ownership of 22 Bell operating companies (BOCs), which provided both local and long-distance telephone service to over 85 million customers (80 percent of the nation's telephone subscribers), AT&T was vertically integrated through the ownership of its Western Electric manufacturing subsidiary. Western Electric, the tenth largest firm in the United States ranked by sales, manufactured approximately 65 to 75 percent of all the U.S. telecommunications equipment in 1982. Bell Labs, the corporation's research and development subsidiary, owned equally by both AT&T and Western Electric, performed both basic and applied research with an annual budget in excess of $2 billion.

AT&T had been regulated since the Communications Act of 1934, which created the Federal Communications Commission (FCC). The commission reflected a new trend: "Political support for increased government control of the economy developed in the 1930s as more and more people lost confidence in the self-regulating aspect of a market economy."[2] Congress's intent in creating the FCC was to ensure the concept of "universal service"—telephone service available across the nation at a reasonable price. With the country still in the grips of the Depression, Congress had decided that allowing certain suppliers a monopolistic position within the industry was in the public interest.

Over the years, however, the public began to look less favorably on monopolies. AT&T, because of its controlling position within the industry, was often the object of suits alleging violations of the Sherman Act. In 1949 the Department of Justice initiated a legal action against the corporation that sought the divestiture of Western Electric and the open licensing of AT&T technology. The case was dismissed in 1956 when AT&T signed a consent decree that essentially barred the corporation from selling its products in unregulated markets. The agreement also restricted Western Electric to manufacturing for AT&T alone and allowed unlimited, royalty-free access to their portfolio of 8,000 patents. In promoting such open availability of information, the Justice Department hoped to encourage and promote rivalry within the equipment market. By surrendering the patent as an effective barrier to entry, AT&T had, in effect, become "dependent on regulatory decisions for protection from competition."[3]

In the decade following the 1956 case, it was apparent that the terms of the agreement did not create the competitive atmosphere within the industry originally intended by the suit. In 1974, prompted by over 60 different civil suits pending against AT&T, the Justice Department filed its second antitrust action against the corporation. The Justice Department's suit, which was designed to break up AT&T into smaller units, claimed that through its control of access to local telephone lines, AT&T discouraged competition in the long-distance communications and equipment manufacturing businesses, areas which had recently been deregulated by the FCC. The Justice Department believed that, in a free market economic system, a single corporation should not be able to dominate the rapidly growing telecommunications industry. This case was settled in 1982 when AT&T agreed to the divestiture.

---

[2]Gerald Brock, *The Telecommunications Industry* (Cambridge, Mass.: Harvard University Press, 1981), 178.
[3]Ibid., 194.

AT&T—BEFORE THE ERA OF COMPETITION

Competition had little meaning for most AT&T executives prior to the 1970s. Only in microwave transmission had AT&T experienced some competition. The corporation's local and long-distance telephone services, sold to what amounted to a captive market, were protected by the industry's regulatory barriers to entry and by the sheer density of the corporation's market presence. Strategic corporate and product decisions were made with the primary goal of satisfying the regulators and maintaining universal service. The regulatory compromise allowed AT&T to operate free of competition at what were anticipated to be fair prices. The fair price was one that allowed all costs, including the costs of debt and equity, to be covered by prices charged, but no more. Since no competition was allowed, there was virtually no business risk, and the danger of excess profits being gained was removed as the regulators sought to have the cost of equity equal the return on equity.

Regulation affected the business in other ways—for instance, in setting customer's prices. As improved technologies drove down costs in the high-volume long-distance business, these lower costs were averaged with the higher costs of local service where new high-volume technologies were not justified. Average costs benefited many customers, but without regulation, they would have made long-distance service especially vulnerable to competitive price cutting. In addition to pricing, depreciation schedules and accounting practices were quite different from those used by unregulated firms. Corporate marketing efforts, largely nonexistent because of AT&T's dominating position within the industry, were limited to image-building advertisements such as the "One Bell System—It Works" promotional campaign.

As virtually the only equipment supplier for the BOCs, Western Electric provided nearly all Bell System hardware needs. The pace of new product introductions was not dictated by the needs of the marketplace or by the regulators, but rather by the rate at which existing products failed to serve their purposes. Furthermore, the company's regulatory protection allowed the BOCs to require that only AT&T equipment be attached to telephone lines. Up until 1968, it was illegal for a customer to purchase a telephone or any other piece of non-AT&T terminal equipment and attach it themselves to a phone company wire. Phones were rented from the telephone company and were installed in the home by a company technician. This was the era of the plain black telephone.

AT&T's pricing strategy also reflected the lack of competition within the industry. Calls made by urban residents supported the cost of calls made by rural residents. The profitable long-distance and terminal-equipment segments subsidized costly local services. In the early 1970s, over 35 to 40 cents out of each long-distance revenue dollar went to support local service. "The point of this subsidizing was simple: to provide universal telephone service. Those who couldn't afford the true cost of service were underwritten by those who could."[4]

Since there was no need to market products aggressively during this period, AT&T was organized along functional lines, as shown in the following chart.

---

[4]"The Phone Rate Hang Up," *The Wall Street Journal*, September 20, 1983, 36.

The "Functional" Organizational Structure (Pre-Divestiture)

American Telephone & Telegraph

Bell Labs	Western Electric	AT&T Long Lines	Bell Operating Companies (including Yellow Pages)

This structure allowed the corporation to maximize the synergistic benefits that resulted from grouping functional expertise and technology. The local operating companies, because of their unique position in the nation's telecommunications network, provided direct contact between the corporation and its customers.

AT&T's financial strategy had also been designed to operate within the monopolistic environment. Since the FCC based the rates that AT&T could charge on an allowed return on the corporation's assets, there was no incentive to minimize new capital investments or to allow existing assets to depreciate rapidly: rapid depreciation would have raised the rates charged. Consequently, AT&T's customer premises equipment (CPE), the equipment owned and operated at the customer's site by AT&T, was depreciated over its useful life. Since all CPE was designed by Bell Labs and built by Western Electric to be reliable, products commonly lasted 40 years or more. Without the generous cash-flow advantages that resulted from rapid depreciation, AT&T's large capital investment needs frequently exceeded internally generated funds and caused the corporation to make regular trips to the debt and equity markets for additional capital, sometimes in large amounts.

THE ORIGINS OF COMPETITION

The grip that AT&T had on the telecommunications industry in the years immediately following the 1956 consent decree began to erode under pressure from the public and the Justice Department, which was unhappy with the outcome of the 1956 antitrust suit. The FCC changed its interpretation of its regulatory responsibility as a result of the changing sentiments. Several of its decisions in the late 1960s and early 1970s opened to competition markets that had previously been AT&T's alone.

In a 1968 decision dubbed the Carterphone Case, the FCC broadened the opportunities for equipment manufacturers when it ruled against AT&T's claims that its monopolistic control of terminal equipment was in the public interest. Since customers could now purchase equipment from any vendor, new suppliers such as Rolm, Mitel, and Northern Telecom were quick to enter the terminal equipment market.

In another historic 1971 decision, the FCC allowed specialized common carriers (SCCs) to offer competitive services in the long-distance telephone market. Many industry observers believed that this business was the most attractive of the formerly protected segments because of AT&T's historical pricing practices. Consequently, of those segments served by AT&T, the multibillion-dollar long-distance business provided new entrants with the highest potential for reaching profitability.

While the FCC was responsible for removing the industry's barriers to entry, recent advances in communications technology made AT&T's businesses even more vulnerable to competition by increasing the flexibility of the network and by decreasing the required initial capital investment.

At the time of the 1956 consent decree, the separation between AT&T's voice-traffic telephone network and the rapidly emerging computer business was clear. However, changes in product technology soon rendered much of the agreement useless and led many legislators to call for a review of the terms of the agreement. In a 1980 decision known as the Second Computer Inquiry, the FCC officially deregulated the terminal equipment market and permitted AT&T to compete in unregulated markets through a fully separate subsidiary named American Bell. The structural separation of American Bell from the rest of the corporation was intended to prevent the established, regulated parts of AT&T's business from subsidizing the competitive, unregulated operations.

THE IMPACT OF COMPETITION

In 1978, with the election of new AT&T Board Chairman Charles Brown, things began to change, starting with a massive redesign of the corporation's structure. He began to reorganize the firm around lines of business, each with its own financial and marketing resources. Said Mr. Brown, "We needed organizational changes to facilitate our ability to move quickly in new areas."[5] The company was organized first into business, residence, and network divisions, with an increased emphasis on marketing and sales. By 1981 AT&T was organized generally as:

The "Lines of Business" Organizational Structure (Post-Divestiture)

American Telephone & Telegraph

AT&T Communications   AT&T Technologies

Long Distance   AT&T Information Systems
                           AT&T Consumer Products
                           AT&T Network Systems
                           AT&T Components & Electronic Systems
                           AT&T Computers
                           AT&T Federal Systems
                           AT&T International

AT&T's unregulated subsidiary, American Bell (renamed, in a later reorganization, AT&T Information Systems), was established as a result of the freedoms gained through the Second Computer Inquiry. Patterned after IBM's National Accounts Division, the separate domestic marketing subsidiary was part of a strategy to prepare AT&T for its entry into unregulated markets. After years of pleasing the regulators, AT&T would now try to please the customer. "They are now [beginning to] sell solutions rather than communications,"[6] remarked a vice president of Federal Express.

---

[5]"Telecommunications—AT&T's Bold Bid to Stay on Top," *Business Week*, October 11, 1982.
[6]Ibid., 66.

The technologically superior and lower-priced products built by many of its new competitors forced the corporation, and its Bell Labs subsidiary, to increase the flow of new products and services. For example, in 1979 new modular AT&T telephones were introduced. Customers could go to one of almost 500 Phone Center stores, choose a phone from a wide array of styles and colors, and install it themselves. This change from leasing to selling equipment meant that the corporation would be free from the burden of financing this huge equipment base. However, the accelerated introduction of new products meant that old assets, some barely beginning their long product lives, would not be fully depreciated because of the conservative accounting policies dictated by the FCC to maintain low local rates. Mr. Brown and his supporters argued that this competition-induced change in strategy dramatically reduced cash flow and increased outside financing in the 1970s.

Competition also affected other areas of the well-worn corporate strategy. In AT&T's 1980 *Annual Report*, Mr. Brown stated that "the pricing of local services to support the goal of universal service, long the main objective of the Bell System, would no longer be considered tenable due to competitive pressures."[7] The price of local service, through a series of rate increases, would slowly bear more of its true cost. These actions indicated to many observers that many past AT&T pricing strategies, such as using high-volume products and services with greater economies of scale to subsidize the less-efficient, low-volume products, would be discarded.

AT&T's efforts in establishing a marketing presence were hampered by the watchful eye of the FCC. For example, the introduction of a new product such as the "Snoopy" phone, a phone shaped like a character in a popular comic strip, required approval by 54 different regulatory bodies. As a result of this bureaucratic nightmare, competitors, free from the regulatory hassles, were often able to examine AT&T's product and service proposals and prepare a response before AT&T could even get to the market.

SIGNIFICANT INDUSTRY TRENDS

The telecommunications industry was undergoing a change of its own. New digital hardware was rapidly replacing the analog technology, while optical fibers, satellites, and microwave systems were being introduced to replace traditional copper wire as the means of carrying telecommunications signals. The digital microprocessor, the heart of the computer, began to appear in telecommunications switching gear and even in telephones. Telephone switches resembled large-scale computers, and required almost identical manufacturing, design, and service systems.

The computer industry was also in the midst of an evolution away from stand-alone, isolated systems toward such new concepts as local area networks. This new method required telecommunications technologies that enabled users at all levels of an organization to create, store, retrieve, transmit, receive, and distribute information electronically between different locations within a building. Furthermore, distinctions between the industries were disappearing. IBM,

---

[7]AT&T, 1980 *Annual Report*.

long a benign technological rival, became a potentially aggressive competitor with its entry into the newly deregulated satellite communications business in 1974.

THE DECISION TO DIVEST

In 1982, facing prospects of reduced profitability from increasing competition, further deregulation, and continued antitrust battles, AT&T signed a second consent decree with the Justice Department. In return for the dismissal of the 1974 suit, AT&T agreed to divest itself of the local portions of 22 wholly owned operating companies and the Yellow Pages. Relieved of the most capital- and labor-intensive portions of its business, AT&T could concentrate on the most profitable segments and could venture into unregulated markets. "This was not our idea," noted Chairman Brown. "We just agreed to it."[8] He elaborated on the pending divestiture:

> it seemed to coincide with a national consensus that competition rather than regulation should be the dominant force in this industry. . . . [It] was offered by the Justice Department and after weighing all the issues, we decided that we wanted to get this [antitrust suit] behind us and start running a business.[9]

Many security analysts hailed the agreement. "For AT&T, this is a superb move," noted a Lehman Bros. telecommunications analyst. "It lets them keep all the neat stuff, and they don't have to dicker around with local distribution."[10] Others were not as optimistic about the divestiture. "[It] is a corporate gamble to top all corporate gambles,"[11] concluded another communications industry consultant. Nonetheless, just as AT&T had left the telegraph business in 1913 to enter the more promising telephone industry, now it would turn away from the telephone industry to enter more profitable markets.

THE IMPACT OF THE DIVESTITURE ON OUTSTANDING AT&T COMMON SHARES

On January 1, 1984, the former wholly owned local telephone companies and the Yellow Pages would be divested to form seven regional holding companies, each of which would continue to supply local telephone service to their customers. The plan called for each AT&T shareholder to retain his or her holdings of AT&T shares and receive one share in each of the newly formed regional holding companies (RHCs) for every ten AT&T shares held. The new AT&T would emerge with the same number of shares (approximately 925 million) and shareholders (3.2 million) as before. The RHCs, because of the 1-for-10 reverse

---

[8]"Going Forward with Arch McGill," *Datamation,* January 1983, 54.
[9]Charles Nadler, "Interview with Charles Brown," *Organizational Dynamics,* Summer 1982, 31.
[10]"Telecommunications—AT&T's Bold Bid to Stay on Top," *Business Week,* October 11, 1982, 66.
[11]Ibid.

split, would each end up with about 92.5 million shares outstanding. Since the plan called for a cash payment in lieu of RHC shares for holders of less than ten AT&T shares, the regionals would have their oustanding shares held by a smaller number of investors.

THE REGIONAL HOLDING COMPANIES

Under the divestiture plan, the 22 Bell operating companies (BOCs), representing about 75 percent of the corporation's assets, would be organized into seven RHCs that would continue to provide local telephone services under the control of their local public utility commissions and the FCC. The RHCs would all rank among the ten largest U.S. utilities (shown in Exhibit 1) and among the largest companies in the S&P 500. In addition to supplying local service, the RHCs would have the Yellow Pages and the rights to over 50 percent of the cellular mobile telephone licenses granted by that date by the FCC. Cellular phone service, a new type of advanced mobile radio telephone service, was forecasted to be a $6-billion market by 1990. Industry experts believed that revenues from the Yellow Pages and cellular telephones, in addition to the prospects of non-AT&T telecommunications equipment sales, would more than compensate for revenues lost when the RHCs relinquished to the new AT&T ownership of customer premises equipment that had been put into service before January 1, 1983.

Equally owned by each of the seven RHCs would be the Central Services Organization (CSO) (later called Bell Communications Research), which was established to provide many of the services formerly provided by AT&T to the 22 BOCs. With over 8,000 employees (over 4,000 drawn from Western Electric and Bell Labs), the CSO would furnish the new local companies with technical assistance on such topics as local area network planning, product and customer engineering, and software development. The subsidiary was jointly operated in order to coordinate the efforts of the RHCs in meeting the technical needs of the residential, business, and government customers.

To assist in the start-up, Bell Labs would be available to the RHCs for technical support for the first year after the divestiture and would supply any resources needed to help non-AT&T carriers, such as MCI and Sprint, plug into the local network until 1987.

Each operating company, as a division of a RHC, would retain its original identity and would continue to serve the same territory. The regions would be roughly comparable in terms of assets (ranging from $15 to $20 billion) and similar in terms of population served. The geographical sizes of the territories, however, ranged from 2 to 14 states. For example, US West, the 14-state RHC that served much of the Midwest and Pacific Northwest, extended nearly a million square miles, while NYNEX, the New York and New England RHC, covered less than a quarter of that territory (see map).

THE "NEW" AT&T

After the spinoff of the RHCs, the "new" AT&T would lose its position as the world's largest corporation, falling to the number-four spot behind Exxon, GM, and Mobil. However, it would remain the largest utility in the United States, when measured by assets (as shown in Exhibit 1).

Seven-Region Planning Model

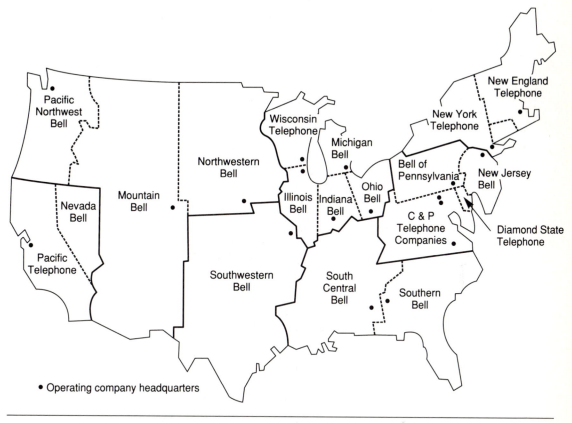

Source: Merrill Lynch Research Department Report, June 23, 1983.

The "new" AT&T would be divided into two business sectors: AT&T Communications (AT&TC) and AT&T Technologies (AT&TT). AT&TC would essentially be an expanded version of the old AT&T Long Lines, the long-distance service unit. With nearly $15 to $20 billion in assets and expected 1984 revenues in excess of $30 billion, AT&TC was expected to be the cash generator that would finance AT&T's entry into unregulated markets. Analysts predicted AT&TC to be the source of most, if not all, of the corporation's profits in the first several years of its existence.

AT&TT, the unregulated side of the corporation, would consist of seven vertically integrated lines of business formed from the original American Bell, Western Electric, and Bell Labs subsidiaries. AT&TT's customers would fall into four major categories: residential telecommunications subscribers, institutional subscribers (businesses), operators of communications networks (including the RHCs), and U.S. and foreign government agencies.

The major task that Mr. Brown and his staff faced would be the transformation of a regulated monopoly into a corporation capable of operating in the highly competitive $75-billion telecommunications business—a business some analysts expected to double in size during the next five years. Many industry analysts had expressed concern that AT&T executives, accustomed to a regulated environment, would have trouble developing competitive instincts. Making the transition even more difficult was the fact that AT&T's long-distance business, the biggest source of the post-divestiture corporation's profits, would still be partially regulated. For Mr. Brown, the most important aspect of the transformation was the definition of the ground rules under which the new AT&T could compete: "the complexity of trying to change ourselves, when we don't know what the future rules are going to be, injects a degree of uncertainty that creates a lot of anxiety."[12]

The divestiture would also have a major impact on AT&T's 1 million employees, of which almost 700,000 were unionized. Some 53 percent of the union membership were assigned to what would become the RHCs. While the majority of the membership favored the divestiture since it would allow the corporation to expand into new businesses and create new jobs, there was concern that the divestiture might be complicated by the August 1983 expiration of their current contract. Competition from nonunion firms was likely to put added pressure on wages, a topic of major concern for the unions that were unhappy about the terms of their present agreement. Their last strike in 1971 lasted several months. Many observers considered AT&T labor to be relatively militant.

The consent decree specified that employee displacement because of the divestiture was to be minimized: just 15 to 20 percent of the total employee population would be reassigned. For example, 3,700 engineers from Bell Labs were transferred to the AT&T Information Systems division to design and market customer premises equipment to be made by Western Electric. Many employees could face a major cultural trauma as a result of the divestiture. Both blue- and white-collar personnel, who were used to job assignments that moved them throughout the corporation during their careers, had to deal with the shock of seeing much of their career efforts divested.

THE COMPETITIVE POSITION OF THE "NEW" AT&T

AT&T faced the challenge of developing marketing expertise in an organization that had never concerned itself with competition in the past. Although the new AT&T would remain the largest single company in the telecommunications industry, its role would be less dominant than it had been before, largely because the number of competitors had grown as the industry's barriers to entry had fallen.

At the time of the divestiture, however, AT&T would not be totally inexperienced in dealing with competition within its formerly protected segments. Since the landmark FCC decisions of the 1960s and 1970s first opened markets within the telecommunications industry to competition, AT&T had been affected by new entrants within both the long-distance and the terminal equipment markets.

The Long-Distance Marketplace.
For many years, the telephone company network had been the sole medium for long-distance communications. However, the increase in the number of SCCs created more alternatives to the

---

[12]Charles Nadler, "Conversation with Charles Brown," *Organizational Dynamics*, Summer 1982, 31.

traditional long-distance network in this increasingly commodity-like segment. By connecting its network to the switched telephone network, a customer could dial the SCC's microwave station through the local telephone system rather than via a private line. Then the SCC, not AT&T, would transmit the call over its network and would return it to the local telephone system at the call's destination for a fraction of what AT&T charged to transmit the same call, since AT&T's prices included local rate support.

The SCCs provided non-telephone company networks of telecommunications services (video, voice, or data). By avoiding low-usage markets and concentrating on high-volume routes, the SCCs took advantage of economies of scale that provided opportunities for price discounting from AT&T's artificially high rates; this was dubbed cream skimming. However, there were disadvantages to using the SCCs' networks. Many of the carriers could only provide service to selected areas of the country. Furthermore, customers often had to dial as many as 26 extra digits when making a long-distance call through an SCC. These conditions were expected to improve after the divestiture as the new carriers expanded their service areas and the BOCs improved the connection to the SCCs. These changes meant that SCC customers would have to dial, at most, four additional digits.

Despite the apparent weaknesses in the level of service that the SCCs provided, AT&T argued that local rates would have to increase substantially if the SCCs were permitted to capture a major share of the long-distance market. Thus, many experts believed that the SCCs would ultimately be required to pay far higher access charges to keep local rates low.

Competition from SCCs had already begun to affect AT&T's position in the growing long-distance market: AT&T's share of the over $30-billion market had dropped from 99 percent in 1978 to 94 percent in 1982 and 92 percent in mid-1983. Analysts predicted that AT&T's share might fall to 65 percent within ten years. Even so, the 10 to 12 percent growth in the total long-distance market was expected to prevent a significant drop in the corporation's revenues.

In the future, SCCs were expected to diversify into other communications media and networks, such as satellites and data transmission. Presently, 80 percent of all communications were voice and just 20 percent were data. While AT&T's network carried most data transmission, primarily owing to its universal availability, the principal transmission mode was analog, a medium not particularly well-suited for digital data transmission. Digital data transmitted via phone lines had to be converted, or modulated, to analog form and then demodulated back into digital form at the receiving end. One of the major changes noticeable after the divestiture would be the long-awaited digital conversion of the remainder of AT&T's long-distance network.

The Terminal Equipment Marketplace.

After 1968, many firms manufactured, marketed, and serviced equipment designed to terminate a telephone line on the customer's premises. Equipment, in addition to the most common product—telephones—included modems, which enabled a computer terminal to communicate via telephone to another computer; key telephone sets (KTS), a small telephone switch used by businesses with few phone lines; and private branch exchanges (PBXs), larger telephone switches used by businesses with a substantial number of lines and telephone sets.

The largest and most important part of the equipment business was the PBX market, expected to reach $6 billion by 1986. The PBX, originally designed as an automated replacement for the traditional switchboard, routed signals for voice and data transmissions. PBX suppliers depended on market penetration in hopes of becoming entrenched in the customer's equipment base. Because of its central position in the on-site telecommunications system, many experts considered the PBX market to be the most critical. "He who controls the switch controls the customer,"[13] noted an industry consultant. (See the diagram shown in Exhibit 2.)

AT&T's Western Electric subsidiary provided equipment for approximately 30 percent of the business market and 70 percent of the residential market. The huge manufacturer, whose sales to AT&T subsidiaries represented over 80 percent of the entire equipment market in 1982, had traditionally supplied transmission and switching gear and other types of equipment to the local operating companies. Since the divestiture would allow the BOCs to do business with other suppliers, some expected AT&T's share of the equipment market to decline. They based their claim on the fact that Western Electric's share of the business PBX market (shown in the following table) had fallen from around 75 percent in the early 1970s to 33 percent by 1983, and the fact that several of the BOCs had already signed long-term supply contracts with AT&T competitors. On the other hand, many believed that the long and close ties between the BOCs and their original supplier would not be quickly severed.

Western Electric's Share of Installed PBX Market

1978	1979	1980	1981	1982	1983 (Est.)
57%	51%	46%	39%	38%	33%

Source: Eastern Management Group.

The Information Processing Market—The Major Uncertainty Facing the "New" AT&T.
Just as regulation accounted for the principal risks that had faced the old AT&T, divestiture and the resulting entry of AT&T into new, unregulated markets were changing the basic nature of the corporation's risk. Most observers thought that information processing, the largest and most competitive segment within the industry, would be the principal target of AT&T's unregulated units. During the past decade, the emphasis on improving white-collar productivity had led to the office automation explosion. Over the next five years, office automation manufacturers were estimated to ship approximately $118 billion worth of equipment. The spectacular growth prospects of this segment were a major determinant in AT&T's ultimate decision to divest the operating company assets. Without the ability to compete in unregulated markets, AT&T would have been effectively locked out of this market, which was so closely tied in to many of its established product areas.

Like those in the mainframe computer business, participants in the information processing and storage business relied on successful market penetration, hoping to get a large installed product base. Their well-trained sales force would then push high-margin items (such as peripherals, software, and service con-

---

[13]Brian O'Reilly, "A Bell System Stepchild Cuts Loose," *Fortune*, November 14, 1983, 110.

tracts) for the customers' networks, thereby increasing the cost of switching to another supplier's products. An article in *Datamation* used IBM to describe this phenomenon:

> The more IBM applications that are put up on a system, the more terminals, memory and CPU's IBM sells; the more computing power and terminals there are, the more software and services IBM sells, and so on.[14]

AT&T would have to play catch-up in order to become a significant participant within this segment. "To be important in office automation," noted a leading communications securities analyst in a recent *Fortune* article, "you need data processing, telecommunications, word processing, and imaging. AT&T has only one of those strengths."[15] Furthermore, none of the main competitors within the segment was significantly involved in any regulated business activity—a distinct disadvantage for AT&T, still dependent on regulated (long-distance) activities for a sizable portion of its income.

The major problem facing the new AT&T was the lack of marketable products for this segment. AT&T had the year before internally introduced a minicomputer that many thought was comparable to Digital Equipment's top-of-the-line model, and some experts believed AT&T had already developed suitable products and was waiting for the right moment. Others were more skeptical, believing that the decade-long product-development cycle typical of the past would continue to plague the corporation as it entered new markets that demanded suppliers to be nimble.

AT&T'S COST OF CAPITAL

As a regulated monopoly, AT&T's allowed rate of return had been partly based on its cost of capital, which over the years its staff of financial analysts had developed considerable expertise in calculating. Dividends, stock price data, betas, price/earnings ratios, growth rates, and the market price of risk figured prominently in estimating the corporation's cost of capital. Analysts typically used the kind of data found in Exhibits 3 through 8 for estimating the costs of debt and equity for AT&T.

In an earlier rate-relief case involving AT&T, the FCC had outlined the following guiding principles for establishing a rate of return for companies under its jurisdiction.

> Generally, the rate of return should be sufficient to enable a utility to maintain its credit and cover the cost of capital already committed to the enterprise as well as to attract additional capital. . . . A return which is too low could impair the ability of a utility to raise additional capital, thus imperiling the integrity of existing investment, with adverse effects on the quality of service. A return which is set too high results in charges to the ratepayer above the just and reasonable level.[16]

---

[14]Jan Johnson, "Strategies in the Services Realm," *Datamation,* January 1983, 27.
[15]Steven Flax, "The Orphan Called Baby Bell," *Fortune,* June 27, 1983, 88.
[16]AT&T, 9 FCC 2nd at 51–52.

Determining a cost of equity for AT&T had always been a struggle. With the divestiture just six months away, the securities markets were treating AT&T much differently than they had in the past, making the estimation of AT&T's cost of equity and capital even more difficult than before. AT&T had always been the conservative investment with which the relative price volatility of other firms' securities could be compared. However, the uncertainty surrounding the divestiture had changed all that. How risky was AT&T, and what was its corporate cost of capital early in the summer of 1983—six months before the divestiture?

American Telephone & Telegraph (A)

EXHIBIT 1
■

The Ten Largest Utilities in 1982
(ranked by assets, dollars in thousands)

As They Were		As They Would Be after Divestiture	
AT&T	$148,185,500	AT&T	$40,487,075
GTE	22,293,550	GTE	22,293,550
Pacific Gas & Electric	13,635,318	Bell South[a]	19,692,750
Commonwealth Edison	12,582,004	NYNEX[a]	16,157,372
Southern Co.	12,301,201	Bell Atlantic[a]	15,415,400
American Electric Power	12,223,786	Ameritech[a]	15,398,460
Mid South Utilities	10,364,653	Pacific Telesis[a]	15,272,257
Southern Cal Edison	10,157,564	Southwestern Bell[a]	14,821,653
Texas Utilities	8,021,407	US West[a]	14,353,262
Public Service Electric	7,906,967	Pacific Gas & Electric	13,635,318

[a]Regional Holding Company.
Source: Carol Loomis, "Valuing the Pieces of Eight," *Fortune,* June 27, 1983, 72.

American Telephone & Telegraph (A)

EXHIBIT 2
■
A Typical Telecommunications System Configuration in 1983[a]

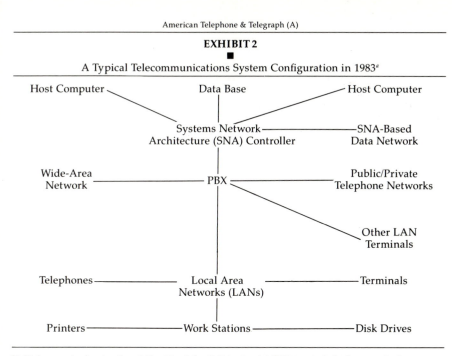

[a]A likely scenario showing the relationship of the digital voice data/PBX to a typical telecommunications system. Attached to the PBX would be all local voice, video, and data devices, all local and wide-area networks (public, private, terrestrial, and satellite), and an SNA communications controller.

American Telephone & Telegraph (A)

EXHIBIT 3
■

Statement of Income and Reinvested Earnings
(millions of dollars, except per share amounts)

| | December 31 | | | | |
	1978	1979	1980	1981	1982
Operating revenues					
Local service					
Service and equipment charges	$15,653	$16,872	$18,972	$21,728	$24,634
Message charges	1,988	2,173	2,185	2,325	2,619
Public telephones	712	779	800	862	946
Private lines	332	384	492	638	787
Long distance					
Message charges	16,325	18,231	20,083	22,233	23,357
WATS	2,745	3,176	3,724	4,488	5,565
Private lines	1,699	1,965	2,244	3,468	4,335
Directory advertising	1,881	2,288	2,652	2,913	3,623
Uncollectibles	(342)	(460)	(494)	(589)	(773)
Total operating revenues	40,993	45,408	50,658	58,066	65,093
Operating expenses					
Maintenance	8,460	9,687	10,917	12,988	14,986
Depreciation	5,540	6,130	7,040	7,900	8,735
Network and operator expenses	2,920	3,157	3,253	3,580	3,910
Marketing and customer service	2,908	3,555	4,320	5,192	6,127
Financial operations	1,092	1,237	1,547	1,671	1,882
Directory	765	855	918	1,049	1,218
Research and systems engineering	320	362	419	507	610
Pension provision	3,600	4,082	4,461	4,773	5,405
Other expenses	900	1,140	1,430	1,684	2,152
Total operating expenses	26,505	30,205	34,305	39,344	45,025
Net operating revenues	14,488	15,203	16,353	18,720	20,068
Operating taxes					
Federal	3,495	3,260	3,241	3,685	4,411
State and local	343	358	339	433	519
Property	1,678	1,626	1,723	1,846	1,949
Other	1,760	1,976	2,206	2,585	2,930
Total operating taxes	7,276	7,220	7,509	8,549	9,809
Operating income	$ 7,212	$ 7,983	$ 8,844	$10,171	$10,259

EXHIBIT 3 *continued*

	December 31				
	1978	*1979*	*1980*	*1981*	*1982*
Operating income	$ 7,212	$ 7,983	$ 8,844	$10,171	$10,258
Other income					
Western Electric	561	636	693	711	337
Construction interest	271	222	271	288	318
Miscellaneous	(81)	(83)	(72)	16	9
Total other income	751	775	892	1,015	664
Income before interest expense	7,963	8,758	9,736	11,186	10,922
Interest expense					
Long-term debt	2,346	2,610	3,055	3,608	3,867
Notes payable	227	343	505	523	416
Other	118	131	208	232	(353)
Total interest expense	2,691	3,084	3,768	4,363	3,930
Income before change in accounting principles	5,272	5,674	5,968	6,823	6,992
Cumulative effect of change in accounting principles	—	—	—	—	287
Net income	5,272	5,674	5,968	6,823	7,279
Less: preferred dividends	163	156	151	146	142
Net income to common shares	$ 5,109	$ 5,518	$ 5,817	$ 6,677	$ 7,137
Average common shares outstanding	659,843	686,109	723,516	788,178	849,550
Earnings per common share	$7.74	$8.04	$8.04	$8.47	$8.40
Dividends per common share	$4.60	$5.00	$5.00	$5.40	$5.40
Value Line beta (7/30)	0.75	0.75	0.70	0.65	0.65
Market price (high–low–close)	64–57–61	64–52–54	56–45–50	61–47–58	64–50–63
Average annual P/E	8	7	6	7	7

Sources: AT&T 1980–1982 and 1978–1982 *Annual Reports;* and *Value Line Investment Survey,* Arnold Bernhard & Co., 1978–1982, New York.

American Telephone & Telegraph (A)

EXHIBIT 4

■

Balance Sheets (millions of dollars, except per share amounts)

	December 31				
	1978	*1979*	*1980*	*1981*	*1982*
Assets					
Telephone plant (at cost)					
In service	$107,468	$117,594	$128,832	$141,419	$152,726
Under construction	3,624	4,326	4,685	5,094	5,230
Held for future use	34	30	68	51	91
	111,126	121,950	133,585	146,564	158,047
Less: accumulated depreciation	20,774	22,092	23,563	26,581	29,983
Net telephone plant	90,352	99,858	110,022	119,983	128,064
Investments					
At equity					
Western Electric	3,512	4,021	4,449	4,991	4,757
Other	376	427	569	564	662
At cost	154	240	315	322	307
Total investments	4,042	4,688	5,333	5,877	5,726
Current assets					
Cash	317	307	268	283	138
Marketable securities	1,656	1,119	1,273	1,776	2,970
	1,973	1,426	1,541	2,059	3,108
Less: drafts outstanding	552	564	541	796	654
Net cash and marketable securities	1,421	862	1,000	1,263	2,454
Receivables					
Customers and agents	4,963	5,507	6,211	7,418	8,067
Other	452	496	725	651	815
Less: uncollectibles	131	170	206	238	302
Net receivables	5,284	5,833	6,730	7,831	8,580
Materials and supplies	775	907	972	1,172	1,179
Prepaid expenses	176	178	203	227	246
Total current assets	7,656	7,780	8,905	10,492	12,459
Deferred charges	1,277	1,142	1,295	1,397	1,938
Total assets	$103,327	$113,768	$125,555	$137,750	$148,186

EXHIBIT 4 *continued*

	December 31				
	1978	*1979*	*1980*	*1981*	*1982*
Equity, Liabilities, and Deferred Credits					
Common shareowners' equity ($16.67 par value)	$ 11,159	$ 11,689	$ 12,580	$ 13,585	$ 14,940
Paid-in capital	9,687	10,942	12,704	14,929	18,084
Reinvested earnings	19,772	21,857	24,037	26,521	28,889
Total common equity	40,618	44,488	49,321	55,035	61,913
Convertible $4 preferred shares	501	432	385	336	301
Redeemable preferred shares	1,600	1,588	1,575	1,563	1,550
Investments in subsidiaries					
Shareholders' equity	981	1,063	394	416	—
Preferred shares	417	500	553	553	536
	1,398	1,563	947	969	536
Total shareowners' equity	44,117	48,071	52,228	57,903	64,300
Long-term debt	34,501	37,495	41,255	43,877	44,105
Current liabilities					
Accounts payable to unconsolidated subsidiaries	974	1,132	1,184	1,330	1,340
Payrolls	432	493	550	632	696
Others	1,587	1,630	1,787	1,829	2,929
Debt maturing within one year	3,772	4,106	4,342	4,019	3,045
Taxes accrued	1,353	1,058	1,215	1,575	1,669
Advance billings	955	1,088	1,279	1,477	1,668
Dividends payable	831	936	984	1,146	1,223
Interest accrued	735	850	995	1,094	1,127
California rate order taxes	1,005	1,304	1,423	1,620	—
Total current liabilities	11,644	12,597	13,759	14,722	13,697
Deferred credits					
Accumulated deferred taxes	9,051	10,784	12,451	14,386	18,068
Unamortized tax credits	3,841	4,613	5,574	6,543	7,590
Other	173	208	288	319	426
Total deferred credits	13,065	15,605	18,313	21,248	26,084
Total equity, liabilities, and deferred credits	$103,327	$113,768	$125,555	$137,750	$148,186

Note: Numbers may not add due to rounding.
Sources: AT&T, 1980–1982 *Annual Reports.*

American Telephone & Telegraph (A)

EXHIBIT 5

■

Amounts of Long- and Intermediate-Term
Debt by Coupon (millions of dollars)

Maturities	Coupons			Total
	2⅝%–6⅞%	7%–8⅞%	9%–17%	
1984	$ 355.0	$ 50.0	$ 150.0	$ 555.0
1985	445.0	50.0	200.0	695.0
1986	235.0	—	326.0	561.0
1987	375.0	—	—	375.0
1988–1997	3,767.0	375.0	2,534.0	6,676.0
1998–2007	825.0	5,423.1	61.5	10,261.6
2008–2017	—	11,147.0	3,749.5	15,721.5
2018–2021	—	1,075.0	8,570.0	9,645.0
Total	$10,779.0	$18,120.1	$15,591.0	$44,490.1

Source: AT&T, 1982 *Annual Report.*

American Telephone & Telegraph (A)

EXHIBIT 6

■

AT&T Forecasts As If Divestiture Did Not Occur

	1983	1984	1986–1988
Revenues (millions)	$ 70,000	$ 76,000	$ 95,000
Net profit (millions)	1,680[a]	7,550	9,900
Net plant (millions)	134,000	142,000	170,000
Capitalization (millions)	106,500	111,000	153,000
Common shares outstanding (millions)	930	960	1,100
Capital spending per share	18.00	20.00	22.00
Earnings per share	1.70[a]	7.75	9.00
Dividends per share	5.40	5.40	5.40
Cash flow per share	12.20	19.15	22.00
Book value per share	65.00	67.40	81.80
Income tax rate	30%	37%	40%
Net profit margin	2.4	10.0	10.4
Long-term debt ratio	41.5	40.5	41.0
Common equity ratio	57.0	58.0	58.0
Return on common equity	2.5	11.5	11.0
Return on capital	3.5	10.5	10.4

[a]Adjusted for extraordinary $5.50 per share write-down of book value.
Source: *Value Line Investment Survey,* October 28, 1983.

EXHIBIT 7
■
Comparison of Yields

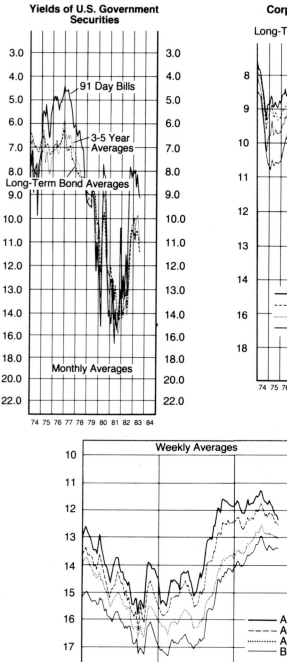

Yields of U.S. Government Securities

91 Day Bills

3-5 Year Averages

Long-Term Bond Averages

Monthly Averages

74 75 76 77 78 79 80 81 82 83 84

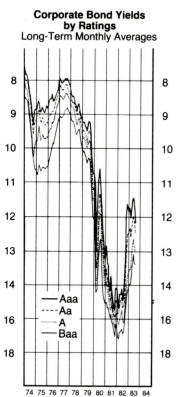

Corporate Bond Yields by Ratings
Long-Term Monthly Averages

Aaa
Aa
A
Baa

74 75 76 77 78 79 80 81 82 83 84

Weekly Averages

Aaa
Aa
A
Bbb

J F M A M J J A S O N D J F M A M J J A S O N D J F M A M J J A S O N D

1981   1982   1983

EXHIBIT 8

■

AT&T Betas

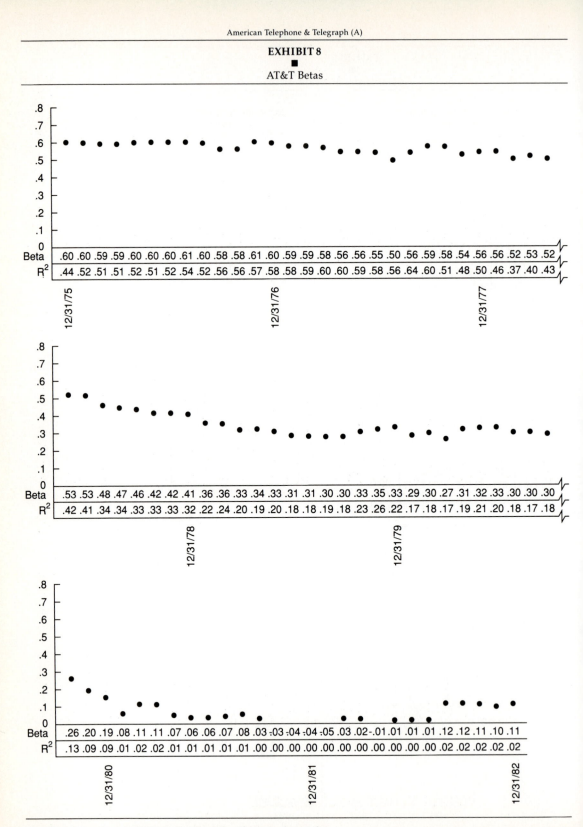

Note: These betas were each calculated using 36 months of total rate-of-return data.

American Telephone & Telegraph (B)

Since the terms of the American Telephone & Telegraph (AT&T) divestiture had been announced [for details see AT&T (A)], analysts and investors alike had been poring over articles for information on what would happen to their holdings. Of particular concern were the value and the riskiness of each of the eight pieces to be divested. For the shareholder considering what to do with the various pieces of AT&T stock that he or she owned in mid-1983, the question was significant. For AT&T, which would be making substantial investments in some of these businesses over the next few years, it was critical to have an estimate of the returns that could be expected from each of these investments.

Estimating a corporate cost of capital for any company was difficult. For AT&T the only clear consensus thus far was that each of the pieces had differing levels of risk. Because there was so much uncertainty, some believed it might be easier to estimate required rates of return (hurdle rates) for each of the eight pieces and then combine the individual rates to arrive at an estimate for AT&T's corporate cost of capital. Although in the summer of 1983 there was considerable speculation about some of the pieces (such as AT&T Technologies, the unregulated portion of the "new" AT&T), more information was available for some of the units (such as Southwestern Bell, the only regional holding company formed from just one Bell operating company). Using this information [and that contained in American Telephone & Telegraph (A)], one could estimate a cost of capital for such segments as AT&T Technologies and Southwestern Bell.

AT&T TECHNOLOGIES

AT&T Technologies (AT&TT), part of which was originally chartered in April 1980 as American Bell, was the unregulated side of the "new" AT&T. After the divestiture, AT&TT would be responsible for designing, manufacturing, marketing, selling, and distributing telecommunications equipment and services to its business, residential, and government customers through seven divisions (see Overview). In addition, AT&TT was scheduled to take ownership of the installed phones and other equipment previously owned by the local telephone compa-

This case as prepared as a basis for class discussion rather than to illustrate either effective or ineffective handling of an administrative situation. Copyright © 1983 by the Darden Graduate Business School Sponsors, University of Virginia, Charlottesville, Virginia.

nies. Despite the fact that this wealth of equipment, valued at $8.5 billion, could be rented, leased, or sold to the customer, industry analysts estimated that near-term losses for several of AT&TT's divisions could exceed $500 million.

Overview of AT&T Technologies' Lines of Business

Business Sector	1984 Revenue (estimated billions of dollars)	Estimated Growth Rate, 1984–1987	Products/Services	Employees
AT&T Information Systems	$ 8.3	5–10%	Business communications systems	110,000
AT&T Consumer Products	2.6	(5)– 5%	Residential equipment	45,000
AT&T Network Systems	6.6	5–10%	Transmission and switching equipment	80,000
Components	0.3	0–10%	Electronic components	15,000
Processors	0.1	100%	Mini- and microcomputers	2,000
Government	0.6	20–50%	Defense electrical and government services	3,000
AT&T International	0.4	25%	Overseas sales of network system	2,000
Total	$18.9	8–10%		377,000

Source: "The 'New' AT&T," Cowen & Co., Institutional Services Research Dept. Report, October 1983.

Within AT&TT's new organizational structure, designed to enhance the synergies between the corporation's unregulated activities, the two largest divisions were expected immediately to account for over 80 percent of AT&TT's post-divestiture revenues. Analysts examining AT&T's post-divestiture competitive capabilities faced big questions about these relatively unproven divisions, AT&T Information Systems and AT&T Network Systems. Little was known about their ability to develop, build, and sell products for a demanding and unpredictable marketplace. Furthermore, the formation of the new divisions caused a great deal of employee displacement from the original corporation's structure. The true impact of this massive physical and cultural change was an unknown that would, like so many other uncertainties surrounding the new corporation, remain unanswered for some time to come. (Pro forma financial projections for the "new" AT&T are shown in Exhibit 1.)

Competitive Position.   The environment in which AT&T Information Systems and AT&T Network Systems would be competing was going through a transformation of its own. As a result of the divestiture and the rapid advances in product technology, competition within the marketplace for strategic position was fierce. Consumers in both the business and residential markets were overwhelmed with what seemed to be a never-ending stream of media pieces, eye-catching ads, and new product choices. Instead of the limited marketing opportunities caused by regulation and AT&T's tight grip on the industry, the divestiture had contributed significantly to the vigorous development of two areas of concentrated activity in which AT&T Technologies would be involved: telecommunications equipment and information processing and storage.

Only a handful of the larger, vertically integrated companies with positions in transmission equipment manufacturing and information processing, such as

AT&T, GTE, and IBM, would be able to compete effectively in both of these segments as well as in the traditional voice and data-transmission segments. As a result, the companies that many experts believed would give AT&TT its biggest challenges were small, aggressive corporations that served narrower market segments. "We don't believe it's our lot in life to go into competition with the AT&Ts or the IBMs of the world," said Paul Henson, chairman of United Tele-communications, Inc. "We are selecting what we consider to be fairly well de-fined market niches."[1]

The key to success in this post-divestiture maze, according to the head of corporate planning for Southern New England Telephone, "[would be] identify-ing the functions needed, where they [were] needed, and then designing sys-tems, at the right price, to meet those needs."[2] Furthermore, noted a leading industry analyst, "the [successful] companies will need distribution, marketing, and development. These are traditional disciplines needed for success, but are skills nobody [in telecommunications] needed before."[3]

AT&T Network Systems—Telecommunications Equipment.

For many years, AT&T's hold on this segment of the telecommunications indus-try had been guaranteed by its monopolistic grip on its telephone network. Western Electric, its huge manufacturing subsidiary, had supplied over 80 per-cent of the nation's telecommunications equipment needs. However, after the FCC decision in 1968 to open this market to competition, new suppliers began seriously threatening the market. At the heart of the telecommunications equip-ment segment was the large-scale PBX market, the largest and most strategically important piece of hardware within a customer's system. Since the PBX was, in fact, the heart of a large telecommunications system, the manufacturer who sold a customer a large PBX often received a large share of follow-up business because of the close technical and service relationships already established with the customer.

Rolm, Western Electric's main competition within this segment before the divestiture, was the world's second largest manufacturer of digital PBXs. Now, AT&T Network Systems, the new AT&T's entrant into this segment, was charged with the same task of competing with this formidable opponent. "Of the nation's 23 largest corporations, 22 [were] Rolm customers."[4] Rolm, one of the dream stories to come out of California's Silicon Valley, was not about to take previous market triumphs sitting down. Aware of the limitations of selling a low sales–turnover product such as a PBX, they had intensified their efforts to add some-thing extra to their PBX business, such as office products.

Other competitors would also be fighting for a piece of this multibillion-dollar market. Northern Telecom, a Canadian equipment manufacturer, expected to be a serious contender for the equipment sales to operating companies. They had been very successful the past year ($300 million in sales) in penetrating the previously closed local operating company market. Other contenders included Mitel, another Canadian-based supplier, whose PBX equipment sales repre-

---

[1]"Telecommunications—Everybody's Favorite Growth Business," *Business Week*, October 11, 1982, 63.
[2]Ibid., 62.
[3]Ibid., 63.
[4]Edward Yasaki, "Rolm—Voicing its Data Desires," *Datamation*, January 1983, 58.

sented 90 percent of their 1982 sales, and Harris, a producer of highly sophisticated telecommunications and information-processing equipment.

	1982 PBX Shipments
Supplier	*Share of 1982 Shipments*
AT&T	37%
Northern Telecom	16
Rolm	14
Mitel	15
Nippon Electric (NEC)	4
Others	14

Source: International Data Corporation.

While no one competitor was strong in all segments of the PBX market, Northern Telecom and Rolm both were powerful in the large PBX market, and Mitel dominated the small PBX market. Future success within this segment would most likely go to the suppliers who could successfully integrate (internally or through joint ventures) their telecommunications efforts with information-processing capabilities. (Historical financial and market results for each of the competitors mentioned within the terminal equipment marketplace are shown in Exhibit 2.)

In the six months immediately prior to the divestiture, it was apparent that AT&T Network Systems was not in an ideal competitive position. Limited by an antiquated product line and its very long product-introduction cycle geared toward the corporation's historic strategy, Network Systems had a way to go before regaining its previously dominant position in the marketplace. At the heart of this problem, experts believed, was the aging market strategy that the old corporation had used for years. Basically, the strategy called for a controlled migration of customers from older switches to the newer digital switches. Without competition, the plan worked beautifully. New products, already developed for use in the marketplace, were introduced only after existing products had been fully depreciated. Unfortunately, the rise in the number of superior, competing products caused many of AT&T's customers to defect, leaving AT&T with a rapidly evaporating customer base and billions of dollars in unamortized research and development investments. While the future did look bright for AT&T Network Systems, many believed that it would take an entire product generation to regain its market dominance.

AT&T Information Systems—Information Processing and Storage.
During the previous decade, the emphasis on improving white-collar and office productivity had led to the office automation revolution. From 1983 to 1987, it was estimated that office automation manufacturers would ship over $118 billion worth of equipment, with personal computers and network systems representing the fastest areas of growth.

U.S. Office Automation Market—
Cumulative Dollar Shipments, 1983–1987

Market Segment	Share of 1983–1987 Market	Estimated Annual Growth Rate
Private branch exchanges (PBXs)	16%	7.5%
Copiers	15	(4.0)
Personal computers	42	30.0
Word processors and electronic typewriters	19	13.0
Multifunction systems and local area networks	8	40.0

Source: International Data Corporation.

In 1983, the leading supplier of office automation products was Wang Labs, whose best-selling local area network "Wangnet" had boosted the sales of its multiterminal word-processing systems to over half of their 1982 revenues and placed them in a formidable market position with a 50-percent share of installed units; IBM, with its commanding position in data processing, also had a steadily increasing share of the office market. Other competitors included Hewlett Packard, the second largest manufacturer of minicomputers in the world with a growing emphasis on business minis and desk-top personal computers, and Xerox, probably the most highly integrated supplier within the segment. Xerox offered its customers a wide array of LAN-based word processors and management work stations as part of their commitment to the office of the future. Xerox had been hindered by its overwhelming dependence on a single line; its copier line accounted for nearly 75 percent of the past year's $8.5 billion in revenues. Their office systems group had lost $120 million in 1982, and it was expected by some to lose as much as $80 million in 1983. (Historical financial and market results for each of the competitors are shown in Exhibit 3.)

Most believed the big confrontation within this segment, which included office automation products, software, and LANs, would be IBM versus AT&T. Both companies had been anticipating the bout for years, and each had taken steps to ensure that it was well-prepared for the fight. IBM had reorganized itself to capitalize on its strengths—its influence with the large mainframe corporate user, and its highly sophisticated sales force. AT&T's reorganization, by virtue of its universal market presence in homes and offices and its over 4,500 retail outlets, positioned the corporation in the very small business and consumer segment. "AT&T has a brand-name presence in every office, factory, and home in America,"[5] noted a leading securities analyst with Morgan Stanley. Most experts agreed that while it was unlikely that AT&T would ever stray into IBM's large-user market, a fierce battle would be fought for the lower and middle ground. "AT&T will attack from [its installed] communications [base], while IBM will leverage its installed computers,"[6] concluded one researcher.

In spite of its position as the apparent underdog within this segment, AT&T appeared to want to participate in most, if not all, areas of information

---

[5]"The Odds in a Bell–IBM Fight," *Business Week*, January 25, 1983, 83.
[6]Ibid.

processing. John Malone, a former AT&T manager turned consultant, theorized, "[AT&T] may not want to capture a major market position [in all areas of office automation], but they definitely have ambitions of providing full-system solutions for meeting the needs of the office."[7]

The Consumer Products division faced less technological uncertainty than did the other major divisions with AT&T Technologies. This would be the world of the low-variable-cost producer of integrated, interactive systems for the home. Through AT&T's traditional market strength in the retail segment, it had targeted the residential and small business end of the market—historically, a weakness of most of the other telecommunications suppliers. By the end of 1983, the division hoped to have 5,000 retail outlets. These included 461 Phone Center stores and over 1,200 Sears, Bradlees, and True Value Hardware store outlets.

Uncertainties Facing AT&T Technologies.   The major uncertainty facing every division within AT&T Technologies was its sales force, which was having difficulty adapting to the new environment. "They are still marketing under the old concept which is 'We're the only one on the block and you've got to do business with us.' "[8] The lack of expertise in this area was not a surprise to some: "It will take years for AT&T to develop the marketing experience IBM has."[9]

Efforts had been made to improve the poor initial showing of the divisions' sales forces. "We're training our people in what problem-solving is all about and putting in support systems designed toward that focus,"[10] said the president of an AT&T subsidiary's marketing and sales division. In addition to training, the sales force had tried to learn from its previous mistakes. "When we lose a sale, we do a review to figure out why. It's like combat—you analyze the other guy's offerings and see what he's using to beat us,"[11] said the chairman of AT&T Information Systems.

The new products in development were creating the most excitement and apprehension at all the divisions within AT&T Technologies. "We didn't go through this agonizing legal process to provide the same capability," said the vice president for market development at Western Electric, the manufacturing arm of AT&TT. "We did it because we wanted to get into new and exciting businesses."[12] With the combination of its sales force and the talented team of Western Electric and Bell Labs, both parts of AT&TT, most believed that AT&T possessed "all the elements of a successful entry into the computer business."[13] There were indications that the corporation had several personal-computer products ready for introduction but was waiting for the right moment. However, questions still remained: "most [AT&T] employees don't understand the concept of risk analysis as it applies to a competitive marketplace. They have always been in a win/win situation,"[14] noted an ex-AT&T manager. Nonetheless, competitors still had a great deal of respect for AT&T. "Anyone who discounts AT&T and

---

[7]Jan Johnson, "Strategies in the Services Realm," *Datamation*, January 1983, 28.

[8]Ibid.

[9]"The Odds in a Bell–IBM Bout," *Business Week*, January 25, 1982, 23.

[10]"Changing Phone Habits," *Business Week*, September 5, 1983, 70.

[11]Ibid., 71.

[12]Ibid.

[13]Ibid.

[14]Jan Johnson, "Strategies in the Services Realm," *Datamation*, January 1983, 30.

Western Electric is crazy,"[15] said the president of Southern New England Telephone.

THE REGIONAL HOLDING COMPANIES

As a result of the divestiture agreement, AT&T would spin off its 22 Bell Operating Companies, representing about 75 percent of the corporation's assets, to form seven regional holding companies (RHCs). These RHCs would continue to provide regulated telephone services in addition to other services that would be out from under the watchful eyes of the regulators.

Part of the divestiture agreement specified that the RHCs would be spun off in "sound financial condition." As a result, they would all have debt/capital ratios of approximately 45 percent. Even though this debt level would compare favorably with similar utilities, Standard & Poor's and Moody's had expressed doubts about the RHCs maintaining the AAA bond ratings that most of the Bell Operating Companies had previously enjoyed. Exhibit 4 provides other financial estimates for the seven RHCs.

There were indications that the new operating companies, still driven largely by financial, not operating, risks, would need far less outside financing than had their parent company. Recent changes made it possible for the local companies to adopt faster depreciation schedules, which could generate enough cash to permit dramatically reduced external funding. For example, Pacific Telephone, considered one of the financially weakest operating companies, funded 70 percent of its capital investment needs internally in 1982, up from 45 percent in 1980.

Sample RHC Balance Sheet, January 1, 1984

Assets		Liabilities and Equity	
Current assets	$ 1,875	Current liabilities	$ 1,500
Other assets	525	Long-term debt	4,900
Telephone plant	13,300	Common equity	6,200
		Other liabilities	3,100
Total assets	$15,700	Total liabilities and equity	$15,700

Debt ratio: 4,900/(4,900 + 6,200) = 44.9%

Source: Adaptation of Lehman Brothers, Kuhn Loeb Research Department estimate.

Most analysts expected the securities marketplace to view the RHCs as "moderately attractive income vehicles, [treating] them as utilities, judging each company by earnings, dividends, regulation, attractiveness of service area, and financial status."[16] What would differentiate the individual companies would be how they managed the resources at their disposal. (Exhibit 4 contains estimates

---

[15]"Changing Phone Habits," *Business Week*, September 5, 1983, 71.
[16]"AT&T," Merrill Lynch Research Department Report, June 23, 1983.

of 1984 financial performance for each of the seven RHCs, while Exhibits 5 and 6 contain financial data for selected competitors and the telephone industry.)

Changes Brought about by the Divestiture.

As a result of the divestiture agreement, customers would begin to see immediately many changes that otherwise might have taken years. The most dramatic of these would be the switch to what was called *usage sensitive pricing*—charging separately for customer access and usage. The prices of local calls, part of what had been subsidized by interstate-call revenues, would be determined on the basis of duration, distance, and time of day. Access charges that more closely approximated the true cost of providing local service would be implemented so that incentives for other carriers to bypass telephone company services would be eliminated. Currently, "without measured service, a computer user can tie up a [local] phone line for hours—without paying one cent more than a customer making a three-minute call."[17]

Another major change would be the modernization of the operating company's equipment. The assets to be received from AT&T as part of the agreement were the oldest in the corporation's asset base. "The most modern pieces of equipment are in the long-haul segment, where the highest traffic is,"[18] noted an industry expert. In order to prepare for equal access and competition, the RHCs would be installing such new equipment as computerized switching gear, optical fiber networks, and digital switches.

The trend toward digital switching of calls would be likely to have the greatest impact on the local networks. More than half of the trunk lines in metropolitan areas were digital in 1983. Digital switching would enable local phone company networks to participate to a much greater extent in the growing data transmission business by allowing both data and voice signals to be more efficiently carried along the same network. "The home information age is going to dawn on us soon, and the more usage [of local phone lines for carrying data], the higher our profits."[19] By 1990, 90 percent of all trunk lines were expected to be digital.

Competitive Characteristics of the Seven RHCs.

Each of the seven new operating companies was likely to emerge "as the leading supplier of local communications services in their region."[20] Many experts believed that the RHCs would be in advantageous positions as they entered the telecommunications industry on their own. With more than 182 million telephones installed, they had direct access to nearly 80 percent of the nation's telephone users. The RHCs would function as the gateway to the customer by distributing a variety of communications equipment and services. All suppliers would have to rely on the local operating company's network for the final connection to the customer. Therefore, the RHCs would profit not only from the services they provided, but also from those of other vendors.

In addition to being the local distributors of equipment and services, the RHCs would be able to share in the growth of long-distance services through

---

[17]"Changing Phone Habits," *Business Week*, September 5, 1983, 72.
[18]"The Operating Companies' Strategy for Survival," *Business Week*, October 11, 1982, 70.
[19]"What the Spinoff Will Mean to the Customer," *Business Week*, September 5, 1983, 71.
[20]Ibid.

access charges. Furthermore, their extensive billing and collection system could be marketed to long-distance and equipment vendors.

The RHCs would also play a major role in providing cellular mobile phone service. Cellular telephone service

> is composed of cell sites [served by transmitters connected to] a mobile telephone switching office, and [the] subscriber's mobile equipment. . . . Each cell site serves [an area] 2–10 miles wide and is designated a set of frequencies allowing multiple re-use of each channel for many different simultaneous conversations in any given area. When a user places a call, the closest transmitter relays it to the mobile telephone switching office which connects it to the local telephone system. When the caller moves from one cell to another, the switching center [transfers the call to] the next cell.[21]

Cellular service was expected to be a significant revenue source for the local companies in the future. Although development thus far had been primarily in the vehicular phone segment of the market, cellular technology had the potential of being the voice and data transmission medium for the traveling business person. The Federal Communications Commission regulated this industry and had begun to issue licenses. The RHC's formidable positions worried many cellular market hopefuls such as MCI and Western Union.

The divestiture agreement also allowed the operating companies the opportunity of broadening the scope of their businesses beyond regulated local services. While the concept of allowing regulated utilities to compete in unregulated markets had been encouraged by many economists as a means of maintaining rate levels, permission by the courts would be required. Many experts believed that the new RHCs, because of their established local presence, could become AT&T's biggest competitors in the business communications market.

Uncertainties Facing the RHCs.
"The break-up will force a dizzying array of decisions. Many customers will receive as many as three phone bills—one for long distance, another for local calls, and a third for equipment rental and repair."[22] Despite their dominant positions as the leading suppliers of local telecommunications services, the operating companies faced the challenge of establishing their new corporate identities with their customers who were used to writing just one check a month for their telephone services. Many experts thought this task would be toughened by the fact that many competitors, eager to capitalize on the confusion brought about by the divestiture, were attempting to accomplish the same thing.

The biggest hurdle that many observers believed lay ahead for the new operating companies was providing consumers with reasonably priced quality phone service without the benefits of long-distance subsidies. If local phone rates failed to keep pace with higher costs, new investment could decline and the level of service could deteriorate. At the same time, it was possible that increases in local rates could provide enough incentive for some customers, primarily those

---

[21]Standard & Poor's *1983 Industry Surveys* (New York: Standard & Poor's Corp., © 1983), T–21.
[22]"The Bell Breakup," *US News & World Report,* October 24, 1983, 55.

involved in data transmission, to find lower-cost alternative services. For example, the New York Stock Exchange had tested a microwave-based system designed to transmit transaction data between the exchange and its data-processing facility. Advances in technology in the future could eventually permit even the smallest of users to develop alternative methods of communication transmission.

Southwestern Bell.

Southwestern Bell, the only operating company to go through the divestiture intact, served a five-state region made up of Texas, Arkansas, Kansas, Oklahoma, and Missouri. Zane Barnes, Southwestern's president and CEO and head of Southwestern for the past decade, earned the distinction of being the only RHC chief executive that analysts thought had significant experience running an operating company.

The territory Southwestern served contained some of the fastest-growing regions in the country. "In 1980, for the first time in the history of the United States, more Americans were living in the South and West than in the North and East."[23] Furthermore, two of the ten cities that possessed the greatest growth opportunities for the next decade, San Antonio and Austin, were served by Southwestern Bell.

Southwestern Bell not only had spectacular growth prospects, but state regulators in the region seemed to be well aware of the need for healthy, periodic rate increases in order to allow utilities continued access to sources of capital. "We have to allow Southwestern [Bell] to be competitive in the financial markets with NYNEX and US West"[24] (two other RHCs), said the chairman of the Texas Public Utilities Commission. However, the region that Southwestern served was considered one of the two toughest regulatory challenges facing any of the RHCs. Because of the loss of a large share of long-distance revenue, Southwestern had the unpleasant task of generating compensating funds through rate increases in what had proved to be a fairly hostile regulatory climate at times. Analysts examining 1984 forecasts had pointed out that $3.4 billion of Southwestern's total $7.8 billion in revenues was expected to come from rate increases currently pending. Any shortfall from this figure would have a serious impact on Southwestern's 1984 performance.

Southwestern had issued debt securities in early 1983. The assignment of an A2 rating by Moody's and a AA rating by Standard & Poor's indicated the rating services' belief that the questions facing Southwestern added too much uncertainty for its highest ratings. Financial and market information on publicly traded telephone companies is in Exhibits 5 and 6.

Top managers at Southwestern were actively examining the possibilities of entering nonregulated markets as soon as possible. "We want to be there when office automation explodes,"[25] said their vice president of strategic planning. Entry into unregulated markets could prove to be extremely important for the RHCs. "There is no part of the divested BOC revenue stream that is not subject to competition,"[26] conceded a member of a special AT&T task force that completed an RHC marketing plan before the divestiture agreement was signed.

---

[23]John Naisbit, *Megatrends* (New York: Warner Books, 1982).
[24]"What the Spinoff Will Mean to the Customer," *Business Week*, September 5, 1983, 71.
[25]Ibid.
[26]"The Operating Companies' Strategy for Survival," *Business Week*, October 11, 1982, 70.

COST OF CAPITAL

Normally, the process of arriving at an estimate for the cost of capital for an established company or division involved examining historical financial statements, market returns, future projections, and estimates of the levels of risk associated with the enterprise. Complicating the cases of AT&T Technologies and Southwestern Bell were the facts that neither was publicly traded and little historical information that could be applied to their new competitive status was available in the year immediately preceding the divestiture. Adding to the difficulty of the situation was the almost overwhelming complexity of the dynamic environment in which they would be competing. Nevertheless, projected levels of risk and cost of capital estimates were of significant importance to both internal analysts, external investors, and regulators.

How risky were AT&T Technologies and Southwestern Bell, and what were their respective costs of capital early in the summer of 1983—six months before the divestiture?

American Telephone & Telegraph (B)

EXHIBIT 1
■

Estimated AT&T Consolidated Income Statement
(millions of dollars, except per share amounts)

	1981R	1982R	1983E	1984P	1985P
AT&T Communications					
Revenues					
Interstate					
Toll	$12,145	$13,203	$15,051	$17,346	$18,250
WATS	2,992	3,252	4,520	6,284	7,810
Private line	2,464	2,679	3,394	3,840	4,800
Intrastate	5,408	5,926	6,495	7,188	7,801
International	1,820	1,770	1,800	1,850	1,940
Total revenues	$24,829	$26,830	$31,260	$36,472	$40,601
Operating profit	$ 7,449	$ 8,049	$ 9,378	$10,942	$12,180
AT&T Technologies					
Revenues					
AT&T Information Systems	$ 6,820	$ 7,500	$ 8,002	$ 8,270	$ 8,340
AT&T Consumer Products	2,510	2,525	2,575	2,630	2,680
AT&T Network Systems	6,087	6,313	6,283	6,620	7,101
Components	0	0	0	310	320
Processors	0	0	5	37	63
Government systems	325	374	467	584	730
AT&T International	50	100	200	400	500
Total revenues	$15,792	$16,812	$17,532	$18,851	$19,733
Operating profit	$ 714	$ 650	$ 244	$ 717	$ 1,141
Total revenues	$40,621	$43,642	$48,792	$55,323	$60,334
Operating profit	8,163	8,699	9,622	11,658	13,322
Corporate expense	3,772	4,010	5,130	6,036	6,733
Interest expense	800	700	800	900	1,000
Pre-tax income	3,591	3,989	3,692	4,722	5,589
Tax rate	40%	40%	40%	40%	40%
Net income	$ 2,155	$ 2,393	$ 2,215	$ 2,833	$ 3,353
Shares outstanding (millions)	788	850	933	950	1,000
Earnings per share	$2.73	$2.82	$2.37	$2.98	$3.35

R = revised, E = estimated, P = preliminary.
Source: Adapted from "The New AT&T: A Framework for Analysis," Cowen & Co. Institutional Services Research Report, October 1983.

American Telephone & Telegraph (B)

EXHIBIT 2
■
Selected Terminal Equipment Suppliers' Performance, 1979–1982

Company and Year	Primary EPS	Dividend/ Share	Book Value/ Share	Market Price High–Low–Close	Average Annual P/E	Long-Term Debt/Capital[a]	Net Income/ Revenue	Return on Equity
Rolm (Value Line Beta at 7/29/83: 1.35)								
1979	$0.75	N.Ap.	$ 1.90	$23–10–21	22	18.9%	9.9%	52.3%
1980	1.09	N.Ap.	3.22	50–17–47	31	34.2	8.6	43.5
1981	1.39	N.Ap.	7.07	50–25–32	27	22.4	8.1	26.8
1982	1.70	N.Ap.	9.10	55–20–23	22	18.0	7.8	21.0
Northern Telecom (Value Line Beta at 7/29/83: 1.15)								
1979	1.06	0.24	6.88	15–10–14	12	15.8	6.0	14.0
1980	(0.18)	0.28	5.71	16– 8–10	N.Av.	28.0	N.Av.	N.Av.
1981	0.98	0.27	6.65	17– 9–16	13	20.7	4.7	15.2
1982	1.17	0.26	7.48	24–10–23	15	18.3	5.0	15.9
Mitel (Value Line Beta at 7/29/83: 0.95)								
1979	0.16	N.Ap.	0.69	N.Av.	N.Av.	14.6	12.8	32.4
1980	0.44	N.Ap.	1.49	26– 5–25	35	21.4	15.5	39.0
1981	0.77	N.Ap.	5.52	41–18–30	36	11.0	16.8	21.3
1982	0.32	N.Ap.	5.94	30–12–30	60	39.9	5.8	5.6
Harris Corp. (Value Line Beta at 7/29/83: 1.10)								
1979	2.45	0.60	12.95	34–25–34	12	20.7	6.4	19.8
1980	2.63	0.72	14.25	56–27–56	16	28.2	6.1	18.6
1981	3.37	0.80	17.22	60–37–44	15	23.5	6.7	20.4
1982	2.42	0.88	18.44	41–20–41	12	22.8	4.4	13.1

N.Ap. = not applicable; N.Av. = not available
[a] At book value.
Source: Standard & Poor's NYSE Stock Reports, July 20, 1983, © 1983. Standard & Poor's Corp., New York; and Value Line Investment Survey, New York: Arnold Bernhard & Co., Inc., © 1983.

American Telephone & Telegraph (B)

EXHIBIT 3

■

Selected Information Processing Companies' Performance, 1979–1982

Company and Year	Primary EPS	Dividend/ Share	Book Value/ Share	Market Price High–Low–Close	Average Annual P/E	Long-Term Debt/Capital[a]	Net Income/ Revenue	Return on Equity
IBM (Value Line Beta at 8/12/83: 1.00)								
1979	$5.16	$3.44	$25.64	$80–61–64	14	9.5%	13.2%	21.2%
1980	6.10	3.44	28.18	72–50–68	10	11.2	13.6	22.7
1981	5.63	3.44	30.66	71–48–58	11	12.7	11.4	19.0
1982	7.39	3.44	33.16	98–55–96	11	12.3	12.8	22.9
Xerox (Value Line Beta at 8/12/83: 1.05)								
1979	6.69	2.40	38.29	69–52–62	9	19.2	8.0	18.4
1980	7.33	2.80	42.90	71–48–60	8	17.2	7.6	18.1
1981	7.08	3.00	44.11	64–37–41	7	16.0	6.9	16.3
1982	4.34	3.00	43.96	41–27–37	8	15.9	4.3	9.9
Wang Labs (Value Line Beta at 8/12/83: 1.65)								
1979	0.30	0.02	1.23	8– 3– 8	20	47.4	8.9	29.6
1980	0.50	0.04	1.88	22– 7–21	30	50.4	9.6	33.0
1981	0.68	0.05	3.91	23–12–14	16	33.5	9.1	22.6
1982	0.88	0.06	4.82	31–12–30	25	34.8	9.2	20.5
Hewlett Packard (Value Line Beta at 5/13/83: 1.20)								
1979	0.86	0.09	5.22	16–10–15	15	1.2	8.6	18.0
1980	1.12	0.10	6.42	24–13–24	17	1.8	8.7	19.2
1981	1.28	0.11	7.83	27–19–22	18	1.3	8.7	17.9
1982	1.53	0.12	9.37	41–18–38	19	1.5	9.0	17.8

[a]At book value.

Source: Standard & Poor's *NYSE & ASE Stock Reports*, July 20, 1983, © 1983. Standard & Poor Corp., New York; and *Value Line Investment Survey*, New

York: Arnold Bernhard & Co., © 1983.

EXHIBIT 4
■

Estimated Regional Holding Companies' Information, 1984
(billions of dollars, except as noted)

	Ameritech	Bell South	Bell Atlantic	Southwestern Bell	NYNEX	Pacific Telesis	US West
Revenues	$ 8.30	$ 9.80	$ 8.30	$ 7.80	$ 9.90	$ 8.10	$ 7.40
Net income	0.92	1.40	0.93	0.88	0.98	0.82	0.88
Earnings per share	9.47	12.21	9.69	8.93	9.54	8.00	8.96
Assets	17.00	21.50	17.10	15.00	18.70	16.00	15.00
1984 Employees, (thousands)	80	101	80	80	98	82	80
Return on capital	10.0%	11.0%	9.9%	10.1%	10.2%	9.6%	10.5%
Anticipated first quarter dividend	$ 1.50	$ 1.95	$ 1.60	$ 1.40	$ 1.50	$ 1.35	$ 1.35

Source: "Changing Phone Habits," *Business Week,* September 5, 1983, 72; and "The Breakup of AT&T," *The Wall Street Journal,* November 17, 1983, 24, 25.

EXHIBIT 5
■

Selected Telephone Companies' Performance, 1979–1982

Company and Year	Primary EPS	Dividend/ Share	Book Value/ Share	Market Price High–Low–Close	Average Annual P/E	Long-Term Debt/Capital[a]	Net Income/ Revenue	Return on Equity
Southern New England Telephone (Value Line Beta at 7/29/83: 0.65)								
1979	$5.24	$3.60	$48.78	$41–33–36	7	38.3%	9.6%	10.8%
1980	5.60	3.72	50.21	36–29–36	6	44.0	9.4	11.4
1981	7.68	4.20	53.06	47–33–46	5	41.8	10.9	14.9
1982	6.12	4.68	54.13	62–40–60	8	40.5	8.5	11.4
Cincinnati Bell (Value Line Beta at 7/29/83: 0.50)								
1979	5.16	2.42	35.22	30–27–30	6	36.0	14.0	15.2
1980	4.25	2.52	36.40	29–23–25	6	34.3	11.5	11.9
1981	4.12	2.62	37.17	28–24–28	7	37.6	10.4	11.2
1982	4.27	2.72	38.20	34–27–33	7	36.0	10.2	11.4
Centel (Value Line Beta at 7/29/83: 0.70)								
1979	3.34	1.88	20.31	28–23–25	8	43.9	11.1	16.8
1980	3.51	2.02	20.30	27–21–25	7	44.5	10.4	16.8
1981	3.89	2.12	21.60	35–23–31	8	43.8	10.2	17.6
1982	3.96	2.21	22.91	38–27–37	8	42.0	9.4	16.9
Continental Telecom (Value Line Beta at 7/29/83: 0.70)								
1979	2.15	1.33	15.13	18–14–15	7	57.2	10.7	14.6
1980	2.13	1.38	15.51	16–13–16	7	58.5	10.2	13.9
1981	2.34	1.47	16.10	19–15–18	7	55.5	9.5	14.9
1982	2.32	1.56	16.73	20–15–17	8	56.5	8.7	14.1

[a] At book value.

Source: Standard & Poor's *NYSE Stock Reports,* July 20, 1983, © 1983. Standard & Poor Corp., New York; and *Value Line Investment Survey,* New York: Arnold Bernhard & Co., Inc., © 1983.

American Telephone & Telegraph (B)

EXHIBIT 6
■

Selected Telephone Company Industry Averages, 1978–1982
(billions of dollars, except per share amounts)

	1978	1979	1980	1981	1982
Income Statement					
Sales	$53.80	$60.30	$66.30	$76.00	$85.20
Net income	6.30	6.80	7.10	8.30	8.90
Earnings/common share	6.00	6.15	6.03	6.58	6.52
Dividends/common share	3.50	3.73	3.83	3.99	4.06
Balance Sheet					
Assets	$ 130	$ 144	$ 158	$ 173	$ 187
Net plant	112	124	137	149	160
Common equity	48	52	58	64	73
Long-term debt	45	49	54	57	59
Market price (high–low)	51–45	51–41	45–36	51–38	55–39
Average annual price/earnings ratio	8	7	7	7	8

Source: *Standard & Poor's Industry Composite,* July 1983.

P A R T

4

FINANCING CAPITAL INVESTMENTS

New Hampshire

Savings Bank Corporation

After operating for over 150 years as a state-chartered mutual institution, the New Hampshire Savings Bank decided to convert to a stockholder-owned bank in 1982. A number of other mutual savings banks and mutual savings and loan institutions had completed or were planning conversions for similar reasons— increased flexibility with and access to capital. A mutual institution, owned by its depositors, could only increase its equity base through additions to retained earnings. Conversion offered the opportunity to raise capital through the sale of stock. Furthermore, being a stock corporation would facilitate the bank's execution of its plans for gradual expansion through acquisition of other banks, particularly commercial banks that were also organized as stock corporations. (The company had recently entered into an agreement to purchase all the outstanding common shares of Rockingham County Trust Company of Salem, N.H., at a purchase price of $80 per share, for a total of $3.2 million.)

The conversion, which had occurred on March 4, 1983 with a public offering, raised a question that had previously never been an issue for New Hampshire Savings Bank's management or directors: whether to pay a cash dividend, and if so, how much? The bank's president, John Hardie, who was particularly anxious to settle the matter, had made the dividend-policy issue the first item on the agenda for the August 9 meeting of the bank's board of directors.

THE THRIFT INDUSTRY

Historically, the savings and loan, or "thrift," industry had been involved in attracting savings deposits from the general public and making loans secured by first mortgage liens on residential and other real estate. A number of variables influenced the savings flows of thrifts: interest rates, personal income levels, and regulatory ceilings on interest rates payable on savings accounts along with other government policies and regulations. Lending activities had been influenced by such factors as demand for and supply of housing, conditions in the construction industry, and availability of funds. Because of its strong correlation with poten-

Copyright Professor J. Peter Williamson, Amos Tuck Graduate School of Management, Dartmouth College, Hanover, N.H., © 1984.

Note: Names of individual directors have been disguised.

tially volatile economic measures, the industry was also considered to be quite sensitive to changes in economic conditions.

The October 1979 decision by the board of governors of the Federal Reserve System to shift its focus in controlling the rate of inflation from short-term interest rates and commercial bank reserves to the rate of growth of certain monetary aggregates had a significant impact on the performance of the thrift industry. This policy change, combined with persistently high levels of inflation and interest rate volatility, had both increased the cost and reduced the availability of funds to thrifts. The recent drop in the inflation rate as a result of the economic recovery and more relaxed Federal Reserve Board policies had helped to reduce the levels of interest rates and, consequently, increased the amount of funds available to thrifts.

EARNINGS

The earnings of thrifts had largely depended on the difference, or spread, between the average yield received from loans and investments and the average cost of maintaining savings accounts and of borrowings. Because lending activities of the thrifts had been limited primarily to long-term, fixed-rate mortgage loans secured by real estate, the average rate of interest realized by a thrift on its loan portfolio could not adjust as quickly to changes in interest rates as could the cost of its savings accounts and borrowings.

The relatively large operating losses common in the thrift industry during the last decade had been attributed to several key factors. Competing investment securities, offering higher yields and greater liquidity than those of thrifts, reduced deposit inflows and increased outflows. In addition, rapidly rising interest rates reduced the spread, adversely affecting the performance of the traditional areas of business within the thrift industry. While changes in regulation had broadened their lending and borrowing powers by allowing them into different types of investments and mortgage loans, thrifts' earnings and operations were still tightly linked to changes in the level of interest rates, financial market conditions, and most thrifts' relatively large investments in long-term, low-yielding mortgage loans.

RECENT LEGISLATIVE DEVELOPMENTS

The deregulation of the industry had enhanced thrifts' competitive position with other financial institutions. Several federal and state legislative actions within the past few years had eliminated many of the distinctions between commercial banks and thrifts:

1. Since December 1982, thrifts had been authorized to offer new insured money market accounts with no required minimum maturity period or interest ceiling (but with a minimum deposit of $2,500)—accounts which were directly equivalent to, and competitive with, money market mutual funds.

2. Since January 1983, insured Super NOW accounts, with a minimum deposit of $2,500, no interest ceiling, and no limit on the number of transactions in any given period, had been authorized.

3. No later than January 1984, all interest rate differentials favoring thrifts would be eliminated; all interest rate ceilings would be eliminated by April 1986.

New Hampshire state laws regulating state-chartered thrift institutions were less restrictive than comparable federal laws for federally chartered thrifts. For example, New Hampshire state-chartered thrifts might invest a higher percentage of their assets in commercial loans and in the equity and debt securities of unrelated companies.

NEW HAMPSHIRE SAVINGS BANK

Originally established in 1830, the New Hampshire Savings Bank (NHSB) was a state-chartered mutual savings bank operating with six offices and one remote service facility in central New Hampshire. With total assets of approximately $295 million, NHSB was ranked third in asset size among all thrifts and savings banks in New Hampshire. NHSB had consistently been among the most profitable thrifts in the United States in recent years, and its ratio of net worth to deposits, a popular measure of financial stability, was well above the industry average. NHSB's net interest spread, another key comparative measure, had not dropped below 1.04 percent for any quarter since the beginning of 1979. Highlights of NHSB's financial progress are shown in Exhibits 1 to 3.

      NHSB's principal business consisted of investing its funds in first mortgage loans on residential and commercial properties, on small- to medium-sized businesses, and in an unusually large number of consumer loans, including education, mobile home, and home improvement loans. The bank had been expanding its commercial activities for some time, and it intended to consider further expansion, subject to regulatory limitations. As a thrift institution, NHSB was subject to supervision and regulation by the Federal Deposit Insurance Corporation (FDIC), the bank commissioner of the state of New Hampshire, and the Federal Home Loan Bank of Boston (FHLB). As was typical in thrifts, the capital-to-deposit ratio was 3 percent, although it had been as high as 5 percent in the recent past.

      The bank had three primary sources of funds: savings deposits from the general public; advances from the FHLB; and sales of loans in the secondary market, particularly residential and commercial first mortgage and education loans.

      In an attempt to protect itself from violent fluctuations in the cost of its funds, NHSB had chosen to limit the growth of higher cost funds, such as high-rate certificates, and had originated adjustable-rate and short-term, fixed-rate mortgages to replace long-term, fixed-rate mortgages. Furthermore, the bank consciously limited its growth during periods of high interest rates in order to manage both its liabilities and its assets better. Savings deposit growth was reduced substantially by offering less-than-market rates on long-term deposits. In addition, the bank structured its mortgage loans to facilitate their resale in the secondary market. As a result of its emphasis on adjustable-rate and short-term, fixed-rate mortgages, only 59 percent of its year-end 1982 mortgage loan portfolio was interest rate-sensitive.

      In 1981 and 1982, NHSB had operated at a loss, primarily because of the portfolio restructuring it had done late in those years. During December 1981, the bank sold low-rate mortgage loans at a pre-tax loss of $1,183,000 (resulting in an income tax benefit of $355,000) and pass-through securities at a pre-tax loss of $1,487,000 (resulting in an income tax benefit of $446,000). During December 1982, the bank sold additional low-rate mortgage instruments at a pre-tax loss of $7,097,000 (resulting in an income tax benefit of $2,200,000). The proceeds from these sales of low-yielding assets were reinvested at higher rates and for shorter terms, primarily in commercial real-estate loans, with three principal effects on the bank's asset portfolio: the yield was increased; the composition was diversified away from residential first mortgage loans; and the average maturity was shortened, improving the matching of asset and liability maturities. In essence, the bank exchanged assets yielding 11.9 percent with an average maturity of 17.9 years for assets yielding 13.3 percent with an average maturity of 10.4 years. In the absence of these sales, net income in 1981 would have been approximately $2,205,000, and net income in 1982 would have been approximately $996,000.

NHSB's relatively high current level of profitability was a direct result of its unusually large short-term, rate-sensitive consumer loan portfolio, its substantial activity as originator of education loans (subsequently sold in the secondary market), its strong capital position, and its excellent management. Furthermore, the bank's commitment to computer-based forecasting enhanced its managers' ability to estimate the consequences of interest rate changes and assisted them in using such innovative portfolio management techniques as option writing and investing in financial futures.

COMPETITION

In attracting deposits, NHSB faced strong competition from a number of sources. Historically, competition had come from other thrifts and commercial banks located in its primary market area of Merrimack and Belknap Counties in central New Hampshire. Recently, short-term money market funds and other corporate and government securities yielding higher interest rates than those allowed to be paid by the bank under federal regulations had significantly cut into NHSB's available funds. Although this additional competition had reduced the bank's recent deposit growth, the forthcoming elimination of federal regulatory controls on savings deposits and interest rates was expected to improve the competitive position of the thrifts.

NHSB's strategy for attracting new customers in the highly competitive thrift industry had been to offer depositors a wide variety of savings programs, convenient branch locations, a wide network of automated teller machines, and pre-authorized payment and withdrawal systems. In addition, NHSB offered its customers new personal investment products such as tax-deferred retirement plans, individual retirement accounts (IRAs), and Keogh plans as well as such traditional services as money orders, traveler's checks, and safe-deposit boxes.

Within NHSB's real-estate lending business, the bank's main competition came principally from mortgage banking companies, other thrifts, commercial banks, insurance companies, and other institutional lenders. NHSB's strategy in this segment had been to provide high-quality, efficient service while varying the interest rates and loan fees it charged borrowers, real-estate brokers, and builders.

BACKGROUND TO THE CONVERSION

The Federal Home Loan Bank Board (FHLBB), the government institution that regulated savings and loan banks, had established a procedure for the conversion of mutual savings banks to stockholder-owned banks. After an independent appraisal of the market value of the institution, a public offering of shares could be arranged with an underwriter who would, based on this valuation, set a maximum price on the shares to be issued. Before the shares were offered to the public, however, the bank's depositors were given an opportunity to subscribe for shares at the maximum price. The remaining shares were publicly sold at a fair price (less than or equal to the maximum price) determined by the underwriter. If the public offering price was lower than the price offered to the depositors, the depositors were entitled to purchase their shares at the lower price. In a few instances, 70 percent or more of the shares issued in a conversion had been subscribed for by the bank's depositors. More commonly, about 20 percent to 30 percent were purchased by depositors with the balance going to the general public.

The only advantage enjoyed by a depositor of the bank over a member of the general public, therefore, was having the first opportunity to subscribe for shares. Before the FHLBB developed its rules, there had been cases where depositors were given shares in their banks without payment on the grounds that a mutual bank belonged to its depositors and that, when it converted to a stock corporation, the depositors should be given the entire stock ownership. However, the amended rules prohibited giving shares of stock to depositors or even offering them a discount from the public offering price.

The conversion of the NHSB involved one feature that had not been tried before. Rather than simply being converted from a state-chartered mutual institution to a state-chartered corporation, the bank itself was converted to a stock corporation with all of its stock held by a simultaneously created holding company. The holding company then offered its stock to the bank depositors and to the general public. The result was a stockholder-owned holding company, New Hampshire Savings Bank Corporation, which in turn held all the stock of the NHSB. The conversion of NHSB was completed without incident at a price of $13.75 per share for each of the 1,563,984 shares distributed in March 1983. Since then, NHSB's common stock had been traded over the counter and was included in the National Association of Security Dealers daily quotes (in *The Wall Street Journal*, for example). Exhibit 4 contains the NASD report on trading in NHSB stock for the month of July 1983, and Exhibit 5 shows the price performance and trading volume for the stock since it was first issued.

The August 9 Directors' Meeting. **Management's Perspective.** The first item on the agenda for the bank's directors was the discussion of a dividend policy. The president, John Hardie, opened the subject by observing that he and Robert Dustin, the executive vice president (evp), held quite different opinions with respect to dividends. Mr. Hardie favored the declaration of a dividend of about 15 cents a share in the third quarter of 1983. This would represent an annual rate of 60 cents, or about 4.3 percent of the $13.75 issue price of the shares. He observed that Merchants Savings Bank, a major competitor, had just converted from a mutual savings bank to a stockholder-owned institution and had established a dividend of a little over 5 percent on the issue price of its shares. In urging the cash dividend, Mr. Hardie commented that he believed the shareholders of NHSB expected a dividend, noting that some had withdrawn money from savings accounts that were paying them 5½ percent interest per year in order to buy their shares. He believed that these stockholder/depositors would be very disappointed if there were no dividend to replace the interest they had once earned on their savings. After stressing the importance of inspiring loyalty among the stockholders who were also bank customers, he invited the evp to state his opinion.

Mr. Dustin opposed the payment of any cash dividends. He believed that many of the stockholders were more interested in capital gains than in dividends, and he observed that a dividend of 5 percent on the original issue price would amount to over $1 million a year, an amount he believed NHSB could make better use of by investing in the business.

With respect to the dividends paid by the Merchants Savings Bank, Mr. Dustin said the board should not be stampeded by what Merchants had decided to do. Because the stock price of both Merchants and NHSB had dropped in the past few days (NHSB had declined from $18 to $17 per share while Merchants lost $2 down to $23), he believed that the payment of a cash dividend would not offer any extra protection from a market decline. Mr. Dustin added that, while the initial offering prospectus had mentioned a dividend, it made no promise of a cash dividend, and there was no evidence that the shareholders were counting on such a dividend. Furthermore, once NHSB began paying cash dividends, he did not believe that it would be able to stop.

The Directors' Perspectives.   Most of the directors had ideas to express about the dividend-policy question. One director, Martin Long, expressed the opinion that many shareholders were anticipating a dividend and would be disappointed if none were paid. He suggested, however, that it was not necessary to pay as much as a 5 percent dividend; perhaps the shareholders would be satisfied with a lesser amount that would still allow NHSB to reinvest a substantial portion of its earnings in the business.

Another director, Catherine Johanson, disagreed. She believed that, although the prospectus did not explicitly promise a cash dividend, it did strongly indicate that, if there were to be a dividend, it would be 5 percent of the issue price of the shares. (See Exhibit 6 for excerpts from the prospectus.)

A third director, Jennings Wilson, observed that he thought the bank and its earnings belonged to the shareholders. It was only fair, he believed, to distribute the earnings to the shareholders in the form of dividends and let the shareholders decide whether they wanted to spend this money or to reinvest it in the stock of the bank or in that of another company. Noting that there was a substantial personal income tax burden on dividends, another director, Fred Piel, expressed the belief that any shareholder who wanted to reinvest dividends in NHSB stock would be better off if no dividends were paid. Mr. Wilson called this idea a rather sophisticated view of dividends, one that he doubted many of the shareholders would understand.

Another director, Ross Byrd, flatly stated that he would vote against the payment of cash dividends. He did not believe the shareholders had purchased stock in the bank for the sake of dividends. If they had been looking for dividends, they would have purchased stock in a utility with a proven high-dividend yield.

At this point, Mr. Dustin commented that whatever was to be done should be simple. His conclusion, based on several conversations with NHSB depositors when the stock was first offered, was that many of those depositors had only a vague idea of what it meant to become a stockholder of the bank. The president supported this point. He stressed that the depositors were enthusiastic about their bank and were interested in buying stock because of their loyalty to the bank rather than because they thought the stock would be a profitable investment.

The bank's legal counsel, Sharon Marino, also a director, observed that the investment banking firm that had underwritten the offering of stock had suggested that dividends would have little effect on the stock price. Exhibits 7 and 8 contain excerpts from two of the investment bankers' publications that had been distributed to NHSB account executives about the time of the offering.

Mr. Wilson, who had suggested a modest dividend payout, repeated his argument that many of the stockholders had probably purchased their stock in anticipation of at least some dividends. He was supported by Ms. Marino, who said she thought that many of the stockholders were probably quite unsophisticated but were loyal to the bank and deserved some dividend, although it might not be necessary to pay the entire 60 cents. Mr. Wilson underlined the importance of building loyalty to the bank, saying that shareholder/depositors would bring more business to NHSB if they were paid dividends.

In response to Mr. Wilson's question about how many of the bank shares were held by depositors, Mr. Hardie replied that most of the shares were held in street names, and it just was not possible to identify the true ownership. However, some blocks of stock were known to be held by other savings banks and by at least one mutual fund. At that point, the president tabled the discussion. He said he was glad the subject had been aired but thought that at least one more meeting would be needed before the board was ready to vote on a dividend policy. He therefore proposed putting the topic on the agenda for the following month's meeting.

The Investment Committee's Meeting. A week after the August directors' meeting, the NHSB investment committee met to discuss the investment policy of the bank, its liquidity position, and the maturity structure of its assets and liabilities. As was customary at these meetings, the committee heard a brief presentation from its consultant on financial planning, B. D. Turner. Toward the end of the meeting, the question of an appropriate dividend policy came up.

Mr. Turner, who had been involved in the decision to convert the bank from a mutual institution to a stockholder-owned bank, observed that he believed the prospectus had held out a strong expectation that the bank would begin paying dividends fairly soon. Were dividends to be declared, he thought that the prospectus had provided assurance that stockholders would be paid at an annual rate of at least 5 percent of the original offering price. On the other hand, he also agreed that a stock dividend might be appropriate. He noted that more recent conversions of mutual to stock savings banks had prospectuses that specifically disclaimed any intention of paying cash dividends in the near future. This, he said, did not seem to have hurt the attractiveness of their shares.

Still opposed to cash dividends, Mr. Dustin nevertheless described a conversation he had had with a stockbroker that morning. The broker had urged NHSB to pay cash dividends becaue NHSB was a particularly strong bank with a successful earnings record and should demonstrate that strength publicly. The broker had also pointed out that a number of institutions, especially bank trust departments, would probably buy the bank's stock if cash dividends were declared (in some cases, institutions and trust departments were simply not permitted to buy stocks that did not pay cash dividends). Finally, the broker had said that, in his opinion, bank stock investors did expect cash dividends.

After a brief conversation, Mr. Turner agreed with Mr. Dustin that the stock price performance of Merchants Bank had been no better than that of NHSB despite Merchants' cash dividend policy. Furthermore, he noted that he understood a good deal of the NHSB stock issue had been purchased by other savings banks. Their interest was presumably not in dividends but in ready access to all of the information distributed to stockholders. Mr. Dustin said that he had received that same information, and he knew of a number of mutual funds that had purchased a portion of the offering. They both concluded that it was extremely difficult to analyze the dividend preferences of the stockholder group at this point.

As the president closed the discussion, he commented that when he presided over the coming November's special stockholders' meeting called to authorize a stock-option program for NHSB senior executives, he would like to be able to announce the establishment of a cash dividend policy.

The September 13 Directors' Meeting.   On September 13, 1983, several months after NHSB had published its second-quarter earnings report, the directors met for their final discussion of the dividend-policy question. Mr. Byrd said that he was very impressed by a letter received from Moseley, Hallgarten (Exhibit 9), an investment organization, which had strongly urged the bank to pay a cash dividend. "That letter seems to say it all," he observed. However, Mr. Piel said that he did not see why the NHSB had to follow the pattern set by other savings banks and added that cash dividends usually involved significant income taxes to shareholders.

As the discussion continued, Mr. Wilson reiterated his earlier support for a dividend and said that instituting cash dividend payments might increase NHSB's stock price, so that the shareholder looking for capital gains would benefit from this action. Agreeing, Ms. Johanson reminded the board of the dividend statement in the prospectus and added, "I suppose we could be in some trouble with the SEC if we did not initiate the cash dividend soon."

The president reported that he had recently had a conversation with a local depositor who had subscribed for an unusually large number of shares. This shareholder said that he had no personal desire for cash dividends, but he believed that most bank shareholders did; at least this is what he had been told by stockbrokers. Mr. Hardie added that approximately 900 depositors of the bank had subscribed for shares in the original offering. As a group, they had purchased about 20 percent of the offering. (Approximately 34,000 depositors were eligible and had been invited to subscribe. Another 20,000 had account balances below $50 and were not eligible to participate.)

Finally, Mr. Wilson said that he could understand why a newly formed company might not pay dividends. "But," he said, "we're a mature institution more than 150 years old. How can we possibly justify not paying a dividend?"

The president called for a vote.

New Hampshire Savings Bank Corporation

EXHIBIT 1
■

Financial Highlights
(dollars in thousands, except per share amounts)

	June 30, 1982	June 30, 1983
For the Quarter Ended June 30:		
Increase in deposits	$ 2,660	$ 7,315
Increase in loan originations	29,444	46,877
Increase in loan receivables	6,221	17,136
Total income	2,231	3,664
Net income	416	1,249
For the Six Months Ended June 30:		
Increase in deposits	5,469	13,321
Increase in loan originations	44,569	77,647
Increase in loan receivables	(1,006)	22,132
Total income	3,585	6,570
Net income	488	2,487
Weighted-Average Yield and Costs at June 30:		
Yield on total loans	11.68%	12.40%
Yield on investments	10.24	8.90
Combined weighted-average yields	11.28	11.47
Cost of deposit accounts	8.96	8.04
Cost of borrowings	10.76	10.21
Combined weighted-average costs	9.16	8.27
Per Share Data:		
Earnings per share for quarter	N.Ap.	0.80
Book value per share at end of quarter	N.Ap.	28.77

N.Ap. = not applicable.

EXHIBIT 2
■

New Hampshire Savings Bank Corporation and
Subsidiaries Consolidated Statements of Financial Position
(thousands of dollars, unaudited)

	June 30, 1982	June 30, 1983
Assets		
Cash and due from banks	$ 4,136	$ 14,526
Federal funds sold	7,456	8,493
Investment securities		
U.S. government and federal agency securities	10,999	23,430
Mortgage-secured investments	14,697	4,763
Certificates of deposit	3,278	3,998
Other securities	32,041	38,633
Total investment securities	61,015	70,824
Loans	215,977	236,809
Less: unearned discount	(5,887)	(5,827)
Less: reserved for loan losses	(591)	(739)
Net loans	209,499	230,243
Accrued interest receivable on loans	1,825	1,662
Property, furniture, and equipment, net	5,089	6,025
Other real estate owned	795	385
Other assets	4,451	4,396
Total assets	$294,266	$336,554
Liabilities and Stockholders' Equity		
Deposits		
Savings	$ 92,229	$ 86,557
Money market accounts	—	43,681
Six-month money market CDs	68,884	47,078
Other term deposits	74,933	76,142
Total deposits	236,046	253,458
Liabilities under repurchase agreements	1,342	—
Other borrowed funds	25,898	33,866
Accrued expenses and other liabilities	3,581	4,236
Total liabilities	266,867	291,560
Stockholders' equity		
Common stock, $1 par value/share	—	1,564
Paid-in surplus	—	17,933
Guarantee fund	12,000	12,000
Retained earnings	15,399	13,497
Total stockholders' equity	27,399	44,994
Total liabilities and stockholders' equity	$294,266	$336,554

New Hampshire Savings Bank Corporation

EXHIBIT 3

■

New Hampshire Savings Bank Corporation and
Subsidiaries Consolidated Statements of Income
(thousands of dollars, except per share amounts, unaudited)

	Three Months Ended		Six Months Ended	
	June 30, 1982	June 30, 1983	June 30, 1982	June 30, 1983
Interest and dividend income				
Interest on loans	$5,963	$6,972	$11,548	$13,289
Interest on bonds and other investments	1,353	1,402	2,503	2,694
Dividends on stock investments	217	178	424	323
Interest on federal funds sold	304	262	483	572
Total interest and dividend income	7,837	8,814	14,958	16,878
Interest expense				
Regular savings	1,266	1,116	2,410	2,229
Time deposits	4,052	2,982	8,246	6,063
Money market accounts	—	872	—	1,569
Borrowed funds	722	766	1,405	1,602
Total interest expense	6,040	5,736	12,061	11,463
Net interest and dividend income	1,797	3,078	2,897	5,415
Provision for possible loan losses	37	81	75	42
Net interest and dividend income after provision for possible loan losses	1,760	2,997	2,822	5,373
Other income				
Income from fees and service charges	423	599	660	1,015
Other	48	69	103	182
Total other income	471	668	763	1,297
Total income	2,231	3,665	3,585	6,570
Operating expenses				
Salaries and benefits	785	1,028	1,607	1,961
Occupancy costs	240	208	379	387
Other operating costs	586	975	1,442	1,993
Total operating expenses	1,611	2,211	3,428	4,341
Income (loss) before provision for federal income taxes and securities transactions	620	1,454	157	2,229
Provision (benefit) for income taxes	191	574	47	799
Income (loss) before securities transactions	429	880	110	1,430
Net gain (loss) on sale of securities	(13)	369	378	1,057
Net income	$ 416	$1,249	$ 488	$ 2,487
Earnings per share				
Income before securities transactions	N.Ap.	0.56	N.Ap.	0.91
Net income	N.Ap.	$0.80	N.Ap.	$1.59
Weighted-average shares outstanding	N.Ap.	1,563,984	N.Ap.	1,563,984

N.Ap. = not applicable.

New Hampshire Savings Bank Corporation

EXHIBIT 4

■

NASDAQ System Statistics

	Composite Index	Assigned Index (Other Finance)
High	321.58	279.43
Low	303.09	268.74
Close	303.96	272.80
Previous close	318.70	269.96
Percentage change	+4.62	+1.05
Total NASDAQ volume	1,294,387,100	
Average daily volume	64,719,355	
Total market value	$229,384,748,000	

NASDAQ symbol :	NHSB
Security description	Common stock ($1.00 par value)
Total shares outstanding	1,563,984

Please notify NASD of any change in company contact or address.

New Hampshire Savings Bank Corp.
John Hardie
President
27 North State Street
Concord, NH 03301

Summary for this Security

1. Quote range: High bid 18⅝ Low bid 17⅝
   High ask 18¾ Low ask 17⅞
2. Closing bid (JUN) 18⅛
   (JUL) 18½ Percentage change +2.07
3. Volume for month 185,453

Daily Statistical Report

Date	*High Bid*	*Low Bid*	*Close Bid*	*High Ask*	*Low Ask*	*Close Ask*	*Change (Bid)*	*Volume*	*NASDAQ Volume*	*Composite Close*
Fri. 1	18⅛	18⅛	18⅛	18⅜	18⅜	18⅜	0	5,850	62,996,300	321.58
Week	18⅛	18⅛	18⅛	18⅜	18⅜	18⅜	0	5,850	62,996,300	321.58
Mon. 4	Holiday							0		
Tue. 5	18⅛	17⅝	17⅝	18⅜	17⅞	17⅞	−½	13,873	58,190,100	317.15
Wed. 6	17⅝	17⅝	17⅝	17⅞	17⅞	17⅞	0	2,100	63,383,400	319.14
Thu. 7	17¾	17⅝	17¾	18	17⅞	18	+⅛	2,285	72,620,100	320.30
Fri. 8	17¾	17⅝	17⅝	18	17⅞	18	−⅛	3,620	62,055,200	319.57
Week	18⅛	17⅝	17⅝	18⅜	17⅞	18	−½	21,878	256,248,800	319.57
Mon. 11	18	17⅝	18	18⅛	18	18⅛	+⅜	14,925	60,917,100	320.38
Tue. 12	18	17⅝	17⅝	18¼	17⅞	17⅞	−⅜	8,250	72,131,800	316.93
Wed. 13	17¾	17⅝	17¾	18	18	18	+⅛	2,885	65,863,200	314.59
Thu. 14	18¼	17¾	18¼	18½	18	18½	+½	9,800	65,024,700	315.49
Fri. 15	18¼	18¼	18¼	18½	18½	18½	0	2,700	57,384,700	312.87
Week	18¼	17⅝	18¼	18½	17⅞	18½	+⅝	38,560	321,321,500	312.87
Mon. 18	18¼	18	18	18½	18½	18½	−¼	3,715	54,151,900	310.29
Tue. 19	18⅛	17⅞	17⅞	18½	18¼	18¼	−⅛	10,350	69,379,200	311.17
Wed. 20	18	17⅞	18	18¼	18¼	18¼	+⅛	3,400	76,078,200	316.76
Thu. 21	18¼	18	18¼	18½	18¼	18½	+¼	27,400	77,995,900	319.29
Fri. 22	18⅜	18¼	18¼	18½	18½	18½	0	14,400	64,634,700	320.71
Week	18⅜	17⅞	18¼	18½	18¼	18½	0	59,265	342,239,900	320.71
Mon. 25	18¼	18¼	18¼	18½	18⅜	18½	0	1,300	54,044,000	320.84
Tue. 26	18¼	18¼	18¼	18½	18½	18½	0	3,000	62,549,400	320.38
Wed. 27	18½	18¼	18½	18¾	18½	18¾	+¼	18,700	71,025,000	315.04
Thu. 28	18⅝	18⅝	18⅝	18¾	18¾	18¾	+⅛	2,400	65,496,800	308.47
Fri. 29	18½	18½	18½	18¾	18¾	18¾	−⅛	34,500	58,525,400	303.96
Week	18⅝	18¼	18½	18¾	18⅜	18¾	−¼	59,900	311,640,600	303.96

NASDAQ Market Makers in this Security as of 07/15/83: Carl P. Sherr and Company; Tucker, Anthony & R. L. Day; Smith Barney/Harris Upham; E. F. Hutton & Company Inc.; Moseley Hallgarten Estabrook; Oppenheimer & Co., Inc.; and Bear, Sterns & Co.

New Hampshire Savings Bank Corporation

EXHIBIT 5
■
Stock Price Performance and Trading Volume, 1983

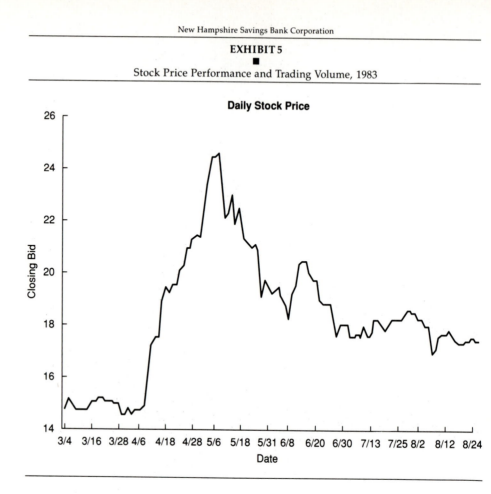

continued

EXHIBIT 5 *continued*

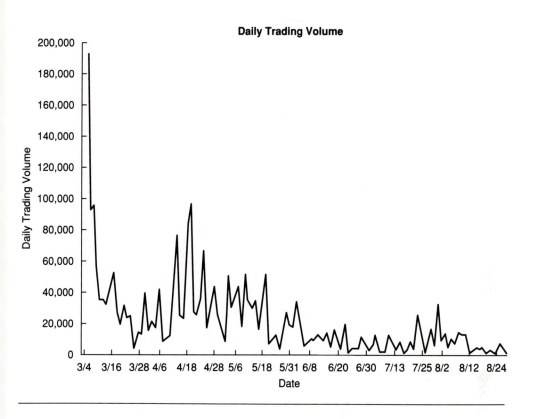

EXHIBIT 6

■

New Hampshire Savings Bank Corporation Prospectus

Prospectus

1,139,836 Shares

New Hampshire Savings Bank Corp.

Common Stock

The above shares constitute a portion of the 1,450,000 shares of the common stock ("Conversion Stock") of New Hampshire Savings Bank Corp. ("Holding Company") to be issued upon the conversion of New Hampshire Savings Bank ("Bank"). The simultaneous conversion of the Bank from mutual to stock form, issuance of all of the Bank's stock to the Holding Company, and offer and sale of the Conversion Stock by the Holding Company is herein referred to as the "Conversion." The remaining shares of Conversion Stock have been subscribed for by savings account holders of the Bank in a subscription offering by the Holding Company (the "Subscription Offering") and will be purchased at the Public Offering Price set forth below.

The Holding Company's common stock has been approved for quotation on the National Association of Securities Dealers Automated Quotation System ("NASDAQ"). Its NASDAQ symbol is "NHSB." Prior to this offering ("Public Offering") there has been no public market for the common stock of the Holding Company, and there can be no assurance that an established market for such stock will develop.

Certain limitations on the purchase of Conversion Stock are described under "The Conversion — Limitations on Conversion Stock Purchases" and "The Conversion — Restrictions on Acquisition of the Holding Company."

THESE SECURITIES HAVE NOT BEEN APPROVED OR DISAPPROVED BY THE SECURITIES AND EXCHANGE COMMISSION NOR HAS THE COMMISSION PASSED UPON THE ACCURACY OR ADEQUACY OF THIS PROSPECTUS. ANY REPRESENTATION TO THE CONTRARY IS A CRIMINAL OFFENSE.

	Public Offering Price	Underwriting Discount(1)	Proceeds to Holding Company(2)(3)
Per Share	$13.75	$ .95	$12.80
Total	$15,672,745	$1,082,844	$14,589,901
Total, as Adjusted(4)	$17,240,025	$1,191,129	$16,048,896

(1) The Holding Company has agreed to indemnify the Underwriters against certain liabilities.

(2) Before deducting expenses payable by the Holding Company which relate to the Conversion, Subscription Offering and Public Offering and which are estimated to be $754,656. Of such amount, $593,230 is allocable on a pro rata basis to the shares offered hereby. See "Use of Proceeds" for the net proceeds available to the Holding Company from the sale of all 1,450,000 shares of Conversion Stock.

(3) Of the proceeds to the Holding Company, approximately 93% will be transferred to the Bank in exchange for all of the capital stock of the Bank. It is expected that the balance of the net proceeds will be retained by the Holding Company.

(4) Assuming exercise of a 30-day over-allotment option granted to the Underwriters to purchase up to an additional 113,984 shares. See "Underwriting."

E. F. Hutton & Company Inc.

March 4, 1983

EXHIBIT 6 *continued*

Use of Proceeds.   Approximately 92 percent of the net proceeds from the sale of the Common Stock will be used by the Holding Company to purchase all of the stock of the Bank. These funds will be added by the Bank to its working capital and used for general business purposes. It is expected that the balance of the net proceeds will be retained by the Holding Company to be used in connection with its efforts to acquire and develop other banks and other businesses as is permitted by New Hampshire law. The Holding Company has not at this time identified any business it intends to acquire or develop, and the net proceeds to be retained by it may not be sufficient for such purposes if and when such businesses are identified. Until the net proceeds are used as indicated, they will be invested by the Holding Company and the Bank in short-term securities.

Dividend Policy.   It is intended that, following the Conversion, the Holding Company will establish a dividend policy to pay cash dividends on the Conversion Stock. The Holding Company may also consider the payment of stock dividends from time to time in addition to, or in lieu of, cash dividends. If a cash dividend policy is established, it is anticipated that dividends would initially be set by the Holding Company at an annual rate of approximately 5 percent of the initial Public Offering Price of the Conversion Stock. Payment of dividends by the Holding Company is, however, subject to determination and declaration by the board of directors of the Holding Company. Since the Holding Company currently has no significant source of income other than dividends from the Bank, Holding Company dividends will depend upon receipt of dividends from the Bank, which in turn will depend on the dividend policy of the Bank. It is intended that the Bank establish a dividend policy following Conversion to pay dividends to the Holding Company in such amounts as will permit the payment of the aforesaid dividends by the Holding Company. In each case, the determination and declaration will take into account the Holding Company's and the Bank's respective financial condition and results of operations, economic conditions, and other factors, including the regulatory restrictions discussed below. No assurances can be given that dividends will in fact be paid or that, if paid, such dividends will not be reduced or eliminated in future periods.

The New Hampshire Business Corporation Act ("Business Corporation Act") permits the Holding Company to pay dividends on its capital stock only from the unreserved and unrestricted earned surplus of the corporation or from unreserved and unrestricted net earnings of the current fiscal year and the next preceding fiscal year taken as a single period. The Bank is not subject to the Business Corporation Act, but the BTCI rules prohibit the payment of a cash dividend if the effect thereof would cause the net worth of the Bank to be reduced below either the amount required for the liquidation account or the net worth requirements imposed by New Hampshire or federal laws or regulations.

The BTCI rules prohibit the Bank, without the approval of the BTCI, from paying a cash dividend for a period of ten years from the effective date of the Conversion in an amount in excess of one half of the greater of (i) the Bank's Net Income for its current fiscal year, or (ii) the average of the Bank's Net Income for its current fiscal year and no more than two of the immediately preceding fiscal years. *Net Income* means all gross income less all expenses, including interest on FHLB advances and borrowed money, interest or dividends on withdrawable and nonwithdrawable accounts (but not on capital stock) and income taxes, if any, and all losses.

Furthermore, the Federal Deposit Insurance Act prohibits the Bank from paying dividends on its capital stock if it is in default in the payment of any assessment to the FDIC.

In addition, the Bank cannot pay dividends if such payment would impair its "guaranty fund," which New Hampshire law requires it to maintain at a level of 3 percent of all deposits.

New Hampshire Savings Bank Corporation

EXHIBIT 7
■
Excerpt from Investment Bankers' Publication
Regional Bank Monthly
August 1983

	Percent Change, 1981–1982	*7/29/83*	*Year-to-Date Percent Change, 1983*
NASDAQ Bank Index	+ 9.27	− 190.88	+ 22.07
S&P 500	+ 14.71	− 162.56	+ 15.54
Dow Jones Utilities	+ 9.60	− 129.77	+ 8.63

In this issue of the "Regional Bank Monthly" we have expanded our traditional "New England Bank Stock Monthly" to include some interesting banks in the Middle Atlantic region from New York to Washington, D.C., and the Sunbelt.

BANKS SHOW STRONG
FIRST HALF EARNINGS

Half of the banks on the Moseley Regional Bank Monthly achieved net earnings for the first six months of 1983 of 20 percent or more. Special note should be taken of the banks listed below, which year to date have achieved higher than 25 percent net earnings growth over the first six months of 1982.

		First Half 83/82 Net Earnings Percent Growth
Connecticut	Colonial Bancorp	+37.8%
Maine	Casco–Northern Corp.	+72.2
	Maine National Corp.	+25.8
	Merrill Bancshares	+56.9
Massachusetts	Bank of Boston	+42.0
	Bank of New England	+29.9
	UST Corp.	+29.0
New Hampshire	Bankeast	+76.7
	Indian Head Banks	+49.1
New Jersey	Citizens First Bankcorp.	+25.9
New York	Key Banks	+35.1

EXHIBIT 7 *continued*

		First Half 83/82 Net Earnings Percent Growth
Pennsylvania	Core States Financial	+30.3
	Dauphin Deposit	+31.5
	Fidelcor	+51.9
Vermont	First Vermont Financial	+47.7
	Howard Bank	+58.3
	Vermont Financial	+31.0

In May and June short-term interest rates rose, increasing costs and putting pressure on second quarter earnings. The recent (August 8) rise in the prime rate should help ease the pressure on margins at many of these banks. The surge in consumer spending which has been leading the national economic recovery is favorable for the consumer-oriented retail banks we follow at Moseley. The good prospects for low inflation and continuing economic recovery should help the banking industry.

BIG SAVINGS BANKS CONVERT

In order to raise capital to strengthen their competitive positions, mutual savings banks are "going public" and converting to stockholder-owned savings banks. Two of the largest such conversions in our region, in July, were *Howard Savings Bank,* New Jersey, with 8.6 million shares, and *The Provident Institution for Savings in the Town of Boston,* Mass., with 3.3 million shares.

In August, the *Philadelphia Savings Fund Society* is planning the largest new offering in history with 32 million shares.

1983 MARKET OUTLOOK

Year to date, the NASDAQ Bank Index (+22.07%) has sharply outperformed the S&P 500 (+15.54%). The regional bank stocks on this list are yielding an average of 4.95 percent and selling at 7.04 times our 1983 earnings estimate and at only 101 percent of book value. The S&P 400 stocks are yielding an average of 4.5 percent and selling at a multiple of 11.1 times 1983 estimates. These bank stocks are still selling at a substantially lower multiple than the industrial stocks. We expect the bank stocks' relative valuation to improve significantly in the next year.

Given the expected multiple expansion and the favorable economic fundamentals, the regional bank stocks should *outperform* the general market again over the next year.

continued

EXHIBIT 7 continued

	Symbol	1982–1983 Range	7/29/83 Bid Price	Percent Price Change from 12/31/82	Percent Price Change from Prior Month	Net Income per Share**			P/E 1983E	Individual Dividend	Yield	Dividend Payout	6/30/83 Book Value	Market Value to Book Value
						1981	1982	1983						
Connecticut														
CBT Corp.[kl]	CBCT*	38–20	$31.25	19%	1%	$4.61	$5.36	$4.90	$6.38×	$1.64	5.25%	33%	$32.68	96%
Citytrust Bancorp[c]	CITR*	43–21	42.00	50	0	4.08	5.20	6.05	6.94	1.48	3.52	24	34.67	121
Colonial Bancorp	CBCN*	28–12	25.50	89	(5)	3.91	(9.43)	2.50	10.20	0.80	3.14	32	22.74	112
First Bancorp	FBAN*	53–21	51.00	62	(3)	4.35	4.78	5.35	9.53	1.60	3.14	30	37.53	136
First Connecticut Bancorp[c]	FCBC*	44–25	42.50	18	1	4.64	5.12	5.60	7.59	1.60[b]	3.76	29	33.68	126
Hartford National Corp.[j]	HNAT*	41–19	36.38	(2)	(1)	4.29	4.46	5.90	6.17	2.00	5.50	34	33.10	110
Northeast Bancorp[cf]	NBIC*	45–26	40.50	16	(2)	4.73	4.72	5.00	8.10	2.29[h]	5.65	46	38.71	105
Maine														
Canal Corp.[cl]	—	26–20	26.00	0	4	1.46	2.30	3.00	11.30	0.50	1.92	22	23.15	112
Casco–Northern Corp.[cl]	CNOB	41–20	25.00	(30)	(30)	2.41	3.18	3.60	6.94	1.40	5.60	39	31.85	78
Depositors Corp.[j]	DEP	30–19	29.50	10	2	3.38	3.79	4.20	7.02	1.90	6.44	45	25.08	118
Maine National Corp.[dh]	MMAC*	24–13	23.50	45	0	1.85	2.48	2.85	8.25	1.00[b]	4.26	35	19.26	122
Merrill Bankshares[g]	MERB*	17–07	16.50	8	(4)	1.59	1.74	2.25	7.33	0.88	5.33	39	13.79	120

Massachusetts

Bank of Boston[ml]	BKB	48–22	39.00	16	(4)	6.25	6.67	7.50	5.20	2.12	5.44	28	51.29	76
Bank of New England[cl]	BKNE*	65–29	52.00	17	1	6.58[a]	7.93	8.75	5.94	2.60	5.00	30	51.70	101
Baybanks	BBNK*	37–19	33.63	12	2	4.99	5.34	5.00	6.73	2.00	5.95	40	39.02	86
Capitol Bancorp[c]	CAPB	25–15	24.75	21	1	3.00	4.17	NE	5.94	1.08	4.36	26	15.55	159
Conifer/Essex Group[c]	CNFG*	40–23	30.00	2	(15)	5.01	5.22	NE	5.75	1.80	6.00	34	32.90	91
Multibank Financial[ce]	MLTF*	40–20	32.50	28	(6)	4.57	5.52	5.73	5.67	1.32	4.06	23	34.70	94
Patriot Bancorp[c]	PATB*	29–17	22.00	33	(12)	3.33	3.18	NE	6.92	1.00	4.55	31	24.61	89
Shawmut Corp.[c]	SHAS*	40–24	36.75	10	17	4.67	5.63	4.75	7.74	1.92	5.22	40	44.64	82
State Street Boston[g]	STBK	47–17	40.00	45	(14)	3.14	4.16[i]	4.55	8.79	0.90	2.25	20	25.86	155
UST Corp.[cg]	USTB	24–09	19.50	24	(9)	2.01	2.31	NE	8.44	0.64	3.28	28	11.91	164

New Hampshire

Bank of New Hampshire[g]	—*	17–08	17.00	48	3	0.73	3.03	3.15	5.40	0.73	4.29	23	19.81	86
Bankeast[c]	BENH*	28–14	27.75	32	7	4.47	3.24	4.15	8.56	1.60	5.77	49	36.11	77
First New Hampshire Banks[o]	FINH*	32–15	29.00	5	0	3.02	3.32	3.80	7.63	1.00[b]	3.45	26	25.97	112
Indian Head Banks[f]	IHBI*	31–14	28.50	11	6	2.81	3.03	3.70	7.70	0.96[b]	3.37	26	28.19	101
Merchants Savings Bank	MBAK*	25–16	19.25	20[r]	(4)	NA	NA	NE	NM	0.80	4.16	NM	28.75	67
New Hampshire Savings Bank	NHSB*	25–13	18.50	35[r]	2	NA	NA	NE	NM	0.00	0.00	NM	28.77	64

continued

EXHIBIT 7 *continued*

	1983 2d Quarter (millions of dollars)				Average Monthly Trading Volume	Common Shares Out (thous.)	Market Capital (millions of dollars)	6/30/83 Average Equity to Average Assets	Last 12 Months Net Earnings	6/30/83 Return on Average Assets	6/30/83 Return on Average Equity
	Average Assets	Average Deposits	Average Net Loans	Average Equity							
Connecticut											
CBT Corp.[kl]	$ 4,809	$ 3,539	$ 2,811	$278.10	267,650	8,662	$268.52	5.78%	$ 35,541	0.74%	12.78%
Citytrust Bancorp[c]	963	812	674	55.50	20,350	1,635	68.67	5.76	8,926	0.93	16.08
Colonial Bancorp	1,265	1,076	842	73.60	127,467	2,236	59.81	5.82	(18,174)	NM	NM
First Bancorp	820	456	523	55.50	24,700	1,473	77.33	6.77	7,638	0.93	13.76
First Connecticut Bancorp[c]	753	602	330	56.90	16,967	1,715	72.03	7.56	8,979	1.19	15.78
Hartford National Corp.[j]	3,943	3,162	2,252	227.00	438,558	5,871	216.49	5.76	29,138	0.74	12.84
Northeast Bancorp[cf]	1,463	1,245	848	105.70	33,492	2,747	114.00	7.22	13,171	0.90	12.46
Maine											
Canal Corp.[cl]	264[†]	198[†]	123[†]	15.30[†]	NA	691	17.28	5.80	1,791	0.68	11.71
Casco–Northern[cl]	663	577	424	37.20	4,325	1,139	40.86	5.61	4,777	0.72	12.84
Depositors Corp.[i]	659	531	321	42.70	11,942	1,777	51.53	6.48	7,314	1.11	17.13
Maine National Corp.[dh]	552[†]	460[†]	263[†]	38.00[†]	NA	2,703	63.52	6.88	5,661	1.03	14.90
Merrill Bankshares[g]	578[†]	446[†]	237[†]	45.00[†]	20,463	3,443	59.39	7.79	7,603	1.32	16.90

Massachusetts

Bank of Boston[ml]	18,122†	11,966†	10,716†	894.00†	658,625	18,280	740.34	4.93	142,203	0.78	15.91
Bank of New England[cl]	5,169	3,390	2,675	251.00	200,500	4,392	226.19	4.86	38,564	0.75	15.36
Baybanks	4,067	3,546	2,129	235.00	305,250	6,318	207.70	5.78	33,660	0.83	14.32
Capitol Bancorp[c]	201†	140†	88†	14.30†	NA	1,020	24.99	7.11	4,418	2.20	30.90
Conifer/Essex Group[c]	995	866	663	57.20	26,592	1,775	63.01	5.75	9,330	0.94	16.31
Multibank Financial[ce]	1,175†	1,010†	764†	64.60†	71,083	1,984	68.45	5.50	11,015	0.94	17.05
Patriot Bancorp[c]	211	172	90	20.60	NA	997	24.93	9.76	3,658	1.73	17.76
Shawmut Corp.[c]	5,223	3,793	2,817	275.00	315,715	6,161	194.07	5.27	31,509	0.60	11.46
State Street Boston[g]	4,043	2,476	1,259	219.00	383,267	8,645	404.15	5.42	50,337	1.25	22.98
UST Corp.[cg]	631†	399†	283†	30.30†	11,018	2,755	59.23	4.80	6,602	1.05	21.79
New Hampshire											
Bank of New Hampshire[g]	293†	241†	164†	17.90†	NA	981	16.68	6.11	3,763	1.28	21.02
Bankeast[c]	482	424	273	35.40	NA	1,076	27.98	7.34	3,846	0.80	10.86
First New Hampshire Banks[o]	602†	500†	381†	39.60	NA	1,533	44.46	6.58	5,845	0.97	14.76
Indian Head Banks[f]	675	579	477	38.60	NA	1,361	36.75	5.72	5,075	0.75	13.15
Merchants Savings Bank	391	303	315	32.60	NA	1,318	26.36	8.34	1,357	0.35	4.16
New Hampshire Savings Bank	326†	244†	225†	45.00†	NA	1,564	28.36	13.80	(913)	NM	NM

continued

EXHIBIT 7 continued

	Symbol	1982–1983 Range	7/29/83 Bid Price	Percent Price Change from 12/31/82	Percent Price Change from Prior Month	Net Income per Share** 1981	1982	1983	P/E 1983E	Individual Dividend	Yield	Dividend Payout	6/30/83 Book Value	Market Value to Book Value
Rhode Island														
Fleet Financial Group^c	FLT	51–23	$47.13	37%	3%	$ 5.30	$6.28	$7.00	6.73×	$2.20	4.67%	31%	$37.52	126%
Old Stone Corp.^c	OSTN*	28–17	25.25	10	(10)	(8.56)	3.69	3.50	7.21	2.08	8.24	59	29.56	85
RIHT Financial^cn	RIHT*	49–22	45.00	58	(2)	6.06	3.18	NE	14.15	2.32	5.16	73	45.82	98
Vermont														
Chittenden Corp.	CNDN*	23–11	19.25	4	(13)	2.19	2.38	2.65	7.26	1.00^b	5.19	38	20.37	95
First Vermont Financial	FIVT*	18–13	18.00	20	3	2.37	2.11	2.75	6.55	1.20	6.67	44	20.69	87
Howard Bank^c	HOBK*	23–12	21.00	25	0	2.03	2.85	3.65	5.75	1.09^b	5.19	30	21.40	98
Merchants Bank	—*	20–11	20.00	38	0	2.91	3.52	3.85	5.19	1.20^b	6.00	31	18.50	108
Vermont Financial Services^p	VFSC*	20–11	20.00	33	5	2.68	3.13	3.50	5.71	1.10^b	5.50	31	24.74	81

	1983 2d Quarter (millions of dollars) Average Assets	Average Deposits	Average Net Loans	Average Equity	Average Monthly Trading Volume	Common Shares Out (thous.)	Market Capital (millions of dollars)	6/30/83 Average Equity to Average Assets	Last 12 Months Net Earnings	6/30/83 Return on Average Assets	6/30/83 Return on Average Equity
Rhode Island											
Fleet Financial Group^c	$4,214†	$2,683	$2,667	$255.40	181,892	6,189	$282.37	6.06%	$40,052	0.95%	15.68%
Old Stone Corp.^c	1,976†	1,574†	1,454†	91.40†	45,625	2,223	62.24	4.63	8,348	0.42	9.13
RIHT Financial^cn	1,938	1,429	1,149	97.00	111,158	2,127	97.84	5.01	5,845	0.30	6.03
Vermont											
Chittenden Corp.	535†	480†	386†	29.20†	37,308	1,488	32.74	5.46	3,678	0.69	12.60
First Vermont Financial	329†	294†	215†	25.00†	NA	1,248	21.84	7.60	3,074	0.93	12.30
Howard Bank^c	338†	292†	244†	18.00†	NA	896	18.82	5.33	3,050	0.90	16.94
Merchants Bank	248†	217†	179†	14.00†	NA	828	16.56	5.65	3,108	1.25	22.20
Vermont Financial Services^p	321†	284†	220†	18.10†	NA	789	14.99	5.64	2,756	0.86	15.23

Middle Atlantic Region

	Symbol	1982–1983 Range	7/29/83 Bid Price	Percent Price Change from 12/31/82	Percent Price Change from Prior Month	Net Income per Share**			P/E 1983E	Individual Dividend	Yield	Dividend Payout	6/30/83 Book Value	Market Value to Book Value
						1981	1982	1983						
New Jersey														
Citizens First Bancorp[g]	CFB	23–10	$23.25	47%	11%	$0.75	$2.46	$3.40	6.84×	$1.00	4.30%	29%	$17.88	130%
Commercial Bancshares[c]	CBNJ*	31–13	29.75	70	(3)	2.75	3.72	4.30	6.92	1.68	5.65	39	33.09	90
First National State Bancorp[cl]	FNS	42–22	36.25	16	(8)	5.66	6.59	NE	5.50	2.40	6.62	36	43.34	84
Heritage Bancorp[c]	HRTG*	26–12	25.25	38	(1)	3.45	3.36	3.70	6.82	1.52	6.02	41	28.58	88
Horizon Bancorp	HZB	27–14	25.75	32	(1)	3.48	3.35	4.00	6.44	1.52	5.90	38	24.82	104
Midlantic Banks[cl]	MIDL*	42–20	42.25	50	7	4.89	5.94	6.70	7.11	1.88	4.45	28	38.52	110
Summit Bancorp[c]	SUBN	27–17	22.50	(16)	2	4.05	4.60	NE	4.89	1.20	5.33	26	19.09	118
United Jersey Banks	UJB	30–12	28.63	56	8	2.90	3.17	NE	9.03	1.24	4.33	39	26.04	110
New York														
Bank of New York	BK	62–37	61.25	23	3	7.61	8.30	9.20	6.66	3.40	5.55	37	72.14	85
First Empire State	FEMP*	33–17	29.50	22	(6)	3.60	4.11	NE	7.18	1.00	3.39	24	44.22	67
Key Banks[cl]	KEY	29–12	29.00	84	20	2.78	3.50	4.00	7.25	1.50	5.17	38	27.73	105
Lincoln First Banks[c]	LFBK*	40–24	36.00	0	(3)	4.84	6.61	NE	5.45	2.00	5.56	30	59.14	61
Norstar Bancorp[cl]	NOR	38–22	36.38	21	6	3.99	4.62	4.80	7.58	2.20[b]	6.05	46	30.79	118
Security New York State[cl]	SNYK*	33–12	32.75	90	(1)	3.21	3.47	NE	9.44	1.50	4.58	43	28.09	117
Pennsylvania														
Commonwealth National[c]	CMHC	34–24	28.50	(2)	20	2.06	1.40	NE	20.36	2.32	8.14	166	46.39	61
Continental Bancorp[c]	CBRP	30–22	27.75	(3)	(4)	4.07	4.65	4.00	6.94	2.04	7.35	51	26.96	103
Core States Financial[c]	CSFN	66–32	66.38	29	6	6.13	9.73	11.00	6.03	3.52	5.30	32	68.50	97
Dauphin Deposit[cg]	DAPN	34–21	33.50	29	16	3.24	3.52	NE	9.52	1.64	4.90	47	27.04	124
Fidelcor[c]	FICR	37–17	35.50	41	1	5.91	5.47	6.50	5.46	2.00	5.63	31	43.63	81
First Pennsylvania Corp.	FPA	09–02	7.13	43	(14)	0.02	(1.66)	NE	NM	0.00	0.00	NM	11.28	63
Independence Bancorp[cl]	—*	30–20	29.50	28	(2)	3.77	4.21	4.80	6.15	1.72	5.83	36	26.42	112
Industrial Valley Bk. & Tr.[c]	IBKT	25–16	23.50	11	6	3.32	3.18	3.20	7.34	2.20	9.36	69	32.02	73
Mellon National[l]	MEL	57–27	51.50	36	2	5.88	6.83	8.00	6.44	2.44	4.74	31	51.35	100
Meridian Bancorp[g]	MRDN	36–24	31.75	27	(2)	4.45	4.71	4.87	6.52	2.20	6.93	45	36.00	88
PNC Financial[cl]	PNCF	45–24	44.50	39	11	4.71	5.09	5.80	7.67	1.92	4.31	33	33.85	131
Washington, D.C.														
American Security Corp.[c]	ASEC*	30–18	28.25	15	3	3.62	3.93	4.60	6.14	1.40	4.96	30	28.93	98

continued

EXHIBIT 7 continued

| | 1983 2d Quarter (millions of dollars) | | | | Average Monthly Trading Volume | Common Shares Out (thous.) | Market Capital (millions of dollars) | 6/30/83 Average Equity to Average Assets | Last 12 Months Net Earnings | 6/30/83 Return on Average Assets | 6/30/83 Return on Average Equity |
	Average Assets	Average Deposits	Average Net Loans	Average Equity							
New Jersey											
Citizens First Bancorp[g]	$ 832†	$ 707†	$ 414†	$ 43.40†	15,808	2,559	$ 53.42	5.22%	$ 7,085	0.85%	16.32%
Commercial Bancshares[c]	569†	441†	220†	44.90†	35,967	1,402	43.11	7.89	5,389	0.95	12.00
First National State Bancorp[cl]	4,295†	3,336†	2,247†	236.00†	99,508	5,794	227.41	5.49	37,223	0.87	15.77
Heritage Bancorp[c]	1,645†	1,389†	866†	114.50†	1,100,558	4,272	109.47	6.96	20,674	1.26	18.06
Horizon Bancorp	1,572†	1,247†	952†	99.80†	57,650	4,189	108.91	6.35	15,022	0.96	15.05
Midlantic Banks[cl]	4,145†	3,223†	2,230†	237.00†	219,617	5,134	202.79	5.72	40,431	0.98	17.06
Summit Bancorp[c]	1,024†	875†	555†	79.60†	NA	3,225	70.95	7.77	11,394	1.11	14.31
United Jersey Banks	3,416†	2,540†	1,602†	59.60†	182,142	5,797	154.35	4.67	20,379	0.60	12.77
New York											
Bank of New York	12,822	9,062	7,796	597.70	481,592	7,247	429.38	4.66	73,256	0.57	12.26
First Empire State	1,946†	1,578†	1,211†	123.40†	71,942	2,868	89.63	6.34	9,532	0.49	7.72
Key Banks[cl]	2,765	2,323	1,428	204.10	187,292	7,410	178.77	7.38	27,830	1.01	13.64
Lincoln First Banks[c]	3,909	3,047	2,176	206.90	230,200	3,402	126.72	5.29	24,531	0.63	11.86
Norstar Bancorp[cl]	3,720	3,078	1,627†	327.40†	104,900	9,427	324.05	8.80	46,654	1.25	14.25
Security New York State[cl]	1,633†	1,323†	863†	76.70	34,092	1,695	55.94	4.70	8,001	0.49	10.43
Pennsylvania											
Commonwealth National[c]	1,233†	935†	735†	68.50†	NA	1,490	35.39	5.56	4,348	0.35	6.35
Continental Bancorp[c]	2,907	2,477	1,898	210.90	90,800	7,908	229.33	7.25	34,234	1.18	16.23
Core States Financial[c]	6,253	4,205	3,298†	396.00†	369,717	5,824	365.46	6.33	59,133	0.95	14.93
Dauphin Deposit[cg]	1,270†	1,057†	518†	97.80	27,242	3,775	109.48	7.70	14,172	1.12	14.49
Fidelcor[c]	4,062	2,969	1,709	218.70	460,467	5,180	181.30	5.38	42,170	1.04	19.28
First Pennsylvania Corp.	5,149†	3,294†	3,011†	194.60†	1,118,867	16,218	133.80	3.78	(23,477)	NM	NM
Independence Bancorp[cl]	420†	327†	179†	26.10†	NA	1,042	31.26	6.21	4,179	1.12	18.08
Industrial Valley Bank & Trust[c]	1,778†	1,416†	878†	88.80†	60,067	2,864	63.72	4.99	11,559	0.65	13.02
Mellon National[l]	24,956	14,988	14,672	1,268.00	778,150	25,316	1,275.29	5.08	160,246	0.64	12.64
Meridian Bancorp[s]	3,403†	2,768†	2,303†	234.70†	329,308	6,852	111.35	6.90	34,250	1.01	14.59
PNC Financial[cl]	11,317	7,058	5,098	697.00	628,642	20,621	830.00	6.16	106,873	0.94	15.33
Washington, D.C.											
American Security Corp.[c]	3,272	2,329	1,781	211.00	68,542	7,386	203.12	6.45	29,072	0.89	13.78

Averages for All Regions

	Percent Price Change from 12/31/82	Percent Price Change from Prior Month	P/E 1983E	Yield	Dividend Payout	Market Value to Book Value	Average Equity to Average Assets	Return on Average Assets	Return on Average Equity
Averages:									
All Regions	27%	0.10%	7.04 ×	4.95%	36%	101%	6.26%	0.86%	13.92%

ªEPS do not include $53 million ($1.21 per share) after-tax gain on sale of aircraft.
ᵇPlus stock.
ᶜBased on March 31, 1983, balances.
ᵈReorganized into bank holding company. Old stock exchanged for new stock on 2 for 1 basis.
ᵉAdjusted for 50 percent stock dividend 1983.
ᶠAdjusted for 5 percent stock dividend 1983.
ᵍAdjusted for 2 for 1 split 1983.
ʰAdjusted for 20 percent dividend 1983.
ⁱEPS excludes nonrecurring gain of $1.68 per share on sale of real-estate purchase options.
ʲIncludes pooling of interest with Connecticut National Bank.
ᵏIncludes merger with State National Bancorp.
ˡMerger pending.
ᵐName change from First National Boston.
ⁿName change from Hospital Trust Corp.
ᵒName change from First Bancorp of New Hampshire.
ᵖName change from Vermont National Bank.
ᵠPercent price change from initial offering date.
ʳName change from American Bancorp as a result of consolidation with Central Penn National.
*Moseley makes a market in this stock.
†Simple average.
NE No estimate.
NA Not available.
NM Not meaningful.
**All earnings have been restated to reflect an SEC ruling requiring banks to report earnings on a one-line basis.

New Hampshire Savings Bank Corporation

EXHIBIT 8

∎

Excerpt from Investment Bankers' Publication

Valuing S&L Stocks

Investors use two basic ratios to value publicly traded thrift institution stocks:

Market price to book value per share.

Market price to total assets per share.

The chart below shows that, based on price to book value, NHSB's stock will be priced at a significant discount to industry averages, despite its extraordinary yield spread and superior profitability. NHSB's ratio of price to assets is somewhat better than industry averages, reflecting its unusually strong net worth position.

Note also the percentage increases in price from initial offering to present. Thrift stocks in today's market are consistently doing well for their investors.

Institution	Symbol	Initial Offering Price(s)	Current Market Price 2/15/83	Percentage Change in Market Price(s)	Market Price to Book Value		Market Price to Total Assets		Most Recent Yield Spread	Total Assets (thousands)
					Initial	Current	Initial	Current		
New Hampshire	NHSB	$13.75	—	—	48.62%[b]	—	6.35%[c]	—	2.24%	$ 313,831
		12.00	—	—	45.06[b]	—	5.59[c]	—		311,436
		10.25	—	—	41.03[b]	—	4.81[c]	—		309,040
Recent Offerings										
Fortune Federal	FORF	14.00	$14.00	—	44.93	44.93%	2.38%	2.38%	(0.51)	1,293,099
Mid-State Federal	MSSL	13.75	16.25	18.18%	59.24	70.01	3.64	4.30	0.92	472,025
Washington Federal	WFSL	11.75	23.25	97.87	39.91	83.18	4.59	9.09	0.55	695,921
Puget Sound	SBFS	12.00	20.00	66.67	48.02	82.58	7.03	11.72	0.71	467,998

FN Financial	FNFC	18.00	18.75	4.17	97.88	101.96	3.74	3.89	(2.48)	7,163,398
Westside Federal	WFHC	11.50	15.00	30.43	46.13	60.17	3.95	5.15	0.09	262,342
University Federal	UFSL	12.00	20.75	72.92	29.15	53.19	2.28	3.94	(0.58)	294,758
Fidelity Federal	FFED	10.00	12.125	21.25	36.11	46.53	1.86	2.26	(0.44)	1,705,439
Other Thrifts										
Napies Federal	NAF	11.125	26.50	106.37	63.57	118.09	5.74	7.44	NA[d]	783,718
City Federal (NJ)	CTYF	11.00	18.50	253.18	33.48	77.57	1.50	2.65	1.32	4,440,606
American Federal—Colorado	AFSL	11.00	25.00	127.27	43.93	94.63	3.08	3.88	NA	322,457
First Financial—Stevens Pt.	FFIN	11.00	14.50	31.82	57.86	92.24	3.35	3.66	0.90	277,206
Land of Lincoln	LOLS	7.50	9.00	20.00	38.54	31.19	2.99	2.26	0.46	600,149
Sooner Federal	SFOK	11.50	21.25	84.78	29.03	61.86	1.75	2.87	(0.27)	1,313,717
Texas Federal	TXSL	10.75	13.75	27.91	33.86	59.83	2.01	2.52	NA	818,287
Industry Averages										
Recent offerings						67.82		5.34		
All other publicly traded institutions										
NYSE						140.91		4.69		
ASE						159.33		2.25		
OTC						70.60		3.20		
All publicly traded institutions						96.04		3.97		

[a] Adjusted for stock splits.
[b] Based on pro forma stockholders' equity.
[c] Based on pro forma total assets.
[d] Not available.

New Hampshire Savings Bank Corporation

EXHIBIT 9

■

Dividend Policy Statement from Investment Advisory Service

Moseley, Hallgarten, Eastabrook & Weeden, Inc.

Investments Since 1850

Post Office Box One

60 State Street

Boston, Massachusetts 02101

(617) 367–2400

August 19, 1983

Mr. Robert E. Dustin

Executive Vice President

New Hampshire Savings Bank

27 N. State Street

Concord, New Hampshire 03301

Dear Bob,

I have enclosed for your perusal our most recent publication of the Moseley Regional Bank Stock Monthly. For the first time, we have included the New Hampshire Savings Bank and as you can see your numbers compare rather favorably with the rest of the group, particularly your capital ratio.

It would be especially helpful to us in our work if you could provide us with some earnings projection for 1983 to assist in the computation of our data base.

As you can see, yours is the only company in this group that does not currently pay a dividend. Since this is a shortcoming, it does make marketing efforts on your behalf somewhat more difficult. If NHSBC were to initiate even a nominal dividend, the marketing potential for the stock would be opened up to a myriad of new investors.

For instance, most trust department and money managers across the country require that before any company be put on their approved list it must pay some sort of cash dividend, however nominal. Additionally, many of the state and municipal retirement systems across the United States function under a prudent-man rule which also requires a cash dividend from stock investments.

Such investors—in the long run—are the advantageous ones for us to seek out. Two illustrations that immediately come to mind are, first, when Texas Instruments declared a nominal dividend of 20¢ per year. It was immediately placed on most trust department buy lists and the price of the stock more than doubled in the ensuing year.

Closer to home, when Compugraphic Corp. initiated a small dividend, they also were placed on the recommended list of a number of trust departments and the price of the stock more than tripled in the next 12 months. Granted, a cash dividend is not the only determinant in evaluating the market price of a stock, but certainly reaching out to new investors should help your market performance over the long run.

Should your strategy be one whereby you might be considering an aggressive acquisition policy both intra and interstate, certainly a higher market evaluation for NHSBC's stock would be beneficial in this endeavor.

Another sound point regarding a quarterly dividend: it provides you with the opportunity to communicate with shareholders on a regular basis and sometimes this type of communication inspires your shareholders to consider extending their investment in your company. I would suggest a February, May, August and November 15th payment date in conjunction with your quarterly releases.

Further, should you initiate a cash dividend, I would strongly recommend a dividend reinvestment program which in all probability would be favorably received by your shareholders. This would provide a small means of acquiring new capital for your company.

To conclude, we are delighted that we can include your company on our Monthly, and feel that it will be useful to NHSBC and its shareholders. I do hope that we might have a chat soon, since there are a number of other comments I should like to offer to help explain further why your consideration of a cash dividend can be a most effective and beneficial move for NHSBC, its shareholders, and the marketability of the stock. And when you are able to decide to take such action, we will be delighted to let our followers know that you have declared a cash dividend which can only mean that the outlook for your company is a good one!

Sincerely,

James E. Moynihan, Jr.,
Senior Vice President—Investments
JEM/hh
encl.

Kelly Services, Inc.

As part of his rotation training, William Murry, a new analyst with Shack, Stripes, & Roam Securities (SS&R), had been assigned a portfolio of service companies. Three of the companies provided temporary help, and of the three, he found one, Kelly Services, Inc., to be particularly interesting. Kelly's growth and profitability record, and lack of debt, were what caught Mr. Murry's attention.

In his MBA program, Mr. Murry had been taught that debt was less expensive than equity, so he wondered whether a company that shied away from borrowing could be successful compared to its competitors. Could it be maximizing value for shareholders? Because interest rates had declined considerably over the previous couple of years (as shown in Exhibit 1), reducing the cost of debt even further, Mr. Murry wondered how Kelly might have been affected if the company had taken on some debt either in 1985 or early in 1986. Had Kelly's shareholders penalized the company for losing debt-derived value by keeping the share price lower than it would otherwise have been?

In contrast to Mr. Murry's MBA teachings, many of his colleagues at SS&R believed that Kelly had been a superior performer because it had no debt, and that it needed no debt now.

THE INDUSTRY

Temporary employed in the United States is booming. According to the Bureau of Labor Statistics, employment growth in the temporary help services industry has averaged 11 percent a year over the last 13 years, compared with a 2.1 percent growth rate for non-agricultural jobs throughout the economy.[1]

The increasing use of temporary help could be attributed to at least three factors. First, such help was used as an employment buffer; it would decline

---

[1] The quote and statistics in this section are from Cherlyn S. Granrose and Eileen Appelbaum, "The Efficiency of Temporary Help and Part-Time Employment," *Personnel Administrator*, January 1986, 71.

This case was prepared as a basis for class discussion rather than to illustrate either effective or ineffective handling of an administrative situation. Copyright © 1986 by the Darden Graduate Business School Sponsors, University of Virginia, Charlottesville, Virginia.

early in a recession, but would rebound rapidly in an economic recovery. In 1983, the first year of recovery from a recession, the use of temporary help had increased by 17.5 percent.

Second, companies had begun to hire temporary workers under long-term contracts. According to labor economist Audrey Freedman,

> "What the companies are doing is organizing so they don't have to pay for vacation, holidays, health benefits or pensions. In addition, they don't have to allocate money for training and for promotion." The savings can be large, and some firms are now building temporary work into their employment strategies.[2]

Third, temporary workers had expanded beyond secretaries and clerical workers to include engineers, accountants, nurses, and even lawyers and doctors costing up to $150 per hour. Ms. Freedman said,

> "In the make-or-buy decision, a lot of companies are deciding to buy, rather than make, something they need." Renting a professional instead of hiring one fits in with this trend, she says. The new temps choose temporary work to get money and experience at the beginning of a career, a lighter work load at the end, or a more relaxed lifestyle along the way.[3]

By 1982, 46 percent of temporary employment and 57 percent of receipts of temporary help services firms were earned at non-office jobs.

A 1985 survey indicated that, of temporary help hired for office jobs, 58 percent were used in clerical positions and 25 percent were used for secretarial duties; the remaining 17 percent were used for such tasks as word and data processing and accounting functions. About half were hired to alleviate work overloads, and one-third were hired to cover for absent employees.

THE COMPANY

Kelly Services, Inc. was founded in 1946 in Detroit, Michigan and had remained under family management, with William R. Kelly as chief executive officer. The company emphasized clerical and secretarial services, but also provided some marketing, light industrial, technical, and nursing and home health-care temporary help services through over 650 offices in the United States, Canada, the United Kingdom, and France. Kelly opened 64 new offices in 1985 and 47 in 1984, but most of the company's growth had come from increased business from existing markets and customers.

As shown in Exhibit 2, Kelly's sales and profits had more than quintupled between 1976 and 1985 and had more than doubled since 1982. Kelly's sales had grown more rapidly than its assets and equity base and had done so with no long-term debt.

---

[2]Ibid., 72.
[3]"These 'Temps' Don't Just Answer the Phone," *Business Week*, June 2, 1986, 74.

Wages and salaries (cost of goods sold) amounted to about 74 percent of Kelly's total revenues, and accounts receivable from businesses constituted about 55 percent of total assets. On the other side of the balance sheet, wages, payroll taxes, and insurance constituted 71 percent of current and total liabilities. In 1985, Kelly had $17.6 million in common stock and $11.5 million of treasury stock; retained earnings had increased from $102.1 million in 1984 to $123.0 million in 1985.

Kelly had split its stock ten times since 1962, when it first issued shares to the public. In June 1984, to improve the stock's marketability, each common share was split and reclassified as 1½ shares of nonvoting Class A and one-half share of voting Class B common stock. A five-for-four stock split took place in August 1985. Insiders controlled 60 percent of the Class A and 76 percent of the Class B shares. In 1985, dividends averaged 54 cents per share, representing the 14th consecutive and 23d overall annual increase in dividends since 1962. Exhibit 3 provides stock price data for Kelly Services between 1980 and 1985.

THE COMPETITION

Mr. Murry had similar information in his portfolio on two of Kelly Services' competitors, Volt Information Sciences, Inc. and Olsten Corporation. Olsten was the more successful of the two firms. (Manpower, Inc., better known than Volt or Olsten, had been sold recently, and public data were no longer available for it.)

Olsten Corporation was the third largest temporary help company in North America, with 119,000 personnel available through 322 offices in 39 states and Canada. About 31 percent of Olsten's offices were operated under franchise. The company had no long-term debt, and the Olsten family owned 40 percent of the stock.

Volt Information Sciences, Inc., earned about 60 percent of its revenues through its temporary help operations and 32 percent through typesetting equipment sales and service; the remaining 8 percent was earned through the installation of automatic directory assistance systems and the sale of technical manuals. Volt employed 13,800 people, 70 percent of whom were temporary workers. The company had a long-term debt/equity ratio of 124 percent and a long-term debt/assets ratio of 42 percent. Insiders owned 32 percent of Volt stock.

Financial data for Volt, Olsten, and Kelly Services are compared in Exhibit 4.

PROJECTIONS

Being curious about the effect that debt might have on Kelly Services, Mr. Murry created three pro forma financial statements based on the company's 1985 figures. He had worked out some rough figures for different capital structures (shown in Exhibit 5) by assuming that,

1. The debt would be used to repurchase stock in January 1985 at $25 per share
2. The interest rate on the long-term debt would be 12.5 percent

3. The tax rate would be 50 percent, close to the average of the past 10 years

4. The payout ratio would be 28 percent

From this analysis he found earnings would decrease as leverage increased, but earnings per share would increase, with no negative impact on dividends, as shown below:

	Proportion of Debt to Equity			
	Actual	*30 Percent*	*50 Percent*	*70 Percent*
Net income (millions)	$32.6	$29.6	$27.9	$26.3
Earnings/share	2.01	2.03	2.06	2.10
Dividends/share	0.56	0.57	0.58	0.59

These results seemed in conflict to Mr. Murry. In addition, he was certain that whatever the shareholders perceived about the company would be reflected in its share price. The stock price was $25 per share at the beginning of 1985. What would it be if debt increased? Did these same results hold true for Olsten and Volt? Was his business school lesson that leverage increased performance right or wrong? Did these data, or would further analysis, prove his professor's techniques correct?

Mr. Murry was determined to solve this enigma and show others at SS&R the exact source of the value of leverage—if he could determine whether increasing debt increased shareholder value.

Kelly Services, Inc.

EXHIBIT 1
■

Interest Rates on Debt of Different Quality

Year/Month		Prime Rate	U.S. Treasury Bonds		Corporate Bonds			
			3-Year	10-Year	Aaa	Aa	A	Baa
1980		15.27%	11.55%	11.46%	11.94%	12.50%	12.89%	13.67%
1981		18.87	14.44	13.91	14.17	14.75	15.29	16.04
1982		14.86	12.92	13.00	13.79	14.41	15.43	16.11
1983		10.79	10.45	11.10	12.04	12.42	13.10	13.55
1984		12.04	11.89	12.44	12.71	13.31	13.74	14.19
1985	1	10.61	10.43	11.38	11.37	11.82	12.28	12.72
	2	10.50	10.55	11.51	12.13	12.49	12.80	13.23
	3	10.50	11.05	11.86	12.56	12.91	13.36	13.69
	4	10.50	10.49	11.43	12.23	12.69	13.14	13.51
	5	10.31	9.75	10.85	11.72	12.30	12.70	13.15
	6	9.78	9.05	10.16	10.94	11.46	11.98	12.40
	7	9.50	9.18	10.31	10.97	11.42	11.92	12.43
	8	9.50	9.31	10.33	11.05	11.47	12.00	12.50
	9	9.50	9.37	10.37	11.07	11.46	11.99	12.48
	10	9.50	9.25	10.24	11.02	11.45	11.94	12.36
	11	9.50	8.88	9.78	10.55	11.07	11.54	11.99
	12	9.50	8.40	9.26	10.16	10.63	11.19	11.58

Sources: *Federal Reserve Bulletin*, various issues; and *Economic Report of the President*, 1986.

EXHIBIT 2

Financial Data (dollars in millions, except per share data)

	1976	1977	1978	1979	1980	1981	1982	1983	1984	1985
Sales	$152.4	$202.6	$279.0	$369.3	$409.7	$462.6	$419.9	$524.4	$741.2	$876.4
Net income	5.7	7.3	12.6	15.0	15.2	18.2	12.0	17.5	26.7	32.6
Earnings/share	0.35	0.45	0.67	0.91	0.92	1.10	0.72	1.07	1.65	2.01
Dividends/share										
Common	0.09	0.10	0.14	0.19	0.26	0.30	0.36	0.38	0.20	N.Ap.
Class A common	N.Av.	N.Av.	N.Av.	N.Av.	N.Av.	N.Av.	N.Av.	N.Av.	0.26	0.56
Class B common	N.Av.	N.Av.	N.Av.	N.Av.	N.Av.	N.Av.	N.Av.	N.Av.	0.21	0.46
Assets	$ 37.0	$ 44.5	$ 60.3	$ 75.1	$ 87.9	$104.2	$108.8	$124.2	$148.9	$178.6
Cash	—	—	—	9.8	22.5	37.9	47.7	35.7	39.5	48.1
Net working capital	22.0	20.1	27.5	38.0	48.3	60.9	67.0	71.5	86.0	102.4
Stockholders' equity	27.4	32.8	42.8	54.7	65.7	78.4	84.2	89.4	108.8	129.1
Average P/E ratio	5.5	6.9	6.8	6.1	8.6	10.6	15.1	15.0	10.9	12.8
Average dividend yield	4.5%	3.5%	3.2%	3.5%	3.4%	2.5%	3.3%	2.4%	2.5%	2.2%
Return on sales	3.7	3.6	4.5	4.1	3.7	3.9	2.9	3.3	3.6	3.7
Return on assets	15.4	16.4	20.9	20.0	17.3	17.5	11.0	14.1	17.9	18.3
Return on equity	20.4	21.8	25.3	27.1	23.0	23.2	14.2	19.6	24.6	25.3
Shares outstanding (000)[a]										
Common	16,266	16,303	16,365	16,489	16,563	16,553	16,539	16,174	16,192	16,147
Class A	N.Av.	N.Av.	N.Av.	N.Av.	N.Av.	N.Av.	N.Av.	N.Av.	12,716	12,845
Class B	N.Av.	N.Av.	N.Av.	N.Av.	N.Av.	N.Av.	N.Av.	N.Av.	3,476	3,302
Beta	N.Av.	N.Av.	N.Av.	N.Av.	N.Av.	N.Av.	N.Av.	N.Av.	0.75	0.75

N.Av. = not available.
N.Ap. = not applicable.
[a] Adjusted for stock splits and reclassification.

Kelly Services, Inc.

EXHIBIT 3
■

Stock Price[a] Quarterly Average

			Kelly					
			Common		Class A		Class B	
Year/ Quarter		S&P 500	High	Low	High	Low	High	Low
1980	1	102.9	$20⅔	$15⅓				
	2	114.2	17⅔	15⅓				
	3	125.5	23⅔	17⅓				
	4	135.8	22⅔	20¾				
1981	1	136.0	27	21⅓				
	2	131.2	33	26⅔				
	3	116.2	33	27⅓				
	4	122.6	32⅓	28				
1982	1	111.9	30	25¾				
	2	109.6	30½	23				
	3	122.4	25½	19¼				
	4	139.4	34	24¼				
1983	1	151.9	37½	30½				
	2	166.4	41	35				
	3	167.2	47½	41				
	4	164.4	47	40				
1984	1	159.2	18	15½				
	2	168.1	16⅜	15⅛				
	3	166.1			$27½	$22½	$27	$21
	4	165.0			28½	22½	27½	23
1985	1	153.2			30¾	20¾	30⅜	21⅛
	2	166.1			34½	25¾	37⅛	27⅛
	3	167.2			38¾	32¾	38¾	33½
	4	180.7			46½	34⅛	42½	34

[a]Kelly data adjusted for the 1987 split.

Kelly Services, Inc.

EXHIBIT 4
■

Comparative Financial Statements, 1984–1985
(dollars in millions, except per share data)

	Kelly (December 31)		Olsten (December 31)		Volt (October 31)	
	1984	1985	1984	1985	1984	1985
Sales	$741.2	$876.4	$218.8	$262.9	$391.7	$389.8
5-year growth	16.2%	17.6%	24.4%	25.0%	22.3%	18.6%
Net profit	$ 26.7	$ 32.6	$ 6.0	$ 7.3	$ 13.0	$ (6.0)
5-year growth	17.1%	21.2%	23.2%	31.0%	9.6%	C/C
Earnings/share	$ 1.65[a]	$ 2.01[a]	$ 0.74	$ 0.90	$ 1.70	$ (0.84)
5-year growth	17.1%	21.2%	17.5%	24.7%	4.4%	(5.5)%
Dividends/share	$ 0.46[a]	$ 0.56[a]	$ 0.12	$ 0.16	0	0
5-year growth	20.1%	16.0%	15.7%	22.4%	0	0
Average annual P/E	10.9	16.5	10.5	15.9	11.9	N.Ap.
Dividend payout ratio	27.0%	27.0%	16.0%	18.0%	0	0
Cash	$ 39.5	$ 47.9	$ 15.6	$ 20.8	$ 37.2	$ 27.2
Total current assets	126.2	151.9	55.0	63.5	190.2	159.4
Total assets	148.9	178.6	59.8	71.8	361.0	309.0
Total current liabilities	40.2	49.5	23.6	29.4	115.0	73.9
Long-term debt	0.0	0.0	0.0	0.0	125.9	125.9
Long-term debt and capital leases	0.0	0.0	0.0	0.0	127.3	127.3
Net worth	$108.8	$129.1	$ 36.2	$ 42.3	$115.5	$102.8
5-year average tax rate	49.5%	49.4%	48.0%	47.7%	46.1%	45.7%[b]
Stock price (end of year)	$28	$44	$18	$30	$17	$20
Beta	0.75	0.75	1.25	1.25	1.40	1.40
Return on sales	3.6%	3.7%	2.7%	2.8%	3.3%	(1.8)%
Return on assets	17.9	18.3	10.0	10.2	3.6	(2.3)
Return on capital	24.6	25.3	16.6	17.3	5.4	0.9
Return on equity	24.6	25.3	16.6	17.3	11.3	(6.8)
Common shares (millions)	16.19	16.15	8.11	8.13	7.35	7.05

C/C = cannot calculate because of a loss in at least one year.
N.Ap. = not applicable.
[a]Class A common stock.
[b]Four-year average because of loss during period.

Kelly Services, Inc.

EXHIBIT 5

∎

Pro Forma 1985 Results for Alternative Capital Structures
(dollars in millions, except per share data)

| | Actual | Pro Forma Debt/Total Capital | | |
		30 Percent	50 Percent	70 Percent
Sales	$876.4	$876.4	$876.4	$876.4
Earnings before interest and taxes	64.0	64.0	64.0	64.0
Interest	0.0	4.8	8.1	11.3
Earnings before taxes	64.0	59.2	55.9	52.7
Taxes	31.4	29.6	28.0	26.4
Net earnings	$ 32.6	$ 29.6	$ 27.9	$ 26.3
Dividends	$ 9.1	$ 8.3	$ 7.8	$ 7.4
Shares outstanding (millions)	16.15	14.60	13.57	12.53
Earnings/share[a]	$ 2.01	$ 2.03	$ 2.06	$ 2.10
Price/earnings ratio	16.50×	N.Av.	N.Av.	N.Av.
Dividends/share	$ 0.56	$ 0.57	$ 0.58	$ 0.59
Dividend yield[b]	2.00%	N.Av.	N.Av.	N.Av.
Beginning of year				
Debt	$ 0.0	$ 38.7	$ 64.5	$ 90.4
Net worth	129.1	90.4	64.6	38.7
Stock price/share	25.0	N.Av.	N.Av.	N.Av.

N.Av. = not available.
[a] At a 50-percent tax rate the EPS would be $1.98.
[b] End of year.

Marriott Corporation

In January 1980, the management of the Marriott Corporation found itself in an interesting dilemma: not only did the corporation have considerable excess debt capacity, but projections of future operations and cash flows indicated that this capacity would increase during the upcoming year. Management had stated that unused debt capacity was inconsistent with the goal of maximizing shareholder wealth. Excess debt capacity was viewed as comparable to unused plant capacity because the existing equity base could support additional productive assets.

Management's negative view of excess debt capacity had been strengthened by the rising inflation rates of the late 1970s, which were thought to increase the costs of unused debt capacity both directly and indirectly. As stated in Marriott's 1979 *Annual Report:*

> Both the cost of equity and the cost of debt increase with inflation. However, as inflation accelerates, tax deductibility partially offsets the rising cost of debt. On the other hand, business absorbs the full inflationary impact of equity cost increases. A firm which prudently utilizes its full debt capacity substitutes marginally cheaper debt for more expensive equity, thus optimizing the weighted cost of capital.

High inflation rates also had subtle effects on the firm's capital structure. Measured by its current value, debt previously committed at comparatively low interest rates actually declined in value. When the company's balance sheet was recast on a current-value basis, the debt-to-total capital ratio actually declined, implying an increase in debt capacity.

Management was therefore faced with two problems. First, it needed to determine the amount of funds that would be available if Marriott's full debt capacity were utilized. Second, management needed to decide whether to invest the excess funds in new or existing businesses, or to return them to the company's shareholders by paying higher cash dividends or repurchasing stock.

This case was prepared as a basis for class discussion rather than to illustrate either effective or ineffective handling of an administrative situation. Copyright © 1982 by the Darden Graduate Business School Sponsors, University of Virginia, Charlottesville, Virginia.

MARRIOTT CORPORATION: BACKGROUND

Operations through 1974.   The Marriott Corporation (MC) was founded by J. Willard Marriott in 1927, beginning as a root beer stand. The family first broadened its operation in 1937 when it pioneered in the field of airline catering, and again in the 1950s when it entered the hotel business and began providing food-service management to hospitals. The corporation's period of greatest diversification occurred in the late 1960s when, in addition to expanding the company's existing businesses, MC management made the following moves: (1) acquired several foreign airline catering kitchens; (2) bought the Big Boy coffee shop chain; (3) obtained the rights to use Roy Rogers's name on a chain of family restaurants; (4) entered the amusement business by initiating plans to develop up to three theme parks; and (5) purchased a cruise ship business, the Sun Line Shipping Co.

The corporation's aggressive growth proceeded unchecked until 1975. From 1968 to 1974, both sales and net income increased at an average annual rate of 22 percent, while earnings per share nearly tripled. The absolute growth in the size of the corporation was perhaps best reflected in the quadrupling of its capital base in this seven-year period, as shown in Exhibit 1. By the end of 1975, the Marriott Corporation had been organized into the five operating groups described in Exhibit 2: restaurant operations; the business and professional services group; the hotels group; Sun Line Cruises; and theme parks.

In 1975, Marriott's profits declined for the first time in 20 years. While domestic sales and profits had grown during the year, their rates of growth were slowed and profit margins were eroded by the combined effects of inflation and recession. In addition, the rapid business expansion resulting from management's targeted growth rate of 20 percent per year had generated sizable new-venture start-up costs and significant increases in interest expenses. However, the major factor that affected Marriott's 1975 performance was the $5.8 million loss incurred by Sun Line Cruises. Inflation had a devastating effect on this business, as rapidly escalating oil prices increased costs and declining consumer interest in cruise vacations reduced sales. The outbreak of the Greek–Turkish war on Cyprus, one of the company's areas of operation, further reduced the company's revenues.

The combined effect of all of these problems was a 12.6 percent decline in Marriott's 1975 net income and a 14 percent drop in earnings per share. The company's return on average equity reached a new low of 8.8 percent.[1]

Reappraisal, 1975–1976.   In view of the company's 1975 performance, MC management reassessed its long-term goals and developed the following objective: to continue the company's growth by renewing the corporation's historic emphasis on the hotel business. However, management believed that the company was too highly leveraged and too dependent on inflexible secured debt to reach this goal easily.

---

[1]Marriott changed the end of its operating year in 1978 from July to December to accommodate the seasonality of the theme parks. The financial statements for the five preceding years, 1974–1977, when restated to the new operating year, showed the following results for 1974–1975: net income increased 0.2 percent; earnings per share declined 1.4 percent; and return on average equity reached a low of 9.5 percent.

Until 1975, MC had relied on the traditional mortgage markets for most of its long-term financing. By the end of 1975, 63 percent of Marriott's long-term obligations (about 81 percent of the company's net worth) was in the form of secured debt. Roughly 54 percent of Marriott's net property, plant, and equipment was pledged against this debt, making any significant modification to or disposition of these assets extremely difficult. This situation was regarded by Marriott management as a constraint on the company's maneuverability.

Furthermore, the corporation's continued expansion into the restaurant, catering, and amusement businesses had changed the composition of its assets. The assets associated with these new businesses could not be readily mortgaged. For instance, lenders were unwilling to grant mortgages on the assets associated with Marriott's theme parks. Originally estimated to cost $80 million, these assets had a final cost of $160 million. Lastly, the mortgage markets had shown wide swings in both interest rates and availability of funds. These variations raised additional questions about the future costs and availability of long-term mortgage debt financing.

In short, MC management viewed its continued reliance on the mortgage markets as a constraint on the company's growth and its ability to capitalize rapidly on high-return investments. Consequently, management decided to diversify the company's source of debt by making MC an A-rated unsecured borrower and by developing a wider market for the debt associated with its hotels. Before it could take these steps, however, MC had to improve its returns and restructure its liabilities.

To increase the rate of growth in revenues, MC management accelerated the corporation's marketing efforts. Concurrently, cost-control programs were initiated to improve margins. Moreover, about $100 million of marginally productive assets were disposed of. Reflecting management's renewed commitment to the hotel business, the dispositions included several foreign airline catering kitchens, the majority interest in an idle cruise ship, a security company, excess land around the existing theme parks, and land originally purchased in anticipation of a third theme park. Exhibit 2 details the changes in Marriott's operating units between 1975 and 1979.

MC management also reduced planned capital expenditures and increased its hurdle rates for new investments. Some existing hotels were sold to counteract the capital intensity of the hotel business, although MC retained management contracts for these hotels, thereby keeping operational control of the units. MC also increased its reliance on off-balance-sheet financing as a further means of reducing the company's capital intensity.[2] Finally, the company issued 1.25 million shares of common stock, the first equity issue since 1975.

Results through December 1978.

The results of management's actions were almost immediately apparent. All key performance ratios had shown improvement as early as 1976, and the corporation's cash flow had increased strongly, up 25 percent over the 1975 level. In addition, both the proportion of mortgage notes payable to total capital and the ratio of assets pledged to net property, plant, and equipment had declined, while the corporation's debt maturities had been lengthened. Management had decided that the corporation's

---

[2] By keeping its investments in ventures to less than 50 percent, management could, for accounting purposes, record its investments using the equity method, thereby increasing the rates of return earned.

annual cash flow should, at a minimum, equal the sum of the next 5 years' debt maturities. It was able to meet this self-imposed debt limit as early as 1976, when Marriott's cash flow exceeded its 5-year debt maturities by 6 percent. Continued strong returns through 1977 allowed the corporation to place $40 million of 20-year unsecured debt.

Several further steps were taken during 1978. First, MC initiated the payment of cash dividends. In addition, management redefined its debt criterion: long-term debt was, at a minimum, to equal 45 percent of total capital.[3] And last, management adjusted the corporation's target debt rating from A to BBB. An A rating, management believed, was not all that desirable for growth-oriented companies that required financial flexibility. Furthermore, in the case of companies such as Marriott that used borrowed funds to meet restrictive loan covenants relative to working capital requirements, the higher credit rating could also be more expensive. MC management had decided that the interest payments saved by less restrictive loan covenants relative to working-capital balances would more than offset the increased interest rates resulting from the lower credit rating.

By the end of 1978, management believed that Marriott Corporation was in a financially liquid and flexible position. Sales had increased 15 percent, but earnings were up 39 percent, more than double management's goal of 15 percent per year earnings' growth. Marriott's cash flows had increased 22 percent, boosted both by the increased earnings as well as by the receipt of $35 million in after-tax proceeds from the sale of assets. The return on average equity had increased from the 1975 low of 9.5 to 14 percent. The return on total capital had risen from 13 to 16 percent.

For the most part, each of the corporation's business segments had done well during the period. While operating margins in the contract food service and restaurant groups had eroded slightly, those of the hotel group had increased, resulting in an overall 2 percent improvement in the corporate operating margin from 9 percent in 1975 to 11 percent in 1978. The major profit gains came from the theme parks, which began operations in 1976, and from a turnaround in the cruise ship business. Exhibit 3 provides operating results for Marriott's five business groups.

Long-term debt was at an all-time low of 37.5 percent of total capital, and the 1978 cash flow exceeded the sum of the next 5 years' debt maturities by 11 percent. These improvements led management to believe that it had $150 million in excess debt capacity.

Operating Year 1979.

On the basis of Marriott's 1978 returns and those projected for 1979, management increased the company's capital budget for the year by 14 percent and repurchased 5 million shares of common stock at a cost of $74 million. This purchase was intended to offset the dilutive effects of the company's stock option plan.

Despite these major investments, Marriott's 1979 performance exceeded that of 1978, as shown in Exhibits 4 and 5. As a result, management continued to believe that the corporation was significantly underleveraged despite the increase in debt to 41 percent of total capital.

---

[3]Long-term debt was defined as senior debt plus capital-lease obligations. Total capital was defined as total assets less current liabilities.

In 1979, the Financial Accounting Standards Board required firms of Marriott's size to report the effects of inflation on their financial statements for the first time. The results of recasting Marriott's financial statements into constant dollar and current value bases are shown in Exhibit 6. MC management favored the current value approach over the constant-dollar method for several reasons: (1) the company's assets were largely real-estate based and tended to appreciate rather than depreciate in value; (2) the assets were not subject to any major technological or competitive obsolescence that might necessitate their replacement; and (3) the company's annual repair and replacement costs traditionally averaged only 50 percent of the yearly depreciation charge. Management concluded that its reliance on the company's historical financial statements had caused it to undervalue MC's assets and to overstate its liabilities. Once again, management believed that the company's debt capacity had been underestimated.

At the same time, management concluded that the debt-to-total capital ratio was not the best measure of debt capacity. This ratio ignored the market value of assets and liabilities, the reliability and size of cash flows, and the structural differences among competitors within an industry. Instead, management chose to measure debt capacity in terms of earnings' coverage of net interest. Specifically, they concluded that earnings before interest and taxes, adjusted for actual repair and replacement expenses rather than by the income statement's depreciation charge, should cover net interest five times. (Exhibit 7 displays the results of applying this and other debt criteria to the company's historical financial data.)

The uncertainty about the best measure of the company's debt capacity spilled over into MC management's investment and capital-budgeting processes. Originally very project-oriented in its investment and financing decisions, management had taken a broader perspective when it diversified away from the mortgage markets. The use of unsecured debt had allowed management to separate the investment and financing decisions. However, it was still faced with determining the relationship between the corporation's debt capacity and the earning power of a given project. Management thought that MC's debt capacity was directly related to a project's ability to generate a reliable stream of cash to cover the interest charges associated with its financing. This view implied that the corporation's prevailing debt criterion should be applied project by project in the capital-budgeting procedure.

MARRIOTT'S 1979
INVESTMENT ALTERNATIVES

While management did have considerable discretion in determining the best investments for the corporation,[4] each of the preceding decisions and factors, as well as the prevailing capital market conditions detailed in Exhibit 8, contributed to the complexity of the 1979 investment decision. Management had identified two general categories of investments: (1) promoting growth by expanding exist-

---

[4]Management's decision-making abilities were constrained only by the corporation's articles of incorporation, which required the approval of two-thirds of the outstanding shares for any merger, sale, or exchange of substantially all of the assets or businesses of the company.

ing operations or diversifying into new businesses; or (2) returning capital to the shareholders by increasing the company's dividends or by buying back some of the outstanding stock.

I. PROMOTE GROWTH

Alternative 1. Accelerate Expansion of Existing Businesses.
MC Management could increase its rate of investment in existing operations. The most promising area for investment was the hotel business. Although a mild recession was anticipated for early 1980, its effects on the lodging industry in general and on Marriott in particular were expected to be mild. Marriott hotels catered to business people and convention-goers whose travel plans were less subject to change than those of vacationers. MC hotels had come through the 1970 recession and the even more severe one in 1974 to 1975 with healthy earnings increases. Prevailing trends in the lodging industry also appeared to favor rapid room expansion. Industrywide construction had been somewhat constrained recently because of high interest rates, rising construction costs, and selective institutional lending.

An increase in the rate of hotel-room expansion also made sense from a competitive viewpoint. During the latter half of the 1970s, both Hilton and Holiday Inn, two of Marriott's major competitors, had diversified their investments away from the pure lodging business into gambling and casino ventures. MC management had decided to avoid the gambling business for ethical reasons and was in a good position to expand in the more traditional markets.

At the end of 1979, Marriott had 50 hotels in various stages of development. Completion of these units would result in about a 20 to 25 percent annual rate of growth in hotel rooms. More than half of these planned hotels were to be managed rather than wholly owned by the Marriott Corp. The large proportion of managed hotels among the planned units reflected management's emphasis on higher returns on invested capital rather than increased margins. The operating margin on a managed hotel was lower than that of an owned property—8 to 10 percent versus 15 percent, on average.[5]

If Marriott management chose to invest additional funds in the hotel business, it could do so in one of the following ways:[6]

1. Limited capital investment: MC could take up to a 50-percent equity position, thus minimizing its capital investment while maximizing the probability of being awarded the management contract on the property.

2. Full capital investment in a property with high and reasonably well-assured returns: MC could expand existing MC hotels where occupancy rates were high and the local market's demand was known and readily forecast.

3. Full capital investment, but low entry cost: MC could acquire an existing hotel where the Marriott name, management expertise, and referral systems were expected to improve the property's results.

4. Capital put fully at risk in a new hotel at a new location.

---

[5]Joseph J. Doyle, "Marriott Corporation–Lodging and Restaurants–1/3/79." Research Report for Smith Barney Harris Upham & Co., Inc., New York.
[6]Ibid.

Details regarding hotel life cycles and average construction costs for hotel properties are shown in Exhibit 9. In 1979, the average annual occupancy rate in the U.S. lodging industry was about 73 percent, slightly higher than the 1978 level of 72 percent. Marriott hotels, however, had an average occupancy rate of over 80 percent in 1979, well above the industry average.

Alternative 2. Diversify through Acquisition.

MC management could also use the company's funds to acquire another company. Management had every reason to believe that it could identify a company and a situation that would benefit from Marriott's principal asset: the operating expertise that cut across a broad range of food-service, lodging, and entertainment businesses.

Exhibit 10 displays recent data on merger and acquisition activity in the market.

II. RETURN SHAREHOLDERS' CAPITAL

Alternative 3. Increase Dividends.

MC management could also increase the company's cash dividends. Although a single lump-sum payment could be paid to the shareholders, this tactic would offer only a short-term solution to the company's problem of excess debt capacity and steadily increasing cash flows. A permanent increase in the company's payout ratio seemed a more reasonable alternative.

A major increase in cash dividends had significant ramifications for existing shareholders as well as for potential investors.

Per share data and other financial data for Marriott and its principal competitors are shown in Exhibits 11 and 12.

Alternative 4. Repurchase Shares of Common Stock.

A repurchase of common stock carried with it many of the same advantages and disadvantages as the previous alternative. Most serious, potentially, was the possible market interpretation of the move: the idea that Marriott had fully utilized its growth opportunities. The fact that management had only recently repurchased about five million shares on the open market was also of some significance. By shrinking the company in this manner, however, management had expected that the company's earnings per share and return on equity would increase enough to offset any negative interpretation of the strategy. Trends in Marriott's stock price relative to those of its major competitors are shown in Exhibit 12.

If management selected this alternative, it would need to make several decisions: (1) how many shares to tender, (2) at what price, and (3) whether or not to retire the shares repurchased.

At the end of 1979, the Marriott family owned about 6.5 million shares of the company's common stock. Nonfamily members of management owned an additional 1.5 million shares through the company's stock option and profit-sharing plans. Ownership of the remaining shares was largely dispersed among about 50,000 shareholders.

Marriott Corporation

EXHIBIT 1
■
Marriott Corporation: Historical Performance[a]

	Sales—Percentage Change/Yr.	Net Income—Percentage Change/Yr.	PAT/Avg. Equity/Yr.	Pre-Debt Cash Flow[b] Percentage Change/Yr.	Average Capital[c] Percentage Change/Yr.	Pre-Debt Cash Flow/ Avg. Capital	Debt/ Total Capital[d]
1968	35.0%	23.1%	N.Av.[e]	N.Av.	N.Av.	N.Av.	49.0%
1969	31.0	20.6	12.9%	28.0%	N.Av.	13.1%	43.4
1970[e]	23.0	23.9	12.9	36.2	32.6%	13.4	49.4
1971	10.6	24.3	12.4	27.4	25.9	13.6	48.0
1972	20.2	28.7	11.6	22.3	23.9	13.4	49.7
1973	27.3	18.3	11.2	20.0	21.6	13.2	53.4
1974	19.0	15.8	11.4	25.3	20.1	13.8	50.4
1975	14.4	(12.6)	8.8	10.0	18.9	12.8	54.1
1976[e]	21.6	43.1	10.7	23.0	15.9	13.5	50.5
1977	15.3	17.5	10.7	11.2	6.9	14.1	45.3
1978	14.6	29.9	12.3	15.1	0.4	16.1	38.2

[a]Marriott changed its year end in 1978 from the last Friday in July to the Friday closest to December 31, to accommodate the seasonality of the theme park business better. At that time, the corporation restated its financial statements for the four preceding years (1974–1978) to reflect the change in its operating year. However, the data shown above have not been restated to reflect more accurately the corporation's historical performance and the results management was faced with in 1975 when it changed its business and financial strategies. All data were taken from the *1978 Annual Report* (7/28/78) but reflect the effects of changes in accounting policies instituted subsequent to 1975 (e.g., accounting for leases).
[b]Pre-debt cash flows = PAT + Depreciation and other non-cash charges + After-tax interest payments.
[c]Average capital = Two-year average of total assets − Current liabilities.
[d]Debt = End-of-year senior debt + Capital leases. Total capital = End-of-year total assets − Current liabilities.
[e]The year is 53 weeks long.
N.Av. = not available.

Marriott Corporation

EXHIBIT 2
■
Marriott Activities, 1975 and 1979

	Number of Units	
Operating Group	7/25/75	12/28/79
A. Restaurant Operations Group		
1. Company-owned restaurants	407	476
a. Dinner houses and restaurants	18	9
b. Ice cream parlour restaurants (Farrells)	83	77
c. Cafeterias (principally Hot Shoppes)	40	16
d. Coffee shops (principally Bob's Big Boy)	132	180
e. Fast foods (principally Roy Rogers)	124	194

EXHIBIT 2 *continued*

	Number of Units	
Operating Group	7/25/75	12/28/79
2. Franchised restaurants	846	1,013
a. Coffee shops (Big Boys)	746	901
b. Ice cream parlour restaurants (Farrells)	22	32
c. Fast foods (Roy Rogers)	78	80
3. Production facilities		
a. Kitchens providing food research and production for Marriott restaurants, hotels, and flight kitchens as well as for sale to the food-service industry and retail food chains.	2	0
B. *Business and Professional Services Group* (subsequently named Contract Food Services)		
1. Domestic flight kitchens (airline catering)	40	39
2. International flight kitchens (airline catering)	20	23
3. Management contracts: Provision of food service to business and industry, health care and educational institutions, highway restaurants, etc.	168	217
4. Airline terminal contracts	10	12
5. Special services (including institutional catering from in-flight kitchens and food service to auto-train passengers)	19	0
6. Security systems	12	0
C. *Hotels Group*		
1. Company-owned properties		
a. Hotels	19[a]	20
b. Rooms	8,371[a]	8,348
2. Company-managed properties		
a. Hotels	11[a]	27
b. Rooms	4,616[a]	12,608
3. Franchised Marriott Inns		
a. Inns	12	18
b. Rooms	2,841	5,328
4. Resort/hotel condominiums		
a. Properties with condominiums held for retail sale	2	1
5. Full-service travel bureau	1	0
D. *Sun Line Cruises*		
a. Number of ships	3	3
E. *Theme Parks* (parks completed in 1976)	0	2

[a]Hotel data have been revised to a calendar-year basis and show units in operation at end of December 1975.
Source: Marriott Corporation, 1975 and 1979 *Annual Reports.*

EXHIBIT 3

■

Segment Data (dollars in millions)

Fiscal Years

	Unaudited											
	1975		1976		1977		1978		1979[a]	
	Dollars	Percent	Dollars	Percent	Dollars	Percent	Dollars	Percent	Dollars	Percent
Sales										
Hotel group	$238.3	31%	$281.3	30%	$334.7	31%	$ 408.3	33%	$ 535.0	35%
Contract food services	256.3	33	289.4	30	342.6	31	388.0	31	479.8	32
Restaurant group	267.3	34	295.4	31	316.9	29	347.2	28	377.3	25
Theme parks	0	0	64.1	7	71.9	7	75.5	6	83.9	6
Cruise ships and other	14.0	2	16.5	2	24.2	2	30.6	2	34.0	2
Total sales	$775.9	100%	$946.7	100%	$1,090.3	100%	$1,249.6	100%	$1,510.0	100%
Operating profit[a]										
Hotel group	$ 33.3	47%	$ 38.1	41%	$ 54.1	47%	$ 66.5	49%	$ 86.6	51%
Contract food services	18.7	26	19.2	20	21.2	18	23.5	17	31.6	18
Restaurant group	21.7	31	20.2	22	26.1	23	27.6	21	28.5	17
Theme parks[b]	0.0	0	14.7	16	10.0	9	11.8	9	17.5	10
Cruise ships and other	(2.6)	(4)	0.9	1	4.0	3	4.8	4	6.4	4
Total operating profit	$ 71.1	100%	$ 93.1	100%	$ 115.4	100%	$ 134.2	100%	$ 170.6	100%
Gross Margin: Operating Profit/Sales										
Hotel group	14.0%		13.5%		16.2%		16.3%		16.2%	
Contract food services	7.3		6.6		6.2		6.1		6.6	
Restaurant group	8.1		6.8		8.2		8.0		7.6	
Theme parks[b]	—		22.9		13.9		15.6		20.9	
Cruise ships and other	(18.6)		5.5		16.5		15.7		18.8	
Total Marriott	9.1%		9.8%		10.6%		10.7%		11.3%	

Segment	Identifiable Assets			Net Assets Employed		
	1977	1978	1979	1977	1978	1979
Hotel group	$379.1	$ 351.2	$ 434.3	$353.7	$303.6	$371.9
Contract food services	127.9	138.6	163.2	99.3	99.3	124.0
Restaurant group	162.0	184.9	198.8	143.8	161.7	175.4
Theme parks[b]	169.0	167.5	162.9	164.0	161.4	158.0
Cruise ships and other	45.1	43.9	45.3	36.0	32.0	32.0
Corporate	66.4	114.2	75.9	32.9	68.9	30.6
Total	$949.5	$1,000.3	$1,080.4	$823.7	$826.9	$891.9

Segment	Capital Expenditures and Acquisitions			Depreciation and Amortization		
	1977	1978	1979	1977	1978	1979
Hotel group	$43.1	$ 62.9	$ 80.6	$17.7	$16.0	$16.0
Contract food services	9.9	10.8	20.3	7.4	7.9	7.6
Restaurant group	23.7	34.1	45.0	11.8	12.5	14.7
Theme parks[b]	9.7	9.2	6.3	7.9	8.0	9.2
Cruise ships and other	0.8	0.4	1.2	1.7	1.8	1.4
Corporate	11.2	21.7	5.1	0.8	0.9	1.7
Total	$98.4	$139.1	$158.5	$47.3	$47.1	$50.6

Segment	Sales/Total Capital[ac]			Return on Capital (Operating Profit/Total Capital)[ac]		
	1977	1978	1979	1977	1978	1979
Hotel group	0.95×	1.34×	1.44×	15.3%	21.9%	23.3%
Contract food services	3.67	3.91	3.87	22.7	23.7	25.5
Restaurant group	2.20	2.15	2.15	18.2	17.1	16.3
Theme parks[b]	0.44	0.47	0.53	6.1	7.3	11.1
Cruise ships and other	0.67	0.96	1.06	11.1	15.0	20.0
Total Marriott	1.32	1.51	1.69	14.0	16.2	19.1

Source: Marriott Corporation, 12/28/79 and 12/29/78 *Annual Reports*. The company changed its year end in 1978 to the Friday closest to December 31. The segment results are presented on the new fiscal-year basis. The unaudited data for 1975 and 1976 as restated were prepared using the same procedures employed to obtain the audited 1977 and 1978 results.

[a]Operating profit represents total operating results before interest, corporate administrative expense, unallocated corporate charges, and dispositions of business and idle property.
[b]Theme park operating results for 1976 are not comparable with subsequent years because the initial year did not bear the full burden of off-season costs and included charges for depreciation and real estate taxes only from the opening of the parks.
[c]Net identifiable assets = Total identifiable assets − Identifiable current liabilities = Total capital.

Marriott Corporation

EXHIBIT 4
■
Consolidated Income Statements
(thousands of dollars, except per share data)

	Year Ending				
	7/25/75[a]	7/30/76[a]	12/30/77	12/29/78	12/28/79
Sales	$732,396	$890,403	$1,090,313	$1,249,595	$1,509,957
Costs and Expenses					
Cost of sales and operating expenses	533,222	647,044	815,510	935,504	1,135,855
General and administrative expenses	31,469	35,023	43,935	50,182	53,616
Rent	30,427	34,146	—	—	—
Taxes—payroll, etc.	28,455	35,929	45,246	50,300	56,495
Depreciation and amortization[b]	30,637	36,119	47,279	47,144	50,623
Advertising and promotion	12,289	18,858	28,518	34,901	46,535
Gross interest	28,328	31,187	32,565	28,454	32,545
Interest capitalized	(10,353)	(10,432)	(2,359)	(4,766)	(4,705)
Net interest	17,975	20,755	30,206	23,688	27,840
Profit-sharing contributions	3,604	4,582	5,730	7,792	10,337
Pre-opening and development expenses	5,911	6,183	4,766	4,785	5,511
Total costs and expenses	693,989	838,639	1,021,190	1,154,296	1,386,812
Profit before taxes	38,407	51,764	69,123	95,299	123,145
Gross taxes	19,564	26,819	34,638	46,334	58,879
Investment tax credit (flow-through)[c]	(2,975)	(5,900)	(4,565)	(5,335)	(6,734)
Net taxes	16,589	20,919	30,073	40,999	52,145
Profit after taxes	21,818	30,845	39,050	54,300	71,000
Primary EPS	$0.66	$0.90	$1.04	$1.43	$1.96
Fully diluted EPS	N.Av.	N.Av.	1.04	1.43	1.95
Cash dividends/share[d]	N.Av.	N.Av.	0.30	0.13	0.17
Funds from operations[e]	70,320	87,543	99,834	121,588	140,934
Capital expenditures	$159,178	$143,235	$81,887	$134,738	$149,000

Footnotes for Exhibit 4:
[a]Data for 1975 to 1976, if restated to an operating year ending in December, would show the following summarized results, unaudited (in millions of dollars).

	12/75	12/76
Sales	$775.9	$946.7
Operating expenses	704.8	853.6
Gross interest	33.5	33.2
Interest capitalized	(10.5)	(6.4)
Net interest	23.0	26.8
Corporate expenses + Income + Dispositions	8.0	13.4
Profit before taxes	40.1	52.9
Gross taxes	20.3	26.0
Investment tax credit	(4.4)	(5.1)
Net taxes	15.9	20.9
Profit after taxes	$ 24.2	$ 32.0
Fully diluted earnings per share	$ 0.69	$ 0.86
Funds provided from operations	$ 77.6	$ 92.2
Capital expenditures	154.6	113.4

[b]Depreciation and amortization are accounted for on a straight-line basis.
[c]Investment tax credits are accounted for using the flow-through method.
[d] Marriott used 2.5 percent stock dividends annually from 1970 to 1977, except in 1972 when the stock split two for one.
[e]Funds provided from operation = Net income + Depreciation, Deferred taxes, and Other items not requiring current outlay of working capital.
Source: Marriott Corporation, 1976 Annual Report.

Marriott Corporation

EXHIBIT 5

■

Consolidated Balance Sheets[a] (thousands of dollars)

	Year Ending				
	7/25/75[a]	7/30/76[a]	12/30/77	12/29/78	12/28/79
Assets					
Current Assets					
Cash and equivalent	$ 18,318	$ 17,760	$ 16,990	$ 14,747	$ 12,445
Marketable securities at cost	6,490	2,993	—	38,510	8,825
Accounts receivable	43,588	50,293	61,484	76,774	99,955
Inventories (FIFO)	27,667	35,504	41,498	41,108	46,629
Prepaid expenses	4,492	7,580	9,444	9,571	9,868
Total current assets	100,555	114,130	129,416	180,710	177,722
Lincolnshire Hotel (net assets under sale/leaseback)	7,282	—	—	—	—
Property and Equipment					
Land	58,932	73,784	106,919	100,053	103,009
Buildings and improvements	174,053	270,686	293,679	264,038	323,059
Leasehold improvements	165,742	198,280	213,118	213,791	251,409
Furniture/equipment	164,967	228,401	248,066	250,265	284,733
Capital leases	—	—	53,408	29,243	29,724
Cruise ships	11,219	11,367	11,441	11,814	11,903
Idle land and ship	33,262	37,610	—	—	—
Construction in progress	98,044	16,483	29,441	88,270	62,501
Total property and equipment	706,219	836,611	956,072	957,474	1,066,338
Depreciation and amortization	(128,169)	(155,218)	(204,152)	(212,430)	(241,160)
Net property and equipment	578,050	681,393	751,920	745,044	825,178
Other Assets					
Investment in/advances to affiliates[b]	11,557	10,467	26,548	25,506	27,160
Goodwill	18,960	18,656	17,549	19,257	19,106
Notes receivable	—	—	11,670	17,805	16,284
Deferred pre-opening costs	5,636	5,388	—	—	—
Other	14,470	14,192	12,407	11,933	14,915
Total other assets	50,623	48,703	68,174	74,501	77,465
Total assets	$736,510	$844,226	$949,510	$1,000,255	$1,080,365

[a]Data for 1975 to 1976 do not reflect changes in accounting requirements relative to capital leases which were adopted in subsequent years. When instituted in the July 1978 financial statements, the change had the cumulative effect of a $2.4-million decline in the 1976 retained earnings balance of $63.6 million.

[b]The aggregated numbers (dollars in millions) and balance sheet characteristics of Marriott's affiliates in 1975 and 1979 are summarized below:

	Nos. of Investments	Total Assets	Total Liabilities	Total Equity
July 1975	2	$ 53	$ 46	9
Dec. 1979 (5 of 11 investments)	11	211	155	56

Source: Marriott Corporation, *Annual Reports.*

EXHIBIT 5 *continued*

	Year Ending				
	7/25/75[a]	7/30/76[a]	12/30/77	12/29/78	12/28/79
Liabilities and Shareholders' Equity					
Current Liabilities					
Short-term loans	$ 2,752	$ 2,989	$ 3,976	$ 3,473	$ 4,054
Accounts payable	33,111	41,503	46,666	66,960	71,528
Accrued liabilities	37,843	43,653	51,376	72,509	79,909
Income taxes payable	—	—	13,034	18,672	22,511
Current portion of debt and capitalized leases	11,424	10,119	10,813	11,758	10,497
Total current liabilities	85,130	98,264	125,865	173,372	188,499
Senior Debt					
Interim construction financing	4,948	16,000	—	—	—
Mortgage notes payable[c]	207,135	219,906	214,090	175,565	163,520
Unsecured notes payable	117,941	115,022	107,332	110,457	178,075
Total senior debt	330,024	350,928	321,422	286,022	341,595
Capital lease obligations	—	—	48,092	23,877	23,684
Deferred income taxes	34,514	47,343	56,385	59,903	65,597
Deferred income and other liabilities	866	1,007	2,435	10,260	20,569
Convertible subordinated debentures	32,240	31,340	29,515	28,165	26,918
Shareholders' Equity					
Common stock ($1 par)[d]	32,507	35,567	36,674	36,891	36,900
Capital surplus	169,974	212,250	222,785	224,915	224,533
Net deferred compensation payable in stock	3,256	3,952	4,967	6,350	7,670
Retained earnings	47,999	63,575	103,037	152,555	217,779
Treasury stock at cost	N.Av.	N.Av.	(1,667)	(2,055)	(73,379)
Total equity	253,736	315,344	365,796	418,656	413,503
Total liabilities and shareholders' equity	$736,510	$844,226	$949,510	$1,000,255	$1,080,365

N.Av. = not available.
[c]The value of the net assets pledged against this debt was estimated at $243 million in 1975 and $293 million in 1979.
[d]Changes in Marriott's common stock accounts are summarized below (figures in thousands):

	7/26/74–7/25/75	7/25/75–7/30/76	7/30/76–7/29/77	12/30/77–12/29/78	12/29/78–12/28/79
Opening number of shares	31,183	32,507	35,567	36,507	36,715
Shares issued	1,324	3,060	1,101	385	235
Shares repurchased	—	—	—	177	4,851
Closing number of shares	32,507	35,567	36,668	36,715	32,098
Estimated number of shareholders, end of period	43,200	47,000	52,800	50,700	N.Av.

Marriott Corporation

EXHIBIT 6
■

Inflation-Adjusted Financial Statements (thousands of dollars)

A. *Current Value Accounting*

Changes in Shareholders' Equity[a]

Current value, December 29, 1978	$767,719
Discretionary cash flow	99,123
Reduction in current value of debt	25,287
Increase in current value of assets	77,227
Purchase of treasury stock	(74,187)
Cash dividends	(5,776)
Common stock issued and other	3,810
Current value, December 28, 1979	$893,203[b]

Shareholders' Equity—12/28/79	*Historical Cost*	*Current Value*
Non-monetary assets (primarily property and equipment)	$927,287	$1,356,244
Less net monetary liabilities		
Senior debt and capital leases	365,279	320,736
Convertible debt	26,918	20,718
Other monetary liabilities, net	121,587	121,587
Total net monetary liabilities	513,784	463,011
Shareholders' equity	$413,503	$ 893,203
Senior debt and capital leases to total capital	41%	24%

Gain from Decline in Purchasing Power of Net Monetary Liabilities

Negative working capital	$ 6,322
Debt and other monetary liabilities	48,787
Total gain	$ 55,109

B. *Total Constant-Dollar Accounting (average 1979 dollars)*

	12/28/79
Net income as reported	$ 71,000
Constant-dollar adjustments	
Cost of sales	(5,203)
Depreciation and amortization of property and equipment	(18,427)
Total constant-dollar adjustments	(23,630)
Constant-dollar net income	$ 47,370
Constant-dollar gain from decline in purchasing power of net amounts owed	$ 55,109
Constant-dollar net income per share (excluding gain from decline in purchasing power of net amounts owed)	$1.31
Shareholders' equity (constant 1979 dollars)	$ 703,598
Effective 1979 income tax rate	52.4%

EXHIBIT 6 *continued*

C. *Five-Year Comparison of Selected Supplementary Financial Data Adjusted for the Effects of Changing Prices (average 1979 dollars)*

Fiscal Years Ended	Net Sales and Other Operating Revenue	Cash Dividends Declared per Common Share	Market Price per Common Share at Year End	Average Consumer Price Index
1975	$1,045,878	$—	$20.17	161.2
1976	1,206,576	—	16.88	170.5
1977	1,305,371	.04	13.73	181.5
1978	1,389,647	.14	12.99	195.4
1979	1,509,957	.17	16.53	217.4

[a]Property and equipment and investments in affiliates are valued on a discounted cash flow basis. Projections of future cash flows are adjusted to reflect anticipated asset-maintenance requirements. Goodwill is assigned no value. The interest rates used to discount the cash flows reflect current market rates.
[b]If the current value of existing hotel management agreements were included in the data, this figure would increase by about $275.8 million to $1,169 million.
Source: Marriott Corporation, 1979 *Annual Report.*

Marriott Corporation

EXHIBIT 7
■
Alternative Measurements of Debt and Marriott Results

	1974	1975	1976	1977	1978	1979
1. Cash flow/Year/5-year debt maturities[a]	0.63	0.84	1.06	1.11	1.15·	N.Av.
2. (Senior debt + Capital leases)/(Total assets − Current liabilities)[b]	53%	55%	48%	45%	38%	41%
3. EBIT/Net interest[b]	3.06	2.74	2.98	3.29	5.02	5.42
4. EBIT adjusted/Net interest[bc]	3.74(est.)	3.51	3.80	4.27	6.43	6.64
5. EBIT adjusted/Gross interest[b]	2.65(est.)	2.40	3.07	3.95	5.35	5.66

N.Av. = not available.
[a]Data reflect July fiscal year. Figure for 1978, if restated to December calendar year, would be 1.19.
[b]Data reflect December calendar year.
[c]EBIT adjusted = EBIT + Depreciation − Actual repairs/replacements.

Marriott Corporation

EXHIBIT 8
■
Market Data, 1975–1979

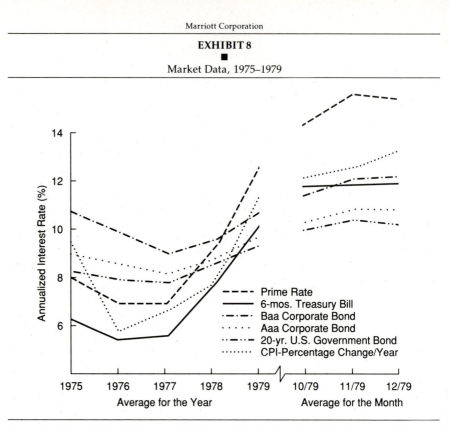

Source: *Federal Reserve Bulletin*. CPI data compiled by Economic Studies Center, Tayloe Murphy Institute, University of Virginia.

Marriott Corporation

EXHIBIT 9
■
Typical Life Cycle, 150-Room Motel

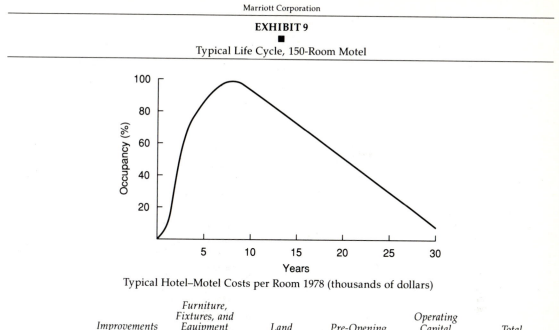

Typical Hotel–Motel Costs per Room 1978 (thousands of dollars)

	Improvements	Furniture, Fixtures, and Equipment	Land	Pre-Opening	Operating Capital	Total
Luxury	$32–55	$5–10	$4.0–12.0	$1.0 –2.0	$1.0 –1.50	$43.0–80.5
Standard	20–32	3–6	2.5– 7.0	0.75–1.5	0.75–1.00	27.0–47.5
Economy	8–15	2–4	1.0– 3.5	0.5 –1.0	0.5 –0.75	12.0–24.23

Source: "The Appraisal of Lodging Facilities," by Stephen Rushmore, *The Cornell Hotel and Restaurant Administration Quarterly,* August 1978. Life-cycle data have been adjusted to show occupancy rather than operating-income data.

Marriott Corporation

EXHIBIT 10

∎

Data on the Merger and Acquisition Market, 1975–1978

Year and Market Value of Companies Receiving Tender Offers (millions of dollars)	Number of Tender Offers Received	Average 5-Year Sales Growth per Year[a]	Average 5-Year Earnings Growth per Year[a]	Market Price/Book Value[b] (average)	Market Price/Earnings Ratio[b] (average)	Market Price/Cash Flow[b] (average)	Average Return on Equity[b]	Average Total Debt/Equity[b]	Average Tender Price/Market Value = Premium[b]
1975									
$20	6	5.5%	11.3%	0.52	7.72	4.06	7.5%	0.94	43.97%
$20–250	6	19.8	29.2	1.03	6.60	4.87	15.6	0.75	44.65
$250	—	—	—	—	—	—	—	—	—
1976									
$20	2	8.9	N.Av.	0.45	7.60	4.39	6.0	0.46	29.56
$20–250	11	17.3	20.7	1.45	11.81	6.83	16.6	1.43	28.98
$250	3	13.8	13.2	1.37	10.77	7.30	12.8	0.99	43.25
1977									
$20	1	4.2	N.Av.	0.72	10.69	3.55	7.0	1.76	36.50
$20–250	12	12.7	12.8	1.52	9.43	5.46	16.7	1.19	39.64
$250	6	12.9	19.9	1.56	9.29	7.99	14.9	0.71	62.55
1978									
$20	—	—	—	—	—	—	—	—	—
$20–250	10	11.5	3.7	1.15	7.37	4.17	18.6	1.70	60.05
$250	3	10.9	17.9	1.32	6.38	4.58	19.7	1.13	35.30
Control Group 1978[c]									
$20	—	18.8	6.3	1.05	9.0	4.30	6.0	1.32	N.Ap.
$20–250	—	14.1	13.5	1.74	8.9	6.46	19.2	0.54	N.Ap.
$250	—	18.3	10.2	1.49	8.8	5.80	17.3	1.07	N.Ap.

N.Av. = not available.
N.Ap. = not applicable.
[a]Five years prior to tender offer.
[b]All numbers reflect actual data two weeks prior to receipt of tender offer.
[c]Control group is random sample of companies in operation in 1978.

Marriott Corporation

EXHIBIT 11

∎

Travel Services Industry Competitors: Historical Data
(millions of dollars, except per share data or as noted)

Company and Year	Annual Revenues	Annual Profit after Tax	Return on Average Equity	Debt/ Total Capital	Primary Earnings per Share	Cash Flow per Share	Dividends per Share	Average Equity/ Average Shares	Average Market Price	Beta
Holiday Inns										
1975	$ 912	$41.0	9.4%	36.9%	$1.36	$3.43	$0.35	$14.73	$11.65	1.50
1978	1,188	63.0	11.9	33.3	2.04	4.17	0.56	17.74	18.77	1.55
1979	1,092	71.0	12.0	31.1	2.25	3.47	0.66	19.03	18.48	1.60
Hilton Hotels										
1975	351	42.0	20.5	34.7	1.43	2.35	0.28	7.26	6.05	1.40
1978	444	68.0	26.6	36.0	2.62	3.72	0.74	10.88	20.70	1.45
1979	484	99.0	29.1	23.4	3.76	4.77	1.09	13.51	29.33	1.40
Ramada Inns										
1975	212	1.0	0.8	67.0	0.04	0.59	0.06	4.88	4.00[a]	1.70
1978	308	10.2	7.1	63.7	0.40	1.09	0.12	5.54	7.56	1.55
1979	348	15.5	10.2	63.3	0.57	1.39	0.12	5.66	10.43	1.50
Marriott										
1975	732	21.8	9.0	55.5	0.65	1.54	N.Ap.	7.12	10.99	1.55
1978	1,250	54.3	14.0	40.9	1.43	2.57	0.13	10.22	11.34	1.55
1979	1,510	71.0	17.1	44.0	1.96	3.79	0.17	11.75	14.90	1.50
S&P 500										
1975	999.7 bil.	50.9 bil.	12.4	31.0	2.31	4.22	1.01	19.14	22.80	1.00
1978	1,454.0 bil.	82.7 bil.	15.1	29.0	3.52	6.00	1.44	23.97	27.43	1.00
1979	1,725.6 bil.	101.2 bil.	16.7	29.0	4.25	7.04	1.61	26.19	29.29	1.00

N.Ap. = not applicable.

[a]Estimated.

Sources include *Value Line; Standard & Poor's Computer Services, Inc.; and S&P Standard NYSE Stock Reports.*

Marriott Corporation

EXHIBIT 12
■

Comparative Common Stock Data, 1978–1979
(monthly closing price)

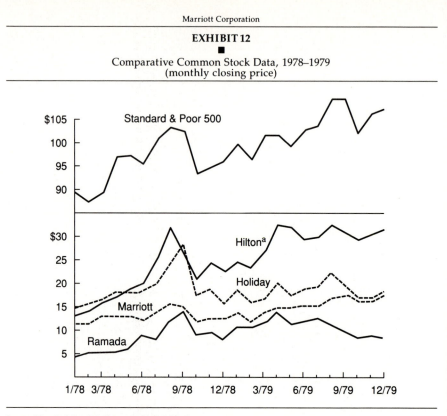

Source: New York Stock Exchange Daily Stock Index.
[a]Market price per share for Hilton has been adjusted for a two-for-one stock split in December 1978.

Hop-In Food Stores, Incorporated

In early March 1977, Charles Merriman was attempting to set a price for the first public offering of stock by Hop-In Food Stores, Incorporated, a regional convenience food store chain headquartered in Roanoke, Virginia. Mr. Merriman, who was vice president of corporate finance for Scott and Stringfellow, a small investment banking firm located in Richmond, Virginia, had agreed to underwrite 60,000 shares of Hop-In's common stock at a price bringing not less than $10 per share to the company. The underwriter's commission was to fall somewhere between 6 and 7 percent of the aggregate offering price, making $10.60 per share the minimum acceptable market price. Under this agreement, Scott and Stringfellow was required to purchase the entire issue from Hop-In, thereby assuming the risk that they would be unable to resell the issue to the public at something more than $10.60 per share. Beyond the $10 commitment, however, Scott and Stringfellow had no legal liability and was given leeway to price the issue at whatever level seemed appropriate.

COMPANY BACKGROUND

Hop-In Food Stores, incorporated on June 23, 1966 by John M. Hudgins, Jr., started in Roanoke as a single store selling a broad line of foodstuff and convenience items. Since 1966, sales had grown at a 55-percent annual rate, and by the end of 1976, the company operated 84 stores in two states. Table 1 shows the increase in the number of stores over the 5 fiscal years and 6 months ended December 31, 1976.

Hop-In had grown primarily through the acquisition of established stores rather than by internal expansion; of the 84 stores operating at the end of 1977, 58 had been acquired. The company pursued this policy of growth by acquisition because experience had proven both the costs and risks of operating a new store to be greater than those of purchasing an established one. New store sites were selected on the basis of residence density, the extent of street and highway access, and the proximity of competing stores.

This case was prepared as a basis for class discussion rather than to illustrate either effective or ineffective handling of an administrative situation. Copyright © 1979 by the Darden Graduate Business School Sponsors, University of Virginia, Charlottesville, Virginia.

TABLE 1
■
Change in Number of Stores

Period	Stores Added during Period	Stores Closed during Period	Stores Operating at End of Period
Fiscal 1972	9	0	19
Fiscal 1973	4	1	22
Fiscal 1974	5	0	27
Fiscal 1975	10	1	36
Fiscal 1976	41	1	76
Six months ended December 31, 1976	10	2	84

Source: Preliminary *Prospectus,* March 1977.

PRODUCT LINE AND COMPETITION

Hop-In stores emphasized the sale of traffic-building items, such as beer, soft drinks, cigarettes, wine, bread, milk, and other dairy and bakery products. Only nationally advertised brands in the grocery field and better-known local or regional brands of dairy and bakery products and meats were sold. Prices on staple foodstuff and convenience items were slightly higher than at conventional supermarkets, but competitive with other convenience food stores. Because of the nature of the product line, advertising was kept to a minimum except in connection with new store openings.

Gasoline was sold at 68 of Hop-In's 84 store locations. Pumping and storage facilities at 19 of the stores offering gasoline were owned by Hop-In. Facilities

TABLE 2
■
Convenience Stores' Sales by Product Category
(fiscal year ended June 30)

	1973	1976
Beer and wine	26.2%	23.4%
Gasoline	1.9	18.3
Grocery	15.2	12.3
Soft drinks	11.5	8.7
Tobacco	11.3	8.3
Health, beauty, household	7.1	7.1
Milk and dairy	11.0	7.1
Chips and snacks	4.6	3.6
Sandwiches and salads	3.9	3.8
Publications	1.5	3.8
Bakery	5.1	3.4
Miscellaneous	0.7	0.2
Total	100.0	100.0

Source: Preliminary *Prospectus,* March 1977.

at the remaining 49 stores were owned by suppliers under arrangements whereby Hop-In received a rental commission from the supplier based on the amount of gasoline sold. Traditionally, gasoline prices at these stores had been lower than those charged by stations selling nationally branded gasoline and competitive with those charged by independent stations in the area. However, this pricing policy had been possible only to the extent permitted by the company's and supplier's costs of gasoline.

In the past several years, sales of grocery and other staple items had declined as a percentage of sales primarily because of increased gasoline sales. Also, the company had made an effort to emphasize the sale of faster moving and more profitable items. Table 2 shows the breakdown of sales by product category.

Another factor contributing to the decline in sales of grocery and other staple items was the increasing competition within the retail-food industry. Hop-In's stores competed with local and national chain groceries, supermarkets, drugstores, and similar retail outlets, most of which had extended operating hours and expanded product lines in response to competition provided by convenience stores. Hop-In's most direct competition, however, came from other convenience food stores. The three major convenience food store chains with which Hop-In competed in Virginia and North Carolina were Seven-Eleven, Munford, and L'il General. Several of these competitors, because of their greater size, had developed competitive advantages including greater financial resources, economies of scale in purchasing, and national advertising. Exhibit 1 presents financial data on two of these competitors. Exhibit 2 provides information on six publicly held convenience food store companies.

FINANCIAL HISTORY

Mr. Hudgins operated the company as a closed corporation until November 1968 when a 60,000-share intrastate offering of common stock was made. By 1976, primarily as a result of a two-for-one split in 1972, the number of shares outstanding had grown to 124,657, of which 34 percent was owned by insiders and 13 percent was owned by the company's employee stock ownership plan; the remaining shares were held by outsiders. No single individual owned more than 10 percent of the oustanding shares. Hop-In stock was traded informally and only within the state of Virginia. In March 1977, it was selling at $9.50 per share.

Since the 1968 offering, Hop-In had been operating as much like a public company as possible. Financial statements had been prepared according to generally accepted accounting principles, and annual reports had been published each fiscal year. Exhibit 3 presents the statement of earnings for the fiscal years from 1972 to 1976 and the 6 months ended December 31, 1975 and 1976. Exhibit 4 shows Hop-In's financial position.

Prior to fiscal year 1976, Hop-In's cash flow from operations had provided enough working capital to support operations, while capital expenditures were supported by long-term borrowings or small injections of equity capital. This balance was threatened by the increasing number of acquisitions. During the 18 months ended December 31, 1976, the company purchased the assets (inventory and equipment) of 45 convenience food stores for a total of $1,396,945. Although the majority of funds required for these acquisitions was provided by internal sources, an additional $539,000 was short-term debt. As of December 31, 1976, $400,000 of this balance outstanding was payable to a bank under a line of credit totaling $550,000. Because Mr. Hudgins was expecting additional working capital needs in anticipation of the seasonal increase in sales generally experienced during the late spring and summer months, he wanted to reduce the level of short-term debt to provide some debt capacity should the need for additional funds arise.

GOING PUBLIC

For some time Mr. Hudgins had been contemplating the move to issue stock—to go public. Up until 1976, however, Hop-In's need for funds had not exceeded internal sources to the extent that they could not be covered by small stock purchases by management. However, the growth which Hop-In had experienced in 1975 and 1976 suggested that a new financing strategy was needed.

In addition to the need for external funds to finance growth, a number of considerations made going public attractive to Mr. Hudgins: (1) publicly traded stock would be a more effective tool for use in acquisitions; (2) it would establish a trading market for managers, directors, and employees who participated in the company's employee stock ownership plan (ESOP); (3) it would simplify estate settlement in the case of death of a major stockholder; and (4) it would strengthen the company's bargaining power with its lenders.

Having balanced these advantages of a public offering against the possible disadvantages, which included initial high costs and the risk of a poor after-market, Mr. Hudgins decided that the time to go public had come. Subsequently, contact was made with Mr. Merriman, and the offering was scheduled for late March 1977.

CURRENT SITUATION

The decision facing Mr. Merriman was a delicate one; there were risks associated with either an underpricing or an overpricing of the equity issue. If the new stock were overpriced, there was a chance that a market would not develop, leaving the securities "on the banker's shelf." Such a delay in the sale of stock would not only tie up Scott and Stringfellow's capital, but would also increase their exposure to potential downturns in the market, which might have further lowered the stock's value, forcing sale at reduced prices or even at a loss. If this occurred, goodwill among the selling group and investors who had purchased the stock at issue price would be damaged, thereby weakening Scott and Stringfellow's distribution network for future new issues. An underpriced issue, on the other hand, might be equally damaging. Scott and Stringfellow would draw criticism for not obtaining maximum value for Hop-In, leading to possible loss of underwriting business, not only with Hop-In, but with other corporate clients.

Before preparing the offer price, Mr. Merriman reviewed the economic and equity market conditions of March 1977. In early 1977, the general feeling about the nation's economy was one of optimism. A newly elected president had just taken office, and all indicators pointed toward recovery from the lull that followed the 1975 recession. Although the consumer price index for January rose by a seasonally adjusted annual rate of 9.6 percent, the largest increase in 18 months, most forecasters predicted an inflation rate of no more than 6 percent, and interest and bond coupon rates were falling. It was expected that the declining interest rates would draw investors' funds away from the fixed-income securities market and into the equity securities market, creating a favorable equity market climate. Stock market observers were cautiously optimistic about

1977, expecting market price growth of 10 to 20 percent followed by a leveling off or a partial reversal of growth to occur by the end of the year.

As a supplement to the comparative market and financial statistics shown in Exhibits 1 and 2, Mr. Merriman collected the following data: operating ratios on the retail grocery industry shown in Exhibit 5, a listing of recent equity issues and their respective prices shown in Exhibit 6, and some stock price indexes shown in Exhibit 7.

Additional considerations that concerned Mr. Merriman were (1) prospective problems with the SEC and shareholders because Hop-In's auditors were not one of the big eight firms; (2) the limited extent to which the new shares could be distributed geographically; and (3) Hop-In's lack of an established dividend policy. Finally, one other factor interested Mr. Merriman as he sought a pricing benchmark. He had heard that major petroleum companies were buying companies with gasoline sales facilities similar to Hop-In for roughly book value.

Hop-In Food Stores, Incorporated

EXHIBIT 1
∎

Comparative Financial Data: Industry Leaders, Years Ended December 31
(dollars in millions, except per share data)

	Net Sales	Net Working Capital	Current Ratio	Operating Income	Net Income before Taxes	Net Income	Earnings/ Share	Dividends/ Share	Price Range (Calendar Years)	Book Value/ Share[a]
Southland Corporation (Seven-Eleven)										
1966	$ 449.80	$ 41.20	2.3	$ 15.10	$10.91	$ 5.63	$0.50	$0.10	$ 8⅝–6⅝	$ 2.69
1967	527.30	41.10	2.0	21.53	14.26	7.21	0.62	0.11	12⅝–5¾	3.26
1968	621.10	56.60	2.1	29.03	19.60	9.35	0.73	0.12	22⅜–11½	5.48
1969	840.80	76.70	2.2	39.24	24.82	12.10	0.81	0.12	22–15½	6.45
1970	980.90	79.90	2.1	45.28	30.09	14.90	0.96	0.12	18¼–13	7.28
1971	1,079.80	83.60	2.1	51.32	34.56	17.30	1.09	0.15	29⅛–14½	8.39
1972	1,226.10	107.90	2.1	59.12	39.34	20.37	1.14	0.19	34½–22½	10.52
1973	1,393.60	96.00	2.0	68.05	44.15	23.33	1.26	0.22	27⅞–11	11.57
1974	1,609.30	89.80	1.8	87.03	57.84	29.74	1.60	0.31	19½–11¾	12.78
1975	1,789.70	94.70	1.8	103.63	68.18	34.32	1.80	0.37	26⅞–14⅜	14.21
Munford, Inc.										
1966	75.46	—	—	5.34	2.62	1.55	0.67	0.60	15½–8⅛	13.36
1967	90.99	8.00	1.9	6.37	3.95	2.17	0.87	0.60	25¼–9⅜	14.02
1968	99.31	12.44	2.3	6.41	3.81	2.06	0.80	0.51	35½–14⅜	4.84
1969	116.41	9.83	1.9	7.40	3.91	2.03	0.78	0.24	31⅜–11⅝	6.05
1970	127.99	11.38	1.9	7.62	4.01	1.97	0.82	0.24	14⅞–5½	6.44
1971	140.81	17.32	2.5	8.44	8.78	2.69	1.03	0.24	19¼–8⅝	6.81
1972	155.22	19.59	2.5	8.91	5.56	3.15	1.20	0.24	19⅞–13	8.78
1973	198.52	22.43	2.4	10.11	6.31	3.57	1.36	0.28	14⅛–5	10.15
1974	227.26	20.33	2.1	11.17	7.00	3.89	1.48	0.32	8½–4	11.52
1975	273.16	24.64	1.8	12.38	7.64	4.29	1.63	0.36	8¾–4¼	13.00

Source: *Standard and Poor's Industry Survey.*
[a]Two-for-one stock split in 1966.

Hop-In Food Stores, Incorporated

EXHIBIT 2
■
Comparative Financial Data on Selected Companies

	Hop-In	Southland	Munford	Dillon	Sunshine Junior	National Convenience Stores	Circle K
Latest complete fiscal year	6/30/76	12/31/75	1/1/76	7/3/76	12/31/75	6/30/76	4/30/76
Sales (thousands)	$14,078	$1,789,754	$273,161	$1,148,399	$58,050	$212,606	$302,600
Net income (thousands)	$ 281	$ 34,319	$ 4,287	$ 22,433	$ 1,300	$ 2,652	$ 6,910
Net income/sales	1.99%	1.92%	1.56%	1.9%	2.2%	1.25%	2.3%
Net income/net worth	22.38%	12.63%	11.63%	23.73%	14.94%	15.41%	18.03%
Earnings per share (primary)							
1971	N.Ap.	$1.09	$1.03	$0.78	$0.59	N.Av.	$0.84
1972	$0.55	1.14	1.20	0.95	0.48	$0.82	0.94
1973	1.11	1.26	1.36	1.28	0.62	0.90	0.99
1974	1.61	1.60	1.48	1.53	1.04	1.24	0.99
1975	1.73	1.80	1.63	1.97	0.95	0.67	1.07
1976	3.34	2.10	1.30	2.50	0.82	1.37	1.43
Market price, 10/29/76	N.Ap.	$26⅛	$9⅜	$31⅝	$6	$9¾	$7½
Price/earnings ratio, 10/29/76	N.Ap.	14.5×	6×	13×	6×	7×	5×
Price/earnings range							
1972	N.Ap.	20–30	11–17	18–25	17–32	17–28	27–43
1973	N.Ap.	9–22	4–10	12–18	5–18	4–16	6–37
1974	N.Ap.	7–12	3–6	10–14	3–7	3–7	5–10
1975	N.Ap.	6–15×	3–5×	8–17×	4–11×	4–9×	5–8×

Current cash dividend rate	N.Ap.	$0.37	$0.35	$0.96	$0.20	0	$0.51
Current cash yield	N.Ap.	1.4%	3.7%	2.3%	3.3%	0	6.8%
Where traded	N.Ap.	NYSE	NYSE	NYSE	AMEX	OTC	AMEX
Number of shares outstanding, 10/29/76	124,657	18,061,047	2,107,455	8,601,539	1,237,880	1,583,766	4,814,938
Book value/share	$10.06	$14.21	$13.00	$9.30	$7.03	$10.87	$7.95
Book value/market value	N.Ap.	54%	138%	30%	117%	111%	106%
Capitalization (thousands)							
Short-term debt[a]	$ 551	$ 4,627	$ 2,090	$ 3,995	0	$ 363	$ 170
Long-term debt	577	119,911	26,448	13,769	0	6,085	13,846
Shareholders' equity	1,254	271,821	36,847	94,519	$8,700	17,210	38,316
	$ 2,382	$ 396,359	$ 65,385	$ 112,283	$ 8,700	$ 23,658	$ 52,332
Percentage short-term debt	23%	1%	3%	4%	0	2%	1%
Percentage long-term debt	24	30	40	12	0	26	26
Percentage equity	53	69	57	84	100%	72	73

N.Ap. = not applicable.
N.Av. = not available.
[a] Includes current maturities of long-term debt.
Sources: Company annual reports; company 10-K Reports; and Standard & Poor's Stock Report.

EXHIBIT 2 *continued*

SOUTHLAND CORPORATION

The Southland Corporation, incorporated in Texas in 1961 as the successor to an ice business organized in 1927, was the country's largest operator and franchiser of convenience stores and a major processor and distributor of dairy products. On December 31, 1975, the company's operations included 5,579 convenience stores, 124 Gristede's and Charles & Co. food stores and sandwich shops, 20 Barricini and Loft's candy shops, dairy distribution under 12 regional brand names, and chemical, ice, truck-leasing, and food-processing operations in a total of 41 states, the District of Columbia, and four provinces of Canada.

MUNFORD, INC

Munford, Inc., an Atlanta-based company operating in 26 states, was primarily engaged in the retail marketing of goods through convenience food stores, import stores, and building material stores. On January 1, 1976, the company's operations included 1,304 convenience food stores, 42 import stores specializing in imported gift and home-furnishing items; 14 building material stores; 19 refrigerated warehouses, and 25 ice facilities. The company had also franchised 33 fast-food operations and 38 convenience food stores.

DILLON COMPANIES

Dillon Companies was primarily engaged in retail food distribution, operating 185 supermarkets and 186 convenience stores serving all or part of 11 states under a number of different trade names. This Kansas-based company also operated several junior department stores and a real-estate company.

SUNSHINE-JR. STORES, INC.

Sunshine-Jr. Stores, Inc. was engaged in the business of operating food supermarkets and convenience food stores in Florida, Alabama, Georgia, and Mississippi. All stores were supplied by a company-owned 112,200 square foot distribution center in Panama City, Florida. The company also operated a bakery that supplied the supermarkets and a commissary that prepared prepackaged salads and sandwich items for the Florida stores. The company initially was in the supermarket business exclusively, but since 1961, convenience food stores had become an increasing factor in company operations. On December 31, 1975, the company operated 7 supermarkets and 236 convenience food stores.

NATIONAL CONVENIENCE STORES, INC.

National Convenience Stores, Inc. and its consolidated subsidiaries operated convenience food stores under the names STOP N GO and SHOP N GO. As of June 30, 1976, 743 stores were operating in the states of Arizona, California, Colorado, Florida, Georgia, Kansas, Louisiana, Mississippi, Missouri, Nevada, Oklahoma, Tennessee, and Texas. Of this number, 729 were operated by the company directly and 14 were operated by its franchisees.

continued

CIRCLE K FOOD STORES, INC.

Circle K Corporation, incorporated in Texas in 1951, operated 1,049 convenience food stores in the West and Southwest. In addition to selling food and food-related items, 540 of the stores had self-service gasoline pumps.

Source: Company *10–K Reports.*

Hop-In Food Stores, Incorporated

EXHIBIT 3
■

Statement of Earnings, 1972–1976

	Year Ended June 30					Six Months Ended December 31 (Unaudited)	
	1972	1973	1974	1975	1976	1975	1976
Revenue							
Net grocery sales	$2,359,352	$4,346,235	$6,565,500	$8,565,668	$11,466,085	$5,048,806	$9,163,641
Net gasoline sales		28,737	321,596	1,445,826	2,477,427	1,149,062	1,532,188
Gasoline commissions	18,925	56,570	68,213	87,389	95,846	41,229	82,561
Net equipment sales			210,170	231,905	17,095	9,714	12,133
Money order commissions	3,080	7,592	10,455	11,260	21,431	8,270	16,120
Total revenue	2,381,357	4,439,134	7,175,934	10,342,048	14,077,884	6,257,081	10,806,643
Costs and expenses							
Cost of sales							
Grocery	1,742,885	3,205,151	4,752,908	5,936,491	7,685,318	3,429,247	6,148,906
Gasoline		25,714	278,955	1,298,581	2,317,334	1,072,408	1,457,866
Equipment			200,668	204,186	14,082	9,057	11,615
Total cost of sales	1,742,885	3,230,865	5,232,531	7,439,258	10,016,734	4,510,712	7,618,387
Operating, general, and administrative	550,724	1,031,452	1,611,855	2,497,104	3,364,258	1,426,799	2,721,043
Depreciation	34,667	60,565	105,732	148,991	202,761	80,560	140,201
Total costs and expenses	2,328,276	4,322,882	6,950,118	10,085,353	13,583,753	6,018,071	10,479,631
Operating profit	53,081	116,252	225,816	256,695	494,131	239,010	327,012
Other expense (income)							
Interest expense	17,435	32,630	50,252	78,785	86,433	32,256	44,347
Other	(3,713)	(5,811)	(12,096)	(24,964)	(45,864)	(16,280)	(41,246)
Total other	13,722	26,819	38,156	53,821	40,569	15,976	3,101
Earnings before income taxes and extraordinary credit	39,359	89,433	187,660	202,874	453,562	223,034	323,911
Federal and state income taxes							
Current	13,951	12,650	48,544	111,270	64,000	33,705	110,000
Deferred	0	5,133	19,581	(44,380)	109,000	57,389	22,318
Total taxes	13,951	17,783	68,125	66,890	173,000	91,094	132,318

continued

EXHIBIT 3 *continued*

	Year Ended June 30					Six Months Ended December 31 (Unaudited)	
	1972	1973	1974	1975	1976	1975	1976
Earnings before extraordinary credit	25,408	71,650	119,535	135,984	280,562	131,940	191,593
Extraordinary credit	11,900	6,682	0	0	0	0	0
Net earnings	$ 37,308	$ 78,332	$ 119,535	$ 135,984	$ 280,562	$ 131,940	$ 191,593
Earnings per share							
Primary							
Earnings before extraordinary credit	$0.37	$1.01	$1.61	$1.73	$2.26	$1.58	$1.54
Extraordinary credit	0.18	0.10	0	0	0	0	0
Net earnings	$0.55	$1.11	$1.61	$1.73	$2.26	$1.58	$1.54
Fully diluted							
Earnings before extraordinary credit	$0.37	$0.80	$1.19	$1.35	$1.55	$1.25	$1.54
Extraordinary credit	0.18	0.07	0	0	0	0	0
Net earnings	$0.55	$0.87	$1.19	$1.35	$1.55	$1.25	$1.54

Source: Preliminary *Prospectus,* March 1977.

Hop-In Food Stores, Incorporated

EXHIBIT 4
■
Balance Sheet

	June 30, 1976	December 31, 1976 (Unaudited)
Assets		
Current assets		
Cash	$ 209,930	$ 106,154
Accounts receivable		
Trade	51,942	71,279
Employees and other	11,816	19,034
Note receivable	18,516	19,269
Inventories	1,364,465	1,495,518
Prepaid expenses	109,511	152,784
Total current assets	1,766,180	1,864,038

EXHIBIT 4 *continued*

	June 30, 1976	December 31, 1976 (Unaudited)
Property and equipment		
Equipment and fixtures	2,252,513	2,531,446
Office furniture and fixtures	66,164	69,090
Leasehold improvements	325,485	330,008
Total property, plant, and equipment	2,644,162	2,930,544
Less accumulated depreciation and amortization	584,366	724,567
Net property and equipment	2,059,796	2,205,977
Other assets		
Note receivable	77,766	67,939
Miscellaneous	37,894	49,764
Total other assets	115,660	117,703
Total assets	$3,941,636	$4,187,718
Liabilities and Stockholders' Equity		
Current liabilities		
Notes payable—unsecured		
Banks	$ 500,000	$ 400,000
Others	39,000	25,000
Current installments of long-term debt	141,010	125,977
Accounts payable	1,244,672	1,379,152
Accrued expenses		
Salaries and bonuses	188,220	111,529
Other	38,451	121,613
Federal and state income taxes	3,166	81,984
Total current liabilities	2,154,519	2,245,255
Long-term debt—less current maturities	635,590	577,027
Deferred income taxes	89,335	111,653
Stockholders' equity		
Common stock: $2.50 par value per share: Authorized 300,000 shares; issued and outstanding 124,657 shares	311,642	311,642
Additional paid-in capital	154,220	154,220
Retained earnings	596,330	787,923
Total stockholders' equity	1,062,192	1,253,785
Total liabilities and stockholders' equity	$3,941,636	$4,187,720

Source: Preliminary *Prospectus,* March 1977.

Hop-In Food Stores, Incorporated

EXHIBIT 5
■
Retail Grocery Industry Comparative Financial Data

132 Statements Ended on or about June 30, 1975
152 Statements Ended on or about December 31, 1975

	Under $250M[a]	Between $250M and $1MM	Between $1MM and $10MM	Between $10MM and $50MM	All Sizes
Number of Statements	67	89	90	38	284
Assets (percentages)					
Cash	10.6%	11.6%	8.9%	8.5%	8.7%
Marketable securities	1.3	0.8	0.9	0.4	0.5
Receivables, net	6.0	5.3	5.0	4.8	4.9
Inventory, net	36.3	34.5	36.3	39.5	38.6
All other current	1.2	2.8	1.9	1.9	1.9
Total current	55.4	54.9	53.1	55.1	54.7
Fixed assets, net	33.6	33.0	37.7	38.6	38.1
All other noncurrent	11.1	12.0	9.2	6.3	7.2
Total assets	100.0	100.0	100.0	100.0	100.0
Liabilities and Net Worth (percentages)					
Due to banks—short-term	2.3	5.6	3.2	1.6	2.1
Due to trade	20.2	20.0	28.6	26.5	26.6
Income taxes	1.5	1.7	2.3	1.5	1.7
Current maturities long-term debt	4.9	5.1	3.6	2.2	2.7
All other current	7.3	10.5	8.2	8.4	8.4
Total current debt	36.1	42.9	45.9	40.2	41.5
Noncurrent debt, unsubordinated	21.7	18.9	19.6	18.5	18.8
Total unsubordinated debt	57.8	61.8	65.5	58.8	60.3
Subordinated debt	1.1	1.3	1.5	0.3	0.6
Tangible net worth	41.1	36.9	33.0	40.9	39.1
Total liabilities and net worth	100.0	100.0	100.0	100.0	100.0
Income Data (percentages)					
Net sales	100.0	100.0	100.0	100.0	100.0
Cost of sales	80.0	81.2	80.7	79.2	79.6
Gross profit	20.0	18.8	19.3	20.8	20.4
All other expense, net	18.0	17.2	18.0	19.1	18.8
Profit before taxes	2.0	1.6	1.3	1.7	1.6
Ratios[b]					
Quick	0.8	0.7	0.5	0.5	0.6
	0.3	0.4	0.3	0.3	0.3
	0.1	0.2	0.2	0.3	0.2

EXHIBIT 5 *continued*

	Under $250M[a]	Between $250M and $1MM	Between $1MM and $10MM	Between $10MM and $50MM	All Sizes
			132 Statements Ended on or about June 30, 1975		
			152 Statements Ended on or about December 31, 1975		
Current	2.6	2.0	1.5	1.8	1.8
	1.4	1.4	1.1	1.4	1.3
	1.1	0.9	0.9	1.1	1.0
Fixed/worth	0.4	0.5	0.8	0.6	0.6
	0.8	0.9	1.1	0.8	1.0
	1.8	1.7	1.9	1.4	1.8
Debt/worth	0.5	0.8	1.3	0.9	0.9
	1.4	1.8	2.1	1.7	1.7
	2.9	3.3	3.9	2.1	3.2
Unsubordinated debt/capital funds	0.5	0.8	1.2	0.8	0.8
	1.3	1.5	2.0	1.6	1.7
	2.9	3.2	3.5	2.1	3.1
Sales/receivables[c]	**0** INF	**0** 999.8	**1** 578.8	**1** 326.4	**0** 999.8
	1 412.0	**1** 449.8	**1** 309.6	**2** 178.2	**1** 303.6
	3 106.9	**3** 115.1	**3** 142.5	**3** 106.7	**3** 110.5
Cost of sales/inventory[d]	**16** 22.8	**15** 23.6	**16** 21.9	**21** 17.6	**16** 22.0
	23 15.8	**22** 16.3	**24** 14.8	**29** 12.4	**23** 15.7
	33 10.9	**29** 12.4	**34** 10.6	**34** 10.5	**33** 10.9
Sales/working capital	56.4	45.3	78.7	80.8	59.4
	17.9	20.0	26.8	30.9	24.4
	2.0	−182.0	−170.2	22.2	−999.8
Sales/worth	24.8	28.2	35.1	22.9	27.1
	11.4	16.4	19.1	15.1	16.2
	7.6	9.2	11.6	10.9	9.4
Percentage profit before taxes/worth	67.0	46.8	47.5	37.0	46.2
	31.6	30.3	27.4	25.0	28.5
	13.6	15.6	13.3	17.6	14.0
Percentage profit before taxes/total assets	24.9	19.0	16.2	15.1	18.7
	15.1	9.6	8.9	10.7	10.1
	4.6	3.8	4.0	6.0	4.3
Net Sales	$61,747M	$339,002M	$1,843,562M	$5,701,526M	$7,945,837M
Total Assets	9,161M	47,152M	267,002M	923,519M	1,246,834M

[a]Asset size M = thousands of dollars; MM = millions of dollars.
[b]Ratios are given for upper quartile, median, and lower quartile.
[c]Boldfaced number is receivables turnover in days.
[d]Boldfaced number is inventory turnover in days.
Source: *1976 Annual Statement Studies,* Robert Morris Associates.

Hop-In Food Stores, Incorporated

EXHIBIT 6

■

Recent Common Equity Issues

Offering Date	Company	Offer Price	Recent Bid
1977			
1/6	Madison Gas & Electric Co.	16⅜	16⅛
1/6	Tetra Tec, Inc.	8	8¼
1/11	Middle South Utilities, Inc.	16¾	16¾
1/11	Wacoal Corp.	22⅝	22⅜
1/12	Iowa Public Service Co.	21½	21⅝
1/13	Surgicot, Inc.	7⅛	6¾
1/18	Freemont General Corp.	14½	14⅛
1/19	Intermountain Gas Co.	16¾	17½
1/25	Omega Optical Co.	10	8¾
1/25	Grow Chemical Corp.	10¼	10⅜
1/27	Brougham Industries, Inc.	7½	7¾
1/27	Makita Electric Works, Ltd.	33⅞	33⅝
2/1	Continuous Curve Contact Lenses, Inc.	10	10¾
2/8	Kennametal, Inc.	25¼	24⅝
2/9	New York State Electric and Gas Corp.	29½	29⅛
2/9	St. Jude Medical, Inc.	3½	6½

Source: *Investment Dealer's Digest.*

Hop-In Food Stores, Incorporated

EXHIBIT 7
■
Stock Price Indexes

		OTC NBQ 35 Stock Industrials[a]	OTC NASDAQ Composite[b]	S&P 500 Composite	Dow Jones 30 Industrials
1976					
High		461.02(2/26)	92.52(7/15)	107.83(9/21)	1,014.79(9/21)
Low		374.31(11/11)	78.06(1/2)	90.90(1/2)	858.71(1/2)
November	11	374.31	88.15	99.64	931.43
	18	383.75	89.81	101.89	950.13
	24	386.41	90.69	102.41	950.96
December	2	394.51	91.84	102.12	946.64
	9	412.28	94.10	104.51	970.74
	16	411.01	94.93	104.80	981.30
	23	409.68	95.22	104.84	985.62
	29	417.03	96.29	106.34	994.93
1977					
January	6	418.58	97.20	105.02	979.89
	13	408.90	96.84	104.20	976.15
	20	414.48	97.08	102.97	959.03
	27	420.79	96.04	101.79	954.54
February	3	424.28	96.33	101.85	947.14
	10	420.30	96.29	100.82	937.92
	17	419.57	96.56	100.92	943.73
	24	411.23	94.84	99.60	932.60
March	3	402.47	95.53	100.88	948.64

[a]National Quotation Bureau.
[b]National Association of Security Dealers Automated Quotations.
Source: *Investment Dealer's Digest.*

Bearings, Inc.

In late November 1983, Raymond Smiley, vice president of finance for Bearings, Inc., was focusing his thoughts on the upcoming Finance Committee meeting. Since joining Bearings 2 years earlier, Mr. Smiley had become convinced that the company's capital structure needed to be altered to facilitate funding of the growth planned for the company by John R. Cunin, chairman of the board. While Mr. Smiley's most immediate concern was to determine the best method of funding the company's $45-million need, he had two general questions on his mind: (1) what funding alternatives were open to him, given the company's historically conservative management philosophy, and (2) what funding options needed to be available to fund future growth requirements.

He wanted to begin discussion of these topics at the meeting. Before recommending a significant change in the financial structure, Mr. Smiley knew he should carefully think through his ideas.

PRODUCTS AND CUSTOMERS

Bearings was the leading national distributor of ball, roller, linear, and thrust bearings, power transmission equipment, and other industrial supplies. The company did not manufacture any of the products it sold; it bought bearings and bearing accessories from over one hundred manufacturers, such as Timken, SKF, Fafnir, Torrington, and MRC/TRW. Bearings stocked over 145,000 types and sizes of bearings. Sales were made through an extensive network of 262 service centers located across the United States.

In the fiscal year ended June 30, 1983, Bearings reported $5.4 million in net income on $351.2 million of sales—its first sales decline in 25 years. (Exhibit 1 presents recent financial statements.) A breakdown of 1983 sales showed that ball, roller, thrust, and linear bearings amounted to 55 percent of sales, power transmission equipment to 32 percent, and specialty products such as seals, lubricants, and bearing-related devices to 13 percent. The fiscal year 1976 breakdown had been 67 percent, 20 percent, and 13 percent, respectively.

Bearings had more than 175,000 customers, and its average order was $180. About 10 percent of the company's sales came from the forest products industry, followed by primary metals, food processing, mining, and textiles. These top five industry groups accounted for just under 30 percent of Bearings' 1983 revenues.

In keeping with its founder's original strategy, 85 percent of the company's business was from the replacement and maintenance markets. Only 15 percent was from the original equipment market (OEM), which bearing manufacturers dominated.

This case was prepared as a basis for class discussion rather than to illustrate either effective or ineffective handling of an administrative situation. Copyright © 1986 by the Darden Graduate Business School Sponsors, University of Virginia, Charlottesville, Virginia.

HISTORY

Bearings, Inc. was founded in 1923 by Joseph M. Bruening when he was 27. He borrowed $5,000 and started selling replacement parts for cars and trucks. Over the next 6 decades, the company grew through product-line expansion and acquisition of regional distribution companies. By 1983, Bearings had total assets of nearly $200 million and an equity base of $120 million. Management owned 14 percent of the common stock; institutions held about 50 percent.

Bearings' business philosophy clearly reflected Mr. Bruening's spartan management style; the company prided itself on its lean profile. It had only two vice presidents when its revenues reached $275 million in 1978. As one observer noted, "Bruening ran a metal-desk, linoleum-floor kind of company." This conservative attitude could also be seen in the company's balance sheet, where long-term debt was seldom greater than 7 percent of equity. The strength of the company's balance sheet made it a very attractive takeover candidate, however, and several times in the 1970s, Mr. Bruening had been approached by conglomerates seeking to acquire Bearings. Mr. Bruening always responded that his most important goal was to maintain Bearings as an independent company.

In 1980, Mr. Bruening, then 84 years old, decided that the time had come for him to step down from the day-to-day management of Bearings. While retaining the position of chairman of the board, he transferred the responsibility of president and chief executive officer to Mr. Cunin, a 35-year company veteran. In 1983, Mr. Cunin assumed the position of chairman and chief executive officer. Although trained in the Bruening school of management, he and the new president brought more aggressive leadership to the company. First, they increased the number of corporate officers, hiring Mr. Smiley among others. Second, they expanded the number of sales offices. Third, and perhaps most important, Mr. Cunin established a corporate goal of $1 billion in sales by 1988. Exhibit 2 provides projected income statements reflecting Mr. Cunin's sales goal.

THE INDUSTRIAL DISTRIBUTION INDUSTRY

Bearings, Inc. competed in the very fragmented industrial distribution industry. This $40 to $45 billion market included sales of machinery, tools, pulleys, chains, power transmission equipment, and bearings. Highly cyclical, sales for the industry declined by 10 percent during the 1982 recession. As of November 1983, sales were down an additional 2 percent. Prior to the 1982 recession, however, the industry had shown solid growth of 12.7 percent per year from 1975 through 1981 (see Exhibit 3).

The sale of bearings and other antifriction components totaled $2.9 billion in 1982. This figure represented a 20-percent drop from the $3.6 billion of bearing sales in 1981. Sales data for 1958 to 1983 are shown in Exhibit 4. Power transmission items accounted for another $4.5 billion in sales in 1982. Over 3,400 independent distributors handled nearly 80 percent of all bearings sold.

Although the industrial distribution industry was highly fragmented, and competition tended to be regional, Bearings, Inc. management viewed two companies as its primary national rivals: Motion Industries and Kaman Bearing and Supply.

Motion Industries, a division of Genuine Parts Company, sold a product line comparable to Bearings' to 100,000 customers in 20 states through 160 branches and distribution centers. Genuine Parts had entered the industrial parts replacement business in 1976 with the acquisition of Motion Industries. By 1982, Genuine Parts had acquired three more industrial distribution concerns and was second in the industry behind Bearings. In 1982, Genuine Parts' Industrial Parts Group had sales of $374 million, an operating profit of $22 million, and assets of $156 million.

Kaman Corporation was a diversified, technology-oriented company with strengths in precision measurement, aerospace manufacturing, and military software and systems. In addition, Kaman had a major presence in industrial distribution as both a bearing manufacturer and distributor. Kaman Bearing and Supply was formed in the early 1970s in order to expand the corporation's bearing-manufacturing capability and to balance its exposure to the aerospace market. In 1982, Kaman's industrial distribution division recorded $199 million in revenues and operating profits of $9.2 million on an asset base of $65 million. That division accounted for roughly 40 percent of Kaman Corporation's total sales and operating profits. Data for both Kaman and Genuine Parts are presented in Exhibit 5.

Bearings' current strategy was to compete as the highest priced, highest value-added player. Genuine's strategy was similar to Bearings', but it offered a slightly lower price with noticeably less service. Kaman, on the other hand, aimed at offering the lowest cost product with little value-added service. Kaman's low-cost products were imported from Japan, a source that Bearings and Genuine had avoided.

RECENT DEVELOPMENTS

The fiscal year that ended on June 30, 1983 had been Bearings' most difficult in recent memory. As a result of the overall economic downturn of 1982 and 1983, Bearings posted quarterly income results below those of the previous year for 6 consecutive quarters. (Exhibit 6 presents quarterly earnings and market price information.) While most of the company's situation could be attributed to the business cycle, some internal decisions had also adversely affected results during this period.

On June 30, 1982, Bearings made its first acquisition in more than 15 years when it purchased Advance Bearing and Supply Company of Worcester, Massachusetts. This move provided Bearings with an immediate position in the New England market, which the company previously had not tapped. In November 1982, the company purchased the Cottingham Bearing Corporation of Dallas for $12 million cash. As it had in New England, Bearings penetrated the southwestern regional market more quickly than would have been possible through internal growth. However, the startup costs associated with the acquisitions had an adverse impact on the financial statements: inventory buildups increased interest expenses.

Bearings' stock price had remained remarkably strong during the recessionary period and as it made its acquisitions. Mr. Smiley attributed the strength partly to the market's approval of the new management and partly to the market's implicit endorsement of the company's new momentum. He wondered, however, whether the two acquisitions had caused Bearings to be identified as a possible takeover candidate. Its strong balance sheet and solid cash flows could attract a raider. Although Mr. Smiley knew of no effort to accumulate a position in Bearings' shares, any institutional holder might be prepared to sell if an attractive takeover offer were made.

FUNDING OPTIONS

Because of the capital market's lack of familiarity with Bearings, Mr. Smiley wished to raise enough external funds to last the company for the next several years. Previous external financing raised by Bearings had been in the form of a term loan through a local bank. Mr. Smiley wanted to repay the $7-million long-term note (due in 1986); to cover refinancing the two recent acquisitions, which had been funded through short-term debt totaling $15.5 million; and to provide the company with another $22 million to finance the next several years' working-capital and capital-expenditure needs. By raising $45 million in this first trip into the capital markets, Mr. Smiley believed Bearings would be in a strong position to move toward Mr. Cunin's $1 billion sales goal.

As Mr. Smiley pondered the upcoming Finance Committee meeting where he would make a recommendation to Mr. Cunin, he reviewed the list of funding alternatives presented by the company's investment banker. Management's initial inclination had been to make an equity issue. Although Bearings' common stock was currently trading just below its recent all-time high of almost $41 a share, Mr. Smiley was confident the company could net $36 a share after discounts and issuing costs. The strong market price and the belief that an equity issue would best maintain Bearings' reputation as a conservatively financed company were the major arguments in favor of the stock issue. Mr. Smiley believed that the company would maintain its $0.25 quarterly dividend policy except under the most dire circumstances.

He had one other funding option to consider. The company could contract a 20-year debenture for $45 million. Although the current yield for a Baa-rated corporate bond was 13.61 percent, Mr. Smiley believed that Bearings could line up funding at 13.00 percent. Annual sinking-fund payments of $3 million would begin in 1989. Exhibit 7 provides data on historical interest rates.

With this information in hand, Mr. Smiley set out to draft his recommendation for the Finance Committee meeting.

Bearings, Inc. (A)

EXHIBIT 1
■

Financial Information, Fiscal Years Ended June 30, 1980–1983
(millions of dollars, except per share data)

	1980	1981	1982	1983
Income Statements				
Sales	$332.9	$358.2	$370.2	$351.2
Cost of goods sold	234.4	252.8	262.6	247.2
Gross profit	98.5	105.4	107.6	104.0
Selling, general, and administrative	68.8	73.0	80.4	89.8
Depreciation	1.6	1.7	1.8	2.6
Earnings before interest and taxes	28.1	29.8	25.4	11.6

EXHIBIT 1 *continued*

■

Financial Information, Fiscal Years Ended June 30, 1980–1983
(millions of dollars, except per share data)

	1980	1981	1982	1983
Interest	2.5	2.3	2.6	2.1
Profit before taxes	25.6	27.5	22.8	9.5
Taxes	12.4	13.3	10.8	4.1
Net income	$ 13.2	$ 14.2	$ 12.0	$ 5.4
Assets Balance Sheets				
Cash	$ 2.3	$ 2.2	$ 1.5	$ 3.4
Accounts receivable	40.0	47.0	41.4	44.1
Inventories	84.4	81.7	90.2	107.2
Other current assets	2.2	1.6	4.2	4.5
Total current assets	128.9	132.5	137.3	159.2
Property, plant, and equipment	27.8	30.7	37.3	46.7
Less depreciation	8.8	10.3	11.8	14.1
	19.0	20.4	25.5	32.6
Other assets	0.3	0.3	0.3	0.7
Total assets	$148.2	$153.2	$163.1	$192.5
Liabilities and Equity				
Notes payable	$ 9.6	$ 5.2	$ 5.5	$ 23.0
Accounts payable	23.8	20.4	22.6	30.8
Other current liabilities	6.7	9.3	8.4	10.0
Total current liabilities	40.1	34.9	36.5	63.8
Long-term debt	7.0	7.0	7.0	7.0
Deferred taxes	0.0	0.0	0.3	0.9
Total liabilities	47.1	41.9	43.8	71.7
Common stock	10.0	10.0	10.0	10.0
Retained earnings	91.2	101.4	109.4	110.9
Treasury stock	(0.1)	(0.1)	(0.1)	(0.1)
Total equity	101.1	111.3	119.3	120.8
Total liabilities and equity	$148.2	$153.2	$163.1	$192.5
Other Relevant Data				
Common shares (millions)	3.99	3.99	3.99	3.99
Earnings per share	$ 3.30	$ 3.55	$ 3.01	$ 1.36
Dividends per share	0.96	1.00	1.00	1.00
Average market price	28.50	26.50	29.25	32.88
Price/earnings ratio	8.6×	7.5×	9.7×	24.2×
Dividend yield	3.4%	3.8%	3.4%	3.0%

Bearings, Inc. (A)

EXHIBIT 2
■

Summary Projected Income Statements, 1984–1988
(millions of dollars)

	1984	1985	1986	1987	1988
Sales	$431	$530	$652	$802	$1,000
Gross profit	121	148	183	225	280
Selling, general, and administrative (includes depreciation)	95	117	143	176	220
Earnings before interest and taxes	$ 26	$ 31	$ 40	$ 49	$ 60

Assumptions

Sales growth of 23 percent per year

Gross profit margin of 28 percent

Selling, general, and administrative at 22 percent of sales includes depreciation of $2.9, $3.2, $3.8, $4.2, and $4.5 (millions) for 1984–1988

Bearings, Inc. (A)

EXHIBIT 3
■

Industrial Distributor Sales

	Distributor Sales (billions)	Percentage Change from Previous Year
1972	$16.4	N.Ap.
1973	20.8	26.8%
1974	23.5	13.9
1975	23.3	(0.9)
1976	24.9	6.9
1977	29.4	18.1
1978	33.2	12.9
1979	37.8	13.9
1980	41.6	10.1
1981	47.8	14.9
1982	43.3	(9.4)

N.Ap. = not applicable.
Source: *Industrial Distribution*, July 1983.

Bearings, Inc. (A)

EXHIBIT 4
■

Total Value of U.S. Sales of Antifriction Bearings and Components
(millions of dollars)

	Total Value	Annual Change (percent)	Value in 1967 Dollars	Annual Change (percent)
1958	$ 636.8	N.Ap.	N.Ap.	N.Ap.
1963	961.0	N.Ap.	N.Ap.	N.Ap.
1967	1,292.2	N.Ap.	$1,292.2	N.Ap.
1968	1,293.7	0.1%	1,274.6	(1.4)%
1969	1,396.0	7.9	1,350.1	5.9
1970	1,295.3	(7.2)	1,186.2	(12.1)
1971	1,258.2	(2.9)	1,101.8	(7.1)
1972	1,418.7	12.8	1,212.6	10.1
1973	1,695.7	19.5	1,403.7	15.8
1974	1,960.7	15.6	1,395.5	(0.6)
1975	2,046.3	4.4	1,246.2	(10.7)
1976	2,195.2	7.3	1,243.0	(0.3)
1977	2,444.5	11.4	1,277.2	2.8
1978	2,799.3	14.5	1,356.9	6.2
1979	3,260.5	17.3	1,438.9	6.0
1980	3,284.5	0.7	1,239.0	(13.9)
1981	3,607.7	9.8	1,183.6	(4.5)
1982	2,888.7	(19.9)	871.4	(26.4)
1983 (est.)	2,746.3	(4.9)	826.9	(5.1)

N.Ap. = not applicable.
Source: *Industrial Distribution*, October 1983.

Bearings, Inc. (A)

EXHIBIT 5
■

Selected Data on Competitors
(millions of dollars)

	1981	1982
Sales		
Genuine Parts Company	$1,875.7	$1,936.5
Industrial Parts Group	413.7	374.1
Kaman Corporation	416.5	475.4
Industrial Distribution Division	162.4	198.5
Operating Profit		
Genuine Parts Company	200.1	200.8
Industrial Parts Group	30.7	22.1
Kaman Corporation	26.5	33.9
Industrial Distribution Division	9.2	8.6
Identifiable Assets		
Genuine Parts Company	705.8	754.4
Industrial Parts Group	159.6	155.6
Kaman Corporation	160.3	170.5
Industrial Distribution Division	63.8	65.0

Bearings, Inc. (A)

EXHIBIT 6
■
Quarterly Summary Income Data and Stock Prices

Year/ Quarter	Sales (millions)	Earnings per Share	Stock Price Range (high–low)	S&P 500 Index Closing Price
1980				
3	$76.4	$0.79	$35½–29	$102.9
4	80.6	0.81	32⅛–28½	114.2
1981				
1	89.3	0.92	33⅜–22¾	125.5
2	86.6	0.78	25⅛–21½	135.8
3	79.6	0.65	29¾–23¾	136.0
4	85.3	0.75	27⅞–23¾	131.2
1982				
1	94.4	1.01	29½–22½	116.2
2	98.8	1.14	29⅝–25¾	122.6
3	95.6	0.94	27 –25⅛	111.9
4	91.8	0.79	36 –26⅝	109.6
1983				
1	92.9	0.75	35⅛–27¾	122.4
2	90.0	0.53	29⅝–26¾	139.5
3	81.3	0.37	30 –26	151.9
4	82.0	0.17	36 –28¼	166.4
1984				
1	90.6	0.34	39 –32	164.4
2	97.2	0.48	40⅜–31¼	167.4
3	98.9	0.50	41 –33	159.2

Note: Bearings' beta was 0.75 at the end of 1984.
Source: New York Stock Exchange, *Stock Price Guides—1980–1984.*

Bearings, Inc. (A)

EXHIBIT 7
■
Interest Rates[a]

		Corporate Bonds	
	Prime Bank Rate	Aaa	Baa
1978	9.06%	8.43%	9.36%
1979	12.67	9.55	10.65
1980	14.88	11.75	13.48
1981	19.10	14.23	16.23
1982	15.00	13.68	15.76
1983 Jan.	11.50	11.00	12.38
Feb.	11.00	11.13	12.25
March	10.50	10.50	11.88
April	10.50	11.00	11.75
May	10.50	10.60	11.25
June	10.50	11.25	12.13
July	10.50	11.38	12.13
Aug.	10.50	12.20	13.00
Sept.	11.00	12.38	13.25
Oct.	11.00	11.85	12.50
Nov.	11.00	12.00	12.88

[a] Average for the period.
Sources: *Economic Report of the President*, 1985; and *Federal Reserve Bulletin*, various issues.

Philip Morris, Incorporated:

Swiss Franc Financing

On October 24, 1980, Hans Storr, vice president and chief financial officer of Philip Morris, Inc., knew that he had a difficult selling job ahead of him. After much analysis and discussion with investment bankers and other Philip Morris financial officers, he still believed that the company should undertake a major financing in the Swiss franc (SFr) Eurobond market. He knew that not everyone in the company shared his enthusiasm for the opportunities in the Euromarkets, and should he decide to issue SFr bonds, he would need to convince other members of senior management that this was the best course of action.

In any event, the company would require significant external funding over the next few years. Although the company was more leveraged than some outside analysts thought appropriate, management was comfortable with the current debt/equity ratio and intended to continue the current financing mix. Given the projected profitability of the company, management believed that additional funding should be raised in the debt markets. Thus, the decision facing Mr. Storr was where to issue debt at the most favorable terms.

COMPANY BACKGROUND

Philip Morris was founded in the 19th century and was incorporated in Virginia in 1919. Originally a cigarette manufacturer, the company began a series of diversification moves in the late 1960s. In 1970, Philip Morris acquired the Miller Brewing Company, and in 1978, it purchased the Seven-Up Company. In addition, the company diversified into specialty chemicals and papers, tissue papers, packaging materials, and real-estate and community development.

By 1980, Philip Morris was one of the largest industrial companies in the United States. The company had achieved the enviable record of 26 consecutive years of growth in revenues, net profits, and earnings per share. The financial statements for 1978 and 1979 are shown in Exhibits 1 and 2.

As a result of the diversification and growth of the company, Philip Morris had six operating divisions:

- Philip Morris U.S.A. (tobacco products)
- Philip Morris International (tobacco products and Seven-Up)

This case was prepared as a basis for class discussion rather than to illustrate either effective or ineffective handling of an administrative situation. Copyright © 1982, by the Darden Graduate Business School Sponsors, University of Virginia, Charlottesville, Virginia.

■ Miller Brewing Company (beer)
■ The Seven-Up Company (Seven-Up, North America only)
■ Philip Morris Industrial (specialty papers and chemicals)
■ Mission Viejo Company (community development)

A breakdown of the operating companies' performance, along with other financial highlights, is shown in Exhibit 3.

The company's growth had not been limited to the domestic U.S. market. Philip Morris marketed cigarettes in over 160 countries and, in addition to being the largest cigarette exporter in the United States, the company had offshore manufacturing facilities as well as joint venture and licensing arrangements. Seven-Up was also a significant international product marketed in approximately 90 countries. In these international markets, the distribution was primarily through franchised bottlers and distributors.

International operations had sales and profits growth records matching their domestic counterparts: operating revenues for 1979 increased 42.5 percent over 1978 results and operating income by 38.2 percent. This growth was expected to continue. Financial results for 1978 and 1979 by region are shown in Exhibit 4. Foreign operations accounted for about 25 percent of the operating revenues, but only about 9 percent of operating income in 1979. About 18 percent of the identifiable assets of the consolidated subsidiaries were held offshore. Further financial data for the consolidated and unconsolidated subsidiaries are shown in Exhibit 5.

Although the international operations had contributed to the growth of the company, they had also created a financial reporting problem. This resulted from the company's adoption on January 1, 1976 of the Financial Accounting Standard (FAS) #8.

TRANSLATING FOREIGN SUBSIDIARY STATEMENTS

FAS #8 required all U.S. companies to use the temporal method of translating the financial statements of foreign subsidiaries for consolidated reporting purposes. The temporal method prescribed which exchange rate to use for translating assets and liabilities denominated in foreign currencies. Historical exchange rates (i.e., those in existence at the time of acquisition) were to be used for all fixed assets. Inventories were to be valued at the lower of (1) cost translated at historic rates or (2) market value translated at current rates (i.e., those in existence at the date of the balance sheet). In almost all cases, inventories were translated at historic exchange rates. All other accounts were to be translated at the current exchange rates. This being the case, the temporal method produced results virtually equivalent to the monetary/nonmonetary translation method that translated monetary items at current rates and nonmonetary items at historic rates.

Whether the company experienced a gain or loss depended on the difference between the assets and the liabilities that were translated at the current exchange rate. For companies with a net monetary asset position (i.e., with assets exceeding the liabilities translated at current rates), a strengthening foreign currency resulted in a foreign exchange translation gain. The gain occurred because the value of the assets stated in U.S. dollars had increased by an amount greater than the increased value of the foreign liabilities stated in U.S. dollars.

Conversely, a net monetary liability position in the same situation yielded a translation loss. The impact of the translation process was reversed if the foreign currency weakened (devalued) against the U.S. dollar.

FAS #8 directed that these translation gains or losses be included in the income statement for the reporting period, even though they were only paper gains or losses and had not actually been realized in the cash flows of the multinational company. This requirement for immediately including the translation results in the income statement, along with other concerns about the appropriateness of the exchange rate assigned to various balance sheet accounts, had caused much discussion in the accounting and financial community. Most of the discussion had suggested that FAS #8 was unacceptable and should be changed.

FAS #8 at Philip Morris.

Philip Morris had concurred with the arguments that FAS #8 distorted the company's financial reporting. In an effort to eliminate the impact of the translation gains and losses, Mr. Storr had undertaken regular balance sheet hedging in the forward currency markets. This policy was pursued with some reluctance because it involved taking economic positions to hedge noneconomic positions. Nevertheless, management was justifiably proud of the earnings record of Philip Morris and believed that the FAS #8 requirements were a potential threat to the continuation of annual and quarterly income gains.

Philip Morris was particularly vulnerable to translation gains and losses. Foreign currency debt incurred to finance its large tobacco inventories held offshore and its plant and equipment investments in foreign subsidiaries resulted in an exposed liability position for the company.

Although the FAS #8 reporting requirements had caused considerable earnings fluctuations in the ensuing years, Mr. Storr had been reasonably successful in mitigating these fluctuations through the hedging operations. Operating primarily on the foreign exchange market with currency futures, the company had attempted to forecast the future exchange rates for the major currencies. When Mr. Storr's forecasts differed from the markets' forward exchange rates, he would enter into open contracts to buy or sell currencies in the future. In essence, the company was speculating against the market. Mr. Storr believed that he and his staff were successful in forecasting the results of normal economic factors, but political and other shocks were difficult, if not impossible, to predict.

Potential FAS Changes.

Because of the controversy surrounding FAS #8, the FASB had announced in January 1979 that they would evaluate proposed changes to the standard. Although FAS #8 had not yet been officially superseded, Mr. Storr had received in late August an exposure draft of some proposed changes. If the exposure draft were accepted, the revisions to FAS #8 would be significant.

The exposure draft proposed replacing the temporal translation method of FAS #8 with an all-current method. All balance sheet accounts would be translated at the current or most recent exchange rate. This change would eliminate the need to translate any accounts at historic rates, even though the accounts reflected on the subsidiaries' balance sheets might still be recorded at historic costs.

A further change would be to eliminate the inclusion of translation gains and losses in the income statement for the parent. Instead they would be recorded as a separate component of stockholders' equity. Any transaction gains or losses would continue to be included in the income statement just as they were under FAS #8.

Although these changes would eliminate the provisions of FAS #8 that had received the most opposition, the proposed standard was not without its critics. The FASB had approved the exposure draft by only a four-to-three vote. In the short time since the exposure draft had been issued, many accountants and financial managers had voiced their displeasure with various aspects of the proposed standards. First, some managers were content with FAS #8 and believed that it was consistent with long-time accounting methods and theories. Second, the exposure draft proposed a departure from the tradition of having all changes in the owners' equity accounts flow through the income statement. Third, because of the use of current exchange rates, some argued that the proposed standard would result in an unacceptable mix of historic and inflation accounting.

The FASB had scheduled a public meeting for December 1980 to discuss the proposed accounting standard. Although the exposure draft specified that the new standard would become effective in December 1981, the growing opposition to the proposed standard made its adoption uncertain.

PREVIOUS FOREIGN FINANCING

In 1972 Philip Morris had been attracted by the lower borrowing rates in Switzerland and other European countries. With US$ long-term bond rates at about 7½ percent, corporations could benefit from a 75-basis-point spread by financing in Swiss francs at 6¾ percent. Philip Morris decided to take advantage of this interest rate differential and had floated and sold some Swiss franc bonds in 1972. Taking advantage of similar spreads, the company also issued Deutsche mark and Dutch guilder bonds.

This decision proved to be disastrous for Philip Morris and the other U.S. corporations that had undertaken similar financings. After the change to floating exchange rates in 1973, the Swiss franc strengthened appreciably from the SFr 3.20/US$ exchange rate that had existed in 1972. The effective cost of the SFr bonds was thus very high. Exhibit 6 shows historic SFr/US$ exchange rates. Exhibit 7 provides information on Swiss and U.S. inflation and interest rates.

Even though this initial foray into the foreign debt markets had proven to be less than satisfactory and the SFr bonds had been called in 1978, the earliest date possible, Mr. Storr was convinced that the current SFr situation was an excellent opportunity to obtain low-cost financing.

CURRENT SITUATION

Because of the need to raise debt funds, Mr. Storr had investigated the available rates in several markets. US$ rates for a US$ 60 million, 7-year, A-rated bond were about 14½ percent. A comparable issue in the Swiss franc market would be priced at about 6½ percent. This 8-percent interest rate differential was reflected in the forward exchange rates, where the SFr was selling at a substantial premium over the spot rate of SFr 1.6755/US$. The 30-, 60-, and 180-day forward rates were SFr 1.6608, SFr 1.6405, and SFr 1.6088, respectively.

The foreign exchange markets had recently entered a period of hectic trading that resulted in significant volatility in exchange rates. This volatility was at least partially fueled by the uncertain political environment caused by continued speculation about the fate of the U.S. hostages in Iran. Mr. Storr believed that the markets' volatility overshadowed the underlying economic situation. Based on his analysis, he believed that the high forward premium for the Swiss franc was unwarranted and the strength of the franc was therefore overstated.

Although he believed that the franc would probably strengthen against the dollar, he believed that the 8-percent interest rate differential was a sufficient cushion. The SFr would need to appreciate by more than 8 percent before the SFr debt would become more expensive than the alternative US$ financing. His view of the economic factors led him to think that an 8-percent devaluation of the dollar against the Swiss franc was unlikely. Information about the Swiss and U.S. balance of payments and currencies are contained in Exhibits 8, 9, and 10.

Some uncertainties were connected with the sale of the SFr debt, however. The European debt markets evaluated issuers differently than U.S. markets did. Rather than relying on rating agencies to grade the quality of the borrower, the European markets relied primarily on the reputation of the borrower. For this reason, most of the borrowers in the Euromarkets were governments or governmental agencies. The corporations that tapped the Euromarkets were large, well-known companies.

Since Philip Morris had not been a regular participant in the Euromarkets, Mr. Storr did not know how an issue would be accepted. He thought that being a major multinational company would work in his favor, however.

Given the uncertainties associated with the SFr Eurobond, Mr. Storr wondered if he shouldn't just resign himself to the more conservative approach and issue U.S. dollar debt. If he were right about the Swiss franc, the company would benefit from substantial interest savings. If wrong, however, he would be opening himself to a repeat of the last SFr financing fiasco.

Philip Morris, Incorporated: Swiss Franc Financing

EXHIBIT 1
■
Consolidated Statements of Earnings for the Years Ending December 31
(thousands of dollars, except per share amounts)

	1978	1979
Operating revenues	$6,632,463	$8,302,892
Cost of sales		
Cost of products sold	3,072,134	3,778,737
Federal and foreign excise taxes on products sold	1,663,600	2,158,801
Gross profit	1,896,729	2,365,354
Marketing, administration, and research costs	931,978	1,195,667
	964,751	1,169,687
Equity in net earnings of unconsolidated foreign subsidiaries and affiliates	3,331	20,947
Operating income of operating companies	968,082	1,190,634
Corporate expense	54,106	70,207
Interest expense (excluding capitalized interest of $23,680,000 in 1979 and $13,425,000 in 1978)	149,794	205,476
Other deductions, net	18,685	9,515
Earnings before income taxes	745,497	905,436
Provision for income taxes	336,916	397,555
Net earnings	$ 408,581	$ 507,881
Earnings per common share	$ 3.38	$ 4.08

Philip Morris, Incorporated: Swiss Franc Financing

EXHIBIT 2
■
Consolidated Balance Sheets for the Years Ending December 31
(thousands of dollars)

	1978	1979
Assets		
Cash and cash equivalents	$ 72,930	$ 59,060
Receivables	473,586	576,858
Inventories		
Leaf tobacco	1,459,048	1,548,422
Other raw materials	198,541	253,767
Work in process and finished goods	419,551	432,614
Housing programs under construction	111,413	136,497
Total inventories	2,188,553	2,371,300
Prepaid expenses	21,688	21,097
Total current assets	2,756,757	3,028,315
Investments in and advances to unconsolidated foreign subsidiaries and affiliates	243,271	260,172

EXHIBIT 2 *continued*

	1978	1979
Land and offtract improvements	72,836	114,445
Property, plant, and equipment, at cost		
Land and land improvements	101,256	133,980
Buildings and building equipment	476,152	562,489
Machinery and equipment	1,231,438	1,547,558
Construction in progress	408,485	581,069
Total property, plant, and equipment at cost	2,217,331	2,825,096
Less accumulated depreciation	479,726	595,594
Net property, plant, and equipment	1,737,605	2,229,502
Brands, trademarks, patents, and goodwill	652,368	645,586
Long-term receivables	66,258	51,534
Other assets	79,070	49,298
Total assets	$5,608,165	$6,378,852
Liabilities and Stockholders' Equity		
Notes payable	$ 211,345	$ 59,909
Current portion of long-term debt	13,866	8,699
Accounts payable and accrued liabilities	785,201	897,415
Federal and other income taxes	129,388	190,186
Dividends payable	31,867	38,920
Total current liabilities	1,171,667	1,195,129
Long-term debt	2,146,968	2,447,761
Deferred income taxes	149,952	233,604
Other liabilities	24,918	31,403
Total liabilities	3,493,505	3,907,897
Cumulative preferred stock, par value $100 per share	7,693	—
Common stock, par value $1 per share	62,136	124,544
Additional paid-in capital	439,443	385,085
Earnings reinvested in the business	1,608,954	1,961,326
Total stockholders' equity	2,118,226	2,470,955
Less cost of treasury stock	3,566	—
Net stockholders' equity	2,114,660	2,470,955
Total liabilities and stockholders' equity	$5,608,165	$6,378,852

Philip Morris, Incorporated: Swiss Franc Financing

EXHIBIT 3
■

Financial Highlights (thousands of dollars, except per share amounts)

	1975	1976	1977	1978	1979
Operating revenues	$3,642,414	$4,293,782	$5,201,977	$6,632,463	$8,302,892
Net earnings	211,638	265,675	334,926	408,581	507,881
Earnings per common share	1.810	2.240	2.800	3.380	4.08
Dividends declared per common share	0.463	0.575	0.781	1.025	1.25
Percentage Increase over Prior Year					
Operating revenues	21.0%	17.9%	21.2%	27.5%	25.2%
Net earnings	20.6	25.5	26.1	22.0	24.3
Earnings per common share	14.9	23.8	25.0	20.7	20.7
Dividends declared per common share	19.4	24.2	35.8	31.2	22.0
Operating Companies' Revenues					
Philip Morris U.S.A.	$1,721,549	$1,963,144	$2,160,362	$2,437,465	$2,767,035
Philip Morris International	1,040,002	1,083,970	1,349,280	1,810,861	2,581,270
Miller Brewing Company	658,268	982,810	1,327,619	1,834,526	2,236,481
The Seven-Up Company	—	—	—	186,494	295,480
Philip Morris Industrial	151,960	169,096	216,699	237,165	268,847
Mission Viejo Company	70,635	94,762	148,017	125,952	153,779
Consolidated operating revenues	$3,642,414	$4,293,782	$5,201,977	$6,632,463	$8,302,892
Operating Companies' Income					
Philip Morris U.S.A.	$ 337,314	$ 401,426	$ 474,400	$ 568,145	$ 701,340
Philip Morris International	112,975	130,104	153,791	188,561	260,620
Miller Brewing Company	28,628	76,056	106,456	150,300	180,894
The Seven-Up Company	—	—	—	26,291	6,985
Philip Morris Industrial	8,052	10,620	14,860	15,024	18,268
Mission Viejo Company	5,875	16,333	33,225	19,761	22,437
Consolidated operating income	$ 492,844	$ 634,539	$ 787,732	$ 968,082	$1,190,634

Compounded Average Annual Growth Rate

	1954–1979	1964–1979	1969–1979	1974–1979
Operating revenues	13.5%	18.6%	21.9%	22.5%
Net earnings	15.8	23.1	24.2	23.7
Primary earnings per share	14.4	20.5	20.4	20.9

Philip Morris, Incorporated: Swiss Franc Financing

EXHIBIT 4
■

Consolidated Financial Data by Geographic Region
(thousands of dollars)

	1978	1979
Operating revenues		
United States	$5,230,535	$6,228,752
Europe	1,268,127	1,736,002
Other foreign	133,801	338,138
	6,632,463	8,302,892
Operating profit		
United States	877,947	1,067,265
Europe	67,991	102,911
Other foreign	11,129	(12,754)
	957,067	1,157,422
Reconciliation		
Equity in net earnings of unconsolidated foreign subsidiaries and affiliates	3,331	20,947
Amortization of goodwill and trademarks	7,684	12,265
Operating income of operating companies	968,082	1,190,634
Identifiable assets		
United States	4,394,028	4,984,037
Europe	765,760	927,350
Other foreign	129,671	140,956
	5,289,459	6,052,343
Investments in and advances to unconsolidated foreign subsidiaries and affiliates	243,271	260,172
Corporate assets	75,435	66,337
Total assets	$5,608,165	$6,378,852

Philip Morris, Incorporated: Swiss Franc Financing

EXHIBIT 5
■
Principal Financial Data of Foreign Subsidiaries and Affiliates (thousands of dollars)

	Consolidated (wholly owned)	Unconsolidated (partially owned)
1978		
Assets	$ 944,956	$ 667,850
Liabilities	552,052	346,099
Net assets	392,904	321,751
Equity and advances	392,904	226,871
Operating revenues	1,401,928	1,099,767
Net earnings	58,398	13,561
Equity	58,398	3,331
1979		
Assets	1,087,005	776,255
Liabilities	588,811	421,391
Net assets	498,194	354,864
Equity and advances	498,194	242,808
Operating revenues	2,074,140	1,269,794
Net earnings	56,638	34,433
Equity	56,638	20,947

Philip Morris, Incorporated: Swiss Franc Financing

EXHIBIT 6
■
Swiss Franc Exchange Rates

	SFr/US$
1973[a]	3.2440
1974	2.5400
1975	2.6200
1976	2.4505
1977	2.0000
1978	1.6200
1979	1.5800
1980–July 31	1.6500
1980–October 24	1.6755

[a]Annual exchange rates are those existing at the end of the year.
Source: *The Wall Street Journal* and IMF, *International Financial Statistics.*

Philip Morris, Incorporated: Swiss Franc Financing

EXHIBIT 7
■
Interest and Inflation Rates for Switzerland and the United States

	Switzerland		United States	
	Consumer Price Index[a]	Government Bond Yield[b]	Consumer Price Index[a]	Government Bond Yield[b]
1973	85.4	5.60%	82.6	6.95%
1974	93.7	7.15	91.6	7.82
1975	100.0	6.44	100.0	7.49
1976	101.7	4.99	105.8	6.77
1977	103.3	4.05	112.7	6.69
1978	104.1	3.33	121.2	8.29
1979	107.9	3.45	134.9	9.71
1980–July	112.5	4.60	153.6	9.27

[a]CPI is for the end of the period.
[b]Yields are averages for the period.
Source: IMF, *International Financial Statistics*, September 1980.

Philip Morris, Incorporated: Swiss Franc Financing

EXHIBIT 8
■
Balance of Payments, Switzerland (millions of US$)

	1973	1974	1975	1976	1977	1978	1979
Exports	9,626	12,056	13,109	14,907	17,695	23,618	N.Av.
Imports	(11,404)	(14,256)	(13,118)	(14,597)	(17,690)	(23,623)	N.Av.
Other goods and services	2,727	3,078	3,292	3,788	4,435	5,363	N.Av.
Unrequited transfers	(670)	(705)	(693)	(598)	(665)	(923)	(1,020)
Direct investment	—	—	—	—	—	—	—
Portfolio investment	(1,755)	(954)	(3,503)	(5,172)	(4,760)	(6,210)	N.Av.
Other long-term capital	(1,001)	(630)	(962)	(2,067)	(2,190)	(4,734)	(7,150)
Other short-term capital	508	(489)	(2,897)	2,632	598	4,674	924
Errors and omissions	2,346	2,331	6,293	4,089	3,610	8,619	N.Av.
Foreign government holdings	6	(61)	23	3	14	538	755
Other official	190	107	—	(1)	20	36	(8)
Change in reserves	(574)	(476)	(1,543)	(2,986)	(1,066)	(7,354)	(1,859)

Note: Parentheses indicate a debit.
N.Av. = not available.
Source: IMF, *International Financial Statistics*, September 1980.

Philip Morris, Incorporated: Swiss Franc Financing

EXHIBIT 9
■
Balance of Payments, United States (billions of US$)

	1973	1974	1975	1976	1977	1978	1979
Exports	71.42	98.31	107.13	114.76	120.82	142.05	182.05
Imports	(70.47)	(103.64)	(98.06)	(124.04)	(151.71)	(175.83)	(211.50)
Other goods and services	10.20	14.87	14.10	18.96	21.76	25.02	34.93
Unrequited transfers	(4.15)	(7.40)	(4.88)	(5.33)	(4.99)	(5.52)	(6.13)
Direct investment	(8.53)	(4.27)	(11.59)	(7.62)	(9.23)	(8.47)	(14.62)
Portfolio investment	3.20	(1.38)	(3.32)	(4.62)	(0.32)	0.40	(0.69)
Other long-term capital	(1.59)	(1.84)	(4.74)	(2.95)	(4.15)	(3.45)	(2.92)
Other short-term capital	(2.78)	(1.76)	(8.99)	(10.08)	(6.57)	(18.98)	5.06
Errors and omissions	(2.54)	(1.66)	5.68	10.43	(0.69)	11.44	23.66
Foreign government holdings	5.10	10.24	5.51	13.05	35.43	31.06	(13.56)
Other official	0.21	0.02	(0.50)	(0.04)	0.22	0.89	1.23
Change in reserves	(0.07)	(1.49)	(0.35)	(2.52)	(0.58)	1.39	2.47

Note: Parentheses indicate a debit.
Source: IMF, *International Financial Statistics*, September 1980.

Philip Morris, Incorporated: Swiss Franc Financing

EXHIBIT 10
■
Excerpts from Articles Discussing Economic Conditions in Switzerland and the United States in Late 1980

INTERNATIONAL CURRENCY REVIEW 12, NO. 5

U.S. Dollar.   A brief pre-election period of improving morale during the third quarter, fostered by wishful thinking on the part of certain senior U.S. officials, punctuated the pervasive pessimism which has gripped the business community in the United States this year. The euphoria was quickly smothered, however, by rising interest rates and friction between the discredited Carter regime and the Federal Reserve Board following accusations from the White House that the central bank had been interfering with "the recovery." In practice, despite the speed with which the U.S. economy responds to monetary initiatives, the Federal Reserve system is in no better position to stabilise this inflationary economy than the man in the moon. But at least its preoccupation with domestic economic matters has been relatively unhampered by serious dollar crises in recent months, despite the grave turn of events in the Middle East—a point which officials have been anxious to stress. Indeed the dollar's "stability" has been just about the only positive development they have been able to report.

As severe inflationary distortions have multiplied, it has become increasingly difficult for officials, let alone outside observers, to monitor accurately what has been happening in the U.S. economy. Spokesmen sometimes employ misleading short-hand methods of making economic and political scoring points which merely confuse matters further. Use is also typically made of unreliable statistics as a basis for doubtful conclusions.

It is our considered view that, with economies so distorted, the international financial system swamped with capital flows and abruptly transferable liquidity, and political instability mounting, it has become impossible to anticipate how the dollar is likely to perform other than on a bilateral basis. All we know for sure is that the Federal Government has embarked on an unprecedented orgy of deficit spending which reached a peak in election year—a fact which, when considered in the context of the continued proliferation of external dollar-denominated liquidity, cannot fail to undermine the eventual purchasing power of the dollar both at home and abroad.

Yet in response to pressures resulting from the clash between the Federal sector's borrowing needs and those of private borrowers, market rates have risen and any early correction seems unlikely in the absence of drastic public spending reductions. Perversely, therefore, the medium-term outlook for the dollar is for continued artificial "strength," as the worldwide transactions demand for dollars persists at inflated levels to pay for sky-high oil bills. With spot oil prices under upward pressure and another oil price explosion perhaps only months away, this artificial "strength" looks like [it is] becoming a semi-permanent feature of the international economic environment.

Swiss Franc. Although the current account of the Swiss balance-of-payments will be in deficit this year for the first time since 1965, the Swiss franc will not be unsettled. Indeed with inflation falling to a negligible level, the franc has fully recovered from the weakness it demonstrated during the first quarter of 1980; and it may again be facing a period of appreciation, especially as it is no longer protected by a battery of controls warding off foreign money.

Economic growth in Switzerland was fairly brisk during the first half of 1980. Although signs of a slowdown are now becoming more apparent (stocks are rising, and foreign orders are less buoyant), private consumption has recovered from last year's fall, while fixed investment seems likely to be the most vigorous sector of domestic demand. Business expenditure on plant and equipment is expected to rise by 5% in real terms this year . . .

Certainly, the 1981 budget announced in early October gave no indication of any stresses and strains in the allocation of resources. Even the budget deficit, the most intractable of all aggregates in the affairs of practically every other developed country, is diminishing in line with a medium-term programme—which specifies that it will be no greater than SFr 1500 million in 1983. Next year's budget deficit is estimated SFr 1.17 billion against SFr 1.29 billion in the current year and SFr 1.17 billion in 1979.

During the first quarter of 1980, the Swiss franc was seriously weakened by the combined impact of mounting inflation and a widening trade deficit. The elimination of most of the remaining controls on capital inflows had little immediate impact—although, at the time, the Swiss authorities made no attempt to match the higher interest rates that were on offer in all other financial centres. Only at the end of February was the discount rate raised by 1%, to 3%; now that rates in other financial centres are generally lower than they were 6 months ago, the differential against Switzerland is obviously less marked. Even so, Swiss rates are still much lower than elsewhere.

The attraction appears to be that 3% earned on a deposit in Switzerland is very close to providing a real rate of return (as well as the renewed prospect of a capital gain through the currency's appreciation), while 15–20% earned in certain other European centres is still less than the current rate of reported or presumed inflation.

However there would not appear to be any serious chance that the old problem of unwanted appreciation will return. Next year, when the current account may be in balance and inflation negligible, the attraction of the Swiss franc, no longer surrounded by a barricade of controls, may well prove irresistible. . . . There seems little doubt that many treasurers, either in national Treasuries or within multinational corporations, would welcome the opportunity to diversify at least a proportion of their dollar portfolios into Swiss francs, should appropriate opportunities become available.

NIGEL BANCE, "THE WORLD ECONOMY IN 1981," *EUROMONEY*, OCTOBER 1980

There will be a sharp increase in world unemployment next year, matched by a sharp fall in world inflation. Economic growth rates will decline, but on the whole will be positive.

That is the summary of the average of more than 300 forecasts for 33 major economies that *Euromoney* has collected for our annual survey of the world economy.

As it turns out, the average of these forecasts—or if you like, the forecast of forecasts—has been a remarkably accurate guide to world growth, inflation, and unemployment. In the August issue of its *Monitor*, Dillon, Read analyzed the forecasts in our annual surveys on the world economy for 1977, 1978, and 1979. The analysis showed that average forecasts are a much better indicator of actual performance than individual forecasts. On economic growth, for example, the average error of the forecasts of forecasts for all countries in the survey was only 0.5%, that for inflation 1.1%.

The forecasters' expectations for this year and next are set out in the tables in this survey. But here's a brief summary of the major economies:

United States.   All 32 forecasters expect an absolute decline in GNP this year. The average forecast is a negative 1.4%, coinciding exactly with the official forecast from the Council of Economic Advisors. But a modest recovery is expected in the first half of 1981 and the average forecast for next year is a positive 1%, although the Council of Economic Advisors expects only 0.3%. Inflation is expected to decline to below 10% in 1981, from 13% this year. And *all* forecasters expect U.S. unemployment to rise next year from an average of 7.6%, in 1980, to 8.6%.

	Real GNP (percent)		Consumer Prices (percent)		Unemployment Rate (percent)	
	1980	1981	1980	1981	1980	1981
United States						
Highest forecast	−0.5	4.0	14.0	11.7	7.9	9.3
Average forecast	−1.4	1.0	13.0	9.5	7.6	8.6
Lowest forecast	−3.0	−1.0	11.0	7.5	7.0	7.6
Switzerland						
Highest forecast	2.5	2.0	7.1	5.7	0.9	1.2
Average forecast	1.5	1.1	4.4	3.6	0.4	0.6
Lowest forecast	0.4	0.5	3.5	2.5	0.2	0.2

Van Dusen Air, Inc.

In June 1985, Gordon Foster, the chief financial officer at Van Dusen Air, Inc., studied the alternatives for financing the company's most recent acquisition. Acquisitions were normal for Van Dusen, because its historical strategy had been to grow through friendly purchases of smaller firms. The $14.5 million purchase of Burlington Northern Airmotive, however, was by far the largest the company had ever made. Its size and Van Dusen management's desire to maintain financial flexibility in order to grow would require careful financing; Van Dusen had already begun analyzing its next potential acquisition.

THE INDUSTRY

Van Dusen provided repair service, fuel, and replacement parts to both the general and commercial aviation markets. The U.S. general aviation market consisted of over 200,000 aircraft, all of which required maintenance, periodic engine overhauls, and replacement parts. The commercial aviation market consisted of approximately 2,700 aircraft; service to commercial carriers was restricted almost entirely to refueling at major airports, because the airlines generally performed the other services themselves.

The industry served everyone from the private pilot needing a new tire for a plane through companies in need of engine overhauls for corporate aircraft to major commercial airlines in need of fuel. Thus, the aviation services industry was highly fragmented, with small aircraft maintenance shops scattered throughout the United States.

The demand for services in the industry depended on airport activity. In 1984, the Federal Aviation Administration (FAA) reported that control-tower activity was up 5 percent for general aviation and 12 percent for commercial aviation from the prior year. The FAA projected that the activity level of general aviation aircraft would increase at low-to-moderate rates through the early 1990s, but that the use of the more sophisticated aircraft (generally those with turbine engines) would more than double by the mid-1990s.

Van Dusen had a broad customer base. In fiscal year 1985, the company's top 10 customers accounted for 6.4 percent of total revenue, and the top 40

This case was prepared as a basis for class discussion rather than to illustrate either effective or ineffective handling of an administrative situation. Copyright © 1986 by the Darden Graduate Business School Sponsors, University of Virginia, Charlottesville, Virginia.

provided only 12.1 percent of the total. Van Dusen was thought to have a 10-percent share of the market, which was enough to dominate it because the nearest competitor had only a 2-percent share of part of the market (the piston-overhaul business). Van Dusen's share of the turbine overhaul market was small because it had only recently entered this segment of the industry. The wholesale price of an overhaul on a piston engine was $8,000, while that for a turbine engine was $65,000.

Given its broad range of services in the general aviation industry, few companies were in full competition with Van Dusen. As Exhibit 1 shows, however, some competitors did have considerable resources. Van Dusen occasionally had to compete with parts manufacturers, many with superior financial resources, that sold their goods directly to the end user. Thus, while Van Dusen was thought to be an overall leader in the industry, it did face substantial competition in nearly all phases of its operations.

Although many manufacturers of parts and supplies for general aviation aircraft sold directly to end users, the majority sold through independent distributors like Van Dusen. The parts manufacturers relied on these distributors to provide much of the advertising and servicing for their products. These parts were sold both as original equipment and as replacement parts.

The wholesale side of the general aviation parts and supplies industry was also fragmented. Van Dusen purchased roughly 10 percent of its parts from its largest supplier and thought that other distributors purchased from an equally diverse range of suppliers.

THE COMPANY

Van Dusen Air, Inc. was a multinational company serving the worldwide aviation market. The company had been incorporated in 1942 when G. B. Van Dusen started selling parts at the Minneapolis–St. Paul International Airport. The company currently had operations in over 30 domestic locations with 20 international branches and roughly 1,100 employees.

The three operating divisions at Van Dusen were Domestic Parts, International Parts, and Aviation Services. Both parts divisions distributed parts and supplies, primarily to corporate and general aviation customers, in their respective regions. The Aviation Services Division provided maintenance, engine overhaul, and fueling services to the general aviation market throughout the United States.

Van Dusen had recently begun to shift some emphasis from its parts-distribution business to its Aviation Services Division's fixed-base operations (FBO) locations. In 1980, parts and supplies represented nearly 80 percent of Van Dusen's total revenue; in 1985, the company projected 70 percent of total revenue would come from parts and supplies. Management expected this trend to continue. The repair market was growing faster than the parts market, and management thought that the FBOs were a way to tap into the growing market for repairs. The company wanted to maintain its parts business, but integrate it into the FBOs.

As it suffered through the recession and the air traffic controllers' strike of 1982, the company's net income fell from $4.6 million in 1981 to $361,000 in 1983. Van Dusen had not been hit as hard by previous recessions, and it was largely because of this drop in earnings that it had begun to emphasize the faster-growing FBO side of the business.

At the same time, the company's strategy had included growth through the friendly acquisition of smaller companies in the general aviation industry, many of which consisted of FBOs. Recent acquisitions included Burlington Northern Airmotive (FBO) in April 1985, Mattituck Airbase, Inc. (FBO) in June 1984, and Universal Export Corporation (parts manufacturer) and Hughes Aviation Services Aircraft Products Division (FBO), both in fiscal year 1983.

This strategy had been very successful for Van Dusen. Revenue had grown from $52 million in 1976 to an estimated $126 million in 1985. The company's net income over that same time period had grown from $1.7 million to an estimated $4.3 million. Exhibits 2 and 3 show the company's financial statements for the years 1976 to 1984. To continue strong growth, management had concluded that both geographic expansion and expansion into the FBO market (both by aggressive acquisition) were necessary.

In addition to this expansionary strategy, Van Dusen also planned to emphasize further the maintenance and overhaul of turbine-type engines of general aviation aircraft. The company was in a good position in the piston market because, except for piston and engine manufacturers, it had the largest piston-overhaul facilities in the industry. The number of turbine engines in use was significantly lower than that of piston engines, but as noted, the use of turbine engines with their more advanced technology was expected to increase at a higher rate. Exhibit 4 contains forecasts of piston and turbine engine use. Management believed that a strong presence in the turbine market, coupled with the company's advanced capabilities, would increase maintenance revenues and parts sales.

Van Dusen had a goal of reaching over half a billion dollars in total revenues by 1990 through its expansionary strategy. Exhibits 5 and 6 contain the company's financial-statement projections through 1990. As Exhibit 6 shows, management expected the parts business to grow at a steady rate, but expectations were much higher for the Aviation Services Division.

BURLINGTON NORTHERN AIRMOTIVE

In April 1985, Van Dusen agreed to acquire Burlington Northern Airmotive (BNA), which had been a subsidiary of Burlington Northern, Inc., for $14.5 million in cash. BNA was strategically attractive to Van Dusen for several reasons. First, its broad range of services and excellent reputation would definitely increase Van Dusen's presence in the FBO industry. Its location at Minneapolis–St. Paul International Airport gave Van Dusen an FBO to serve the upper Midwest. One of the top 20 FBO locations in the United States, the area was thought to account for 5 percent of the total U.S. general aviation market. Van Dusen currently had a parts distribution outlet in Minneapolis, but no FBO. In addition to the FBO operation for fueling and storage of general aviation aircraft, BNA specialized in the maintenance and overhaul of turbine engines. Furthermore, BNA's long profit history fit with Van Dusen's strategy to purchase only companies that required no extensive turnaround efforts.

Mr. Foster had secured short-term funds to pay for the purchase in April, but these notes were fast coming due. He was uncertain how to achieve the flexible long-term financing Van Dusen wanted.

FINANCING ALTERNATIVES

Van Dusen Air already had a 9.4 percent, $6.5 million term loan due in 1992, capitalized leases with a principal value of $1.2 million due in varying amounts through 1988, and a $10-million revolving credit arrangement with an insurance company,[1] of which $7.5 million had been drawn down. Van Dusen was in compliance with all covenants, including one from the revolver that prohibited Van Dusen from incurring any unsubordinated debt in excess of 75 percent of its consolidated tangible net worth.[2]

The acquisition of BNA had looked good not only to Van Dusen, but to many bankers and investment bankers, as well. Mr. Foster had been approached by several different companies who wanted to provide Van Dusen with the long-term financing needed. He had narrowed the choices down to four alternatives he found most attractive:

1.   The first alternative was a straight equity issue for a total of $15 million. Although Mr. Foster was not sure what price per share would be placed on the offering, he had been told by the investment banker proposing the issue that (after fees) the proceeds to the company would most likely be $13 per share, which could be compared with a high stock price of $15 in the prior year and a current price of $14. The company would have to issue 1,153,846 new shares to obtain the funds needed. Exhibit 7 provides Van Dusen's stock price history.

2.   Mr. Foster had also received a proposal that offered a new seven-year term loan for $22.5 million at an interest rate of 13.3 percent per year. Payments would be made semiannually. A covenant of the current revolver loan restricted Van Dusen to an additional $8.6 million of long-term debt unless the revolver was fully repaid.

3.   The third proposal Mr. Foster evaluated was a private placement of subordinated convertible debentures for $15 million. Mr. Foster expected the coupon rate to be 12 percent and the fees 1 percent of the total offering. A sinking fund would begin after the fifth year, with equal payments (at par value) made until the bonds matured in 15 years (if they had not been converted). Each bond was convertible into 57 shares of common stock. The conversion price of $17.50 was 25 percent over the current $14 stock price. After the third year, Van Dusen could call the bonds for $24.50 in cash.

4.   The fourth option was similar to the third, except that it would be a publicly placed subordinated convertible debenture. The coupon for this offering would be 11 percent, and the fee paid would be 4 percent of the total issue. The public placement would have the same sinking fund, maturity, and conversion provisions that the private issue would have.

---

[1]The interest rate on the revolver was 1⅞ percent over the 30-day certificate of deposit rate and 0.5 percent on the undrawn portion. In 1980, the 30-day certificate of deposit rate averaged 12.91 percent; in 1981, it averaged 15.91 percent. The rate dropped back to 12.04 percent in 1982 and to an average of 8.96 percent in 1983. In 1984, it rose to 10.17 percent, but in May 1985, it averaged 7.83 percent. In early June 1985, the 30-day U.S. Treasury bill rate was 6.2 percent
[2]Consolidated tangible net worth = Stockholders' equity − Intangible (other) assets.

Van Dusen Air, Inc.

EXHIBIT 1

■

Selected Data for Competitors in the General Aviation Parts and Supplies Industry
(in thousands, except per share amounts)

	Van Dusen	AAR	Aviall	Butler
Revenues				
1982	$143,097	$175,924	$221,754	$343,808
1983	137,460	155,006	299,933	342,587
1984	144,902	177,762	400,520	313,745[a]
Net Income				
1982	3,086	1,225	2,960[b]	6,311
1983	361	2,795	1,891	5,112
1984	1,792	4,487	8,140	6,266
Long-term Debt				
1983	9,384	23,504	154,000	15,764
1984	15,391	13,040	150,000	11,100
Stockholders' Equity				
1982				
1983	33,056	43,225	5,773	67,683
1984	33,302	81,085	13,794	64,600
Dividends per Share				
1984	0.40	0.44	0.0	0.52
Earnings per Share				
1982	1.01	0.33	0.79	1.13
1983	0.12	0.71	(0.06)	0.82
1984	0.59[c]	0.97	1.59	0.96
Recent Stock Prices[d]				
1982 High	20.50	14.75	N.Av.	17.38
Low	9.50	6.13	N.Av.	7.88
1983 High	12.50	9.88	N.Av.	24.50
Low	8.25	5.75	N.Av.	14.88
1984 High	15.00	17.75	15.00	20.75
Low	10.25	8.63	10.00	12.13

N.Av. = not available (because Aviall was privately held before 1984).
[a]Total before extraordinary items.
[b]Butler 1984 totals exclude discontinued operations.
[c]Van Dusen was not extremely closely held. G. B. Van Dusen and his family controlled roughly 16 percent of the company's stock, the largest block of shares outstanding.
[d]A comparable index, Standard & Poor's 500, was 119.71 in 1982, 160.41 in 1983, and 160.39 in 1984.

Van Dusen Air, Inc.

EXHIBIT 2

∎

Balance Sheets for Years Ended December 31 (thousands of dollars)

	1976	1977	1978	1979	1980	1981	1982	1983	1984
Assets									
Cash	$ 3,418	$ 1,323	$ 1,492	$ 1,836	$ 1,775	$ 5,602	$ 671	$ 2,748	$ 2,312
Accounts receivable	9,657	10,970	13,414	17,384	21,719	23,633	24,549	17,469	22,233
Inventories	14,853	16,522	15,397	18,811	24,259	23,486	25,743	20,519	27,865
Prepaid expenses	185	330	438	301	581	799	909	900	923
Federal tax refunds	0	0	0	0	0	0	0	1,236	447
Total current assets	28,113	29,145	30,741	38,332	48,334	53,520	51,872	42,872	53,780
Buildings	1,430	1,501	1,588	1,508	2,740	2,750	3,534	3,987	4,413
Leasehold improvements	3,126	2,706	2,911	3,044	3,887	4,575	5,236	5,553	4,992
Airplanes and equipment	2,201	2,364	3,049	3,372	4,370	5,074	7,814	9,988	9,794
Accumulated depreciation	(2,144)	(2,297)	(2,517)	(2,756)	(3,239)	(4,206)	(5,446)	(7,091)	(7,953)
Net property, plant, equipment	4,613	4,274	5,031	5,168	7,758	8,193	11,138	12,437	11,246
Other assets	697	234	316	310	224	390	736	1,571	2,066
Total assets	$33,423	$33,653	$36,088	$43,810	$56,316	$62,103	$63,746	$56,880	$67,092

Liabilities and Stockholders' Equity

Notes payable	$ 0	$ 76	$ 0	$ 0	$ 8,201	$ 341	$ 2,808	$ 34	$ 4
Current maturities	597	820	670	674	781	1,989	1,374	1,734	1,679
Accounts payable	6,689	6,278	5,563	8,665	8,739	9,352	6,937	6,410	8,810
Accrued salaries	1,170	1,231	1,457	2,313	2,560	3,349	2,133	2,124	2,514
Other accrued liabilities	0	0	0	0	0	0	1,482	1,018	1,705
Accrued taxes	1,782	911	1,512	1,291	1,202	2,033	820	595	935
Total current liabilities	10,238	9,316	9,202	12,943	21,483	17,064	15,554	11,915	15,647
Deferred taxes	804	948	1,389	1,872	2,263	2,366	2,580	2,298	2,304
Long-term debt	12,563	11,953	12,321	11,559	11,919	10,377	10,949	9,384	15,391
Accrued pensions	0	0	0	0	0	0	13	227	448
Long-term liabilities	$13,367	$12,901	$13,710	$13,431	$14,182	$12,743	$13,542	$11,909	$18,143
Common stock	1,161	1,161	1,328	1,725	2,453	3,014	3,069	3,149	3,149
Paid-in capital	1,835	2,192	3,327	8,049	8,095	15,441	15,772	15,702	15,702
Retained earnings	6,822	8,083	8,521	7,662	10,103	13,841	15,809	15,026	15,596
Treasury stock	0	0	0	0	0	0	0	(821)	(1,145)
Stockholders' equity	9,818	11,436	13,176	17,436	20,651	32,296	34,650	33,056	33,302
Total liabilities and stockholders' equity	$33,423	$33,653	$36,088	$43,810	$56,316	$62,103	$63,746	$56,880	$67,092

Van Dusen Air, Inc.

EXHIBIT 3

■

Income Statements (in thousands)

	1976	1977	1978	1979	1980	1981	1982	1983	1984
Revenues									
Parts and supplies	$52,709	$61,369	$72,915	$86,059	$104,157	$114,701	$119,041	$116,261	$123,438
Fuel and airplanes	4,238	4,965	6,137	7,313	11,364	14,770	16,540	13,751	12,396
Airport services	5,249	4,887	5,459	5,886	6,138	7,080	7,516	7,448	9,068
Total revenues	62,196	71,221	84,511	99,258	121,659	136,551	143,097	137,460	144,902
Operating expenses									
Cost of parts and supplies	38,494	44,999	54,079	64,056	77,218	82,275	85,407	84,658	91,356
Cost of fuel and airplanes	8,765	8,905	10,472	11,892	15,402	19,631	22,205	19,804	19,549
Selling and warehousing	8,813	10,077	11,675	12,585	16,047	20,174	23,206	23,607	22,586
Total operating expenses	56,072	63,981	76,226	88,533	108,667	122,080	130,818	128,069	133,491
Operating income	6,124	7,240	8,285	10,725	12,992	14,471	12,279	9,391	11,411
Corporate expenses and other income									
Administrative expenses	1,544	1,719	1,886	3,198	3,755	4,081	5,875	6,879	7,025
Interest expense	1,305	1,967	1,551	1,132	1,831	1,937	1,087	2,229	1,271
Interest income	246	842	504	167	28	122	88	40	258
Total corporate expenses	2,603	2,844	2,933	4,163	5,558	5,896	6,874	9,068	8,038
Income before taxes	3,521	4,396	5,352	6,562	7,434	8,575	5,405	323	3,373
Taxes	1,759	2,313	2,826	3,353	3,518	4,001	2,319	-38	1,581
Net income	$ 1,762	$ 2,083	$ 2,526	$ 3,209	$ 3,916	$ 4,574	$ 3,086	$ 361	$ 1,792
Dividends	$ 324	$ 373	$ 449	$ 584	$ 788	$ 836	$ 1,118	$ 1,251	$ 1,222
Common shares outstanding	2,101	2,121	2,151	2,301	2,493	2,598	3,069	3,108	3,045

Van Dusen Air, Inc.

EXHIBIT 4
■

Forecasted General Aviation Aircraft by Type of Aircraft
(in thousands)

	Piston		Turbine	
	Single Engine	Multi- Engine	Turboprop	Turbojet
1985	162.9	25.0	6.0	4.5
1986	166.7	25.6	6.6	4.9
1987	172.0	26.5	7.1	5.2
1988	178.7	27.5	7.6	5.5
1989	187.1	28.8	8.1	5.7
1990	192.2	29.6	8.6	5.9
1991	197.0	30.5	9.1	6.2
1992	202.4	31.4	9.6	6.5
1993	207.7	32.2	10.1	6.7
1994	212.6	33.0	10.5	6.9
1995	216.8	33.7	10.9	7.1

Source: Van Dusen Air management estimate.

Van Dusen Air, Inc.

EXHIBIT 5
■

Balance Sheet Projections (in thousands)

	1985	1986	1987	1988	1989	1990
Assets						
Current assets	$65,159	$73,284	$ 82,482	$ 98,845	$115,656	$125,922
Net property and other assets	14,654	20,233	24,097	27,015	32,717	39,176
Total assets	$79,813	$93,517	$106,579	$125,860	$148,373	$165,098
Liabilities and stockholders' equity						
Current liabilities	$26,659	$41,108	$ 47,659	$ 58,125	$ 68,891	$ 69,871
Long-term liabilities	16,746	13,049	13,650	14,382	14,528	13,380
Stockholders' equity	36,408	39,360	45,270	53,353	64,954	81,847
Total liabilities and stockholders' equity	$79,813	$93,517	$106,579	$125,860	$148,373	$165,098

Assumptions
1. As a result of programs in place to reduce receivables and inventories and extend payables, current assets will grow at an annual rate of 14 percent and current liabilities at 21 percent.
2. Property and other assets will increase at 22 percent per year as a result of acquisitions.
3. Long-term liabilities were used as the plug for the balance sheet.

Van Dusen Air, Inc.

EXHIBIT 6
■

Income Statement Projections (in thousands)

	1985	1986	1987	1988	1989	1990
Revenues						
Parts and supplies	$126,312	$141,126	$158,176	$175,047	$191,211	$209,380
Aviation services	45,897	101,874	142,462	190,436	247,652	315,454
Total revenues	172,209	243,000	300,638	365,483	438,863	524,834
Operating income	14,971	23,072	28,464	37,197	44,756	55,774
Administrative expense	7,061	10,807	12,928	16,246	16,508	18,818
Earnings before interest and taxes	7,910	12,265	15,536	20,951	28,248	36,956
Interest expense	2,523	4,180	4,060	4,667	5,135	4,153
Earnings before taxes	5,387	8,085	11,476	16,284	23,113	32,803
Taxes	1,069	3,921	5,566	7,898	11,210	15,910
Net income	$ 4,318	$ 4,164	$ 5,910	$ 8,386	$ 11,903	$ 16,893
Dividends	$ 1,212	$ 1,212	$ 1,212	$ 1,515	$ 1,817	$ 1,817

Assumptions

1. Total revenue will grow at 25 percent per year. The majority of that growth will come from the Aviation Services Division's future acquisitions.

2. Cost of goods sold and administrative expense/revenue will gradually decrease because of the synergy experienced with future acquisitions.

3. Interest expense will remain fairly stable as new debt used to make acquisitions replaces existing long-term debt.

4. Dividends will be $0.40/share through 1987, $0.50/share in 1988, and $0.60/share for 1989 to 1990.

Van Dusen Air, Inc.

EXHIBIT 7
■

Stock Price History
(in thousands)

Date	High	Low	Close	Date	High	Low	Close
1/80	$16.00	$14.00	$15.00	10/82	$10.25	$ 8.25	$ 9.25
2/80	14.00	13.25	13.63	11/82	10.00	8.50	9.13
3/80	13.25	10.00	11.63	12/82	11.25	10.25	10.75
4/80	10.75	10.00	10.38	1/83	14.00	10.75	12.38
5/80	12.25	10.25	11.25	2/83	12.75	12.75	13.25
6/80	12.25	11.75	12.00	3/83	13.25	12.75	13.00
7/80	13.25	12.25	12.75	4/83	14.75	13.00	13.38
8/80	13.75	13.00	13.38	5/83	15.00	14.00	14.50
9/80	14.00	13.25	13.38	6/83	14.00	13.50	13.75
10/80	16.00	13.25	14.75	7/83	15.00	13.75	14.38
11/80	20.00	15.75	17.38	8/83	13.75	13.50	13.63
12/80	18.75	16.75	17.75	9/83	13.75	13.50	13.63
1/81	17.25	14.25	15.75	10/83	13.75	13.00	13.38
2/81	16.75	16.00	16.38	11/83	12.50	10.25	11.38
3/81	17.50	16.00	16.75	12/83	14.75	12.25	13.50
4/81	19.25	17.25	18.25	1/84	14.75	14.00	14.38
5/81	19.25	19.00	19.13	2/84	14.00	13.50	13.75
6/81	20.50	16.75	18.63	3/84	14.25	14.00	14.13
7/81	18.25	16.50	17.38	4/84	14.25	14.25	14.25
8/81	16.75	15.75	16.25	5/84	16.50	13.75	15.13
9/81	16.00	15.00	15.50	6/84	14.00	13.75	13.38
10/81	14.50	12.25	13.38	7/84	14.25	13.75	14.00
11/81	12.25	9.50	10.38	8/84	15.25	14.25	14.38
12/81	11.75	9.50	10.63	9/84	15.25	15.50	15.50
2/82	9.75	9.00	9.38	10/84	15.75	15.50	15.63
3/82	10.50	8.25	9.38	11/84	15.75	15.50	15.63
4/82	11.25	10.00	10.63	12/84	15.25	11.50	13.38
5/82	12.50	10.25	11.38	1/85	13.75	13.00	13.38
6/82	10.25	8.75	9.50	2/85	13.00	13.00	13.00
7/82	9.00	8.75	8.38	3/85	13.25	13.00	13.13
8/82	9.75	8.50	9.13	4/85	13.75	11.75	12.25
9/82	9.75	9.25	9.50	5/85	13.50	11.75	12.63

National Industrial Bridge, Inc.

Late in June 1982, Donald Reardon, assistant treasurer of National Industrial Bridge, Inc., was searching for a way of retiring two debt issues that NIB had placed privately several years earlier. Various scenarios had been discussed, and two alternatives had surfaced as most promising: (1) early retirement of the debts at the 8-percent premiums provided for in the indenture contracts, and (2) the possibility of defeasance. Defeasance had just been used successfully by Exxon, Kellogg, and several other companies.

COMPANY HISTORY AND SITUATION

In 1982, NIB was active in a variety of businesses: construction products, engineering and construction services, financial services, industrial products, special products, and steel products and services. Over the previous ten years, growth had come mainly from acquisitions under the strong leadership of Chairman of the Board David Burkhart. Since 1978, debt had been used to finance all acquisitions and represented a significant portion of the firm's long-term capital. Financial statements for 1980 and 1981 are shown in Exhibits 1 through 4.

Mr. Burkhart believed that the opportunities for acquiring another firm were quite favorable, because quality firms with solid, long-term track records were selling at market prices significantly below book values. In late 1981, NIB had lost a contest for a large machine-tool manufacturer, but during 1982, the company purchased another machine-tool manufacturer, Upper Midwest Tool & Die, because it seemed extremely undervalued. The purchase price of $300 million represented about ten times UMT's 1981 earnings and was financed with working capital from UMT and $225 million in long-term debt drawn from NIB's evergreen revolving credit line.

Earnings for NIB in 1982 were expected to be far below the original prediction of 10 percent growth over 1981. Unfortunately, neither its international nor its domestic business was expected to improve in 1983 because of a delay in world economic recovery. The poor earnings prospects and recent increases in long-term debt were contributing to increased chances for violation of its private-placement indenture agreements.

Copyright by J. Peter Williamson, Amos Tuck Graduate School of Management, Dartmouth College, Hanover, New Hampshire © 1984.

The $36.9-million private placements had been made to effect an acquisition in 1978. The covenants accompanying this debt were intended for the acquired firm, as Mr. Reardon saw it, and seemed unnecessary, indeed unsuited, for NIB, since the subsidiary had been fully assimilated by 1982 into the operations of NIB, except for reporting purposes. The loan covenants required the preparation of separate financial reports for the subsidiary and restricted dividends from it to the parent. Because of the low reported earnings of the subsidiary, no dividends had been declared to the parent. Thus, cash transfers from the subsidiary to the parent took the form of loans, with full documentation and evidence that the terms of the loans were those of an arm's length transaction. Mr. Reardon wanted to rid NIB of those covenants.

THE ALTERNATIVES

Normal prepayment.   When originally issued, the privately placed debt contained provisions for prepayment. Unfortunately, the 8-percent premium associated with the prepayment was significant. Mr. Reardon had wanted to renegotiate the premium with the insurance company lender, but it offered no concessions. In addition, Mr. Reardon believed that NIB could save approximately $100,000 annually in fees and overhead by eliminating the separate divisional audits and reports required by the covenants. In light of NIB's current financial position, he wondered whether he should continue to negotiate, pay the prepayment penalty, or pursue the alternative, defeasance.

Defeasance.   Defeasance or "nullification" had recently become popular with firms wishing to reduce debt levels on their balance sheets. Nullification could be accomplished in several ways, but it always involved the allocation of certain cash-flow-generating assets to service the liability. This step usually called for establishing an escrow or trust account that held agency or government securities. The cash flow from the government securities (interest and principal) would be used to meet the company's originally scheduled debt service. Once a portfolio of these assets, usually called a "dedicated portfolio," had been established, even though the debt was not repaid, the company could stop reporting both the debt and the value of the dedicated portfolio.

The accounting treatment in 1982 of a defeasance was as follows: The debt that was defeased would disappear from the balance sheet, as would the agency or government securities transferred to the trustee. The book value of the debt less the cost of the securities would be reported in the year of the defeasance as gain, but this gain would be reduced by the amount of capital gains tax the company could expect to pay at the maturities of the government bonds (capital gain results from redemption at par of bonds purchased at less than par). Each year until the debt was actually paid off, the company would report the net of interest paid on the debt and interest received from the securities as operating income or expense for the year.

Defeasance was commonly written into the contracts of industrial revenue bonds, but in recent years had spread beyond its use with these bonds because defeasance offered certain advantages over prepayment. To begin with, the buyers of a bond issue might be more willing to authorize a defeasance than a prepayment, since prepayment during a period of low interest rates would force them to take a reduction in interest income. In some cases, the consent of the bond holders was not necessary to effect an "in-substance" defeasance: even though the bond indenture might make no explicit provision for a defeasance, the issuing company could effectively defease the issue. When interest rates were low, the cost of defeasing a bond issue might be substantially below the face value of the issue. In this case, the issuing company would be able, under existing Financial Accounting Standards Board rules, to include in its reported income an extraordinary gain on debt retirement. This gain would not be immediately subject to income tax, since the bonds were not actually paid off. For income tax purposes, the company would continue to deduct interest payments on its bonds, but it would have to report as income any taxable interest and gains at maturity on the U.S. government securities held by the trustee.

The August 9, 1982 issue of *Business Week* reported on defeasance transactions carried out by Kellogg and Exxon. In the first publicly announced corporate example of a defeasance, Exxon transferred $312 million worth of U.S. government securities to its trustee, The Morgan Guaranty Trust Company, to defease six issues of debt totaling $515 million. Exxon was able to report a $130-million after-tax gain on the transaction. Kellogg transferred $65.6 million to Morgan Guaranty Bank; Morgan would make all debt service payments on Kellogg's bonds with a face value of $75 million.

Mr. Reardon thought that the spread between the rate on the private placements and the market yield on government securities was wide enough to result in a reported financial gain from defeasance. Although the gains were attractive to NIB in light of near-term projected earnings, Mr. Reardon had several questions about defeasance: Were any real economies reflected in the gains from defeasance? Would it make any difference if assets to defease the private placements were purchased using new debt financing (7-year debt with a balloon maturity and a coupon of 13 percent) or an equity offering (proceeds derived from $100 million of common stock sold at approximately $19 per share with dividends of $1 per share)? Mr. Reardon was aware that defeasance was looked upon skeptically by accounting authorities and the Securities and Exchange Commission. Moreover, the FASB was about to issue a statement of possible changes in the accounting treatment of defeasances. The statement appears in Exhibit 5.

The debt-service schedules for the two privately placed issues of debentures are shown in Exhibits 6 and 7. Arranging a defeasance would involve assembling a portfolio of U.S. government or agency securities that would match, or nearly match, the debt service of the debt being defeased. Mr. Reardon had discussed the defeasance of the 9-percent debenture with a representative of a major investment banking firm, which recommended the list of U.S. government bonds shown in Exhibit 8.

Exhibit 9 provides an analysis of the cash flows associated with the defeasance. After-tax cash flows were calculated by applying a 50-percent tax rate to interest payments and receipts and a 30-percent rate to the gain recognized as the U.S. government bonds matured. The investment bankers recommended a list of bonds with face values totaling $26,232,694 to defease the 9½ percent debenture issue.

Mr. Reardon was very much aware of market-rate movements and the potential for reporting significant financial gains. The recession and low inflationary expectations had placed downward pressure on the existing high interest rates. He was worried that, if the decision for defeasance were delayed, the beneficial market spreads might disappear. He also was concerned about what the true benefits of defeasance were and whether defeasing the 9-percent issue was better than paying the 8-percent prepayment penalty and retiring the issue.

National Industrial Bridge, Inc.

EXHIBIT 1
■
Income Statements

	1980	1981
Income Statements		
Sales	$1,061,511	$1,562,378
Equity in pre-tax earnings of unconsolidated subsidiaries and affiliates	1,602	10,606
Total sales and equity interest	1,063,113	1,572,984
Costs and expenses		
Cost of sales and operating expenses	967,333	1,389,461
Depreciation and amortization	18,139	24,061
Interest, net	7,345	44,248
Foreign-currency transaction loss (gain)	283	(1,986)
Total costs and expenses	993,100	1,455,784
Operating income before income taxes	70,013	117,200
Provision for income taxes		
Current	32,884	47,166
Deferred	(8,114)	1,078
Total tax provision	24,770	48,244
Net income before extraordinary items	45,243	68,956
Gain on sale of assets, net of income tax of $757 in 1981 and $965 in 1980	3,534	1,274
Net income	$ 48,777	$ 70,230
Per Share Data		
Operating income	$1.69	$2.56
Gain on sale of assets, net of income tax	0.13	0.05
Net income	1.82	2.61
Dividends	0.85	1.00
Retained Earnings		
Balance at beginning of year		
As previously reported	$ 223,966	$ 248,414
Foreign currency translation adjustment	5,506	7,012
As restated	229,472	255,426
Net income	48,777	70,230
Dividends (per share: 1980, $0.85; 1981, $1.00)	22,823	26,870
Balance at end of year	$ 255,426	$ 298,786

National Industrial Bridge, Inc.

EXHIBIT 2
■
Balance Sheet

	1980	1981
Assets		
Current assets		
Cash and short-term deposits	$ 96,340	$ 176,601
Accounts and notes receivable	220,980	277,178
Inventories	332,119	392,788
Other current assets	11,032	9,152
Total current assets	660,471	855,719
Investments in unconsolidated subsidiaries and affiliates	53,286	69,010
Fixed assets	180,883	198,353
Goodwill	57,196	55,626
Other assets	18,294	33,667
Total assets	$970,130	$1,212,375
Liabilities and Shareholders' Equity		
Short-term borrowings	$ 58,029	$ 100,812
Accounts payable and accrued liabilities	218,940	250,256
Customer advances	58,373	77,864
Income taxes		
Current	40,313	19,035
Deferred	34,248	45,681
Current installments on long-term debt	15,096	16,112
Total current liabilities	424,999	509,760
Long-term debt	163,393	296,803
Other deferred liabilities		
Deferred income taxes	32,757	22,962
Pension plans	12,273	10,205
Other	2,920	4,215
Total liabilities	$636,342	$ 843,945
Capital stock (issued 1980, 26,852,922 shares; 1981, 26,890,722)	93,016	93,343
Retained earnings	255,426	298,786
Equity adjustment from foreign currency translation	(14,654)	(23,699)
Total shareholders' equity	333,788	368,430
Total liabilities and shareholders' equity	$970,130	$1,212,375

National Industrial Bridge, Inc.

EXHIBIT 3
■
Changes in Financial Position

	1980	1981
Sources of Working Capital		
Operations		
Net income	$ 48,777	$ 70,230
Add (deduct) items not affecting working capital		
Depreciation	15,389	21,446
Amortization	2,750	2,615
Increase (decrease) in deferred income taxes (noncurrent)	(1,768)	(1,154)
Pre-tax gain on sale of assets	(4,842)	(2,859)
Equity in net income of unconsolidated subsidiaries and affiliates	(765)	(5,427)
Other	(575)	1,320
Working capital provided from operations	58,966	88,479
Proceeds from long-term debt	0	156,309
Proceeds from sale of assets, net of working capital ($2,540 in 1980; $177 in 1981)	7,314	10,182
Issue of share capital	1,727	327
Other	7,942	547
Total working capital provided	$ 75,949	$255,844
Applications of Working Capital		
Acquisition of net noncurrent assets of Koehring		
Fixed assets	66,200	0
Investment in unconsolidated subsidiaries and affiliates	42,188	0
Assumption of long-term debt	(62,310)	0
Other	13,689	0
Total from Koehring acquisition	32,389	0
Advances to unconsolidated subsidiaries	0	9,502
Decrease in deferred income taxes	0	10,949
Purchase of fixed assets	28,031	50,517
Payment of long-term debt	13,432	23,985
Dividends	22,823	26,870
Increase in other assets	4,326	16,814
Adjustment from translation of foreign currency	2,653	6,720
Total working capital applied	$103,654	$145,357
Increase (decrease) in working capital	$ (27,705)	$110,487
Working Capital at Beginning of Year		
As previously reported	$262,811	$236,049
Foreign-currency translation adjustment	366	(577)
As restated	263,177	235,472
Working capital, end of year	$235,472	$245,959

National Industrial Bridge, Inc.

EXHIBIT 4
■
Five-Year Statistical Summary[a] (in millions, except as noted)

	1977	1978	1979	1980	1981
Operating Results					
Sales	$ 581	$ 883	$ 934	$1,062	$1,562
Operating income before income taxes	52	68	63	70	117
Income taxes	19	32	23	25	48
Operating income	33	36	40	45	69
Gain on sale of assets (net of income tax)	0	0	13	4	1
Net income	33	36	53	49	70
Dividends	9	11	17	23	27
Income retained	24	25	36	26	43
Financial Condition					
Working capital	$ 107	$ 171	$ 263	$ 235	$ 346
Cash flow from operations	45	52	51	59	88
Net fixed assets	128	124	106	181	198
Depreciation	10	14	14	15	21
Additions to fixed assets	9	18	13	28	51
Long-term debt	104	139	115	163	297
Shareholders' equity	181	198	309	334	368
Return on average shareholder's equity	19.3%	19.0%	20.9%	15.2%	20.0%
Net income on sales	5.7%	4.1%	5.7%	4.6%	4.5%
Per Share Data[b]					
Sales	$27.29	$41.42	$40.06	$39.60	$58.15
Operating income	1.55	1.69	1.72	1.69	2.56
Gain on sale of assets (net of income tax)	—	—	0.57	0.13	0.05
Net income	1.55	1.69	2.29	1.82	2.61
Dividends	0.44	0.51	0.71	0.85	1.00
Income retained	1.11	1.18	1.58	.97	1.61
Cash flow from operations	2.12	2.43	2.19	2.20	3.29
Equity at year end	8.51	9.28	11.61	12.43	13.70
Shareholders and Employees (in thousands)					
Number of shareholders	3.85	3.85	4.40	5.81	5.73
Number of employees	8.99	13.59	13.34	16.24	17.30
Number of shares outstanding	21.27	21.33	26.63	26.85	26.89

[a]Data for all years have been adjusted to reflect the two-for-one stock subdivisions in November 1974, October 1976, and December 1979. Years 1977 through 1980 have been restated to adopt and comply with the provisions of U.S. FASB Statement #52.
[b]Per share data, except equity at year end, has been calculated based on the weighted-average shares outstanding during the year.

National Industrial Bridge, Inc.

EXHIBIT 5

■

Expected Acceptable FASB Defeasance Treatment

1. Under most circumstances the process of matching assets with specific liabilities is unacceptable, but for the purpose of defeasance, the rule is overlooked.

2. Interest income in the escrow account will be matched or netted against the interest expense of the original debt. The net will be treated as operating income or expense in that period.

3. The Internal Revenue Service will require that the net in 2 be taxed as ordinary income or deductible as expense of the period.

4. The extraordinary gain will no longer be totally recognizable in the period of execution but will be amortized over the life of the defeased debt, and is not taxable.

5. The capital gains that accrue in the escrow account will be taxable in the period in which they occur.

6. Defeasance must be either written into the indenture agreement or one must have confirmation of the lender.

Source: FASB Exposure Draft, *Extinguishment of Debt and the Offsetting of Restricted Assets against Related Debt*, December 13, 1982.

National Industrial Bridge, Inc.

EXHIBIT 6
■

Debt Service Schedule, Private Placement of $5-Million
Unsecured Debentures Due in 1977 with 9-Percent Interest

Due Date	Principal	Interest	Total
11/30/81	0	$ 225,000.00	$ 225,000.00
05/31/82	0	225,000.00	225,000.00
11/30/82	0	225,000.00	225,000.00
05/31/83	0	225,000.00	225,000.00
11/30/83	$ 172,500	225,000.00	397,500.00
05/31/84	172,500	217,237.50	389,737.50
11/30/84	172,500	209,475.00	381,975.00
05/31/85	172,500	201,712.50	374,212.50
11/30/85	172,500	193,950.00	366,450.00
05/31/86	172,500	186,187.50	358,687.50
11/30/86	172,500	178,425.00	350,925.00
05/31/87	172,500	170,662.50	343,162.50
11/30/87	172,500	162,900.00	335,400.00
05/31/88	172,500	155,137.50	327,637.50
11/30/88	172,500	147,375.00	319,875.00
05/31/89	172,500	139,612.50	312,112.50
11/30/89	172,500	131,850.00	304,350.00
05/31/90	172,500	124,087.50	296,587.50
11/30/90	172,500	116,325.00	288,825.00
05/31/91	172,500	108,562.50	281,062.50
11/30/91	172,500	100,800.00	273,300.00
05/31/92	172,500	93,037.50	265,537.50
11/30/92	172,500	85,275.00	257,775.00
05/31/93	172,500	77,512.50	250,012.50
11/30/93	172,500	69,750.00	242,250.00
05/31/94	172,500	61,987.50	234,487.50
11/30/94	172,500	54,225.00	226,725.00
05/31/95	172,500	46,462.50	218,962.50
11/30/95	172,500	38,700.00	211,200.00
05/31/96	172,500	30,937.50	203,437.50
11/30/96	172,500	23,175.00	195,675.00
05/31/97	172,500	15,412.50	187,912.50
11/30/97	170,000	7,650.00	177,650.00
Total as of 6/7/81	$5,000,000	$4,273,425.00	$9,273,425.00

National Industrial Bridge, Inc.

EXHIBIT 7
■

Debt Service Schedule, Private Placement of $31,900,000
Unsecured Debentures Due in 1992 with 9.5-Percent Interest

Due Date	Principal	Interest	Total
10/31/82	$ 2,900,000	$ 1,355,750	$ 4,255,750
04/30/83	0	1,232,500	1,232,500
10/31/83	2,900,000	1,232,500	4,132,500
04/30/84	0	1,109,250	1,109,250
10/31/84	2,900,000	1,109,250	4,009,250
04/30/85	0	986,000	986,000
10/31/85	2,900,000	986,000	3,886,000
04/30/86	0	862,750	862,750
10/31/86	2,900,000	862,750	3,762,750
04/30/87	0	739,500	739,500
10/31/87	2,900,000	739,500	3,639,500
04/30/88	0	616,250	616,250
10/31/88	2,900,000	616,250	3,516,250
04/30/89	0	493,000	493,000
10/31/89	2,900,000	493,000	3,393,000
04/30/90	0	369,750	369,750
10/31/90	2,900,000	369,750	3,269,750
04/30/91	0	246,500	246,500
10/31/91	2,900,000	246,500	3,146,500
04/30/92	0	123,250	123,250
10/31/92	2,900,000	123,250	3,023,250
Total as of 6/7/81	$31,900,000	$14,940,500	$46,840,500

National Industrial Bridge, Inc.

EXHIBIT 8
■
Dedicated Portfolio to Defease 9-Percent Debentures

	Face Value	Coupon	Semiannual Interest	Price	Purchase Cost	Maturity
T-Bond 1	$ 170,000	8.375%	$ 7,118.75	$ 67.30	$ 114,410	11/97
T-Bond 2	170,000	8.500	7,225.00	69.21	117,657	05/97
T-Bond 3	180,000	8.375	7,537.50	67.30	121,140	11/96
T-Bond 4	170,000	8.500	7,225.00	69.21	117,657	05/96
T-Bond 5	180,000	8.375	7,537.50	67.30	121,140	11/95
T-Bond 6	170,000	8.500	7,225.00	69.21	117,657	05/95
T-Bond 7	180,000	10.125	9,112.50	80.28	144,504	11/94
T-Bond 8	170,000	9.000	7,650.00	75.16	127,772	05/94
T-Bond 9	170,000	8.625	7,331.25	73.17	124,389	11/93
T-Bond 10	180,000	7.875	7,087.50	70.12	126,216	05/93
T-Bond 11	180,000	7.250	6,525.00	68.18	122,724	11/92
T-Bond 12	170,000	13.750	11,687.50	100.16	170,272	05/92
T-Bond 13	170,000	14.250	12,112.50	102.24	173,808	11/91
T-Bond 14	160,000	14.500	11,600.00	103.27	165,232	05/91
T-Bond 15	160,000	13.000	10,400.00	97.12	155,392	11/90
T-Bond 16	160,000	8.250	6,600.00	78.60	125,760	05/90
T-Bond 17	160,000	10.750	8,600.00	87.30	139,680	11/89
T-Bond 18	160,000	9.250	7,400.00	83.10	132,960	05/89
T-Bond 19	170,000	8.750	7,437.50	81.18	138,006	11/88
T-Bond 20	160,000	8.250	6,600.00	81.60	130,560	05/88
T-Bond 21	170,000	7.625	6,481.00	80.60	137,020	11/87
T-Bond 22	160,000	12.000	9,600.00	95.20	152,320	05/87
T-Bond 23	160,000	13.875	11,100.00	100.31	160,496	11/86
T-Bond 24	160,000	13.750	11,000.00	100.18	160,288	05/86
T-Bond 25	150,000	11.750	8,812.50	95.17	142,755	11/85
T-Bond 26	150,000	10.375	7,781.25	93.18	139,770	05/85
T-Bond 27	160,000	12.125	9,700.00	98.10	156,960	11/84
T-Bond 28	150,000	9.250	6,937.50	94.80	142,200	05/84
T-Bond 29	130,000	9.875	6,418.75	96.18	125,034	11/83
Total	$4,780,000				$4,003,779	

EXHIBIT 9

■

Cash Flows from Defeasance of 9-Percent Debentures

	Nov. 1982	May 1983	Nov. 1983	May 1984
9-Percent Debentures				
Interest payment	$225,000	$225,000	$225,000	$217,238
Principal payment	0	0	172,500	172,500
Total payment	225,000	225,000	397,500	389,738
U.S. T-Bonds				
Principal received	0	0	130,000	150,000
T-Bond 1	7,119	7,119	7,119	7,119
T-Bond 2	7,225	7,225	7,225	7,225
T-Bond 3	7,538	7,538	7,538	7,538
T-Bond 4	7,225	7,225	7,225	7,225
T-Bond 5	7,538	7,538	7,538	7,538
T-Bond 6	7,225	7,225	7,225	7,225
T-Bond 7	9,113	9,113	9,113	9,113
T-Bond 8	7,650	7,650	7,650	7,650
T-Bond 9	7,331	7,331	7,331	7,331
T-Bond 10	7,088	7,088	7,088	7,088
T-Bond 11	6,525	6,525	6,525	6,525
T-Bond 12	11,688	11,688	11,688	11,688
T-Bond 13	12,113	12,113	12,113	12,113
T-Bond 14	11,600	11,600	11,600	11,600
T-Bond 15	10,400	10,400	10,400	10,400
T-Bond 16	6,600	6,600	6,600	6,600
T-Bond 17	8,600	8,600	8,600	8,600
T-Bond 18	7,400	7,400	7,400	7,400
T-Bond 19	7,438	7,438	7,438	7,438
T-Bond 20	6,600	6,600	6,600	6,600
T-Bond 21	6,481	6,481	6,481	6,481
T-Bond 22	9,600	9,600	9,600	9,600
T-Bond 23	11,100	11,100	11,100	11,100
T-Bond 24	11,000	11,000	11,000	11,000
T-Bond 25	8,813	8,813	8,813	8,813
T-Bond 26	7,781	7,781	7,781	7,781
T-Bond 27	9,700	9,700	9,700	9,700
T-Bond 28	6,938	6,938	6,938	6,938
T-Bond 29	6,419	6,419	6,419	0
Total interest received	241,844	241,844	241,844	235,425

Nov. 1984	May 1985	Nov. 1985	May 1986	Nov. 1986	May 1987	Nov. 1987
$209,475	$201,713	$193,950	$186,188	$178,425	$170,668	$162,900
172,500	172,500	172,500	172,500	172,500	172,500	172,500
381,975	374,213	366,450	358,688	350,925	343,163	335,400
160,000	150,000	150,000	160,000	160,000	160,000	170,000
7,119	7,119	7,119	7,119	7,119	7,119	7,119
7,225	7,225	7,225	7,225	7,225	7,225	7,225
7,538	7,538	7,538	7,538	7,538	7,538	7,538
7,225	7,225	7,225	7,225	7,225	7,225	7,225
7,538	7,538	7,538	7,538	7,538	7,538	7,538
7,225	7,225	7,225	7,225	7,225	7,225	7,225
9,113	9,113	9,113	9,113	9,113	9,113	9,113
7,650	7,650	7,650	7,650	7,650	7,650	7,650
7,331	7,331	7,331	7,331	7,331	7,331	7,331
7,088	7,088	7,088	7,088	7,088	7,088	7,088
6,525	6,525	6,525	6,525	6,525	6,525	6,525
11,688	11,688	11,688	11,688	11,688	11,688	11,688
12,113	12,113	12,113	12,113	12,113	12,113	12,113
11,600	11,600	11,600	11,600	11,600	11,600	11,600
10,400	10,400	10,400	10,400	10,400	10,400	10,400
6,600	6,600	6,600	6,600	6,600	6,600	6,600
8,600	8,600	8,600	8,600	8,600	8,600	8,600
7,400	7,400	7,400	7,400	7,400	7,400	7,400
7,438	7,438	7,438	7,438	7,438	7,438	7,438
6,600	6,600	6,600	6,600	6,600	6,600	6,600
6,481	6,481	6,481	6,481	6,481	6,481	6,481
9,600	9,600	9,600	9,600	9,600	9,600	0
11,100	11,100	11,100	11,100	11,100	0	0
11,000	11,000	11,000	11,000	0	0	0
8,813	8,813	8,813	0	0	0	0
7,781	7,781	0	0	0	0	0
9,700	0	0	0	0	0	0
0	0	0	0	0	0	0
0	0	0	0	0	0	0
228,488	218,788	211,006	202,194	191,194	180,094	170,494

EXHIBIT 9 *continued*

■

Cash Flows from Defeasance of 9-Percent Debentures

	May 1988	Nov. 1988	May 1989	Nov. 1989
9-Percent Debentures				
Interest payment	$155,138	$147,375	$139,613	$131,850
Principal payment	172,500	172,500	172,500	172,500
Total payment	327,638	319,875	312,113	304,350
U.S. T-Bonds				
Principal received	160,000	170,000	160,000	160,000
T-Bond 1	7,119	7,119	7,119	7,119
T-Bond 2	7,225	7,225	7,225	7,225
T-Bond 3	7,538	7,538	7,538	7,538
T-Bond 4	7,225	7,225	7,225	7,225
T-Bond 5	7,538	7,538	7,538	7,538
T-Bond 6	7,225	7,225	7,225	7,225
T-Bond 7	9,113	9,113	9,113	9,113
T-Bond 8	7,650	7,650	7,650	7,650
T-Bond 9	7,331	7,331	7,331	7,331
T-Bond 10	7,088	7,088	7,088	7,088
T-Bond 11	6,525	6,525	6,525	6,525
T-Bond 12	11,688	11,688	11,688	11,688
T-Bond 13	12,113	12,113	12,113	12,113
T-Bond 14	11,600	11,600	11,600	11,600
T-Bond 15	10,400	10,400	10,400	10,400
T-Bond 16	6,600	6,600	6,600	6,600
T-Bond 17	8,600	8,600	8,600	8,600
T-Bond 18	7,400	7,400	7,400	0
T-Bond 19	7,438	7,438	0	0
T-Bond 20	6,600	0	0	0
T-Bond 21	0	0	0	0
T-Bond 22	0	0	0	0
T-Bond 23	0	0	0	0
T-Bond 24	0	0	0	0
T-Bond 25	0	0	0	0
T-Bond 26	0	0	0	0
T-Bond 27	0	0	0	0
T-Bond 28	0	0	0	0
T-Bond 29	0	0	0	0
Total interest received	164,013	157,413	149,975	142,575

May 1990	Nov. 1990	May 1991	Nov. 1991	May 1992	Nov. 1992	May 1993
$124,088	$116,385	$108,563	$100,800	$ 93,038	$ 85,275	$ 77,513
172,500	172,500	172,500	172,500	172,500	172,500	172,500
296,588	288,825	281,063	273,300	265,588	257,775	250,013
160,000	160,000	160,000	170,000	170,000	180,000	180,000
7,119	7,119	7,119	7,119	7,119	7,119	7,119
7,225	7,225	7,225	7,225	7,225	7,225	7,225
7,538	7,538	7,538	7,538	7,538	7,538	7,538
7,225	7,225	7,225	7,225	7,225	7,225	7,225
7,538	7,538	7,538	7,538	7,538	7,538	7,538
7,225	7,225	7,225	7,225	7,225	7,225	7,225
9,113	9,113	9,113	9,113	9,113	9,113	9,113
7,650	7,650	7,650	7,650	7,650	7,650	7,650
7,331	7,331	7,331	7,331	7,331	7,331	7,331
7,088	7,088	7,088	7,088	7,088	7,088	7,088
6,525	6,525	6,525	6,525	6,525	6,525	0
11,688	11,688	11,688	11,688	11,688	0	0
12,113	12,113	12,113	12,113	0	0	0
11,600	11,600	11,600	0	0	0	0
10,400	10,400	0	0	0	0	0
6,600	0	0	0	0	0	0
0	0	0	0	0	0	0
0	0	0	0	0	0	0
0	0	0	0	0	0	0
0	0	0	0	0	0	0
0	0	0	0	0	0	0
0	0	0	0	0	0	0
0	0	0	0	0	0	0
0	0	0	0	0	0	0
0	0	0	0	0	0	0
0	0	0	0	0	0	0
0	0	0	0	0	0	0
0	0	0	0	0	0	0
133,975	127,375	116,975	105,375	93,263	81,575	75,050

EXHIBIT 9 *continued*

■

Cash Flows from Defeasance of 9-Percent Debentures

	Nov. 1993	May 1994	Nov. 1994	May 1995
9-Percent Debentures				
Interest payment	$ 69,750	$ 61,988	$ 54,225	$ 46,463
Principal payment	172,500	172,500	172,500	172,500
Total payment	242,250	234,488	226,725	218,963
U.S. T-Bonds				
Principal received	170,000	170,000	180,000	170,000
T-Bond 1	7,119	7,119	7,119	7,119
T-Bond 2	7,225	7,225	7,225	7,225
T-Bond 3	7,538	7,538	7,538	7,538
T-Bond 4	7,225	7,225	7,225	7,225
T-Bond 5	7,538	7,538	7,538	7,538
T-Bond 6	7,225	7,225	7,225	7,225
T-Bond 7	9,113	9,113	9,113	0
T-Bond 8	7,650	7,650	0	0
T-Bond 9	7,331	0	0	0
T-Bond 10	0	0	0	0
T-Bond 11	0	0	0	0
T-Bond 12	0	0	0	0
T-Bond 13	0	0	0	0
T-Bond 14	0	0	0	0
T-Bond 15	0	0	0	0
T-Bond 16	0	0	0	0
T-Bond 17	0	0	0	0
T-Bond 18	0	0	0	0
T-Bond 19	0	0	0	0
T-Bond 20	0	0	0	0
T-Bond 21	0	0	0	0
T-Bond 22	0	0	0	0
T-Bond 23	0	0	0	0
T-Bond 24	0	0	0	0
T-Bond 25	0	0	0	0
T-Bond 26	0	0	0	0
T-Bond 27	0	0	0	0
T-Bond 28	0	0	0	0
T-Bond 29	0	0	0	0
Total interest received	67,963	60,631	52,981	43,869

Nov. 1995	May 1996	Nov. 1996	May 1997	Nov. 1997	Totals
$ 38,700	$ 30,938	$ 23,175	$ 15,413	$ 7,650	$3,823,425
172,500	172,500	172,500	172,500	170,000	5,000,000
211,200	203,438	195,675	187,913	177,650	8,823,425
180,000	170,000	180,000	170,000	170,000	4,780,000
7,119	7,119	7,119	7,119	7,119	220,681
7,225	7,225	7,225	7,225	0	216,750
7,538	7,538	7,538	0	0	218,588
7,225	7,225	0	0	0	202,300
7,538	0	0	0	0	203,513
0	0	0	0	0	187,850
0	0	0	0	0	227,813
0	0	0	0	0	183,600
0	0	0	0	0	168,619
0	0	0	0	0	155,925
0	0	0	0	0	137,025
0	0	0	0	0	233,750
0	0	0	0	0	230,138
0	0	0	0	0	208,800
0	0	0	0	0	176,800
0	0	0	0	0	105,600
0	0	0	0	0	129,000
0	0	0	0	0	103,600
0	0	0	0	0	96,688
0	0	0	0	0	79,200
0	0	0	0	0	71,294
0	0	0	0	0	96,000
0	0	0	0	0	99,900
0	0	0	0	0	88,000
0	0	0	0	0	61,688
0	0	0	0	0	46,688
0	0	0	0	0	48,500
0	0	0	0	0	27,750
0	0	0	0	0	19,256
36,644	29,106	21,881	14,344	7,119	4,045,313

Green Mountain Power Corporation

In May 1984, Green Mountain Power Corporation was considering petitioning the Vermont Public Service Board (PSB) for permission to enter into a sale-and-leaseback transaction involving its head office building and two service buildings. Negotiations for the sale and leaseback had begun in the middle of 1983, and all that remained was for Green Mountain's board to give its approval. Once the board had made that decision, approval by the PSB would be necessary. Should the PSB refuse to approve the transaction, Green Mountain Power would probably have to keep the properties and would have to convert the short-term debt that had been used to finance them into permanent capital.

THE CORPORATION

Green Mountain Power Corporation, with about 64,000 customers, was the second largest electric utility in the state of Vermont. The company's rates were subject to approval by the PSB, as was permission for any long-term financing and for any short-term borrowing beyond 20 percent of total assets. Whether the lease transaction Green Mountain was contemplating required PSB approval was a matter of dispute. The company claimed that, while Public Service Board approval was necessary for most ordinary long-term financing, it was not required under the Vermont statutes for a lease like the one proposed. Rather than argue the jurisdictional issue to a final conclusion, however, since that might seriously delay the transaction, the company decided to seek the PSB's approval.

THE PROPERTIES

Green Mountain Power Corporation had established a wholly owned subsidiary, GMP Real Estate Corporation (GMPREC), to hold its real estate. Financial statements are shown in Exhibits 1 through 4. In August 1982, GMPREC purchased the land and buildings of the Bellows Falls Service Center for $660,000. In December 1982, GMPREC purchased the land and buildings of the Wilmington Service Center for $150,000. In both cases, the funds were loaned to GMPREC by Green Mountain Corporation.

Copyright by J. Peter Williamson, Amos Tuck Graduate School of Management, Dartmouth College, Hanover, New Hampshire © 1985.

In 1975, GMPREC purchased land for the construction of a new head office building for $100,000, and again, the funds were loaned by the parent corporation. In 1983, the Bank of New England extended a line of credit to GMPREC to refinance the acquisition of all three properties and to finance construction of the new head office building. With the funds borrowed from the Bank of New England, GMPREC repaid all its loans from Green Mountain Power. The line of credit was to extend until December 31, 1984. By late 1983, the head office had been constructed. The cost of all three buildings (not including land) had come to $6,690,000.

THE PROPOSED SALE AND LEASEBACK

In 1983, Green Mountain began to negotiate a sale and leaseback of the three properties with Shearson/American Express, and by late 1983 the terms of the transaction had been settled. A limited partnership would be organized, to be known as Burlington Associates, to which GMPREC would lease the land at the three locations. This lease, the "ground lease," would be for 75 years from June 29, 1984 to June 30, 2059. Burlington Associates would pay rent on this ground lease of $6,139 per month from July 1, 1984 to June 30, 2034, in arrears (that is, the first payment would be due August 1, 1984). From July 1, 2034 through June 30, 2059, the rent would be based on the fair rental value of the land.

GMPREC would sell the buildings (but not the land) to Burlington Associates for a cash purchase price of $6,690,000. Of the total price, $5,943,396 was allocated to the headquarters building, $606,783 to the Bellows Falls building, and $139,821 to the Wilmington building. The sale was scheduled for June 29, 1984.

Burlington Associates would lease the buildings and sublease the land to Green Mountain Power Corporation. The building lease would be a net lease with an initial term of 25 years, with five 5-year renewal terms. The initial term would begin June 29, 1984. Green Mountain Power would have the option to extend the lease for each renewal term, giving 14 months notice in each case.

The yearly rental was based on the expectation that Burlington Associates would be able to use 15-year public utility ACRS depreciation (shown in Exhibit 5) for tax purposes. On this assumption, the rent would initially be $593,403 per year. The rent would be as follows over the term of the lease:

Years	Rent/Year
1–5	$ 593,403
6–25	983,430
26–35	1,179,113
36–50	1,538,700

Rent would be payable monthly, in arrears. The rent would be allocated 88.84 percent to the headquarters building, 9.07 percent to the Bellows Falls building, and 2.09 percent to the Wilmington building. In addition to this rent, Green Mountain Power would be required to pay the rent on the ground lease payable by Burlington Associates to GMPREC. In fact, Green Mountain would pay this rent directly to the subsidiary. Green Mountain Power would also be responsible for all expenses associated with ownership, maintenance, and occupancy of the property, including taxes.

Under the building lease, Green Mountain Power would have an option to purchase the buildings at their fair market values at the end of the 25-year initial term or at the end of any renewal term. In establishing that value, an appraiser would have to take into consideration the existing lease, that is, what the value of the buildings would be if Green Mountain Power occupied them for the balance of the renewal periods up to 2059 at the stipulated rental figures. (This figure would cap the fair market value of the buildings.) Shearson/American Express estimated that the appraised value at the end of 25 years would be approximately 125 percent of the $6,690,000 purchase price.

Burlington Associates would finance its purchase of the buildings with a loan for $6,690,000 from Teachers Insurance Company, which had entered into the loan commitment in October 1983 and agreed to an interest rate of 13.625 percent. The commitment to make the loan at this rate would expire on July 2, 1984, and interest rates had risen since the date of the commitment. The loan from Teachers would be secured by (1) a mortgage on Burlington Associates' interests in the buildings, the building lease, and the ground lease; (2) an assignment of Burlington Associates' interests in the building lease; and (3) a mortgage from GMPREC securing performance by Green Mountain Power Corporation of its lease obligations. Teachers would have no recourse against the Burlington Associates partnership or against any partner in the event the loan payments were not made. The loan would require semiannual (January 1 and July 1) interest payments for 5 years, and then level semiannual payments of principal and interest for 25 years. Burlington Associates would be permitted to prepay principal, subject to a premium, after June 30, 1999. The premium on July 1, 1999 would be 5.450 percent and would be reduced on a sliding scale to 0.545 percent on July 1, 2008. After that date, there would be no prepayment premium.

In the event that Green Mountain Power elected not to extend its lease on the buildings, Burlington Associates had the right to terminate the ground lease. If Green Mountain Power were to choose not to extend its lease and not to purchase the buildings, Burlington Associates would have the right to purchase the land subject to the ground lease at fair market value, its value with no buildings on it.

THE ALTERNATIVE
TO A SALE AND LEASEBACK

GMPREC owed approximately $6,600,000 to the Bank of New England in March 1984. If the sale-and-leaseback transaction did not go through, GMPREC or Green Mountain Power could arrange permanent financing in order to repay the bank loans. As of May 1984, Green Mountain Power could expect to pay about 15.5 percent for conventional long-term debt financing. The company had no public debt outstanding; all its bond issues had been sold privately to insurance companies. For tax purposes, the company would expect to base depreciation on the buildings on a 15-year ACRS schedule. No investment tax credit was available. Approximately 95.1 percent of the $6,690,000 worth of buildings would be depreciable for tax purposes, because $329,300 of the $6,690,000 represented the capitalizing of financing costs during construction rather than cash spent on construction.

THE ANALYSIS

Management of Green Mountain Power, considering its average cost of capital, believed that the sale and leaseback was preferable to ownership of the buildings. In making its ownership analysis, management had made these assumptions: (1) Depreciation would be claimed over 15 years on the ACRS basis (Exhibit 5). (2) The buildings' actual useful life would be 40 years. (3) There would be no investment tax credit. (4) The rent for the ground lease could be ignored because, in essence, Green Mountain Power would be paying the rent to itself. (5) Under the lease arrangement, Green Mountain Power Corporation would exercise its purchase option at the end of 25 years and would pay 200 percent of the original $6,690,000 price.

In evaluating ownership, management also assumed that the buildings would be financed in accordance with Green Mountain's current capital structure: 46.4 percent debt, 16.8 percent preferred stock, and 36.8 percent common stock; debt payments would be spread over 40 years.[1]

For the lease alternative, (1) the rent payments would be offset by the benefit of the tax deduction for rent, and (2) at the end of year 25, there would be a cash outflow to repurchase the buildings at twice their sale price.

CONCLUSION

The sale and leaseback was complicated. Therefore, Green Mountain's board would want to be certain of the value of the process before management went to the Public Service Board.

---

[1]The embedded costs of debt and preferred stock were 13.625 percent and 13.5 percent, respectively. The marginal cost of common equity was believed to be 16.5 percent, and that of preferred equity, 15.5 percent. The marginal tax rate was 50 percent.

Green Mountain Power Corporation

EXHIBIT 1
■
Statements of Consolidated Income for the Years Ended December 31

	1981	1982	1983
Operating revenues (principally sales of electric energy)	$67,926,767	$79,603,299	$85,156,555
Operating expenses			
Power supply expenses	16,066,275	19,706,253	18,376,687
Vermont Yankee Nuclear Power Corporation	2,024,583	4,068,444	4,356,241
Company-owned generation	23,453,066	25,084,918	27,767,555
Other operating expenses	8,551,613	10,007,491	12,046,349
Maintenance	2,016,987	2,577,584	2,713,416
Depreciation and amortization	2,301,751	2,787,615	2,974,034
Taxes other than income	2,643,880	2,861,626	3,060,748
Provision for income taxes	1,715,831	4,892,216	4,841,296
Total operating expenses	58,773,986	71,986,147	76,136,326
Operating income	9,152,781	7,617,152	9,020,229
Other income (deductions)			
Equity in earnings of unconsolidated associated companies	1,247,962	1,060,395	1,093,620
Other, net	71,479	(18,820)	(6,751)
Total other income	1,319,441	1,041,575	1,086,869
Income before interest charges (credits)	10,472,222	8,658,727	10,107,098
Long-term debt	2,605,389	2,553,024	2,702,850
Other	4,067,338	2,651,036	1,642,585
Allowance for borrowed funds used during construction	(480,322)	(214,625)	(473,955)
Total interest charges	6,192,405	4,989,435	3,871,480
Net income	4,279,817	3,669,292	6,235,618
Annual redeemable cumulative preferred stock dividend requirements	471,619	1,095,209	1,949,354
Balance applicable to common stock	$ 3,808,198	$ 2,574,083	$ 4,286,264
Earnings per share of common stock, after annual redeemable cumulative preferred stock dividend requirements	$2.31	$1.23	$1.95
Cash dividends declared per share of common stock	1.44	1.52	1.60
Average number of shares of common stock outstanding	1,647,711	2,096,397	2,199,396

Green Mountain Power Corporation

EXHIBIT 2

■

Statements of Changes in Consolidated Financial Position
for the Years Ended December 31

	1981	1982	1983
Source of Funds			
From operations			
Net income	$ 4,279,817	$ 3,669,292	$ 6,235,618
Add (deduct) noncash items			
Depreciation and amortization	2,301,751	2,787,615	2,974,034
Recoupment revenue	(6,648,523)	(5,407,981)	0
Dividends received from associated companies in excess of equity in earnings	(54,276)	88,950	58,599
Allowance for funds used during construction	(480,322)	(214,625)	(473,955)
Amortization of purchased power costs	3,632,043	3,414,767	5,238,598
Deferred income taxes	470,849	3,914,550	3,137,662
Investment tax credits, net	1,142,660	901,582	234,597
Other	662,249	908,195	814,926
Billed revenue surcharge	843,154	4,595,082	4,864,565
Total from operations	6,149,402	14,657,427	23,084,644
From financing transactions, net of expenses			
Sale of preferred stock	0	8,892,794	0
Sale of debentures	0	0	4,886,902
Sale of common stock	311,010	5,718,676	939,497
Notes payable to banks (reductions)	7,900,000	(3,045,000)	(405,000)
Energy thrift certificates (reductions)	238,600	(2,478,400)	(3,281,200)
Customer advances for construction	920,461	709,542	1,243,129
Total source of funds	$15,519,473	$24,455,039	$26,467,972
Application of Funds			
Plant additions[a]	$ 7,483,147	$10,287,303	$ 9,238,365
Investment in nonutility property	462,215	309,309	299,069
Cash dividends declared	2,837,761	4,582,513	5,455,750
Reduction in			
Redeemable cumulative preferred stock	287,300	220,000	287,300
Long-term debt	550,000	599,000	566,000
Deferred purchased power costs	3,329,481	0	10,151,129
Other, net[a]	138,708	149,276	965,889
Subtotal	15,088,612	16,147,401	26,963,502
Working capital increase (decrease), excluding short-term borrowings	430,861	8,307,638	(495,530)
Total application of funds	$15,519,471	$24,455,039	$26,467,972

EXHIBIT 2 *continued*

	1981	1982	1983
Components of Working Capital Increase (Decrease) Excluding Short-Term Borrowings			
Cash and special deposits	$ (960,247)	$ (324,332)	$ 42,880
Accounts receivable, net	925,857	1,439,346	1,518,376
Accrued utility revenues, excluding recoupment	859,214	458,625	201,900
Fuel, materials, and supplies	859,214	83,432	309,407
Prepayments	149,896	(508,153)	681,355
Current maturities of long-term debt	431,929	(16,000)	0
Accounts payable	992,830	7,055,009	(3,279,135)
Taxes accrued	(100,830)	142,197	55,669
Other	(25,982)	(22,486)	(362,128)
Total	$ 430,861	$ 8,307,638	$ 430,861

[a]Includes allowance for funds used during construction.

Green Mountain Power Corporation

EXHIBIT 3
■
Consolidated Balance Sheets, December 31

	1982	1983
Assets		
Utility plant, at original cost	$ 83,655,832	$ 87,310,885
Less accumulated provision for depreciation	22,102,176	24,434,543
	61,553,656	62,876,342
Construction work in progress	5,094,134	8,706,565
Net utility plant	66,647,790	71,582,907
Other investments		
Associated companies, at equity	11,993,556	12,165,262
Nonutility property, less accumulated depreciation ($1,433,922 and $1,224,646, respectively) at cost	2,228,800	2,309,490
	14,222,356	14,474,752
Current assets		
Cash (see note)	434,419	477,299
Special deposits	182,085	182,085
Accounts receivable, customers and others, less allowance for doubtful accounts	7,851,235	9,369,611
Unbilled recoupment revenue surcharge	6,174,600	5,271,112
Accrued utility revenues	3,784,561	3,986,461
Fuel, materials, and supplies, at average cost	1,753,967	2,063,374
Prepayments	73,202	754,557
Other	71,608	181,855
	20,325,677	22,286,354
Deferred charges		
Unbilled recoupment revenue surcharge, noncurrent	5,289,337	1,328,260
Purchased power costs	3,769,067	8,681,598
Other (see note)	2,521,099	3,334,480
	11,579,503	13,344,338
Total assets	$112,775,326	$121,688,351
Capitalization and Liabilities		
Capitalization (see capitalization data)		
Common stock, $3.33⅓ par value, authorized 5,000,000 shares, outstanding 2,241,702 shares in 1983, 2,167,394 shares in 1982	$ 7,224,639	$ 7,472,333
Additional paid-in capital	12,046,529	12,730,257
Reinvested earnings	10,842,477	11,623,551
Reacquired capital stock, 850 shares in 1982, at cost	(8,075)	—
Total common stock equity	30,105,570	31,826,141
Redeemable cumulative preferred stock	14,400,500	14,113,200
Long-term debt, less current maturities	34,454,000	38,888,000
Total capitalization	78,960,070	84,827,341

EXHIBIT 3 *continued*

	1982	1983
Current liabilities		
Current maturities of long-term debt	566,000	566,000
Short-term debt		
Notes payable to banks	14,205,000	13,800,000
Energy Thrift Certificates	4,776,000	1,494,800
Accounts payable		
Trade	3,377,816	4,606,398
Associated companies	419,846	2,470,399
Dividends declared	487,800	482,262
Customer deposits	400,623	457,893
Taxes accrued	410,967	355,298
Interest accrued	1,158,886	1,001,215
Other	173,824	388,765
	25,976,762	25,623,030
Deferred credits		
Accumulated deferred income tax	4,796,192	7,933,854
Unamortized investment tax credits	2,791,383	3,025,980
Other	250,919	278,146
	7,838,494	11,237,980
Commitments and contingencies	0	0
Total capitalization and liabilities	$112,775,326	$121,688,351

Note: Commitments and Contingencies

1. Construction Commitments

The cash construction requirements for 1984 are estimated to be $8,365,000.

The company has a joint-ownership agreement with the Burlington Electric Department (BED) in a 12 MW hydroelectric generating station proposed to be constructed on the Winooski River in Burlington, Vermont. The company and BED each have a 50-percent interest in the project. The project has been subject to prolonged licensing proceedings.

The company and BED have discussed and are considering a proposal to amend the joint-ownership agreement in order to provide for sole ownership of the project by BED. If such an amendment is consummated, BED would assume substantially all capital construction costs, and the company would purchase approximately one-half of the generation output under a life-of-the-unit contract.

2. GMP Real Estate Corporation

GMP Real Estate Corporation, a wholly owned subsidiary of the company, which is accounted for on the equity basis, has constructed a new corporate headquarters building for the company in South Burlington, and has acquired and refurbished buildings for service centers in Wilmington and Bellows Falls at a cost of $6,857,600, including the cost of the real estate purchased. In connection with construction financing arranged through the subsidiary, the company executed a lease agreement with the subsidiary covering these buildings. The agreement has been assigned to the bank. A long-term sale-and-leaseback arrangement for the buildings is expected to be formalized in mid-1984.

Green Mountain Power Corporation

EXHIBIT 4
■
Consolidated Capitalization Data for the Years Ended December 31

	1982	1983
Capital Stock		
Common stock, $3.33⅓ par value; authorized, 6,000,000 shares; issued and outstanding, 2,241,702 shares in 1983, 2,167,394 in 1982	$ 7,224,639	$ 7,472,339
Redeemable cumulative preferred stock, $100 par value		
5 percent, Class A. Originally authorized and issued, 12,430 shares; oustanding, 2,732 shares in 1983, 3,105 shares in 1982.	$ 310,500	$ 273,200
4.75 percent, Class B. Originally authorized and issued, 15,000 shares; outstanding, 7,650 shares in 1983, 8,100 shares in 1982.	810,000	765,000
7 percent, Class C. Originally authorized and issued, 15,000 shares; outstanding, 9,150 shares in 1983, 9,600 shares in 1982.	960,000	915,000
9.375 percent, Class D, Series 1. Originally authorized, 40,000 shares; issued and outstanding, 31,600 in 1983, 33,200 in 1982.	3,320,000	3,160,000
16.875 percent, Class D, Series 2. Originally authorized, 90,000 shares; issued and outstanding, 90,000 shares in 1983; 90,000 shares in 1982.	9,900,000	9,000,000
	$14,400,500	$14,113,200

The holders of common stock have authorized 200,000 shares of preferred stock, $100 par value, Class D, of which 70,000 shares remain unissued. In addition, the holders of common stock have authorized 50,000 shares of preferred stock, $100 par value.

Purchase and sinking fund requirement for all redeemable cumulative preferred classes: 3 percent annually for Class A, B, and C; 4 percent annually for Class D, Series 1; Class D, Series 2 is entitled to a sinking fund commencing on June 1, 1987 that will retire 15,000 shares ($1,500,000) per year through maturity in 1992. (Shares purchased are to be cancelled and not reissued.)

Redemption provisions: The outstanding series are currently redeemable, in whole or in part, at the option of the company or in the case of voluntary liquidation at $101.00 per share (plus accrued dividends) for the Class A 5-percent series, Class B 4.75-percent series, and Class C 7-percent series, and at $107.28 per share (plus accrued dividends) for the Class D, Series 1, 9.375-percent series. Class D, Series 2 will not be redeemable by the company until June 1, 1989. Thereafter, the issue will be redeemable at the option of the company at the following prices:

■ If redeemed during 12-month period beginning June 1, 1989, at $103.38 per share
■ If redeemed during 12-month period beginning June 1, 1990, at $101.69 per share
■ If redeemed thereafter, at $100.00 per share

Voting Rights: The holders of the common stock have full voting power for the election of directors and for all other purposes. The preferred stockholders are entitled to special voting rights in respect to certain corporate actions and are entitled to elect the smallest number of directors necessary to constitute a majority of the board of directors in the event of a default in payment of four quarterly dividends on the redeemable cumulative preferred stock.

EXHIBIT 4 *continued*

	1982	1983
Long-Term Debt		
First Mortgage Bonds		
3.35-percent series due 1985	$ 8,000,000	$ 8,000,000
4⅝-percent series due 1991	2,000,000	2,000,000
5⅛-percent series due 1996	3,000,000	3,000,000
7-percent series due 1998	3,000,000	3,000,000
8⅝-percent series due 1999	600,000	600,000
9⅛-percent series due 2003—cash sinking fund, $100,000 annually	4,300,000	4,400,000
10¼-percent series due 1996—cash sinking fund, $140,000 annually	2,800,000	2,940,000
10⅝-percent series due 1986	4,000,000	4,000,000
Debentures		
7⅛ percent due 1992—cash sinking fund, $80,000 annually	1,960,000	2,040,000
8⅞ percent due 1994—cash sinking fund, $86,000 annually	1,754,000	1,840,000
9⅜ percent due 1996—cash sinking fund, $160,000 annually	3,040,000	3,200,000
12⅝ percent due 1998—cash sinking fund, commences 1988	5,000,000	0
Total long-term debt outstanding	39,454,000	35,020,000
Less amount due within one year, included in balance sheet under current maturities of long-term debt	566,000	566,000
Long-term debt, less current maturities	$38,888,000	$34,454,000

Substantially all of the property and franchises of the company are subject to lien of the indenture under which first mortgage bonds have been issued.

The aggregate annual sinking fund requirements of long-term debt for each of the years 1984 through 1988 are $732,000, $652,000, $652,000, $652,000, and $1,152,000, respectively. With the exception of the cash requirements noted above, sinking funds on bond indebtedness are usually satisfied by property additions.

Green Mountain Power Corporation

EXHIBIT 5
■

ACRS Depreciation, 15-Year, All Real Estate, except Low-Income Housing,
Placed in Service after December 31, 1980

Use the Column for the Month in the First Year the Property Is Placed in Service

Ownership Year	1	2	3	4	5	6	7	8	9	10	11	12
1	12%	11%	10%	9%	8%	7%	6%	5%	4%	3%	2%	1%
2	10	10	11	11	11	11	11	11	11	11	11	12
3	9	9	9	9	10	10	10	10	10	10	10	10
4	8	8	8	8	8	8	9	9	9	9	9	9
5	7	7	7	7	7	7	8	8	8	8	8	8
6	6	6	6	6	7	7	7	7	7	7	7	7
7	6	6	6	6	6	6	6	6	6	6	6	6
8	6	6	6	6	6	6	5	6	6	6	6	6
9	6	6	6	6	5	6	5	5	5	6	6	6
10	5	6	5	6	5	5	5	5	5	5	6	5
11	5	5	5	5	5	5	5	5	5	5	5	5
12	5	5	5	5	5	5	5	5	5	5	5	5
13	5	5	5	5	5	5	5	5	5	5	5	5
14	5	5	5	5	5	5	5	5	5	5	5	5
15	5	5	5	5	5	5	5	5	5	5	5	5
16	—	—	1	1	2	2	3	3	4	4	4	5
	100%	100%	100%	100%	100%	100%	100%	100%	100%	100%	100%	100%

5

STRATEGIC INVESTMENT

AND FINANCING DECISIONS

Diamond Shamrock Corporation

During early 1981, the management of Diamond Shamrock faced a critical set of decisions regarding the very nature of the company. Historically, Diamond Shamrock had been a major chemicals firm with a moderately sized, regional oil and gas unit. However, increased emphasis on oil and gas coupled with rising energy prices and stagnant growth in the industrial economy had made oil and gas the company's greatest source of revenues. An in-depth strategic analysis indicated that the 1980s would be a time of intense competition in chemicals, and many of Diamond's chemical businesses would face continued low growth and reduced return on investment. The company's energy businesses would be its primary source of growth.

It appeared to management that the company's changing business mix had depressed the price of Diamond Shamrock's shares in the marketplace. Chemical analysts continued to follow the company and, as a result, investors seeking shares in companies with good prospects in energy were unlikely to know about Diamond Shamrock. To understand the company, traditional chemicals-oriented investors now had to become much more knowledgeable about oil and gas in order to evaluate their investment.

Two primary courses of action had been proposed. First, management could continue to oversee an evolutionary change in the company, emphasizing oil and gas. This approach would be coupled with an effort to inform Wall Street about their oil and gas business, but management knew it might take some time, and some believed it might not be successful: one of Diamond's staff had suggested that the company might be viewed as a conglomerate, a type of corporation that recent academic research indicated had a history of undervalued stock prices.

The second course was much more dramatic: they could selectively divest the chemical businesses (which were underperforming or were not significant) and become an oil and gas company. While management thought this course would focus Diamond Shamrock's resources on its strengths, the company's stock had no following among oil investors or analysts. Thus this move would mean changing from a well-known, leading chemicals firm to an unknown, middle-sized oil company.

The two alternatives were quite different, and the latter would change the very nature of the company. Management was determined to examine the choices carefully before taking action.

This case was prepared as a basis for class discussion rather than to illustrate either effective or ineffective handling of an administrative situation. Copyright © 1984 by the Darden Graduate Business School Sponsors, University of Virginia, Charlottesville, Virginia.

TABLE 1
■
Business Segment Results, 1976

Segment	Percentage of Sales	Percentage of Profits
Chemicals	45%	56%
Plastics	13	5
Oil and gas	38	33

BACKGROUND

Diamond Shamrock was formed in December 1967 through a merger between Diamond Alkali Company, a Cleveland-based producer of inorganic commodity chemicals, and Shamrock Oil and Gas Corporation of Amarillo, Texas, an independent oil and and gas producer with regional downstream operations, refining plants, and retail distribution networks. By emphasizing the chemical portion of the company, Diamond Shamrock was able to participate in the growth of the chemical industry during the first half of the 1970s. By 1976, sales had grown to $1,374 million with, as shown in Table 1, 45 percent of sales and 56 percent of profits coming from chemicals.

During the mid-1970s, however, the world and domestic economic environments changed, affecting all of Diamond's businesses. First, the oil embargo in late 1973 created an energy crisis and caused worldwide oil prices to skyrocket. The U.S. response was not only to conserve energy, but also to pass legislation that encouraged production of domestic crude oil. While Diamond was positioned to participate in the increased production of domestic oil, the oil business had not been the company's primary emphasis, and thus participation was limited.

Also during the mid-1970s the United States increased regulation governing proprietary chemicals. This legislation required additional testing for new chemicals, thus increasing the initial development costs and reducing the profitability of Diamond's specialty and proprietary chemical division. While Diamond also manufactured commodity chemicals, patents had historically protected the profitability of proprietary chemicals.

Although Diamond's managers had previously emphasized the chemical business, top management believed the company should be in businesses that had high earnings potentials. Management had a history of using acquisitions and divestitures as one way of changing corporate focus. The Falcon Seaboard acquisition in 1979 began to move the company toward the energy industry. Recent acquisitions and divestitures of assets toward this end are listed in Exhibit 1. These changes were accompanied by a 23-percent compound growth rate in sales and a 10.5-percent compound growth rate in operating profit over the period 1976 to 1980. Exhibit 2 contains financial statements for the 5-year period.

CURRENT SITUATION

By 1980 Diamond Shamrock had four separate businesses—oil and gas, industrial chemicals and plastics, proprietary and specialty chemicals, and coal. The oil and gas unit was predominantly committed to the exploration and production of crude oil and natural gas. However, the unit also refined crude oil into motor fuels, which were sold through branded service stations operated by jobbers and independent dealers in the Southwest and Rocky Mountain areas.

The industrial chemicals and plastics unit produced commodity chemicals and continued to be supported by efficient production processes and a strong marketing staff. The plastics division, a part of this unit, produced products for ultimate use primarily in the construction and automotive industries. The proprietary chemicals and technology unit included agricultural chemicals, electrolytic systems, and specialty chemicals. These segments each produced proprietary products requiring research and development. Finally, a coal unit had been initiated with the purchase of Falcon Seaboard Inc. in 1979. This unit was not expected to be a major part of the business until the mid-1980s.

The oil and gas unit dominated the company, contributing 52 percent of the company's sales and 63 percent of the operating profits in 1980. Exhibit 3 contains data for each of the business segments. The focus of the company had clearly shifted from chemicals to oil and gas, but security analysts still included Diamond Shamrock in the financially diverse chemical industry. Selected financial data for Diamond Shamrock, similar chemical companies, and domestic oil companies are presented in Exhibit 4.

Confusion regarding Diamond Shamrock was also reflected in the company's stock price. A comparison of Diamond's stock price to indexes of chemical and domestic oil companies, found in Exhibit 5, illustrated that Diamond Shamrock was frequently priced between the two indexes. Exhibit 6 contains monthly returns on Diamond Shamrock's common stock and Standard & Poor's 500 Index. Whether the market price accurately reflected the company's business mix was of concern to management. They believed that being followed by the wrong analysts contributed to the stock's undervaluation; only 2 of the 19 security research firms following Diamond categorized it as an oil company.

CORPORATE FINANCIAL GOALS

Management continued to believe that Diamond Shamrock should invest in those businesses that had a high earnings potential and, if necessary, divest assets that had not and were not expected to earn a fair return for the shareholders. In order to make these decisions, management established a financial strategy for the 1980s. They required a corporate return on shareholders' equity (ROSE) of 20 percent. The 20-percent return was based on an assumed 7-percent inflation rate, a 3-percent real rate of return, a 5-percent premium for equity, and a 5-percent premium for Diamond Shamrock stock. Management also selected a target range for the total debt/capitalization of 35 to 37 percent. A return on capital employed (ROCE[1]) of 10.6 to 11.0 percent was computed by management from these measures. Assuming 30 percent of capital spending was noneconomic, management established hurdle rates for new projects of 15.1 to 15.7 percent.[2] A goal for growth in net income was set at a minimum of 13 percent (ROSE of 20 percent and a target dividend payout ratio of 25 to 35 percent).

---

[1]ROCE = ROSE × Percentage of equity in total capital structure.
Percentage equity = [1 − (Percentage of debt + Percentage of deferred taxes)]
Deferred taxes = 10 percent of capital.

[2]Hurdle rate = ROCE/Percentage of economic projects.

Finally, knowing they wanted a ROCE of 10.6 percent, management targeted a divisional pre-tax operating profit return on capital employed of 25.8 percent.

FORECASTS FOR EACH DIVISION

As part of the 1980 business plan, management reviewed each of the divisions in light of corporate objectives, each division's ability to generate or use cash, its sales growth versus operating profit, and its competitive position in relation to its industry's maturity. Results of the analysis, presented in Exhibit 7, indicated that the energy divisions would maintain high sales growth and high operating returns, while the chemical divisions' returns would be low.

Forecasted income statements for each of the individual units through 1988 were also provided by unit managers. As shown in Exhibit 8, the oil and gas and the coal units were expected to meet the required ROCE measure but chemicals were not.

In a Standard & Poor's debt rating seminar on March 17, 1980, Roy Taub, vice president of corporate ratings for Standard & Poor's, commented on the future of the chemical industry.

> The chemical industry has had a lot of downgradings. We are concerned about two things: There have been declining margins in commodity chemicals and the forecast for the energy costs indicates this pressure will continue. Many companies have the bulk of their assets in below average return products and if the company has chosen not to spend money to maintain its plant, returns will get even worse eventually. However, with some price relief and a good 1979, ratings in chemicals are not under the extreme pressure that they were recently.

Gerald Unterman, also from Standard & Poor's, commented on the oil industry.

> We see only modest volume growth in oil in the 1980s, but price will continue to go up fast. The key rating issues are that domestic reserves are steadily declining and it is extremely costly and difficult to replenish spent reserves. In our opinion, ownership of domestic oil reserves is most important in determining quality of the firm's earnings.
>
> We are not interested in oil companies' attempts to diversify since a recent analysis showed that they were only able to earn 2.2% on businesses other than oil.
>
> We are very positive about the short-term prospects of domestic oil producers.

ALTERNATIVE SOLUTIONS

Diamond Shamrock's management believed the company's changing business mix had caused its stock to be undervalued. Strategically, they were considering two most likely courses of action. The conservative approach involved maintaining the status quo as revenues continued to shift toward energy and mounting an educational campaign designed to tell existing security analysts and investors about the "new" Diamond Shamrock. The dramatic strategy involved the divestiture of some or all of Diamond's chemical segments, an increased investment in oil and gas, and building an entirely new investor and analyst following from scratch. Both strategies had risks.

Diamond Shamrock Corporation

EXHIBIT 1
■
Acquisitions and Divestitures, 1976–1980

1976

Acquired Julian Laboratories, a producer of Vitamin D-3 intermediate. Became part of Animal Nutrition Division.

1977

Acquired Federal Yeast Company. Became part of Foods Division.

Acquired Lankro Chemicals Group, Ltd. Name changed to Diamond Shamrock Europe, Ltd.

Acquired remaining 50 percent in Dia Prosim S.A.

Sold polypropylene plastics business.

1978

Acquired 21 percent interest in Sigmor Corporation.

Sold Chemetals Division.

Sold 320 service stations.

1979

Acquired Falcon Seaboard, Inc.

Acquired Shell's animal health business.

Sold Harte and Co.

Sold Mexia Tank Co. (a subsidiary of Falcon Seaboard).

1980

Acquired Fallek Chemical Co. (Assets were primarily cash and cash equivalents.)

Sold Ardco (a subsidiary of Falcon Seaboard).

Diamond Shamrock Corporation

EXHIBIT 2

■

Financial Statements, 1976–1980 (thousands of dollars)

	1976	1977	1978	1979	1980
Revenues	$1,374,644	$1,553,336	$1,851,851	$2,393,935	$3,181,878
Cost of products sold	965,177	1,112,829	1,419,472	1,811,787	2,517,904
Selling and administrative	111,092	122,964	156,950	192,782	220,107
Research and development	24,046	29,266	36,131	41,842	49,964
Interest	33,300	44,089	59,154	71,301	64,374
Facility sales and shutdowns	5,000	(9,300)	(13,323)	—	—
Income before taxes	236,029	253,488	193,467	276,223	329,529
Taxes	97,305	91,365	54,335	98,100	128,315
Net income	$ 138,724	$ 162,123	$ 139,132	$ 178,123	$ 201,214
Assets					
Current assets					
Cash	$ 30,465	$ 33,523	$ 45,758	$ 31,347	$ 28,368
Receivables	206,181	267,102	318,614	443,051	484,600
Inventories	195,850	201,487	239,474	316,168	387,730
Prepaid insurance, etc.	3,582	5,248	5,694	7,150	10,855
Total current assets	436,078	507,360	609,540	797,716	911,553
Property, plant, and equipment	935,307	1,140,768	1,318,299	1,382,931	1,600,250
Investments	32,908	58,918	85,614	134,534	177,142
Intangible assets	91,496	91,700	89,187	87,673	85,764
Deferred charges	8,449	11,722	18,541	14,711	18,339
Total assets	$1,504,238	$1,810,468	$2,121,181	$2,417,565	$2,793,048

EXHIBIT 2 *continued*

	1976	1977	1978	1979	1980
Liabilities and shareholders' equity					
Current liabilities					
Notes payable	$ 19,419	$ 10,258	$ 38,821	$ 28,192	$ 13,464
Accounts payable	95,356	131,776	158,645	232,225	263,644
Long-term debt due within 1 year	6,897	6,366	13,149	7,495	7,464
Accrued interest, taxes, etc.	103,649	106,739	98,720	145,775	138,451
Total current liabilities	225,321	255,139	309,335	413,687	423,023
Long-term debt	428,730	540,497	672,628	712,544	809,847
Long-term capital lease obligations	39,226	41,629	40,783	38,372	35,128
Deferred taxes	126,993	167,895	183,435	224,959	275,989
Other	13,632	12,429	11,434	9,073	7,347
Stockholders' equity					
Preferred stock	7,115	—	—	—	—
Common stock	183,926	200,322	222,950	237,039	348,267
Retained earnings	479,420	592,668	680,715	781,981	893,515
Less: common treasury shares	125	111	99	80	68
Total shareholders' equity	670,336	792,879	903,566	1,018,940	1,241,714
Total liabilities and shareholders' equity	$1,504,238	$1,810,468	$2,121,181	$2,417,575	$2,793,048

Diamond Shamrock Corporation

EXHIBIT 3

■

Business Segment Data, 1976–1980 (millions of dollars)[a]

	Energy		Chemicals			Technology	
	Oil and Gas	Coal	Industrial Chemicals	Plastics	Electrolytic Systems	Specialty Chemicals	Ag Chemicals and Health Products
1976							
Revenue	$ 515.5	$ 0	$403.2	$180.3	$ 39.9	$121.1	$122.2
Operating profit	96.2	0	138.0	14.3	16.0	14.9	13.2
Assets	561.7	0	354.5	176.0	100.0	119.5	87.3
Expenditures for plant and equipment	138.7	0	53.1	64.9	5.8	7.5	16.2
Depreciation, depletion, and amortization	32.8	0	20.6	5.5	6.8	3.9	2.3
1977							
Revenue	630.9	0	411.8	183.1	46.9	150.3	140.2
Operating profit	131.4	0	115.8	8.5	13.5	17.0	16.8
Assets	639.7	0	380.4	233.6	93.8	174.7	131.6
Expenditures for plant and equipment	110.1	0	53.8	126.3	2.4	38.8	27.8
Depreciation, depletion, and amortization	42.2	0	17.6	4.3	9.4	4.9	3.5
1978							
Revenue	669.1	110.9	407.1	184.2	48.1	261.1	191.1
Operating profit	99.0	14.6	80.5	11.5	14.0	17.8	12.7
Assets	659.9	92.2	419.0	283.2	87.9	202.1	189.9
Expenditures for plant and equipment	128.9	20.9	50.9	50.5	2.5	14.2	40.4
Depreciation, depletion, and amortization	65.2	8.4	21.7	12.8	8.6	9.1	5.8

1979

Revenue	969.2	155.9	498.4	264.4	52.9	289.2	231.4
Operating profit	163.0	32.6	89.4	27.0	16.7	19.4	17.8
Assets	794.3	94.8	452.7	268.9	107.0	218.8	274.0
Expenditures for plant and equipment	135.6	11.8	35.1	11.8	5.5	8.6	42.3
Depreciation, depletion, and amortization	67.2	11.9	24.8	15.6	8.2	10.7	11.2

1980

Revenue	1,691.4	158.3	553.2	184.6	63.1	329.1	286.7
Operating profit	275.5	33.4	86.6	(9.9)	21.3	15.6	8.6
Assets	1,027.9	116.9	512.3	276.0	114.9	237.8	322.6
Expenditures for plant and equipment	219.3	7.9	77.3	9.4	10.9	13.6	25.9
Depreciation, depletion, and amortization	74.9	9.0	26.0	15.2	6.0	9.1	13.9

[a]Totals do not include corporate and other.

Diamond Shamrock Corporation

EXHIBIT 4
∎

Comparison with Chemical and Oil Companies' 5–Year Averages, 1975–1979

	Sales Growth Rate	Net Income Growth Rate	Net Profit Margin	Earnings per Share Growth Rate
Chemicals				
Diamond Shamrock	18.4%	13.6%	9.3%	22.8%
Allied	13.6	3.1	4.5	2.8
Dow	17.6	6.0	9.8	18.8
Hercules	11.3	12.9	5.0	4.3
Monsanto	13.6	0.5	6.9	13.0
Rohm & Hass	12.1	5.1	4.3	−3.7
Stauffer	15.2	12.9	9.7	20.8
Oils				
Cities Service	16.5	11.3	4.5	6.2
Getty Oil	15.0	16.6	9.8	17.4
Phillips Petroleum	16.6	15.7	8.3	21.6
Shell Oil	16.5	12.7	7.3	15.5
Standard Oil of Indiana	18.1	9.2	7.7	14.4
Standard Oil of Ohio	22.0	9.2	7.7	26.9
Sun Company	22.7	13.1	5.7	12.2
Union Oil of California	16.3	11.7	5.7	11.4

Source: *Standard & Poor's Industry Surveys,* 1980.

Dividend Payout	ROSE	ROCE	Debt/Capital	P/E	
				High	Low
34.0%	23.5%	13.5%	37%	9.2	5.6
40.2	8.8	6.4	36	9.8	6.6
32.5	23.1	14.2	39	12.8	8.2
56.4	12.3	9.4	27	19.2	11.6
34.5	15.1	11.2	28	9.0	6.0
32.8	7.5	6.3	33	20.0	11.2
30.2	20.3	14.3	32	9.0	4.8
43.8	10.0	7.7	29	9.2	6.6
21.2	14.2	12.1	6	12.6	8.4
29.4	19.5	14.7	20	10.4	7.2
31.4	15.8	12.3	22	7.8	5.0
36.0	16.7	12.7	23	9.0	6.4
29.8	19.5	8.7	62	17.8	11.4
28.6	16.1	10.6	19	7.0	4.8
27.2	15.8	10.9	27	7.8	5.4

continued

EXHIBIT 4 *continued*

	Sales Growth Rate	Net Income Growth Rate	Net Profit Margin	Earnings per Share
Chemicals				
Diamond Shamrock	33.3%	12.9%	6.4%	$ 3.66
Allied	27.4	64.2	5.2	8.15
Dow	14.9	2.7	7.6	4.42
Hercules	6.1	(34.1)	4.6	2.60
Monsanto	6.1	(55.0)	2.3	4.10
Rohm & Hass	8.7	(1.9)	5.4	7.26
Stauffer	11.1	0.7	8.1	3.11
Oils				
Cities Service	32.1	26.5	5.7	8.82
Getty Oil	10.1	44.4	8.6	10.60
Phillips Petroleum	40.9	20.1	8.0	7.01
Shell Oil	37.4	36.9	7.8	4.99
Standard Oil of Indiana	40.4	27.1	7.3	6.54
Standard Oil of Ohio	39.3	52.7	16.4	7.37
Sun Company	21.5	3.3	5.6	5.92
Union Oil of California	31.9	29.1	6.5	3.73

Source: *Standard & Poor's Industry Surveys,* 1980.

Dividend Payout	ROSE	ROCE	Debt/Capital	P/E		Book Value	Debt Rating	Beta
				High	Low			
45%	17.4%	7.5%	36%	11	6	$20.56	A −	1.15
27	17.2	6.1	28	8	5	47.81	A	1.20
37	19.2	7.4	40	9	6	23.71	A +	1.25
45	11.7	6.2	23	10	6	23.79	A	1.30
87	5.3	2.6	30	17	10	77.52	A	1.00
30	14.0	7.7	25	8	5	54.49	A	1.10
28	15.3	6.8	25	8	5	20.70	A	0.90
23	41.4	11.1	26	4	2	24.28	AA	1.15
18	23.1	12.2	11	10	6	50.44	AAA	1.10
26	23.4	11.7	12	9	5	32.44	AA +	1.15
29	20.4	9.0	33	13	5	26.21	AA +	1.05
31	21.8	10.4	19	5	6	32.10	AAA	1.00
19	47.3	17.0	40	12	5	18.57	AA	1.15
29	18.1	7.8	35	10	5	34.38	AA	1.00
19	20.1	10.1	22	15	6	20.04	AA	1.10

Diamond Shamrock Corporation

EXHIBIT 5
■
Stock Price Comparison

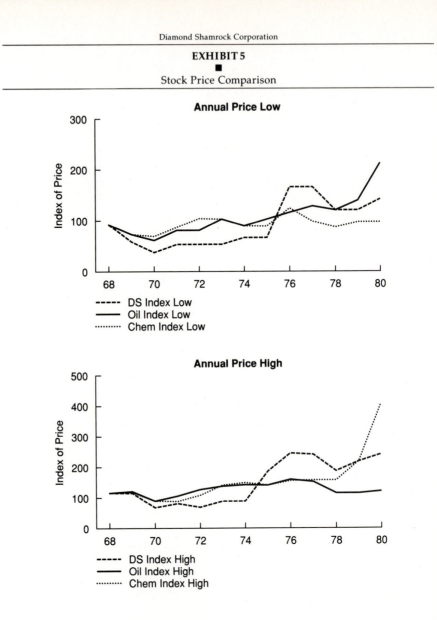

EXHIBIT 5 *continued*

	Annual High/Share	Annual Low/Share
1968	$18.7	$14.2
1969	17.9	9.0
1970	11.6	5.9
1971	12.6	8.3
1972	11.0	8.5
1973	14.4	8.4
1974	14.7	10.3
1975	29.0	10.9
1976	40.0	26.6
1977	38.6	26.4
1978	29.8	19.0
1979	35.1	19.1
1980	38.9	23.2

Diamond Shamrock Corporation

EXHIBIT 6
■
Monthly Returns on Diamond Shamrock Stock and Standard & Poor's 500

Date	Diamond Shamrock	S&P 500	Date	Diamond Shamrock	S&P 500
1976			*1979*		
Jan.	−28.34%	11.99%	Jan.	3.90%	4.21%
Feb.	8.32	−0.58	Feb.	−0.65	−2.84
March	−7.29	3.26	March	15.39	5.75
April	0.18	−0.99	April	−1.11	0.36
May	2.48	−0.73	May	−0.02	−1.68
June	12.90	4.27	June	14.29	4.10
July	−0.79	−0.68	July	−0.50	1.09
Aug.	−9.02	0.14	Aug.	6.01	6.11
Sept.	−4.60	2.47	Sept.	1.44	0.25
Oct.	−0.37	−2.06	Oct.	−6.16	−6.56
Nov.	−2.53	−0.09	Nov.	8.18	5.14
Dec.	5.59	5.40	Dec.	19.43	1.92
1977			*1980*		
Jan.	6.57	−4.89	Jan.	5.95	6.10
Feb.	−0.96	−1.51	Feb.	4.94	0.31
March	−2.79	−1.19	March	−24.55	−9.87
April	1.43	0.14	April	8.13	4.29
May	−0.28	−1.50	May	4.51	5.62
June	−8.57	4.75	June	0.86	2.96
July	−6.25	−1.51	July	7.66	6.76
Aug.	−1.17	−1.33	Aug.	−1.11	1.31
Sept.	3.40	0	Sept.	6.48	2.81
Oct.	−8.23	−4.15	Oct.	−2.66	1.86
Nov.	3.95	3.70	Nov.	14.59	10.95
Dec.	3.49	0.48	Dec.	−2.41	−3.15
1978					
Jan.	−8.02	−5.96			
Feb.	−6.51	−1.61			
March	−7.46	2.76			
April	14.52	8.70			
May	12.11	1.36			
June	−13.14	−1.52			
July	1.46	5.60			
Aug.	8.56	3.40			
Sept.	−9.87	−0.48			
Oct.	−17.91	−8.91			
Nov.	−4.27	2.60			
Dec.	−0.65	1.72			

Diamond Shamrock Corporation

EXHIBIT 7

■

Comparison of Divisions
Divisional Pre-Tax Operating Profit Returns

	Historic Period	Average Historic Return	1979	1980	Average, 1980–1982
Energy					
Oil and gas unit					
Exploration and Production (E&P)	70–78	10%	21%	24%	25%
Refining and Marketing (R&M)	70–78	34	57	61	72
Natural Gas Processing	70–78	43	25	73	68
Ammonia	70–78	50	38	13	14
Coal division	76–78	33	36	33	—
Chemicals					
Industrial chemicals					
Electro chemicals	70–78	35	19	19	23
Soda products	70–78	32	61	62	60
Plastics division	70–78	14	13	15	19
Technology					
Electrolytic systems	76–78	28	28	30	36
Specialty chemicals					
Process chemicals	76–78	32	36	37	43
Functional polymers	76–78	12	0	5	7
Metal coatings	76–78	96	51	74	85
Agricultural chemicals and health products					
Agricultural chemicals	71–78	23	17	15	18
Nutrition and Animal Health (NAH)	76–78	13	12	14	21
Health group	76–78	(30)	(71)	(67)	—
Foods	76–78	32	23	31	36

continued

EXHIBIT 7 *continued*

Segments
Energy
Oil and Gas Unit
 9 = Exploration and Production (E&P)
11 = Refining and Marketing (R&M)
10 = Natural Gas Processing (NGP)
12 = Ammonia
15 = Coal Unit
Chemicals
Industrial Chemicals
 1 = Electro Chemicals
 2 = Soda Products
 3 = Plastics Division
Technology
 5 = Electrolytic Systems
       Speciality Chemicals
 4 = Process Chemicals
14 = Functional Polymers
13 = Metal Coatings
Agricultural Chemicals and Health Products
 6 = Agricultural Chemicals (Ag Chem)
 7 = Nutrition and Animal Health (NAH)
16 = Health Group
 8 = Foods

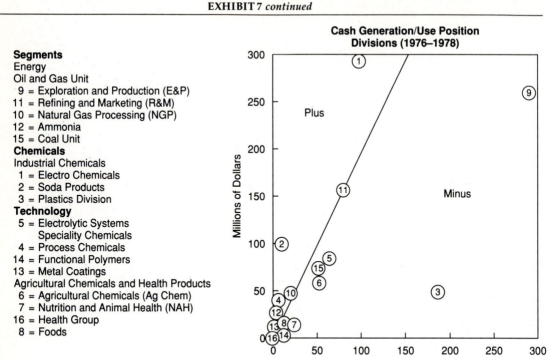

Cash Generation/Use Position
Divisions (1976–1978)

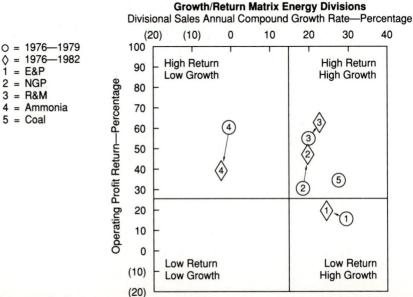

Growth/Return Matrix Energy Divisions
Divisional Sales Annual Compound Growth Rate—Percentage

O = 1976—1979
◊ = 1976—1982
1 = E&P
2 = NGP
3 = R&M
4 = Ammonia
5 = Coal

EXHIBIT 7 *continued*

Competitive Position/Industry Maturity Matrix
Energy Segments Industry Maturity

Segments
Oil and Gas
1 = R&M
2 = E&P
3 = NGP
Coal
4 = Eastern Steam
     Coal
5 = Lignite

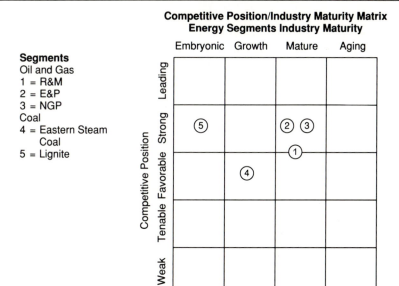

Growth/Return Matrix Chemical Divisions

O = 1976–1979
◊ = 1976–1982
1 = Electro Chem
2 = Soda Products
3 = Plastics

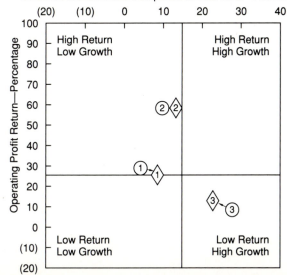

EXHIBIT 7 *continued*

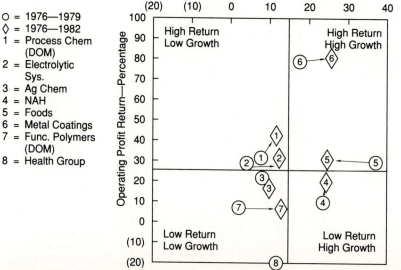

Competitive Position/Industry Maturity Matrix
Chemical Segments Industry Maturity

Segments
Electro Chemicals
1 = CL₂/H₂
2 = Liq. Caustic
3 = Dry Caustic
4 = Pot. Chem.
5 = Solvents–PCE
6 = Solvents–EDC
7 = Solvents–MEC
8 = Solvents–CFM
9 = Chlorowax
10 = TCl
Plastics
11 = PVC
12 = VCM
Soda Products
13 = Chrome
14 = Det. Silicates
15 = Liq. Silicates

Growth/Return Matrix Technology Divisions
Divisional Sales Annual Compound Growth Rate—Percentage

O = 1976—1979
◊ = 1976—1982
1 = Process Chem (DOM)
2 = Electrolytic Sys.
3 = Ag Chem
4 = NAH
5 = Foods
6 = Metal Coatings
7 = Func. Polymers (DOM)
8 = Health Group

EXHIBIT 7 *continued*

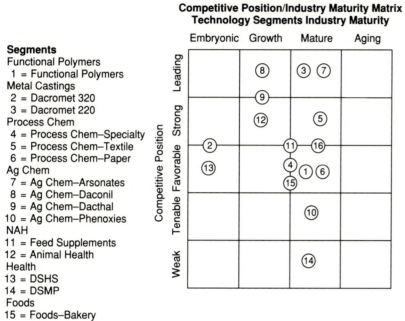

Competitive Position/Industry Maturity Matrix
Technology Segments Industry Maturity

Segments
Functional Polymers
 1 = Functional Polymers
Metal Castings
 2 = Dacromet 320
 3 = Dacromet 220
Process Chem
 4 = Process Chem–Specialty
 5 = Process Chem–Textile
 6 = Process Chem–Paper
Ag Chem
 7 = Ag Chem–Arsonates
 8 = Ag Chem–Daconil
 9 = Ag Chem–Dacthal
 10 = Ag Chem–Phenoxies
NAH
 11 = Feed Supplements
 12 = Animal Health
Health
 13 = DSHS
 14 = DSMP
Foods
 15 = Foods–Bakery
 16 = Foods–Dairy

Diamond Shamrock Corporation

EXHIBIT 8

■

Forecasts for Divisions, 1980

Industrial Chemicals and Plastics Unit ROCE Report from Unit's Plans (dollars in millions)

	1979	1980	1981	1982	1983	1984	1985	1986	1987	1989
Net sales	$609.9	$652.1	$794.6	$889.0	$989.6	$1,100.0	$1,224.0	$1,362.0	$1,517.0	$1,689.0
Gross profit	150.0	160.4	189.3	229.0	237.5	262.9	291.6	321.9	358.5	396.4
Gross margin	24.6%	24.6%	23.8%	25.8%	24.0%	23.9%	23.8%	23.6%	23.6%	23.5%
Operating profit	$124.2	$130.6	$159.2	$206.9	$190.0	$ 210.1	$ 232.8	$ 256.5	$ 285.7	$ 315.1
Corporate allocations	35.5	27.7	31.1	34.5	38.4	46.2	55.8	64.6	73.1	82.7
Profit before tax	88.7	102.9	128.1	172.4	151.6	163.9	177.0	191.9	212.6	232.4
Taxes	29.8	42.2	52.5	70.7	62.2	67.2	72.6	78.7	87.2	95.3
Net income	$ 58.9	$ 60.7	$ 75.6	$101.7	$ 89.4	$ 96.7	$ 104.4	$ 113.2	$ 125.4	$ 137.1
Average capital employed	$672.3	$683.1	$725.7	$818.4	$946.5	$1,109.1	$1,287.4	$1,474.0	$1,675.4	$1,900.2
ROCE	8.76%	8.98%	10.42%	12.43%	9.45%	8.72%	8.11%	7.68%	7.48%	7.22%

Technology Unit ROCE Report from Unit's Plans (dollars in millions)

	1979	1980	1981	1982	1983	1984	1985	1986	1987	1989
Net sales	$500.0	$604.5	$719.0	$826.4	$911.0	$1,002.0	$1,103.0	$1,213.0	$1,334.0	$1,468.0
Gross profit	133.9	159.1	207.7	241.4	244.0	269.0	296.0	325.0	350.0	393.0
Gross margin	26.8%	26.3%	28.9%	29.2%	26.8%	26.8%	26.8%	26.8%	26.8%	26.8%
Operating profit	$ 30.0	$ 36.5	$ 45.6	$ 54.5	$ 63.8	$ 70.1	$ 77.2	$ 84.9	$ 93.4	$ 103.0
Corporate allocations	13.8	12.2	14.2	15.9	17.8	21.4	25.7	29.7	33.5	37.8
Profit before tax	16.2	24.3	31.4	38.6	46.0	48.7	51.5	55.2	59.9	65.2
Taxes	5.7	10.2	13.2	16.2	18.8	20.0	21.1	22.5	24.6	26.7
Net income	$ 10.5	$ 14.1	$ 18.2	$ 22.4	$ 27.2	$ 28.8	$ 30.4	$ 32.6	$ 35.4	$ 38.5
Average capital employed	$245.0	$283.4	$326.0	$375.3	$436.9	$ 513.4	$ 595.0	$ 678.8	$ 768.4	$ 868.1
ROCE	4.29%	4.97%	5.58%	5.97%	6.23%	5.60%	5.11%	4.80%	4.61%	4.43%

Oil and Gas Unit ROCE Report from Unit's Plans (dollars in millions)

Net sales	$969.1	$1,443.7	$1,595.9	$1,033.2	$2,024.0	$2,231.0	$2,460.0	$2,115.0	$2,997.0	$3,311.0
Gross profit	169.4	257.4	308.2	354.7	390.8	434.3	487.3	543.8	609.0	401.5
Gross margin	17.5%	17.8%	19.3%	19.3%	19.3%	19.4%	19.8%	20.0%	20.3%	20.4%
Operating profit	$173.0	$ 225.1	$ 289.1	$ 333.0	$ 340.2	$ 380.5	$ 425.8	$ 475.9	$ 534.1	$ 598.7
Corporate allocations	37.2	34.5	40.3	49.2	56.5	69.7	85.8	100.7	114.4	130.1
Profit before tax	135.8	190.6	248.8	283.8	283.7	310.8	340.0	375.2	419.7	468.6
Taxes	51.3	81.4	106.3	121.4	122.0	133.7	146.2	161.3	180.5	201.5
Net income	$ 84.5	$ 109.2	$ 142.6	$ 162.4	$ 161.7	$ 177.1	$ 193.8	$ 213.9	$ 239.2	$ 267.1
Average capital employed	$668.5	$ 783.1	$ 922.2	$1,147.4	$1,373.0	$1,665.4	$1,963.9	$2,284.2	$2,617.7	$2,997.3
ROCE	12.64%	13.95%	15.46%	14.15%	11.78%	10.63%	9.87%	9.36%	9.14%	8.91%

Coal Unit ROCE Report from Unit's Plans (dollars in millions)

Net Sales	$155.9	$150.0	$158.0	$198.0	$220.0	$249.0	$279.0	$313.0	$351.0	$393.0
Gross profit	37.0	35.0	38.5	47.0	52.2	58.5	65.6	73.6	82.5	92.4
Gross margin	23.7%	23.3%	24.4%	23.7%	237.3%	23.5%	23.5%	23.5%	23.5%	23.5%
Operating profit	$ 33.1	$ 31.0	$ 34.0	$ 42.0	$ 46.7	$ 52.5	$ 59.1	$ 66.6	$ 75.0	$ 84.4
Corporate allocations	5.1	3.9	4.1	5.7	5.0	8.6	10.6	12.4	14.2	16.3
Profit before tax	28.0	27.1	29.9	36.3	41.7	43.9	48.5	54.2	60.8	68.1
Taxes	8.6	6.7	7.3	9.0	10.3	10.8	11.9	13.3	15.0	16.7
Net income	$ 19.4	$ 20.4	$ 22.6	$ 27.3	$ 31.4	$ 33.1	$ 36.6	$ 40.9	$ 45.8	$ 51.4
Average capital employed	$ 92.9	$ 97.7	$ 99.3	$123.4	$139.3	$178.2	$242.2	$281.5	$324.1	$371.1
ROCE	21.87%	20.88%	22.76%	22.12%	22.54%	18.57%	15.11%	14.53%	14.14%	13.85%

Piedmont Transmission Co.

As of July 16, 1980, the future relationship of Piedmont Transmission Co. (PTC) to its parent corporation could best be described as uncertain. PTC's most recent 5-year performance appeared respectable, although not spectacular. Sales had grown at 12 percent per year, while profits before tax had increased 14 percent per year. In fact, PTC's average 15-percent return (EBIT/total capital) had exceeded the comparable 10-percent return of Standard & Poor's 500 (1975–1979).

PTC was not, however, a discrete entity. It was only one of six subsidiaries of the Virginia Southern Corporation (VSC), a diversified business enterprise. While Piedmont's contribution to the parent's total profit before tax had been about 80 percent in 1975, this figure had declined to less than 35 percent by 1979. The reduction resulted from both acquisitions made by VSC during the period and faster rates of growth in the original and new subsidiaries.

Concern about Piedmont's future with VSC had come to a head in July 1980, following the subsidiary's submission of its 5-year forecasts. These showed an anticipated 5 percent per year increase in sales over the 5-year period and an even lower 1 percent per year increase in profits before tax. VSC management, intent on increasing the corporation's stock price and convinced that its upward movement was directly correlated to rapid rates of growth in sales and earnings, considered Piedmont's projections unsatisfactory. It was, therefore, seriously considering the divestiture of Piedmont, previously one of its star performers.

HISTORY OF VIRGINIA SOUTHERN CORPORATION

The Virginia Southern Corp. was established in 1978. It succeeded and replaced the Virginia Company, a wholly owned subsidiary of the Virginia Southern Systems Corporation. Virginia Southern Systems filed for bankruptcy in the early 1970s and was subsequently dissolved as a corporate entity. The corporation's major business, utility operations, was transferred to a new entity, which left the Virginia Company (later renamed the Virginia Southern Corp.) as its sole continuing operation. No changes were made in the three subsidiaries of the

This case was prepared as a basis for class discussion rather than to illustrate either effective or ineffective handling of an administrative situation. Copyright © 1981 by the Darden Graduate Business School Sponsors, University of Virginia, Charlottesville, Virginia.

Virginia Company (VACO), Piedmont Transmission Co., Oceanview Corp., and Gambol Corp. These subsidiaries were transferred to the Virginia Southern Corp. upon its creation.

Company Structure Prior to Bankruptcy:

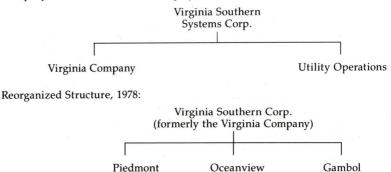

Reorganized Structure, 1978:

Piedmont Transmission Co. had historically been the Virginia Company's major subsidiary and, as such, represented a significant portion of the company's assets, earnings, and growth. Throughout the bankruptcy proceedings, PTC's cash flow and stability provided the financial resources to sustain Virginia Company's two other ailing subsidiaries, Oceanview Corp. and Gambol Corp.

Virginia Southern Systems, however, had been primarily involved in public utility operations. It was required to continue providing these services until the operations could be transferred to a newly established government entity. While assets pertaining to the utility functions had subsequently been sold (transferred) to this entity, Virginia Southern Corp. (VSC) had incurred significant operating losses in the interim. VSC management anticipated that these losses would effectively shield earnings through 1984.

Throughout the years of the bankruptcy proceedings, the Virginia Company adopted goals of increasing its asset base and improving its financial liquidity and flexibility. In the period from 1975 to 1977, the company's asset base increased 22 percent, while liabilities increased only 7 percent, its current ratio improved from 1x to 1.9x, and long-term debt as a percentage of total capitalization declined from 64 percent to 55 percent. These improvements, together with approval of the original company's reorganization plan, led to the 1978 creation of the Virginia Southern Corp. By the end of the year, VSC's stock was being traded on the NYSE.

In fact, VSC started business in 1978 in a good position to grow. In addition to its large tax-loss carry-forwards, VSC management believed that the company's internally generated funds exceeded the limited growth opportunities of its constituent business. As a result, the company managers began considering possible acquisitions. The objective of VSC's acquisition program was to acquire quality companies of significant size in industries to which VSC could contribute managerial expertise or financial resources. The candidates were evaluated on the basis of the following desired characteristics:

1. Predictable and maintainable earnings
2. Ability to increase earnings

3. Potential ability to use VSC's tax-loss carry-forwards

4. Strong management

5. Favorable cash flows

6. Reasonable capital structure

7. Market leadership

8. Attractive return on capital

9. Manageable level of government regulation

VSC made two acquisitions in 1979: Fuel Products Company acquired at the beginning of the year, and Deep Sea Engineering Co. acquired at the end of the year. (The Southwest Refinery Co. had been acquired in 1976.) As of July 1980, the company consisted of the six subsidiaries described below.

1. Piedmont Transmission Co., operator of one of the largest independent petroleum pipelines in the United States

2. Oceanview Corp., developer of residential, resort, commercial, and recreational properties

3. Gambol Corp., developer and operator of several recreational/amusement centers

4. Southwest Refinery Co., refiner of petroleum products, principally asphalt

5. Deep Sea Engineering Co., world's largest producer of mobile, self-elevating oil rigs

6. Fuel Products Co., distributor of liquid petroleum gas and refined petroleum products

Financial data for the parent and its component parts are shown in Exhibits 1 through 7. The comparative performance of VSC and its subsidiaries is shown in Exhibit 8.

VSC's reorientation following its creation was also reflected in changes in its top management. As depicted in Exhibit 9, VSC appointed a new chairman of the board in 1978 and a new chief operating officer the following fall. Because of their diverse backgrounds in governmental regulations and marketing, these two people together were expected (1) to keep VSC abreast of any further legal or regulatory proceedings against VSC arising out of its bankruptcy and (2) to lead VSC into a period of growth, prosperity, and long-term gains.

FINANCIAL STRATEGY

VSC's primary strategy in the years immediately following the bankruptcy proceedings was essentially a defensive one. Major emphasis was placed on maximizing financial liquidity and flexibility through improvements to its balance sheet and earnings.

The company's objectives changed, however, following the issuance of its common stock. Implicitly, this change altered the manner in which VSC management evaluated the performance of its subsidiaries. However, this change did not become explicit until PTC submitted its 5-year operating projections in 1980. At that point, it was made clear that management's objectives had been broadened from the mere guarantee of solvency to the goal of maximizing the return to the company's shareholders. Because VSC did not pay dividends (and had no immediate plans to do so), increases in the value of the shareholders' investments could only be realized through an appreciation in VSC's stock price. VSC's stock prices since the commencement of trading in 1978 are shown in Exhibit 10. Management thought that improvements in the stock's price depended on high rates of growth in sales, earnings, and ROI (measured by EBIT/total invested capital). These indexes had, therefore, become the principal criteria by which the various subsidiaries were evaluated.

The elucidation of VSC management's position generated an as-yet-unresolved debate: Was it appropriate to evaluate each of the six subsidiaries on the basis of the same performance criteria, or should differences among the subsidiaries' operating characteristics be taken into consideration? There were significant differences of opinion over this issue.

Fred Short, VSC's vice president of finance, was a strong supporter of management's position. He believed that the subsidiaries should be evaluated on the basis of the current performance measure, EBIT/total invested capital, or on the basis of the corporate weighted-average cost of capital. He maintained that investors in VSC were not interested in the returns generated by each of the subsidiaries, but were concerned solely with the return offered by the corporation as a whole. This belief led logically to the conclusion that all the subsidiaries should be required to earn the expected corporate rate of return regardless of any differences among them.

This conclusion was strengthened in Mr. Short's mind by his belief that investors desiring to diversify their portfolios were in a better position to do so than was VSC through its subsidiaries. He thought that VSC's adoption of multiple performance measures would ultimately lower the company's expected rate of return and reduce investor interest, with a commensurate reduction in the stock's price.

Mr. Short's bottom line was that each subsidiary should be evaluated against the same criteria and that each should be required to meet or exceed the same minimum growth requirements. As a result, he viewed Piedmont's most recent projections in an extremely negative light. Unless convinced otherwise, he would probably recommend divesting the subsidiary.

Martin Palmer, Piedmont's chief executive officer, was the main proponent of the other side of the argument. While Mr. Palmer had a great deal at stake in the current controversy, his position did have a base in financial theory. As shown in Exhibit 9, Mr. Palmer had been associated with Piedmont for more than 20 years, rising up the corporate ladder to his current position as CEO. Although his career with VSC was not in jeopardy, divestiture of Piedmont would significantly alter the level of his responsibility within the corporation and could possibly affect the size and growth of his compensation package with VSC.

Mr. Palmer's primary allegiance was, however, to the parent company. Through his long association with both VSC and Piedmont, Mr. Palmer had not only prospered himself, he had also worked through an extremely large bankruptcy case. Partly because of his help, VSC was now a strong, growing corporation. Mr. Palmer wanted to see VSC adopt a long-term strategy that would use the strengths of its subsidiaries to the greatest extent possible. Regardless of his own feelings for Piedmont, divestiture was an alternative which Mr. Palmer would endorse if he could be convinced that the subsidiary no longer fit within VSC's overall strategy. Mr. Palmer was not convinced, however, that Piedmont's low projected rates of growth signaled the end of Piedmont's usefulness to the parent.

It seemed to Mr. Palmer that a single set of performance criteria ignored two important points:

1. Each of the subsidiaries operated within a different industry, each of which had different characteristics.
2. The subsidiaries varied in terms of the positions they held within their respective industries.

Mr. Palmer believed that these two points implied the need for each of the subsidiaries to develop its own business strategy. Mr. Palmer wondered whether ignoring this implication wouldn't cause the divisions to take actions that might alter their operating characteristics and/or cause them to make suboptimal strategic decisions. For example, should a utility and a high-technology division each be required to earn the same rate of return? Was it desirable for them to earn the same return? Wouldn't their efforts to do so result in undesirable modifications to each of their underlying strengths?

Mr. Palmer reasoned that a firm must, at a minimum, earn a rate of return commensurate with its risk characteristics in order to continue to attract debt and equity capital. The lower the perceived risk level of the firm in the eyes of investors, the lower the expected return and, therefore, the lower the weighted-average cost of capital. The converse was also true. Because of the differences among VSC's subsidiaries, it seemed more appropriate to view them as a collection of independent businesses, each with its own risk characteristics, strategies, and weighted-average costs of capital. He believed that each division should be evaluated against criteria specific to its particular situation and industry.

To determine the ramifications of his hypotheses, Mr. Palmer decided to do two things: (1) assess the different futures projected by each of the subsidiaries based on their strategic plans and (2) develop weighted-average costs of capital for VSC as a whole as well as for PTC and for one of the more rapidly growing divisions, Deep Sea Engineering Co. To begin his first task, Mr. Palmer consulted the outlook section of each subsidiary's operating projections, reprinted in the appendix to this case.

The second task would be more difficult. The problem of developing reasonably accurate costs of debt and equity was particularly vexing, especially as those costs pertained to the two subsidiaries. Mr. Palmer thought that he would need to identify and compile data on companies with operating characteristics comparable to those of the two subsidiaries in order to develop a cost of capital specific to each of them. He believed he could then use these data to develop the necessary costs of debt and equity. The results of his research efforts are shown in Exhibits 11 through 13. After gathering these data, faced with compiling the appropriate costs of debt and equity and the proper capital structure to use in each of his calculations, Mr. Palmer was unsure whether he had used the correct parameters to identify comparable companies for his analysis.

1. Cost of Debt.   Mr. Palmer was unsure of whose marginal cost of debt to use with respect to Piedmont and Deep Sea. Should he use VSC's marginal cost or those of companies comparable to the subsidiaries? Using the latter figures would relate the subsidiaries directly to their respective industries. However, couldn't VSC, with its larger size and diversified structure, issue debt at a lower rate? In fact, wasn't this one of the advantages of a diversified company, and, as such, shouldn't it be reflected in the computation of a cost of capital?

Additionally, Mr. Palmer was unsure of how to handle VSC's massive tax-loss carry-forwards. The development of a weighted-average cost of capital required all figures to be computed on an after-tax basis to recognize the tax benefits associated with debt-related interest payments. However, it was unlikely that VSC would have to pay any taxes for the next 5 years. Mr. Palmer was unsure of how to handle VSC's particular situation. He had always assumed that tax-loss carry-forwards were good for a company's earnings. The fact that a company's cost of capital would go up if they were considered in the computation of a weighted-average cost of capital didn't seem consistent.

2. Cost of Equity.
Developing appropriate costs of equity also created problems, because none of the subsidiaries traded its own stock. Mr. Palmer had identified three methods of computing a firm's cost of equity: (1) the dividend valuation model, (2) the earnings/price ratio, and (3) the capital asset pricing model (CAPM). (See Exhibit 14 for a brief description of each.) Mr. Palmer realized that if he used either of the first two methods, he would be limited to developing a cost of equity for VSC and applying that rate to each of the subsidiaries. Alternatively, the CAPM would allow him to incorporate into his analysis the data he had gathered on companies comparable to the parent and subsidiaries. The validity of this approach hinged, however, on the success of his research efforts, described in Point 4, below.

3. Weighted Capital Structure.
Mr. Palmer was uncertain about whose capital structure he should incorporate into his analysis. By using the subsidiaries', wasn't he ignoring the strong role VSC played in determining their capital structure? Conversely, if he used the capital structures of the companies he had identified as surrogates, wasn't he ignoring the possibility that a diversified company could frequently issue more debt in the aggregate than its subsidiaries could individually? Since this possibility was frequently a motive behind diversification, shouldn't it be reflected in his analysis?

4. Comparability of Data.
Lastly, Mr. Palmer was uncertain of the true comparability of VSC and the two subsidiaries to the companies he had identified. While he had tried to identify companies operating in similar lines of business, he wasn't at all sure that this made them comparable, per se, to VSC, Piedmont, and Deep Sea. Wasn't it possible for two companies in the same business not to be comparable because of differences in the strategies they had undertaken, as reflected in their financial data? He wondered if he shouldn't have tried to identify companies with similar operating characteristics and strategies rather than similar operations and products.

CONCLUSION

Mr. Palmer realized that it was up to him to resolve these uncertainties. Looking down the road, however, he wasn't sure that even when he had done so, the most difficult task wouldn't still remain: the presentation of his findings to VSC management. It seemed reasonable to expect that Mr. Short and the rest of the financial staff would at least be receptive to his ideas, regardless of whether they agreed with his conclusions. However, he wasn't at all sure of how to approach Frank Major, the new chief operating officer, and Robert Platt, the new chairman of the board. He recognized the danger that the necessary complexity of his analysis might exceed their level of financial sophistication and be overshadowed by their focus on the big picture, VSC's bottom line.

Muttering under his breath, Mr. Palmer wondered if times of prosperity weren't tougher on a manager than times of bankruptcy.

Piedmont Transmission Co.

EXHIBIT 1

■

Virginia Southern Corp. Consolidated Operating Statements
(millions of dollars)

	1975	1976	1977	1978	1979
Balance Sheet					
Assets					
Current assets	$108.4	$152.6	$223.9	$ 247.4	$ 561.8
Net property, plant, and equipment	288.9	322.5	401.9	448.0	752.4
Other assets	285.0	227.8	209.6	210.0	357.0
Assets from discontinued operations	—	—	—	3,806.5	3,721.2
Total assets	$682.3	$702.9	$835.4	$4,711.9	$5,392.4
Liabilities and Stockholders' Equity					
Current liabilities	$106.2	$ 81.9	$120.4	$ 155.0	$ 353.4
Long-term debt	305.9	326.0	352.2	319.2	461.4
Other liabilities	95.3	71.3	69.0	73.3	74.9
Liabilities associated with discontinued operations	—	—	—	3,247.5	3,167.7
Total liabilities	507.4	479.2	541.6	3,795.0	4,057.4
Stockholders' equity	174.9	223.7	293.8	916.9	1,335.0
Total liabilities and stockholders' equity	$682.3	$702.9	$835.4	$4,711.9	$5,392.4
Income Statement					
Net sales	$198.5	$287.1	$504.7	$ 667.1	$1,087.3
Interest expense	9.3	27.9	26.3	30.8	40.2
Depreciation	24.7	26.3	26.4	30.6	52.0
Other expenses	138.4	194.2	380.0	508.5	894.5
Profit before tax	$ 26.1	$ 38.7	$ 72.0	$ 97.2	$ 100.6

Piedmont Transmission Co.

EXHIBIT 2

■

Piedmont Transmission Company Operating Statements
(thousands of dollars)

	1975	1976	1977	1978	1979
Balance Sheet					
Assets					
Current assets	$ 17,908	$ 20,899	$ 25,883	$ 17,237	$ 19,342
Net property, plant, and equipment	205,798	210,228	227,074	231,587	237,656
Other assets	1,658	1,522	1,909	2,676	1,615
Total assets	$225,364	$232,649	$254,866	$251,500	$258,613
Liabilities and Stockholders' Equity					
Current liabilities	$ 28,509	$ 15,825	$ 18,993	$ 16,878	$ 19,315
Long-term debt	81,330	86,680	102,900	95,488	81,963
Other liabilities	18,206	17,207	16,762	15,498	15,919
Total liabilities	128,045	119,712	138,655	127,864	117,197
Stockholders' equity	97,319	112,937	116,211	123,636	141,416
Total liabilities and stockholders' equity	$225,364	$232,649	$254,866	$251,500	$258,613
Income Statement					
Net sales	$ 62,307	$ 72,819	$ 84,455	$ 99,263	$ 96,622
Interest expense	4,932	7,049	7,893	7,822	8,227
Depreciation	10,556	10,702	10,800	11,800	12,274
Other expenses	26,060	31,399	38,199	40,144	41,398
Profit before tax	$ 20,759	$ 23,669	$ 27,563	$ 39,497	$ 34,723

Piedmont Transmission Co.

EXHIBIT 3
■
Oceanview Corp. Operating Statements
(thousands of dollars)

	1975	1976	1977	1978	1979
Balance Sheet					
Assets					
Current assets	$ 27,900	$ 28,100	$ 46,400	$ 50,600	$ 82,300
Net property, plant, and equipment	33,200	30,000	35,700	42,300	63,700
Other assets	98,900	91,200	84,600	101,300	114,200
Total assets	$160,000	$149,300	$166,700	$194,200	$260,200
Liabilities and Stockholders' Equity					
Current liabilities	$ 10,500	$ 11,100	$ 19,200	$ 31,000	$ 65,800
Long-term debt	40,800	36,800	31,400	34,700	46,400
Other liabilities	20,200	13,500	13,100	10,900	8,700
Total liabilities	71,500	61,400	63,700	76,600	120,900
Stockholders' equity	88,500	87,900	103,000	117,600	139,300
Total liabilities and stockholders' equity	$160,000	$149,300	$166,700	$194,200	$260,200
Income Statement					
Net sales	$ 44,300	$ 55,200	$ 91,100	$ 97,900	$133,700
Interest expense	1,748	1,800	1,200	1,500[a]	2,010[a]
Depreciation	3,485	3,200	3,400	3,000	3,850
Other expenses	37,267	44,500	71,400	68,300	96,140
Profit before tax	$ 1,800	$ 5,700	$ 15,100	$ 25,100	$ 31,700

[a]Imputed interest expense based on past average relationship.

Piedmont Transmission Co.

EXHIBIT 4
■

Gambol Corp. Operating Statements
(thousands of dollars)

	1975	1976	1977	1978	1979
Balance Sheet					
Assets					
Current assets	$ 17,400	$ 22,600	$ 30,000	$ 54,100	$ 58,200
Net property, plant, and equipment	41,600	41,500	41,700	128,800	186,400
Other assets	63,300	58,700	60,900	67,100	90,100
Total assets	$122,300	$122,800	$132,600	$250,000	$334,700
Liabilities and Stockholders' Equity					
Current liabilities	$ 19,700	$ 20,200	$ 29,000	$ 42,800	$102,400
Long-term debt	122,100	113,000	94,900	139,600	129,000
Other liabilities	8,500	4,700	6,500	4,600	7,600
Total liabilities	150,300	137,900	130,400	187,000	239,000
Stockholders' equity	(28,000)	(15,100)	2,200	63,000	95,700
Total liabilities and stockholders' equity	$122,300	$122,800	$132,600	$250,000	$334,700
Income Statement					
Net sales	$ 87,000	$108,900	$124,300	$214,800	$249,700
Interest expense	11,139	10,400	8,900	10,000[a]	9,300[a]
Depreciation	10,296	10,442	10,209	10,800	31,814
Other expenses	58,065	74,458	87,491	158,100	176,586
Profit before tax	$ 7,500	$ 13,600	$ 17,700	$ 35,900	$ 32,000

[a]Interest expense for 1978 to 1979 imputed from past relationship.

Piedmont Transmission Co.

EXHIBIT 5
■

Southwest Refinery Co.[a] Operating Statements
(thousands of dollars)

	1976	1977	1978	1979
Balance Sheet				
Assets				
Current assets	$ 41,800	$ 63,400	$ 90,300	$ 81,800
Net property, plant, and equipment	32,700	35,100	38,500	51,700
Other assets	1,400	1,600	1,400	1,100
Total assets	$ 75,900	$100,100	$130,200	$134,600
Liabilities and Stockholders' Equity				
Current liabilities	$ 26,500	$ 34,800	$ 54,100	$ 47,300
Long-term debt	30,100	22,800	6,400	1,300
Other liabilities	0	0	0	0
Total liabilities	56,600	57,600	60,500	48,600
Stockholders' equity	19,300	42,500	69,700	86,000
Total liabilities and stockholders' equity	$ 75,900	$100,100	$130,200	$134,600
Income Statement				
Net sales	$137,200	$197,200	$239,000	$283,000
Interest expense	1,100	835[b]	237[b]	48[b]
Depreciation	1,536	1,570	1,720	1,964
Other expenses	114,064	167,895	207,043	246,588
Profit before tax	$ 20,500	$ 26,900	$ 30,000	$ 34,400

[a]Acquired by VSC in 1976.
[b]Imputed from 1976 relationship to debt outstanding.

Piedmont Transmission Co.

EXHIBIT 6
■
Deep Sea Engineering Co.[a] Operating Statements
(thousands of dollars)

	1975	1976	1977	1978	1979
Balance Sheet					
Assets					
Current assets	$138,500	$126,200	$121,400	$158,300	$208,300
Net property, plant, and equipment	78,500	77,200	74,500	78,000	85,800
Other assets	10,700	9,600	7,100	4,800	6,200
Total assets	$227,700	$213,000	$203,000	$241,000	$300,300
Liabilities and Stockholders' Equity					
Current liabilities	$ 68,100	$ 64,100	$ 52,900	$ 84,000	$126,700
Long-term debt	78,400	51,700	40,000	30,600	25,300
Other liabilities	12,500	16,400	15,200	17,500	17,400
Total liabilities	159,000	132,200	108,100	132,100	169,400
Stockholders' equity	68,700	80,800	94,900	109,000	130,900
Total liabilities and stockholders' equity	$227,700	$213,000	$203,000	$241,100	$300,300
Income Statement					
Net sales	$272,200	$292,300	$291,000	$306,100	$406,000
Interest expense	5,805	5,169	3,214	3,085	3,100
Depreciation	4,572	3,766	3,958	4,000	4,391
Other expenses	242,636	255,044	254,540	265,313	349,610
Profit before tax	$ 19,187	$ 28,361	$ 29,288	$ 33,702	$ 48,899

[a]Operating statements for 1975 to 1979 are prior to the VSC acquisition in late 1979.

Piedmont Transmission Co.

EXHIBIT 7

■

Fuel Products Co.[a] Operating Statements
(thousands of dollars)

	1975[b]	1976[b]	1977[b]	1978	1979[c]
Balance Sheet					
Assets					
Current assets				$ 35,500	$ 79,858
Net property, plant, and equipment				36,100	54,144
Other assets				25,100	4,985
Total assets				$ 96,700	$138,987
Liabilities and Stockholders' Equity					
Current liabilities				$ 20,500	$ 47,285
Long-term debt				19,200	30,137
Other liabilities				—	29,181
Total liabilities				39,700	106,603
Stockholders' equity				57,000	32,384
Total liabilities and stockholders' equity				$ 96,700	$138,987
Income Statement					
Net sales	$144,600	$185,400	$209,900	$220,200	$220,395
Depreciation	N.Av.	N.Av.	N.Av.	N.Av.	1,732
Other expenses	133,000	172,600	201,900	210,300	211,769
Profit before tax	$ 11,600	$ 12,800	$ 8,000	$ 9,900	$ 6,894

N.Av. = not available.
[a]Figures for 1978 to 1979 extracted from consolidated reports.
[b]Data not available for balance sheet figures.
[c]Purchased by VSC.

Piedmont Transmission Company

EXHIBIT 8
■
Comparative Performance: VSC and Its Subsidiaries, 1975–1979 (dollars in millions)

Operating Entity	Revenues		Profit before Tax		Pre-Tax Cash Flow		EBIT/ Total Capital[a]		Pre-Tax Return on Equity		Debt/ Total Capital	
	1979	5-Year Growth/Yr.	1979	5-Year Growth/Yr.	1979	5-Year Cumulative	1979	5-Year Avg.	1979	5-Year Avg.[b]	1979	5-Year Avg.
VSC[c]	$1,087.3	53%	$100.6	40%	$152.6	$494.6	7.8%	10.6	8%	15%	26%	46%
Piedmont Transmission Co.	96.6	12	34.7	14	47.0	202.3	19.2	17.0	25	25	37	43
Oceanview Corp.	133.7	32	31.7	105	35.6	96.3	18.1	12.0	23	14	25	27
Gambol Corp.	249.7	30	32.0	44	63.8	180.3	18.0	23.0	33	175	57	99
Southwest Refinery Co.[d]	283.0	27	34.4	19	36.3	118.8	40.0	41.0	40	63	2	26
Deep Sea Engineering Co.[e]	406.0	11	48.9	26	53.3	180.1	33.4	25.0	37	32	16	32
Fuel Products Co.[f]	220.4	11	6.9	−12	8.6	50.9[g]	11.0[h]	N.Av.	21	N.Av.	48	N.Av.

N.Av. = not available.
[a] Total capital = Long-term debt plus Owners' equity.
[b] Sum of profit before tax, 5 years ÷ Sum of equity, 5 years.
[c] Corporate totals may not equal sum of subsidiaries because of losses and/or gains from other operations.
[d] Acquired by VSC in 1976. Figures shown cover four-year period from 1976 to 1979.
[e] Acquired by VSC in 1979. Figures shown reflect pre-acquisition operations in 5-year period from 1974 to 1978.
[f] Acquired by VSC in 1979. Historic data reflect results of pre-acquisition operations, from 1975 to 1978, and post-acquisition 1979.
[g] No depreciation data available for the period from 1975 to 1978; figure represents sum of PBT 1975–1979 and 1979 depreciation.
[h] No interest data available; figure shown = PBT/TC.

Piedmont Transmission Co.

EXHIBIT 9
■
VSC Organization Chart, 1980: Managers and Their Backgrounds

VSC Board of Directors

Chairman—R. Platt	Age 66; Elected chairman 1978. Previously VP and general counsel to large insurance company. Served as chairman of institutional investors of VSCC throughout bankruptcy proceedings. Primary orientation: legal and regulatory environment.
COO—Frank Major	Age 46; Became COO fall of 1979. Previous experience, 20+ years with large consumer goods corporation. Primary orientation: marketing.
VSC VP of Finance—Fred Short	Age 39; Appointed VP fall of 1979. Previously VP with Oceanview Corp. MBA degree. Primary orientation: finance.
VP Investor Relations—George Perkins	Age 40; Appointed summer of 1979. Previously involved in investor relations with an investment consulting firm. Primary orientation: finance.
VP Treasurer—Arnold Robinson	Age 37: Five years experience with VACO/VSC. Primary orientation: finance.
VP Corporate Development— Clay Jorgens	Age 37; Appointed 1979. Previously VP business development at PTC. More than 5 years experience with PTC. Primary orientation: finance.
CEO Piedmont Transmission Co.—Martin Palmer	Age 51; Appointed 1979. More than 20 years experience with PTC: asst. controller, subsequently VP finance—PTC, 1959–1969; asst. VP finance accounting—VSCC, 1969–1971; sr. VP and chief admin. officer—VACO, 1971–1973; director—PTC, 1971 to present; executive VP and COO—PTC, 1973–1976; and president—PTC, 1976–1979. Primary orientation: finance.

Piedmont Transmission Co.

EXHIBIT 10
■
Virginia Southern Corp. Stock Prices

| | *Virginia Southern Corp.* | | | |
	Common Stock	Pfd. Stock Series A_1 Conv.	Pfd. Stock Series B_1 Conv.	S&P 500 Composite Index
January 1979	$15⅞	$10⅜	$6	99.93
February	17½	10⅛	5⅜	96.28
March	21¼	10⅛	5¾	101.59
April	21⅜	10½	5⅞	101.76
May	20⅝	10⅜	5⅞	99.08
June	17¼	10½	5⅛	102.91
July	18	11⅛	5¾	103.81
August	18¼	11⅞	6	109.32
September	17⅛	11⅝	5⅝	109.32
October	17¼	11	5¼	101.82
November	21⅝	11¾	6¼	106.16
December	23⅛	12⅛	6¼	107.94
January 1980	24⅝	12⅝	6¼	114.16
February	21⅞	12¾	5⅞	113.66
March	15⅞	11¼	4⅝	102.09
April	17¼	12⅛	5	106.29
May	17¾	13¾	5¾	111.24
June	20	14⅜	6½	114.24

Piedmont Transmission Co.

EXHIBIT 11
■

Operating Characteristics: Virginia Southern Corp. and Comparable Companies

Name of Company	Revenues (millions of dollars)		Net Income (millions of dollars)		Total Assets (millions of dollars)		Return on Equity (percent)	
	1979	5-Yr. Grth./Yr. (percent)	1979	5-Yr. Grth./Yr. (percent)	1979	5-Yr. Grth./Yr. (percent)	1979	5-Yr. Average
A. Real-Estate Companies								
1. Deltona Corp. Develops residential and business communities; sells home sites and homes in Fla.; co. owns utilities serving developed communities.	$ 104	9%	$ (9)	—	$ 298	−3%	—	1%
2. GDV, Inc. Owns Fla.'s largest community builder.	1,224	92	48	50%	1,155	35	17%	11
3. Newhall Land and Farming Co. Owns 125k acres California real estate; activities including farming, exploration for and sale of oil and natural gas, construction and leasing of commercial properties, and construction and sale of homes.	105	5	18	22	170	6	20	19
B. Integrated Oil Companies								
1. The Charter Co. Engages in oil production and marketing, commercial printing, insurance, publishing, and broadcasting.	4,250	43	368	146	1,729	32	70	25
2. Mobil Corp. Owns Mobil Oil Corp., Montgomery Ward, and Container Corp. of America.	44,721	21	2,007	26	27,506	16	21	14
3. Sigmor Corp. Largest independent gasoline retailer in U.S.; also operates refinery, markets new and used pipe, owns two intrastate pipelines, operates trucking warehousing facilities, and owns six radio stations. (traded OTC)	782	30	21	11	300	36	17	19

N.Av. = not available.

N.Ap. = not applicable.

[a]Total capital = Total assets − Current liabilities.

[b]At 6/27/80, AAA long-term corp. bonds yielded 11 percent; AA bonds, 11.5 percent; A bonds, 12 percent; and BBB bonds 13 percent.

[c]Figures shown are profits before tax, as Virginia Southern Corp. pays no taxes.

Debt/Total Capital^a (percent)		S&P Bond Ratings^b	Effective Tax Rate (percent)		Common Shares Outstanding (millions)		Stock Price		Payout Ratio (percent)		P/E Ratio		Beta
1979	5-Yr. Average	1979	1979	5-Yr. Average	1979	5-Yr. Average	1979 Range	5-Yr. Range	1979	5-Yr. Average	1979	5-Yr. Average	1979
60%	70%	N.Av.	N.Av.	15%	4	4	14¾–8⅝	15¼–3¼	N.Ap.	N.Ap.	—	17–7	1.55
57	36	N.Av.	46%	48	15	11	14⅛–6⅞	14⅛–2¾	N.Ap.	N.Ap.	4–2	6–3	1.60
16	30	N.Av.	45	42	9	10	24–12¼	24–4⅛	22	22	12–6	9–6	0.80
42	50	B	18	58	25	22	5–50	3⅛–50	3	12	3–0	7–3	1.35
21	24	AA	71	74	424	418	30¼–17	30¼–8⅝	27	30	6–4	6–5	1.10
38	31	N.Av.	36	43	17	14	19¼–5½	19¼–3½	26	33	15–4	9–5	1.25

continued

EXHIBIT 11 *continued*

Name of Company	Revenues (millions of dollars) 1979	Revenues 5-Yr. Grth./Yr. (percent)	Net Income (millions of dollars) 1979	Net Income 5-Yr. Grth./Yr. (percent)	Total Assets (millions of dollars) 1979	Total Assets 5-Yr. Grth./Yr. (percent)	Return on Equity (percent) 1979	Return on Equity 5-Yr. Average
C. Recreation and Leisure Companies								
1. **AMF, Inc.** Two lines of business: leisure (bowling equipment, bicycles, yachts, etc.) and industrial (machinery for industrial use, process equipment for petroleum and other industries, etc.)	$1,438	9%	$ 53	13%	$ 939	5%	13%	12%
2. **Columbia Pictures Industries, Inc.** Produces and distributes movies and TV series, owns radio stations.	613	17	39	65	456	11	24	39
3. **Walt Disney Productions.** Makes and distributes movies, operates theme parks, develops residential and recreational real estate.	797	11	114	17	1,196	11	13	12
4. **Marriott Corp.** Diversified hotel and food-service company, operates theme parks.	1,510	20	71	34	1,080	10	18	13
D. Oil-Field Services and Equipment Companies								
1. **Petrolane Inc.** Leading independent retail marketer of LPG; offers specialized offshore drilling tools and services; charters a fleet of deep-drilling land rigs; operates 90 supermarkets and 64 auto service centers and rents uniforms.	1,143	19	60	22	595	20	23	22
2. **Zapata Corp.** Contract drilling and supply vessel services, dredging, coal mining, oil and natural gas production.	525	11	21	− 9	908	3	9	8

N.Av. = not available.

N.Ap. = not applicable.

[a]Total capital = Total assets − Current liabilities.

[b]At 6/27/80, AAA long-term corp. bonds yielded 11 percent; AA bonds, 11.5 percent; A bonds, 12 percent; and BBB bonds 13 percent.

[c]Figures shown are profits before tax, as Virginia Southern Corp. pays no taxes.

Debt/Total Capital[a] (percent)		S&P Bond Ratings[b]	Effective Tax Rate (percent)		Common Shares Outstanding (millions)		Stock Price		Payout Ratio (percent)		P/E Ratio		Beta
1979	5-Yr. Average	1979	1979	5-Yr. Average	1979	5-Yr. Average	1979 Range	5-Yr. Range	1979	5-Yr. Average	1979	5-Yr. Average	1979
29%	35%	BBB	45%	46%	20	20	14½–18¾	9⅝–24⅜	48%	59%	7–6	11–7	1.10
41	64	B	29	42	10	9	37¼–18⅛	37¼–2⅜	20	N.Ap.	9–5	9–3	1.05
Nil	1	N.Av.	47	47	33	32	45½–33	60¼–19¾	10	7	13–9	20–12	1.10
45	48	N.Av.	42	42	36	36	18¾–11⅝	18¾–6	8	N.Ap.	9–6	16–9	1.25
32	30	N.Av.	43	47	50	44	15–7	15–2¼	23	21	13–6	10–6	1.15
62	63	B	20	28	18	18	14⅞–5¼	14⅞–4¼	13	24	13–5	16–8	1.35

continued

EXHIBIT 11 *continued*

Name of Company	Revenues (millions of dollars)		Net Income (millions of dollars)		Total Assets (millions of dollars)		Return on Equity (percent)	
	1979	5-Yr. Grth./Yr. (percent)	1979	5-Yr. Grth./Yr. (percent)	1979	5-Yr. Grth./Yr. (percent)	1979	5-Yr. Average
E. Multiform Companies								
1. **Alco Standard Corp.** Manufactures electrical, metallurgical, and chemical products; distributes paper, leisure-time products and alcoholic beverages; mines coal and produces coal mining equipment.	$1,917	20%	$ 50	13%	$ 693	13%	21%	22%
2. **Avco Corp.** Offers financial services (conumer finance and mortgage loans); makes gas turbine and other industrial equipment; distributes motion pictures; develops real estate for sale.	1,932	34	128	41	5,300	43	15	14
3. **Fuqua Industries, Inc.** Manufactures lawn and garden equipment, sporting goods, and steel products; operates farm stores and movie theater circuit; and distributes petroleum products.	2,057	40	67	204	925	24	29	12
4. **Gulf and Western Industries.** Manufactures automotive, energy, and capital goods products; operates in leisure area through Paramount Pictures; provides financial services; sugar growing and processing; natural resources, etc.	5,288	19	227	13	5,160	12	18	18
F. Virginia Southern Corp.	1,087	53	101[c]	40[c]	5,392	68	8	15

N.Av. = not available.
N.Ap. = not applicable.
[a]Total capital = Total assets − Current liabilities.
[b]At 6/27/80, AAA long-term corp. bonds yielded 11 percent; AA bonds, 11.5 percent; A bonds, 12 percent; and BBB bonds 13 percent.
[c]Figures shown are profits before tax, as Virginia Southern Corp. pays no taxes.

Debt/Total Capital[a] (percent)		S&P Bond Ratings[b]	Effective Tax Rate (percent)		Common Shares Outstanding (millions)		Stock Price		Payout Ratio (percent)		P/E Ratio		Beta
1979	5-Yr. Average	1979	1979	5-Yr. Average	1979	5-Yr. Average	1979 Range	5-Yr. Range	1979	5-Yr. Average	1979	5-Yr. Average	1979
30%	27%	N.Av.	46%	44%	20	21	18⅝–11⅜	18⅝–3⅞	27%	22%	7–4	6–4	0.75
72	62	B	39	38	16	17	29¼–18⅝	35–2¾	16	N.Ap.	4–2	4–2	1.45
54	50	B	47	40	13	11	19¼–8¾	19¼–3¼	9	12	4–2	5–2	1.35
52	54	B	31	27	60	61	15¾–10⅞	17¼–6⅞	15	16	4–3	5–3	1.25
9	34	N.Av.	N.Av.	N.Av.	23	N.Av.	19.10	N.Av.	N.Av.	N.Av.	7–9	N.Av.	N.Av.

Piedmont Transmission Co.

EXHIBIT 12
■

Operating Characteristics: Piedmont Transmission Co. and Comparable Companies

Name of Company	Revenues (millions of dollars)		Net Income (millions of dollars)		Total Assets (millions of dollars)		Return on Equity (percent)	
	1979	5-Yr. Grth./Yr. (percent)	1979	5-Yr. Grth./Yr. (percent)	1979	5-Yr. Grth./Yr. (percent)	1979	5-Yr. Average
Telephone Companies								
Rochester Telephone	$ 172	12%	$ 27	22%	$ 361[d]	4%	14%	13%
Mid-Continent Telephone[c]	219	15	35	21	722[d]	15	17	16
Continental Telephone	1,135	20	121	20	2,488[d]	10	15	13
United Telecommunications	1,282	15	181	19	3,410[d]	11	14	14
Natural Gas Transmission Companies								
Panhandle Eastern Corp.	1,968	31	148	20	1,992[d]	11	15	14
Southern Resources, Inc.	1,446	23	110	12	1,794	11	17	17
Texas Eastern Corp.	2,944	22	181	12	3,237	4	19	16
Texas Gas Transmission Co.	1,687	24	79	16	1,341	11	16	15
Westcoast Transmission Co., Ltd.	1,098	27	50	11	905[d]	12	13	13
Electric Utilities								
Atlantic City Electric	283	9	34	5	682[d]	5	12	13
Citizens Utilities (traded OTC)	130	16	23	10	373[d]	14	11	12
El Paso Electric (traded OTC)	160	15	23	23	488[d]	25	14	13
Empire District Electric	74	17	8	20	187[d]	18	12	11
Sierra Pacific Power	178	16	22	23	441[d]	12	13	12
Piedmont Transmission Co. (5–5)	97	12	35	14	259	4	25[e]	4

N.Av. = not available.

N.Ap. = not applicable.

[a]Total capital = Total assets − Current liabilities.

[b]At 6/27/80, AAA long-term corp. bonds yielded 11 percent; AA bonds 11.5 percent; A bonds 12 percent; and BBB bonds 13 percent.

[c]Data shown are for four-year period from 1976 to 1979.

[d]Numbers shown = Net assets = Sum of plant at cost, Work in progress, and Nuclear fuel − Depreciation.

[e]All earnings and ROE figures shown are based on profit before tax, as Piedmont Transmission Co. does not pay taxes.

Debt/Total Capital[a] *(percent)*		*S&P Bond Ratings*[b]	*Effective Tax Rate (percent)*		*Common Shares Outstanding (millions)*		*Stock Price*		*Payout Ratio (percent)*		*P/E Ratio*		*Beta*
1979	*5-Yr. Average*	*1979*	*1979*	*5-Yr. Average*	*1979*	*5-Yr. Average*	*1979 Range*	*5-Yr. Range*	*1979*	*5-Yr. Average*	*1979*	*5-Yr. Average*	*1979*
43%	48%	AA	37%	24%	10	10	20⅞–16	20⅞–9⅞	58%	52%	8–6	8–6	0.75
47	51	N.Av.	36	39	12	11	22⅝–16½	22⅝–10¾	54	57	8–6	8–6	0.65
49	52	BBB	43	42	56	48	17⅝–13⅞	17⅞–10	62	65	8–6	10–7	0.80
46	49	BBB	56	59	70	60	21⅜–16⅝	21⅜–12½	57	58	8–6	9–7	0.65
41	46	A	43	48	37	34	33–20	33–13½	38	40	8–5	8–6	0.80
31	39	N.Av.	44	43	20	20	55¾–31¾	55¾–20⅜	25	23	10–6	8–6	0.95
36	42	A/BBB	53	46	25	25	69¼–33⅝	69¼–25⅜	35	39	10–5	9–6	1.05
35	41	A	41	43	21	21	29–17⅝	29–11¾	37	39	8–5	8–6	0.95
46	47	N.Av.	45	33	38	36	14–9⅜	14–6⅛	60	58	11–7	9–7	0.70
39	45	A+	34	32	15	13	20⅜–16¾	24⅝–12⅝	75	71	9–7	10–7	0.60
27	30	AA+	N.Av.	N.Av.	7	6	36¾–27¾	36¾–21½	81	76	12–9	12–10	0.55
39	43	AA−	N.Av.	N.Av.	16	11	11–9	12⅝–8½	74	77	8–6	9–8	0.65
44	45	A	29	42	5	4	14½–11⅛	17¼–11⅛	82	81	8–6	9–8	0.60
47	47	A	39	44	11	9	14¼–12	14⅞–8¼	65	64	7–6	8–6	0.65
41	44	N.Av.	N.Ap.	N.Ap.	N.Ap.	N.Ap.	N.Ap.	N.Ap.	N.Ap.	N.Ap.	N.Ap.	N.Ap.	N.Ap.

Piedmont Transmission Co.

EXHIBIT 13

■

Operating Characteristics: Deep Sea Engineering Co. and Comparable Companies

Name of Company	Revenues (millions of dollars)		Net Income (millions of dollars)		Total Assets (millions of dollars)		Return on Equity (percent)	
	1979	5-Yr. Grth./Yr. (percent)	1979	5-Yr. Grth./Yr. (percent)	1979	5-Yr. Grth./Yr. (percent)	1979	5-Yr. Average
1. **Global Marine, Inc.** Engages in contract offshore drilling, marine engineering and design; has interests in unproven oil, gas, and mineral properties; owns ships, jack-ups, and platforms; provides drilling, transportation services, and construction systems.	$ 155	10%	$ 21	68%	$ 360	20%	27%	10%
2. **Haliburton Co.** Provides diversified oil-field and engineering/construction services, including offshore drilling platforms.	7,766	17	377	14	3,923	17	18	22
3. **Hughes Tool Co.** World's largest manufacturer of drilling bits, used mainly in oil-well equipment (offshore platforms) and servicing.	805	23	85	18	982	27	18	17
4. **McDermott, Inc.** Provides oil industry with construction services, principally offshore production facilities.	3,283	31	88	− 13	3,301	34	6	20
5. **Newpark Resources, Inc.** Serves oil and gas industry by preparing drilling sites and manufacturing, selling, and leasing drilling equipment.	117	42	7	53	147	65	17	17
6. **Ocean Drilling and Exploration Co.** Owns world's largest fleet of offshore drilling barges; explores and produces oil and gas for its own account; and provides diving services.	407	21	53	10	927	13	16	14
7. **Deep Sea Engineering Co.**	406	11	49[c]	26	300	7	37	32

N.Av. = not available.
N.Ap. = not applicable.
[a]Total capital = Total assets − Current liabilities.
[b]At 6/27/80, long-term AAA Corp. bonds yielded 11 percent; AA bonds 11.5 percent; A bonds 12 percent; and BBB bonds 13 percent.
[c]Data shown reflect Deep Sea's pre-acquisition results for the period from 1974 to 1978. All numbers reflect pre-tax results.

Debt/Total Capital[a] (percent)		S&P Bond Ratings[b]	Effective Tax Rate (percent)		Common Shares Outstanding (millions)		Stock Price		Payout Ratio (percent)		P/E Ratio		Beta
1979	5-Yr. Average	1979	1979	5-Yr. Average	1979	5-Yr. Average	1979 Range	5-Yr. Range	1979	5-Yr. Average	1979	5-Yr. Average	1979
65%	68%	B	17%	20%	20	17	10¾–3½	10¾–1¾	2%	N.Ap.	10–3	10–4	1.55
11	15	AA	40	44	117	117	42½–29⅞	42½–19¼	29	19	13–9	13–9	1.20
27	17	A+	38	42	44	41	26⅞–13⅞	26⅞–9⅝	17	13	14–7	14–8	1.35
21	33	A	42	37	50	38	41¾–15⅞	41¾–14⅞	78	33	15–9	10–6	1.20
49	54	N.Av.	38	34	9	7	10⅝–4⅛	10⅝–1⅝	7	N.Ap.	14–5	10–4	1.60
34	38	N.Av.	64	44	50	49	22½–8½	22½–5⅞	19	11	21–8	17–10	1.30
16	32	N.Ap.	N.Ap.	N.Ap.	N.Ap.	N.Ap.	N.Ap.	N.Ap.	N.Ap.	N.Ap.	N.Ap.	N.Ap.	N.Ap.

Piedmont Transmission Co.

EXHIBIT 14

■

Alternative Cost of Equity Models

1. Dividend Valuation Model.

$$K = \frac{D_1}{P_0} + g,$$

where:

K = Estimated cost of equity
D_1 = Dividends/share at end of period 1
P_0 = Price/share at time 0
g = Dividend growth/year (with earnings growth often used as surrogate).

2. Earnings Price Ratio.

$$K = \frac{\text{earnings/share}}{\text{price/share}}.$$

3. Capital Asset Pricing Model.

$$K = R_f + \beta (R_m - R_f),$$

where:

K = Estimated cost of equity
R_f = Risk-free rate of return (This is often based on current Treasury bill rate. At 7/80, this figure was 6.5 percent.)
R_m = Expected market return (R_m less R_f has historically averaged 7 to 8 percent up to 7/80.)
β = Beta, the level of systematic risk associated with a given firm's stock.

Piedmont Transmission Co.

■

APPENDIX
Strategic Outlook for VSC Subsidiaries:[1] Dateline, 1980

1. Piedmont Transmission Co.—Oil-Distribution Industry

a. Description of Operations

PTC, originally founded in 1886, was acquired in 1964. It is one of the largest independent pipelines in the United States, operating about 4,400 miles of pipeline throughout the north and mideast. Close to 1 million barrels per day of petroleum products are transported through three product systems: (1) Refined Products Systems, 88 percent of 1979 revenues; (2) Crude Trunk System, 4 percent of 1979 revenues; and (3) Crude Gathering System, 4 percent of 1979 revenues.

PTC is a common carrier and conducts its business without the benefits of exclusive franchises from government entities or long-term customer contracts. (Most contracts are for 30 days.) It faces competition from barges, trucks, and other pipelines.

b. Industry Outlook

Demand for industry services in the 1980s is projected to grow at 1.5 percent per year. This growth rate is down from the 4 percent per year growth rates experienced during the 1960s and early 1970s. In light of this slow growth in primary demand, it is anticipated that there will continue to be tight competition among industry participants. Such competition, together with the federal government's continued regulation of industry profitability, is expected to keep overall returns down, although it also guarantees a certain minimum return to the industry.

Other factors affecting the industry's future profitability include (1) the continued availability and supply of crude oil and refined products for distribution; (2) governmental success in energy conservation programs and in the development of alternate energy sources; and (3) the possibility of increased or changing government regulation of the industry.

c. PTC's Outlook

PTC's position within the industry appears to be strong heading into the 1980s. PTC, which began operation in the late 1800s, is well-established within its market area and enjoys favorable relations with its shipping customers. The company has an impressive record of steadily rising revenues and earnings.

---

[1]Taken from "VSC's Outlook on the 80s," a presentation to the board of directors in July 1980.

These are expected to grow, largely because of management's continued tight control over costs.

PTC operates a large system of fixed assets. The majority of these are in good condition, requiring only minimum annual upkeep. The high financial costs and numerous environmental barriers associated with recreating a pipeline system comparable to PTC's make it extremely unlikely that any new competitors will enter the market in the near future.

2. Oceanview Corp.—Living/Leisure Industry

   a. Description of Operations

   Oceanview, a community and real-estate development company, handles residential, resort, commercial, and recreational properties. The company's major strategy is to develop communities that have a comprehensive master plan, architectural and land-use controls, recreational facilities, and other amenities that contribute to the quality of living or the overall resort experience. Oceanview also provides ancillary financial and real-estate services.

   Oceanview's projects are principally located in Florida and the southeast. In addition to properties already developed, Oceanview also owns 10,000 acres of choice Florida real estate and is holding it for future expansion.

   b. Industry Outlook

   The real-estate development market, while subject to the wide cyclical fluctuations of the general economy, is expected to remain strong in the southeast during the next 10 years. Demographic analyses project a population growth of 2.8 million people in Florida alone during this period. Housing will be required for this growth, and, given Florida's traditional emphasis on recreation and retirement facilities, the high demand for resort communities is expected to continue.

   The 1979 market was estimated at $1.4 billion. Competition within the resort/recreational segment is based on the amenities provided rather than on their prices. As a result, overall profitability is expected to continue to be strong.

   While Florida's total real-estate development industry is fragmented (at least 14 firms share the market), the planned resort community segment is much less so. The high costs associated with developing resort communities provide a significant barrier to entry, thus somewhat restricting competition and creating the potential for higher margins.

   c. Oceanview's Outlook

   Oceanview has the financial resources, the resort strategy, and the planning capability to grow at a rate faster than that projected for Florida as a whole. Oceanview's position as an acknowledged leader in the development and management of resort properties, together with its unique portfolio of prime real estate and operating properties, is expected to provide the basis for this growth.

3. Gambol Corp.—Recreation Industry

   a. Description of Operations

   Gambol operates seven major recreation/amusement centers in six states. Each center is located near a major metropolitan area and contains multi-interest activities ranging from thrill rides to restaurant facilities.

   b. Industry Outlook

   Future demand for services provided by the recreation industry will hinge on three factors: (1) future levels of personal discretionary income; (2) continued gasoline availability; and (3) the ability of industry competitors to continue satisfying consumer recreation/amusement needs. Continued high inflation as well as persistent gasoline shortages could have a significant negative effect on future demand.

Profitability within the amusement park segment is directly related to attendance. The high capital costs associated with both the centers' original construction and the biennial introduction of new rides make the centers extremely capital intensive.

Competition for the American public's recreation dollar is extremely tight and ranges from the $1 parking permit paid at the local park to the $5,000 paid for a seven-day trip to Bermuda. Recreation is an extremely fragmented, competitive market. There are, however, relatively few large amusement centers in the country. The high capital costs associated with their development imply that this will remain the case in the near future.

c. Gambol's Outlook

Only moderate growth is predicted for Gambol because of both the mature nature of certain of its parks and the necessity of continued high levels of capital investment. While Gambol's facilities are strategically located near major urban areas, it is anticipated that heavy advertising and marketing expenditures will be required to maintain high attendance.

In an effort to overcome the public's fears concerning gasoline availability, Gambol has installed retail gas pumps in all centers.

It should be noted that the principal factors affecting Gambol's attendance figures—inflation and gasoline availability—are also critical to the company's profitability. Profit margins at the centers have been subjected to significant squeezes, although management controls are expected to keep costs down in the near term.

4. Southwest Refinery Co.—Oil-Refining Industry

a. Description of Operations

Southwest Refinery Co., purchased by VSC in 1976, refines several petroleum products, principally asphalt. It is one of the largest producers of asphalt in the southwest.

b. Industry Outlook

The outlook for the oil-refining industry is only moderately favorable. Demand for refined petroleum products is expected to grow at a low 1.5 percent per year. Future demand for asphalt is difficult to project and will depend on both seasonal and cyclical factors. Asphalt is used principally by the construction industry, whose activity is determined by seasonal weather conditions as well as by national economic cycles.

In the past, federal entitlement programs have protected the independent refiners from both supply constraints and high crude oil costs.

Changing regulations have reduced this protection and resulted in higher costs. It is likely that profit margins will be reduced in the future as extreme industry competition precludes price increases as a means to pass the costs along.

c. SRC's Outlook

The outlook for SRC's current operations is only moderate. The demand for asphalt in the southwest is expected to continue growing steadily due to population increases expected in that area. Strategically, SRC is well-located to service this growth in demand. However, SRC's future profitability will be limited because of the aftereffects of price decontrols, extreme competition, and the nature of asphalt—that of a commodity.

There are 35 competitors within SRC's relevant market. Ten of these are major integrated oil companies with their own supply sources, refineries, and marketing facilities. Although competition is, consequently, very tight, the high capital costs associated with entering the market imply an absence of future entrants.

5. Deep Sea Engineering Co.—Oil-Services Industry

   a. Description of Operations

   Deep Sea, acquired by VSC in 1979, is the world's largest designer and producer of mobile, self-elevating, offshore oil rigs.

   b. Industry Outlook

   The demand for offshore oil drilling rigs is growing rapidly and is expected to continue strong throughout the 1980s. Demand for the rigs is directly related to continued high worldwide oil prices, continued uncertainties surrounding future oil and gas supplies, oil company exploration budgets, government lease sales of offshore properties, and retirement/casualty rates in the offshore rig fleet.

   The price sensitivity of rig customers is low. Competition among manufacturers is based primarily on reputation, quality, technological innovation, dependability, and service. As a result, the industry's profitability is attractive.

   The factors determining the industry's competitive structure also create a barrier to entry. There are currently only a few competitors active in the industry; new entrants are not anticipated.

   c. Deep Sea's Outlook

   Deep Sea's competitive position is believed to be strong because of its demonstrated strength in design and construction, its capability to service customers worldwide, and the fortuitous location of its production facilities on the Gulf of Mexico and in Singapore and Scotland. Deep Sea received 36 percent of the orders placed in 1979.

   Deep Sea's order backlog is anticipated to fill capacity through 1983. It is expected that capital expenditures will be required during the 1980s to handle additional growth.

6. Fuel Products Co.—Refined Products Marketing Industry

   a. Description of Operations

   Fuel Products Co. (FPC), acquired by VSC in 1979, markets liquid petroleum gas (LPG) retail in 27 states to almost 200,000 end consumers. In addition, it sells bulk LPG to commercial, agricultural, and industrial consumers; engages in LPG trading; and sells refined petroleum products to both wholesale and retail customers in those states served by PTC.

   b. Industry Outlook

   Demand for LPG is expected to increase in the 1980s, primarily because of the government's efforts to reduce domestic reliance on imported oil. It is expected that LPG will become increasingly financially competitive with other energy sources as price controls are lifted on them by the federal government. Additionally, it is anticipated that the supply of LPG will increase and keep pace with the rises in demand.

   Both the costs and prices of LPG are currently regulated by the government. While industry margins are relatively low, they are fairly constant and offer an attractive return on the capital invested.

   The industry's market has, historically, been very fragmented, with 5,000 dealers nationwide vying for the estimated $3 billion worth of business. There is a current trend toward consolidation in the industry. The smaller firms are dropping out of the market as a result of the increasing costs of federal regulation. Additionally, the integrated oil companies are consolidating their operations in their major geographic markets. As a result of these trends, various geographic areas are opening up, creating additional markets for the medium-sized firms.

c.   FPC's Outlook

FPC has high hopes for the 1980s. By taking advantage of the current trend toward industry consolidation, FPC plans to become a major national marketer of LPG and related products. It is anticipated that FPC's current market area (primarily the Midwest, which accounts for 55 percent of the nation's LPG demand) will provide a strong base from which to expand. FPC has demonstrated its ability to operate within the industry's tight regulatory environment. As a result, the regulatory costs associated with expansion are not expected to be onerous.

Omni Services, Incorporated

This was not the first time someone had shown an interest in buying Omni Services, Inc., a rental linen service headquartered in Culpeper, Virginia. In 1975, a Minnesota firm offered to buy the Omni stock and to pay for it with notes, but Omni's major shareholders objected to holding notes of the other company. Since then, other offers had been rejected. Each time, the major shareholders had expressed concern over the strength of the potential purchaser or the terms of the offer: those making the offers were either too small, had too much debt, or were in a different line of business. But now, the interest of Jean Leducq, the owner of The Société Générale de Location et Services Textiles (Textiles), a large, strong French firm that was also in the rental linen business, seemed more promising. Mr. Leducq was considering buying a majority interest in Omni, with his eventual ownership position to reach two-thirds or better.

Although there had been considerable correspondence and many visits by Textiles employees, Mr. Leducq himself had never visited Omni's headquarters until mid-April. Now he was in the midst of meeting the Omni management and visiting the Culpeper plant. Knowing that Mr. Leducq had engaged a New York firm to value Omni's closely held stock, N. B. Martin, Omni's founder and president, was sure the Frenchman was serious about his proposal. In preparation for the visit, Mr. Martin had asked Omni's comptroller, Larry Thomson, to determine a fair price for a majority of Omni's stock and to consider a method that could be used now to place a price on the remaining shares for sale in 1985.

OMNI SERVICES, INC.

Omni Services, Inc. was a holding company for the 12 companies listed in Exhibit 1. Each of the subsidiaries was called Rental Uniform Service and was located in the eastern United States. Firms like Omni were traditionally considered to be part of the industrial laundry business, but the industry had recently become known as textile lessors.

The industrial laundry business was fragmented. Multidivisional firms that manufactured, rented, and laundered garments were in direct competition with local businesses that bought their uniforms and serviced their customers in a

This case was prepared as a basis for class discussion rather than to illustrate either effective or ineffective handling of an administrative situation. Copyright © 1984 by the Darden Graduate Business School Sponsors, University of Virginia, Charlottesville, Virginia.

limited geographical area. Many of Omni's major competitors were closely held, and little financial information was available about those operations. Of the firms that were public, the five described in Exhibits 2 and 3 were most similar to Omni.

Mr. Martin had learned about the business while working for an industrial laundry in Cincinnati, Ohio. In 1954, he went into partnership with his father-in-law to operate a small ($2,000 per week volume) uniform rental business in Roanoke, Virginia. In partnership with his father-in-law, he opened the Culpeper plant in 1959, and Mr. Martin moved to Culpeper to operate it. It was quickly successful, and sales had grown at a rate of 20 percent almost every year since its founding. The only thing that seemed to stem growth of that operation had been a plant fire in 1974.

By 1968, Mr. Martin had started new operations in Hanover, Pennsylvania, and Morgantown, West Virginia. The three plants, each called Rental Uniform Service (RUS), were separately incorporated. Even though the shareholders and board members were virtually identical, the Internal Revenue Service had treated them as separate entities, and the combined taxes were thus somewhat lower. By 1972, nine RUSs had been added, the separate incorporation tax advantages had disappeared, and the 11 separate operations had become subsidiaries of the newly formed Omni Services, Inc.

Omni supplied industrial uniforms to 75,000 people. Four days a week, a total of 150 trucks left the plants operated by Omni's 12 Rental Uniform Services. Each day every truck had an established route in a nearby metropolitan area. The driver stopped at such places as service stations, garages, and automobile dealerships to deliver six prepackaged shirts and trousers for each employee. Since employees needed specific sizes, the shirts and trousers delivered were the same as those that the driver had picked up the previous week. The employees' names, and often the names of the companies, were stitched on the shirts. The soiled uniforms were returned to the plant for washing or dry cleaning and mending. In addition, Omni provided executive garments for office and management personnel, shop towels, walk mats, fender covers, and linen roll towels.

Most of Omni's business was in large metropolitan areas, and 11 of its 12 subsidiaries were located on the fringes of those areas. For example, the largest and oldest operation, the plant in Culpeper, served the Washington, D.C. area, as well as several less populated areas—Culpeper, Charlottesville, and Lynchburg, Virginia. While these nonmetropolitan processing plants tended to increase transportation time and costs, Mr. Martin had always believed their locations allowed them to attract employees that were more dependable and productive than the more transient and higher-paid city worker. Mr. Martin thought much of Omni's success came from the edge loyal employees gave the firm.

Over the years Omni had been innovative in managing these employees. By 1971, a four-day work week had been instituted. In 1975, Omni was the first firm of any size in Virginia to offer an employee stock ownership plan (ESOP), a kind of profit-sharing plan in which Omni stock was purchased and held in trust for each employee. None of Omni's 600 employees belonged to a union.

Omni had a total of 48 investors, although three were of primary importance: N. B. Martin, the founder, president, and chairman of the board, with 56 percent of the stock; T. Y. Martin, N. B.'s brother, Omni's secretary–treasurer, and president of the Culpeper RUS, who held 23 percent; and the Omni ESOP with 12.5 percent.

Mr. Martin was quite pleased with Omni's present position. Except for the time of the 1974 Culpeper plant fire, when destroyed uniforms had to be replaced and Washington, D.C. laundry and dry cleaning had to be trucked to Hanover, Pennsylvania and back, the firm had prospered and grown. Exhibits 4 and 5 summarize Omni's operations over the previous 7 years. Compared with the other rental uniform services shown in Exhibits 2 and 3, Omni had reason to be proud. The industry average profit before taxes was about 5.5 percent, while Omni's was almost double that figure. Even with this past success, Mr. Martin had begun to plan changes for Omni's future.

Mr. Martin wanted to be less involved in the daily operations and concentrate more on the future for the firm. As a first step, he had in 1978 appointed two regional managers to oversee the 12 individual RUS managers.

In the fall of 1979, Mr. Martin had put together a 5-year plan for Omni with the following goals:

1. Double profits by 1984
2. Double sales by 1984
3. Reduce the debt-to-equity ratio substantially

Capital would be reinvested in new services, except for the following planned dividend payments and annual contributions to the ESOP of 7 to 10 percent of the payroll.

	1980	1981	1982	1983	1984
Total dividends	$216,000	$240,000	$264,000	$288,000	$336,000
Dividends per share	0.36	0.40	0.44	0.48	0.56
Payout ratio (estimated)	14.8%	14.3%	13.5%	12.7%	12.8%

Two other goals, subject to yearly revision, had been spelled out by Omni management:

1. The formation of two or three new RUSs by 1984

2. The potential acquisition of one or two industrial laundries with annual sales of $500,000 to $2 million by 1984

If the possibility of selling or merging the firm developed, Mr. Martin stated, "We will examine any serious offer made to us during the next 5 years. . . . [But] at this time, we do not plan to seek out buyers."

Before the 5-year plan could be formally reviewed and approved by Omni's board in January 1980, the contact with Textiles had been established.

THE TEXTILES OFFER

In September 1979, Mr. Martin had received a letter from an old friend, the president of Workwear, Inc., which manufactured uniforms and until 1976 had been in the rental business. The two men had known each other through the Textile Rental Services Association, a trade group. The letter to Mr. Martin had introduced Jean Leducq, the owner of Textiles, the largest linen supply company in France. One-third of Textiles' $120 million in sales came from the rental of linen roll towels. Mr. Leducq, the letter said, would like to talk to Mr. Martin about the possibility of a merger.

By mid-October, Mr. Leducq's nephew and heir apparent, Christian Colas, a 40-year-old ex-test pilot and Stanford MBA, had visited several of Omni's plants with two other Textiles employees. While in the United States, the trio had also visited other industrial laundry firms. Textiles was obviously serious about investing in a U.S. firm in the rental uniform or industrial laundry business.

When Mr. Martin visited several of Textiles' operations in France in November, he was treated royally. He and Mr. Leducq had talked at length about the differences between the U.S. and French industrial laundry businesses. Mr. Leducq believed that the rental uniform market in France was about where the U.S. market had been in the early 1950s—quite a different business from what it was today.

Up to the late 1940s, U.S. launderers would wait outside the gates of manufacturing plants so they could collect the heavily soiled garments of the workers. These garments were laundered, often in crude processing facilities, and returned several days later. Family laundries and linen supply companies were uninterested in processing heavily soiled garments, and since there were few home washers, housewives were happy to rid themselves of this task. In the late 1940s, the firms found that they could purchase work garments at wholesale prices, add a laundering charge, and still compete with the nonrental laundries handling these garments. In addition, the rental laundry operations could schedule production more efficiently, adding a further cost advantage.

By 1980, 95 percent of the industry's U.S. sales volume was in the rental business. In contrast, about 50 percent of the French market sales were in uniform rentals. Textiles predominantly supplied linens to hotels, hospitals, and restaurants—a very competitive, low-profit business. Mr. Leducq considered uniform rental to hold great promise in France. Furthermore, he believed Textiles' skill in the roll towel business might be useful to Omni, which had little expertise in linen towel sales.

Mr. Martin had carefully explained Omni's relations with its employees to Mr. Leducq and Mr. Colas. He had taken care to explain exactly what the ESOP was and why the firm had started it. He emphasized that he thought the ESOP was very important to the employees and served to make them more involved and committed to Omni. Mr. Leducq had stated that if Textiles did buy a majority of Omni's stock, they would want to set the maximum ESOP ownership at 25 percent of the stock. Although Mr. Martin had briefly mentioned a per share price "in the thirties," the discussion of price had gone little further.

Mr. Leducq said he would want assurances from Mr. Martin that he and the rest of Omni management would stay. Since Mr. Martin would continue to operate Omni as he had in the past, Mr. Martin could offer management contracts to current Omni managers if he wished—it was up to him. Mr. Leducq also wanted assurances that Mr. Martin would continue to operate the business as had been planned: seeking new businesses, and making the capital investment outlays and dividend payments detailed in the 5-year plan.

After Mr. Martin's return from France, he had talked with the other shareholders, Omni management, and the board of directors. One board member recalled that when his firm had been sold 10 years earlier, the buyer had moved right in and taken over. Several years later, after the firm had deteriorated, he had managed to repurchase it and recover the lost business. He then sold it once again 3 years previously, but the circumstances were different. He kept his job; the new owners were investors and not interested in managing the firm. In fact, they seldom even came to Culpeper; he ran the business and also had the cash from the sale. He noted that the same sort of thing had happened to a rental uniform business in Roanoke, Virginia. The ex-owner said the new owner moved right in and "made monkeys of us." The key to success, they all agreed, would be very little operating interference by Textiles' management. Mr. Martin told them that he felt sure that Mr. Leducq had no intention of actively managing Omni.

By mid-March, Mr. Martin felt sure that most of the details could be worked out. Mr. Leducq wanted him to sign a 5-year management contract. Mr. Martin had toyed with the idea of looking for a new challenge, but he wasn't ready to leave the company entirely. He liked the idea of being the CEO of a $20-million business, having the company airplane at his disposal, and being needed by the business. On the other hand, selling some of his stock would provide enough cash to allow him to pay off all his debts, including the mortgage on the new house he was building. Taking Textiles' offer seemed ideal, but the price of the stock had yet to be resolved.

Mr. Leducq had proposed that Textiles purchase 51 percent of Omni's shares in 1980. In 1985, Textiles would make an additional purchase of 90,000 shares, bringing its total ownership position to 66 percent. Of the remaining shares, up to 170,000 more could be sold to Textiles in 1985 at the previously agreed price, if any shareholder wished to sell.

Because this agreement would spread the purchase over 5 years, the French government required that Textiles show the ability to honor the contract by pledging stock or having a line of credit for the full amount of the contractual obligation. Thus, Textiles would have to secure the current price plus whatever it agreed to pay for additional shares in 1985 before the initial purchase.

The 1985 price would be determined by a formula worked out during the current negotiations. Mr. Leducq's objective was to limit his obligation, and hence the amount of security required by the French government, until 1985. Thus he wanted a maximum 1985 price established, regardless of the formula outcome. Since the initial understanding was that the shares necessary to make up the purchase would be solicited from all other shareholders first, with Mr. Martin selling only enough shares to reach the 306,000-share, 51-percent total, Mr. Martin wanted a floor price set, below which the 1985 price would not drop.

Mr. Leducq had engaged Hudson Securities, a New York firm, to value Omni's shares and devise the formula for pricing the remaining shares in 1985. Their report had been expected in time for the April 11 visit to Culpeper. That visit, Mr. Martin had expected, would resolve all remaining questions—except price. The price was to be negotiated later by Mr. Martin, Omni's comptroller Mr. Thomson, and a team composed of people from Hudson Securities and Textiles. In preparation for the pricing meeting, Mr. Thomson asked a consultant who had valued Omni's ESOP shares in the past for a valuation of the Omni stock. That report was to be completed on April 14.

MR. LEDUCQ'S APRIL 11 VISIT

On April 11, Mr. Martin, Mr. Leducq, and Mr. Thomson spent the afternoon visiting the Culpeper plant. Mr. Martin wanted to return the courtesy he had been shown during his visit to France, and it looked like they had succeeded.

The talk, for the most part, centered around how Omni's Culpeper operation differed from the uniform rental business in France. As the day wore on, Mr. Leducq had gotten more and more excited about the prospects of Textiles aggressively expanding into uniform rental, which was Omni's strength.

As the men returned to Omni's headquarters, the tone of the conversation changed. Before, it had been process, market, and growth. Now it was merger. Hudson Securities, however, had been dragging their heels. Already they had broken two appointments. Mr. Martin and Mr. Thomson knew that the valuation would drag on for some time when Mr. Leducq blurted out: "N. B., what's your lowest price? We want this merger to be amicable; we want the company to continue just like it is with you at the head. We don't want you or your employees dissatisfied. But we don't want to feel we've paid too much for the company, either. Give me your lowest price and the 1985 range. We will either agree right now, or we will drop our talks of merger and I'll leave this afternoon."

Omni Services, Incorporated

EXHIBIT 1
■
Location of Omni Subsidiaries

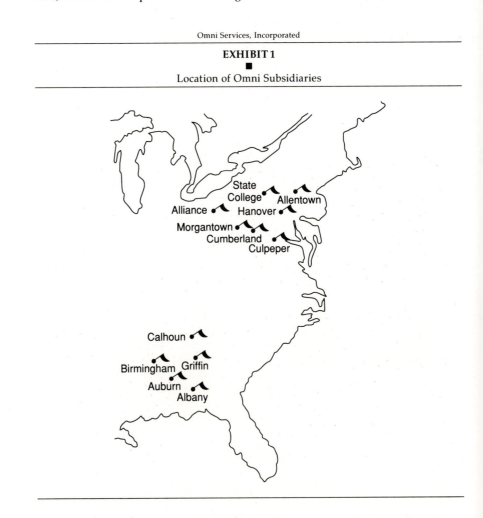

Omni Services, Incorporated

EXHIBIT 2
■

Similar Rental Uniform Service Firms

Unitog manufactured, rented, and sold heavy-duty, soil-resistant uniforms for service-station employees, route drivers, and salesmen. Rental business operated out of nine locations and comprised 38 percent of revenues. Headquarters in Kansas City, Missouri. Approximately 420 stockholders and 2,189 employees.

Rentex provided laundry and rental services, linen-supply services, and dust-control services through nine facilities. Rentals comprised 100 percent of revenues. There were 640 stockholders and 950 employees. Headquarters in Philadelphia, Pennsylvania.

Means Services provided textile maintenance services by rental to businesses in midwestern states, with a concentration on providing work garments, industrial wiping cloths, dust-control textiles, bed and table linens, towels, aprons, uniforms, and continuous towel cabinets. The rental business was 100 percent of its revenue. It had 25 processing plants, 2,718 stockholders, and 3,900 employees. Headquarters in Chicago, Illinois.

Servisco manufactured, rented, and laundered work clothes and uniforms, machine-wiping towels, fender covers, and linens. It also provided contract building maintenance, housekeeping consultant services, and guard (security) services. Its main office was in Hillside, New Jersey, and it operated through 27 full-service rental plants. There were 1,501 stockholders and 6,300 employees.

National Service Industries obtained 26 percent of revenues from renting table linen, bed linen, operating-room packs, towels, uniforms, and dust-control materials, but lighting equipment and chemical products were also manufactured. NSI was further diversified into insulation service, men's apparel, envelopes, furniture marketing services, safety products, furniture leasing, and amusement parks. NSI headquarters were in Atlanta, Georgia, and it had 10,994 stockholders and 19,200 employees.

Omni Services, Incorporated

EXHIBIT 3

∎

Financial Data—Similar Rental Uniform Service Firms

	5-Year Growth in After-Tax Net Profit	5-Year Growth in Revenues	Current Ratio	1978-1979 Growth in Net Worth	Net Profit on Sales	Debt to Common Equity	EPS	Dividend Payout Ratio	Average Yield	Book Value per Share	Return on Common Equity	Sales (in millions)	P/E Ratio	Percent of Sales in Laundry
Omni	27.2%	19.2%	1.5	17.8%	6.1%	35.6%	$2.05	15.6%	N.Av.	$11.48	17.9%	$ 20.0	N.Av.	99%
Rentex	6.6	8.6	1.7	3.9	2.0	60.0	0.60	32.9	4.5%	15.33	5.5	30.7	6.0	100
Servisco	20.4	8.4	3.7	9.3	3.7	29.5	1.60	24.0	5.9	11.84	11.6	92.4	4.0	57
Means Services	10.2	7.0	2.0	5.6	4.4	2.6	2.95	41.0	6.3	25.22	11.0	113.6	6.5	100
NSI	11.8	8.4	2.4	14.4	5.6	5.4	3.12	33.0	5.9	16.48	19.8	708.1	6.0	26
Unitog	(2.8)	10.2	2.9	9.6	3.0	37.6	3.12	26.0	5.3	29.80	10.6	56.4	5.0	38

N.Av. = not available.

Omni Services, Incorporated

EXHIBIT 4
■
Statements of Consolidated Income and Retained Earnings,
Years Ending December 31 (thousands of dollars, except per share data)

	1973	1974	1975	1976	1977	1978	1979	First Quarter 1980
Operating revenues	$7,048	$8,383	$10,247	$12,467	$15,008	$16,785	$20,178	$5,493
Costs and expenses								
Cost of products and plant operations	3,609	4,587	5,231	6,677	7,799	8,738	10,898	2,866
Selling and delivery	1,291	1,610	2,040	2,450	3,092	3,350	3,930	1,051
General and administrative	947	1,243	1,483	1,804	2,129	2,476	3,038	859
Total costs and expenses	5,847	7,440	8,754	10,931	13,020	14,564	17,866	4,776
Income from operations	1,201	943	1,493	1,536	1,988	2,221	2,312	717
Other income (expense)	(102)	(317)	(89)	(117)	(224)	(215)	(242)	0
Income before taxes	1,099	626	1,404	1,419	1,764	2,006	2,070	717
Provision for income taxes	543	293	669	653	784	956	840	315
Income before extraordinary item	556	333	735	766	980	1,050	1,230	402
Extraordinary item	27	37	19	0	0	0	0	0
Net income	$ 583	$ 370	754	$ 766	$ 980	$ 1,050	$ 1,230	$ 402
Less: Dividends paid	$ 96	$ 96	$ 132	$ 144	$ 150	$ 168	$ 192	$ 48
Plus: Retained earnings, beginning of year	1,530	2,017	1,291	2,913	3,535	4,365	5,247	6,285
Retained earnings, end of year[a]	2,017	2,291	2,913	3,535	4,365	5,247	6,285	6,639
Per Share Data								
Income before extraordinary item	$ 0.93	$ 0.56	$ 1.23	$ 1.28	$ 1.63	$ 1.75	$ 2.05	$ 0.67
Extraordinary item	0.04	0.06	0.03	0	0	0	0	0
Net income	0.97	0.62	1.26	1.28	1.63	1.75	2.05	0.67
Dividends	0.16	0.16	0.22	0.24	0.25	0.28	0.32	0.08

[a]Does not include common stock account, but does include the $6,930 paid-in surplus.

Omni Services, Incorporated

EXHIBIT 5
■
Consolidated Balance Sheets, Years Ending December 31 (thousands of dollars)

	1973	1974	1975	1976	1977	1978	1979
Assets							
Cash	$ 222	$ 859	$ 968	$ 686	$ 781	$ 619	$ 824
Accounts receivable	478	604	729	819	978	1,152	1,464
Due from employees	9	22	21	18	4	6	4
Income taxes refundable	23	69	0	54	0	0	0
Inventory	456	485	468	719	531	804	646
Prepaid expenses	22	39	40	53	66	104	101
Total current assets	1,210	2,078	2,226	2,349	2,360	2,685	3,039
Land	154	154	154	334	387	524	581
Buildings	1,604	1,262	1,857	2,727	3,470	3,760	4,396
Equipment	2,717	2,472	3,134	3,969	4,913	5,842	7,688
Aircraft	104	104	104	416	434	544	544
Total plant, property, and equipment	4,579	3,992	5,249	7,446	9,204	10,670	13,209
Less: Accumulated depreciation	1,507	1,368	1,801	2,330	3,042	3,903	4,897
Net plant, property, and equipment	3,072	2,624	3,448	5,116	6,162	6,767	8,312
Goodwill	346	310	274	246	207	168	130
Noncompetition agreements	424	330	236	172	59	0	0
Other assets	10	16	7	10	17	22	31
Total other	780	656	517	428	283	190	161
Total assets	$5,062	$5,358	$6,191	$7,893	$8,805	$9,642	$11,512
Liabilities and Stockholders' Equity							
Accounts payable	330	468	251	410	317	518	617
Current portion of long-term debt	235	248	270	516	542	567	623
Accrued salaries and wages	75	102	179	129	154	174	231
Other accrued expenses	50	59	315	356	348	398	481
Income taxes payable	13	12	357	33	109	201	108
Total current liabilities	703	889	1,372	1,444	1,470	1,858	2,060
Long-term debt	1,742	1,482	1,215	2,212	2,244	1,813	2,452
Deferred income taxes	0	96	91	102	126	124	115
Stockholders' equity (3,000,000 shares authorized of $1 par value; 600,000 shares outstanding)	600	600	600	600	600	600	600
Retained earnings	2,017	2,291	2,913	3,535	4,365	5,247	6,285
Total stockholders' equity	2,617	2,891	3,513	4,135	4,965	5,847	6,885
Total liabilities and stockholders' equity	$5,062	$5,358	$6,191	$7,893	$8,805	$9,642	$11,512

Cities Service Company

The directors of Occidental Petroleum Corporation met early in the second week of August 1982 to discuss a potential acquisition. In an attempt to stave off an unfriendly takeover by corporate raiders at a low market price, Cities Service Company (Cities), a petroleum and chemicals manufacturer, had approached several oil, chemical, and heavy industry companies to determine whether any might be interested in acquiring Cities. Occidental Petroleum was attracted to the company, so this meeting of the board was called to discuss whether Occidental should make a bid for Cities, and if so, at what price.[1]

THE PETROLEUM INDUSTRY

The petroleum industry had been in a state of flux since the mid-1970s, when the Organization of Petroleum Exporting Countries (OPEC) first exerted its power. Prices rose from about $8 per barrel in 1974 to over $35 in 1982, causing the industrialized West to scramble to improve industrial and automotive efficiency. The increased prices often squeezed oil-company profit margins, as firms fought for business. Petroleum companies were caught between the whims of OPEC, which could shift world oil prices by altering production quotas, and lower relative demand on the part of increasingly cost-conscious and energy-efficient industrial and household consumers. The overall state of the economy also played a large part in determining the demand for petroleum products. A recession meant decreased industrial production, less construction, less driving, and more efficient energy use in the home. Petroleum production and price data are shown in Exhibit 1.

In 1982, the petroleum industry was suffering through what was hoped would be the end of the recession. A tight U.S. money supply, high government spending leading to record budget deficits, high unemployment, and increased crude-oil prices had combined to reduce petroleum demand. Although oil was a necessity, and demand was therefore very price-inelastic, a price hike and lower demand meant trouble for the industry as competitors cut profit margins to gain

---

[1]*The Wall Street Journal,* August 16, 1982, 7.

This case was prepared as a basis for class discussion rather than to illustrate either effective or ineffective handling of an administrative situation. Copyright © 1986 by the Darden Graduate Business School Sponsors, University of Virginia, Charlottesville, Virginia.

business. A 48-percent price increase occurred in 1980, followed by a 44-percent increase in 1981. U.S. demand fell 8 percent and 6 percent over the same period.

Bad omens for the U.S. oil market had actually appeared in 1978. Housing starts in the United States fell from an annualized peak of 2.1 million at one point in 1978 to 900,000 at one point in early 1982, meaning lower growth in the demand for heating oil. Over the same period, automobile sales dropped from 11.8 million to 7.0 million on an annualized basis.

In 1980, industrial usage accounted for 39 percent of oil demand, residential usage for 33 percent, and transportation for 28 percent. Greater efficiency in all three areas was eroding demand, however. By 1982, industry required 38 percent less oil per unit of production than it had in 1974. Between 1972 and 1982, residential demand fell 8 percent. Given the increased efficiency of automobiles, it was expected that by 1990, a given number of gallons would fuel a car for 43 percent more miles than in 1981.

Given this scenario, by 1990 industrial demand as a percentage of total demand for oil was expected to drop 7 percentage points to 32 percent; residential use was projected to fall 1 percentage point to 32 percent, as households replaced old, inefficient furnaces. This trend left 36 percent of total demand, an increase of 8 percentage points, to be taken up by the increasingly efficient transportation market. In short, if total petroleum demand was to increase, GNP growth would have to be strong, and more automobiles would have to be driven further.

Demand for petroleum had fallen over 5 percent in the first half of 1982 from the same period the previous year. Between 50 percent and 70 percent of this decline was considered to be the result of the recession rather than conservation. Crude-oil stocks were at record high levels—the sign of an oil glut. Operating margins within the industry had fallen from 19.0 percent in 1979 to 14.3 percent in 1981. The industry's net profit margin fell from 7.5 percent to 4.9 percent over the same period.[2]

Any hope for the sagging petroleum industry lay in two areas: improvement in the world economy and OPEC cooperation. A looser money supply was expected to spur economic recovery in the United States between the second and third quarters of 1983. Housing starts and auto sales were projected to rise, which would increase petroleum demand and could decrease stocks and increase prices. A recovery in the oil industry required OPEC's support of prices, but OPEC would have to control its production to eliminate the oil glut.

THE CHEMICAL INDUSTRY

The chemical industry was also suffering as a result of the recession. As shown in Exhibit 2, industry earnings in the first half of 1982 were off 34 percent from the first half of 1981. The length of the economic recession was blamed for the worst profit drop and lowest margins in decades. Capital spending as a percentage of chemical sales had declined for almost 7 straight years and was expected to fall again in 1983. Some industry economists believed that an upturn would begin in the third quarter of 1982, but most held to a more pessimistic view:

---

[2]All figures are from *Business Week*, November 8, 1982, 32–33; *World Oil*, October 1982, 118–133; and *Value Line Investment Survey*.

Even if the rosier view prevails and economic recovery begins soon, it will take some time to make itself felt in the chemical industry. The problem is that industries such as textiles, autos, and construction—leading chemical outlets—remain depressed, with little relief in sight. These industries are at their lowest levels in years, and even if they stir slightly, upturns will take time to restore chemicals to normal earnings.[3]

OCCIDENTAL PETROLEUM CORPORATION

Occidental, steered by its indefatigable 83-year-old chairman, Armand Hammer, started on its present course in 1957 when Dr. Hammer forsook medicine for a 10-percent stake and managerial control of a tiny oil exploration company. By 1981, Occidental was the 13th largest oil company in the country, with a net worth of $3.5 billion and sales approaching $15 billion, as shown in Exhibits 3 and 4. Exhibits 5 through 7 provide comparative company and industry data. The company was primarily a producer and marketer of crude oil and natural gas, but it also had large chemical, coal, and agribusiness operations, as shown in Exhibit 8.

Dr. Hammer was concerned about the fact that 75 percent of Occidental's oil and gas operations, with assets totaling $3.6 billion, were in countries outside of North America, primarily the United Kingdom, Libya, Peru, and Bolivia. Exhibits 9 and 10 provide information on the company's holdings of developed and undeveloped acreage and productive oil and gas wells around the world. Occidental was interested in increasing its U.S. operations in order to diversify and decrease risk. "We're pretty well set overseas, but not much domestically. Here's a chance, overnight, to achieve some balance. In fact, if this [Cities Service acquisition] goes through, we'll be two-thirds domestic and just one-third foreign," said Dr. Hammer.[4]

Occidental's nonenergy operations were also extensive. Through its subsidiary, Hooker Chemical Corporation, Occidental manufactured a variety of industrial chemicals, plastics, metal-finishing, and agricultural chemical products, both domestically and abroad. Hooker Chemical had received notoriety, however, through litigation stemming from its toxic waste dump near Love Canal in Niagara, New York. Occidental's Island Creek Coal, Inc. owned 21 active bituminous coal mines in Kentucky, West Virginia, and Virginia, 5 inactive mines, and 3 mines under development. Occidental was involved in agribusiness through its ownership of Iowa Beef Processors, Inc., the largest beef packer in the country, and Zoecon Corporation, a manufacturer of tick and flea collars, insect foggers, and roach traps. Shadow Isle, Inc., a purebred cattle breeder, was also an Occidental subsidiary.

CITIES SERVICE COMPANY

Cities Service Company, the 19th largest oil producer in the country, was similar to Occidental in many ways. The company's most important lines of business

---

[3]"Chemical Company Earnings Continue Plunge," *Chemical and Engineering News,* August 8, 1982, 15.

[4]*The Wall Street Journal,* August 16, 1982, 7.

were its integrated oil and natural-gas operations, but it was also involved in the production of industrial chemicals and minerals. The most important difference between the two companies, in Dr. Hammer's eyes, was Cities' extensive holdings of domestic acreage devoted to oil and gas exploration and production. (Exhibits 11 through 19 provide the company's financial statements and selected notes.) Of Cities' oil production, 73 percent was in the United States—a high figure relative to the industry average, as shown in Exhibit 11. Cities produced about half of its petroleum needs and purchased the rest on the open market.

Exhibit 14 details the financial results for each of Cities' divisions over the previous 3 years. Poor operating performance in 1981 was caused by low margins in downstream petroleum operations (especially in Citgo, Cities' marketing arm), by reduced demand for natural gas, and by low copper prices. Oil and gas exploration and production profits had increased, however, in spite of higher exploration costs, because of higher prices for crude oil and natural gas.

The loss of $49 million in 1981 was a result of both poor operating performance and a one-time after-tax write-off of $290 million from the company's discontinued plastics operation. Similar economic conditions led to a reported 17-percent decrease in second-quarter 1982 earnings from continuing operations, down to $74.4 million or 95 cents per share. This decrease caused net income for the first 6 months of the year to drop to $127.7 million or $1.64 per share, down 14 percent from the same period in 1981.

Cities Service had been both the object and instigator of much takeover speculation for several months. On May 31, 1982, Mesa Petroleum, chaired by T. Boone Pickens, offered Cities $50 per share. Mesa already owned 5.3 percent of the company's stock, but wanted at least 51 percent. Mesa was thought to want to increase its domestic reserves. Some analysts also believed that Mr. Pickens was unhappy:

> . . . [with] the marginal costs of carrying more than a three-million-share position in Cities Service that was purchased at a cost estimated at $10 a share higher than the current market price. Mr. Pickens is said to be eager to get something—almost anything—going, to put Cities Service on the selling block so that he can get out of that big investment.[5]

Cities' management, in turn, offered $17 per share for at least 51 percent of Mesa's stock. On June 2 and 3, the companies filed countersuits, each claiming fraudulent behavior and stock price manipulation on the part of the other. Within a week, Mesa made a lower, unfriendly open-market offer of $45 per share for 15 percent of Cities (hoping that far more shares would be tendered), and Cities made a friendly offer of $21 per share for 52 percent of Mesa. Some Wall Street analysts believed Cities may have been interested in selling itself to another company for more than $50 per share if it was unable to escape a takeover by Mesa in any other way. The management of Cities Service had tired of dealing with the specter of Mr. Pickens: "Sometimes I feel like I'm doing battle with P. T. Barnum," said Cities' Chairman Charles Waidelich.[6]

On June 17, Gulf Oil, acting as a white knight, offered $63 per share ($4.8 billion) for Cities. The Federal Trade Commission (FTC) temporarily blocked the

---

[5]*The Wall Street Journal,* May 28, 1982, 4.

[6]*The Wall Street Journal,* June 11, 1982, 14.

acquisition on antitrust grounds, however. The FTC needed time to study possible complications regarding regional concentration in gasoline distribution, jet-fuel production and distribution, and pipeline transportation. On August 7, 1982, having reconsidered its options, Gulf withdrew its bid under the banner of antitrust problems, leaving Cities Service to fend for itself.

By August 10, the remaining six of the large "Seven Sisters" oil companies, as well as several chemical, heavy industry, and other petroleum companies, had been approached by Cities Service through the investment banking firms of First Boston Corp. and Lehman Brothers Kuhn Loeb, Inc. in its attempt to find a friendly buyer. Cities intimated that, if it was unable to find a suitable buyer, it might liquidate its assets, which it considered a better option than leaving itself open to a corporate raider at a price per share in the low- to mid-20s.[7]

Over the previous several months, Cities Service's stock prices had risen and fallen with the company's fortunes in the acquisition market, as shown in Exhibit 6.

CONCLUSION

Now, on August 12, 1982, Occidental's managers knew that they would have to decide and act quickly. Cities Service had approached quite a few firms in its search for a buyer, and Occidental did not want the rug pulled out from under it before it was able to make a decision. On the surface, the acquisition seemed intelligent: Cities' domestic operations would offset Occidental's reliance on overseas production of oil and natural gas. For this reason, antitrust problems were not expected to be an issue, even though the acquisition would make Occidental the eighth largest oil company in the country.

Cities' mining and chemicals operations were of some concern, however. At issue was the question of whether they could be managed profitably or sold at reasonable prices; some believed that Occidental considered the latter option preferable, if it were possible.[8] For now, the decision whether to buy Cities Service depended largely on Occidental managers' ability to settle on a fair price. In light of recent events and Cities' apparent anxiety over finding a friendly buyer, what price would Cities' management be likely accept, should Occidental make such an offer, and how should the company pay for the acquisition if it materialized?

---

[7]*The Wall Street Journal,* August 11, 1982, 2.
[8]*The Wall Street Journal,* August 16, 1982, 7; *Business Week,* August 30, 1982, 23.

Cities Service Company

EXHIBIT 1
■
Petroleum Production Data (millions of barrels)

	Petroleum Producer Price Index (1967 = 100)	U.S. Crude-Oil Production	Crude-Oil Stocks	U.S. Demand, All Oils
1970	106.1	3,517.4	276.4	5,458.9
1971	113.2	3,453.9	259.6	5,634.4
1972	113.8	3,455.4	246.4	6,071.7
1973	126.0	3,360.9	242.5	6,401.7
1974	211.8	3,202.6	265.0	6,158.7
1975	245.7	3,056.8	271.4	6,033.9
1976	253.6	2,976.2	285.5	6,472.3
1977	274.2	3,009.3	347.7[a]	6,816.1
1978	300.1	3,178.2	376.3	7,011.1
1979	376.5	3,121.3	430.3	6,928.9
1980	556.4	3,146.4	482.9	6,441.7
1981	803.5	3,128.6	593.8	6,078.1
1982 1	787.2	263.8	606.2	525.5
2	770.3	243.7	613.0	470.5
3	744.8	268.7	609.2	509.7
4	717.9	257.7	610.4	505.0
5	717.8	269.2	609.5	485.2
6	718.2	259.4	608.3	471.0
7	718.4	268.4	612.8	482.4

[a]Data after 1976 are not strictly comparable with prior data.
Source: Department of Commerce, *Business Statistics 1982*, 116–117.

Cities Service Company

EXHIBIT 2

∎

Earnings for 40 Largest Chemical Companies, Second Quarter of 1982

| | Second Quarter of 1982 | | | | | | First Half of 1982 | | | |
| | Sales ($ millions) | Earnings ($ millions) | Change from 1981 | | Profit Margin[b] | | Sales ($ millions) | Earnings[c] ($ millions) | Change from 1981 | |
			Sales	Earnings	1981	1982			Sales	Earnings
Dow Chemical[d]	$ 2,728.0	$ 77.0	(11)%	(54)%	5.5%	2.8%	$ 5,509.0	$174.0	(8)%	(50)%
Union Carbide	2,299.4	118.2	(14)	(35)	6.8	5.1	4,611.5	209.0	(13)	(40)
W. R. Grace[e]	1,630.2	76.9	(4)	(23)	5.9	4.7	3,093.4	156.0	(3)	(14)
Monsanto	1,623.4	86.2	(13)	(8)	5.1	5.3	3,355.1	233.7	(11)	(13)
Allied	1,595.0	82.0	(1)	(6)	5.5	5.1	3,209.0	145.0	(1)	(15)
FMC	904.8	39.0	8	(13)	5.4	4.3	1,749.4	69.5	6	(23)
American Cyanamid[f]	901.1	31.4	0	(35)	5.0	3.5	1,746.6	59.8	(2)	(36)
PPG Industries[g]	882.1	45.7	(1)	(29)	7.2	5.2	1,600.0	62.2	(6)	(48)
B. F. Goodrich[h]	793.5	15.0	(4)	(43)	3.2	1.9	1,500.0	(3.4)	(6)	def
Celanese	778.0	18.0	(21)	(55)	4.0	2.3	1,638.0	38.0	(14)	(50)
Hercules	651.0	22.3	(9)	(46)	5.8	3.4	1,291.0	44.2	(6)	(48)
Williams Cos.	558.0	19.4	(3)	(49)	6.6	3.5	952.0	25.3	(11)	(72)
Rohm & Haas[i]	528.0	28.0	(3)	(17)	6.2	5.3	1,003.3	44.0	(2)	(28)
Olin	474.2	23.4	(13)	(29)	6.0	4.9	973.9	45.4	(9)	(26)
National Distillers[j]	464.9	22.3	(11)	(37)	6.8	4.8	929.3	(39.2)	(10)	(44)
Ethyl[k]	417.6	27.9	(8)	14	5.4	6.7	820.3	45.1	(7)	2
International Minerals[l]	400.7	4.7	(15)	(84)	6.3	1.2	819.8	28.2	(19)	(63)
Air Products[m]	380.7	24.2	(2)	(14)	7.2	6.4	779.7	53.5	(3)	(18)
Witco Chemical	335.9	8.9	0	(14)	3.1	2.7	669.9	12.8	2	(21)
Stauffer Chemical	305.6	17.2	(19)	(25)	6.1	5.6	935.9	99.3	(7)	(11)
Akzona	254.8	(4.3)	(19)	def	1.8	def	545.4	(7.0)	(12)	def
Pennwalt	253.7	11.0	(9)	(30)	5.6	4.3	500.4	17.2	(9)	(33)
Lubrizol	220.7	13.6	(8)	(48)	10.8	6.2	422.5	29.2	(9)	(42)
Reichhold Chemicals	218.8	3.8	(14)	(46)	2.8	1.7	432.7	7.1	(12)	(39)
Thiokol	210.7	9.5	19	8	5.0	4.5	413.6	18.5	18	9

continued

EXHIBIT 2 continued

| | Second Quarter of 1982 | | | | Profit Margin[b] | | First Half of 1982[a] | | | |
| | Sales ($ millions) | Earnings ($ millions) | Change from 1981 | | 1981 | 1982 | Sales ($ millions) | Earnings[c] ($ millions) | Change from 1981 | |
			Sales	Earnings					Sales	Earnings
Freeport-McMoRan	175.0	15.4	(16)	(64)	20.5	8.8	369.9	49.1	(15)	(54)
Nalco Chemical	166.1	16.4	1	(16)	11.9	9.9	324.9	31.8	1	(18)
GAF[j]	163.4	8.9	(6)	107	2.5	5.4	302.9	5.1	(14)	(31)
International Flavors	123.5	19.8	3	(8)	17.9	16.0	242.1	37.8	(1)	(10)
Liquid Air	120.3	7.8	10	3	6.9	6.4	223.8	15.6	2	(8)
H. B. Fuller[n]	83.0	3.0	(2)	(21)	4.5	3.6	155.6	4.0	(4)	(38)
Petrolite	74.9	7.3	0	(3)	10.0	9.7	157.3	15.8	8	9
Chemed	64.8	4.0	2	(30)	10.9	6.2	124.7	9.2	2	(14)
First Mississippi	62.1	3.5	(4)	(72)	19.4	5.6	113.8	4.7	(12)	(64)
Crompton & Knowles	55.9	1.3	(15)	(46)	3.6	2.3	110.0	2.1	(13)	(50)
Loctite	54.4	3.2	(3)	10	4.7	5.9	109.2	6.5	(3)	16
Stepan Chemical	52.4	1.4	(6)	(25)	3.3	2.7	106.5	2.4	1	(20)
Essex Chemical	47.1	2.6	(10)	4	4.8	5.5	84.8	3.4	(8)	21
Great Lakes Chemical	40.1	3.2	16	(32)	13.6	8.0	82.8	7.1	19	(29)
Philip A. Hunt	29.7	2.0	4	8	6.6	6.7	59.8	4.0	9	38
Total 20 largest companies	$18,652.1	$787.7	(7.9)%	(35.6)%	6.0%	4.2%	$37,186.9	$1,580.8	(6.9)%	(34.6)%
Total 20 other companies	2,471.4	133.4	(4.6)	(34.7)	7.9	5.4	4,882.7	263.6	(5.5)	(31.3)
Grand total	$21,123.5	$921.1	(7.6)	(35.5)	6.2	4.4	$42,069.6	$1,844.4	(6.8)	(34.1)

[a]As of July 30.

[b]After-tax as a percentage of sales.

[c]Fully diluted before nonrecurring and extraordinary items.

[d]Excludes $120 million nonrecurring gain in second quarter of 1982, $54 million extraordinary credit in first quarter of 1982, and $20 million nonrecurring gain in second quarter of 1981.

[e]Excludes $65.1 million nonrecurring gain in first half of 1982.

[f]Excludes net nonrecurring charge of $3.4 million in second quarter of 1982, net gain of $3.4 million in second quarter and first half of 1981, and net gain of $6.2 million in first half of 1982.

[g]Excludes $7.2 million nonrecurring gain in first half of 1982.

[h]Excludes nonrecurring gains of $4.4 million in second quarter of 1982 and $18 million in first half of 1981.

[i]Excludes nonrecurring charge of $13.4 million in second quarter of 1981 and net nonrecurring charge of $9.0 million for first half of 1981.

[j]Excludes net nonrecurring loss of $4.3 million in second quarter of 1982 and net nonrecurring gain of $7.2 million in first half of 1982.

[k]Second quarter of 1982 includes results from First Colony Life Insurance from May 14.

[l]Includes nonrecurring items.

[m]Excludes $9.3 million nonrecurring charge in second quarter of 1982.

[n]Excludes $0.9 million extraordinary gain in first half of 1982.

def = deficit.

Source: *Chemical & Engineering News*, August 16, 1982, 12.

Cities Service Company

EXHIBIT 3
■

Occidental Petroleum Consolidated Income Statement
(millions of dollars, except per share data)

	1976	1977	1978	1979	1980	1981
Revenues						
Net sales	$5,534	$6,017	$6,253	$9,555	$12,476	$14,708
Interest and other	76	63	63	83	250	627
	5,610	6,080	6,316	9,638	12,726	15,335
Expenses						
Cost of sales	4,448	4,674	4,668	6,863	9,057	11,241
Selling and administrative	334	475	563	724	833	766
Interest	110	119	113	137	129	203
Other (income)	(20)	(15)	131	(20)	12	673
	4,872	5,253	5,475	7,704	10,031	12,883
Income before taxes	738	827	841	1,934	2,695	2,452
Tax provision	554	673	834	1,372	1,984	1,730
Net income	$ 184	$ 154	$ 7	$ 562	$ 711	$ 722
Earnings (loss) per share	$ 3.20	$ 2.26	$ 0.10	$ 7.72	$ 8.91	$ 7.59
Dividends per share	1.00	1.19	1.25	1.31	1.93	2.43

Cities Service Company

EXHIBIT 4
■

Occidental Petroleum, Consolidated Balance Sheet (millions of dollars)

	1976[a]	1977	1978	1979	1980	1981
Assets						
Cash and securities	$ 238	$ 170	$ 190	$ 246	$ 275	$ 252
Receivables	766	594	944	1,299	1,498	1,445
Inventories	325	359	410	497	627	804
Other	25	28	28	28	34	51
Total current assets	1,354	1,151	1,572	2,070	2,434	2,552
Long-term receivables	21	17	41	27	31	80
Investments	133	129	119	113	98	470
Property, plant, and equipment, net	2,327	2,365	2,732	3,182	3,931	4,494
Other	70	94	145	168	136	479
Total assets	$3,905	$3,756	$4,609	$5,560	$6,630	$8,075
Liabilities and Equity						
Current maturities of debt	$ 165	$ 97	$ 155	$ 143	$ 183	$ 405
Accounts payable	541	523	845	905	1,007	1,036
Accrued liabilities	136	136	238	306	392	428
Other	72	46	328	504	595	526
Total current liabilities	914	802	1,566	1,858	2,177	2,395
Long-term debt and capital leases	1,197	789	1,064	1,096	1,002	1,013
Other	364	744	584	771	1,054	1,122
Equity						
Minority equity	125	124	128	133	117	114
Redeemable preferred shares	3	173	241	239	226	567
Nonredeemable preferred shares	3	310	258	213	103	65
Common shares	12	14	14	15	16	19
Additional paid-in capital	574	327	395	442	605	1,045
Retained earnings	725	485	369	802	1,333	1,735
Treasury shares	(12)	(12)	(10)	(9)	(3)	0
Total equity	1,430	1,421	1,395	1,835	2,397	3,545
Total liabilities and equity	$3,905	$3,756	$4,609	$5,560	$6,630	$8,075
Common shares outstanding (000)	57,526	68,057	71,121	72,776	79,766	95,186

[a]Equipment and equity data for 1976 not comparable with later years.

Cities Service Company

EXHIBIT 5
■
Comparative Data

	ROE	ROA	ROS	Debt/Capital	Debt/Assets	Beta	Debt Rating	Average Annual P/E Ratio	Dividends per Share	Average Annual Dividend Yield[a]
1976										
Occidental	12.9%	4.7%	3.3%	47.8%	30.6%	1.00	Baa	7.7	$1.00	4.1%
Cities	12.0	6.0	5.4	31.1	21.9	0.80	A	2.1	0.87	5.2
Industry	14.1	6.4	5.2	27.6	17.2	N.Ap.	N.Ap.	6.8	0.80	5.6
1977										
Occidental	10.8	4.1	2.5	38.3	21.0	1.10	A	9.9	1.19	5.3
Cities	10.8	5.6	4.7	32.9	25.4	0.85	A	2.5	1.00	5.3
Industry	13.7	6.1	4.9	28.0	18.2	N.Ap.	N.Ap.	6.7	0.91	6.1
1978										
Occidental	0.5	0.1	0.1	45.6	23.1	1.15	A	0	1.25	7.9
Cities	6.0	2.9	2.5	34.9	26.3	0.85	A	4.0	1.03	6.1
Industry	13.1	6.1	4.6	30.0	17.8	N.Ap.	N.Ap.	6.2	1.01	7.0
1979										
Occidental	30.6	10.1	5.8	39.2	19.7	1.10	A	3.4	1.31	5.0
Cities	15.5	7.3	5.7	31.5	21.5	0.85	A	1.8	1.13	5.0
Industry	23.0	9.1	7.5	28.1	15.6	N.Ap.	N.Ap.	3.7	1.16	6.5
1980										
Occidental	29.7	10.7	5.6	30.5	15.0	1.25	A	3.4	1.93	6.4
Cities	18.4	8.9	6.3	31.3	21.9	0.80	A	6.8	1.53	4.0
Industry	20.5	9.3	6.1	26.5	14.3	N.Ap.	N.Ap.	5.3	1.54	5.4
1981										
Occidental	20.4	8.9	4.7	22.8	13.0	1.25	A	3.7	2.43	8.7
Cities	(2.3)	(0.8)	(0.6)	44.7	28.1	1.10	A	N.Ap.	1.60	3.3
Industry	16.7	7.9	4.9	27.5	14.4	N.Ap.	N.Ap.	5.7	1.91	6.2

N.Ap. = not applicable.

[a]Data for dividend yield is year-end.

Source: *Value Line Investment Survey;* Standard and Poor's Compustat Services Industry Composite.

Cities Service Company

EXHIBIT 6
■
Petroleum Industry Stock Market Data

		Domestic Petroleum Industry Index (1943 = 10)		Stock Price		Earnings per Share		
	Standard & Poor's 500 Index	High	Low	Occidental	Cities Service	Occidental	Cities Service[a]	Industry
1975	90.19	166.68	119.21	14.00	38.75	$2.20	$1.71	$2.18
1976	107.46	191.55	137.07	24.00	59.50	3.20	2.66	2.52
1977	95.10	186.08	155.50	23.25	53.37	2.26	2.54	2.67
1978	96.10	177.74	146.93	15.75	53.87	0.10	1.42	2.88
1979	107.94	271.61	168.23	27.12	83.50	7.72	4.19	5.17
1980	135.76	503.96	258.52	34.62	47.75	8.91	5.64	6.30
1981	122.55	422.73	295.89	24.00	46.00	7.59	(0.58)	5.75
1982 5/7	119.47	N.Av.	N.Av.	20.12	36.50	N.Av.	N.Av.	N.Av.
5/14	118.01	N.Av.	N.Av.	20.50	35.62	N.Av.	N.Av.	N.Av.
5/21	114.89	N.Av.	N.Av.	20.37	37.00	N.Av.	N.Av.	N.Av.
5/28	111.88	N.Av.	N.Av.	20.12	37.00	N.Av.	N.Av.	N.Av.
6/4	110.09	N.Av.	N.Av.	19.50	38.00	N.Av.	N.Av.	N.Av.
6/11	111.24	N.Av.	N.Av.	19.25	34.75	N.Av.	N.Av.	N.Av.
6/18	107.28	N.Av.	N.Av.	18.75	53.12	N.Av.	N.Av.	N.Av.
6/25	109.14	292.73	265.30	18.87	55.00	N.Av.	N.Av.	N.Av.
7/2	107.65	N.Av.	N.Av.	18.00	54.75	N.Av.	N.Av.	N.Av.
7/9	108.83	N.Av.	N.Av.	18.00	52.00	N.Av.	N.Av.	N.Av.
7/16	111.07	N.Av.	N.Av.	17.87	53.75	N.Av.	N.Av.	N.Av.
7/23	111.17	N.Av.	N.Av.	17.75	55.25	N.Av.	N.Av.	N.Av.
7/30	107.09	N.Av.	N.Av.	17.25	Not traded	N.Av.	N.Av.	N.Av.
8/6	103.71	N.Av.	N.Av.	17.12	37.25	N.Av.	N.Av.	N.Av.

N.Av. = not available.
[a]Accounts for a three-for-one stock split in 1980.
Sources: New York Stock Exchange; Standard & Poor's Compustat Services Industry Composite; *Value Line Investment Survey;* and Standard & Poor's *Analyst's Handbook.*

Cities Service Company

EXHIBIT 7

∎

Net Crude Oil Production (barrels per day)

	Domestic		Foreign		Total	
	1980	*1981*	*1980*	*1981*	*1980*	*1981*
Amerada Hess	88,305	82,357	101,899	73,745	190,204	156,102
American Petrofina	18,162	18,036	—	—	18,162	18,036
Ashland Oil	3,100	2,800	9,600	9,500	12,700	12,300
Atlantic Richfield	555,700	539,900	33,600	32,800	589,300	572,700
Diamond Shamrock	29,730	30,287	39	33	29,769	30,320
Exxon	787,000	752,000	3,221,000	3,044,000	4,008,000	3,796,000
Getty Oil	271,000	277,700	145,400	145,900	416,400	393,600
Gulf Oil	364,200	345,400	279,800	269,400	644,000	614,800
Kerr-McGee	32,613	33,827	8,233	N.Av.	40,846	N.Av.
Marathon	168,275	165,874	116,521	64,912	284,796	230,786
Mobil	318,000	316,000	466,000	274,000	784,000	590,000
Murphy	18,032	13,992	41,651	47,577	59,683	61,569
Phillips	270,000	268,000	180,000	141,000	450,000	409,000
Shell	511,000	514,000	21,000	23,000	532,000	537,000
Standard California	373,000	378,000	2,636,000	2,435,000	3,009,000	2,813,000
Standard Indiana	464,000	437,000	372,000	357,000	836,000	794,000
Standard Ohio	715,784	717,291	0	0	715,784	717,291
Sun	206,107	217,321	28,637	27,433	234,744	244,754
Tenneco	72,526	83,101	N.Av.	N.Av.	N.Av.	N.Av.
Texaco	413,000	381,000	2,760,000	2,672,000	3,173,000	3,053,000
Union	171,200	165,800	79,300	70,300	250,500	236,100
Total	5,851,000	5,739,600	10,502,000	9,717,700	16,353,000	15,458,000
Percentage of total produced by these firms	36.3%	37.7%	63.7%	62.3%		

N.Av. = not available.
Source: *National Petroleum News*, Factbook Issue, January 1982, 16–17.

Cities Service Company

EXHIBIT 8

■

Occidental Petroleum: Property, Plant, and Equipment, December 31, 1979–1981
(in thousands)

	1978	1979	1980	1981
Oil and Gas Operations				
International production and exploration				
Leases, exploration costs, and lease and well equipment	$ 439,980	$ 615,122	$ 809,059	$1,060,527
Pipelines and terminals	405,783	468,945	490,861	519,387
Gas plant and other equipment	660,557	770,487	888,973	1,011,488
Other	30,013	47,143	64,426	89,360
Total	1,536,333	1,901,697	2,253,319	2,680,762
International refining, marketing, and transportation				
Refineries and terminals	155,933	106,478	106,001	106,001
Other	73,691	81,894	90,021	95,912
Total	229,624	188,372	196,022	201,913
North America				
Leases, exploration costs, and lease and well equipment	281,719	361,580	578,056	700,165
Pipelines, terminals, and gas plants	63,039	66,851	68,460	73,762
Rolling stock	17,757	16,118	15,757	15,493
Other	61,699	67,414	78,649	90,113
Total	424,214	511,963	740,922	879,533
Chemical Operations				
Land and land improvements	17,454	19,478	36,406	41,581
Buildings	190,014	220,139	274,897	280,320
Machinery and equipment	795,452	850,788	1,093,505	1,173,463
Lease, exploration, and development costs	56,815	66,167	66,209	82,891
Construction in progress	65,891	166,362	196,264	161,962
Leased property under capital leases	55,416	56,948	56,305	79,444
Total	1,181,042	1,329,382	1,723,586	1,819,661
Coal Operations				
Coal, timber, and surface lands	69,154	80,187	81,029	94,921
Mine-development costs	253,380	314,024	463,813	446,506
Mining equipment and related facilities	352,998	389,732	472,115	475,597
Construction in progress	232,526	276,904	194,373	148,857
Total	908,058	1,060,847	1,211,330	1,165,881
Agribusiness Operations				
Land and land improvements	2,291	2,301	1,453	34,749
Buildings	6,780	7,358	11,275	101,786
Machinery and equipment	17,417	18,563	19,680	201,246
Construction in progress	1,135	6,285	3,669	22,896
Total	27,623	34,507	36,077	360,677
Total gross property, plant, and equipment	$4,306,894	$5,027,268	$6,161,256	$7,108,427
Depreciation	$1,574,444	$1,844,793	$2,229,839	$2,614,313
Total property, plant, and equipment	$2,732,450	$3,182,475	$3,931,417	$4,494,114

Cities Service Company

EXHIBIT 9
■
Occidental Petroleum: Oil and Gas Acreage, December 31, 1981
(thousands of acres)

	Developed Acreage[a]		Undeveloped Acreage[b]	
	Gross[c]	Net[d]	Gross[c]	Net[d]
Eastern hemisphere				
Libya				
Concessions	282	138	—	—
Production sharing	1,827	347	10,098	1,380
Total	2,109	485	10,098	1,380
United Kingdom	32	10	510	117
Australia	—	—	17,478	7,126
Pakistan	—	—	77	24
Oman	—	—	3,200	288
Abu Dhabi	—	—	1,898	253
Tunisia	—	—	810	397
Madagascar	—	—	5,313	2,231
Spain	—	—	245	29
Ireland	—	—	243	49
Total eastern hemisphere	2,141	495	39,872	11,894
United States	308	44	1,947	1,535
Other western hemisphere				
Peru	2,658	1,336	1,238	619
Bolivia	1,982	991	—	—
Trinidad	—	—	166	66
Argentina	—	—	519	195
Colombia	—	—	4,942	1,977
Paraguay	—	—	27,065	6,902
Canada	986	457	74,323	25,493
Total other western hemisphere	5,626	2,784	108,253	35,252
Total acreage	8,075	3,323	150,072	46,681

[a]Acres spaced or assignable to productive wells.
[b]Acres on which wells have not been drilled or completed to a point that would permit the production of commercial quantities of oil and gas, regardless of whether the acreage contains proved reserves.
[c]The total acres in which interests are held.
[d]The sum of the fractional interests owned, based on working interests or shares of production, if under production-sharing agreements.

Cities Service Company

EXHIBIT 10
■

Occidental Petroleum, December 31, 1981
(number in parentheses indicates the number of wells with multiple completions)

	Oil				Gas			
Productive Oil and Gas Wells	Gross[a]		Net[b]		Gross[a]		Net[b]	
Eastern hemisphere								
Libya	120	(0)	37.9	(0.0)	—	—	—	—
United Kingdom	48	(0)	17.5	(0.0)	—	—	—	—
Australia	1	(0)	.2	(0.0)	—	—	—	—
Total eastern hemisphere	169	(0)	55.6	(0.0)	—	—	—	—
United States	677	(23)	487.0	(9.0)	253	(47)	78.5	(16.2)
Other western hemisphere								
Peru	1,270	(58)	1,032.5	(29.0)	—	—	—	—
Bolivia	1	(1)	.5	(0.5)	22	(22)	11.0	(11.0)
Canada	113	(0)	25.6	(0.0)	280	(0)	87.1	(0.0)
Total other western hemisphere	1,384	(59)	1,058.6	(29.5)	302	(22)	98.1	(11.0)
Total	2,230	(82)	1,601.2	(38.5)	555	(69)	176.6	(27.2)

	Participation in Exploratory and Development Wells		Pressure Maintenance and Water Flood Installations	
	Gross[a]	Net[b]	Gross[a]	Net[b]
Eastern hemisphere				
United Kingdom	3	1.2	17	6.2
Oman	1	.5	—	—
Australia	1	.7	—	—
Pakistan	1	.9	—	—
Ireland	1	.2	—	—
Total eastern hemisphere	7	3.5	17	6.2
United States	51	10.0	38	9.2
Other western hemisphere				
Peru	19	15.0	406	341.1
Bolivia	2	1.0	—	—
Canada	1	.5	11	3.1
Argentina	1	.4	—	—
Total other western hemisphere	23	16.9	417	344.2
Total	81	30.4	472	359.6

[a]The total number of wells in which interests are owned.
[b]The sum of the fractional interests owned, based on working interests or shares of production, if under production-sharing agreements.

Cities Service Company

EXHIBIT 11
■

Consolidated Income Statements for Cities Service Company, December 13, 1976–1981[a]
(millions of dollars, except per share data)

	1976	1977	1978	1979	1980	1981
Gross income						
Sales income	$3,965	$4,388	$4,661	$5,971	$7,442	$8,546
Investment income	41	48	52	87	115	97
Total income	4,006	4,436	4,713	6,058	7,557	8,643
Costs						
Operating expenses	2,964	3,365	3,582	4,579	5,604	6,538
Exploration	173	179	231	211	294	375
Selling and administrative	158	165	174	180	220	255
Depreciation	148	166	182	230	249	322
Interest	77	72	76	92	79	158.
Taxes	263	268	182	393	611	696
Other	6	11	168	12	11	13
Total costs	3,789	4,226	4,595	5,697	7,068	8,357
Income from operations	217	210	118	361	489	286
Discontinued operations	0	0	0	(13)	(11)	(335)
Net income (loss)	$ 217	$ 210	$ 118	$ 348	$ 478	$ (49)
Net income per share	$ 7.98	$ 7.61	$ 4.26	$12.56	$ 5.64	$(0.58)
Net income accounting for three-for-one stock split in 1980	2.66	2.54	1.42	4.19	5.64	0.58
Dividends per share	0.87	1.00	1.03	1.13	1.53	1.60

[a]Various notes to financial statements are found in Exhibits 13 to 19.

Cities Service Company

EXHIBIT 12
■

Consolidated Balance Sheets for Cities Service Company, December 13, 1976–1981[a]
(dollars in millions)

	1976	1977	1978	1979	1980	1981
Assets						
Cash and securities	$ 348	$ 174	$ 194	$ 444	$ 168	$ 128
Accounts receivable	431	427	500	733	806	782
Inventories	241	316	298	272	359	382
Other	112	104	116	144	184	543
Total current assets	1,132	1,021	1,108	1,593	1,517	1,836
Notes receivable	60	35	30	31	32	20
Other	100	126	64	75	87	91
Property, plant, and equipment, net	2,329	2,537	2,776	3,032	3,670	4,026
Deferred charges	23	21	27	42	52	76
Total assets	$3,644	$3,740	$4,005	$4,773	$5,358	$6,049
Liabilities and Equity						
Notes payable	$ 86	$ 48	$ 44	$ 39	$ 67	$ 374
Accounts payable and accrued liabilities	510	486	560	858	864	1,191
Taxes	95	27	43	195	137	29
Total current liabilities	691	561	647	1,092	1,068	1,594
Long-term debt	669	787	946	922	1,066	1,592
Capitalized leases	153	151	109	104	108	110
Other	328	295	322	416	523	629
Minority interest	7	8	10	12	15	17
Common stock	140	141	141	141	170	170
Capital surplus	150	163	164	167	140	155
Retained earnings	1,526	1,654	1,686	1,939	2,289	2,109
Treasury stock	(20)	(20)	(20)	(20)	(20)	(327)
Total equity	1,796	1,938	1,971	2,227	2,578	2,107
Total liabilities and equity	$3,644	$3,740	$4,005	$4,773	$5,358	$6,049
Common shares outstanding (000)	27,202	27,593	27,668	27,708	84,742[a]	85,125

[a]Various notes to financial statements found in Exhibits 13 to 19.

Cities Service Company

EXHIBIT 13
■

Notes to Cities Service's Financial Statements: Financial Data by
Industry Segments, 1979–1981 (in millions)

	1979	1980	1981
Sales to Unaffiliated Customers			
Energy resources	$1,117.0	$1,340.3	$1,534.3
Refining, marketing, and transportation	3,841.6	4,987.9	5,607.0
Natural-gas transmission	514.0	668.7	885.7
Minerals	276.3	232.7	239.7
Other	222.3	212.4	279.7
Total sales to unaffiliated customers	5,971.2	7,442.0	8,546.4
United States	5,629.9	6,956.4	8,111.9
Canada	147.5	241.8	253.4
Other international	183.8	243.8	181.1
Intersegment sales (eliminated)			
Energy resources	506.9	777.5	933.3
Refining, marketing, and transportation	73.0	95.6	81.9
Natural-gas transmission	56.7	72.6	84.8
Other	1.1	1.3	1.7
Total intersegment sales	637.7	947.0	1,101.7
Intergeographic sales (eliminated)			
United States	4.7	5.9	4.2
Canada	1.0	0.9	2.0
Other international	715.1	757.8	393.3
Total intergeographic sales	$ 720.8	$ 764.6	$ 399.5
Operating Profit (Loss)			
Energy resources	$ 488.5	$ 635.2	$ 530.5
Refining, marketing, and transportation	129.3	170.8	(12.8)
Natural-gas transmission	63.5	82.6	95.0
Minerals	25.4	15.7	5.2
Other	22.1	18.3	23.2
Intersegment (eliminations)	(0.2)	(1.7)	(2.0)
Total operating profit	728.6	920.9	639.1
Equity income			
Energy resources	1.9	6.8	7.5
Refining, marketing, and transporation	15.1	14.7	15.0
Other and general corporate	7.9	5.7	(1.9)
Total equity income	24.9	27.2	20.6

continued

EXHIBIT 13 *continued*

	1979	1980	1981
Other nonoperating income (net) and general corporate expenses			
Energy resources	(0.4)	4.6	9.1
Refining, marketing, and transportation	9.1	17.3	0.4
Natural-gas transmission	0.8	1.6	1.0
Minerals	0.4	(0.2)	(3.3)
Other and general corporate	6.8	16.8	18.1
Total other nonoperating income	16.7	40.1	25.3
Contribution to profit			
Energy resources	$ 490.0	$ 646.6	$ 547.1
Refining, marketing, and transportation	153.3	202.8	2.6
Natural-gas transmission	64.3	84.2	96.0
Minerals	25.8	15.5	1.9
Other and general corporate	36.6	39.1	37.4
Total contribution to profit	770.2	988.2	685.0
Interest expense	(91.6)	(78.8)	(158.4)
Federal, state, and foreign income taxes	(304.2)	(407.5)	(227.6)
Income applicable to minority interests	(13.8)	(13.3)	(12.6)
Income from continuing operations	$ 360.6	$ 488.6	$ 286.4
Contribution to Profit by Region			
United States	$748.5	$904.7	$685.3
Canada	1.0	58.9	37.6
Other international	20.7	24.6	(37.9)
Total contribution to profit	$ 770.2	$ 988.2	$ 685.0
Identifiable Assets			
Energy resources	$1,868.6	$2,333.4	$2,852.8
Refining, marketing, and transportation	985.3	1,141.6	1,251.1
Natural-gas transmission	532.4	637.0	700.2
Minerals	298.6	280.7	339.6
Other	113.4	139.0	159.7
Total identifiable assets	$3,798.3	$4,531.7	$5,303.4
Distribution of identifiable assets			
United States	3,157.4	3,826.6	4,648.4
Canada	514.5	542.0	502.1
Other international	126.4	163.1	152.9
Equity investments			
Energy resources	4.5	11.3	15.3
Refining, marketing, and transportation	8.4	6.5	7.5
Other and general corporate	60.2	68.6	68.1
Total equity investments	73.1	86.4	90.9

EXHIBIT 13 *continued*

	1979	1980	1981
United States	8.8	7.9	9.8
Other international	64.3	78.5	81.1
Corporate assets	613.9	362.7	347.7
Assets of discontinued operations (including deferred taxes receivable in 1981)	287.7	377.2	306.5
Total assets	$4,773.0	$5,358.0	$6,048.5
Capital Expenditures			
Property, plant, and equipment			
Energy resources	$ 412.8	$ 663.7	$ 800.2
Refining, marketing, and transportation	53.1	114.9	175.4
Natural-gas transmission	156.5	120.4	171.6
Minerals	10.9	23.5	36.3
Other and general corporate	33.9	86.5	66.3
Discontinued operations	88.4	71.9	111.6
Total property, plant, and equipment	755.6	1,080.9	1,361.4
Investments and advances	2.1	10.1	7.3
Total capital expenditures	$ 757.7	$1,091.0	$1,368.7
Capital expenditures by region			
United States	$ 653.8	$ 967.1	$1,182.1
Canada	46.1	56.0	84.3
Other international	57.8	67.9	102.3
	$ 757.7	$1,091.0	$1,368.7
Depreciation, Depletion, and Amortization			
Energy resources	$ 132.7	$ 144.2	$ 168.1
Refining, marketing, and transportation	50.5	33.4	30.7
Natural-gas transmission	21.3	48.3	90.9
Minerals	13.9	11.0	14.0
Other and general corporate	11.1	11.6	18.0
Total depreciation, depletion, and amortization	$ 229.5	$ 248.5	$ 321.7
Dry-Hole and Unproved Lease Costs			
Impairment			
Energy resources	$ 105.7	$ 151.1	$ 193.3
Natural-gas transmission	6.1	4.5	7.0
Total dry-hole costs and unproved lease	$ 111.8	$ 155.6	$ 200.3

Cities Service Company

EXHIBIT 14

■

Notes to Cities Service's Financial Statements: Sales by Segment

	1976	*1977*	*1978*	*1979*	*1980*	*1981*
Natural gas liquids (thousands of barrels per day)						
Public sales	75.1	80.4	67.8	85.2	67.9	48.8
Intersegment sales (principally to discontinued operations)	43.9	40.9	35.2	40.3	37.5	36.9
Helium (million cubic feet)	225.3	279.8	250.2	230.3	288.9	307.7

Cities Service Company

EXHIBIT 15
■
Notes to Cities Service's Financial Statements: Energy Resources

	1976	1977	1978	1979	1980	1981
Net acreage held at year end (millions)[a]						
United States	12.5	11.0	11.8	11.9	12.2	12.4
Canada	4.4	2.8	2.7	2.8	2.8	1.9
Other international	18.3	10.7	12.0	9.0	11.4	22.8
Net wells completed[a]						
Oil	106	74	82	120	189	208
Gas	84	102	132	129	99	160
Dry	64	79	111	89	104	129
Total wells completed	254	255	325	338	392	497
Net wells producing at year end[a]						
Oil	4,860	4,957	5,024	5,036	5,243	5,474
Gas	2,147	2,239	2,370	2,432	2,510	2,546

[a]Includes international contract operations where applicable.

Cities Service Company

EXHIBIT 16
■
Notes to Cities Service's Financial Statements: Production

	1976	1977	1978	1979	1980	1981
Crude oil, net barrels per day (000)						
Texas	51.4	47.8	43.3	40.8	38.1	36.7
Louisiana	28.0	25.0	21.7	19.2	17.3	17.8
Kansas	9.8	9.6	9.1	8.8	8.4	8.7
Oklahoma	7.4	6.9	6.0	5.5	5.3	4.8
Wyoming	1.1	3.1	4.8	3.4	3.3	3.7
New Mexico	4.9	4.7	4.2	3.8	3.4	3.1
California	1.5	1.3	1.5	1.4	1.5	1.2
Other states	1.7	1.5	1.5	1.5	1.5	1.7
Canada	5.6	4.7	4.5	4.9	4.9	5.1
Other international[a]	23.6	23.9	21.6	30.2	25.8	23.8
Total crude oil	135.0	128.5	118.2	119.5	109.5	106.6
Natural-gas liquids, net barrels per day (000)						
United States	89.2	84.3	88.3	83.0	75.9	71.4
Canada	0.4	0.8	1.1	1.0	1.1	0.9
Other international	0.3	0.3	0.3	0.3	0.3	0.3
Total natural-gas liquids[b]						
Natural gas, net cubic feet per day (million)						
Louisiana	351.3	324.5	294.8	254.4	227.1	239.2
Texas	250.2	200.4	199.8	228.3	222.0	200.2
Kansas	202.8	196.4	211.9	192.9	163.3	157.9
Oklahoma	128.9	123.1	123.3	105.5	92.1	91.3
Wyoming	3.4	10.1	18.1	26.1	53.7	85.5
New Mexico	53.8	48.7	39.2	36.0	28.8	27.3
West Virginia	15.0	14.4	12.9	12.9	14.1	13.7
Other states	8.7	7.9	8.0	10.0	10.2	9.6
Canada	21.9	25.7	30.4	33.0	29.7	26.8
Other international (including equity interest)	6.0	6.3	9.1	15.7	22.0	25.1
Total natural gas[c]	1,042.0	957.5	947.5	914.8	803.0	876.6
Synthetic crude oil from Canadian tar sands, net barrels per day (000)	N.Ap.	N.Ap.	5.0	10.1	12.6	12.2

N.Ap. = not applicable.
[a]Includes international contract production.
[b]Excludes volumes processed by others.
[c]Wet gas basis.

Cities Service Company

EXHIBIT 17

■

Notes to Cities Service's Financial Statements: Average Sales Prices and Average Lifting Costs[a]

	United States				Canada				Other International			
	1978	1979	1980	1981	1978	1979	1980	1981	1978	1979	1980	1981
Average sales prices												
Crude oil and condensate (per bbl.)	$8.96	$12.13	$21.01	$34.37	$10.35	$10.76	$12.56	$14.76	$4.92	$10.74	$12.26	$10.14
Natural gas ($/mcf)	0.72	0.94	1.24	1.63	1.31	1.43	2.09	2.23	0.45	0.45	0.50	0.69
Average lifting costs ($ per equivalent barrel of crude oil condensate and natural gas)	1.33	1.68	3.63	7.11	2.00	2.06	3.17	6.17	1.68	1.57	2.84	3.09
Other average sales prices ($/bbl.)												
Synthetic crude oil	0.00	0.00	0.00	0.00	0.00	19.80	31.97	35.29	0.00	0.00	0.00	0.00
Natural-gas liquids	9.06	13.80	19.69	28.58	8.42	9.22	15.79	14.66	0.00	0.00	0.00	0.00

[a]Lifting costs are the costs incurred in lifting the oil and gas to the surface and include windfall profits tax, gathering, treating, primary processing, field storage, property taxes, and insurance on improved properties. Lifting costs do not include any exploration expenses, amortization of capitalized acquisition, exploration and development costs, transportation costs, income taxes, or interest expense.

It should be noted that the net revenues do not represent profits to oil companies, since lifting costs include only a portion of operating expenses. For the same reason, the average sales price less the average lifting cost should not be taken to represent the profit per equivalent barrel of production.

For purposes of calculating average lifting cost, data for natural gas have been converted to a liquid equivalent using 3,600 cubic feet of natural gas to one barrel of oil.

In determining the average sales prices, transfers to affiliates and to other segments of the company are valued at estimated market prices, natural gas volumes are expressed on a wet gas basis, and international sales prices are an average of the prices of the various countries, including service contract fees.

Cities Service Company

EXHIBIT 18

■

Notes to Cities Service's Financial Statements:
Estimated Future Net Revenues from Production of Proved Oil and
Gas Reserves at December 31, 1981 ($ millions)

| | Proved Developed and Undeveloped | | | | | Proved Developed | | | | |
	United States	Canada	Other International	Total	Equity Interest—Netherlands	United States	Canada	Other International	Total	Equity Interest—Netherlands
1982	$1,001	$61	$ (9)	$1,053	$ 20	$1,020	$ 56	$ 8	$1,084	$ 20
1983	769	54	4	827	17	772	49	1	822	20
1984	696	48	36	780	20	674	44	2	720	20
Remainder	6,209	402	69	6,680	97	5,982	316	6	6,304	91
Total	$8,675	$565	$100	$9,340	$154	$8,448	$465	$17	$8,930	$151

Present Values of Estimated Future Net Revenues from Production of Proved Oil and Gas Reserves[a]
(as estimated at year ends, $ millions)

	Proved Developed and Undeveloped	Proved Developed	Equity Interest—Netherlands
United States			
1978	$1,800	$1,870	0
1979	3,141	3,093	0
1980	4,071	3,911	0
1981	4,295	4,195	0

Canada			
1978	203	195	0
1979	214	210	0
1980	256	250	0
1981	304	264	0
Other International			
1978	79	11	$ 51
1979	47	47	75
1980	61	47	81
1981	66	14	105
Total			
1978	$2,182	$2,076	$ 51
1979	3,402	3,350	75
1980	4,388	4,208	81
1981	4,665	4,473	105

*a*Disclosures of estimated future net revenues and the related present values are based on the volume of leasehold reserves. Future net revenues are based on projected production at year-end prices less lifting costs (including the windfall profits tax), future development and reclamation costs, all projected at year-end levels. As required, a discount factor of 10 percent was used in calculating present values.

The development of the present value data forces a number of key assumptions and judgments about the future, some of which may be critically flawed. Among the many measurement and forecasting problems, the uncertainties involved with estimating volumes of oil and gas reserves and their production rates into the future are paramount. Management cautions that any projection of estimated future net revenues is highly subjective and has the potential to result in misunderstanding and misleading inferences. While the information presented was calculated in accordance with the SEC guidelines, there are various other equally valid assumptions under which these calculations and estimates could be made that would produce substantially different results.

Cities Service Company

EXHIBIT 19
■

Notes on Cities Service's Financial Statements: Pension Plan

The company and its subsidiaries cover substantially all employees with noncontributory pension plans. Total pension expense, including the amortization of past service costs, most of which are being amortized over a period of approximately 30 years, was $39.3 million for 1981, $43.1 million for 1980, and $37.7 million for 1979. Pension cost is generally funded as accrued.

The actuarial present value of accumulated benefits to participants of the plans and the net assets available for those benefits at the most recent actuarial valuation dates (January 1 of each year) are (in millions):

	1980	1981
Actuarial present value[a] of accumulated plan benefits		
Vested	$363.5	$385.2
Nonvested	34.8	33.0
Total	418.2	398.3
Net assets available for benefits	$641.5	$517.8

[a]The average rate of return assumed in determining the actuarial present value of accumulated plan benefits was 8 percent.

Company contributions are determined by a projected benefit actuarial cost method that recognizes future plan benefit increases expected to result from future increases in members' salaries. This contribution method results naturally in the accumulation of funds in excess of the present value of accumulated plan benefits. In accordance with FASB Statement No. 36, the calculation of the present value of accumulated plan benefits shown above does not include provision for future salary increases.

Philip Morris, Incorporated:

Seven-Up Acquisition (A)

The decision had been made. Philip Morris, Inc. (PM) was going to make a takeover bid for the Seven-Up Company. The difficulties and intricacies of that decision paled, however, in the face of the next one: at what price should PM management make its tender offer?

It was the latter half of April 1978, and in the face of an increasingly active merger/acquisition market, PM management recognized the need for the utmost speed and secrecy in developing its bidding strategy.

BACKGROUND

Philip Morris, Inc. was one of the 50 largest companies in the United States in 1977 with revenues of $5.2 billion and an asset base of $4 billion. The company had achieved record increases in sales and earnings over the 5 years ending 1977, as shown in Exhibit 1, and its stock was extremely highly rated. However, while market analysts predicted that PM's annual sales growth would continue at 13 to 14 percent between 1977 and 1982, earnings were expected to increase by only 12 to 13 percent per year.

Philip Morris, originally founded in the 19th century, had primarily manufactured and sold cigarettes until the late 1960s. What diversification the company had undertaken was largely vertical and included manufacturing paper, packaging, and chemical products used in making cigarettes.

In the late 1960s, the first reports regarding the potential dangers of smoking began to emerge, and by the early 1970s, cigarette advertising was banned from television. These events led PM management to modify its corporate strategy by diversifying into new businesses. PM's experience with its early acquisitions eventually led the company's managers to the following conclusion: future acquisition targets should be significant players within large industries, i.e., relatively large companies whose performance could make a significant contribution to that of the corporation as a whole. Because of the healthy cash flows of the cigarette business, management was willing to forgo strong early returns

---

This case was prepared as a basis for class discussion rather than to illustrate either effective or ineffective handling of an administrative situation. Copyright © 1982 by the Darden Graduate Business School Sponsors, University of Virginia, Charlottesville, Virginia.

from an acquired company if its long-term potential appeared attractive. Management decided, however, to limit its diversification to companies that produced consumer goods, hoping for synergies from the broader use of PM's existing marketing expertise.

The first major step in this strategy was the acquisition of Miller Brewing Co. in 1970. PM management used essentially the same consumer-driven strategy with its beer products as it had with its cigarette products. Sophisticated marketing programs were undertaken that included (1) detailed market studies identifying target consumer groups and their salient characteristics, (2) the identification of existing, or the development of new, products for the groups so identified, and (3) the creation of a product packaging, distribution, and advertising program suitable for the product and the specific consumer group. Concurrently, management committed itself to constructing modern, efficient production facilities adequate for the volume that PM's marketing programs were expected to generate.

While PM management's strategies for beer and tobacco products were procedurally similar, they differed in terms of their practical applications. Specific cigarette brands were being marketed to increasingly well-defined (and, therefore, smaller) consumer groups, but PM management redefined Miller beer's target market in a dramatic move that greatly increased the number of the product's potential consumers. When PM acquired the Miller Brewing Co., that company marketed one major product, Miller Beer, which, with a 4 percent share of market, was the seventh largest selling beer in the country. The company had annual sales of 5 million barrels, making it the fifth largest brewer in the United States.

PM management refocused Miller's marketing program away from the female, upper-income consumer implicitly targeted by the "Champagne of Bottled Beer" theme. Management believed that the use of *champagne* isolated the beverage from the mainstream of the beer market and implied that the beer should be offered only on special occasions. Instead, the beer was now targeted toward the male, blue-collar, heavy beer-drinking segment of the market.

By 1977, Miller's share of market exceeded 15 percent, the second largest share in the industry. In addition, PM management had increased the company's production capacity to 30 million barrels per year, making Miller the second largest U.S. brewer. Plans to increase this capacity to 50 million barrels per year by 1982 had already been approved.

In addition, PM management developed and introduced two new products: Miller Lite and domestically brewed Lowenbrau. The latter product was targeted at the super premium-priced segment historically dominated by Michelob. Miller Lite, however, was a relatively new concept in the beer industry. Although most other national brewers subsequently introduced competitive products of their own, Miller Lite retained its position as the leading low-calorie beer in the United States through 1977. The financial and share-of-market results of PM management's strategy are shown in Exhibit 2.

The success of PM management's marketing strategy in both the beer and the cigarette industries was reflected in its financial statements. In 1977 alone, Philip Morris's net earnings increased 26 percent on a sales increase of 21 percent, and the return on average equity reached a 10-year high of 22 percent. Total debt to equity was at a 10-year low of 0.93, and the company's net cash flow (after-tax cash flow less common and preferred dividends) exceeded planned capital expenditures by 19 percent. PM's most recent financial statements are shown in Exhibits 3 and 4.

At the end of 1977, Philip Morris's operations were divided into five groups:

1. Philip Morris U.S.A. (cigarettes)
2. Philip Morris International (cigarettes)
3. Miller Brewing Company (beer)
4. Philip Morris Industrial (specialty papers, chemicals, etc.)
5. The Mission Viejo Company (real estate and community development)

Each group's contribution to Philip Morris's revenues and operating income is shown in Exhibit 1.

On the basis of the increasing share-of-market success and the returns of its existing products and operations, PM management decided to make another acquisition. Management settled on the soft-drink industry, focusing on the Seven-Up Company as the most likely target.

SOFT-DRINK INDUSTRY

The soft-drink industry was large and growing. Soft-drink sales of the top five competitors alone were about $4.7 billion in 1977, up 16 percent from the 1976 figure of $4.0 billion. In the 5-year period from 1973 to 1977, these companies generally outperformed the S&P 500 composite average, as shown in Exhibits 5 and 6. Detailed financial statements for the Seven-Up Company appear in Exhibits 7 through 9.

Soft-Drink Product.   Soft drinks were the quintessential consumer product. They were a low-cost, multipurchase consumer item, the sales of which were highly influenced by sophisticated marketing programs. The industry's successful combination of advertising, promotional efforts, packaging, and distribution had, by the end of 1977, made the drinks the most popular beverage in the United States. There was every indication that the drinks were well on their way to acquiring the same status worldwide.

Soft drinks traced their origin to two different sources, both medicinal. On the one hand, research into the therapeutic properties of naturally effervescent spring waters had begun as early as the 1600s in Europe. By the beginning of the 19th century, artificially carbonated soda water was being bottled and sold commercially in both the United States and Europe. Concurrently, various syrups were being developed to cure a wide range of ills. Among these was Coca-Cola, invented in May 1886. Coke was originally marketed as a medicinal syrup, whose chief components, cocaine and opium, would cure a wide range of nervous afflictions, such as neuralgia and hysteria. By chance, the product was mixed with soda water by the end of 1886, giving rise to the soft-drink product known in 1977. (The major intervening modifications to the product were the deletions of the cocaine and opium.)

Similarly, Seven-Up, introduced in 1929 as "Bib-Label Lithiated Lemon-Lime Soda," was advertised as a hangover cure for home and hospital use. The fact that Seven-Up was also widely perceived as an excellent mixer for alcoholic drinks provided an added boost to sales. In fact, Seven-Up management did not consciously redefine and market Seven-Up as a soft drink until 1968.

Soft drinks were deceptively simple in their composition, which included only four basic categories of ingredients: a base-flavor concentrate or extract, such as cola, a sweetener, water, and carbonation. However, the base concentrates contained numerous flavorings, the specific names and proportions of which were secrets closely guarded by the concentrate manufacturers. The type of sweetener used in the soft drink was also variable. At the end of 1977, saccharin was the major sugar substitute used in diet drinks, while either sugar or high-fructose corn syrup (HFCS)[1] might be used in the production of regular soft drinks.

Soft drinks came in numerous flavors: cola, orange, root beer, lemon-lime, etc. Cola-flavored drinks were the most popular in the United States, enjoying a 62 percent share of the total domestic soft-drink market (regular and diet drinks). Coca-Cola and Pepsi-Cola were the two top-selling cola products, with 39 percent and 28 percent of this segment's volume. Lemon-lime drinks constituted the next largest flavor category with a 12 percent share of the total market. Seven-Up and Sprite (a Coca-Cola Co. product) were the leading competitors within the segment, holding 49 percent and 23 percent of the segment, respectively. The distance between the cola and lemon-lime segments was slightly less in the international market, where lemon-lime drinks had a 15 percent share of the total market.

Since their introduction, diet drinks had enjoyed increasing popularity. By 1977, sales of diet drinks had grown to roughly 11 percent of the total market. Each of the top soft-drink companies had introduced one or more diet products. The success of the different flavor categories within the diet-drink market paralleled the patterns in the total market. Cola-flavored products of the Coca-Cola Co. and PepsiCo. Inc., Tab and Diet Pepsi, dominated the market with 23 percent and 19 percent shares of the diet-drink market. Diet Seven-Up was the only major lemon-lime product in the diet market and, with an 11 percent share, was the third largest selling diet drink in the country.

Market data for the soft-drink industry and its leading competitors are shown in Exhibits 10 and 11.

Market-Growth Analysis.

By 1977, soft drinks had surpassed coffee as the most popular beverage in the United States. In the period between 1963 and 1977, soft-drink consumption grew from 3.4 billion gallons per year to 7.9 billion gallons, representing an increase in consumption of from 191 to 389 12-oz. cans per person per year, roughly comparable to 20 percent of the average daily liquid intake.

Numerous factors contributed to the phenomenal growth in soft-drink sales. In the early years, the United States' rapid rate of population growth provided a steadily increasing number of consumers. Per capita consumption was spurred by the product's relatively low price, by intensive marketing efforts, and by the spread of distribution networks across the country.

---

[1]HFCS was sold at a 20 percent discount to sugar for an equivalent sweetening power. At the end of 1977, most concentrate manufacturers (except Coca-Cola and PepsiCo) had authorized its use in whole or in part in the production of soft drinks. Seven-Up, which required less sweetener than the colas, derived a special economic advantage from the substitution of HFCS for sugar.

By the 1960s, the wide availability of soft drinks was forcing competition to proceed along other dimensions:

> The frontiers of the American market had been conquered, and henceforth domestic growth would come by priming the market with new products and using new ways to market the old ones. The need for a complete soft-drink line was underscored by the widespread acceptance of the multiple-flavor vending machine and the triple-drink fountain dispenser. To avoid being outflanked by competitors, each manufacturer introduced a spate of new containers intended to make soft-drink consumption as convenient as possible. The most noticeable trend was nonreturnable bottles and cans, the latter particularly after the introduction of the easy opening flip-top in 1962.[2]

Further constraints on the industry's growth appeared in the latter half of the 1970s as America's population growth rate gradually declined. Down to about 1 percent per year by 1977, the decline implied a major demographic shift toward an older population. Whether or not America's teenagers, historically the industry's primary target market, would carry their soft-drink consumption patterns with them into their twenties and thirties was a question of major concern to both concentrate manufacturers and other industry participants.

The increasing saturation of the market, together with the country's changing demographics, led to greatly increased competition among the soft-drink companies, as each strove to maintain and improve its historical growth record. Media advertising budgets were sharply increased (as shown in Exhibit 12), and price discounting became commonplace.

Internationally, soft drinks were meeting the same acceptance that they had received in the United States. Although per capita consumption was considerably less than that in the United States, this phenomenon resulted largely from the products' later entry into the international market. Furthermore, the growth rates in certain countries were roughly comparable to patterns experienced earlier in the United States.

Industry Structure.   There were four major groups of participants in the soft-drink industry: concentrate or extract manufacturers, raw material and packaging suppliers, bottling and distribution companies, and retailers. The general relationships between these groups are outlined below.

Concentrate Manufacturers.   More than 30 companies manufactured branded products and marketed them regionally or nationally, while numerous food chains produced private-label soft drinks. Sales within the industry were, however, highly concentrated. Five companies (Coca-Cola Co.; PepsiCo., Inc.; Seven-Up Co.; Dr. Pepper Co.; and Royal Crown Cos.) accounted for 75 percent of the 1977 sales volume, as shown in Exhibit 10. The leading brands of each of these companies (Coca-Cola, Pepsi-Cola, Seven-Up, etc.) accounted for 56 percent of the total industry volume.

Each of the top five competitors could trace its origin to the turn of the century. By the end of World War II, each had begun to market its product

---

[2]J. C. Louis and Harvey Z. Yazijian, *The Cola Wars* (New York: Everest House, Publishers, 1980), 107–108.

internationally. In fact, Coca-Cola was being distributed through 64 bottlers in 28 countries as early as 1930. By the end of 1977, Coke was available in more than 135 countries, Pepsi-Cola in 140 countries, Seven-Up in 86 countries, and Royal Crown products in 51 countries.

The industry leaders had also grown by expanding their product lines (as highlighted in Exhibit 10) and by diversifying into other products. As shown in Exhibit 13, by 1977 only the Dr. Pepper Co. derived 100 percent of its revenues from the sale of soft drinks.

Soft-Drink Bottlers and Distributors.   The distribution system in the soft-drink industry was almost as old as the products themselves. The system had been established by the Coca-Cola Co. in 1899 and subsequently adopted by other soft-drink companies. Briefly, Coca-Cola's owner, Asa Candler, had signed a contract with Benjamin Franklin Thomas and Joseph Brown Whitehead, giving them the right to set up bottling plants throughout the nation at no expense or liability to the Coca-Cola Co. In addition, Mr. Candler agreed to sell the syrup exclusively to the two men, to furnish labels and advertising materials, and to grant them the sole rights to use the Coca-Cola trademark. Mr. Thomas and Mr.

Soft-Drink Industry: General Structure

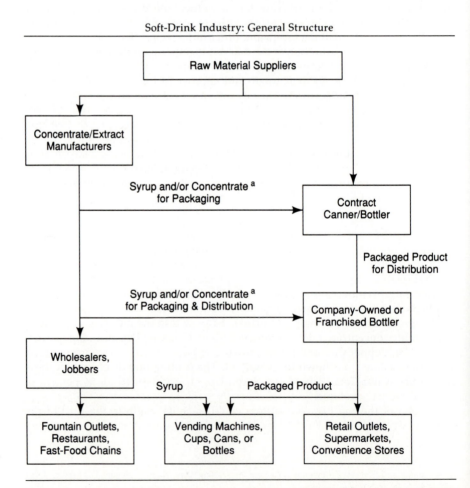

[a]Concentrate, when combined with the sweetener, was referred to as *syrup*. Only Coca-Cola and PepsiCo. sold syrup to their bottlers.

Whitehead promptly set out to find enterprising individuals with adequate capital for their own bottling operations. In exchange for their investment, each franchisee was granted the exclusive right to bottle and market a given product within a certain geographic market.[3] Typically, in the early years, family members would use the earnings from one franchise territory to set up a relative in an adjacent area. Because the franchises were granted in perpetuity, the arrangement fostered a closed system within which franchises were passed from parent to child through the years.

The franchised bottlers operated under certain contractual constraints. Bottlers had to maintain quality standards, provide adequate bottling and distributing facilities, and participate in marketing programs. Furthermore, they were not allowed to sell in other franchised territories (or to sell to second parties who were likely to sell the product in another territory), nor could they sell directly competing products. However, a bottler was under no legal obligation to handle the full product line of any single concentrate manufacturer and could select which product to distribute within a given flavor category. Thus, for example, an independent Pepsi franchisee could distribute Seven-Up within the lemon-lime segment, rather than Teem, PepsiCo.'s competitive entry.

The franchise bottling system had originally evolved because of economic necessity. The concentrate manufacturers needed to maximize their products' distribution and availability, while the bottlers needed some guarantee of territorial exclusivity to make it worth their while to invest in the necessary capital equipment. The result, early in the industry's history, was a multiplicity of small bottlers. As time passed, a plethora of container sizes and shapes put many small bottlers at an economic disadvantage: they could not invest in all of the production lines necessary to ensure a complete line of any given product. Many bottlers therefore entered into joint ventures with one another to share production facilities. Alternatively, several concentrate manufacturers, such as the Seven-Up Company, made separate contracts with independent canners which guaranteed the provision of the full line of products to the company's franchised bottlers.

Regardless of the production system used, all products were still distributed through the territorially franchised bottlers. The numbers of bottlers were declining, however, while their territories were expanding. Of the estimated 5,200 domestic bottlers in operation in 1947, only 2,300 were thought to remain in business in 1970.[4] This change derived in part from mergers among the individual bottlers as one means of providing the necessary production equipment. However, the trend was also caused by the acquisition of certain bottlers by larger corporate entities, which included newcomers to the soft-drink industry as well as certain concentrate manufacturers themselves. In the former case, the trend toward acquisitions by outsiders started in the late 1960s when certain medium-sized conglomerates such as RKO General and General Cinema, started buying bottlers. By the late 1970s, however, larger conglomerates were making the acquisitions, the size of the purchasers reflecting the attractive cash flows of many bottlers. In the case of the concentrate manufacturers, the primary goal was to maintain or increase their control over marketing and distribution. The

---

[3]The bottlers' specific production responsibilities included (1) purchasing raw materials, principally sweeteners and packaging materials; (2) mixing the concentrate, sweetener, water, and carbonation; and (3) packaging the finished product.

[4]J. C. Louis and Harvey Z. Yazijian, *The Cola Wars* (New York: Everest House, Publishers, 1980), 334.

results of the increased concentration among the bottlers and concentrate manufacturers are shown in the table of domestic sales by bottler.

Breakdown of 1977 Domestic Sales by Type of Bottler				
	Company-Owned Bottlers		Franchised Bottlers	
Company	Nos.	Percent Sales	Nos.	Percent Sales
Coca-Cola Co.	11	10%	555	90%
PepsiCo., Inc.	13	22	404	78
Seven-Up Co.	1[a]	3	473[b]	97
Dr. Pepper Co.	5	12	494	88
Royal Crown Cos.	13	25	272	75

[a]The Seven-Up Bottling Co. of Phoenix, Ariz., was acquired in 1972. The company also owned a second bottling operation in Ontario, Canada.
[b]It was estimated that only three bottlers handled the Seven-Up line exclusively: all others marketed one or more competitive products. Industry analysts also estimated that about 330 of Seven-Up's bottlers (70 percent of the total) handled Coca-Cola or Pepsi-Cola.
Source: Company annual reports and 10–K's, *Value Line*, and industry reports.

The increasing concentration among soft-drink bottlers and concentrate manufacturers did not go unnoticed. In the mid-1970s, the Federal Trade Commission brought an antitrust action against the industry in general and against the territorial franchise system in particular. Although a decision on the case was not imminent at the end of 1977, the industry was lobbying strongly against the action. Dissolution of the franchise system, the industry argued, would cause irreparable economic damage to the independent bottlers by opening the door for a warehouse distribution system along the lines of that used in the beer industry.

Competitive Environment.

The soft-drink industry had long been dominated by its two leading competitors, the Coca-Cola Co. and PepsiCo., Inc. These two companies, through their competition with each other, determined the industry's pricing schedules and marketing programs.

For instance, until 1975 the Coca-Cola Co. was the industry price leader in both the fountain and take-home segments of the market. Coke's pricing schedule was based on the terms originally negotiated with its bottlers at the turn of the century. As a result, the price of the company's base concentrate had remained at 88 cents per gallon for many years.[5] In 1974, however, PepsiCo. initiated an aggressive campaign against Coca-Cola. The company's theme, "the Pepsi Challenge," asked customers to taste test the two beverages. The campaign was supported by heavy consumer discounts as well as increased advertising

---

[5]Coca-Cola charged its bottlers for sugar on the basis of the average price of sugar at the ten largest northeast refiners during the first 10 days of each quarter. Coca-Cola was one of the world's leading purchasers of sugar and procured its needs under futures contracts.

expenditures. With this campaign, PepsiCo. seized the position of industry price leader within the take-home segment.

This escalation of the competition between Coke and Pepsi affected the rest of the industry in two ways. The widespread use of consumer discounts reflected the growing emphasis on volume and share-of-market data rather than earnings. Those concentrate manufacturers electing not to discount their products, such as the Seven-Up Company, ran the risk of weakening their relations with their bottlers. The budgets allocated to marketing were also increasing.

These trends were not expected to abate in the near future. In fact, early in 1978, the Coca-Cola Co. began negotiations with its bottlers to change their fixed-price contracts. Coke's aim was to revise its pricing schedule such that the syrup's price could be raised commensurate with increases in the consumer price index. In return for this concession, Coke promised its bottlers that the company would use a large portion of the anticipated increase in earnings to augment its marketing budget in the Coke–Pepsi dispute. Negotiations on this matter were ongoing in March 1978.

These negotiations had several implications for Coke's competitors. Since most companies strove to approximate Coke's pricing schedule, the negotiations appeared to offer some relief from inflation's negative effect on margins. However, this benefit was largely offset by the specter of the increased marketing budgets Coke had promised its bottlers.

In addition, Coca-Cola Co.'s and PepsiCo.'s marketing programs were becoming more successful, as reflected in the increases in their individual shares of market as well as in the continued preference for cola-flavored products. Both the Seven-Up Company and the Dr. Pepper Co. responded with campaigns highlighting the differences between their products and the colas. Seven-Up management introduced the "Uncola" theme in 1968, while Dr. Pepper relied on "the most misunderstood soft drink" theme. Although Seven-Up introduced modest variations on its Uncola message in the intervening years, the basic theme had not changed substantially by 1977: "7-Up is a drink with a style all its own, and the people who drink it have a style all their own." This theme was re-emphasized and repackaged in 1977 and presented by management as its vehicle to regain its former share of the market. Specifically, management announced its goal of growing at a rate of 1 to 2 percent higher than the industry as a whole.

Early in 1978, however, Seven-Up's president made the following statement to *Advertising Age* (4/17/78): "research has found that the 'Seven-Up image is confused and cloudy.' " The company subsequently terminated its relationship with its advertising agency of 36 years and announced its intent to test market a new graphics program in late 1978 and to increase the product's advertising budget. Market analysts generally approved of this move, thinking that the Uncola campaign had succeeded too well: consumers had come to see Seven-Up as a specialty product.

Competition in the industry was also proceeding along two other major fronts: international expansion and new product development. The Middle East was the major arena of expansion during 1977. The Coca-Cola Co., previously well-established in Israel, was finally granted permission to enter the Egyptian market. Less than 12 months later, Seven-Up management announced its intent to introduce Seven-Up into the Cairo market in May 1978 and to open 11 other bottling operations abroad during the year.

With respect to new product entries, the last major spurt of activity had been in the early 1960s. PepsiCo. acquired and introduced Mountain Dew nationally. PepsiCo. and Coca-Cola introduced Teem and Sprite into the lemon-lime segment, and all companies developed and started marketing diet drinks. In early 1978, the Coca-Cola Co. was test marketing Mello Yello, and the Seven-Up Company introduced Quirst, a new entry into the lemonade market. Quirst, which had been developed by Seven-Up's recently acquired subsidiaries, was to be test marketed in about one-fifth of the U.S. market starting in early May. The product's introductory campaign was to be backed by an annual advertising budget of $5 million.[6]

Industry Outlook.

The outlook for the soft-drink industry in the latter half of the 1970s was mixed. While domestic demographic trends and a tight competitive environment implied reductions in the rates of soft-drink sales growth, the international market appeared to be wide open. According to certain security analysts, "Foreign markets continue to hold great potential for the major producers. Per capita soft-drink consumption in most overseas nations is only a small fraction of the U.S. rate. Although it is highly unlikely that consumption in Third World nations will ever match the U.S. level, there remains great room for growth." Taking the domestic and international markets together, industry analysts predicted a 5 to 6 percent growth rate in the industry over the next 5 years.

There was, however, the possibility that certain other forces might affect future sales levels. The soft-drink industry was under attack on several fronts at the end of 1977. Nutrition experts, alarmed at increasing per capita soft-drink consumption, were vocal in their criticism of the product. Their concerns were reinforced by research into the possible toxic effects of heavy sugar ingestion. Saccharin, the sugar substitute used in diet soft drinks, was also a source of controversy. Saccharin's safety was under continuing study by the federal Food and Drug Administration. Caffeine, a component of most soft drinks but not of Seven-Up, had recently re-emerged as a potential problem. The FDA had initiated a study on the safety of heavy caffeine consumption, particularly as it pertained to children and teenagers, the industry's primary market. Although the caffeine content of soft drinks was considerably less than that of comparable amounts of tea or coffee, the study represented an additional source of uncertainty for the industry.

CONCLUSION

Despite their uncertain futures, little about either the soft-drink industry or the Seven-Up Company reduced their attractiveness to PM management. On the contrary, Seven-Up appeared particularly attractive from both financial and operational points of view. Although the product was new to PM management, the problems of its merchandising were very familiar.

Unfortunately, however, the current status of the merger and acquisition market implied that the Seven-Up Company might well evoke interest among other acquisitive corporations. This realization put additional pressure on PM

---

[6]Shortly after Seven-Up management introduced Quirst, the company was sued by the Squirt Co. for trademark infringement. The outcome of the case had not been determined by April 1978.

management to act quickly and provided an additional consideration in its initial tender offer. On its part, Seven-Up's management recognized that the company was not only attractive, but also potentially vulnerable to a takeover. Seven-Up management proposed and received approval of two actions at the company's April 1978 shareholders' meeting. First, dividends were increased, presumably to strengthen investor interest in and support of the stock. Second, and more telling, the shareholders approved amendments to the company's articles of incorporation providing for the establishment of three classes of directors, each of which would serve a staggered three-year term.

Thus, it appeared that the conditions in the market, as well as the position of Seven-Up's management and shareholders, demanded a very careful, competitive tender offer.

Philip Morris, Inc.: Seven-Up Acquisition (A)

EXHIBIT 1
■

Philip Morris: 5-Year Performance
(dollars in millions, except per share amounts)

	1973	1974	1975	1976	1977
Operating Companies' Revenues (percent)					
Philip Morris U.S.A.	50.1%	49.9%	47.3%	45.7%	41.5%
Philip Morris International	31.6	29.5	28.6	25.2	25.9
Miller Brewing Co.	10.6	13.4	18.1	22.9	25.5
Philip Morris Industrial	5.1	5.2	4.2	3.9	4.2
Mission Viejo	2.6	2.1	1.9	2.2	2.8
Total percentage[a]	100.0	100.0	100.0	100.0	100.0
Total dollars	$2,602.5	$3,011.0	$3,642.4	$4,293.8	$5,202.0
Operating Companies' Income (percent)					
Philip Morris U.S.A.	69.0%	70.9%	68.4%	63.3%	60.6%
Philip Morris International	28.0	23.3	22.9	20.5	19.6
Miller Brewing Co.	(1.0)	1.6	5.8	12.0	13.6
Philip Morris Industrial	2.5	3.0	1.6	1.7	1.9
Mission Viejo	1.3	1.2	1.2	2.6	4.2
Total percentage[a]	100.0	100.0	100.0	100.0	100.0
Total dollars	$ 329.5	$ 403.6	$ 492.8	$ 634.5	$ 782.7
Other Expenses					
Interest expense	$ 51.0	$ 82.7	$ 99.0	$ 102.8	$ 101.6
Provision for income taxes	107.0	122.0	149.2	206.3	290.6
Net Earnings	148.6	175.5	211.6	265.7	334.9
Per Share Data					
Primary earnings	$ 2.71	$ 3.15	$ 3.62	$ 4.47	$ 5.60
Dividends declared	0.67	0.78	0.93	1.15	1.56
Book value	14.66	16.97	20.63	23.99	28.16
Market price of common: High–low					
	68.38–48.75	61.38–34.13	59.25–40.88	63.25–49.75	64.88–51.50
Market price of common: End of year	57.38	48.00	53.00	61.75	61.88
Operating Performance					
Pre-tax profit margin	9.80%	9.90%	9.90%	11.00%	12.00%
Return on average equity	19.70	19.60	19.20	20.00	21.50
Total debt/equity[b]	1.16	1.27	1.18	1.07	0.93
Net cash flow/capital expenditures[c]	0.81	0.79	0.85	1.19	1.19
Beta	1.11	1.15	1.15	1.15	1.10
Date of beta estimate	11/30/73	11/1/74	10/31/75	10/29/76	10/28/77

[a]Numbers many not add to 100 percent due to rounding.
[b]Total debt = Long-term debt + Notes payable + Current portion of long-term debt.
[c]Net cash flow = Profit after tax + Depreciation − Dividends on common and preferred stock.
Source: Philip Morris, Inc., 1977 *Annual Report;* Value Line.

Philip Morris, Inc.: Seven-Up Acquisition (A)

EXHIBIT 2
■

Miller Brewing Company, 1968–1977
(all data in millions)

Operating Performance: 1968–1977

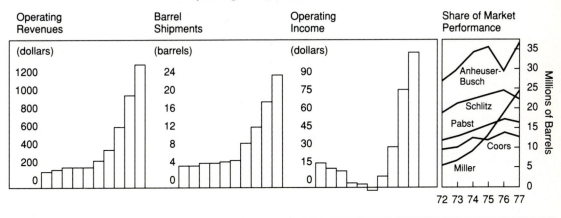

Source: Philip Morris, Inc., *Annual Reports.*
Source: Robert J. Flaherty, "Philip Morris' Year of Decision," *Forbes,* July 10, 1978, 30

Philip Morris, Inc.: Seven-Up Acquisition (A)

EXHIBIT 3
∎
Philip Morris Income Statements
(thousands of dollars, except per share amounts)

	Results for Year Ending December 31		Results for Three Months Ending March 31	
	1976	1977	1977	1978
Operating revenues	$4,293,782	$5,201,977	$1,142,617	$1,390,709
Cost of sales				
Cost of products sold	1,966,871	2,401,680	527,077	638,882
U.S. federal and foreign taxes on goods sold	1,159,286	1,352,487	296,160	371,838
Gross profit	1,167,625	1,447,810	319,380	379,989
Marketing, administrative, and research	547,287	676,772	150,475	178,478
Equity in net earnings of unconsolidated foreign subsidiaries and affiliates	(14,201)	(11,694)	(2,911)	(2,303)
Operating income of operating companies	634,539	782,732	171,816	203,814
Corporate expense	35,229	38,523	11,089	12,491
Gross interest	109,258	108,747	27,007	32,159
Capitalized interest	6,424	7,163	1,273	2,599
Net interest expense	102,834	101,584	25,734	29,560
Net currency translation hedging costs	15,520	11,633	(2,047)	2,645
Other deductions, net	9,028	5,476	4,258	(1,944)
Earnings before income tax	471,928	625,516	132,782	161,062
Provision for federal and other income tax	206,253	290,590	61,365	73,541
Net earnings	$ 265,675	$ 334,926	$ 71,417	$ 87,521
Earnings per common share	$4.47	$5.60	$1.19	$1.46

Source: Philip Morris, Inc., *Annual Reports.*

Philip Morris, Inc.: Seven-Up Acquisition (A)

EXHIBIT 4
∎
Philip Morris Balance Sheets (thousands of dollars)

	Results for Year Ending December 31		Results for Three Months Ending March 31	
	1976	1977	1977	1978
Assets				
Cash and cash equivalents	$ 64,353	$ 72,231	$ 47,070	$ 75,026
Net receivables	267,943	316,723	310,260	332,138
Inventories				
Leaf tobacco	1,089,301	1,271,235	1,083,092	1,256,118
Other raw materials	125,620	142,231	125,855	143,436
Work in process and finished goods	379,446	314,519	393,322	385,699

EXHIBIT 4 *continued*

	Results for Year Ending December 31		Results for Three Months Ending March 31	
	1976	*1977*	*1977*	*1978*
Housing programs under construction	63,137	89,576	74,821	94,317
Total inventories	1,657,504	1,817,561	1,677,090	1,879,570
Prepaid expenses	15,945	14,505	21,582	22,585
Total current assets	2,005,745	2,221,020	2,056,002	2,309,319
Investments in and advances to unconsolidated foreign subsidiaries and affiliates	220,147	229,508	219,158	227,920
Land and offtrack improvements	58,766	69,576	59,648	70,464
Property, plant, and equipment, at cost	1,323,923	1,594,910	1,355,123	1,693,442
Less accumulated depreciation	330,044	392,478	340,157	409,696
Net property, plant, and equipment	993,879	1,202,432	1,014,966	1,283,746
Brands, trademarks, patents, and goodwill	211,570	222,492	211,594	222,183
Long-term receivables	66,463	64,762	65,047	67,073
Other assets	25,639	38,249	42,434	41,435
Total assets	$3,582,209	$4,048,039	$3,668,849	$4,222,140
Liabilities and Shareholders' Equity				
Notes payable	260,131	121,139	N.Av.	N.Av.
Accounts and notes payable	N.Av.	N.Av.	396,581	309,407
Accounts payable and accrued liabilities	402,775	503,767	N.Av.	N.Av.
Accrued liabilities	N.Av.	N.Av.	272,355	390,825
Current portion long-term debt	17,729	15,740	N.Av.	N.Av.
Federal and other income taxes	103,527	139,766	119,917	157,971
Dividends payable	19,359	24,741	19,463	30,737
Total current liabilities	803,521	805,153	808,316	888,940
Long-term debt	1,247,778	1,426,619	1,249,596	1,443,229
Deferred income taxes	77,714	104,429	87,449	119,519
Other liabilities	23,214	21,772	28,878	23,284
Total liabilities	2,152,227	2,357,973	2,174,239	2,474,972
Cumulative preferred stock ($100 par)	8,812	8,262	8,812	7,787
Common stock ($1 par)	59,490	59,922	59,806	59,928
Additional paid-in capital	294,225	300,538	292,947	301,055
Earnings reinvested in business	1,071,488	1,325,149	1,137,148	1,381,934
Less treasury stock, at cost	(4,033)	(3,805)	(4,103)	(3,536)
Total shareholders' equity	1,429,982	1,690,066	1,494,610	1,747,168
Total liabilities and shareholders' equity	$3,582,209	$4,048,039	$3,668,849	$4,222,140

Source: Philip Morris, Inc., *Annual Reports.*
N.Av. = not available.

Philip Morris, Inc.: Seven-Up Acquisition (A)

EXHIBIT 5
∎

Top Four Soft-Drink Companies: Performance, 1973–1977

Company and Year	Primary EPS	Cash Flow per Share	Dividends per Share	Book Value per Share	Return on Equity	Market Price High–Low[a]	Average Annual P/E	Long-Term Debt/ Equity
Coca-Cola[b] Beta @ 3/10/78: 1.20								
1973	$1.80	$2.29	$0.90	$ 7.44	22.7%	$75.0–57.8	38.9	0.9%
1974	1.64	2.13	1.04	8.01	19.2	63.9–22.3	26.8	1.1
1975	2.00	2.55	1.15	9.45	19.5	46.8–26.6	19.9	0.7
1976	2.38	2.95	1.33	10.53	21.0	47.6–36.7	17.7	0.6
1977	2.67	3.33	1.54	11.92	21.0	40.9–35.5	14.3	0.9
PepsiCo., Inc.[b] Beta @ 3/10/78: 1.15								
1973	$1.12	$1.71	$0.38	$ 5.32	16.0%	$29.9–21.3	24.3	44.7%
1974	1.23	1.90	0.43	6.12	15.7	23.9–9.8	13.9	62.7
1975	1.47	2.20	0.50	7.11	16.7	24.8–13.6	14.2	45.0
1976	1.85	2.68	0.63	8.44	18.1	29.2–23.2	14.0	37.0
1977	2.15	3.19	0.83	9.57	19.3	28.6–22.3	11.5	44.0
Seven-Up Co.[b] Beta @ 3/10/78: 1.25								
1973	$1.30	$1.47	$0.43	$ 5.08	21.4%	$37.3–21.8	23.6	4.7%
1974	1.54	1.76	0.61	6.04	21.9	30.8–10.5	14.3	3.6
1975	1.88	2.14	0.75	7.54	23.0	36.0–15.5	16.0	2.4
1976	2.28	2.59	1.13	8.75	24.4	41.0–29.8	15.6	0.9
1977	2.38	2.70 est.	1.25	9.90 est.	23.0 est.	32.8–23.8	11.7 est.	0.6 est.
Dr. Pepper[b] Beta @ 3/10/78: 1.50								
1973	$0.51	$0.60	$0.23	$ 1.99	25.5%	$30.0–18.8	49.2	0.0%
1974	0.52	0.62	0.28	2.27	22.7	22.9–6.5	26.1	0.0
1975	0.62	0.74	0.32	2.58	24.0	15.1–7.0	18.1	0.0
1976	0.81	0.95	0.40	2.80	27.0	17.8–11.0	18.6	0.0
1977	1.01	1.23	0.53	3.42	26.5	17.3–11.0	13.3	0.9
S&P 500: Industry Composite[c]								
1973	$2.27[d]	$3.78[e]	$0.91	$17.26	13.5%	$38–24	13.7[f]	48%
1974	2.46[d]	4.11[e]	0.98	18.55	13.7	31–16	9.7[f]	50
1975	2.29[d]	4.10[e]	1.01	19.71	12.0	30–18	10.0[f]	52
1976	2.85[d]	4.76[e]	1.14	21.37	13.7	34–24	10.0[f]	49
1977	3.11[d]	5.20[e]	1.31	23.07	13.8	32–24	9.4[f]	48

[a]All stocks traded on NYSE except Seven-Up, which trades in the OTC market.
[b] Source: Value Line.
[c]Source: Standard & Poor's Compustat Services, Inc.
[d]Primary EPS includes extraordinary items and discontinued operations.
[e]Estimated by casewriter: [PAT + Depr. + Depl. + Amort.] ÷ Primary nos. of shares.
[f]Computed by casewriter.

EXHIBIT 6

■

Common Stock Movement, January 1977–April 1978
(closing price at end of month or at date shown)

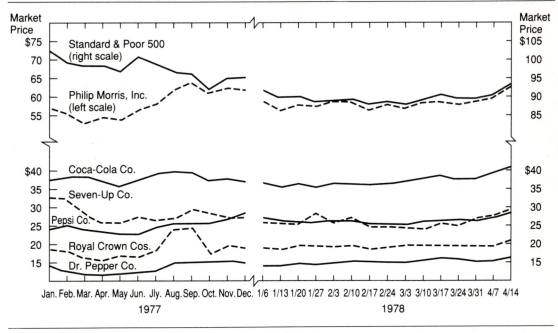

EXHIBIT 7

■

Seven-Up Company Income Statements
(thousands of dollars, except per share amounts)

	Results for Year Ending December 31		Results for Three Months Ending March 31[a]	
	1976	1977	1977	1978[b]
Net sales	$233,283	$250,998	$50,416	$60,271
Cost of products sold	117,166	129,040	24,863	29,878
Gross profit	116,117	121,958	25,553	30,393
Selling, administrative, and general expense	71,482	76,815	17,184	20,004
Interest expense	289	335	37	139
Other expenses, net of other income	(2,800)	(2,401)	(579)	(799)
Earnings before income tax	47,146	47,209	8,911	11,049
Income taxes	22,394	21,420	4,047	5,278
Net earnings	$ 24,752	$ 25,789	$ 4,864	$ 5,771
Earnings per common share	$ 2.28	$ 2.38	$ 0.45	$ 0.53
Dividends per common share	$ 1.13	$ 1.25	$ 0.30	$ 0.35

[a]Quarterly data are unaudited.
[b]Results for 1978 exclude operations of Oregon Freeze Dried Foods, acquired in February 1978. Had the company been included for the entire three-month period, sales at 3/31/78 would have been $62,015,000, net earnings $5,830,000, and earnings per share $0.54.
Source: Seven-Up Company, *Annual Reports.*

Philip Morris, Inc.: Seven-Up Acquisition (A)

EXHIBIT 8
■
Seven-Up Company Balance Sheets (thousands of dollars)

	Results for Year Ending December 31		Results for Three Months Ending March 31[a]	
	1976	1977	1977	1978[a]
Assets				
Cash	$ 5,462	$ 4,517	$ 9,707	$ 13,723
Short-term investments	34,589	42,616	29,704	22,534
Accounts and notes receivable	18,469	20,467	19,991	23,398
Less allowance for doubtful accounts	(275)	(220)	(289)	(220)
Net receivables	18,194	20,267	19,702	23,178
Inventories				
Finished products (FIFO)	12,029	13,067	12,606	16,880
Extract and raw materials (sugar carried at LIFO)	14,025	14,088	16,454	17,515
Total inventories	26,054	27,155	29,060	34,395
Prepaid expenses and other current assets	2,547	2,635	2,861	2,679
Total current assets	86,846	97,190	91,034	96,509
Other assets	2,678	2,330	2,628	2,498
Property, plant, and equipment, at cost				
Land	6,527	6,407	6,464	6,537
Orchards	1,989	2,113	2,146	2,113
Buildings and improvements	15,739	18,866	15,626	19,254
Machinery and equipment	23,942	29,290	24,512	31,044
Orchards under development	1,535	1,706	1,446	1,752
Construction in progress	3,782	2,450	4,639	3,498
Less depreciation (straight-line)	(15,932)	(18,632)	(16,459)	(19,557)
Net property, plant, and equipment	37,582	42,200	38,374	44,641
Net intangible assets: trademarks, formulas, and goodwill	4,144	4,009	4,081	9,726
Total assets	$131,243	$145,729	$136,117	$153,374

EXHIBIT 8 *continued*

	Results for Year Ending December 31		Results for Three Months Ending March 31[a]	
	1976	*1977*	*1977*	*1978[a]*
Liabilities and Shareholders' Equity				
Current liabilities				
Notes payable to foreign banks	489	2,189	2,302	1,998
Accounts payable	7,933	8,653	9,366	9,874
Employee compensation	1,981	2,261	1,785	2,264
Accrued advertising	8,774	9,949	7,761	10,513
Other accrued liabilities	2,317	2,932	2,101	3,425
Income taxes	4,396	3,385	6,308	6,333
Current portion of long-term debt	354	259	352	419
Total current liabilities	26,244	29,628	29,975	34,826
Other liabilities				
Long-term debt (excluding current portion)	943	689	842	703
Deferred income taxes	2,504	1,979	2,539	2,390
Total liabilities	29,691	32,296	33,356	37,919
Shareholders' equity				
6 percent cumulative preferred stock	3,588	3,076	3,076	3,076
Common stock ($1 par value)[b]	10,720	10,722	10,720	10,725
Additional capital	11,150	11,345	11,277	11,389
Retained earnings	76,094	88,290	77,688	90,265
Total shareholders' equity	101,552	113,433	102,761	115,455
Total liabilities and shareholders' equity	$131,243	$145,729	$136,117	$153,374

[a]Quarterly data are unaudited.
[b]The descendants of the Seven-Up Company's three original founders owned 45 percent of Seven-Up's common stock, roughly half of which was held in beneficiary trusts for future generations. Common stock held by unrelated members of management increased the total controlled by the company to about 51 percent. Twenty-one percent of the stock was held by a group of 53 institutional investors, and the remainder was owned by unrelated parties. Although members of the founding families had not taken a particularly active role in the management of the company in recent years, two grandsons of the original founders were elected directors of the company at the April 1978 shareholders' meeting. This brought the total number of family representatives on the board to three and was interpreted as an apparent attempt to strengthen the families' hands in the business.
Source: Seven-Up Company, *Annual Reports.*

EXHIBIT 9

■

Seven-Up Company Historical Data (millions of dollars, except per share amounts)

	1969	1970	1971	1972	1973	1974	1975
Earnings Data							
Net sales	$103.0	$111.6	$124.4	$132.5	$146.7	$190.9	$213.6
Gross profit	48.0	51.6	58.1	62.8	71.0	80.8	101.2
Selling, general, and administrative	30.0	32.5	36.6	40.2	45.2	51.2	61.3
Operating profit	18.0	19.1	21.5	22.6	25.8	29.6	39.9
Net miscellaneous income	0.2	0.5	0.7	0.6	1.3	2.5	(0.1)
Profit before tax	18.2	19.6	22.2	23.2	27.1	32.1	39.8
Income taxes	9.6	9.8	10.9	11.2	13.0	15.5	19.5
Profit after taxes and extraordinary items	8.4[d]	9.8	11.3	12.0	14.1	16.6	20.3
Depreciation and amortization	1.1	1.2	1.1	1.3	1.8	2.3	2.9
Capital expenditures	2.9	1.9	2.6	3.1	7.5	6.8	6.8
Per Share Data							
Earnings[a]	0.75	0.89	1.03	1.10	1.30	1.54	1.88
Dividends[b]	0.24	0.33	0.40	0.42	0.43	0.61	0.75
Book value[b]	2.50	3.08	3.72	4.62	5.50	6.45	7.93

	$22¾–14¼	$30¾–17¾	$36⅛–26¾	$50⅛–33⅜	$37¼–21¾	$30¾–10½	$36–14¾
Market price range[b][c]							
Average number of shares[a]	10,326,961	10,335,038	10,345,034	10,378,538	10,457,812	10,467,739	10,636,841
Balance Sheet Data							
Current assets	$ 35.4	$ 40.7	$ 45.8	$ 52.3	$ 58.8	$ 67.3	$ 86.6
Plant, property, and equipment	14.8	16.0	17.2	19.3	24.6	29.1	32.7
Other	5.2	4.5	4.4	5.8	6.2	7.3	6.7
Total assets	55.4	61.2	67.4	77.4	89.6	103.7	126.0
Current liabilities	14.7	15.2	15.9	17.7	20.1	24.9	34.8
Long-term debt	3.2	2.8	1.7	2.4	3.1	2.7	2.1
Other	0.7	0.4	0.4	0.4	0.4	0.4	0.6
6 percent cumulative preferred stock	3.6	3.6	3.6	3.6	3.6	3.6	3.6
$5.71 convertible Class A preferred stock	7.4	7.3	7.3	5.1	4.9	4.6	—
Owners' equity	25.8	31.8	38.5	48.2	57.5	67.5	84.9
Total liabilities and owners' equity	$ 55.4	$ 61.2	$ 67.4	$ 77.4	$ 89.6	$103.7	$126.0

[a]Based on the weighted-average number of shares outstanding during the year. Data have been adjusted to reflect stock splits in 1969 and 1972 and to reflect those shares issuable upon the exercise of stock options.

[b]Adjusted retroactively for two-for-one stock splits in 1969 and 1972.

[c]High–low bid prices, OTC.

[d]Extraordinary loss of $0.2.

Source: Seven-Up Company, *Annual Reports*. All data have been restated on pooling-of-interest basis to reflect the operations of the Warner Jenkinson Co. and Ventura Coastal Corp. acquired in 1970 and 1973, respectively. Numbers may not add due to rounding.

Philip Morris, Inc.: Seven-Up Acquisition (A)

EXHIBIT 10
■
Volume Sales and Share-of-Market Data:
Top Five Soft-Drink Companies

	1975	1976	1977
Coca-Cola Co.			
Coca-Cola	24.2%	24.3%	24.5%
Sprite	2.5	2.7	2.8
Tab	2.5	2.6	2.6
Fanta	2.1	2.3	2.3
Mr. Pibb	0.8	0.7	0.9
Fresca	0.6	0.6	0.5
Others	0.1	0.2	0.3
Total	32.7	33.4	33.9
PepsiCo., Inc.			
Pepsi-Cola	17.4	17.0	17.2
Mountain Dew	1.1	1.5	1.9
Diet Pepsi	1.6	1.9	2.1
Pepsi Light	0.1	0.5	0.5
Teem	0.3	0.2	0.2
Others	0.3	0.3	0.4
Total	20.8	21.4	22.3
Seven-Up Company[a]			
7-Up	6.6	6.3	6.0
Diet 7-Up	1.0	1.2	1.2
Total	7.6	7.5	7.2
Royal Crown Cos.			
Royal Crown	3.4	3.3	3.2
Diet Rite Cola and RC 100	0.8	0.8	0.8
Nehi and others	1.2	1.2	1.0
Total	5.4	5.3	5.0
Dr. Pepper Co.			
Dr. Pepper	4.9	5.0	5.3
Sugar Free Dr. Pepper	0.6	0.8	1.0
Total	5.5	5.8	6.3
Total SOM, top 5	72.0	73.4	74.7
Millions of cases sold, top 5[b]	3,208.5	3,587.9	3,925.5

[a]Sales of Seven-Up's Howdy Flavors were a negligible proportion of total soft-drink sales in the year shown: case sales are included in the total of the cases sold by the top five companies.
[b]1 case = 24 8-oz. containers or 16 12-oz. cans.
Source: Lehman Brothers Kuhn Loeb Research, as printed in *Beverage Industry,* April 24, 1981. Copyright: John C. Maxwell and *Beverage Industry.* Reprinted by special permission of John C. Maxwell.

Philip Morris, Inc.: Seven-Up Acquisition (A)

EXHIBIT 11
■
Trends in the Soft-Drink Industry

A. Estimated Share of Soft-Drink Market by Flavor Category[a]

	Cola	Lemon-Lime	Pepper Type	Orange	Root Beer	Other
1970	63.0%	12.0%	3.9%	8.3%	4.5%	8.4%
1971	63.0	12.0	3.9	8.4	5.0	7.7
1972	63.0	12.0	4.6	8.4	5.0	7.0
1973	62.5	12.5	5.0	8.2	5.0	6.8
1974	61.7	12.8	5.2	8.0	5.2	7.1
1975	62.1	12.9	5.3	7.9	5.2	6.6
1976	62.2	12.7	6.7	7.8	5.2	5.4
1977	62.4	12.4	7.3	7.4	5.3	5.2

B. Composition of U.S. per Capita Annual Liquid Consumption[b]

	Soft Drinks	Beer	Wine and Distilled Spirits	Coffee[a] and Tea	Milk[d]	Other[d]
1970	14.8%	10.1%	1.7%	22.6%	12.7%	38.1%
1971	15.8	10.6	1.9	22.5	12.6	36.7
1972	16.6	10.8	1.9	22.5	12.7	35.4
1973	17.4	11.3	2.0	22.7	12.5	34.1
1974	17.4	11.8	2.0	21.9	12.2	34.7
1975	17.1	12.0	2.0	21.5	12.4	35.0
1976	18.7	12.1	2.1	19.9	12.3	34.9
1977	20.0	12.5	2.1	19.2	12.2	34.0

[a]Source: *Beverage Industry*, April 24, 1981; Copyright John C. Maxwell and *Beverage Industry*. Based on data from Lehman Brothers Kuhn Loeb Research. Figures include diet drinks in the appropriate flavor category.
[b]Source: *Beverage Industry*, May 22, 1981, p. 19. Data are based on USDA, DSI, USBA, American Bottled Water Assoc., and Lehman Brothers Kuhn Loeb Research estimates.
[c]Coffee data are based on three-year moving average to counterbalance inventory savings.
[d]Data for milk and juice (the latter is included in *Other* category) reflect USDA revisions as of 7/1/80.

Philip Morris, Inc.: Seven-Up Acquisition (A)

EXHIBIT 12

■

Major Media Spending by Top Five Soft-Drink Competitors
(thousands of dollars)

	1973	1974	1975	1977
Coca-Cola Co.				
Coca-Cola	$24,013.4	$22,122.1	$20,261.3	$24,227.1
Tab	5,315.8	5,099.3	6,369.5	4,195.5
Fresca	2,589.9	2,544.5	2,381.3	1,273.0
Sprite	1,738.0	2,463.1	2,542.3	4,188.3
Diet Sprite	N.Av.	N.Av.	10.2	293.4
Fanta beverages	391.8	147.2	74.5	117.6
Mr. Pibb	264.3	911.1	1,297.4	1,208.2
Mr. Pibb Diet	N.Av.	N.Av.	13.0	11.2
Other, general[a]	412.7	817.8	407.4	790.9
Total	34,725.9	34,105.1	33,356.9	36,305.2
Company total[b]	40,980.9	41,605.6	41,931.8	52,385.8
PepsiCo., Inc.				
Pepsi-Cola	13,383.2	14,795.4	14,557.1	24,410.0
Diet Pepsi	4,097.5	4,138.8	3,673.1	6,387.5
Mountain Dew	349.5	634.6	2,577.3	4,457.5
Pepsi-Light	N.Av.	N.Av.	918.2	6,565.0
Teem	0.8	N.Av.	61.2	248.8
Other[a]	466.7	60.8	366.8	1,225.6
Total	18,297.7	19,629.6	22,153.7	43,294.4
Company Total[b]	36,040.1	37,607.0	42,447.6	77,851.8
Seven-Up				
7-Up	10,430.6	10,185.0	9,230.5	12,897.9
Diet 7-Up	2,068.4	1,967.1	743.3	N.Av.
Sugar Free 7-Up	N.Av.	N.Av.	2,482.6	1,489.1
Other[a]	218.4	252.6	949.4	327.2
Total	12,717.4	12,404.7	13,405.8	14,714.2
Company Total[b]	13,048.8	12,911.6	14,013.9	14,714.2

EXHIBIT 12 *continued*

	1973	1974	1975	1977
Dr. Pepper Co.				
Dr. Pepper	5,245.8	5,401.9	4,574.5	6,871.0
Sugar Free Dr. Pepper	95.7	1,739.1	1,547.6	1,771.5
Diet Dr. Pepper	1,113.4	N.Av.	N.Av.	N.Av.
Other[a]	30.8	20.1	297.3	155.4
Total	6,485.7	7,161.1	6,419.4	8,797.9
Company Total[b]	6,604.2	7,279.5	6,506.1	8,881.5
Royal Crown Cos.				
Royal Crown Cola	1,279.9	579.9	486.1	7,418.8
Diet Rite Cola	626.4	2,130.6	3,388.6	2,289.3
Diet Rite beverages	2,351.2	133.5	108.8	4.8
Other[a]	3,605.7	5,116.8	10,088.3	245.5
Total	7,863.2	7,960.8	14,071.8	9,958.4
Company Total[b]	$ 8,064.3	$ 8,094.2	$14,784.8	$17,589.2

N.Av. = not available.

[a]Figures in this category are an aggregate of all nonproduct-specific expenditures, e.g., general company promotions, promotional tie-ins between one or more products (Tab and Fresca or Diet and Regular Dr. Pepper), sweepstakes, youth sports programs, etc. The numbers are included inasmuch as the expenditures are likely generally to support specific products. Expenditures for lower volume products, such as the Dr. Pepper Co.'s Big Red Soft Drink or PepsiCo.'s Rebel beverage, are not included in the *Other* category.

[b]Represents total media spending by the company for all products.

Source: Leading National Advertisers, New York, January–December 1973–1975 and 1977. Figures represent total expenditures in 6 media areas: magazines, newspaper supplements, network television, spot television, network radio, and outdoor advertising. All numbers are estimates.

Philip Morris, Inc.: Seven-Up Acquisition (A)

EXHIBIT 13
■

Five Leading Concentrate Manufacturers:
Analysis of Sales, 1976–1977 (millions of dollars)

Company and Product Line	1976		1977	
	Sales	Earnings	Sales	Earnings
Coca-Cola Co.	$3,033	$586	$3,560	$678
Soft drinks	77%	87%	75%	87%
Other (juices, tea, coffee, wine, etc.)	23	13	25	13
Total	100%	100%	100%	100%
PepsiCo., Inc.	$3,109	$360	$3,649	$412
Beverages	37%	40%	38%	44%
Food products	30	30	29	28
Food service	12	17	14	18
Transportation	13	6	12	6
Sporting goods	8	7	7	5
Total	100%	100%	100%	100%
Seven-Up Company[a]	$ 233	$ 44	$ 251	$ 45
Soft drinks	79%	90%	78%	90%
Lemon products	13	2	14	5
Flavors/colors	8	8	8	4
Total	100%	100%	100%	100%
Dr. Pepper Co.	$ 187	$ 32	$ 227	$ 37
Beverages (total)	100%	100%	100%	100%
Royal Crown Cos.	$ 287	$ 38	$ 350	$ 39
Soft drinks	61%	61%	58%	56%
Citrus	16	17	15	21
Home decorating	21	20	16	12
Fast food	2	2	11	12
Total	100%	100%	100%	100%

[a]Diversification within the Seven-Up Company had occurred fairly steadily in the period from 1970 to 1978, as shown below:

1970   Acquired Warner-Jenkinson Co., the dominant source of Seven-Up extract for over 50 years and a highly respected technical leader in the manufacture of flavors, colors, and fragrances.

1972   Acquired the first company-owned bottling company, subsequently named the Seven-Up Bottling Co. of Phoenix, Ariz.

1973   Acquired Ventura Coastal Corp., which grew, processed, and sold fresh lemons and lemon products, including frozen concentrate for lemonade. Ventura supplied roughly one-third of the lemonade market and provided the Seven-Up Co. with one-fifth of its lemon oil needs. Warner-Jenkinson acquired a small company with operations related to its own.

1974   Ventura Coastal Corp. acquired the Golden Crown Citrus Co., a manufacturer of juices. Golden Crown's product line was subsequently expanded to handle the frozen concentrates being produced by Ventura, and a new powdered lemonade was developed and put into test marketing. Warner-Jenkinson acquired a second small company with related operations.

1978   Oregon Freeze Dried Foods was acquired in February for $9.8 million in cash. The company, which had sales of $10.5 million in the year ending 6/30/77, was touted as the world's leading processor of freeze-dried goods.

Source: Company reports and *Value Line.*

Philip Morris, Incorporated:

Seven-Up Acquisition (B)

It was late April 1978, and the management of Philip Morris, Inc. (PM) expected to make its bid for the Seven-Up Company within several days. Sam Baxter, a recent Stanford MBA, was a member of the acquisition team. As a financial analyst, his job was to help develop the forecasts necessary to support the price to be offered by PM.

Mr. Baxter decided to base his analysis on a discounted cash flow (DCF) model he had used in business school.[1] He believed that this method would be useful in the valuation of the Seven-Up Company for several reasons. First, he regarded the expected cash flows of an investment to be a more realistic indicator of its future potential than its earnings, even though many managers had traditionally based their valuations on earnings and earnings multiples. PM management did use a cash flow approach to rank its capital investment decisions, so the use of the DCF model was a logical extension of current practice.

VALUATION TECHNIQUE

Before starting the process of forecasting Seven-Up's expected cash flows, a critical question had to be answered: from whose point of view should the analysis be done? That of Philip Morris management, Seven-Up management, or the capital markets? Clearly, the current market price of Seven-Up's stock represented one set of expectations for the company's future—expectations that theoretically incorporated estimates of the future performance of the Seven-Up Company, the soft-drink industry, and the market as a whole. However, early in 1978, Seven-Up management had taken certain actions that indicated its dissatisfaction with the company's performance and the value ascribed to it by the market. For instance, management had fired the company's advertising agency of 36 years and had announced a goal of 7 to 8 percent growth in sales for 1978, as compared with the 5 to 6 percent expected for the industry as a whole. Seven-Up management's actions clearly reflected its belief in a bright future for the

---

[1]The model was very similar to one described by Alfred Rappaport in an article published in the *Harvard Business Review* ["Strategic Analysis for More Profitable Acquisitions," *HBR* (July–August, 1979): 99–110.] Quotations subsequently appearing in this case are taken from that article and publication.

This case was prepared as a basis for class discussion rather than to illustrate either effective or ineffective handling of an administrative situation. Copyright © 1982 by the Darden Graduate Business School Sponsors, University of Virginia, Charlottesville, Virginia.

company, perhaps brighter than that envisioned by the stock market. The analysis could also be made from the viewpoint of PM management. The company had a history of introducing innovative changes to newly acquired companies, each of which implied certain costs and benefits that should, perhaps, be reflected in the analysis.

Mr. Baxter recognized that the viewpoint taken in the analysis affected not only the cash flows, but also the discount rate that would be used. Hoping to resolve his uncertainties, he decided to review his notes from business school on the DCF model.

The model defined the cash flows in the following way:

Yearly cash flows = (Earnings before interest and taxes, EBIT) ×
(1 − Income tax rate) + Depreciation and other noncash charges −
Capital expenditures − Cash required for increases in net working capital.

Certain comments were offered on how to estimate some of the cash flow variables. First, the income tax rate used in the analysis should be "the effective cash rate rather than a rate based on the accountant's income tax expense, which often includes a portion that is deferred." Second, the model suggested that both the estimates of future capital expenditures and investments in working capital could, for simplicity's sake, be based on their historical relationship to past increases in sales. With respect to capital expenditures, the analyst could "simply take the sum of all capital investments less depreciation over the past 5 or 10 years and divide this total by the sales increase from the beginning to the end of the period. With this approach, the resulting coefficient not only represents the capital investment historically required per dollar of sales increase but also impounds any cost increases for replacement of existing capacity."

While working capital could be estimated in a similar fashion to capital expenditures, two caveats to the procedure were offered: "1) the year-end balance sheet figures may not reflect the average or normal needs of the business during the year, and 2) both the accounts receivable and inventory accounts may overstate the magnitude of the funds committed by the company." While no specific action other than being careful was recommended with respect to the first problem, the following recommendation was made with respect to the second. "To estimate the additional cash requirements, the increased inventory investment should be measured by the variable costs for any additional units of inventory required and by the receivable investments in terms of the variable costs of the product delivered to generate the receivable rather than the absolute dollar amount of the receivable."

In using a DCF approach, the analyst must select an appropriate horizon and determine the target's residual value at the horizon. Although it was possible to rely simply on gut feel (e.g., "I don't feel comfortable making projections beyond 10 years out"), a more pragmatic approach to the problem had been suggested:

A better approach suggests that the forecast duration for cash flows should continue only as long as the expected rate of return on incremental investment required to support forecasted sales growth exceeds the cost-of-capital rate.

If for subsequent periods one assumes that the company's return on incremental investment equals the cost-of-capital rate, then the market would be indifferent whether management invests earnings in expansion projects or pays cash dividends that shareholders can in turn invest in identically risky opportunities yielding an identical rate of return. In other words, the value of the company is unaffected by growth when the company is investing in projects earning at the cost of capital or at the minimum acceptable risk-adjusted rate of return required by the market.

Thus, for purposes of simplification, we can assume a 100 percent payout of earnings after the horizon date or, equivalently, a zero growth rate without affecting the valuation of the company. (An implied assumption of this model is that the depreciation tax shield can be invested to maintain the company's productive capacity.)[2]

A "simple yet analytical, nonarbitrary" method of determining that period for which the expected rate of return on any incremental investments would exceed the cost-of-capital rate was to:

compute the minimum pretax return on sales *(P min)* needed to earn the minimum acceptable rate of return on the acquisition *(k)* given the investment requirements for working capital *(w)* and fixed assets *(f)* for each additional dollar of sales and given a projected tax rate *(T)*. The formula for *P min* is:[3]

$$P \ min = \frac{(f + w)k}{(1 - T)(1 + k)}.$$

For example, assume one company's management is considering the acquisition of another company with the following characteristics: (1) working capital and fixed-asset requirements per incremental sales dollar are 17 percent and 18 percent, respectively; (2) the tax rate is 48 percent; and (3) the appropriate cost of capital is 15 percent.

$$P \ min = \frac{(.17 + .18)(.15)}{(1 - .48)(1 + .15)} = 8.8\%.$$

Thus, the management of the acquisitor should develop projections only for those years it believes the target can earn a pre-tax return on sales of 8.8 percent or greater.

Having thus established the horizon date to use in the analysis, the determination of the target's residual value became simple: "The residual value is then the present value of the resulting cash flow perpetuity beginning one year after the horizon date."

CONCLUSION

After refreshing his memory as to the mechanics of the discounted cash flow model, Mr. Baxter considered how best to apply it to the Seven-Up Company. Gathering all of the information he had available on the company and the soft-drink industry,[4] he settled down to a long day's and a longer night's work.

---

[2]Ibid.

[3]Ibid.

[4]Philip Morris Incorporated: Seven-Up Acquisition (A) provides all requisite data on the Seven-Up Company and Philip Morris.

Norris Industries

In mid-August 1981, Sam Mencoff, an investment manager at First Chicago Investment Corporation (FCIC), reclined pensively in his chair after his first thorough reading of the prospectus before him. FCIC had been invited to make a major investment in the leveraged buyout of Norris Industries, a large California-based firm engaged in the design and manufacture of industrial, construction, and defense products using metal-working technology. Mr. Mencoff was struck by the purchase price, which at $43.05 per share represented nearly a 50-percent premium over Norris's market price ($29) the day before the announcement and nearly a 90-percent premium over what it had been selling for in 1979 before negotiations began. Norris was listed on the New York Stock Exchange, and its $420-million purchase price would make the buyout one of the largest in history. Much had been written about the supposed "restructuring" of industrial America that Norris exemplified. Would the housing and auto industries, and hence Norris, ever return to their former viability, Mr. Mencoff wondered, or was this the "final" down cycle that spelled the beginning of the end?

The proposed buyout had been arranged and structured by Kohlberg, Kravis, Roberts & Co. (KKR), a leading New York investment firm that specialized in leveraged buyouts. FCIC had worked with KKR in the past, and Mr. Mencoff considered them one of the top performers in the industry. He was far from confident, however, about this particular deal. Since the total purchase price was so large, FCIC would be expected to invest a major sum, close to $9 million, for a "strip" of investment instruments. This would be one of the largest investments in a single company that FCIC had ever made. Furthermore, Norris's business was tied to the housing and auto industries, which had been devastated by the current recession. The timing and extent of those industries' recoveries would in large part determine the safety of FCIC's investment.

COMPANY BACKGROUND

Norris Industries was founded by Kenneth T. Norris in 1930 as Norris Stamping and Manufacturing Company for the purpose of making fabricated metal products. The company was operated as an individual proprietorship until 1940, when it was incorporated. In 1938, Norris won its first military contract, to build

This case was prepared as a basis for class discussion rather than to illustrate either effective or ineffective handling of an administrative situation. Copyright © 1984 by the Darden Graduate Business School Sponsors, University of Virginia, Charlottesville, Virginia.

practice bombs, which was followed by another contract for the manufacture of aluminum cartridge containers. During World War II, the company's defense business dominated what little commercial business remained. Following the war, Norris expanded into automobile wheels, stainless steel cookware, and plumbing fixtures.

In 1950, Norris became a publicly held corporation when the Norris family sold 30 percent of its stock. Thermador Electrical Manufacturing Company, a maker of consumer appliances, and Compressed Gas Cylinders Company were acquired in 1951, and Norris changed its name to Norris–Thermador Corporation to capitalize on the public acceptance of Thermador products. The company's growth in commercial products was halted during the Korean War, when once again the defense business grew sharply and became dominant.

Norris's shares were listed on the New York Stock Exchange in 1960, and during the 1960s, a more active acquisition program expanded the company's commercial product lines at the same time the Vietnam War caused rapid expansion of its defense business. Among the acquisitions made during the 1960s that formed a major part of the current commercial business were: Bowers Manufacturing Company (electrical hardware) in 1963, Trade-Wind Motor Fans (currently part of Thermador–Waste King) in 1965, and Price Pfister Brass Manufacturing Company (household plumbing) in 1969. The company again changed its name in 1966 to Norris Industries to reflect its growing diversification.

The 1970s began with the acquisitions of Artistic Brass and Pressed Steel Tank Company in 1970 and the Automotive Trim Division in 1973. In 1977, Norris acquired the McIntosh Corporation, which significantly added to its automotive product lines. Despite acquisitions during the 1970s, the major emphasis of Norris's strategy (more than a quarter of a billion dollars) was on providing modern equipment and adequate capacity to existing businesses to capitalize on future opportunities. During 1980, the company concentrated more on market and product development and metal-working technology and less on capital expansion.

In 1981, the company operated 38 factories, which were organized into 12 divisions. Norris was a market leader or one of the leaders for most of its product lines. For instance, it held 30 percent of the U.S. residential lock market and 42 percent of the decorative brass market, and was the largest producer of wheel covers in the United States. In defense products, it held a dominant share in cartridge cases and projectile bodies.

Norris's revenues were derived from building and remodeling products (43 percent), from automotive and industrial products (42 percent), and from defense products (15 percent). The company had $599 million in sales in 1980 on $365 million in assets. Because of the company's heavy reliance on cyclical industries, net income was down to $23.8 million in 1980, compared with $35.4 in 1979 and $41.7 in 1978. Capital expenditures had consistently exceeded depreciation in recent years, and the company had little debt. Exhibits 1 to 4 present a more detailed examination of Norris's financial performance. Exhibits 5 and 6 show the impact on the results if Norris had used the proposed financing structure over that same period.

FIRST CHICAGO
INVESTMENT CORPORATION

FCIC was founded in 1972 under the Bank Holding Company Act and was a wholly owned subsidiary of First Chicago Corporation (the parent of The First

National Bank of Chicago). FCIC and the First Chicago Corporation composed the Equity Group at First Chicago, which was the leading institutional investor in the U.S. private equity capital markets. In 1980, the firm's portfolio was roughly $180 million (at cost) invested in 90 companies. These companies generally fell into one of two categories: start-up ventures requiring equity to finance additional growth, or management buyouts where equity was required for the acquisition of operating assets by a management team through the use of significant debt leverage. In analyzing an investment opportunity, the Equity Group at First Chicago emphasized the strength of the management team, the value of a unique market opportunity or competitive advantage, and attractive economics and returns commensurate with the risks.

TERMS OF THE FINANCING

KKR was forming a new company (NEWCO) to acquire all the outstanding stock of Norris. The purchase price was $420.1 million, based on $43.05 per share for approximately 9.8 million outstanding shares. The purchase price was 10.6 times 1981 estimated earnings of $39.8 million, or approximately $4.00 per share. Norris projected excess cash of approximately $60 million, which was to be used as part of this financing. After deducting the cash, the purchase price was approximately $360.1 million, or 9.9 times 1981 estimated earnings.

The funds necessary to finance the acquisition of Norris Industries were to be raised and used as shown in Table 1. The subordinated notes would be sold to institutional investors along with 4.5 million shares of stock at $5.50 per share. Upon completion of the acquisition, and after the exercise of the stock options issued to management, ownership of NEWCO on a fully diluted basis would be as follows:

	Number of Shares	Book Value	Ownership Position
Banks	430,550	$ 2,368,025	4.3%
Institutions	4,505,780	24,781,790	45.4
Management	1,300,000[a]	7,150,000[a]	13.1
KKR	3,700,000	20,350,000	37.2
Total	9,936,330	$54,649,815	100.0%

[a]Management was to purchase approximately 401,500 shares for cash at a price of $5.50 per share and be issued stock options to purchase approximately 576,900 shares at an option exercise price of $5.50 per share at the closing.

TABLE 1
■
Source and Use of Funds in Buyout (millions of dollars)

Funds Available

9-year declining balance revolving bank credit with required annual amortization in years 3 through 9[a]	$275.0
5-year bank credit at 18 percent; interest only in first 5 years; issued with warrants to purchase 430,550 shares at $5.50 per share	12.8

continued

TABLE 1 *continued*

Funds Available continued

19.5 percent subordinated notes with required amortization in years 10 and 11[b]	39.9
Common equity from the sale of 8.6 million shares at $5.50 per share[c]	47.3
Total raised	375.0
Estimated cash on December 31, 1981	60.6
Total funds available	$435.6

Funds Used

Purchase of stock[d]	$420.1
Purchase of deferred stock plan and employee stock options[e]	1.3
Fees and expenses[f]	9.0
Excess cash and working capital	5.2
Total funds used	$435.6

[a]$25 million in years 3 through 6, $45 in years 7 and 8, and a final reduction of $85 at maturity. Mandatory reductions were also to be made with the proceeds from the sale of specific assets held for sale (Exhibit 7). Interest would be at prime plus ¾ percent, with a maximum annual interest payment of 17 percent. Any interest beyond 17 percent would be accrued and added on to the loan, up to a maximum of $40 million. The company would also have available a $30-million line of credit. (U.S. Treasury bills were yielding 15.5 percent.)
[b]Of the 19.5 percent, 16.5 would be payable on a quarterly basis with the balance payable annually and subject to a restrictive payment clause to be negotiated with the banks.
[c]Approximately 9.9 million shares were to be issuable on a fully diluted basis. Banks were to be issued 430,550 warrants at closing, management was to be issued approximately 576,900 options at closing, and approximately 321,600 shares were to be reserved but unissued for future management employees.
[d]9,758,254 shares at $43.05 per share.
[e]148,500 options exercisable at $25.50. Amount shown is net of taxes.
[f]Includes fee to Goldman, Sachs of $3.0 million and to KKR of $4.0 million.

The balance sheets would be as shown in Exhibit 8.

THE INVESTMENT DECISION

As Mr. Mencoff looked again at the pro formas (Exhibits 5, 6 and 8), several concerns came to mind. First and foremost, he pondered the $43.05 price per share. The purchase premium itself did not seem out of line with other leveraged buyouts shown in Exhibits 9 and 10, but he knew that Norris, through Goldman, Sachs, had been seeking a buyer for 2 years without success. He was also aware that the price had been set at $38, but that it had suddenly been raised when another corporation made an unexpected offer of $43.00 per share. All of these things made him want to look at a valuation rather carefully.

The biggest risk that Mr. Mencoff saw was the default risk. Could Norris service its huge debt obligations should the housing and auto markets not perform as projected? (A summary of the loan covenants is shown in Exhibit 11.) How much financial slack did Norris have? How long could Norris survive a prolonged recession? Were there risks that he, Norris, and KKR had overlooked?

Mr. Mencoff decided he would have to generate some estimates of return to FCIC on its investment. It had been suggested by KKR that FCIC invest a total of $8,999,996 in a "strip" of securities—$3,075,000 in the 19.5 percent subordinated notes, $1,909,875 in common stock (347,250 shares), and an additional investment of $4,015,121 in the KKR fund, which would invest directly in the common stock of NEWCO (730,022 shares)—which would bring the total fully diluted ownership to 10.8 percent of NEWCO. Would the returns on this investment vary, Mr. Mencoff wondered, depending on what happened in the economy? What were the critical factors in making this a good investment?

Norris Industries

EXHIBIT 1
■
Consolidated Balance Sheets (dollars in thousands)

	December 31	
	1979	1980
Assets		
Current assets		
Cash	$ 5,411	$ 346
Short-term investments	—	28,193
Accounts receivable	89,802	86,850
Inventories	97,394	86,136
Prepaid expenses	6,926	7,474
Total current assets	199,533	208,999
Property, plant, and equipment	230,090	254,615
Less accumulated depreciation	111,588	128,302
Net property, plant, and equipment	118,502	126,313
Special tooling, net of amortization	3,317	4,916
Total net property, plant, and equipment	121,819	131,229
Other assets		
Leases and contracts receivable	12,171	13,704
Excess cost of businesses over net assets acquired	7,129	4,961
Other	8,438	5,756
Total other assets	27,738	24,421
Total assets	$349,090	$364,649
Liabilities and Shareholders' Equity		
Current liabilities		
Current portion of long-term debt	$ 245	$ 1,521
Accounts payable	27,381	29,002
Other liabilities	36,217	40,161
Total current liabilities	63,843	70,684
Deferred incentive compensation	9,145	11,126
Long-term debt	24,786	23,265
Shareholders' equity		
Common stock—par value $.50 per share (authorized 20,000,000 shares; issued 9,758,254 shares in 1980 and 1979)	5,090	5,090
Additional paid-in capital	8,528	8,528
Retained earnings	237,698	245,956
Total shareholders' equity	251,316	259,574
Total liabilities and shareholders' equity	$349,090	$364,649

Norris Industries

EXHIBIT 2

■

Consolidated Statements of Income and Retained Earnings
(dollars in thousands)

	For the Years Ending December 31		
	1978	1979	1980
Net sales	$628,273	$659,008	$599,179
Costs and expenses			
Cost of sales	487,607	530,091	488,341
Selling and advertising expense	28,775	31,324	32,361
General and administrative expense	27,752	31,255	33,527
Interest expense	2,839	2,818	1,652
Loss on disposition of products	—	—	4,520
Other, net	352	(161)	(3,489)
Total costs and expenses	547,325	595,327	556,912
Income before income taxes	80,948	63,681	42,267
Income taxes	39,256	28,287	18,396
Net income	$ 41,692	$ 35,394	$ 23,871
Retained earnings at beginning of year	$186,374	$215,966	$237,698
Cash dividends to shareholders (per share: $1.24 in 1978; $1.40 in 1979; $1.60 in 1980)	(12,100)	(13,662)	(15,613)
Retained earnings at end of year	$215,966	$237,698	$245,956
Net income per common share	$4.27	$3.63	$2.45

Norris Industries

EXHIBIT 3
■

Revenues and Profits by Industry Segment

	1976	1977	1978	1979	1980	1981[a]
Revenues						
Building and remodeling						
Hardware products	19.8%	19.3%	18.2%	19.5%	19.3%	17.7%
Housing products	12.4	12.5	12.7	13.1	12.8	12.4
Plumbing products	15.4	15.9	15.1	14.5	14.7	13.2
Total	47.6	47.7	46.0	47.1	46.8	43.3
Industrial						
Automotive products	32.3	34.6	36.2	35.6	30.2	36.7
Cylinder products	5.0	5.3	4.5	4.5	5.3	4.8
Total	37.3	39.9	40.7	40.1	35.5	41.5
Defense	15.1	12.4	13.3	12.8	17.7	15.2
Total	100.0%	100.0%	100.0%	100.0%	100.0%	100.0%
Pre-Tax Contribution						
Building and remodeling						
Hardware products	19.4%	19.0%	17.8%	18.3%	11.9%	17.0%
Housing products	6.2	8.2	8.0	10.3	2.0	8.2
Plumbing products	10.0	12.1	11.7	6.8	(1.1)	8.7
Total	35.6	39.3	37.5	35.4	12.8	33.9
Industrial						
Automotive products	45.4	44.0	50.5	49.5	59.2	50.7
Cylinder products	5.2	5.6	3.1	5.8	10.6	2.9
Total	50.6	49.6	53.6	55.3	69.8	53.6
Defense	13.8	11.1	8.9	9.3	17.4	12.5
Total	100.0%	100.0%	100.0%	100.0%	100.0%	100.0%

[a]Estimated.

EXHIBIT 4
■
Depreciation and Capital Expenditures (thousands of dollars)

Industry Segments	Depreciation and Amortization			Capital Expenditures		
	1978	1979	1980	1978	1979	1980
Building and remodeling						
Hardware products	$ 3,723	$ 5,400	$ 5,254	$ 8,007	$ 4,884	$ 4,131
Houseware products	1,395	1,452	1,249	1,614	1,273	2,512
Plumbing products	2,715	2,920	2,968	2,929	4,490	3,294
Total	7,883	9,772	9,471	12,550	10,647	9,937
Industrial						
Automotive products	5,142	6,384	7,862	10,095	17,703	7,303
Cylinder products	464	460	496	714	1,825	9,223
Total	5,606	6,844	8,358	10,809	19,528	16,526
Defense	2,543	969	1,081	2,047	1,883	2,584
General corporate	360	401	451	265	346	252
Total	$16,342	$17,986	$19,361	$25,671	$32,404	$29,299

EXHIBIT 5
■
Pro Forma Historical Income Statement (millions of dollars)

	1976	1977	1978	1979	1980	1981 Estimated
Income before taxes and interest	$75.4	$86.7	$83.8	$66.5	$43.9	$77.7
Interest expense						
Industrial revenue bonds	1.6	1.6	1.6	1.6	1.6	1.6
Senior bank debt (17 percent)[a]	48.8	48.8	48.8	48.8	48.8	48.8
Subordinated notes (19.5 percent)[b]	8.0	8.0	8.0	8.0	8.0	8.0
Total	58.4	58.4	58.4	58.4	58.4	58.4
Pre-tax income	17.0	28.3	25.4	8.1	(14.5)	19.3
Income taxes (50 percent)	8.5	14.1	12.7	4.0	(7.2)	9.6
Net income	$ 8.5	$14.2	$12.7	$ 4.1	$ (7.3)	$ 9.7
Interest coverage ratio						
Senior debt	1.50×	1.72×	1.66×	1.32×	0.87×	1.54×
All debt	1.29×	1.48×	1.43×	1.14×	0.75×	1.33×
Cash flow						
Net income	$ 8.5	$14.2	$12.7	$4.1	$ (7.3)	$ 9.7
Depreciation	12.3	13.0	16.3	18.0	19.4	22.4
Cash flow from operations	$20.8	$27.2	$29.0	$22.1	$12.1	$32.1

[a]17 percent is assumed to reflect a reasonable long-term average bank rate. The actual rate in effect would float, with a cash flow limit of 17 percent per year.
[b]16.5 of the 19.5 percent would be payable on a quarterly basis with the balance payable annually, subject to a restrictive payment clause to be negotiated with the banks.

EXHIBIT 5 *continued*

Pro Forma Historical Balance Sheet,[a] June 30, 1981
(millions of dollars)

	Actual	Adjustments	Pro Forma
Assets			
Cash and equivalents	$ 50.3	$ (55.4)[c]	$ (5.1)[c]
Accounts receivable	98.4		98.4
Inventory (LIFO basis)[b]	73.3		73.3
Prepaid expenses	7.5		7.5
Total current assets	$229.5	(55.4)	$174.1
Net property, plant, and equipment	127.5		127.5
Other assets	27.0	158.5[d]	185.5
Total assets	$384.0	$ 103.1	$487.1
Liabilities and Shareholders' Equity			
Current liabilities	$ 76.9		76.9
Deferred compensation	12.0		12.0
Industrial revenue bonds	23.2		23.2
Revolving credit		286.0[e]	286.0
Subordinated debt		41.0[e]	41.0
Equity	271.9	(223.9)	48.0
Total liabilities and shareholders' equity	$384.0	$ 103.1[d]	$487.1

[a]This assumes that the transaction had occurred on June 30, 1981.
[b]The excess of current cost over the amount determined under LIFO was $52.1 million on June 30, 1981.

[c]Proceeds from financing	$ 375.0
Purchase of stock	(420.1)
Stock options and deferred stock repurchase	(1.3)
Fees and expenses	(9.0)
Net cash	$ (55.4)

Norris's cash balance is projected to increase to $60.6 million by December 31, 1981.
[d]While it is estimated that NEWCO will write up the assets of Norris immediately after completion of the acquisition, thereby eliminating much of the goodwill, the excess purchase price over book value on acquisition would be:

Purchase price		$420.1
Book value	271.9	
Less stock option and deferred stock purchase not previously recorded	(1.3)	
Less fees	(9.0)	
Total	$261.6	
Adjusted book value		261.6
Excess purchase price over book value of assets acquired		$158.5

[e]Proceeds from acquisition financing.

Norris Industries

EXHIBIT 6
■
Pro Forma Income Statement, 1982–1990
(millions of dollars, except per share amounts)

	1982	1983	1984	1985	1986	1987	1988	1989	1990
Income before taxes and interest	$91.6	$100.7	$110.7	$121.7	$133.8	$147.1	$161.8	$177.9	$195.6
Interest expense									
Industrial revenue bonds	1.6	1.6	1.6	1.6	1.6	1.5	1.5	1.4	1.4
Bank debt (17 percent)	48.8	48.8	48.8	44.5	40.2	34.0	29.8	22.1	14.5
Subordinated notes (19.5 percent)	8.0	8.0	8.0	8.0	8.0	8.0	8.0	8.0	8.0
Total	58.4	58.4	58.4	54.1	49.8	43.5	39.3	31.5	23.9
Pre-tax income	33.2	42.3	52.3	67.6	84.0	103.6	122.5	146.4	171.7
Income taxes (50 percent)	16.6	21.1	26.1	33.8	42.0	51.8	61.2	73.2	85.8
Net income	$16.6	$21.2	$26.2	$33.8	$42.0	$51.8	$61.3	$73.2	$85.9
Earnings per share	$1.66	$2.12	$2.62	$3.38	$4.20	$5.18	$6.13	$7.32	$8.59
Book value per share[a]	$7.16	$9.28	$11.90	$15.28	$19.48	$24.66	$30.79	$38.11	$46.70
Interest coverage ratio									
Senior debt	1.8×	2.0×	2.2×	2.6×	3.2×	4.1×	5.2×	7.6×	12.3×
All debt	1.6×	1.7×	1.9×	2.3×	2.7×	3.4×	4.1×	5.7×	8.2×
Capitalization at Year End (millions of dollars)									
Bank debt	$286.0	$286.0	$261.0	$236.0	$200.0	$175.0	$130.0	$ 85.0	$ 0.0
Industrial revenue bonds	23.0	22.7	22.4	21.9	21.3	20.7	20.1	19.7	19.3
Total senior debt	309.0	308.7	283.4	257.9	221.3	195.7	150.1	104.7	19.3
Subordinated debt	41.0	41.0	41.0	41.0	41.0	41.0	41.0	41.0	41.0
Equity	64.6	85.8	112.0	145.8	187.8	239.6	300.9	374.1	460.0
Total subordinated debt and equity	$105.6	$126.8	$153.0	$186.8	$228.8	$280.6	$341.9	$415.1	$501.0

[a] Assumes 10 million shares outstanding at $5.50 per share.

Pro Forma Cash Flows as of Year End, 1982–1990 (millions of dollars)

	1982	1983	1984	1985	1986	1987	1988	1989	1990
Net income	$16.6	$21.1	$26.1	$33.8	$42.0	$51.8	$61.3	$73.2	$85.9
Depreciation	23.0	23.1	23.1	22.0	21.5	21.5	21.5	21.5	21.5
Cash flow from operations	39.6	44.2	49.2	55.8	63.5	73.3	82.8	94.7	107.4
Principal payments									
Bank payments	0.0	0.0	25.0	25.0	36.0	25.0	45.4	45.0	85.0
Industrial revenue bond payments	0.3	0.3	0.3	0.5	0.6	0.6	0.6	0.4	0.4
Subordinated payments—industrial revenue bond payments	0.0	0.0	0.0	0.0	0.0	0.0	0.0	0.0	0.0
Total payments	0.3	0.3	25.3	25.5	36.6	25.6	45.6	45.4	85.4
Cash flow available for working capital and capital expenditures	39.3	43.9	23.9	30.3	26.9	47.7	37.2	49.3	22.0
Capital expenditures	15.0	16.0	17.0	18.0	19.0	25.0	25.0	25.0	25.0
Working capital	12.0	8.0	8.0	5.0	5.0	5.0	5.0	5.0	5.0
Net cash flow	$12.3	$19.9	$(1.1)	$7.3	$2.9	$17.7	$7.2	$19.3	$(8.0)
Beginning cash	5.2	17.5	37.4	36.3	43.6	46.5	64.2	71.4	90.7
Ending cash	$17.5	$37.4	$36.3	$43.6	$46.5	$64.2	$71.4	$90.7	$82.7

Assumptions to Pro Forma Statements for 1982–1990

1. Income before taxes and interest is based on management's estimate for net income before taxes and interest of $91.6 million for 1982 compared with the current estimate of $77.7 for 1981. Principal underlying assumptions include the following:
   a. Domestic automobile and light truck production at 10.3 million units for 1982 versus estimate for 1981 of 9.0 million units.
   b. Residential construction at 1.65 million units for 1982 versus estimate for 1981 of 1.35 million units.
2. Income before taxes and interest beyond 1982 based on projections made by KKR assumption of a 10-percent compounded growth rate.
3. There is no interest income on excess cash.
4. No proceeds from the sale of assets. Norris currently has assets held for sale that could generate $14.1 million.
5. No charges resulting from the revaluation of assets pursuant to Accounting Principles Board #16.
6. Working capital includes net change in receivables, inventories, and accounts payable.
7. Existing industrial revenue bonds will be assumed by NEWCO.

Norris Industries

EXHIBIT 7

■

Assets Held for Sale (millions of dollars)

Description	Action Contemplated	Estimated Price	Net Book Value	Net Cash after Taxes
Sponge Cushion	Sell all assets, including receivables, as going concern	$ 3.8	$ 3.6	$ 3.7
O. L. Anderson plant	Sell inventory and property, plant, and equipment as going concern	2.4	1.7	2.1
Leases and contracts currently financed by the company in-house	Sell to financial institution	14.5[a]	17.0	14.5
Ypsilanti plant currently partially leased to General Motors (205,000 square feet on 20 acres)	Sell	3.0	1.7	2.5
Other miscellaneous property (129,000 square feet of buildings)	Sell	1.7	0.5	1.3
Total		$25.4	$24.5	$24.1

[a]A 15-percent discount rate was used to estimate the value of fixed longer-term low-rate leases and contracts outstanding.

Norris Industries

EXHIBIT 8

■

Balance Sheets before and after Recapitalization as of December 31, 1981
(dollars in millions, except per share amounts)

	Projected Balance Sheet 12/31/1981	Redeem Stock Options	Redeem Share-holders' Equity	Issue NEWCO Stock	Record New Debt Structure	Record Fees and Expenses	NEWCO Pro Forma Balance Sheet 12/31/1981
Assets							
Current assets							
Cash and cash equivalents	$ 60.6	$(1.3)	$(420.1)	$48.0	$327.0	$(9.0)	$ 5.2
Accounts receivable	93.6	0.0	0.0	0.0	0.0	0.0	93.6
Inventories	79.3	0.0	0.0	0.0	0.0	0.0	79.3
Prepaid expenses	7.9	0.0	0.0	0.0	0.0	0.0	7.9
Total current assets	$241.4	$(1.3)	$(420.1)	$48.0	$327.0	$(9.0)	$186.0
Property, plant, and equipment	134.0						134.0
Excess of purchase price over net worth	0.0	0.0	137.6	0.0	0.0	9.0	146.6
Other assets[a]	24.8	0.0	0.0	0.0	0.0	0.0	24.8
Total assets	$400.2	$(1.3)	$(282.5)	$48.0	$327.0	0.0	$491.4
Liabilities and Shareholders' Equity							
Current liabilities	$ 80.8	0.0	0.0	0.0	0.0	0	$ 80.8
Deferred incentive compensation	12.6	0.0	0.0	0.0	0.0	0	12.6
Long-term debt	23.0	0.0	0.0	0.0	$327.0	0	$350.0
Total liabilities	$116.4	0.0	0.0	0.0	$327.0	0	$443.4
Equity							
Common stock	4.1	$(5.1)[b]	48.0	0.0	0.0	0	$ 48.0
Additional paid-in capital	8.5	$(8.5)	0.0	0.0	0.0	0	0.0
Retained earnings	270.2	(1.3)	(268.9)	0.0	0.0	0	0.0
Total equity	$283.8	$(1.3)	$(282.5)	$48.0	0.0	0	$ 48.0
Total liabilities and shareholders' equity	$400.2	$(1.3)	$(282.5)	$48.0	$327.0	0	$491.4
Net working capital	$160.0						$105.2
Current ratio	2.99×						2.30×
Common shares outstanding	9,758,254						10,000,000[c]
Book value per common share	$29.08						$5.50

[a]Includes excess of investment over net assets acquired of $4.9.
[b]To adjust stock to $43.05 per share and record payout net of related income tax effects.
[c]Fully diluted.

Norris Industries

EXHIBIT 9

■

Data on Leveraged Buyouts and Other Acquisitions

Company Acquired	Date	Acquisition of Stock or Assets	Premium/Price One Day Prior to Announcement	Offer as a Percentage of Net Income	Multiple of Book Value	Senior Debt/Total Debt	Subordinated Debt/Total Debt	Subordinated Debt/Total Capital
Houdaille Industries	10/28/78	S	93%	13.9×	2.0×	65.5%	34.5%	29.6%
Bliss & Laughlin	8/10/79	S	23	8.7	1.7	N.Av.	N.Av.	N.Av.
Carrier Corp.	9/16/78	A	39	10.2	1.6	N.Av.	N.Av.	N.Av.
Gardner-Denver	1/22/79	A	46	12.2	2.1	N.Av.	N.Av.	N.Av.
Eltra Corp.	6/29/79	A	25	11.6	1.5	N.Av.	N.Av.	N.Av.
Washington Steel	3/12/79	A	34	7.3	1.3	N.Av.	N.Av.	N.Av.
Studebaker-Northington	7/25/79	A	17	10.7	1.4	N.Av.	N.Av.	N.Av.
Marathon Manufacturing	8/13/79	A	13	11.4	2.1	N.Av.	N.Av.	N.Av.
Congoleum	1980	A/S	50	9.4	2.4	68.6	31.4	27.6

N.Av. = not available.

Norris Industries

EXHIBIT 10
■
Average Market Prices of Norris Shares[a]

Period	High	Low
1977	$31	$19
1978		
First quarter	23¾	19¾
Second quarter	26	21½
Third quarter	27	20⅝
Fourth quarter	26¾	20
1979		
First quarter	25¼	20⅜
Second quarter	28	22¾
Third quarter	28⅞	23¼
Fourth quarter	26⅝	19
1980		
First quarter	26⅜	18¼
Second quarter	23½	19
Third quarter[b]	33½	22⅜
Fourth quarter	32½	23¾
1981		
First quarter	31½	25½
Second quarter	32½	27½
Third quarter[c]	39¾	29

[a]Norris shares currently traded on the New York Stock Exchange and the Pacific Stock Exchange.
[b]On August 4, 1980, the last business day prior to the public announcement of proposals for the acquisition of Norris by KKR and another firm, the closing price per Norris share was $29.
[c]On July 22, 1981, the last business day prior to the public announcement of a proposal for the acquisition of Norris at a price of $38 per share by an investor group to be formed by KKR, the closing price per share of the Norris shares was $29.13. On August 19, 1981, the last business day prior to the announcement that an agreement had been executed with KKR for an increased price of $43.05 per Norris share, the closing market price per share was $36.00.

Norris Industries

EXHIBIT 11
■
Summary of Loan Covenants

1. Working capital minimum of $75,000,000.
2. Current ratio minimum of 1.5 to 1.
3. Tangible net worth minimums of:

Amount	Period
$ 41,000,000	Closing to 12/31/82
52,000,000	12/31/82 to 12/31/83
64,000,000	12/31/83 to 12/31/84
84,000,000	12/31/84 to 12/31/85
109,000,000	12/31/85 to 12/31/86
144,000,000	12/31/86 to 12/31/87
179,000,000	12/31/87 to 12/31/88
219,000,000	12/31/88 and thereafter

4. No prepayment of subordinated debt.
5. Sale of assets is unlimited, except by other financial covenants, and proceeds must be applied to the revolving credit to the extent of:
   a. 50 percent for all assets sold in a single sale or in an integrated series of sales over $1,000,000.
   b. 100 percent for all assets held for sale in excess of $4,000,000.

6

TECHNICAL NOTES

Managing Foreign Exchange Risks

As developments in communications and transportation have increased accessibility to other parts of the world, U.S. companies have increased the business they conduct in foreign markets. Because each country has its own medium of exchange (currency), companies involved in international business must deal with a new dimension not present in domestic activities—that of managing foreign exchange risk. This risk occurs because the exchange rates between currencies fluctuate, causing a change in the value of the company's international activities in terms of its domestic currency.

There are three types of foreign exchange risks: transaction exposure, translation exposure, and economic exposure. Each of these exposures results from different activities of the company and is determined in a different way.

Through astute management (and perhaps a little luck), it is possible to minimize the foreign exchange risks associated with conducting business internationally. This note discusses the nature of the three foreign exchange risks and some methods companies might use to manage them.

ASSESSING FOREIGN EXCHANGE RISKS

Transaction Exposure.   Transaction exposure exists during the normal course of international business transactions whenever two or more currencies are involved and there is a lag between the date a contract is signed or goods delivered and the date of payment. Transaction exposure also exists when there is a time difference between the declaration of a dividend by a foreign subsidiary and its actual payment. The risk associated with transaction exposure is that the exchange rate will fluctuate before the transaction is completed and the currency exchange occurs, thereby changing the amount of domestic currency paid or received.

Transaction exposure would exist, for example, if a U.S. electronics company contracted to sell 10,000 semiconductors to a French computer manufacturer at a sales price of FF (French franc) 10 per unit with delivery in 90 days

This note was prepared as a basis for class discussion from publicly available information. Copyright © 1984 by the Darden Graduate Business School Sponsors, University of Virginia, Charlottesville, Virginia.

and payment due on delivery. If the exchange rate of US$ to FF on the date of the contract signing were US$0.23/FF, then the U.S. company would expect to receive US$23,000 for the sale (i.e., FF10 × 10,000 × US$0.23/FF = US$23,000). If the exchange rate of US$ to FF on the date of delivery were US$0.21/FF, then the U.S. company would receive only US$21,000.

Translation Exposure.   Translation exposure occurs because of the need to translate the financial statements of foreign subsidiaries and affiliates into the currency of the parent company in order to prepare consolidated financial statements. As no exchange of cash or other assets takes place, translation exposure is solely the result of the financial accounting and reporting process.

U.S. companies are required to translate foreign financial statements in accordance with the standards set forth in Statement of Financial Accounting Standards No. 52 (FAS 52), *Foreign Currency Translation,* issued by the Financial Accounting Standards Board (FASB) in December 1981. FAS 52 superseded the highly criticized and controversial FAS 8 that had been in effect about 6 years. FAS 8 had been issued by the FASB in response to the need for more explicit guidance on how foreign operations should be accounted for in the consolidated financial statements of U.S. companies. This need was brought about primarily by three significant developments of the early 1970s: (1) continued expansion of international business activities; (2) extensive changes in the international monetary system; and (3) divergent practices by U.S. companies in accounting for their international activities.

Prior to FAS 8, several translation methods had been generally accepted, and managements could exclude translation adjustments from the determination of income by electing to defer recognition through the use of reserve accounts. FAS 8 specified that the objectives of translation were to measure and express, (a) in dollars and (b) in conformity with U.S. generally accepted accounting principles, the assets, liabilities, revenues, or expenses that were measured or denominated in foreign currency. FAS 8 required the use of the temporal method, and the FASB acknowledged that the financial information generated in accordance with its application might not be compatible with the expected economic effects of an exchange rate change. The board expressed the belief that economic compatibility could not be achieved without major changes in the existing accounting model. This issue subsequently proved to be one of the two major sources of dissatisfaction with FAS 8 by both internal and external users of corporate financial statements.

The other principal complaint about FAS 8 was that its requirement to include all translation gains and losses in the determination of income for the period in which the exchange rate changed caused unnecessary and economically unjustifiable fluctuations in the periodic earnings reported by U.S. companies. In May 1978, the FASB issued an invitation for public comment on the 12 Statements of Financial Accounting Standards that had been in effect for at least two years. The comments received indicated such widespread dissatisfaction with FAS 8 that in January 1979 the board decided to reconsider its position on foreign currency translation.

During its deliberations, the FASB discovered that the issues involved were still as complex and controversial as they had been when FAS 8 was formulated. The process was slow and required the issuance of two exposure drafts prior to the adoption of the revised standard. By a 4 to 3 vote, the FASB approved the issuance of FAS 52, drastically changing the manner in which foreign activities are accounted for.

According to FAS 52, the objectives of translation are to (1) provide information that is generally compatible with the expected economic effects of an exchange rate change on an enterprise's cash flows and equity and (2) reflect in consolidated financial statements the financial results and relationships of the individual consolidated entities as measured in their functional currencies in conformity with U.S. generally accepted accounting principles. Additionally, the board expressed the belief that, to the extent practicable, accounting for foreign currency translation in the United States should harmonize with related practices followed in other industrialized countries around the world. The board also acknowledged that there is probably neither an ideal translation method nor one capable of generating overwhelming support.

As noted in the translation objectives, FAS 52 adopted a functional currency approach to translation. This is a radical departure from the U.S. dollar approach taken in FAS 8, because it permits multiple measurement bases in consolidated financial statements. The FAS 52 approach is based on the premise that the foreign entities in a multinational enterprise operate and generate cash flows in a variety of economic environments and that differences in these environments should be recognized in the translation process. Thus the first step is to identify the functional currency for each entity included in the financial statements of the reporting enterprise. An entity's functional currency is defined as the currency of the primary economic environment in which it operates; normally, that is the currency of the environment in which an entity primarily generates and expends cash. Although FAS 52 provides guidance regarding the determination of the functional currency, considerable judgment will often be necessary. As the resulting translated financial statements can differ significantly, selection of each foreign entity's functional currency is an important managerial decision.

Once the functional currencies have been determined, the accounts of each foreign entity should be brought into conformity with U.S. generally accepted accounting principles and remeasured in their functional currency, with any gains or losses generally treated as adjustments to income. (Remeasurement is not necessary if the foreign financial statements are already stated in the entity's functional currency.) If the functional currency is the U.S. dollar, the foreign entity's financial statements should be remeasured into U.S. dollars so as to produce the same result as if the books had been kept in U.S. dollars. With minor exceptions, the remeasurement process into a U.S. dollar functional currency is the same as the translation process required by FAS 8: the temporal method is used, and any gains or losses resulting from the remeasurement process are reflected in income.

If the functional currency is other than the U.S. dollar, the remeasured financial statements are translated into U.S. dollars using the current rate method. Any translation gains or losses are taken directly to a separate component of stockholders' equity and have no effect on current income. Translation from the functional currency to the U.S. dollar is not necessary when the U.S. dollar is the functional currency, because the remeasurement process previously described converts foreign financial statements into U.S. dollars.

It should be evident that both the objectives and procedures of foreign currency translation are vastly different under FAS 52 from those of FAS 8. Even so, when the U.S. dollar is determined to be the functional currency, the translation process produces similar results to those that would have resulted under FAS 8.

Table 1 provides a comparison of the current rate and temporal methods of foreign currency translation. As can be seen, a company's translation exposure

TABLE 1

■

Comparison of Balance Sheet Translation Methods

Balance Sheet Item	Current Rate Method	Temporal Method
Cash	Current	Current
Receivables	Current	Current
Inventory	Current	Historical[a]
Fixed assets	Current	Historical
Payables	Current	Current
Long-term debt	Current	Current
Owners' equity	Historical	Historical

[a]Unless the lower of cost or market (LCM) rule results in inventory being stated at market, then current.
Note: *Current* means that the item is translated at the exchange rate that existed at the balance sheet date.
Historical means that the item is translated at the exchange rate that existed at the time the asset was acquired, the debt issued, or the capital contributed.

is quite different under these two methods. Under the temporal method (which is essentially a monetary–nonmonetary approach), exposure depends on the relationship between a company's monetary assets and its monetary liabilities. Under the current rate method, a company's exposure depends on the relationship between its total assets and total liabilities. Because companies frequently have net monetary liability positions yet typically have net total asset positions, translation exposure under the current rate method is often the reverse of that under the temporal method.

As an example of balance sheet translation in accordance with FAS 52, assume that the same U.S. electronics company previously discussed established a French subsidiary with the following balance sheet.

French Subsidiary in French Francs (thousands)

Assets		Liabilities and Equity	
Cash	FF 50	Current liabilities	FF 350
Inventory (cost)	300	Long-term debt	50
Plant and equipment (net)	100	Equity	50
Total	FF 450	Total	FF 450

With the initial exchange rate of US$0.23/FF, the translated values of the subsidiary would be as follows.

French Subsidiary in Dollars (thousands)

Assets		Liabilities and Equity	
Cash	US$ 11.5	Current liabilities	US$ 80.5
Inventory (cost)	69.0	Long-term debt	11.5
Plant and equipment (net)	23.0	Equity	11.5
Total	US$ 103.5	Total	US$ 103.5

If the French franc subsequently weakened against the dollar, with the exchange rate falling to US$0.21/FF, and the balance sheet of the French subsidiary remained exactly the same in French francs, the translated values would then be:

French Subsidiary in Dollars (thousands)

Assets		*Liabilities and Equity*	
Cash	US$ 10.5	Current liabilities	US$ 73.5
Inventory (cost)	63.0	Long-term debt	10.5
Plant and equipment (net)	21.0	Equity	10.5
Total	US$ 94.5	Total	US$ 94.5

Although the values attached to the subsidiary's assets and liabilities remain constant when stated in French francs, the translation process produces a loss of US$1,000, the amount of the decrease in the equity account needed to balance the subsidiary's U.S. dollar balance sheet. Assuming the French franc to be the functional currency, the translation loss would appear as a separate component of equity in the consolidated balance sheet.

This example illustrates that a U.S. company's translation exposure is a function of the relationship between a foreign entity's assets and liabilities, because all such accounts are translated at current exchange rates. A loss occurs whenever (as in the example) the foreign currency weakens against the U.S. dollar. Conversely, a gain occurs whenever the foreign currency strengthens against the U.S. dollar, Thus FAS 52 attempts to capture the economic consequences of the change in exchange rates.

The amount of the translation adjustment can also be calculated directly by multiplying a company's exposed asset or liability position by the amount of the currency exchange rate fluctuation. In the preceding example, the French subsidiary had a net asset position of FF 50 determined as follows:

Total assets	FF 450
Less: Total liabilities	400
Position (long)	FF 50

The loss would be calculated as FF 50 × US$0.02/FF = US$1,000.

In addition to changing the manner in which foreign balance sheets are translated, FAS 52 also changed the way foreign income statements are translated. When a foreign entity's local currency is the functional currency, application of the current rate method required by FAS 52 results in translating both cost of sales and depreciation at the weighted-average exchange rate for the period. Under the temporal method required by FAS 8, these two important expenses were translated at historical rates. In the case of the French subsidiary just described, application of FAS 52 would result in smaller translated amounts for cost of sales and depreciation than would have been the case under FAS 8.

In terms of financial reporting disclosures, FAS 52 requires the following:

■ The aggregate *transaction* gain or loss included in determining net income for the period. This includes those resulting from the remeasurement process and those resulting from forward contracts.
■ An analysis of the current year's changes in the separate component of equity reflecting cumulative translation adjustments.
■ If significant, disclosure of the effects of a rate change subsequent to the date of the financial statements on unsettled balances pertaining to foreign currency transactions may be necessary.

Economic Exposure.

Economic exposure is a forward-looking concept because it focuses on the impact of exchange rate fluctuations on the operations of the subsidiary. Economic exposure is based on the concept that the economic value of the subsidiary is the present value of the future cash flows generated by the subsidiary. If the exchange rate fluctuation affects the U.S. dollar cash flows, then the present value of the cash flows will be altered, and the economic value of the subsidiary will be changed.

In the theoretical world of perfectly efficient markets, the exchange rate fluctuations would not have any effect on the present value of the U.S. dollar cash flows, because in the theoretical models, there are no barriers to adjusting prices to reflect the new exchange rates. However, in the real world, managers often encounter constraints in their ability to make adjustments for the changing exchange rates. Price controls are not uncommon, nor are long-term fixed-price contracts and exchange restrictions. Thus, although theoretical models indicate otherwise, the manager must be concerned about the impact of an exchange rate fluctuation on the future cash flows of the subsidiary.

Because future cash flows are primarily the result of future revenues and expenses, they are the first elements to be examined in determining the potential impact of a change in exchange rates. Sales volume should be evaluated at the expected exchange rate. If the subsidiary's sales are made primarily within the subsidiary's currency area, then the unit volume may not be affected. If the subsidiary exports products, an expected exchange rate fluctuation may affect the product prices and thereby the competitiveness of the subsidiary's products. If the foreign currency depreciates, the subsidiary may attempt to increase prices to maintain profit margins. An appreciation of the foreign currency might allow the subsidiary to reduce prices. Any price change, of course, will have an impact on the expected unit sales volume.

From a cost standpoint, if all of the costs are incurred in the subsidiary's currency, then a movement in the exchange rate might have little impact. In this case, the major consideration would be the general inflationary or deflationary impact on the economy of the foreign country and how that would affect the costs of the subsidiary.

On the other hand, if imported raw materials or intermediate goods are required for the subsidiary's production, the new exchange rate might have a direct impact on the costs of production. In addition, if the unit sales volume changes, the efficiency of the production process might be altered with an associated impact on production costs.

The exchange rate fluctuation can also affect the capital required by the foreign subsidiary. Changes in unit sales volume could affect the capital investment necessary for the required production capacity. Changes in unit sales volume and/or sales prices might affect the need for working capital in the subsidiary.

Even if an analysis shows that the expected exchange rates will not result in any changes in the foreign currency cash flows of the subsidiary, the cash flows will still be altered when converted to the currency of the parent company if the respective values of the currencies change. Thus there will always be some impact on the present value of the future cash flows when an exchange rate is changed.

The economic exposure of a subsidiary is the difference between the present value of the cash flows determined at the old or current rates and the present value of the cash flows at the new or expected rates. Evaluation of this exposure is useful in determining what might happen if the exchange rates moved, or after the fact in evaluating the changes in the subsidiary's economic value following a change in the currency value. (See Appendix A on economic exposure.)

THE FUNCTION OF THE FOREIGN EXCHANGE MARKETS

All three types of foreign exchange risks (i.e., transaction, translation, and economic) result from movements in the exchange rates or parity among currencies. Because these changes occur in the currency markets, an understanding of the role and function of the foreign exchange markets is critical to the successful management of foreign exchange risks.

Trading in the foreign exchange markets proceeds through contracts made between banks and buyers or sellers of foreign currency. Two types of exchange markets exist, each distinguished by the type of contract involved. In a spot market, the parties agree to exchange one currency for another at a fixed ratio to be delivered immediately or within one or two business days. In the forward market, the purchaser of foreign currency contracts for delivery in the future of a currency at a specific rate. Traditionally, these forward contracts are negotiated for delivery in 1, 2, 3, 6, and 12 months. Occasionally, contracts involving major currencies (i.e., the British pound, West German mark, Japanese yen, Swiss franc, French franc, and Canadian dollar) can be arranged for delivery at any specified date up to 3 years distant. In New York, the quotations are given in terms of the amount in dollars required to make one unit of foreign exchange. For illustration, here is such a quotation from *The Wall Street Journal.*

	Bid
Japan (yen)	$0.004232
30-Day Futures	0.004253
90-Day Futures	0.004288
180-Day Futures	0.004334
France (franc)	0.2104
30-Day Futures	0.2090
90-Day Futures	0.2071
180-Day Futures	$0.2050

A bid quotation is the price a bank is willing to pay to purchase a currency. The rates of the spot market are the prevailing rates determined by the supply of and demand for the particular currency.

Forward rates differ from spot rates in that they are usually quoted at a certain premium or discount of the spot rate. The difference depends on the financial community's assessment of the future relative strength of that currency. This assessment is based on the country's balance of payments, trade figures, international reserves, GNP, money supply, rate of inflation, and other domestic and international economic indicators. The forward rate also differs from the spot rate because of differences in interest rates in a given country and the rest of the world. The currency with the lower interest rate will sell at a premium, whereas the currency with a higher rate will sell at a discount in the forward markets.

Quite often, exchange rates are expressed in terms of an annual percentage rate derived from the spot rate. The following equation is used:

$$\frac{FR - SR}{SR} \times \frac{12}{N} \times 100 = \text{Discount (or premium) in percent terms,}$$

where

FR = Forward rate
SR = Spot rate
N = Months to maturity.

For example, the purchaser of a yen 90-day future would be buying at a 5.3 percent premium:

$$\frac{0.004288 - 0.004232}{0.004232} \times \frac{12}{3} \times 100\% = 5.3\% \text{ per annum.}$$

However, the purchaser of a franc 90-day future would be buying at a 6.2 percent discount:

$$\frac{0.2071 - 0.2104}{0.2104} \times \frac{12}{3} \times 100\% = (6.2)\% \text{ per annum.}$$

Because of the traders' immediate needs, the spot market is quite active in the foreign exchange market. Although the forward market plays a secondary role, it is nonetheless useful, since it allows traders and investors to deal with risk in the relative future values of currencies traded.

MANAGING FOREIGN EXCHANGE RISKS

Managing Transaction Risks.   **Hedging through Foreign Exchange Market Contracts.**   A hedge in the foreign exchange market simply requires the agreement of two parties to exchange currencies at a stated rate (known when the contract is made) at some future point in time. This forward exchange rate will differ from the present spot rate as previously explained. The contract will cover an exposed transaction by guaranteeing the exchange rate at which the remittance will be made. (For an example, see Appendix B on hedging through foreign exchange market contracts.)

Hedging through Money Market Loans.   A money market hedge is essentially an immediate conversion of loaned funds. Funds are borrowed by the payer in local currency and immediately converted to the recipient's currency (and usually placed in an interest-bearing account). In this manner, the effect of future changes in the exchange rates are avoided altogether. When payment is due, the remittance is transferred from the interest-bearing account to the recipient. Meanwhile, the payer needs only to pay off the original funds loaned (plus interest). (See Appendix C on hedging through loans.)

Leading and Lagging.   Leading and lagging the timing of cash exchanges is one of the simplest ways to control foreign exchange exposure. The process involves speeding up, even prepayment, or slowing down the exchange of funds between companies in order to transfer the funds at, given forecasts of future rates, relatively advantageous (to the exposed party) exchange rates. Many countries have imposed restrictions on the amount of time that funds can be led or lagged. Such laws can seriously impair a manager's ability to apply this technique successfully. (See Appendix D on leading and lagging.)

Invoicing Currency.   In some situations, it may be advantageous for a company to bill customers in a currency other than the customer's local currency to alleviate transaction exposure. Such a technique is especially useful to companies who have a major customer in one country and a major supplier in another. In this case, the customer might be billed in the supplier's currency.

To a lesser extent, this technique may be an aid to decreasing translation exposure as well as enabling the company to hold currencies other than its own local currency, particularly in the case where one is a strong currency and the other is a weak currency. (See Appendix E on invoicing currency.)

Recent Developments.   Recent strategies to manage foreign exchange risk are even more sophisticated than those of the past. These new strategies include using foreign currency swaps, sometimes in conjunction with interest rate swaps to hedge the transaction exposure; currency futures; and options on currency futures to manage risk. Forward markets provide other opportunities for hedging.

Managing Translation Risks.   **Balance Sheet Adjustments.**   This technique involves maintaining a net zero exposure (or, if desired, a net asset or liability exposure) through manipulation of account balances. It can be accomplished by careful management of the size and timing of transactions relating to exposed accounts near a corporate year end, especially monetary accounts. Obviously, such a strategy is limited by the necessity of integrating this technique with normal operations; ideally, asset management will lower translation exposure without interfering with the normal transactions.

Swaps.   Loan swaps, currency swaps, and credit swaps are all basically the same; they allow companies to provide financing to a foreign affiliate without having to channel the funds through the foreign exchange market. A swap entails dual offsetting loans of equal value (at the start of the arrangement) in two different currencies between two companies or institutions. Normally, each consolidated company involved will be a loan recipient in one currency and the lender in the other. (See Appendix F on swaps.)

Currency swaps are similar to the loan swaps described in Appendix F except that no loans are recorded. They are viewed simply as an exchange of one currency for another. In a credit swap, one of the companies involved will be a bank with a foreign office ready to make a loan to a company's subsidiary upon deposit of equivalent currency value in the bank's domestic location.

Licensing.   In some cases where a foreign affiliate may retain high translation exposure to the detriment of the parent company, it may be wise for the corporation to consider licensing its product to an independent foreign company rather than maintaining a subsidiary. Licensing eliminates all translation exposure because there is no affiliate to consolidate, and depending on the licensing agreement, it may alleviate all transaction exposure as well. Ideally, licensing should have been carefully considered prior to the establishment of the foreign affiliate. A decision of this sort is, perhaps, the ultimate in allowing financial reporting to influence business decisions.

Among the advantages of licensing, three stand out as key. First, licensing allows the parent company to increase revenues with relatively low commitment of funds. Licensing provides an alternative to direct investment and direct trade by permitting the licenser to generate revenue through the sale of intangible assets, such as trademarks, patents, technology, and production processes. Licensing allows the licenser to explore and test the growth potential of foreign markets with little direct expense to the company.

Second, licensing can often enhance the product's image in the country where it is licensed, and often the fact that a product is international in scope increases the visibility and enhances the image of the product and company in the home market.

Third, licensing can also afford the licenser protection for a patent, trademark, or a production process by having the licensee legally register the patent, etc., in its home country. This step secures the rights of the parent company.

In addition, licensing allows the building and development of strong international working relationships between companies and countries. Licensing can often be the first step in a process that ends with a foreign company investing directly in the home country of the licensee.

There are, however, some disadvantages to licensing. First, even with strong and detailed licensing agreements, the company may experience great difficulty in insuring proper quality control. Poor quality control can negate many of the advantages of increasing markets and enhancing the image of the product.

Second, licensing limits the profit potential of the licenser. In most instances, the licensee pays only a set percentage of the sales price to the licenser, but determining what price is commensurate with the actual value of the patent, trademark, or process is difficult. The licenser, by accepting a set percentage of revenue, does not participate in the upside potential of a rapidly expanding market. Third, the licenser who delivers patents, etc., to licensees is always vulnerable to the licensee who severs the agreement and then uses the process to develop a competitive product.

Fourth, as previously mentioned, not only is setting the price difficult, it is also extremely difficult to formalize and negotiate agreements between the parties. Renegotiating pre-existing licensing agreements can also be very difficult. In many instances, the licenser in renegotiation has lost some initial bargaining power, as the company's once proprietary knowledge has been in the hands of the licensee for some time.

Finally, the goal of using a licensing agreement as a first step toward foreign direct investment may not be realized. Foreign governments may be defensive about allowing the licenser of a product to discontinue a licensing agreement with a local company so that the foreign company can begin producing the product locally.

Managing Economic Risks.   **Pricing.**   In order to maintain a constant level of domestic-currency cash flow, the subsidiary in a foreign country should adjust prices to reflect changes in the exchange rates. For example, if the foreign currency devalues, the subsidiary should increase the prices charged for its products in the foreign market. This step will provide a greater volume of foreign currency, which when exchanged, will yield a constant level of the domestic currency.

Unfortunately, this alternative may not be available. Often countries with depreciating currency values have internal economic problems. These internal problems are typically caused by inflation and associated increases in prices. One governmental policy tool that is frequently used is to limit price increases through price controls, which restrict the ability of the subsidiary to increase prices to offset the devaluation of the currency.

Operations.   From a long-term standpoint, the best alternative may be to improve the operating efficiencies of the subsidiary. In a devaluing currency, the objective would be to reduce operating expenses while holding the sales price constant. The subsidiary should examine alternative production techniques, lower cost sources of materials, and other methods of improving its operating margins.

CONCLUSION

The size of the company, which includes its diversity of holdings and international activities, dictates the magnitude of foreign exchange risk exposure and therefore the need for foreign exchange risk management. The previous examples of managing risk continually emphasize the necessity of integrating the proposed technique with the normal operations of the company. All the techniques have certain costs attached to them, costs that are often difficult to measure. Only if the costs of the techniques are less than the impact of the unwanted exposure will they be worthwhile. Once the decision is made to manage foreign exchange risks, the approach used will be affected by the size and diversity of foreign operations. If foreign exchange risk management is appropriate, its success requires a logically structured approach that encompasses the entire risk. Coordinated corporate action is required rather than independent action by individual subsidiaries and affiliates.

The management of the different types of risk (i.e., transaction, translation, and economic) also involves the need to rank and weigh their impact on the company. Specifically, transaction risk involves realized gains and losses, while translation risk involves unrealized gains and losses. Measurement of the impact is also complicated by the fact that the elimination of translation gains or losses exposes the company to greater transaction exposure and vice versa. In weighing the impact of risks, one critical factor involved is determining whether the impact of a real gain or loss is more important than an unrealized gain or loss. As in many financial matters, this determination involves many complexities and requires continual review and study.

BIBLIOGRAPHY

Aggarwal, Raj. *Financial Policies for the Multinational Company—The Management of Foreign Exchange.* New York: Praeger Publishers, 1976.

Aliber, Robert Z. *Exchange Risk and Corporate International Finance.* New York: John Wiley & Sons, 1978.

Arinal, Andreas R. *Foreign Exchange Risk.* New York: John Wiley & Sons, 1976.

Eiteman, David K., and Arthur I. Stonehill. *Multinational Business Finance.* 3d ed. Reading, Mass.: Addison-Wesley, 1982.

Ensor, Richard, and Boris Antl, editors. *The Management of Foreign Exchange Risk.* Great Britain: Euromoney Publications, Ltd., 1978.

Kolde, Endel J. *International Business Enterprise.* Englewood Cliffs, N.J.: Prentice-Hall, 1968.

Levich, Richard M., and Clas G. Wihlbord. *Exchange Risk and Exposure.* Lexington, Mass.: Lexington Books, 1979.

Moriscato, Helen G. *Currency Translation and Performance Evaluation in Multinationals.* Ann Arbor, Mich.: UMI Research Press, 1980.

Nehrt, Lee C. *International Finance for Multinational Business.* 2d ed. Scranton, Penn.: International Textbook Company, 1972.

Pippinger, John E. *Fundamentals of International Finance.* Englewood Cliffs, N.J.: Prentice-Hall, Inc., 1984.

Rodriguez, Rita M. *Foreign-Exchange Management in U.S. Multinationals.* Lexington, Mass.: Lexington Books, 1980.

Rodriguez, Rita, and E. Eugene Carter, *International Financial Management.* 3d ed. Englewood Cliffs, N.J.: Prentice-Hall, Inc., 1984.

Solving International and Financial Currency Problems. New York: Business International Corp., 1976.

Spronck, Lambert H. *The Financial Executive's Handbook for Managing Multinational Corporations.* New York: John Wiley & Sons, 1980.

Managing Foreign Exchange Risks

■

APPENDIX A

Economic Exposure

The general formulation for calculating the economic exposure is as follows:
Economic exposure $= PV_0 - PV_a$, where

$$PV_0 = \frac{CF_{0_1} \times R_{0_1}}{1 + K} + \frac{CF_{0_2} \times R_{0_2}}{(1 + K)^2} \cdots + \frac{CF_{0_n} \times R_{0_n}}{(1 + K)^n}$$

$$PV_a = \frac{CF_{a_1} \times R_{a_1}}{1 + K} + \frac{CF_{a_2} \times R_{a_2}}{(1 + K)^2} \cdots + \frac{CF_{a_n} \times R_{a_n}}{(1 + K)^n}$$

where:

PV_0 = Present value of the cash flows at the original exchange rates
PV_a = Present value of the cash flows at the adjusted or new exchange rates
CF_{0_n} = Cash flow from the subsidiary in year n with the original exchange rates
CF_{a_n} = Cash flow from the subsidiary in year n with the adjusted or new
      exchange rates
K = Original exchange rate in year n
R_{a_n} = Adjusted or new exchange rate in year n.

     Using the example of the U.S. electronics company, assume that at the time
of the investment, the U.S. company expected its French subsidiary to generate
the following cash flows.

Year 1	FF100,000
Year 2	120,000
Year 3	130,000
Year 4 and continuing through Year n	150,000

     Assuming a discount rate of 15 percent for the French subsidiary, at the
exchange rate of US$0.23/FF, the present value of the cash flows to the U.S.

parent company would be US$191,890. This figure would be the economic value of the French subsidiary.

With the strengthening of the dollar against the French franc, the expected cash flows might be reduced. This could occur because the French subsidiary would have to pay more in terms of French francs for the raw materials imported to manufacture the semiconductors. Because of an increase in raw material costs, the expected cash flows might be reduced to the following:

Year 1	FF 95,000
Year 2	115,000
Year 3	120,000
Year 4 and continuing through Year n	140,000

With the exchange rate changed to US$0.21/FF, the present value of the cash flows using the same 15 percent discount rate would be US$164,120. The economic value of the subsidiary would be reduced by US$27,770 by the revaluation of the U.S. dollar.

■

APPENDIX B

Hedging through Foreign Exchange Market Contracts

Using the example of the U.S. electronics company, assume the following sequence of events:

> November 28, 1980: Delivery of FF100,000 worth of semiconductors to a French computer manufacturer (FF = French franc; sales price = FF10 per unit). Payment is due on February 26, 1981 in French francs. At November 28, 1980 spot prices of FF4.4685/US$(US$0.2238/FF), the export sale is worth US$22,380.00 if no credit terms are extended. In order to protect against an adverse change in the value of the FF against the US$, the U.S. company sells FF100,000 against the US$ for delivery on February 26, 1981 at FF4.3935/US$(US$0.2276/FF), the market price for 3-month dollars against the French franc. The forward contract will provide US$22,760.
>
> February 26, 1981: The U.S. firm receives a check for FF100,000. The U.S. firm delivers FF100,000 against the forward contract and receives US$22,760.

From the beginning of the transaction, the U.S. firm knows the exact amount of dollars it will receive when the French franc payment is finally realized.

Forward Rate Contracted

1. On November 28, 1980   US$0.2276 × FF100,000 = US$22,760
2. Actual spot rate on February 26, 1981   US$0.2011 × FF100,000 = US$20,110

Gain on November Forward versus February Spot

3. (line 1 − 2)   US$0.0265 × FF100,000 = US$ 2,650

■

APPENDIX C
Hedging through Loans

Again, using the example of the U.S. electronics company, assume the following sequence of events:

November 28, 1980: The U.S. company delivers the FF100,000 worth of semiconductors to the French computer manufacturer. Payment is due on February 26, 1981 in French francs. On November 28, if no credit was extended, the spot price of US$0.2238 would result in an export sale worth US$22,380. In order to protect against an adverse change of the franc against the dollar, the U.S. company borrows FF100,000 from a Paris bank at 13.4 percent on a discount basis, converts the FF96,759 proceeds from the loan into U.S. dollars (FF96,759 × US$0.2238 = US$21,655), and invests the dollars in a 3-month Treasury bill in the United States at 14.84 percent. After 3 months, the bill would be worth US$22,458.

February 26, 1981: The U.S. company receives a check for FF100,000. The French franc revenues from the export sale are used to pay the FF100,000 loan from the Paris bank. The 3-month bill is liquidated, and it yields the anticipated US$22,458. By undertaking this series of actions, the U.S. company knows the exact amount of dollars it will receive when the French franc payment is finally realized.

Liquidation Value of

1. 3-month bill: $US\$21,655 + \dfrac{14.84}{4} (US\$21,655) =$ US$22,458

2. Actual spot rate on February 26, 1981: US$0.2011 × FF100,000 = US$20,110

Gain on November Money Market Loans versus February Spot Price

3. (line 1 − 2) US$ 2,348

∎

APPENDIX D
Leading and Lagging

If the currency is expected to appreciate in value, companies making payments in that currency will accelerate payment of their obligations in that currency (a *lead*). Similarly, if a currency is under pressure, foreign companies making payments in that currency will delay as long as possible (a *lag*). A simple chart outlines the logic.

	Foreign Currency	
Company's Cash Flows	*Strengthen*	*Weaken*
Receipts	Delay	Speed up
Payments	Speed up	Delay

Independent multinational companies necessarily have similar objectives in their leading and lagging activity toward each other. For this reason, leading and lagging activity is most successful between subsidiaries of one company. If intrasubsidiary transfers of this type are used, the parent will need to change its systems for evaluating profits and investment so that units and managers are treated equitably when a lead or a lag, at the expense of a subsidiary but for the good of the company, takes place.

LEADING/LAGGING
BETWEEN TWO SUBSIDIARIES

ABC France owes $22,380 to ABC USA for semiconductors. Normal payment terms are 90 days, and the exchange rates on November 28, 1980, the day of delivery, are FF4.4685/US$(0.2238/FF).

Subsidiary Transactions, 11/28/80

ABC France	FF	ABC USA	US$
Cash	150,000	Accounts receivable	22,380
Inventory	100,000	Equity	22,380
Accounts payable	100,000		
Equity	150,000		

If the FF depreciates by 10 percent before maturity (FF4.9725/US$ or US$0.2011/FF), there is a net pre-tax loss to ABC France of FF11,300.

ABC France	FF	ABC USA	US$
Cash	150,000	Accounts receivable	22,380
Inventory	100,000	Equity	22,380
Accounts payable	111,300		
Equity	138,700		

If the payment from ABC France to ABC USA is accelerated and completed before devaluation, the results would be as follows:

ABC France	FF	ABC USA	US$
Cash	50,000	Cash	22,380
Inventory	100,000	Equity	22,380
Equity	150,000		

Managing Foreign Exchange Risks

■

APPENDIX E
Invoicing Currency

If the U.S. company selling semiconductors to the French computer manufacturer were a distributor of Japanese semiconductors, the U.S. distributor might prefer to be paid in yen. By being paid in yen, the majority of the transaction risk would be transferred away from the U.S. company to the Japanese and French companies. The U.S. company's gross profit, the sales revenue less the cost of goods sold in yen, would reflect the transaction exposure resulting from the sale of semiconductors. The gross profit might then be subject to risk management techniques. Assume the following sequence of events:

November 28, 1980: The U.S. distributor purchases 10,000 semiconductors from a Japanese manufacturer at a price of 404.0523 yen (Y) per unit for a total of Y4,040,523. The U.S. company sells the semiconductors at a 20 percent markup to a French company for Y4,848,627. Both the payable and the receivable are due on February 26, 1981 (90 days). The spot rate for Y/US$ exchange is US$0.004616/Y or Y216.64/US$.

February 26, 1981: The French company pays the U.S. company Y4,848,627. The U.S. company pays the Japanese company Y4,040,523.

1. Accounts receivable	Y4,848,627
2. Accounts payable gross profit subject to exchange	4,040,523
3. Gain or loss (line 1 − 2)	Y 808,104

Managing Foreign Exchange Risks

■

APPENDIX F
Swaps

The structure of a back-to-back, or parallel, loan might be the following:

November 28, 1980

Spot Rate US$0.2238/FF   FF4.4685/US$

U.S. parent agrees to lend a U.S. subsidiary of a French parent US$22,380 in return for the French parent's agreement to lend the French subsidiary of a U.S. parent FF100,000. Both loans to be rolled over on 2/26/81.

USA	*France*
U.S. parent firm loans $22,380 to the French affiliate in the United States.	French parent firm loans FF100,000 to the U.S. affiliate in France.

February 26, 1981

If the franc devalues against the dollar by 10 percent, the French parent would advance additional francs so as to bring the principal value of the two loans back to parity, as agreed upon in the loan terms on February 26, 1981.

Spot Rate US$0.2011/FF   FF4.9725/US$

French parent advances U.S. affiliate FF111,285 to bring the principal value of the two loans back to parity.

USA	*France*
U.S. parent firm loans $22,380 to the French affiliate in the United States	French parent firm loans F111,285 to the U.S. affiliate in France.

Merger and Acquisition Market:

Evolution of Cash Tender Offers to 1978

The pace of activity in the merger and acquisition (M&A) market during the latter half of the 1970s could only be described as frenzied, giving rise to numerous analogies with the merger craze of the 1960s. The total value of the mergers announced during 1976 was estimated at more than $20 billion; preliminary results for 1977 indicated at least a comparable level of activity for that year. These values were only slightly lower than the previous high of $24 billion announced in 1969.[1] Because the actual number of mergers completed per year had been declining since the 1960s, the value per deal had already surpassed the level experienced during that earlier period.

The M&A market of the late 1970s was similar to that of the 1960s in another significant way. Each market was dominated by the use of tender offers—unsolicited surprise offers made directly to the shareholders of a company. In fact, the number of tender offers made in 1976 was estimated to exceed the number of negotiated mergers by a factor of 3,[2] a spread that was expected to continue growing during 1977. More tender offers were made in 1977 alone, 181, than in any preceding year, and the total number of offers made in 1976 and 1977 exceeded the number of those made in the entire preceding decade (313 versus 305).[3]

Most of these tender offers were for cash, primarily because such transactions were fast and effective. If all went smoothly, the offer (and the deal) could be completed within a matter of days. This speed, together with the secrecy necessarily surrounding the development of such an offer, generated considerable unease among companies that perceived themselves as potential targets:

> It seems to happen fast. Very fast. For some the shock comes as a "bear hug." For others, the *Wall Street Journal* announces the terms of a surprise tender offer which was delivered to the SEC offices the preceding day at 4:58 p.m. No matter how top management learns of an unsolicited tender offer, the first reaction is disbelief—even fear.[4]

---

[1]"The Great Takeover Binge," *Business Week*, November 14, 1977, 176.

[2]Ibid., 178.

[3]Douglas V. Austin, "Tender Offer Update: 1978–1979," *Mergers and Acquisitions* (Summer 1980), 14.

[4]*Tender Offers*, Ernst & Whinney, 1980.

This note was prepared as a basis for class discussion from publicly available information. Copyright © 1984 by the Darden Graduate Business School Sponsors, University of Virginia, Charlottesville, Virginia.

The mystery surrounding cash tender offers was also reflected in the jargon they had spawned, such as Saturday night special, sleeping beauty, and white knight. Exhibit 1 defines some of the more prevalent expressions.

The growing use of cash tender offers resulted in the development of new corporate strategies designed either to effect or to foil surprise tender offers. Because all publicly held corporations were potential targets for tender offers, many of the defensive strategies were assimilated into general corporate patterns of behavior. (In fact, the desire to maintain corporate or managerial independence was, in certain cases, stronger than any motivation to maximize either earnings or value for the stockholders.)

This corporate preoccupation with mergers and merger defenses throughout the 1970s makes it critical for the student or practitioner of finance to have more than a cursory knowledge of the motives behind the actions taken. This note provides some of that background, including general information on tender offers per se, a description of the major strategies available to both offering and target management teams, and a discussion of the relationships among the major interest groups involved in any tender offer—the management teams, shareholders, and arbitrageurs.[5]

TENDER OFFERS: BACKGROUND

A tender offer is an offer made directly to the shareholders of a company to purchase all or some portion of their shares of its preferred or common stock at a specified price. Payment for the stock may be in the form of cash, securities (an exchange), or some combination of the two (a combination offer).

The major attraction of tender offers as a takeover tool has been that they allow the offering company to bypass the target company's management. (Other pros and cons of tender offers will be discussed later.) They are therefore extremely useful when resistance to a merger/acquisition proposal is either anticipated or encountered. Using a tender offer thus implies potential resistance on the part of the target's management to the prospect of a takeover, although the actual reaction is largely a function of the offer's specific terms. Offers that the target company tries to fight off are referred to as *unfriendly offers*. Unfriendly offers, if successful, always conclude in a purchase of stock for cash, a transaction that is taxable to the shareholder. Offers that are supported by the target company's management are referred to as *friendly offers*. These may lead to several different kinds of takeovers or business combinations.

Tender offers were not widely used before the mid-1960s. Prior to that time, takeovers were generally associated with corporate raids, the sole aim of which was to liquidate the target companies. The general view held by the business community at large was that both the goal and the tactic were unethical, which initially impeded the widespread use of tender offers. Two general trends supported the subsequent change in perception and the increased use of tender offers: (1) market and economic considerations heightened the attractiveness of tender offers as a financial weapon, and (2) experience began to show that a tender offer did not necessarily lead to a liquidation and was not as disreputable

---

[5]The SEC regulations referred to in this note are those in effect during 1977. Subsequent amendments are reflected in Tender Offers 1978–1979.

a tactic as had been believed. Exhibits 2 and 3 detail the trends in the numbers and kinds of tender offers made during the period. Exhibit 4 provides pertinent market data.

The tender offer market of the 1960s was generally characterized as having been dominated by "freewheeling conglomerateurs." Their goal was straightforward: to show a continuous stream of earnings gains. That this goal was sometimes attained through an uninterrupted stream of takeovers rather than through improvements in underlying productivity or profitability did not particularly help the conglomerateurs' business reputations or the perception of tender offers. Additionally, the fact that a large number of the takeovers were effected through stock exchanges—the actual value of which often came into question subsequently—further increased the uncertainties surrounding the ethics and propriety of the takeovers. These questions attracted the attention of both state and federal regulators toward the latter half of the 1960s. New regulations in turn created uncertainties, which persisted into the 1970s.

The reaction of the federal government to the large number of takeovers in the 1960s was both legislative and judicial. In the late 1960s, the Justice Department brought numerous antitrust actions against corporations trying to grow through acquisitions, a factor contributing to the decline in the number of offers made per year. Although the department's activities tapered off during the early 1970s, an increase in antitrust cases seemed likely by the middle of the decade, as the number of takeovers began to rise again and the size of the corporations involved continued to increase. In fact, by 1977, it was believed that there was a distinct possibility that the Carter administration, through the Justice Department, would try to slow down the takeover wave, using corporate size that created adverse economic concentration as an argument rather than focusing on pure antitrust issues. This possibility was the subject of ongoing debate among economists, politicians, and corporate executives, who believed that the M&A market would change markedly if the federal government accepted the premise that "big is bad."

The federal government reacted to the takeovers of the 1960s also with legislative actions. In 1968, Congress passed the Williams Bill, an amendment to the Securities and Exchange Act of 1934. The bill was designed to respond to the perceived potential for shareholder abuse by acquiring companies, especially by those offering stock exchanges. It placed stringent disclosure requirements on the offering company to ensure that shareholders had an adequate information base on which to decide whether to hold or tender their shares of stock.

The disclosure requirements of the Williams Act were amended both in 1970 and 1977 to include more stringent regulations that applied to the target as well as the offering company. Exhibit 5 summarizes the regulations that became effective in 1977. The fact that these disclosure requirements were more time-consuming and costly for stock exchanges than for cash offerings gave added impetus to the use of cash offers.

In addition to these federal measures, certain states also reacted strongly to the large number of takeovers. Typically, laws were adopted to protect local corporations (and local jobs) or to protect corporations with substantial assets or numbers of shareholders in the state. Most states established commissions that could disapprove a given tender offer by stopping an offering company from soliciting shares in that state. By 1977, at least 30 states had adopted antitakeover laws that could, at a minimum, delay the tender offer long enough for the target company to identify a more desirable merger partner. At the same time, however, the constitutionality of these laws was coming into question. There was a distinct possibility that they would be overthrown, leaving the regulation of the market to the federal government.

The emergence of the new regulations described above was one of the major causes of the decline in the number of tender offers made in the late 1960s and early 1970s, although changes in money market conditions and increasingly strong and effective defenses by target companies also contributed to the decline. Five major factors contributed to the re-emergence of tender offers during the mid-1970s: (1) corporations grew familiar with the regulatory framework, (2) corporate liquidity remained high, (3) the stock market was depressed, (4) inflation's effects on construction costs started tipping the scale toward buy rather than build decisions, and (5) the available supply of willing merger partners continued to decline. In essence, potential offerors had both the motivation and the means to start using tender offers again, which they did in 1975. The mid-1970s market differed in one major respect from that of the previous decade: the primary vehicle was a cash rather than a stock offer.

The economic conditions during the period also led to changes in the types of offering companies as well as in the underlying rationale behind the acquisitions. By the mid-1970s, many Fortune 500 companies had made or anticipated making surprise cash tender offers. What had previously been regarded with disdain had become not only acceptable, but also good business.

> Until only a few years ago, most blue-chip American corporations regarded unfriendly takeover attempts in the same light as crashing a party—totally graceless and nothing a gentleman would do. The unfriendly takeover was, after all, the hallmark of the nouveau riche conglomerateur, the meddlesome upstart who thought that sheer size would bring him corporate respectability much as decorating his newly purchased mansion with Rauschenbergs would give him instant background. Moreover, investment bankers viewed unfriendly takeovers in precisely the same light as their blue-chip clients, and piously refused to engage in them.
>
> But tastes have changed. . . . As the merger and acquisition specialist at an old-line banking house known for its intransigence about handling unfriendly takeovers for clients acknowledged recently: "Contested mergers have become standard corporate procedure, and tender offer techniques are now considered just another tool in the kit to get these things accomplished."[6]

Most of the takeovers effected by these companies were motivated by traditional business strategy—vertical or horizontal integration or product diversification. The underlying goals of improving productivity and profitability were eminently respectable and reflected well on tender offers per se.

Additionally, numerous foreign corporations entered the market during the latter half of the 1970s. Wanting to develop U.S. facilities, they had reached the same conclusion as their American counterparts: a cash tender offer was the fastest, least expensive method of getting established. These foreign corporations were motivated to buy American for any number of reasons:

1. The depressed U.S. stock market represented an attractive investment outlet for surplus dollars.

---

[6]Julie Connelly, "The Boom in Unfriendly Takeovers," *Institutional Investor* (December 1975), 48.

2. The United States was the largest market for the corporation's goods.

3. Labor productivity was higher in the United States than in Europe.

4. The United States was perceived as the last bastion of capitalism, offering political stability and a liberal economic environment.

In 1976, 39 U.S. manufacturing companies were acquired by foreign firms for a total of $338 million. This figure increased to 59 companies for $590 million in the first 9 months of 1977, more than double the level of the preceding year, on an annualized basis.[7,8]

In short, cash tender offers had become the most widespread technique of participating in an increasingly active and competitive merger and acquisition market.

CASH TENDER OFFERS AND THEIR ALTERNATIVES: PROS AND CONS

By 1977, cash tender offers were generally perceived as the fastest, most aggressive, and most effective method of completing a takeover. The actual or threatened use of such an offer presumed the potential for resistance to the takeover. In that context of hostility, alternative methods of gaining control were limited. The acquiring company could either (1) purchase enough of the target's shares on the open market either to gain control outright or to initiate a proxy fight, or (2) directly offer the target's shareholders an exchange of stock or stock and cash. Both approaches had disadvantages.

Purchasing any sizable number of shares on the open market created several problems. To avoid inflating the price of the stock, purchases had to be made over an extended period of time. The acquiring company was thus faced with a choice between a lengthy takeover process at close-to-market prices or a faster process at a higher price. Neither was particularly attractive: there was no guarantee of success, and there was always the possibility that changes in market or business conditions would reduce the target's attractiveness. In addition, SEC regulations required that anyone purchasing more than 5 percent of another corporation's stock had to notify both the SEC and the subject company and had to make certain disclosures regarding his or her intentions. Thus, all elements of surprise were lost, and the chances that the target could develop an effective defense were maximized.

Proxy fights were the most widely used method of effecting an unfriendly takeover prior the the development of tender offers. However, as research has

---

[7]"The Great Takeover Binge," *Business Week*, November 14, 1977, 176.

[8]The first tender offers by foreign corporations for U.S. enterprises occurred in 1973 when five such offers were made. By the next year, the number had increased to 16. Interestingly, the number of offers made between 1972 and 1975 by foreign companies had a lower proportion of total unsuccessful offers than did the aggregate number of tender offers made in the same period in the market at large. Less than 4 percent of the foreign offers were unsuccessful versus a comparable 16 percent for the market as a whole. This higher rate of success might have been the result of differences in the accounting laws governing American and foreign nationals. The latter are not required to amortize the goodwill associated with the purchase of a company as Americans are, thus effectively allowing them to bid higher prices than their American counterparts. For more information, see Douglas V. Austin, "Tender Offer Statistics: New Strategies Are Paying Off," *Mergers and Acquisitions* (Fall 1975), 9.

shown,[9] proxy fights did not have a very good rate of success and were time-consuming and expensive.

The major problem with any offer to exchange stock derived from the SEC regulations governing the transaction. Chief among these was the requirement that the shares to be exchanged be registered with the commission. Not only was this relatively expensive, it was also time-consuming and frequently gave the target company advance notice of the offering company's intentions.

Stock exchanges had other problems: they could dilute the acquiring company's earnings, and they were more difficult to sell to the target's shareholders than a cash offer. The valuation problem derived from two sources: (1) it was difficult for shareholders to interpret the monetary value of a stock offer; as a result, (2) it was easier for the target's management to argue that the offer was inadequate.[10]

Cash tender offers, on the other hand, had none of these disadvantages. On the contrary, factors that operated to the target's advantage under any of the other alternatives favored the acquisitor under a cash tender. The major advantages are summarized below.

1. *Cash tender offers were fast.* The average duration of the largest offers made in 1975 and 1976 was 10 to 14 days from the date of the announcement to the initial termination date of the offer.[11] Not only did the short time frame curtail the target's ability to mount an effective defense, it also minimized the chance that a competitive bidder would, on its own initiative or at the instigation of the target, make a counteroffer. Furthermore, it allowed the offering company to take swift advantage of the market or business conditions that roused its acquisition interest in the first place.

2. *Cash tender offers were relatively inexpensive,* if all went smoothly. Up-front costs were limited to advertising expenses, fees resulting from legal and financial advice received in the development of the offer, and finance charges for the credit lines established to handle the short-term financing of the offer. The offering company's exposure was relatively limited, although the up-front expenses could increase dramatically if the target company initiated lawsuits that the offering company chose to pursue.

3. *An offering bid effectively fixed the market price of the target's stock.* Market speculators would bid the price up to a level slightly less than that bid, a level which

---

[9]A study of proxy fights between 1956 and 1960 showed that of 28 such contests, only 9 were successful. This is less than a 33-percent success rate. The study was conducted by Douglas V. Austin, "Proxy Contest and Corporate Reform," Bureau of Business Research, University of Michigan Graduate School of Business Administration, 1965, as referred to by Samuel L. Hayes, III and Russell A. Taussig, "Tactics of Cash Takeover Bids," *Harvard Business Review* (April 1967), 137.

[10]Interestingly, research has shown that of the tender offers made between 1956–1967, those offering an exchange of stock had a higher success rate than did those offering an exchange of cash, 85 percent successful versus 78 percent. This spread increased further in the period from 1968 to 1972 to an 80 percent success rate for stock exchanges versus only a 61 percent success rate for the cash offers. While no data on the success rate of exchange offers was available for latter periods, the success rate of cash tender offers increased dramatically between 1972 and 1977 to about 82 percent. For more information, see Douglas V. Austin, "Tender Offers Revisited: 1968–1972 Comparison with the Past and Future Trends," *Mergers and Acquisitions* (Fall 1973), 16–27; "Tender Offer Update, 1978–79," *Mergers and Acquisitions* (Summer 1980), 13–24.

[11]Raymond S. Troubh, "Purchased Affections: A Primer on Cash Tender Offers," *Harvard Business Review* (July–August 1976), 80.

would remain fixed unless a competitor entered the bidding. In short, the offering company's liability was limited to the price actually bid. The offering company was thus in a position to select the price it was willing to pay and to develop a bidding strategy around that price.

4. *The monetary value of a cash tender offer was self-evident.* Because the offering price usually incorporated a certain premium, the target's management was immediately put in the undesirable position of arguing that the bid of hard cash was an inadequate reflection of the company's intangible future value. Furthermore, a cash offer for stock was superior to a purchase of assets. The value of the stock was readily identifiable, having been established in an open market. The value of the assets was more difficult to ascertain, and the valuation process could be both time-consuming and expensive for the acquiring company.

5. *The risks associated with cash tender offers were discrete* and largely self-imposed by the acquiring company. In essence, the acquisitor could put whatever conditions on the offer it wanted; it was not legally bound to complete the purchases unless all of the conditions had been met. The offeror's financial liability was, therefore, limited to the up-front costs.

6. *Cash tender offers were very successful.* Of the cash tender offers made between 1972 and 1977, 82 percent were at least partially successful.[12] In cases of partial success, fewer than 100 percent of the shares bid for were actually tendered, but the offeror accepted those shares and would presumably continue to fight for control. Exhibit 2 details partially and totally successful tender offers from 1960 to 1977.

The major disadvantage of the cash tender offer resulted from its major advantage—the element of surprise. Because the offering price was developed in the utmost secrecy, it was, perforce, based entirely on publicly available information. As a result, the offering company was unable to investigate thoroughly the target's operations or financial status and had no contractual protection regarding any of the target's representations. As a result, the premium established by the offering company could be higher than that which would have been arrived at through amicable negotiations. The continued growth in the use of cash tender offers showed, however, that corporate America believed the advantages more than outweighed this disadvantage.

TARGET CHARACTERISTICS

Certain characteristics were considered (1) to heighten a company's financial or economic attractiveness and/or (2) to increase its vulnerability and, therefore, the likelihood of a successful takeover.[13] These characteristics related to:

1. Performance
2. Balance sheets
3. Shareholders
4. General company attributes.

---

[12]Douglas V. Austin, "Tender Offer Update: 1978–1979," *Mergers and Acquisitions* (Summer 1980), 17.

[13]This and the following section draw heavily on *Tender Offers,* a booklet prepared by Ernst & Whinney in 1980.

1. *Performance.* A company could become attractive to another on the basis of either its actual or potential profits. Depending on the perspective of the acquiring company, an already profitable company could be as attractive as a less profitable one with greater turnaround potential. Those companies about to receive the returns of long-term projects or development efforts might be especially attractive targets, as would be those that had not taken advantage of all available business opportunities. Generally, companies with lower earnings growth rates or price/earnings ratios than their competitors were perceived to be relatively more vulnerable. Poor earnings and stock price records not only reduced the price for the offering entity, they also made the tender offer and its premium more attractive to the target's shareholders.

2. *Balance Sheets.* Two major balance sheet characteristics were perceived to increase a company's attractiveness. First, a company with excess liquidity and/ or unused debt capacity could be of particular interest to an offering company, since either or both could be used to fund the offering company's growth or the takeover itself. Secondly, a company was attractive when the monetary value of its net assets exceeded its market value.

3. *Shareholders.* Vulnerability was indicated by both the ownership structure of the company and the attitudes of its shareholders. However, many of the characteristics appeared contradictory. For instance, a company whose stock was held in large blocks by a few investors (e.g., pension funds, trusts, institutions) might be as vulnerable as one whose stock was held by a large number of widely dispersed shareholders. In the first case, the entities holding the stock could be forced to tender their shares to fulfill their fiduciary roles.[14] In the latter case, widely dispersed ownership was seen to imply little long-term commitment to the company. A similar contradiction occurred with respect to the stock's trading patterns: both light and heavy patterns of trading could be seen as evidence of vulnerability. The first situation implied a lack of investor interest in the stock,

---

[14]The levels of preparedness and financial commitment exhibited by target management teams in mounting their defenses against a tender offer were the subject of much debate. While there was a general consensus that a preliminary rejection of a tender offer was an appropriate strategy to elicit a higher bid from the offering company, questions had been raised about the rapid commitment of significant amounts of corporate funds to what some called "knee-jerk reactions" to the potential loss of managerial control. At issue were (a) the nature of the relationship between the managers and directors of a company and its shareholders and (b) the potential for conflict of interest between the two groups. The question of whether a management team was trying to perpetuate itself or to protect the interests of the shareholders had been raised on several occasions.

The relationship between the managers and directors of a company and its shareholders is considered fiduciary in nature and is largely governed by case law. The major underpinning of the cases is that corporate managers and directors are in a better position to make judgments about the enterprise and its future than are the shareholders because of the special positions the former hold. As a result, certain duties had over time been ascribed to managers and directors which governed their relationship with the stockholders. These included the duties to (a) always advance the shareholders' best interests, (b) avoid any conflict of interest, and (c) act in good faith.

The behavior of individuals or institutions holding stock in trust for others was controlled by a body of state and federal law. The fiduciary nature of the relationships was defined in terms of a series of duties owed to the beneficiaries: (a) the duty of care (otherwise known as the "prudent man" rule); (b) the duty of undivided loyalty; and (c) the duty not to delegate certain discretionary powers. Specific authorities delegated to or powers withheld from the trustee would, ordinarily, be detailed in the trust document itself and would vary depending on the trust's function. For instance, a trust set up for charitable purposes would result in a very different set of trustee responsibilities than would one set up to serve one generation of beneficiaries. Trustees were considered to be personally liable to their beneficiaries for any loss or depreciation in the value of the trust, which increased the incentive for the trustee to exercise care.

while the latter implied that the market sensed an imminent improvement in stock price or a tender offer. Heavy trading was interpreted as evidence of vulnerability also because newer shareholders were generally perceived as having a shorter-term orientation than longer-term shareholders.

4. *General Company Attributes.* Certain other general attributes could also increase a company's attractiveness as a takeover candidate. These were generally reflections of the overall trends in the M&A market. In the late 1970s, for instance, as inflation caused construction costs to continue rising, companies with efficient, relatively new production facilities became increasingly attractive. Similarly, corporations with existing brand names and distribution networks became increasingly attractive to those entities desiring to diversify their operations, while those companies with strong products in growth markets were of particular interest to growth-oriented entities.

TARGET COMPANIES: DEFENSIVE STRATEGIES

Defensive strategies became increasingly sophisticated as cash tender offers became more prevalent. These strategies were generally of two types. The first involved changes to a company's operations or performance that were designed to minimize either its attractiveness or vulnerability. The second type of strategy was essentially procedural and had one major goal: to delay events in any takeover attempt such that the optimal deal could be negotiated for the shareholders, whether in the form of a higher price, a merger with a third party, or a rejected bid.

Operational Strategies.   Strategies in this group were designed both to reduce the likelihood that an unsolicited tender offer would be received and to minimize the chances that such an offer, if received, would be completed on the offering company's original timetable. The basic premise was to "know thyself"—to determine how attractive or vulnerable a target the firm was so that the deficiencies could be corrected.

The first step in the corporate self-analysis was to compare the company's performance and operations to the traits described above. Where similarities were found, steps were undertaken to determine the source of the problem. For instance, poor earnings and stock price performance might lead to an evaluation of the company's operations or an in-depth analysis of its market position vis-à-vis those of its major competitors. To correct any weaknesses, firms could:

1. Modify operations to improve returns and/or reduce any competitive disadvantages.

2. Reduce excess liquidity or unused debt capacity by increasing capital investments (new products, new facilities, purchase of treasury stock, etc.) or by increasing dividends (which, potentially, had the added advantage of improving shareholder relations and improving the stock's price/earnings ratio).

3. Dispose of unnecessary assets to reduce the book value per share.

4. Try to develop a broad base of shareholder support by

    a. Identifying the company's shareholders and their geographic dispersion.

b. Communicating with them regularly to maximize their understanding of the company's operations and long-term potential.

c. Identifying the goals of the typical shareholder (e.g., dividends, capital appreciation, etc.).

5. Explore the possibility of placing as much stock as possible with the company's employees, managers, and others having clear long-term interests in the company's continuation.

6. Repurchase shares of stock as a means of reducing both liquidity and the number of shares in the hands of nervous shareholders.[15]

7. Raise the dividends to solidify shareholder support.[16]

The major caveat to the adoption of any defensive strategy was that it have some rational basis in legitimate business strategy. The target's managers' primary duty was to protect and maximize the shareholders' interests. The fact that management's long-term, personal concerns could be at odds with the shareholders' best interests was a potential source of conflict. (See Footnote 14 for further discussion of this point.) By the end of 1977, the courts were beginning to recognize this conflict and to hear cases in which shareholders sued managers who had successfully fought off unsolicited tender offers. This trend represented a major constraint on management's actions.

Procedural Strategies.

Procedural strategies had been designed to perform two functions. On the one hand, they were intended to deter potential offers by making a successful tender offer more difficult to effect. On the other hand, they were also intended to give the target company more flexibility in assessing and reacting to an offer. Procedural strategies were both preventive and reactive.

Preventive Strategies. The major factor in an effective defense was the speed with which the target company's management could react to the offer. To ensure a fast response, most companies created evaluation and response teams of lawyers, investment bankers, and accountants. If the decision were made to fight an offer, additional aid would be required in the form of public relations and proxy solicitation firms. Many companies put representatives of each of these groups on retainer to assure their participation if and when a tender offer was received.

The target's management and defense teams were responsible for familiarizing themselves with all pertinent federal and state laws and regulations, including those of the SEC, the Federal Communications Commission, the Federal Trade Commission, and any pertinent state regulatory commissions. In some cases, these efforts led the target's management to decide that it was in the company's best interests to relocate its headquarters to a state with more restrictive antitakeover statutes.

---

[15]It could be argued further that a stock repurchase could raise a company's price/earnings multiple by an amount greater than that resulting from the reduction in number of outstanding shares. This would in turn, result in a commensurate increase in the stock price, potentially necessitating a higher premium on the tender offer and a greater total purchase price for the offering company.

[16]The strategy of using company funds to increase cash dividends solely for the purpose of garnering shareholder support had raised certain questions. The major issue under debate was the questionable appropriateness of buying off a shareholder with his own profits.

Managers of a company perceived to be vulnerable could also modify the company's charter or bylaws to make any unanticipated change in control of the company more difficult. Examples of charter changes included:

1. Staggering the terms served by the members of the board of directors.

2. Adopting "super-majority" clauses, which required the approval of a large proportion of shareholders for mergers or certain other actions, such as modifications to the board of directors.

Managers could also identify and evaluate prospective merger partners who might come to their company's aid in the event of a tender offer. This foresight often allowed the target to identify a potential partner on the basis of compatibility rather than ready availability.

Reactive Strategies.   There were four possible responses to a tender offer: the managers could (a) oppose it; (b) support it; (c) state their neutrality; or (d) make no comment. The last two options, however, implied consent or indifference and generally facilitated the offer, leaving managers the basic choice of supporting or opposing the tender offer.

Most specialists recommended that a tender offer be opposed only if there was a strong, rational basis for doing so. Otherwise, managers could expose themselves to a shareholder lawsuit. To determine whether an offer should be opposed, the target's management tried to assess the effect of the offer on and its attractiveness to several different groups:

1. The target company's shareholders.

    a.   Was the offer price fair?

    b.   If the deal was a stock exchange, was the offering company an attractive investment opportunity for the target's shareholders?

    c.   If the offer was for less than 100 percent of the target's stock, what protection would be available for remaining minority shareholders?

2. The target company's employees and the surrounding community.

    a.   Were the offering company's personnel policies compatible with the target's?

    b.   Was it likely the offering company would liquidate the target?

    c.   What would be the effect on the local community?

3. The target company's competitors and the consumers of its products.

    a.   Would the acquisitor liquidate the company?

    b.   Were there potential antitrust issues?

Target companies that decided, on the basis of the preceding analysis, to oppose an offer had several defensive strategies available to them. Normally, one of the first steps in opposing an offer was to initiate an aggressive information and publicity program. Such a program would (a) clarify the target's reasons for opposing the offer, and (b) publicize those conditions that were expected to impede the offer's success. The former information (which might highlight the inadequacy of the price, the unattractiveness of the merger partner, etc.) was directed at the target's shareholders. The latter information (which might highlight antitrust or other legal issues slowing down the offer's resolution) was directed at stockbrokers and arbitrageurs. Its dissemination was intended to discourage speculation in the stock.[17]

Concurrently, target companies could also take legal actions to oppose or impede the progress of a tender offer. The major goals of any such actions were (a) to gain time to organize an effective defense, and (b) to reduce the attractiveness of the situation to arbitrageurs and other market speculators. A well-prepared target company generally had ready for filing a petition for a temporary restraining order (usually claiming antitrust violations) and a preliminary injunction. These would be filed in jurisdictions sympathetic to the targets of unfriendly takeover attempts.

Other defensive strategies were also available. Target companies could make it difficult for offering entities to communicate with their shareholders by withholding the list of shareholder names and addresses for as long as was legally allowable. Target companies could also make defensive mergers or, if there was enough time, acquire a company with operations in the same field as the offering company. The successful completion of this move could generate antitrust issues that were sufficient to prevent the successful completion of the original tender offer. There was a side benefit of such a merger. If the acquisition were made for stock, the increase in the number of shares outstanding could discourage the bidder from proceeding with the offer.

Managers of the target companies could also, if there was time, undertake certain of the proactive strategies discussed earlier, such as amending the company's charter or bylaws. Any action undertaken for the sole purpose of fighting off a tender offer could, however, bring shareholder lawsuits against the company's managers.

And last, the emotional side of the tender offer battle should not be ignored. Whether in terms of the publicity campaigns conducted or the lawsuits filed, the reactions of target companies to proposed tender offers could be both highly emotional and personally unpleasant for the managers of the offering company: "The toughest thing for the management of an acquiring company to accept is that they will be named in suits, they will have to testify, and they'll be characterized as raiders. Most people would rather be lovers than fighters."[18] The vehemence of the target company's reaction to a tender offer could be the major factor in the offer's failure. In at least one case, the bidder simply withdrew.

BIDDING COMPANIES: OFFENSIVE STRATEGIES

A corporation that decided to make an acquisition using a surprise cash tender offer was clearly determined to succeed in the shortest time and at the most reasonable price possible. Several types of strategies had been developed to help

---

[17]A discussion of the arbitrage community's role in the merger and acquisition market follows later in this note.

[18]Julie Connelly, "The Boom in Unfriendly Takeovers," *Institutional Investor* (December 1975), 52. The statement was made by a merger specialist familiar with and in reference to an unsuccessful tender offer by Northern Electric for Dictaphone in 1974. The major factor cited in Dictaphone's successful defense was the unexpected vehemence of its response.

realize these goals. They fell into three general groups: (a) pre-offer strategies, (b) strategies for structuring the offer, and (c) post-offer strategies.

Pre-Offer Strategies.

Establishing a strong acquisition team was the major action a bidding company could make prior to the initiation of a tender offer. Similar in composition to the defensive teams established by target companies, the acquisition teams were designed to help the bidder (a) identify a desirable target, (b) structure a suitable bidding strategy for the tender offer, (c) develop contingent responses to the target's anticipated reactions, (d) provide support in the publication of the offer, and (e) provide support and advice in all follow-up activities. For instance, prior to the publication of the tender offer, the bidder's legal staff generally reviewed the target company's bylaws and all pertinent federal and state laws and regulations that might be invoked by the target. The team also prepared a preliminary version of the bidder's rebuttal to the press release that the target was anticipated to make. With only minor editing to meet the specific charges levied, the bidder could get its response to the press within hours.

Bidding companies were legally allowed to buy up to 4.9 percent of a target company's stock before having to disclose the purchases to either the target or the SEC. There were pros and cons to buying stock prior to a tender offer.

1. Such purchases could, perhaps, be made for less than the tender offer price. This potential benefit had to be weighed against two possible dangers. First, heavy buying could raise the stock price, thus increasing the premium required in the tender offer. Alternatively, continuous, low-level buying increased the possibility that both the name of the target and the imminence of the tender offer would be leaked to the market, also greatly increasing the stock's price and the premium required.

2. The purchases reduced the number of shares that had to be tendered for, thus increasing the offer's chance of success. The major question was whether the number of shares purchased was material in light of the potential problems outlined above.

3. The purchases offered a psychological advantage. They allowed the bidding company to address the target's stockholders as "fellow shareholders."

Strategies for Structuring the Offer.

All tender offers incorporated certain basic variables: (a) the length of time for which the offer would be open, (b) the number of shares being sought, and (c) the premium being offered. In addition, certain standard conditions were included to protect the bidder's liability in case of such events as government intervention or war.

The minimum length of time for which an offer could be open was set by the SEC at 10 business days, although the bid could be extended subsequently by the offering company. All shares tendered in the first 10 days had to be accepted on a pro rata basis, although the bidder could stipulate that shares tendered subsequently (assuming the offer was extended) would be accepted on a first-come, first-served basis.

The determination of the number of shares for which to bid was a decision of considerable import. It entailed a trade-off between the financial attractiveness of tendering only for those shares required for control and the strategic advantage of tendering for more. At issue was the role to be played by market arbitrageurs. Arbitrageurs were concerned primarily with the short-term profits to be earned by purchasing a target's stock directly after a tender offer was made and subsequently tendering those shares at the close of the offer period. Tender offer strategists assumed that the shares of the target that were traded subsequent to the tender offer were purchased primarily by arbitrageurs. It was therefore assumed that all such shares would be tendered. Thus, the involvement of arbitrageurs could give a significant advantage to the offering company.

Arbitrageurs based their decision on whether to participate in a given tender offer on their assessments of two factors: (a) the probability of the offer's success, and (b) the amount of time their capital would be tied up. Tender offers for less than 100 percent of a company's stock or which contained certain conditions (e.g., so many shares had to be tendered before any would be purchased) were unattractive to arbitrageurs. They didn't want to commit their capital to a purchase of stock when they had no guarantee that the entire block would be saleable at the higher tender offer price. Furthermore, pro rata offers for less than 100 percent of the stock might also be detrimental to the acquiring company. Once the arbitrageurs sold the pro rata share of their holdings to the bidder, they could liquidate the remainder by dumping it on the market. This usually depressed the company's stock price immediately after the establishment of the new control block. Consequently, there was considerable pressure to tender for more than just those shares necessary to gain control.

The decision of what premium to set on the offer, while not the sole determinant of success,[19] was clearly of critical importance. Over time, certain factors had gained recognition as being important in the premium-setting decision: (a) factors that related to the target company, its competitors, and the stock market in general; and (b) factors that related to the merger and acquisition market. Considering both sets of factors, the offering company had to strike a balance between the price it was willing to pay and the price the target's shareholders would require.

Conventional wisdom, in late 1977, held that the most important company-related determinants of a premium were the historic and current levels of the target's stock price, those of its competitors' stock prices, and that of the stock market as a whole. Holders of a stock whose price was depressed (significantly below its historically normal levels) would require a larger premium than would those whose stock appeared healthy. The rationale appeared simple—why would anyone sell out when a stock was at its historic low? In addition, it was also generally believed that stocks with a lower market price per share would require a higher premium than would those trading at a higher price.

Other factors had also been cited as important in determining the premium. The more dispersed the current ownership, it was argued, the higher the premium would have to be to induce shareholders to tender their stock. Similarly, an imbalance in bargaining positions between the offering company and the target could also affect the size of the premium.[20] The relative bargaining

---

[19]See, for instance, Samuel L. Hayes, III and Russell A. Taussig, "Tactics of Case Takeover Bids," *Harvard Business Review* (March–April 1967), 140; Douglas V. Austin, "Tender Offers Revisited: 1968–1972 Comparisons with the Past and Future Trends," *Mergers and Acquisitions* (Fall 1973), 21; Douglas V. Austin, "Tender Offer Statistics: New Strategies Are Paying Off," *Mergers and Acquisitions* (Fall 1975), 13; and Fred J. Ebeid, "Tender Offers: Characteristics Affecting Their Success," *Mergers and Acquisitions* (Fall 1976), 27.

[20]Kenneth R. Ferris, Arie Melnick, and Alfred Rappaport, "Tender Offer Pricing: An Empirical Analysis," *Mergers and Acquisitions* (Spring 1977), 9–13.

power of the two companies could, it was argued, be estimated on the basis of certain factors: the number of shares already owned by the offering company prior to the tender, the offering company's access to inside information, the respective financial positions of the two companies, and the target's ability to resist.

However, the importance of each of the above factors paled somewhat in the face of the astonishingly high levels of competition in the merger and acquisition market of the late 1970s. Pricing decisions were made as much in response to the fight anticipated as they were on the basis of the target's historical or potential value. By 1977, two trends were becoming apparent. First, the premiums offered over market price had assumed epic proportions. The most commonly cited example was the battle for control of Babcock & Wilcox Co., which J. Ray McDermott & Co. eventually won as the white knight. The deal was concluded at $65 per share, 87 percent higher than the company's pre-offer market price of $34.75 and 55 percent above the initial bid of $42 per share offered by United Technologies.

> The Babcock deal is the one that shook the corporate world most. It demonstrated that buying companies at close to their prices in the stock market is very difficult. Bankers now say that the biggest mistake an acquiring company can make is to bid too low. . . "Brute economic power—the one who is willing to pay the most—usually decides who will win."[21]

The greatly increased competition was the source of the second emerging trend—a movement back toward negotiated mergers.

> The takeover climate has become so competitive that every corporation interested in acquisitions is finding it necessary to arm itself with the best advice and manpower available. Deals that were once negotiated are suddenly turning unfriendly as management searches for better offers elsewhere. Some corporate officers admit that they are now shying away from making bids because the contests can become so fierce. "We considered bidding for a company," says one chief executive, "but a banker confided that once we did, he would have another company offering more money right away. It's getting so we will only do a merger if we can negotiate it."[22]

Certain other factors could be introduced into the structure of the tender offer to increase the likelihood of success. For instance, the offering company could raise the commission offered to the soliciting broker rather than the premium offered to the shareholder. The goal was to increase the effort spent to solicit dispersed shares rather than pay more to attract large shareholders. In other situations, tendering companies assured the target's managers that they would be retained after the merger.

Post-Offer Strategies.

Actions by the tendering company's acquisition team following the offer's publication generally took two forms: (a) rebutting the target's defenses and (b) wooing the target's shareholders. While the former

---

[21]"The Great Takeover Binge," *Business Week*, November 14, 1977, 184.

[22]Ibid, 182.

efforts were frequently restricted to courtroom appearances, the latter held a prominent position in the public eye.

The battle for the shareholders' allegiances was usually waged in the media. The offering company's primary goal was to convince the target's shareholders that:

1. The tender price was both fair and attractive.

2. All markets for the stock would disappear if the tender offer were successful.

3. Future dividends might be reduced or eliminated.

4. The target company could be maneuvered into a forced merger at a later date at an as-yet-unknown, possibly lower, price or for a different medium of exchange (stock).

5. The company's basic business or its prospects could be subject to change.

6. They might never be offered such a value again if the tender offer failed.

7. They might have other, better investments for their money than holding the stock of the target company.

The aggressiveness with which these messages were transmitted was frequently determined by the vigor of the target's defense. Although some tendering companies might withdraw their offers in the face of a belligerent defense, especially one waged on a personal level, others were willing to persevere. As fast and seemingly effective as cash tender offers were, they still required a sizable financial and psychological commitment on the part of the tendering company.

CONCLUSION

Changing economic and market conditions had led to the growth in activity within the merger and acquisition market between the late 1960s and 1970s. These, together with a changing regulatory environment, had elicited the phenomenal growth in cash tender offers as the major vehicle for effecting the desired business combinations. By 1977, the number of such offers was on the rise, spurred in part by increasing levels of foreign corporate participation. The increase in the number of eager offering companies combined with a declining number of willing targets had spurred competition and, not surprisingly, inflated premiums. Whether this situation and the conditions underlying its development would remain unchanged throughout 1978 and the remainder of the decade was of critical interest to both potential tendering companies and target companies.

BIBLIOGRAPHY

Archbold, Pamela. "How to Foil a Raider." *Investor Relations* (November 1977), 33–34.

Austin, Douglas V. "Tender Offers Revisited: 1968–1972 Comparisons with the Past and Future Trends." *Mergers and Acquisitions* (Fall 1973), 16–27.

Austin, Douglas V. "Tender Offer Statistics: New Strategies Are Paying Off." *Mergers and Acquisitions* (Fall 1975), 9–24.

Austin, Douglas V. "Tender Offer Update: 1978–1979." *Mergers and Acquisitions* (Summer 1980), 13–24.

"The Great Takeover Binge." *Business Week*, November 14, 1977, 176–184.

"A Two-Price Bid to Force a Merger." *Business Week*, February 27, 1978, 35–36.

"Will Sun's Raid Set a Pattern?" *Business Week*, February 13, 1978, 99.

Connelly, Julie. "The Boom in Unfriendly Takeovers." *Institutional Investor* (December 1975), 48–52.

"A Difference of Opinion: A Brief against Managements that Fight Off Tender Offers." *Fortune*, March 12, 1979, 159–160.

Ebeid, Fred J. "Tender Offers: Characteristics Affecting Their Success." *Mergers and Acquisitions* (Fall 1976), 21–30.

Tender Offers. Ernst & Whinney, 1980.

Ferris, Kenneth R., Arie Melnick, and Alfred Rappaport. "Cash Tender Offer Pricing: An Empirical Analysis." *Mergers and Acquisitions* (Spring 1977), 9–13.

Fleischer, Arthur, Jr. "The SEC's New Disclosure Rules for Takeovers." *Institutional Investor* (September 1977), 9–10.

Goff, Neal. "Takeover Backlash: The Shareholders Sue." *Financial World*, June 15, 1979, 15.

Hayes, Samuel L., III, and Russell A. Taussig. "Tactics of Cash Takeover Bids," *Harvard Business Review* (March–April 1967), 135–148.

Long, Lynn Thompson. "Pressure on Fiduciary Holders in Premium Cash Offers." *Mergers and Acquisitions* (Winter 1979), 4–11.

Long, Lynn Thompson. "Director Fiduciaries: Protecting Shareholder Interests." *Mergers and Acquisitions* (Winter 1980), 4–9.

McCann, Joseph, and Roderick Gilkey. *Joining Forces: Creating and Managing Successful Mergers and Acquisitions.* Englewood Cliffs, N.J.: Prentice Hall, 1988.

Schwartz, Gabriel B., and Edmund J. Kelly. "Bank Financing of Corporate Acquisitions— The Cash Tender Offer." *The Banking Law Journal* 88, no. 2 (February 1971), 99–111.

Troubh, Raymond S. "Purchased Affection: A Primer on Cash Tender Offers." *Harvard Business Review* (July–August 1976), 79–91.

Merger and Acquisition Market: Evolution of Cash Tender Offers to 1978

EXHIBIT 1
■
Tender Offer Jargon

'White Knights' and 'Shark Repellents'

The argot of tender offers

by Patrick J. Davey
CB Management Research

Up to a decade ago, "tender offers"—a curious, ambiguous phrase, when you come to think of it—stirred little reaction in corporate boardrooms and received scant attention in the press. After all, they seldom surfaced, and then usually only in connection with a company's efforts to repurchase a portion of its outstanding shares.

But now tender offers have become a financial phenomenon. They have demonstrated their potency in a new and more threatening role—the almost total replacement of proxy contests as a means of seizing control of companies from resisting managements. Considerable executive time is devoted to either planning them or devising defenses against them. And the intercompany battles they often provoke are widely discussed and publicized—witness the recent brouhaha in the bidding for control of Avis, Inc.

Because practitioners in the tender offer arena have developed their own argot (as in any other trade: journalism, "bogus type"; subway motormen, "the dead man's button"), descriptions of takeover contests are not always fully comprehensible to the layperson. Here is a glossary that may facilitate understanding of such accounts:

■ *Raid*—an unnegotiated tender offer to wrest control of a company. It is perpetrated by a raider or aggressor on a target.

■ *Saturday Night Special* or *Blitzkrieg*—a variety of raid in which the tender is usually for cash and open for only a very brief period of time.

■ *Bear-hug*—notification of a target's management, but not its shareowners, of a proposed tender offer at a fixed price and subject to specified conditions.

■ *Bisexual*—a type of tender offer in which a target's management maintains a neutral stance; that is, it neither actively supports nor opposes the raid.

■ *Casual Pass*—notification of a target that a merger is desired, but at a price to be negotiated.

■ *Trading Stamp*—a security, e.g., a convertible debenture used as the consideration in an exchange offer.

■ *Showstopper*—an impediment, such as an antitrust violation, that effectively halts a tender offer.

■ *Sleeping Beauty*—a company that possesses a number of characteristics which make it a likely candidate or target for takeover via raid.

■ *Black Book*—a detailed compilation of lists, procedures, and reference materials useful in installing defenses against, and prompting responses to, unnegotiated tender offers. It is sometimes referred to as a *Pearl Harbor File*.

■ *Shark Repellent*—a takeover statute enacted by a state that imposes strict notification and disclosure requirements on originators of tender offers for companies incorporated, domiciled, or transacting business within its boundaries. (Also, generally, any measure designed to frustrate a takeover attempt.)

■ *White Knight*—a company that steps in to thwart a raider by itself acquiring a target company. Sometimes called a *Prince Charming* or *Sweetheart*.

Source: *Across The Board*, September 1977, 90. Reprinted by special permission of *Across The Board*, the Conference Board, and Picture Collections, the Branch Libraries of the New York Public Library.

Merger and Acquisition Market: Evolution of Cash Tender Offers to 1978

EXHIBIT 2
■
Tender Offer Data

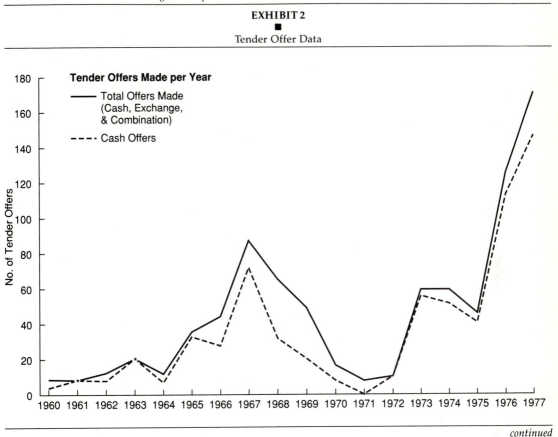

continued

EXHIBIT 2 *continued*

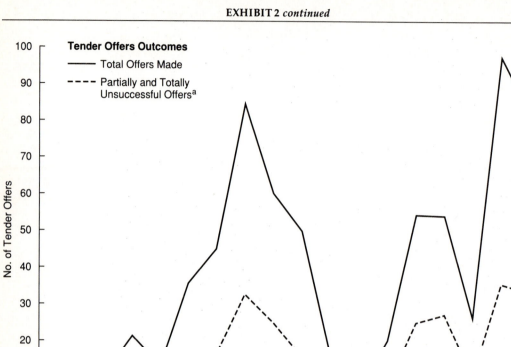

^aSuccessful offer: The bidder receives and accepts shares adequate to gain control of the target. Partially successful offer:
The bidder receives fewer shares than were bid for, but accepts them. Unsuccessful offer: The bidder receives fewer
shares than were bid for and refuses to accept them or withdraws the offer.
Source: Douglas V. Austin, "Tender Offer Update: 1978–1979," *Mergers and Acquisitions* (Summer 1980). The total number
of offers made per year differ on the two graphs due to data limitations.

Merger and Acquisition Market: Evolution of Cash Tender Offers to 1978

EXHIBIT 3

■

Tender Offer Premiums: Bid over Prevailing Market Price

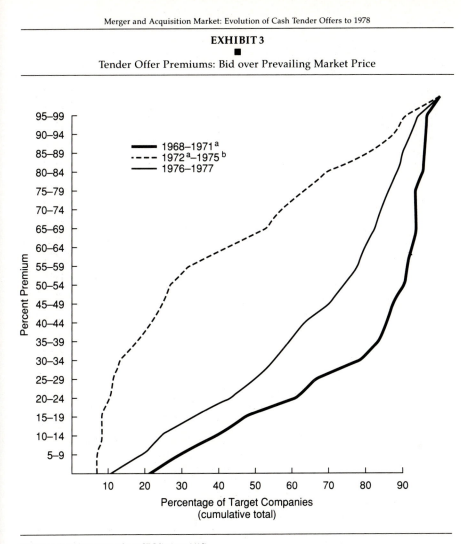

[a]Numbers have been revised per SEC listings 14(d).
[b]Numbers are for 6 months only.
Source: Douglas V. Austin, "Tender Offer Update: 1978–1979," *Mergers and Acquisitions* (Summer 1980), 19. Premiums are based on target's common stock price two weeks prior to bid's announcement.

Merger and Acquisition Market: Evolution of Cash Tender Offers to 1978

EXHIBIT 4
■
Financial and Market Data

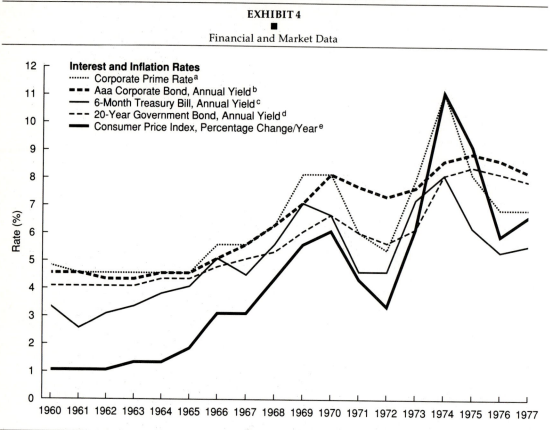

Interest and Inflation Rates
········ Corporate Prime Rate[a]
━ ━ ━ Aaa Corporate Bond, Annual Yield[b]
───── 6-Month Treasury Bill, Annual Yield[c]
─ ─ ─ 20-Year Government Bond, Annual Yield[d]
━━━━ Consumer Price Index, Percentage Change/Year[e]

[a]Figures shown represent averages of daily effective rates on an annualized basis. Source: *Annual Statistical Digest, 1971–1975* and *1974–1978*, Board of Governors of the Federal Reserve System, Washington, D.C.

[b]Rates shown are based on seasoned issues. Numbers represent averages of daily figures from Moody's Investors Service. Source: *Federal Reserve Bulletin, 1976–1978.*

[c]Bills quoted on bank-discount basis. Market yields are used as close approximation of rates on new issues. Source: *Federal Reserve Bulletin, 1976–1978.*

[d]Yields on the more actively traded issues adjusted to constant maturities by U.S. Treasury based on daily closing bid prices. Data for 1960 through 1973 are for long-term bonds and notes, which figures have, historically, been lower than those for 20-year government bonds. Long term includes all bonds neither due nor callable within 10 years. Numbers are unweighted averages for all outstanding notes and bonds based on their daily closing bid prices. Source: *Federal Reserve Bulletin, 1976–1978.*

[e]Figures represent the percentage change from the previous year. Data are for urban wage earners and clerical workers and are not seasonally adjusted. Source: U.S. Department of Labor, Bureau of Labor Statistics: compiled by the Economics Studies Center, Tayloe Murphy Institute, University of Virginia, Charlottesville, Virginia.

Source: Standard & Poor's Corporation, New York, *Analysis Handbook.*

EXHIBIT 4 *continued*

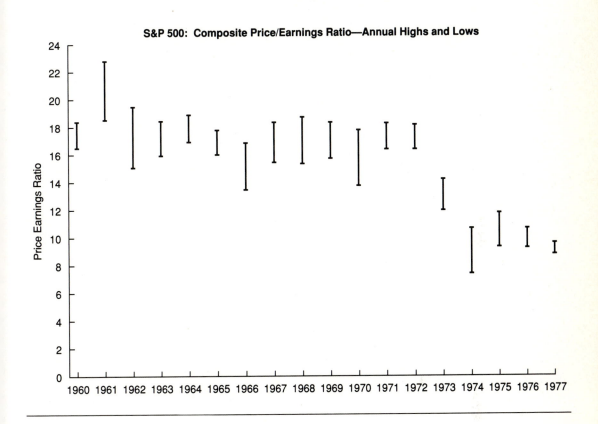

S&P 500: Composite Price/Earnings Ratio—Annual Highs and Lows

Merger and Acquisition Market: Evolution of Cash Tender Offers to 1978

EXHIBIT 5
■

SEC Regulations Governing Takeovers
(effective date 8/31/77)

Effective August 31, 1977, the Securities and Exchange Commission revised its disclosure requirements for companies making takeover offers. Henceforth, all information was to be prepared and presented on the basis of a new Schedule 14D–1.

Bidding companies or persons were required to make the following disclosures:

1. Their principal businesses.

2. Whether they (or their managers and directors) had been subject to any judgments enjoining violations of the securities laws (or any other criminal proceedings) within the previous 5 years.

3. Financial statements of corporate bidders where the "bidder's financial condition is material to a decision by a security holder . . . whether to sell, tender, or hold securities."[a]

4. Past transactions between the bidder and the target, as well as any past negotiations or discussions, including, where appropriate, the nature and approximate dollar value of any transactions effected within the most recent 3-year period.

5. The source and amount of funds to be used by the bidder in effecting the tender offer, including, where appropriate, the material terms and conditions of any loan agreements entered into as a result of the offer.

6. The bidder's plans and proposals for the target, including:

   a. An extraordinary corporate transaction, such as a merger, reorganization, or liquidation.

   b. A sale or transfer of a material portion of the target's assets.

   c. Modifications to the target's management.

   d. Significant changes to the target's capitalization, dividend policy, or other facets of the target's corporate structure or business.

   e. Modifications to the marketability of any of the target's class(es) of securities, e.g., delisting a certain class of security, etc.

7. The number of shares and the proportion of the particular class of the target owned by the bidder.

8. Regulatory requirements that must be complied with prior to the completion of the offer (e.g., approval of the FTC, etc.).

9. Descriptions of any significant pending legal actions pertaining to the tender offer.

10. Information regarding members of the bidder's management team and any other persons exercising control of the company.

---

[a]The determination of when financial statements were or were not required was the subject of continuing debate. The SEC's regulations provided only that the answer to the financial statement disclosure question depended on the specific facts and circumstances of the company's tender offer, including (i) the terms of the tender offer, particularly those concerning the amount of the securities being sought; (ii) whether or not the tender offer was for control of the target; (iii) the bidder's plans and proposals; and (iv) the bidder's ability to pay for the securities sought in the offer or to repay any loans made by the bidder or its affiliates.

Source: Arthur Fleischer, Jr., "The SEC's New Disclosure Rules for Takeovers," *Institutional Investor* (September 1977), 9.

Tender Offers: 1978–1979

Tender offer activity in the merger and acquisition (M&A) market continued unabated between the ends of 1977 and 1979. Although the actual number of cash tender offers made per year declined from the 1977 high of 181, their dollar value continued to increase. In addition, the average premium over market price rose to 73 percent in 1978. The success rate of the offers also continued to rise, reaching 84 percent in the first 6 months of 1979.[1] Not surprisingly, those economic and market conditions that had contributed to the initial growth in the use of cash tender offers (e.g., high inflation rates, depressed stock market) also continued unabated. (See Exhibits 1 through 3 for further data.)

Continued competition in the M&A market gave rise to two related trends, the combined effect of which was to make the cash tender offer an even more formidable weapon than it had been before. First was a movement toward increasingly sophisticated bids—bids that presented a strong carrot to the shareholders, but a stick to the target's managers and certain classes of shareholders. The stick thus created was frequently brandished by the target's shareholders themselves in the form of legal actions against their management teams and reflected the second trend—an increasing number of shareholder lawsuits. The net result of these patterns was not only to make resistance by the managers and directors of a target company more difficult, but also to make it dangerous financially.

In response to the continued widespread use of cash tender offers and the continued increase in their dollar value, efforts were made on both the regulatory and legislative fronts to tighten the rules by which the game was played. In short, acquisitions via cash tender offers were becoming increasingly sophisticated, complex, expensive, and, therefore, risky.

STRUCTURE OF BIDS

The major change in the structure of cash tender offers between 1977 and 1979 was the evolution toward bids designed to trigger the fiduciary responsibilities of the target company's managers, directors, and certain classes of shareholders.

---

[1]All data taken from Douglas V. Austin, "Tender Offer Update: 1978–1979," *Mergers and Acquisitions* (Summer 1980), 13–24.

This note was prepared as a basis for class discussion from publicly available information. Copyright © 1984 by the Darden Graduate Business School Sponsors, University of Virginia, Charlottesville, Virginia.

Two-price bids or bids conditioned on the acquiescence of large or institutional holders of the target's stock exemplified the trend.

One of the earliest reports of the two-price cash tender offer appeared in February 1978, when the Bundy Corporation bid for the shares of Resistoflex Corporation. The bid, termed one of the tightest bear hugs yet, offered $20 per share for each of Resistoflex's 1.7 million shares if the response to the offer was positive. If, however, management resisted the tender, only $18 per share would be offered. The ostensible rationale behind the offer's structure was that resistance would generate expensive legal fees for the bidder, increasing its overall investment in the company and therefore reducing its return. The two-price bid was designed to deduct the anticipated expenses from the total amount offered.

The two-price offer not only increased the attractiveness of the deal to the shareholders, but it also maximized the pressure brought to bear on the target's directors. From the shareholders' perspective, the initial offer of $20 per share was particularly attractive; it was nearly double the stock's pre-tender market price and significantly higher than the average prevailing premium of about 60 percent.

From the directors' perspective, however, the offer presented a no-win situation. They could accept the offer, which, in their opinion, might or might not be in the best interests of the shareholders. Alternatively, they could recommend its disapproval. If the offer was successfully resisted, however, the directors could find themselves the object of a shareholder lawsuit. The two-price bid was

> designed to thwart what some analysts call "an almost knee-jerk reaction to fight" in today's merger environment. "A target company figures that it can fight now and get the money later, anyway," says one dealmaker. "What this deal says is, if you're going to fight, it's going to cost us money so you're going to get less."[2]

While the offer achieved the stated purpose of preventing knee-jerk reactions, it also greatly reduced the courses of action open to the directors and managers of the target and their flexibility in pursuing them.

In addition to the two-price offer, tender offers also appeared that were designed specifically to trigger the fiduciary responsibilities of trustees and other institutional holders of large blocks of the target's stock. The simplest of these forms involved a bid at a level high enough above the pre-offer market price to trigger the institution's legal responsibility to sell. The more sophisticated bid was structured so that the entire offer was conditional on the tender of those shares held by trustees or institutions. Such a bid highlighted the latter groups' legal responsibilities, both to their beneficiaries and, where appropriate, to the target's minority shareholders.

SHAREHOLDER LAWSUITS

The stick behind all the preceding moves was the growing number of shareholder lawsuits against managers and directors who had successfully resisted cash tender offers for their companies. Although no data were available on the

---

[2]"A Two-Price Bid to Force a Merger," *Business Week*, February 27, 1978, 36.

exact number of shareholder lawsuits that had ever been brought, the following actions were underway in June 1979:[3]

1. Eight cases were pending against McGraw-Hill, whose management had rejected American Express's offer of nearly $1 billion during early 1979.

2. Thirteen cases had been filed against Marshall Field and Company after its managers outmaneuvered Carter Hawley Hale Stores in 1978, causing the latter to withdraw its $380-million offer.

3. Two cases were pending against the management of Universal Leaf Tobacco, which resisted a $153-million offer by Congoleum Corporation in 1976.

4. Two lawsuits were pending against the managers of the Woolworth Company, who had successfully fought off a takeover bid in May 1978.

No shareholder lawsuit had yet been found in favor of the plaintiffs. However, the growing number of such cases and the fact that many of them sought to hold the target's directors personally liable for the loss of the premium certainly gave managers of target companies a strong incentive to think things over before rejecting an offer out of hand.

The central issue in each of the lawsuits was the nature of the relationship between the shareholders of a company and its managers and directors. Were the directors responsible solely for providing the shareholders with certain basic information regarding the existence and terms of the offer and advising them as to its attractiveness? Or were managers and directors authorized to make a decision regarding the offer and, on that basis, to commit significant sums of money to resist it? The following question summarizes the issue:

> Suppose I own a delicatessen. One day, when I'm away from the store, a fellow comes in and tells the guy who's sweeping the floor that he'd like to buy the place. Now suppose, when I get back, the guy doesn't bother to pass that offer along to me. Well, if I found out about it, what would I do? I'd kick his butt right out of the store. (Lawyer Abe Pomerantz as quoted in *Financial World*.[4])

The situation was, of course, heightened in those cases where the floor sweeper, whether for fear of losing his job or some other reason, took money out of the cash register on his own initiative to hire a doorman and watchdog to keep the inquisitive stranger from coming back. As the argument went, the owner was clearly owed the right to decide whether or not to sell the company. In those instances where that right was abrogated, the owner could hold the managers liable for the lost income.

LEGAL AND REGULATORY ENVIRONMENT

The persistent high level of corporate merger and acquisition activity and the use of cash tender offers to effect them elicited essentially the same reactions

---

[3]The data are from Neal Goff, "Takeover Backlash: The Shareholders Sue," *Financial World*, June 15, 1979, 16. For further descriptions of the tender offer battles referred to here, see p. 17 of the article.

[4]Ibid., 15.

from the regulatory and legislative bodies. The purposes behind the actions differed significantly, however,

From a regulatory perspective, the major concern was to protect the rights of the companies' shareholders. This function was performed largely by the Securities and Exchange Commission (SEC) via the Securities Exchange Act of 1934 as amended. The most pertinent of the amendments modifying the act was the Williams Bill, adopted in 1968 and itself amended on several occasions. The most recent revisions were adopted in December 1979, and they further refined and tightened the disclosure requirements regarding both bidding and target companies engaged in a tender offer battle. A summary of the disclosure rules governing cash tender offers appears in Exhibit 4.

The SEC's regulatory efforts were generally intended to preserve investor confidence in the capital markets by protecting the interests of all classes of stockholders. Legislative modifications initiated between 1977 and 1979, however, had a different focus. They were concerned with a broader, macroeconomic perspective, which argued that excessive economic concentration (as evidenced by mergers between large corporate entities) was a nonproductive use of the country's capital resources. In March 1979, Senator Edward Kennedy proposed a bill that, if passed, would (a) ban all business combinations between companies with assets or sales greater than $2 billion each and (b) prevent the acquisition of a company with greater than 20 percent of a market or $350 million in assets or sales by any company having $350 million or more in sales or assets, unless the acquisitor could show that the acquisition would result in efficiencies or was willing to divest a comparable amount of assets. Because the bill was such a major departure from the basic principles of free-market enterprise, discussion and resolution of the issues it raised were expected to take several years.

While the general thrust of these regulatory and legislative actions and proposals was to slow and/or curtail merger and acquisition activity in general and cash tender offers in particular, political events implied the possibility of a future reversal in philosophy. Ronald Reagan declared his candidacy for president during 1979 and campaigned on a pro-business platform. There could be no doubt that, if the Republican party won the 1980 elections, the political, regulatory, and legislative climate would be significantly different for corporate America than it had been under President Jimmy Carter and the Democratic party.

CONCLUSION

By the end of 1979, the cash tender offer was one of the most widely used methods of acquiring control of another company. Two factors suggested that the tactic would continue to be used on a widespread basis. First, the economic and market conditions that had made corporate growth through acquisitions both attractive and necessary continued unabated. Second, cash tender offers continued to be one of the fastest and most effective takeover techniques. This situation implied several trends for the future. The number of potential takeover targets would necessarily begin to dwindle over time, giving rise to greater takeover competition and higher premiums. With the stakes thus increasing, the strategies of both offering companies and targets would become increasingly sophisticated. Tactics that had originally evolved to correct perceived sources of vulnerability to a takeover would, in effect, become absorbed into the normal course of business practices.

BIBLIOGRAPHY

Austin, Douglas V. "Tender Offer Update: 1978–1979." *Mergers and Acquisitions* (Summer 1980), 13–24.

"A Difference of Opinion: A Brief against Managements that Fight Off Tender Offers." *Fortune,* March 12, 1979, 159–160.

Tender Offers. Ernst & Whinney, 1980.

Goff, Neal. "Takeover Backlash: The Shareholders Sue." *Financial World,* June 15, 1979, 15+.

Long, Lynn Thompson. "Director Fiduciaries: Protecting Shareholder Interests." *Mergers and Acquisitions* (Winter 1980), 4–9.

Long, Lynn Thompson. "Pressure on Fiduciary Holders in Premium Cash Offers." *Mergers and Acquisitions* (Winter 1979), 4–11.

"A Two-Price Bid to Force a Merger." *Business Week,* February 27, 1978, 35–36.

"Will Sun's Raid Set a Pattern?" *Business Week,* February 14, 1978, 99.

Tender Offers: 1978–1979

EXHIBIT 1
■
Tender Offer Data

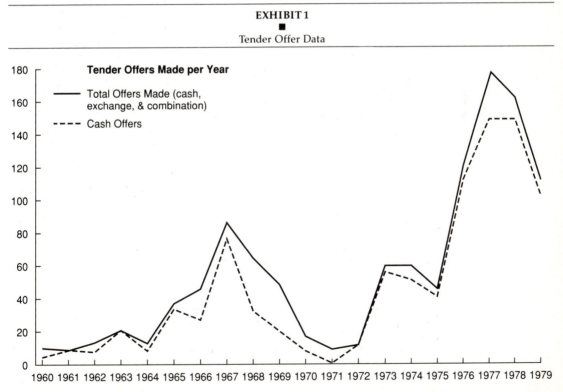

continued

EXHIBIT 1 *continued*

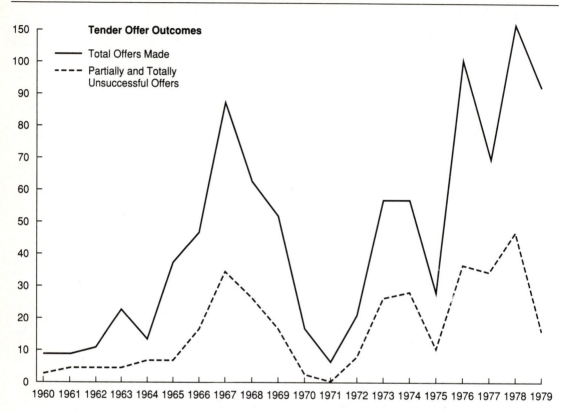

Tender Offer Outcomes

— Total Offers Made

--- Partially and Totally
Unsuccessful Offers

[a]Successful offer: The bidder receives and accepts shares adequate to gain control of the target. Partially successful offer: The bidder receives fewer shares than were bid for, but accepts them. Unsuccessful offer: The bidder receives fewer shares than were bid for and refuses to accept them or withdraws the offer.

Source: Douglas V. Austin, "Tender Offer Update: 1978–1979," *Mergers and Acquisitions* (Summer 1980). The total numbers of offers made per year differ on the two graphs because of data limitations. Figures for 1979 represent 6-month data on an annualized basis.

Tender Offers: 1978–1979

EXHIBIT 2
■
Tender Offer Premiums: Bid over Prevailing Market Price

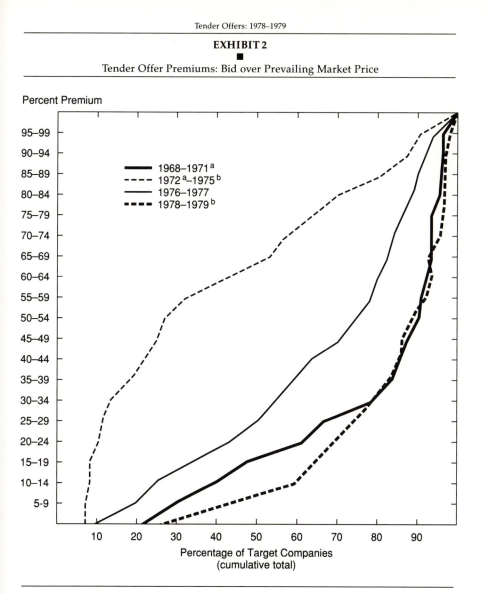

Percent Premium

Legend:
- 1968–1971[a]
- 1972[a]–1975[b]
- 1976–1977
- 1978–1979[b]

Percentage of Target Companies
(cumulative total)

[a]Numbers have been revised as per SEC listings 14 (d).
[b]Numbers are 6-month totals only.
Source: Douglas V. Austin, "Tender Offer Update: 1978–1979," *Mergers and Acquisitions* (Summer 1980), 19. Premiums are based on target's common stock price two weeks prior to bid's announcement.

Tender Offers: 1978–1979

EXHIBIT 3
■

Financial and Market Data

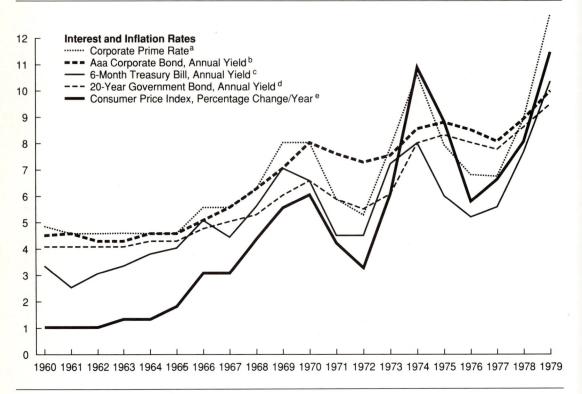

Interest and Inflation Rates
- ·········· Corporate Prime Rate[a]
- ▬ ▬ ▬ Aaa Corporate Bond, Annual Yield[b]
- ———— 6-Month Treasury Bill, Annual Yield[c]
- ▬ ▬ ▬ 20-Year Government Bond, Annual Yield[d]
- ━━━━ Consumer Price Index, Percentage Change/Year[e]

[a]Figures shown represent averages of daily effective rates on an annualized basis. Source: *Annual Statistical Digest*, 1971–1975 and 1974–1978, Board of Governors of the Federal Reserve System, Washington, D.C.

[b]Rates shown are based on seasoned issues. Numbers represent averages of daily figures from Moody's Investors Service. Source: *Federal Reserve Bulletin*, 1976–1978.

[c]Bills quoted on bank-discount basis. Market yields are used as close approximation of rates on new issues. Source: *Federal Reserve Bulletin*, 1976–1978.

[d]Yields on the more actively traded issues adjusted to constant maturities by U.S. Treasury based on daily closing bid prices. Data for 1960 to 1973 are for long-term bonds and notes, which figures have, historically, been lower than those for 20-year government bonds. Long term includes all bonds neither due nor callable within 10 years. Numbers are unweighted averages for all outstanding notes and bonds based on their daily closing bid prices. Source: *Federal Reserve Bulletin*, 1976–1978.

[e]Figures represent the percentage change from the previous year. Data are for urban wage earners and clerical workers and are not seasonally adjusted. Source: U.S. Department of Labor, Bureau of Labor Statistics; compiled by the Economics Studies Center, Tayloe Murphy Institute, University of Virginia, Charlottesville, Virginia.

Source: Standard and Poor's Corporation, New York, *Analysts Handbook*.

EXHIBIT 3 *continued*

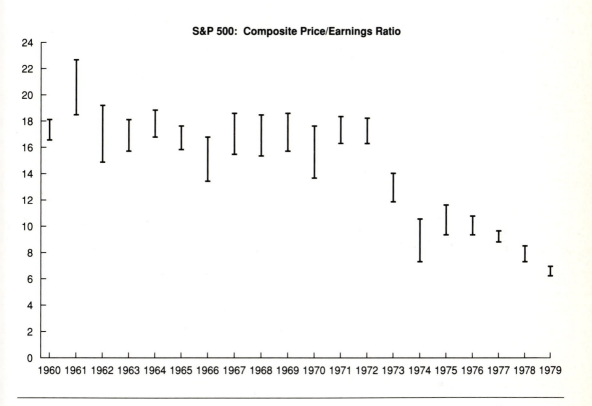

S&P 500: Composite Price/Earnings Ratio

EXHIBIT 4

■

Summary of SEC Disclosure Requirements

A. Schedule 14D–1: Bidder Filing Requirements

A bidder who seeks to acquire 5 percent or more of any equity security of another company must file Schedule 14D–1 before the effective date of the offer. For an unnegotiated cash tender offer, the bidder will normally file late on the day before the offer is announced.

A summary of the required disclosures follows. Basically all the information in Items 1 through 10 must also be included in any of the bidder's announcements or solicitations.

Item 1. Security and Subject Company
Identify the target company, securities sought, consideration being offered, and the market in which the securities are traded.

Item 2. Identity and Background
Identify the bidder corporation (or individual), its officers, their employment history, and any civil or criminal convictions of such officers during the last 5 years.

Item 3. Past Contracts, Transactions, or Negotiations with the Target
(a) State nature and amount of any transactions with the target company or its officers or directors (subject to certain materiality criteria) during the last 3 years.
(b) Describe any acquisition, merger, or tender offer negotiations or contracts with the target company during the past 3 years.

Item 4. Source and Amount of Funds
Describe terms of any loans necessary to finance the tender offer and plans for repayment. The bidder can elect not to disclose publicly the names of financial institutions involved.

Item 5. Purpose of the Tender Offer and Plans of the Bidder
State the purpose or purposes of the tender offer and describe any plans or proposals which would result in: a merger, reorganization, or liquidation; a material sale of assets; changes to the board of directors; changes in the capitalization or dividend policy; material changes in the corporate structure or business; or cause the delisting of the target company securities.

Item 6. Interest in Securities of the Target
Identify target company securities currently held and all transactions in them during the past 60 days.

Item 7. Contracts, Arrangements, Understandings, or Relationships with Respect to the Target Company's Securities
Describe any contract or understanding between the bidder and any person with respect to any securities of the target company, such as an understanding about guaranties of loans, guaranties against loss, or the giving or withholding of proxies.

Item 8. Persons Retained, Employed, or to Be Compensated
Identify all persons paid to make solicitations or recommendations (e.g., public relations specialists and investment bankers) and describe compensation arrangements.

Item 9. Financial Statements of Certain Bidders
Furnish financial information of the bidder when it is material to a decision of the target company shareholders (as with an exchange offer).

Item 10. Additional Information
If material to a security holder's decision whether to sell, tender, or hold his securities, furnish information as to: any present or proposed contracts with target company management (e.g., employment contracts); known regulatory requirements that must be complied with (e.g., FCC approval); applicability of antitrust laws; applicability of margin requirements; and any material legal proceeding relating to the offer.

Item 11. Exhibits to Be Filed
Furnish a copy of:
(a) Tender offer material which is published and provided to security holders on behalf of the bidder.
(b) Any loan agreement referred to in Item 4 of this schedule, agreements referred to in Item 7 or 10, or any written legal opinions on the tax consequences of the offer.

B. Schedule 14D-9: Target Filing Requirements

A target company is required to state its position with respect to a tender offer and file Schedule 14D-9 within 10 days of receiving the offer. This schedule must also be filed by any other person (e.g., a shareholder or officer) who makes a public statement of position.

A summary of the required disclosures follows. Basically, all the information in the schedule (except Item 5 and the exhibits) must be included in any communications to the shareholders.

Item 1. Security and Subject Company
Identify the target company and the securities being sought by the bidder.

Item 2. Tender Offer of the Bidder
Identify the bidder.

Item 3. Identity and Background
State the name and business of the person filing the statement. If material, describe any contracts or agreements between the person filing the statement (e.g., the target company or its management) and the bidder or its management, including any actual or potential conflicts of interest (e.g., informal employment contracts).

Item 4. The Solicitation or Recommendation
State the filer's position with respect to the tender offer *and the reason therefore.* The statement of position can: (1) recommend acceptance, (2) recommend rejection, (3) express no opinion and remain neutral, or (4) be unable to take a position.

Item 5. Persons Retained, Employed, or to Be Compensated
Identify all persons paid to make solicitations or recommendations (e.g., public relations specialists and investment bankers) and describe compensation arrangements.

Item 6. Recent Transactions and Intent with Respect to Securities
Describe any transactions in the target company's stock during the past 60 days involving the person filing the statement or its management. Also, state whether shares that are held by the person filing the statement (assuming it is not the target company itself) will be tendered, sold, or held.

Item 7. Certain Negotiations and Transactions by the Subject Company
Describe any negotiations underway that would result in a merger, recapitalization, sale of a material amount of the assets, or any other extraordinary transaction.

Item 8. Additional Information to Be Furnished
Furnish any additional information necessary to make the required statements not materially misleading.

Item 9. Material to Be Filed as Exhibits
Furnish copies of any written solicitations which are sent to shareholders or published, or the context of any oral solicitation campaigns (e.g., phone calls to major shareholders). Also supply copies of any contract described in Item 5.

Source: *Tender Offers,* Ernst & Whinney, 1980.

Mergers and Acquisitions:

A Market Continuing to Evolve[1]

The 1980s saw the burgeoning of takeover defenses in the M&A arena. Takeover defenses became a part of the planning of major corporations, and takeover defense provisions became part of the structure of most corporations. These takeover defenses ran all the way from legal maneuvering to restructuring of firms in an attempt to make the company less attractive to acquisitive raiders. There were two reasons for managements' increased concern about the possibility of being acquired. First, the number of mergers continued almost unabated, and some of those mergers were very large indeed. No company seemed immune to the threat of takeover. Second, managers were especially worried about the fate of their companies (and their jobs) after the takeover was completed: some acquirors had massively restructured the operations of their targets.

During the 1980s, new words came into use as the result of tactics for acquiring and defending. Poison pill, golden parachute, drop and sweep (all defined in Exhibit 1) entered the jargon. In addition to new words and defensive strategies, a new method of financing allowed larger transactions for participants with different motives. The financing was to use high amounts of debt, usually called junk bonds, and the resulting transaction was called a leveraged buyout. This note briefly reviews the trends in the acquisition market during the 1980s and discusses the role of tender offers and leveraged buyouts in the evolution of that market.

From 1979 on, the number of acquisitions attempted and completed in the United States rose in every year except 1982, when for the first time in many years, the number of transactions declined, as did the value of the completed transactions. Was the bull market for acquisitions over, as many had predicted for some time? Or was the merger wave simply gaining strength for another assault? As shown in Exhibit 2, in 1982, the price/earnings ratio of the average common stock had risen to 12.3 from 9.0 the previous year. Stock prices were up more than earnings, which was a potential sign of a bull market. Such a bull market could bode ill for acquisition activity. As noted in Exhibit 3, however, 1982 was just the calm after the storm of activity in 1981 and before new storms in 1984. Resting in 1983, volume then rose by almost 32 percent, and total consummated mergers reached $125 billion in 1984. This total is large by itself,

---

[1]We use the words merger and acquisition interchangeably in this note. In fact, in the past merger meant the way in which the combination of two or more companies was structured, and acquisition denoted the act of taking over the other firm. Over time the meaning of the two words has blurred.

but when compared with the transactions in 1980 of $32 billion, it becomes huge. Even more important was a change in the size of the average merger: in 1979, the average was $22.3 million; in 1986, it had risen to $47.3 (see Exhibit 4). Moreover, some acquirors completed several transactions in a single year. As shown in the following table, Dart & Kraft completed 18 acquisitions in 1986 alone:

Major Acquirors

Year	Company	No. of Transactions
1987	Borden Inc.	10
1986	Dart & Kraft	18
1985	Merrill Lynch & Co., Inc.	14
1984	Allegheny Beverage Corp.	13
1983	Healthdyne, Inc.	11
1982	New York Times Co.	11

In 1980, the dominant type of acquisition was a U.S. company acquiring another U.S. domestic firm. Goldman Sachs, an investment banking firm, estimated that, on an annualized basis, however, the number of acquisitions made by non-U.S. firms of a U.S. company tripled from 1987 to the first quarter of 1988, while domestic acquisitions of domestic U.S. companies merely doubled.[1] Moreover, a new form of financing an acquisition transaction became large enough to warrant recording, the leveraged buyout (LBO). LBOs were acquisitions made using considerably larger amounts of debt than had been used in the past, and they left the acquired companies with as much as 70 or 80 percent of their capital from debt sources. The debt was generally publicly issued junk bonds—unrated debt sold in the public markets or privately placed. Previously, junk bonds had not been deliberately issued; they developed over time as the company that had issued the debt fell on hard times. The junk bond market in 1986 was dominated by one investment banking company, Drexel Burnham Lambert, and had been devised primarily by one of their principals, Mike Milkin.

Companies considered good candidates for LBOs had stable earnings, little debt, and high-quality assets. As you can see in Exhibit 5, the number of leveraged buyouts rose and the size of the average transaction increased by more than 50 percent from 1983 to 1985. Several partnerships had been formed to acquire firms through the leveraged buyout approach. Using their and others' money leveraged by junk bonds issued by the acquired firm, such companies as Kohlberg Kravis and Forstmann Little became major players in the highly leveraged acquisition market. Even with potential legal problems hanging over Drexel, and concerns about the quality and financial strength of companies that were carrying considerable debt as a result of LBOs, the leveraged buyout activity continued in 1988.

As leveraged buyouts introduced a new method of financing transactions during the early 1980s, another trend was coming to characterize the acquisition

---

[1]The estimates were reported in "An Appraisal: Analysts Wonder if Takeover Pace Will Continue," *The Wall Street Journal* (April 25, 1988), 51.

market: many transactions were made by buyers seeking to earn a quick financial profit through restructuring rather than through strategic investment. Financial buyers, like most of the corporate raiders (e.g., Carl Ican and Ivan Boesky), competed with strategic acquirors (usually corporations) for many of the same transactions and often used considerable leverage in executing their purchases. Many contended that financial buyers were part of the reason acquisition prices rose to record levels—levels strategic buyers often considered unrealistic.

In addition, the tactics of corporate raiders (financial acquirors) before and after mergers were different from those of strategic acquirors. Some financial acquirors did not really want to acquire the targeted company; they wanted to encourage the company management, fearful of a takeover, to repurchase the raiders' shares. To repurchase a raider's entire block of shares, the company would have to offer a price that was higher than the market price and was not offered to other shareholders. This practice is called greenmail. In addition, after a completed transaction, raiders often sold off valuable assets (sometimes whole divisions) or closed unprofitable plants to cut costs. This activity concerned managements hoping to protect their positions and other employees hoping to continue their employment. Thus raiders' activities spurred considerable discussion in the U.S. Congress and defensive activity in corporate boardrooms.

Even with the increase of LBOs and financial raiders, the form of the average transaction had changed little from 1982 through 1986. As shown in Exhibit 6, cash was still the dominant form of payment in 1986. In 1982, 55 percent of the transaction payments were cash. SEC regulations also changed little over the period, as shown in Exhibit 7.

By 1987, even in the face of a strong stock market, many were anticipating little change in the number and size of mergers. Although the emphasis had changed from conglomerate merger (the combination of unrelated or little related businesses) to related merger (the combination of vertically or horizontally integrated companies), purchase of markets and products through acquisition still was perceived to be cheaper and less risky than growing markets and developing products internally. Tender offers, a subset of all merger activity, followed the pattern set in the broader market. The number of tender offers increased throughout the period, as shown in Exhibit 8. The size of the mergers and the premium paid above the market price seemed to achieve some modest equilibrium, as shown in Exhibit 9, even if prices remained high.

In 1987, there were some fundamental changes. The number of all kinds of mergers declined, as seen in Exhibit 5. Increases in the stock market level were assumed to be the culprit, and indeed M&A activity was down for each quarter of the year. The stock market decline on October 19 and 20 precipitated a virtual suspension of activity for the remainder of the year. Arbitrageurs, those trading on potential price changes for announced acquisitions, and junk bond financiers had been hurt and were being more cautious. When activity resumed in early 1988, most mergers were of the related variety, and frequent acquirors were saying that the era of the conglomerate merger was finished. Many believed that merger activity was more related to general economic activity than it had been in the recent past.

Early 1988 activity pointed toward another banner year for merger activity, however. Three causes were cited for the rebirth of activity after the decline in late 1987: the bargain price of stocks; the value of the dollar; and the potential that a new administration would not take the hands-off attitude adopted by the Reagan administration. The precipitous decline in the value of the U.S dollar increased the number of acquisitions of U.S. companies by non-U.S. acquirors, notably the Japanese. Concerns about the "selling of America" began to be heard. In addition, junk bond financing was dampened: increasing interest rates and concerns about the quality of current and future junk-financed companies led to a greater unwillingness of the market to absorb new junk bonds.

What was certain by mid-1988 was that fundamental changes had been wrought in the merger market. Managers were more concerned about the potential for takeover and were defending their companies through legal and strategic activities. Poison pills and golden parachutes characterized the legal strategies. More efficient management, selling off poorly performing divisions, accepting higher leverage, and reducing unused assets such as cash, seemed to be features of strategic defenses. Many corporate raiders, those specializing in financial transactions throughout the 1980s, suggested that new efficiency in corporate America came first as a result of fear—the fear of corporate raids and the loss of managerial control. They believed that this new level of concern boded well for corporate shareholders, indeed for American industry in general. There were those, however, who disagreed.

Mergers and Acquisitions: A Market Continuing to Evolve

EXHIBIT 1

■

New Jargon

Poison-Pill Securities: Securities that place extra burdens, often financial, on the unfriendly acquiror, in an effort to make the acquisition more difficult and costly. Typical poison-pill provisions include an increase in dividends or the addition of voting rights for preferred shareholders, or trigger the immediate call of outstanding bonds. The event that triggers the poison-pill features is the purchase of a prescribed percentage of the company's common shares or a change in the control of the company over the objections of the current directors. Some poison securities have been challenged in court as unfairly discriminating against a particular group of shareholders (those acquiring the triggering shares), and the whole issue of poison securities is being considered in the U.S. Congress.

Drop and Sweep: An acquiror terminates a tender offer and goes directly to the market to purchase large blocks of the company's common stock.

Stock Parking: The potential acquiror uses agents, usually investment bankers, to purchase shares on their behalf. Such stock is registered in the agent's name, and the acquiror thus avoids the SEC notification (Section 13-D) requirement for owners of 5 percent of a company's stock.

Golden Parachute: An employment contract provision allowing for a very generous settlement in the event that senior executive job(s) is terminated as a result of a consummated takeover. In 1987, the top compensation paid a corporate executive, including exercised options, was $26 million. The largest golden parachute was when Viacom was acquired by Sumner Redstone. The CEO of Viacom received an estimated $25 million, and the executive vice president a total of $9.5 million.[a] When such a contract is provided for those below the most senior managment, it is called a silver parachute.

Greenmail: An offer to purchase securities owned by an unfriendly suitor for a price above that currently in the market. The purchase offer is typically limited to those shares owned by the unfriendly suitor. Many believe that such a payment discriminates against the other shareholders. The greenmail practice has generated considerable controversy and attention by the courts and U.S. Congress.

Payment-in-Kind (PIK): Using securities, for instance, preferred stock and warrants, to buy all or a portion of a company. The PIK securities go to the shareholders of the acquired company.

---

[a]Data from John Byrne, Keith Hammonds, Ronald Grover James Treece, and Jo Ellen Davis, "Who Made the Most and Why," *Business Week*, May 2, 1988, 50–56,

Mergers and Acquisitions: A Market Continuing to Evolve

EXHIBIT 2
■
S&P 500 P/E Ratio Annual High and Low

Year	High	Low
1980	9.48	6.63
1981	8.99	7.34
1982	12.31	9.86
1983	10.24	8.88
1984	11.1	8.9
1985	14.5	10.0
1986	17.2	14.0

Source: Standard & Poor's *Analyst Handbook,* December 1985 and 1986.

Mergers and Acquisitions: A Market Continuing to Evolve

EXHIBIT 3
■
Merger and Acquisition Completion Record, 1977–1986

	No. of Transactions	Percentage Change	Value (millions)	Percentage Change	Average Size (millions)
1977	1,209	N.Ap.	N.Av.	N.Av.	N.Av.
1978	1,452	20.1	N.Av.	N.Av.	N.Av.
1979	1,529	5.3	$ 34,177.2	N.Ap.	$22.3
1980	1,565	2.4	32,958.9	−3.6	21.1
1981	2,326	48.6	67,208.9	103.9	28.9
1982	2,297	−1.2	60,402.3	−10.1	26.3
1983	2,385	3.8	52,535.5	−13.0	22.0
1984	3,144	31.8	125,693.0	139.3	40.0
1985	3,397	8.0	144,283.5	14.8	42.5
1986	4,024	18.4	190,512.3	32.0	47.3
1987	3,701	−8.0	N.Av.	N.Av.	N.Av.

N.Av. = not available; N.Ap. = not applicable.
Source: Adapted from "1986 Merger Profile," *Mergers and Acquisitions,* (May/June 1987).

Mergers and Acquisitions: A Market Continuing to Evolve

EXHIBIT 4
■
Values of All Transaction Types

Price Paid (millions)	Percentage of Valued Transactions				
	1982	1983	1984	1985	1986
$ 1.0– 5.0	35.6%	30.7%	30.3%	31.1%	25.9%
$ 5.1–10.0	19.6	18.9	16.7	15.1	14.3
$10.1–15.0	8.8	9.9	9.8	8.4	8.4
$15.1–25.0	9.8	9.2	9.9	9.9	10.8
$25.1–50.0	10.4	12.3	11.6	11.2	11.4
$50.1–99.9	7.2	9.1	8.2	8.3	9.1
$100.0 and over	8.6	9.8	13.5	16.0	20.1

Source: Annual Profiles, *Mergers and Acquisitions.*

Mergers and Acquisitions: A Market Continuing to Evolve

EXHIBIT 5
■
Number of Merger Acquisitions and LBO Completions

All Activity	1982	1983	1984	1985	1986	1987
U.S. firms acquiring U.S. firms	1,960	2,075	2,625	3,001	3,541	3,198
Non-U.S. firms acquiring U.S. firms	222	116	182	212	329	327
U.S. firms acquiring Non-U.S. firms	139	148	139	184	154	176
Total	2,321	2,339	2,946	3,397	4,024	3,701
Divestitures only	N.Av.	657	158	1,019	1,317	1,118
LBOs only	N.Av.	321	245	253	308	259

Value[a] in Millions of Dollars

All Activity	1982	1983	1984	1985	1986
U.S. firms acquiring U.S. firms	$59,579.2	$50,179.2	$113,982.6	$124,291.7	$165,221.9
Non-U.S. firms acquiring U.S. firms	54,984.4	2,218.2	8,040.7	18,838.0	23,348.4
U.S. firms acquiring Non-U.S. firms	1,002.0	1,160.0	2,004.2	1,152.9	1,942.0
Total	6,609.6	53,557.4	124,027.5	144,283.5	190,512.3
Divestitures only	N.Av.	N.Av.	29,749.5	43,030.0	65,736.9
LBOs only	N.Av.	N.Av.	18,606.7	19,339.9	40,610.5

[a]Based on transactions where prices were researched.
N.Av. = not available.
Source: Annual Profiles, *Merger and Acquisitions.*

Mergers and Acquisitions: A Market Continuing to Evolve

EXHIBIT 6
■
Form of Payment, 1986

Price Paid (millions)	All Cash	All Stock	Combination	Undisclosed[a]
$ 1.0– 5.0	48.9%	9.1%	17.6%	24.4%
$ 5.1–10.0	42.2	11.1	21.8	24.9
$10.1–15.0	40.1	13.2	17.8	28.9
$15.1–25.0	39.1	13.7	15.2	32.0
$25.1–50.0	44.7	13.0	16.8	25.5
$50.1–99.9	44.2	10.3	17.6	27.9
$100.0 and over	44.8	8.5	25.9	20.8
Total—1982	55.0	14.0	20.0	11.0
Total—1986	44.4	10.7	19.5	25.4

Note: Based on 1,822 transactions where price data were revealed. Percentages represent the number of deals that fit into the price categories.
[a]Price was given, but the form of payment was not.
Source: Standard and Poor's *Analyst Handbook,* December 1985 and 1986.

Mergers and Acquisitions: A Market Continuing to Evolve

EXHIBIT 7
■
SEC Tender Offer Rule Changes

In December 1982, the SEC amended Rule 14d-8 requiring a bidder in an oversubscribed tender offer to accept securities tendered during the offering period on a pro-rata basis. This effectively extended the proration period from 10 calendar to 20 business days.

In 1983, the SEC Committee on Tender Offers recommended that the minimum offering period for a partial tender offer should be two weeks more than an any-and-all offer, and in 1984, the SEC amended Rule 10b-4 to proscribe hedged tendering. Hedged tendering is quite similar to short tendering, a practice that had been previously proscribed.

Mergers and Acquisitions: A Market Continuing to Evolve

EXHIBIT 8
■
Tender Offers

	Total Offer Made	Cash Offer	Partially and Totally Unsuccessful Offers
1980	83	71	28
1981	128	109	67
1982	96	83	34
1983	77	70	31
1984	142	136	29
1985	121	109	38
1986	183	177	49

Source: Douglas V. Austin, Tender Offer Updates 1980–87, *Mergers and Acquisitions*, Various issues.

Mergers and Acquisitions: A Market Continuing to Evolve

EXHIBIT 9
■
Update: Percentage of Targeting Companies

Percentage	1978–1983	1984	1985	1986
100+	5.5	2.2	0.0	2.0
90–99	1.6	1.1	0.0	0.0
80–89	1.9	1.1	4.2	2.0
70–79	2.9	2.2	1.4	3.4
60–69	4.9	2.2	1.4	2.7
50–59	5.4	9.9	6.9	5.4
40–49	9.6	11.0	8.3	11.5
30–39	13.2	13.2	20.8	12.8
20–29	16.8	19.8	12.5	13.5
10–19	15.4	23.0	27.8	21.0
0.1–9	22.8	14.3	16.7	21.0
<0	0.0	0.0	0.0	4.7

Source: Douglas V. Austin, Tender Offer Updates 1980–87, *Mergers and Acquisitions*, Various issues.

The Business Environment:

A Retrospective, 1929–1987

The cases in this book cover a decade of doing business in this and other countries. Over this period, a number of things changed in the environment in which managers conducted business. For instance, managers of all kinds were affected by inflation at levels not experienced in most countries since the mid-1940s; the maturing of the baby-boom generation in the United States influenced the sale and advertising of products attractive to the young (e.g., soft drinks and fast foods); and worldwide product and capital market integration forced managers to face new competition in unfamiliar environments. These managers found the 1970s and 1980s confusing, frustrating, and, for some, bursting with opportunity.

Many of you were neither active participants nor interested bystanders in the world of business at the times of these cases. The easy approach to analyzing a case set in an unfamiliar period would be to use today's social, economic, and political environment as the context in which the decisions must be made. To do this is dangerous. Decisions based on a particular environment frequently are specific to that environment, and, as we all know, changes occur with surprising rapidity. Thus, confronted with the same problem, rational managers in different economic, political, and social environments could have made different decisions. This is as it should be. The job for the manager, as well as the student, is to gain an understanding of the environmental factors and the interrelationships among those factors that can have a major impact on the decisions he or she will make. To operate in the context of these cases, to understand how these managers made their decisions, and to put yourself in the position of making some of the decisions, you must recreate those environments. This note provides you with some perspective on the various environments in which the managers in these cases made their decisions.

Since most of these cases are set in the United States, this note describes the United States, but with much international data added for the 1980s as international product and capital markets became increasingly integrated. For the cases set outside the United States, the case itself or an appendix to it contains some of the pertinent contextual information, but space necessarily limits that information. The manager in each instance would have conducted and used extensive research and broad experience in his or her particular envi-

This note was prepared as a basis for class discussion from publicly available information. Copyright © 1984 by the Darden Graduate Business School Sponsors, University of Virginia, Charlottesville, Virginia.

ronment in making each decision. To be a good manager requires skill, talent, and insight based on as much information about the environment as can be learned.

While these cases are set in the 1970s and 1980s, the practice of management during those periods was conditioned by what had gone on before. Although one could go back to earliest recorded history and find events that profoundly affect the practice of management today, my choice was to begin with a period that has a recent and continuing impact on business and one for which there is easily obtainable statistical information—the 1930s.

The data used in this note come primarily from readily available sources and can be updated or expanded at most public and all university libraries. Much of the data is presented in graphic form to make casual inspection easy. For each exhibit, the data source is noted so more detailed information can be gathered if needed. The exhibits appear at the end of the note.

THE 1930s

The 1930s was a period of shock to the United States both socially and economically. The period now known as the Great Depression affected every person and business in this country and around the world. Capital markets, lures for the speculator in the 1920s, destroyed the savings of many during the 1930s. Industrial production, which was stagnant for most of the previous decade, dropped precipitously in the early 1930s (Exhibit 1), and investment in new enterprises came to a virtual standstill. As production declined, interest rates dropped as a reaction to the lack of demand; the average work week, which had been declining since the turn of the century, reached a century-long low (Exhibit 2); breadlines became an everyday occurrence for many who had never been without a job and never dreamed they would be. Drought in the Midwest created the dust bowl. Movies and books chronicled the disaster, but not until years later—after the hurt and bewilderment had passed.

Population growth, steadily increasing by more than 1.5 percent per year before 1930, dropped below 0.8 percent, setting the stage for the baby boom of the late 1940s. President Franklin Roosevelt, in response to the crisis, put in place many of the institutions we still know today and many that are parts of our economic and political history—Social Security, Securities and Exchange Commission (SEC), Works Progress Administration (WPA), savings and loans, and laws governing the banking industry (the Glass Steagall Act).

During this period, the gross national product, the sum of goods and services in the whole economy, dropped from $103 billion in 1929 to $56 billion in 1934, before it began a gradual recovery, as shown in Table 1 and Exhibits 3A and 3B.[1]

To fuel the programs designed to pull the country out of the Depression, government spending increased. As a percentage of the GNP, the federal debt rose to a pre-WW II high of 45 percent (Exhibit 4), and the federal government operated at a previously unheard of deficit (Exhibits 5A and 5B). Up to that point, debt in the United States had increased in line with GNP growth (Exhibits 6A and 6B)—a process analogous to a firm financing part of its growth with debt. It was not until the mid-1920s that debt grew more rapidly than the economy itself, and in the early 1930s, the growth in debt significantly outstripped

---

[1]The exhibits and tables in this note contain, for the most part, data from 1930 to 1986.

TABLE 1

■

Gross National Product, 1929–1940

	GNP (billions)	Year-to-Year Change
1929	$103.4	6.6%
1930	90.7	−12.3
1931	76.1	−16.1
1932	58.3	−23.4
1933	55.8	−4.2
1934	65.3	17.0
1935	72.5	11.0
1936	82.7	14.1
1937	90.7	9.7
1938	85.0	−6.4
1939	90.9	7.0
1940	100.0	10.0

economic growth: the real level of debt financing had increased substantially. That growth in debt came largely from the public sector, and private sector debt decreased substantially (Exhibit 7).

As demand for money decreased, the cost of that money decreased as well. In 1929, short-term interest rates were just over 2 percent (Exhibit 8). By 1933, they were 0.5 percent, and in 1940, they reached a low for the decade of just over 0.14 percent. The prime rate, the rate charged by banks to their best customers, declined from 6.0 percent to 1.5 percent over the same period (Exhibit 9). Long-term corporate and government interest rates also declined over the same period (Exhibits 10A and 10B), with Aaa corporate bonds beginning the decade at almost 5 percent and ending it at just over 3 percent. Nominal rates that included expected inflation declined, while real rates—rates net of inflation—first rose precipitously before finally declining, as shown in Exhibit 11. In 1930, the real interest rate was about 5 percent. Because of the disinflation that characterized the Great Depression, by 1932 the real rate was over 10 percent before it began to decline. The *real* interest rate has not been as high since.

The underlying cause of the very high real rate of interest was inflation. The GNP price deflator, one measure of inflation, declined by 11.1 percent in 1932 alone, as shown in Table 2.

Stock prices, always a part of the Great Depression lore, began declining in 1929, but that was only the beginning. Investors were heartened by the short periods of price recovery, shown in Figure 1, only to be hurt once again by the downtrend that continued well into 1932 when the market bottomed at under 60 (Exhibit 12), as measured by the Dow Jones Industrial Average. Volume rose and finally dropped along with price. In 1932 alone, the average investor in the stock market lost more than 40 percent of the value of his or her holdings (Exhibit 13). It was the single worst loss of capital in the history of the U.S. markets. From 1929 to 1933, the average market investor's stock portfolio had declined by more than 60 percent, and investors in small companies saw losses that made the decline in the Standard & Poor's 500 pale in comparison (Exhibit 14). Corporations that survived the decade did so with management embracing a "debt is dangerous—pay cash, extend no credit" philosophy.

TABLE 2
■
Changes in Gross National Product, 1929–1940

	GNP Deflator
1929	0.0%
1930	− 3.2
1931	− 9.2
1932	−11.1
1933	− 2.2
1934	8.5
1935	1.9
1936	0.5
1937	4.8
1938	− 2.4
1939	− 0.7
1940	2.5

Source: *Federal Reserve Bulletin*, Board of Governors of the Federal Reserve System, Washington, D.C.

FIGURE 1
■
Weekly Dow Jones Industrial Average, 1929–1933

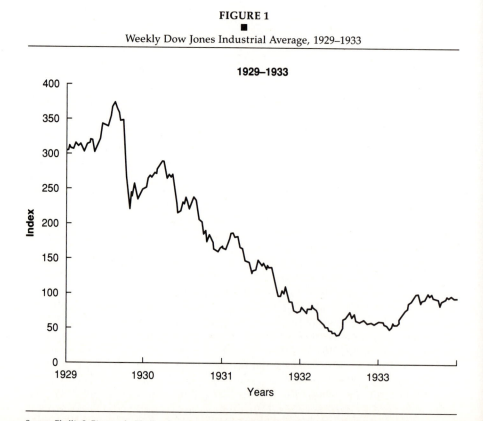

Source: Phyllis S. Pierce, ed., *The Dow Jones Averages 1885–1980* (Homewood, Ill.: Dow Jones-Irwin, 1982).

The economic shocks of the 1930s led the United States and other governments around the world to try to protect their own economies, if they could. Trade protectionism became widespread. Import restrictions were imposed in an effort to build up the domestic economy, and currencies were devalued for competitive reasons. Currency devaluation led to a decrease in the cost of exported goods and an increase in the cost of imports—a concept called *beggar thy neighbor*. These efforts, instead of saving economies, had the effect of shrinking world wealth as nations struggled not to operate at their competitive advantages, but to insulate their economies.

In 1941, the United States entered World War II. Ending the deprivation of the 1930s, the war finished the economic reconstruction that Franklin Roosevelt had started during the decade, but it did so with a speed that could never have been achieved with peaceful solutions. The Japanese attack on the U.S. military installations at Pearl Harbor was a shock to the American people and both a shock and opportunity for American business. The era marked the beginning of many trends that are still affecting business in the 1980s. It was the era that saw women enter the work force in jobs that had never been held by women and would not again be easily open to them until the late 1970s, if then. It represented the first large group of women working by choice rather than from personal economic necessity, and they were the mothers of the working women of the 1970s. It was also the era when the demand for production from industries spawned the defense industry's cost-plus contracts that have endured without real criticism up to the present time. It was a period of radical solutions to potential military defeat: the atom bomb was developed and used, leaving a legacy of nuclear fear and the danger of world annihilation that haunts us still in the 1980s.

The romance and danger of war that began in 1941 left us with legacies that influence our thinking and our ways of doing business today. Understanding that the events of 1941 had, and have, a profound effect on the way managers run their businesses allows one to understand the effect of even more recent events. Table 3 details the major events, economic and political, social and technological, that were important in the 1940s. To provide further perspective on the environment, there is a bit of information about the books, movies, and songs popular at this time.

1940 TO 1949

Even before the United States entered the war in late 1941, industrial production had sped up to satisfy the demands of warring nations. Lend-lease, under which the United States lent war material to countries involved that could not afford outright purchase of the equipment, temporarily kept the United States out of the war while gearing up production. By 1940, industrial production had recovered to well above pre-1929 levels (Exhibit 1). The gross national product, as shown in Table 4 and Exhibit 3A, increased at a pace that, in the beginning, heartened the Depression-ravaged economy.

To fuel this upsurge in production, the federal government increased its debt. At first glance, the increase in debt during this period (Exhibit 4) bears no comparison with the increases that would follow, but as a percentage of the GNP, the debt burden was staggering. Debt increased faster than GNP could follow, and the federal government was the primary borrower. For the first time, the federal debt exceeded nonfederal obligations (Exhibit 7). At the same time, deficit

TABLE 3

The Decade of the 1940s

	Economy	History and Politics	Science and Technology	Popular Culture and Daily Life
1941	Office of Price Administration (OPA) established. Supreme Court upholds federal wage and hour law.	Lend-Lease Bill signed. Pearl Harbor—U.S. enters WWII.	"Manhattan Project" atomic research begins.	Film: *Citizen Kane* F. Scott Fitzgerald, *The Last Tycoon*
1942	OPA freezes rents. War Production Board (WPB) and National War Labor Board (NWLB) established.	War Manpower Commission established with power over all essential workers. American forces land in French North Africa.	First automatic computer developed in U.S. Magnetic recording tape invented.	Popular song: "White Christmas" Gas, sugar, and coffee rationing
1943	Wage and price freeze. Start of income tax withholding.	Eisenhower named supreme commander. Race riots in several major U.S. cities.	Penicillin successfully used.	Film: *Casablanca* Popular dance: Jitterbug
1944	Cost of living in U.S. rises almost 30 percent.	D-Day landings in Normandy. Roosevelt defeats Dewey.	Synthetic quinine developed. First eye bank established.	Film: *Going My Way* Tennessee Williams, *The Glass Menagerie*
1945	Wage Stabilization Board established	FDR dies; Truman becomes president. World War II ends.	First atomic bomb detonated.	"Bebop" comes into fashion. Catchword "Kilroy was here" spreads.
1946	Price and wage controls terminated except on rents, sugar, and rice.	U.S. General Assembly holds first session. Churchill gives Iron Curtain speech.	Xerography process invented.	John Hersey, *Hiroshima* "Ranch" homes become popular.
1947	Taft-Hartley Act passed.	Marshall Plan announced. Truman Doctrine for containment of Soviet expansion.	Transistor invented.	More than 1 million veterans enroll in colleges under G.I. Bill of Rights.
1948	Injunction prevents nationwide rail strike. GM-UAW contract has first cost-of-living clause.	Berlin airlifts begin. Israel comes into existence.	Long-playing record invented.	Alfred C. Kinsey, *Sexual Behavior in the Human Male.*
1949	U.S. Foreign Assistance Bill grants $5.43 billion to Europe.	NATO formed. Communist People's Republic proclaimed in China.	U.S.S.R. tests atomic bomb. U.S. launches guided missile.	George Orwell, *Nineteen Eighty-Four* Arthur Miller, *Death of a Salesman*

Source: *A Horizontal Linkage of People and Events* by Bernard Grun. Copyright 1975, 1979 by Simon & Schuster. Reprinted by permission of Simon & Schuster, Inc.

TABLE 4

■

Gross National Product and Treasury Borrowing Rate, 1940–1949

	GNP (billions)	Annual Change	Change in GNP Deflator	90-Day Treasury Bill Rate
1940	$100.0	10.0%	2.5%	0.014%
1941	125.0	25.0	8.2	0.103
1942	158.5	26.7	10.6	0.326
1943	192.1	21.3	4.6	0.373
1944	210.6	9.6	2.0	0.375
1945	212.4	0.9	2.3	0.375
1946	209.8	−1.2	15.6	0.375
1947	233.1	11.1	13.1	0.594
1948	259.5	11.3	6.9	1.040
1949	258.3	.5	−1.0	1.102

Source: *Federal Reserve Bulletin*, Board of Governors of the Federal Reserve System, Washington, D.C.

spending, a feature of the economic recovery programs of the 1930s, more than doubled (Exhibit 5A).

While the federal government raised debt to finance the increased production for the war, interest rates rose little (Exhibits 8, 9, 10A, and 10B). The 90-day Treasury bill rate, at a low of 0.014 percent at the beginning of the decade, rose to 0.375 percent in 1944 and did not change until 1947. The cause of the stability of interest rates obviously was not a lack of demand. Instead, it resulted because the federal government controlled—pegged—the rate of interest during the war. It was not until 1948 that short-term rates exceeded 1.0 percent, the prime rate rising from 1.5 to 2.0 percent by the end of the decade.

While these rates seem quite low by modern standards, they are in nominal terms. If we examine the rates in real terms, they are not low, but negative, meaning inflation exceeded interest rates, as shown in Exhibit 11. The inflation rate of the mid-1940s was high—so high that it would not be seen again until the 1970s. At one point just after the end of the war, the real rate of interest was more than a negative 13 percent.

Stock market prices increased steadily during this period (Exhibit 12A). Only the end of the war brought the Dow Jones Industrial average down, but even then it was nowhere near the level that had been reached in the previous decade. Volume, however, still had not recovered to pre-1930 levels. The returns that shareholders received during this period (Exhibit 13), with the exception of those in the period immediately following the end of the war, were all positive. Stock prices of smaller firms recovered with particular strength (Exhibit 14).

Business during the early 1940s boomed. Costs lost importance in the demand-driven wartime society. When the war was over, however, many firms found the shift from war to peacetime production difficult. Returning servicemen with pent-up demand created widespread shortages for consumer goods. Rationing of staples and nonstaple consumer goods, driven by wartime necessity and propaganda, exacerbated demand in the late 1940s. As servicemen returned home and lives began to become more normal, autos, homes, home furnishings, and consumer durables were in short supply. Demand drove the retooling of

FIGURE 2

Population Growth

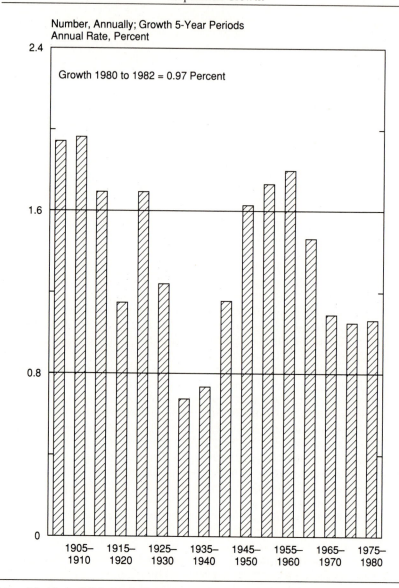

Source: *Federal Reserve Bulletin,* Board of Governors of the Federal Reserve System, Washington, D.C.

many industries, and the recovery of normal personal relationships created the baby boom—a population increase (shown in Figure 2) that did not taper off until 1960.

To stabilize world financial conditions after World War II, international financial leaders met at Bretton Woods, New Hampshire, and established the World Bank to lend money to developing countries for building infrastructure, the International Monetary Fund as a lender of last resort for countries with balance-of-payments problems, a system of fixed exchange rates, and the gold standard for the United States.

THE 1950s

By the end of the 1940s, Rosie the Riveter, the symbol of American working women during the war, was back at home. The United States successfully managed to airlift supplies into Berlin as the Soviet bloc tried to cut the isolated city off from the rest of West Germany; the first cost-of-living clause was written into a union contract; and the Korean "police action" was about to begin. Out of World War II had come radar, the transistor, and a host of useful and destructive inventions. During the 1950s came the oral contraceptive, the hydrogen bomb, color TV, and the polio vaccine, all of which would change American life for some time to come. In this era, the Supreme Court ruled that school segregation violated the Constitution. Joseph McCarthy began a series of congressional hearings on communist influence in the United States that would profoundly affect what we believed about communism and would adversely affect the lives of many prominent and not so prominent people. The McCarthy hearings would later be characterized by many as witch hunts. Table 5 provides more details of this retrospectively conservative decade.

After tapering off in the late 1940s, industrial production began to climb again (Exhibit 1). While the growth was not smooth, it was relentless. Real GNP fluctuated (Exhibits 3A and 3B) as inflation rose (Exhibit 15). These post-war highs would not be exceeded until the late 1960s. Even with the Korean conflict, federal debt leveled off. As a percentage of GNP (Exhibits 6A and 6B), it reached a post-war low of 50 percent by the decade's end. In fact, the government actually operated at a surplus (Exhibits 5A and 5B) for several periods during the decade—a balanced budget that politicians in the 1980s would long to see again. Federal debt not only fell but did so relative to total debt in the United States (Exhibit 7). The increase in total debt even kept pace with the increase in the output of goods and services, the GNP. The worldwide economy was also expanding. Major countries' currencies, which had not been so before, became freely convertible and helped trade to flourish.

As spending for the Korean police action waned, national defense expenditures dropped, while benefit payments for individuals, much of it entitlement benefits to which the government was obliged (i.e., social security and pensions), began their inexorable climb (Exhibit 16).

Interest rates, which were pegged during the war years, began a rise that saw the prime rate in 1959 at 4.5 percent—the highest it had been since before the Depression (Exhibits 8, 9, 10A, and 10B). Treasury bills, long yielding less than 2 percent, reached 3.4 percent in 1959. In real terms, interest rates were positive again (Exhibit 11).

The stock market volume and prices (Exhibits 12A and 12B) rose, and investors had years when their returns from investing in common stocks were as high as 50 percent (Exhibit 13A). Earnings yields (earnings per share/price per share) on common stocks, which began the decade at almost 15 percent, dropped to 2.5 percent. Price/earnings ratios which began at over 7 rose to an average of almost 40 (Exhibit 17). Real stock returns, net of inflation, rose from less than 30 in 1948 to over 50 during the decade (Exhibit 18). All these changes indicate that investors were willing to take more risks and take less in current

TABLE 5

■

The Decade of the 1950s

	Economy	History and Politics	Science and Technology	Popular Culture and Daily Life
1950	Defense Productions Act gives president power to stabilize wages and prices.	Start of Korean War.	Einstein: General Field Theory.	Film: *All about Eve*
1951	Office of Economic Stabilization established.	Internal Security Act restricts communists in United States.	Electric power produced from atomic energy. Color television introduced.	J. D. Salinger, *The Catcher in the Rye* Film: *A Streetcar Named Desire*
1952	Defense Productions Act extended.	Eisenhower elected president. Republicans capture both houses of Congress.	First hydrogen bomb exploded. Oral contraceptive produced.	Ernest Hemingway, *The Old Man and the Sea* John Steinbeck, *East of Eden*
1953	End of price controls. Margin requirements for stock purchases reduced from 75 to 50 percent.	Department of Health, Education, and Welfare created. Korean armistice signed.	Lung cancer reported attributable to cigarette smoking.	Film: *The Robe*—first Cinemascope B. F. Skinner, *Science and Human Behavior*
1954	3.7 million unemployed as result of recession.	*Brown v. Board of Education*—Supreme Court rules that segregation in public schools violates 14th Amendment. Army–McCarthy hearings.	First use of Salk antipolio serum.	Film: *On the Waterfront* First Newport Jazz Festival held.
1955	AFL and CIO merge; new president George Meany.	Montgomery, Alabama bus boycott begins.	Ultra-high frequency waves produced at MIT.	Popular song: "Rock around the Clock" Vladimir Nabokov, *Lolita*

Year				
1956	Economic expansion sparked by government defense spending.	Eisenhower reelected president; Congress is Democratic. Soviet troops march into Hungary.	Transatlantic cable telephone service inaugurated.	Elvis Presley gains popularity. Theater: *My Fair Lady*
1957	Teamsters Union expelled from AFL–CIO when Hoffa refuses to expel criminals.	Troops sent to Little Rock, Arkansas to enforce integration. Eisenhower Doctrine to protect Middle East from communists.	U.S.S.R. launches Sputnik I and II.	Jack Kerouac, *On the Road* Dr. Seuss, *The Cat in the Hat*
1958	1958 recession reaches trough in April; 7.7 percent unemployment.	European Common Market established. John XXIII becomes pope.	U.S. launches Explorer I satellite. Stereo recording comes into use. NASA established.	J. K. Galbraith, *The Affluent Society* Film: *Cat on a Hot Tin Roof*
1959	Four-month steel strike ended when Taft-Hartley Act invoked.	Alaska and Hawaii become states. Castro becomes Premier of Cuba; expropriates U.S.-owned sugar mills.	Nobel Prize for synthesis of RNA and DNA.	Popular song: "Mack the Knife" Philip Roth, *Goodbye Columbus*

Source: *A Horizontal Linkage of People and Events* by Bernard Grun. Copyright 1975, 1979 by Simon & Schuster. Reprinted by permission of Simon & Schuster, Inc.

income. By all accounts, confidence had returned to the stock market. Corporate profits (Exhibit 19) and returns on assets and equity showed significant declines before rising at the end of the decade: return on assets and equity dropped by 35 percent before rebounding. Investment in assets slowed, and internal funds generally kept pace with corporate needs (Exhibit 21). As a result, liquid assets declined, and notably in 1954, the ratio of long-term to short-term debt (Exhibit 22) was at a level that would never again be reached by U.S. corporations.

THE 1960s

In 1960, the United States was in a recession. The president who ushered in the decade was a well-known WWII figure, Dwight D. Eisenhower. By year's end, John Kennedy was president, and perhaps as a portent of things to come, *Psycho* was the movie of the year. The 1960s marked the entry into the Vietnam war, the investment in the social programs of Lyndon Johnson's Great Society, and both manned and unmanned satellites in space. The Beatles came to the U.S. music scene, and riots came to many American cities. Civil rights came, if slowly; Vietnam escalated; and the killing of students at Kent State and Memphis State radicalized a generation. It was also a decade that saw some of the banking regulations that had been imposed during the aftermath of the stock market crash of 1929 began to crack, and that watched the environment become a matter of legislation and government regulation. Table 6 details some of the highlights of the decade.

Industrial production and gross national product increased (Exhibits 1, 3A, and 3B), resulting in a decrease in relative federal debt. The budget, at least in the pre-Vietnam half of the decade, was almost in balance. It wasn't until the later half of the decade that things began to change. The Great Society increased government spending for individual benefits at a dizzying pace (Exhibits 5A, 5B, and 16). While Americans at home watched the Vietnam war in living color on the 6 o'clock news, defense spending growth was transient (Exhibit 16).

The later part of the 1950s and early 1960s was a period of great growth and expansion of U.S. multinational corporations. Some became concerned that unfettered growth of U.S. multinational companies abroad could result in U.S. business dominance of some economies. As a result, some governments attempted to restrict the growth of these firms. In addition, the U.S. government attempted to stem the flow of U.S. investment abroad when it became clear that there were, for the first time, balance of payments deficits (Exhibit 23).

U.S. corporate profits rose faster and further than they had fallen in the 1950s (Exhibit 19). Corporate investment increased from the 1958 low of 8.7 percent of real GNP to 11 percent in 1966—the same year capacity utilization reached 91 percent. Not only did firms increase their investment in capital assets (Exhibit 21), but they invested heavily in research and development: 1963 research and development spending exceeded 2 percent of the real GNP.

As corporations increased their need for funds, they decreased their reluctance to go to the debt markets for capital (Exhibit 24). The markets responded with increased nominal rates of interest (Exhibits 8, 9, 10A, and 10B), and stock prices reacted to increased earnings and went up, thereby rewarding the risk taker (Exhibits 12A and 12B). Real returns from investing in common stocks rose (Exhibit 18), one indication of why the 1960s are often called the "go-go" or golden years of the stock market. From the late 1950s onward, many believed that it was hard not to pick winners (Exhibits 13 and 14). The euphoria of a long upward trend in the stock market, a bull market, led many into a position that the erratic 1970s demonstrated was not inviolate. Indeed, by 1974, many felt as if they had survived a period like the crash of 1929. But in the late 1960s, U.S. business appeared to be strong, the stock market a haven for the prudent investor, and it was believed little could change this inevitable course. The year 1970 itself gave some warning, but one that would not be heeded until after the disastrous oil embargo and price increases changed the sources and uses of capital in the world.

THE 1970s

By 1971, wages and prices were frozen as President Nixon battled inflation that had reached an unacceptable 6 percent. The fixed exchange rate system for currency established at Bretton Woods was abandoned, the U.S. dollar was devalued in 1971 and again in 1973, and wage and price controls that were instituted to curb inflation continued until the year after the landslide reelection of Richard Nixon.

After the ice-cream era of the 1960s, the 1970s shocked, dislocated, and changed the face of business in the United States and around the world. This was the era in which the United States would ignominiously lose a war, would lose a vice president to accusations of graft, and would almost impeach a president. The word *stagflation* was coined as economies struggled to recover from simultaneous inflation and recession brought on by the meteoric rise in oil prices in 1973 and 1974. Table 7 shows some of the events of the 1970s.

Until 1973, most industrialized nations had operated as if fuel were inexhaustible and cheap. Typifying this faith was the all-electric home, with electric appliances for all but the most simple tasks, and automobiles that disregarded fuel consumption as they became more and more like mobile living rooms. The United States, mindful of the costs and relative success of exploring for domestic crude, had increased its dependence on imported oil (Table 8). This dependence on imports was expected to grow, and imports more often than not came from the Middle East, an area that had increasingly become the primary worldwide source of crude. The Organization of Petroleum Exporting Countries (OPEC) changed this way of thought and life almost overnight.

Crude oil prices, all below $4.50 a barrel in January 1973, rose fourfold by year's end. As shown in Table 9, by the beginning of 1975, the prices were up to a high of $15.00 a barrel, and the oil-exporting nations had become the new holders of the world's wealth. In 1974 alone, OPEC earned $95 billion, three times what it had earned in 1973. Of that, $60 billion found its way into capital markets as direct investments, primarily in short-term bank deposits and government securities. Oil importers became vassals to a new master, the countries that exported large amounts of crude. Borrowing to import oil, many nations would become the 1980s debtor nations. The United States' problems with its balance of payments and current account balance (Exhibit 23) were exacerbated by the increase in oil prices.

As a result, industrial production (Exhibit 1), which had leveled off in response to the recession in the early 1970s, nosedived. Gross national product increased (Exhibits 3A and 3B), but the increase was masked by the rate of

TABLE 6

■

The Decade of the 1960s

	Economy	History and Politics	Science and Technology	Popular Culture and Daily Life
1960	Recession. Eisenhower cuts military staff abroad to slow gold drain; $4 billion lost since 1958.	U-2 airplane shot down over U.S.S.R. Kennedy elected president.	Laser device developed. First weather satellite.	Film: *Psycho* John Updike, *Rabbit Run*
1961	Business recovery; GNP up 4.1 percent from 1960.	Bay of Pigs invasion. Berlin Wall constructed.	First U.S. manned space flight.	Joseph Heller, *Catch-22* Film: *West Side Story*
1962	Kennedy forces steel companies to cancel price increases. Trade Expansion Act cuts some tariffs.	Cuban missile crisis. U.S. marshals and troops enforce James Meredith's admittance to Univ. of Mississippi.	Thalidomide causes birth defects.	Rachel Carson, *Silent Spring* Popular song; "Blowing in the Wind"
1963	$380 million U.S. wheat sale to Soviet Union. Congressional act requiring arbitration passed to avoid rail strike.	Nuclear test ban treaty signed by U.S. and U.S.S.R. Kennedy assassinated.	First use of an artificial heart during heart surgery.	John LeCarre, *The Spy Who Came in from the Cold* Film: *Dr. Strangelove*
1964	Tax Reduction Act: Personal income tax rates reduced from 20–91 percent scale to 14–70 percent; corporate from 52 percent to 48 percent over 2 years	Gulf of Tonkin Resolution, escalation of war in Vietnam. Civil Rights Law passed. Johnson defeats Goldwater in Democratic landslide.	Ranger VII takes close-up photographs of the moon's surface.	The Beatles become popular. Films: *Mary Poppins*, *Goldfinger*.

1965	Johnson's budget of $97.7 billion is less than 15 percent of GNP; lowest ratio in 15 years.	Johnson proclaims Great Society; Medicare bill signed. Riots in Watts, Los Angeles.	Momentum increases for antipollution laws on a national scale in United States.	Film: *The Sound of Music* Ralph Nader, *Unsafe at Any Speed*
1966	Rate of inflation doubles from 1965 to 3 percent.	International days of protest agains U.S. policy in Vietnam.	U.S. and U.S.S.R. spacecrafts make soft landing on moon.	William Manchester, *The Death of a President*
1967	Balance of payments deficit over $3.5 billion.	Six-Day War between Israel and Arabs. Riots in Cleveland, Newark, and Detroit.	China explodes first hydrogen bomb. First human heart transplant.	Film: *Bonnie and Clyde* J. K. Galbraith, *The New Industrial State* Miniskirts popular
1968	Tax surcharge passed. Gold crisis—London gold market closed at request of United States to halt heavy selling of gold; two-price system for gold adopted.	Navy intelligence ship Pueblo captured by North Korea. Martin Luther King and Robert Kennedy assassinated. Nixon defeats Humphrey.	James D. Watson: The double helix. AMA sets new standard of death—brain death.	Film: *2001: A Space Odyssey* Popular song: "Mrs. Robinson" Student unrest on university campuses.
1969	Inflation becomes worldwide problem. Prime bank rate at record high 8.5 percent.	Warren Burger appointed Chief Justice of Supreme Court. William Calley charged with murder of civilians at My Lai, Vietnam.	Apollo IX; first manned moon landing. Use of cyclamates and DDT restricted.	Film: *Midnight Cowboy* Popular song: "Aquarius" Woodstock Festival.

Source: *A Horizontal Linkage of People and Events* by Bernard Grun. Copyright 1975, 1979 by Simon & Schuster. Reprinted by permission of Simon & Schuster, Inc.

TABLE 7

■

The Decade of the 1970s

	Economy	History and Politics	Science and Technology	Popular Culture and Daily Life
1970	Dow Jones drops to 631 during recession. Regulation Q limiting interest rate banks can pay is suspended for 30–89-day CDs.	Killing of four students at Kent State by National Guard during Vietnam protest. Environmental Protection Agency created.	First complete synthesis of a gene. First Earth Day.	Film: *Catch-22* Popular song: "Raindrops Keep Falling on My Head"
1971	Nixon orders 90-day freeze on wages and prices. U.S. devalues dollar; Japan and most European countries revalue currencies upwards.	26th Amendment allowing 18-year-olds to vote ratified. Fighting in Indochina spreads to Laos and Cambodia. Prisoner uprising at Attica results in death of 42.	Mariner 9 orbits Mars.	Film: *A Clockwork Orange* Aircraft hijacking becomes major problem.
1972	Dow-Jones Stock Index over 1000 for first time. "Phase II" economic measures continue to control wages, prices, and profits.	Nixon visits China. Nixon defeats McGovern in landslide; Democrats retain majorities in Congress.	Discovery of a 2.5 million-year-old human skull in Kenya.	Film: *The Godfather* "All in the Family" leading TV show
1973	U.S. devalues dollar. Arab oil embargo. End of most wage-price controls. Regulation Q suspended for investments over 90 days.	Vietnam cease-fire agreement. Watergate investigation underway. Agnew resigns as vice president.	Congress authorizes trans-Alaska pipeline.	Film: *Last Tango in Paris* "The Waltons" leading TV show
1974	Worldwide inflation; dramatic increases in cost of fuel, food, and materials. Oil embargo lifted. Dow Jones Index at 12-year low.	Nixon resigns over Watergate. Gerald Ford becomes president. Patty Hearst kidnapped.	Mariner 10 sends pictures of Venus.	Film: *The Exorcist* "Streaking" craze on campus.
1975	Gold sales legal in U.S.; first time in 41 years. Electricity rates rise by 30 percent. Individual and corporate income taxes cut by $22.8 billion. Moratorium on grain sales to Russia.	South Vietnam falls to communists. American merchant ship Mayaguez seized by Cambodia.	First artificial animal gene created. U.S. prepares for voluntary conversion to metric system.	Film: *Jaws* Discos become popular.

Year				
1976	Decline in consumer spending owing to steep increases in retail prices. Lockheed payoffs lead to close scrutiny of business ethics. Prime rate goes below 7 percent. Budget deficit equals $65.6 billion.	Jimmy Carter elected president. Sec. of State Kissinger calls for policy of detente with Soviet Union.	Swine-flu immunization. Red Dye No. 2 banned.	CB radio craze. Bicentennial celebrated. Film: *Network*.
1977	Minimum wage increases from $2.30 to $3.35 per hour by 1981. Dollar weak in foreign exchange. Record trade deficit of $2.82 billion reported in June.	U.S. announces reduction in aid to nations with human rights violations. "Koreagate" scandal of influence buying.	GM introduces its first diesel-powered auto. Alaska pipeline opens.	"Roots" popular TV miniseries Film: *Star Wars* Punk rock popular.
1978	105-day United Mineworkers strike. Prime rate reaches 11¾ percent from 7¾ percent. Humphrey-Hawkins bill approved by Congress legislating 4 percent unemployment and 3 percent inflation by 1983.	Panama Canal treaty ratified. Proposition 13 initiative in California.	First test-tube baby born. Oil drilling begins in Baltimore Canyon region off New Jersey shore.	Films: *Coming Home, Animal House*
1979	Prime rate reaches 15¾ percent. Chrysler receives loan guarantee. Federal Reserve changes monetary policy to control member banks' reserves.	American hostages taken in embassy in Teheran, Iran. Salt II Treaty signed between U.S. and U.S.S.R. Egypt and Israel sign peace treaty.	Three Mile Island nuclear accident occurs.	Film: *Kramer vs. Kramer* Gas shortages create long lines at gas stations.

Source: *A Horizontal Linkage of People and Events* by Bernard Grun. Copyright 1975, 1979 by Simon & Schuster. Reprintd by permission of Simon & Schuster, Inc.

TABLE 8
■
U.S. Foreign Trade: Fuel (billions of U.S. dollars)

	Exports	Imports	Balance
1958	$1.1	$1.6	$ − 0.5
1960	0.8	1.6	− 0.9
1965	0.9	2.2	− 1.3
1970	1.6	3.1	− 1.5
1971	1.5	3.7	− 2.2
1972	1.6	4.8	− 3.2
1973	1.7	8.2	− 6.5
1974	3.4	25.4	−21.9

Source: *International Economic Report of the President*, March 1975, 133.

inflation (Exhibit 15). Real GNP declined, although GNP had declined in only one year since 1947, in 1970. The impact of the change in oil prices on inflation is shown in Table 10.

Oil price rises hurt, and since exchange rates were no longer fixed, the unpredictability of exchange rate changes increased. While unfixing exchange rates better reflected supply and demand, and the game of guessing when and how a currency would be devalued was made less profitable, a new set of problems were created for U.S. companies doing business abroad.

In response to the oil price-induced recession, unemployment began to rise (Exhibit 25). The decline in employment caused by the recession coincided with the coming to age of the majority of the boom babies, exacerbating a problem that would have arisen anyway.

Federal budget deficits (Exhibits 5A and 5B) renewed their climb to levels that in the 1980s would not only reach an all-time high, but would also become politicized. To finance oil imports, the United States increased its borrowing, even though in proportion to GNP, the level of debt did not rise as quickly (Exhibit 4).

The increase in inflation and the change in the structure of wealth worldwide had yet another effect—that of increasing uncertainty. The combined effect

TABLE 9
■
Posted Price: Crude Oil by Origin (dollars per barrel, January 1[a])

	1973	1974	1975
Saudi Arabia	$2.591	$11.651	$11.251
Libya	3.770	15.768	15.768
Nigeria	3.561	14.690	14.691
Venezuela	3.094	13.776	14.312
Canada	4.400	6.600	12.100

[a]42 U.S. gallons per barrel.
Source: *International Economic Report of the President*, March 1975, 157–159.

TABLE 10

■

GNP and Inflation, 1969–1975 (billions of dollars)

	GNP	Constant GNP[a]	GNP Deflator
1969	$ 944.0	$1,087.6	5.0%
1970	992.7	1,085.6	5.4
1971	1,077.6	1,122.4	5.1
1972	1,185.9	1,185.9	4.1
1973	1,326.4	1,254.3	5.8
1974	1,434.2	1,246.3	9.7
1975	1,549.2	1,231.6	9.6

[a]Constant 1972 dollars.
Source: *Federal Reserve Bulletin*, Board of Governors of the Federal Reserve System, Washington, D.C.

of inflation on interest rates could have been devastating. Only because the Federal Reserve Board of Governors policy was to manage interest rates rather than the amount of money available did interest rates remain relatively stable (Exhibits 8, 9, 10A, and 10B). When the policy was changed in 1978, interest rates destabilized and rose.

The effect that the rise in oil prices had on the stock market was profound. The Dow Jones Industrial Average, which had reached an all-time high in 1972, dropped by 200 points by early 1974 (Exhibits 12A and 12B), and real stock returns dropped to a level not realized since the 1930s (Exhibit 18). Some believed that we were on the cusp of a 1929-like depression. At the low point of the market, it was rumored that over 20 percent of all New York Stock Exchange stocks were selling for less than their net working capital.

The effect on the wealth of investors was devastating. Not since the beginning of the 1930s had investors been so affected: the return on the Standard & Poor's 500 was a loss of 14.7 percent in 1973 and 26.5 in 1947, for a two-year loss of 20.8 percent (Exhibit 13). The booming 1960s had done nothing to prepare investors for these losses, particularly since it had been believed that common stocks were inflation hedges. Not unexpectedly, at the same time that market prices dropped, the market for new equity issues was virtually nonexistent. Much of the financing done in 1974 and 1975 was debt (Exhibit 24).

In nominal terms, long-term corporate bondholders suffered less, with an average loss of 1 percent over the same period. Borrowers, in large measure because of the Federal Reserve Board's policy to control the level of interest rates, obtained what amounted to negative interest rates on the money they borrowed (Exhibit 11).

While the market was reacting to changes in the very structure of the world economic order, U.S. corporations began to feel the effect: the stock market's precipitous drop was a forecast of the real returns American corporations would soon earn. Return on assets and equity declined (Exhibit 20), and corporate capital expenditure programs were curtailed (Exhibit 21). In every way, corporate profits suffered, and shareholders suffered another loss as dividends were lowered. Exhibit 19 shows that 1974 to 1975 was the single worst period for corporations in more than 3 decades. Capacity utilization rates dropped to almost 70 percent, and real investment was as low as the period immediately

TABLE 11

■

Selected Items: Corporate Balance Sheets
(as a percentage of total assets and liabilities except as noted)

	1960	1970	1975	1979
Total assets and liabilities (billions)	$1,207	$2,635	$4,287	$6,835
Assets (in percent)				
Cash	8.04%	6.72%	6.76%	6.75%
Notes and accounts receivable	20.05	22.58	23.82	25.91
Inventories	7.54	7.21	7.42	7.36
Mortgage and real estate loans	10.69	12.45	12.78	12.30
Capital assets	24.28	22.77	20.81	19.72
Liabilities (in percent)				
Notes and accounts payable	9.28	12.14	12.50	13.65
Other current liabilities	30.24	33.85	36.32	37.79
Bonded debt and mortgages	12.76	13.78	13.69	12.95
Surplus and individual profits	22.29	20.91	19.66	19.96

Source: "Income Tax Returns of Active Corporations—Assets and Liabilities: 1960–1979," *Statistical Abstract of the U.S., 1982–1983,* 536.

following the Korean War (Exhibit 26). The effect on certain corporate liabilities and assets was clear. As shown in Table 11, cash dropped as inflation ate into assets, and short-term debt rose markedly throughout the decade (Exhibits 27 and 28) as managers sought to put off financing until more favorable circumstances prevailed.

In retrospect, many believe that the effort to control all controllable expenses led many corporations to cut their research and development programs, although the decline seems to have been underway since the early years of the decade, as shown in Figure 3.

As inflation increased the costs of doing business, corporations began to enter the capital markets with renewed interest. There was a substantial increase in borrowing (Exhibits 22 and 24), particularly of short-term capital.

In late 1979, Paul Volcker was appointed the new chairman of the Federal Reserve Board of Governors. Real and nominal rates of interest on borrowed funds rose dramatically; the average rates on new 90-day Treasury bills rose from 7.2 in 1978 to 10.0 percent in 1979 (Exhibit 8) and were poised for further rises in the early 1980s. In April 1980, the prime rate topped 20 percent; inflation was more than 11 percent (Exhibit 15) and was expected to go higher. Oil prices, the source of much of the dislocation in late 1973, doubled once again, but without the same crippling effect. The increase in oil prices was cushioned by the decrease in consumption that came from conservation policies and behavior worldwide—an unexpectedly large decrease.

THE 1980s

By mid-1980, the growth in real GNP (Exhibits 3A and 3B) had dropped below its 1974 bottom. Industrial production (Exhibit 1) had flattened, and real stock

FIGURE 3

■

The Slump in Industrial R&D Spending

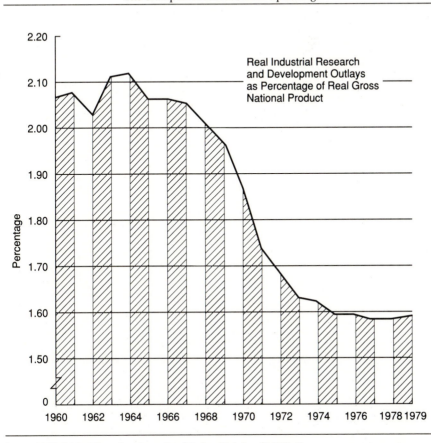

Real Industrial Research
and Development Outlays
as Percentage of Real Gross
National Product

Source: "A Diminished Thrust from Innovation," *Business Week*, June 30, 1980, 61.

returns had reached a decade low (Exhibit 18). Iran held members of the U.S. embassy staff hostage despite President Jimmy Carter's efforts to release them. To add to the difficulty, unemployment (Exhibit 25), which had dropped since its 1975 peak, began to increase. It was in this environment of economic uncertainty and political turmoil that Ronald Reagan was elected president, bringing with him a Republican majority to the Senate.

By July of 1981, President Reagan's controversial trickle-down, supply-side economics had become not just a catch phrase, but a reality. It had been enacted with the Economic Recovery Act of 1981 and was designed to put more capital into the hands of investors, to speed economic recovery, and thereby to increase tax revenues. By 1981, the budget deficit had reached almost $60 billion. Congress increased the debt ceiling and increased it once again; originally estimated in 1981 to reach $91.5 billion by 1983, the actual deficit was $195 billion. Table 12 lists some of the events of 1980 through 1987.

Interest rates, the bête noire of the late 1970s, continued to be both high and volatile (Exhibits 8, 9, 10A, and 10B). Figure 4 shows the level of interest rates and the major events that determined their course from 1979 onwards.

TABLE 12

■

The Decade of the 1980s

	Economy	History and Politics	Science and Technology	Popular Culture and Daily Life
1980	Monetary Control Act approved. Recession. President Carter announces new anti-inflation program. Prime rate exceeds 20 percent: interest rates extremely volatile.	Abscam investigations of congressional influence buying. Reagan defeats Carter; Republican majority in Senate.	Virus-fighting substance made by gene splicing.	Film: *The Empire Strikes Back*
1981	Economy remains depressed. Interest rates remain high and volatile. Dollar strong in foreign exchange. Bankruptcies increase. Inflation falls. Economic Recovery Act of 1981. 1981 budget deficit = $57.9 billion.	Reagan cuts budget. Labor unrest in Poland. Iranian hostages returned. Equal Rights Amendment fails.	Columbia space shuttle in operation.	Film: *On Golden Pond* Baseball players strike.
1982	Prime rate falls to 11.5 percent, unemployment over 10 percent. International lending crisis—over $706 billion owed by troubled developing and Eastern bloc countries. Oil prices decline.	Israel invades Lebanon. Argentina and Great Britain go to war over the Falkland Islands.	First permanent artificial heart implanted into human.	Films: *E.T., Gandhi* More than 3 million personal computers sold.
1983	Inflation drops to 3.6 percent. Federal deficit reaches record $200 billion. WPPSS $2.25 billion is largest municipal bond default in U.S history. Dow-Jones Industrial Average reaches 1287.	More than 200 U.S. Marines killed in Lebanon. Korean Air Lines jet shot down by Soviet Union. U.S. Marines invade Grenada.	Nuclear Magnetic Resonance (NMR) radiation-free X-ray scanner developed. Scientists search for cure for AIDS.	TV movie: *The Day After* Film: *Return of the Jedi* Rock videos become popular.

Year				
1984	Trade deficit hits $100 billion. Grace Commission proposes $424 billion in government savings over 3 years. Oil company mergers begin Texaco/Getty Chevron/Gulf Mobil/Superior. Continental–Illinois Bank bailed out by FDIC.	Reagan/Bush reelected in landslide. Andropov dies, replaced by Chernenko. 2000+ killed in India by Union Carbide plant toxic fumes. Indira Gandhi killed. Marines pull out of Lebanon.	First baby from frozen embryo born. Next mass extinction forecasted in 15 million years.	Film: *The Killing Fields*. Olympics held in Los Angeles.
1985	Uninsured savings and loan crisis in Ohio. Discount rate falls to 7½ percent.	Gramm–Rudman–Hollings bill becomes law. Chernenko dies, replaced by Gorbachev. TWA plane hijacked, one American killed. One American killed when *Achille Lauro* cruise ship is hijacked. Mexican earthquake kills more than 5,000.	*Titanic* found. First septuplets born in United States. Anticancer drug tested.	New Coke introduced. Live-Aid held to feed hungry Africans. Professional wrestling makes it big. Film: *Out of Africa*.
1986	West Texas crude oil prices plummet from $30.90/bbl. in November 1985 to $11.30/bbl. in July 1986, then rebound to $18/bbl. in December 1986. Discount rate falls to 5½ percent. Producer prices fall in 1986 for first decline in 20 years. Unemployment falls to 6.6 percent.	U.S. bombs Libya, killing Qaddafi's daughter. Space Shuttle *Challenger* explodes, killing seven astronauts. Major tax reform becomes law. Reagan administration admits to having traded arms for hostages with Iran. Gramm–Rudman–Hollings ruled unconstitutional. President Marcos flees Philippines, Aquino becomes president.	AIDS drug AZT gets FDA approval Halley's Comet returns on 76-year orbit. Chernobyl nuclear accident kills 23.	Film: *Platoon*.
1987	Volcker resigns. Stock market boom, followed by biggest one-day decline (over 500 points) on October 19.	INF agreement signed by United States and U.S.S.R.	Average age in U.S. 32 +	Films: *Fatal Attraction, The Last Emperor*

FIGURE 4
■
How Interest Rates Behaved during Volcker's Tenure

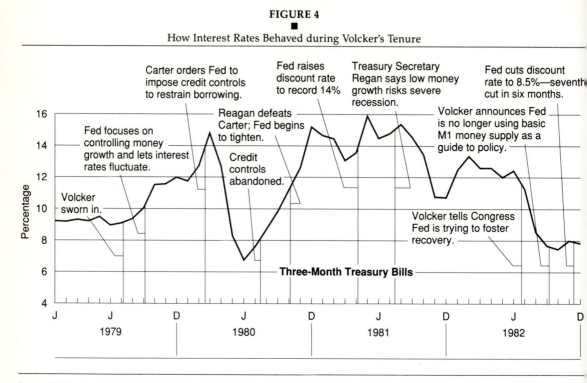

Source: "Washington Debate: Paul Volcker's Report Card," *Business Week,* May 2, 1983, 114; updated from *Economic Report of the President,* January 1987.

Treasury bills reached a high of 16.3 percent in May 1981, and it was not until late 1981 that rates began to decline. By mid-1984, forecasters were divided on the direction the rates, then over 10 percent on 90-day Treasury bills, would go.

In this environment, stock prices languished until they made a whirlwind recovery in late summer 1982. Analysts, who were surprised at the meteoric rise of stock prices—almost 25 percent in the last 6 months of the year—called the market a forecast of good things to come for corporate profits, even as the unemployment rate continued to climb and soup kitchens reappeared. Corporate profitability reached a low in 1982.

There was much to concern the alternately optimistic and pessimistic forecasters in late 1983 and early 1984. U.S. banks had lent many times their capital in some of the most uncertain areas of the world. Oil-price rises in the 1970s had begun the problem. OPEC loaned "petrodollars" short term to banks, and banks loaned money to less developed countries to buy oil from the oil-producing nations. The loans were largely at floating rates, and the less developed countries expected to repay them with income derived largely from commodity exports. Inflation (Table 13), interest rates, and decreased commodity prices, however, put the borrowers in difficult positions. The foreign debt was large (Table 14), and the ability of countries to pay it decreasing. For instance, Argentina's gross domestic product was $199.5 billion, and debt was $58.1 billion; Poland's debt was $80.8 billion, and GDP was $84.6 billion.

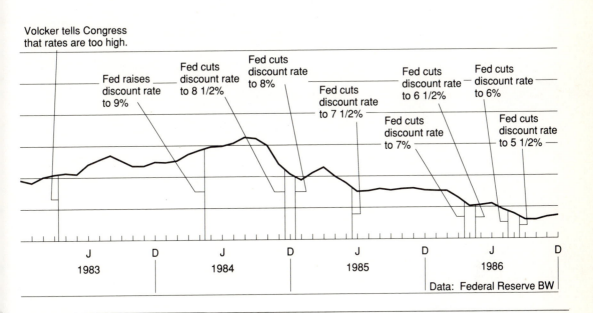

Volcker tells Congress that rates are too high.

Fed raises discount rate to 9%

Fed cuts discount rate to 8 1/2%

Fed cuts discount rate to 8%

Fed cuts discount rate to 7 1/2%

Fed cuts discount rate to 7%

Fed cuts discount rate to 6 1/2%

Fed cuts discount rate to 6%

Fed cuts discount rate to 5 1/2%

Data: Federal Reserve BW

TABLE 13

■

International Rates of Inflation (annual average rate)[a]

Country	1960–1969	1970–1973	1974–1975	1976–1978	1979–1980
Israel	5.2%	12.7%	39.5%	39.2%	103.0%
United States	2.3	4.9	10.1	6.6	12.4
United Kingdom	3.4	8.0	20.0	13.5	15.7
Italy	3.7	6.6	18.1	15.3	17.9
West Germany	2.4	5.3	6.5	3.6	4.8
Argentina	22.2	40.3	86.6	245.7	128.3
Chile	28.5[b]	89.5	436.1	103.1	34.3
Brazil	44.2	17.9	28.3	41.5	67.1
Industrial countries	2.9	5.8	12.2	8.0	10.6
Western hemisphere (excluding United States and Canada)	21.1	20.5	36.1	48.8	51.8
World	4.1	6.8	14.4	10.8	13.5

[a]Based on rates of change for average yearly price levels.
[b]Computed for the 1964 to 1969 period.
Source: *Bulletin*, Federal Reserve Bank of St. Louis, August/September 1982.

TABLE 14

∎

Largest Borrowers—Amount of Outstanding Debt

| Country | Foreign Debt (in billions) | 1985 Interest | | Debt Owed to U.S. Banks (in billions) |
		Amount (in billions)	Estimated Percentage of 1985 GNP	
Brazil	$103.5	$11.8	5.8%	$23.8
Mexico	97.7	10.0	6.3	25.8
Argentina	50.8	5.1	7.9	8.1
Venezuela	32.6	4.1	8.1	10.6
Philippines	27.4	2.1	6.2	5.5
Chile	21.9	2.1	12.9	6.6
Yugoslavia	20.0	1.7	3.6	2.4
Nigeria	18.0	1.8	1.9	1.5
Morocco	14.4	1.0	8.2	0.9
Peru	13.9	1.3	10.8	2.1
Colombia	13.9	1.3	3.3	2.6
Ecuador	7.9	0.7	6.0	2.2
Ivory Coast	6.3	0.6	8.7	0.5
Uruguay	4.9	0.5	9.8	1.0
Bolivia	4.2	0.4	10.0	0.2
Total	$437.4	$44.5	Average 7.3%	$93.8

Source: "Plan Has a Peck of Practical Problems," *Fortune*, December 23, 1985, p. 101. © 1985 Time Inc. All rights reserved. Reprinted with permission.

As borrowers struggled to find ways to pay the interest on their debts, international financial experts struggled to limit the interest payments that had been designed to increase when interest rates rose, as they did in mid-1984. For example, a last-minute rescue by other Latin American countries allowed Argentina, where inflation was raging at 500 percent in the first half of 1984, to keep the interest on its debt current for awhile, but by mid-July, many U.S. banks were finally writing off their Argentine loans as nonperforming, with an unwelcome effect on bank profitability.

Not only did less developed countries increase their debt, but U.S. government debt and accompanying interest payments had risen drastically, as shown in Figure 5. The U.S. current account balance was a distressing deficit of 41.6 billion in 1983.

At the same time, by many indications the economy and corporations were recovering. Real GNP (shown in Figure 6) had increased, and corporate profitability was up.

Along with the precarious position in which the international banking community found itself, the United States struggled with increasing deficits, an exchange rate that favored imports, and a stock market that favored pessimists. Whether the United States could recover from the shocks of the last two decades, as shown in Figure 7, remained to be seen.

A westward- and southern-moving population, aging as the baby-boom generation reached majority, presented new directions for the creative manager. For managers with vision, the integrated world economy offered a challenge, not

FIGURE 5
■
Federal Interest Payments

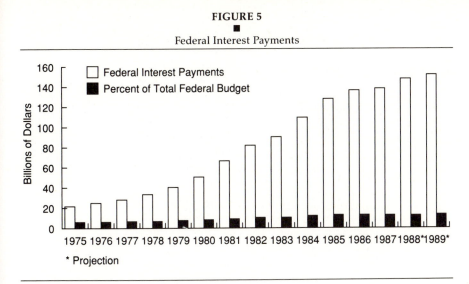

Source: *Economic Report of the President,* January 1988, 338–339.

FIGURE 6
■
Quarterly Change in Real GNP (1982 dollars)

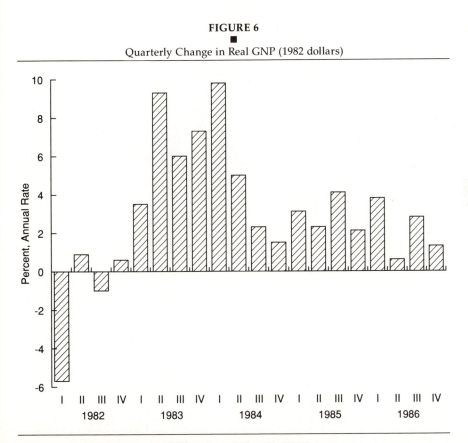

Source: Economic Indicators, February 1987, December 1986, December 1985, 3.

FIGURE 7

Recovering from the Era of Shocks

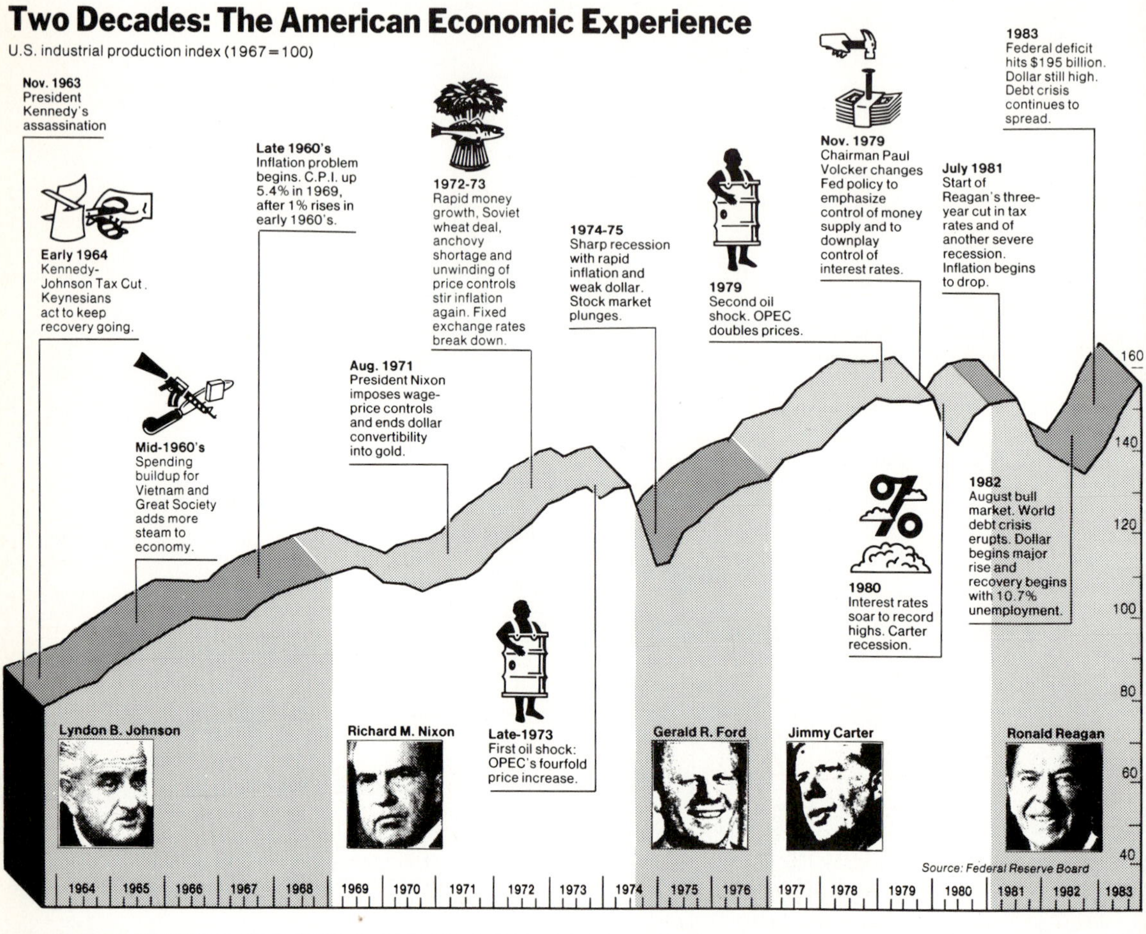
Two Decades: The American Economic Experience
U.S. industrial production index (1967=100)
Nov. 1963 President Kennedy's assassination
Early 1964 Kennedy-Johnson Tax Cut. Keynesians act to keep recovery going.
Mid-1960's Spending buildup for Vietnam and Great Society adds more steam to economy.
Late 1960's Inflation problem begins. C.P.I. up 5.4% in 1969, after 1% rises in early 1960's.
Aug. 1971 President Nixon imposes wage-price controls and ends dollar convertibility into gold.
1972-73 Rapid money growth, Soviet wheat deal, anchovy shortage and unwinding of price controls stir inflation again. Fixed exchange rates break down.
Late-1973 First oil shock: OPEC's fourfold price increase.
1974-75 Sharp recession with rapid inflation and weak dollar. Stock market plunges.
1979 Second oil shock. OPEC doubles prices.
Nov. 1979 Chairman Paul Volcker changes Fed policy to emphasize control of money supply and to downplay control of interest rates.
1980 Interest rates soar to record highs. Carter recession.
July 1981 Start of Reagan's three-year cut in tax rates and of another severe recession. Inflation begins to drop.
1982 August bull market. World debt crisis erupts. Dollar begins major rise and recovery begins with 10.7% unemployment.
1983 Federal deficit hits $195 billion. Dollar still high. Debt crisis continues to spread.
Lyndon B. Johnson
Richard M. Nixon
Gerald R. Ford
Jimmy Carter
Ronald Reagan
160
140
120
100
80
60
40
1964 1965 1966 1967 1968 1969 1970 1971 1972 1973 1974 1975 1976 1977 1978 1979 1980 1981 1982 1983
Source: Federal Reserve Board

Source: Leonard Silk, "Recovering from the Era of Shocks," *The New York Times,* January 8, 1984, p. F1, Section 3.
Copyright © 1984 by The New York Times Company. Reprinted by permission.

just a longing for days when the world seemed to be made up of underdeveloped areas waiting for goods from the U.S. industrial machine.

By 1985, the U.S. economy had rebounded. Industrial production was up, annualized real GNP approached 10 percent in some quarters (Figure 6), and Ronald Reagan had been elected to a second term by a landslide. The vote for Reagan did not, however, carry Republicans into the U.S. Congress as it had in 1980. Supply-side economics, based in the main on stimulative tax cuts rather than spending cuts, seemed to be working—contrary to its vigorous opponents' expectations.

Record employment growth had outstripped that of our major trading partners by 1985, as shown in Figure 8, and the proportion of the U.S. population that was employed showed its first real gains in two decades (Figure 9). Coming out of the deep mid-1970s recession, with its concomitant unemploy-

FIGURE 8

■

Cumulative Change in Employment
since 1959, an International Comparison (annual data)

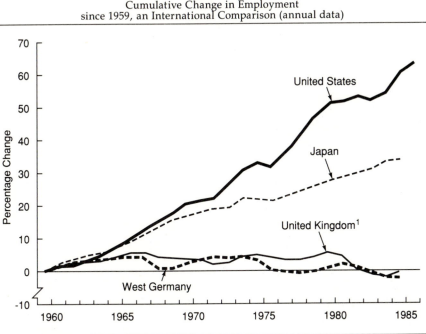

¹Excludes Northern Ireland.
Note: For United States, employment includes resident Armed Forces; data relate to persons 16 years of age and over.
For other countries, data approximate U.S. concepts.
Source: *Economic Report of the President,* January 1987, 42.

ment increase, and the second round of oil-price increases in the early 1980s, employers were operating from strength and used that strength to trim wages: wage growth slowed from 10 percent in 1981 to 2 percent in 1986. Many of the new jobs were being found in a lower paying but growing sector of the economy, service industries. Manufacturing, long the partner of agriculture in U.S. productivity, began to wane (Figure 10), and as Figure 11 shows, employment in the goods-producing industries began to decline.

At the same time that the service sector was showing strong growth, agriculture was facing one of its worst periods. Commodity prices had been in decline for some time, and when they fell further (Figure 12), many farmers were forced into bankruptcy. While some believed that this decline was just the bottom of a long economic cycle, many banks, already reeling from problems with their loans to less developed countries, were hard hit by farm-loan losses and problems in the oil fields.

In 1986, worldwide oil prices suffered their first real decline ever. From November 1985 to April 1986, prices fell by $17.15 per barrel, from a high of $30.90. Some price recovery had stabilized prices at about $18.00 a barrel by December 1986. The price declines sorely affected oil-field loans by banks, which had forecast higher cash flows from their creditors, but the declines also pushed inflation down to its 20-year low (Exhibit 15).

Low inflation helped rescue interest rates. As shown in Figure 13, the Federal Reserve discount rate declined three times during 1986 alone, and in real

FIGURE 9
■
Employment–Population Ratio, an
International Comparison (annual data)

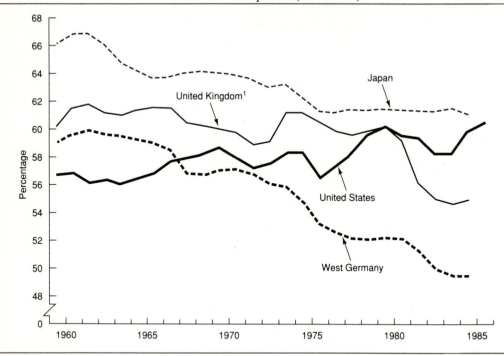

[1]Excludes Northern Ireland.
Note: For United States, employment as percent of noninstitutional population (both include resident Armed Forces); data related to persons 16 years of age and over. For other countries, data approximate U.S. concepts.
Source: *Economic Report of the President*, January 1987, 41.

FIGURE 10
■
Employment Shares—Goods-
Producing and Service-Producing Industries

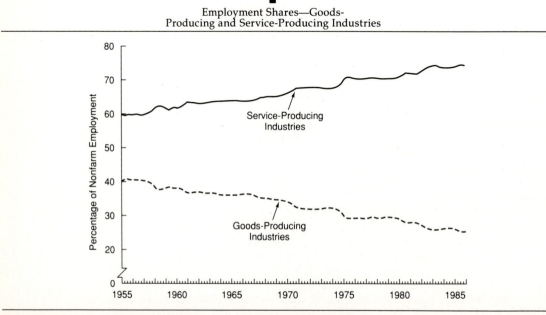

Note: Data relate to all employees on nonfarm payrolls (establishment data), seasonally adjusted.
Source: *Economic Report to the President*, January 1986, 45.

FIGURE 11
■
Manufacturing Shares in Real GDP and Employment

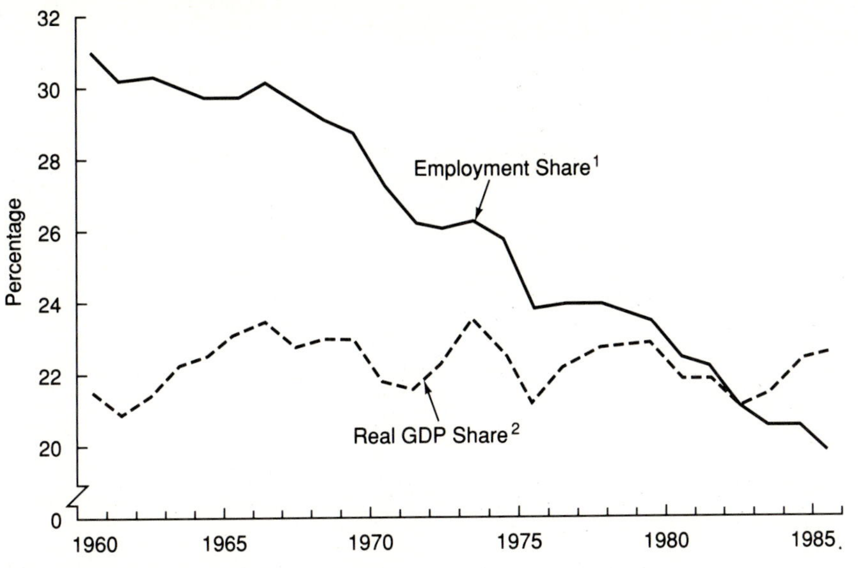

[1]Manufacturing as percent of nonfarm payroll employment.
[2]Manufacturing as percent of real gross domestic product less agriculture, forestry, and fisheries.
Source: *Economic Report of the President*, January 1986, 27.

FIGURE 12
■
Commodity Prices: The Great Decline Returns

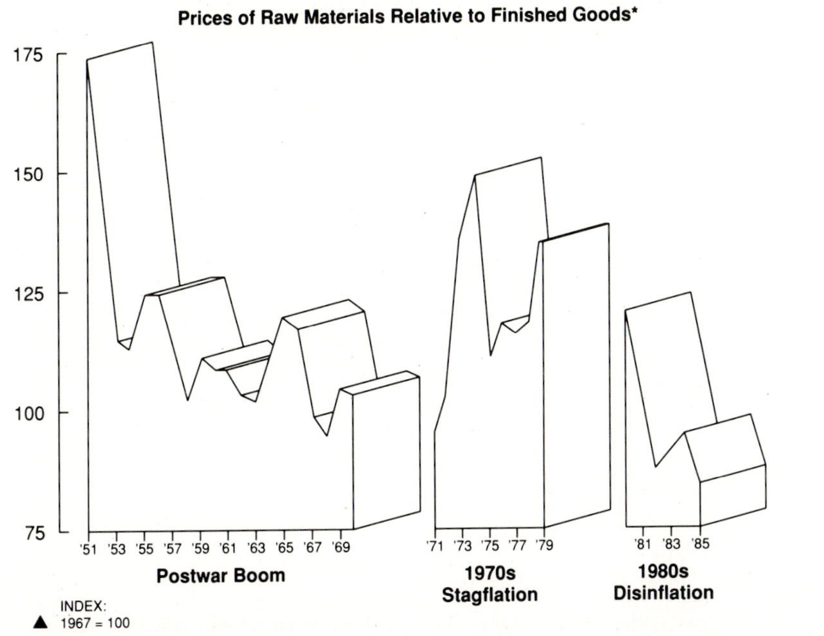

Prices of Raw Materials Relative to Finished Goods*

*Ratio of spot-market price index for raw industrial commodities to producer-price index for finished goods.
Source: Reprinted from May 5, 1986 issue of *Business Week* by special permission "Is the World Economy Riding a Long Wave to Prosperity?" p. 84. Copyright © 1986 by McGraw-Hill, Inc.

FIGURE 13
■
U.S. Jawboning and Lower
Interest Rates Push the Dollar Down

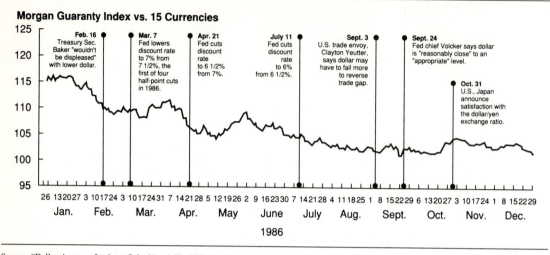

Morgan Guaranty Index vs. 15 Currencies

Source: "Dollar Appears Set for a Calm Year," *The Wall Street Journal*, January 2, 1987, 6B. Reprinted by permission of *The Wall Street Journal*, © Dow Jones & Company, Inc., 1987. All Rights Reserved.

terms, interest rates seemed to fall to their historic levels (Exhibit 11). Mortgage rates, long high enough to discourage home buying and building, descended to 8.5 percent for 30-year mortgages in some places. These rates encouraged rushes to refinance old, high-rate mortgages and stimulated home building.

Even as the interest rates declined, the dollar was dropping from its inflated high (Figures 13 and 14), a high that had spurred foreign travel and the budget deficit shown in Figure 15. While the president was focusing on a supply-side–driven recovery, little tangible evidence could be found that recovery would

FIGURE 14
■
Index of the Dollar's Value against 15
Industrial-Country Currencies (1980–1982 = 100)

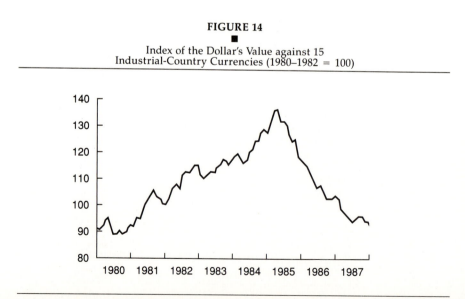

Source: "The Falling Dollar Isn't a Magic Cure," *The Wall Street Journal*, November 23, 1987. Reprinted by permission of *The Wall Street Journal*, © Dow Jones & Company, Inc., 1987. All Rights Reserved.

FIGURE 15
■

Federal Outlays and Receipts as Percent of GNP

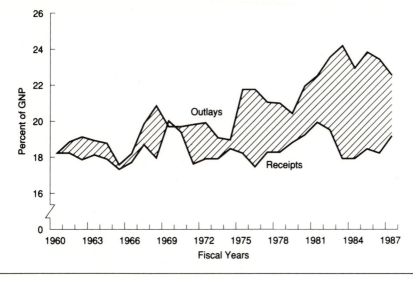

Note: Data for 1987 are estimates.
Source: *Economic Report of the President*, January 1986, 67.

reduce U.S. government debt. Receipts were below average and, worse yet, expenditures were far outstripping reasonable forecasts for revenues (Figure 15). Interest alone was taking 13 percent of government expenditures in 1986, more than double the 1966 level (Figure 16). The deficit had boomed since Reagan had taken office in 1980 (Figure 17). Not since World War II had the U.S. endured large deficits, and never so large as those created in the 1980s.

FIGURE 16
■
Government Expenditures, 1966–1986

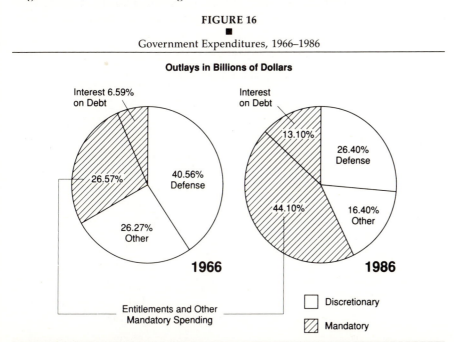

Source: Heidi Mack and Shirley Horn, "How the Government Spends Its Money," *The Christian Science Monitor*, October 27, 1987, 6. © 1987 TCSPS. Reprinted with permission.

FIGURE 17
■
The Federal Budget Deficit

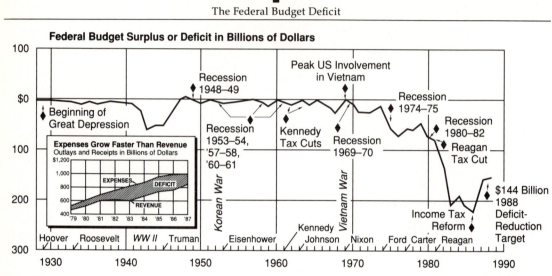

Federal Budget Surplus or Deficit in Billions of Dollars

Note: All figures are for fiscal years. The government's budget years are similar to car model years. Fiscal year 1988 began October 2, 1987 and runs through September 30, 1988.
Source: Shirley Horn's "The Looming Budget Deficit," *The Christian Science Monitor,* October 27, 1987, 6. Copyright © 1987 TCSPS. Reprinted with permission.

To fuel the deficits, massive Treasury financings were undertaken. Foreign purchases of these and other securities increased in spite of the declines in the dollar (see Figure 14 and Table 15). Despite these problems, by the end of 1986, industrial production had increased, durable goods orders had risen, employment was at a record high, interest rates had fallen, and the stock market bulls were raging.

TABLE 15
■
Foreigners' Appetite for U.S. Securities, 1986

	Net Foreign Purchases (billions of dollars)		
	U.S. Treasurys and Agencies	*U.S. Corporates (including Euro issues)*	*U.S. Equities*
1981	7.0	13.2	5.8
1982	12.8	17.0	3.9
1983	16.9	11.0	5.4
1984	26.6	28.6	− 3.0
1985	24.8	44.4	5.0
1986[a]	68.4	47.5	20.0
1987[b]	72.0	50.0	30.0

[a]Estimate
[b]Projection
Source: "U.S. Attracts Foreign Capital," *The Wall Street Journal,* January 2, 1987, p. 8B. Reprinted by permission of *The Wall Street Journal,* © Dow Jones & Company, Inc., 1987. All Rights Reserved.

FIGURE 18

■

Strong Consumer Confidence in Economy

Consumer confidence has stabilized in recent years, compared to the dramatic swings that occurred with recessions in the past. Left scale: Consumer Confidence Index, 1985 equals 100. Right scale: Quarterly percentage changes in real GNP, at annual rates.

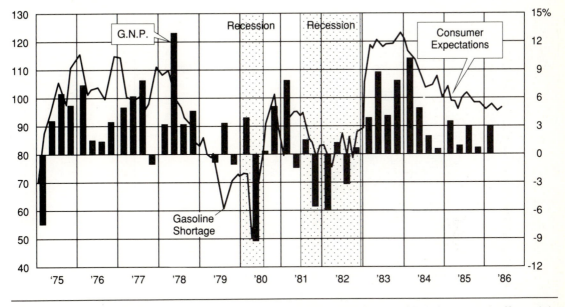

Source: *The New York Times Financial Planning Guide*, September 14, 1987, 12. Copyright © 1987 by The New York Times Company. reprinted by permission.

Consumer confidence (Figure 18) had sparked the rebirth of the basic engines of the U.S. economy, especially the auto industry. By the end of 1986, the Dow Jones Industrial Average had almost doubled (Figure 19) and reached just under 2000 at year's end. The rapid rise in the Dow, and the considerable profits made and expected on Wall Street, brought out both the optimists and the pessimists. This longest and broadest sustained rise in the stock market, when coupled with worries about the budget deficit, the balance of payments, and the high degree of leverage of both companies and individuals—that is, the debtor status of the country and its people—gave rise to a number of market crash forecasts. Others who were more optimistic found reasons for the remarkable recovery that were rooted in forecasts for further economic progress.

The bulls and the optimists won. Although looming and rising deficits were of concern, they did not affect the markets.

As debt continued to rise, interest rates began to climb. Spending was outstripping growth in disposable income, and imports contributed to the balance-of-trade deficit (Figures 20 and 21). In August 1987, the Dow Jones Industrial Average passed 2700. Then on Black Monday October 19, the markets reacted in the most dramatic one-day decline in Wall Street history. The Dow Jones Industrial Average dropped from just under 2300 to just over 1700. A variety of forces led to this severe decline. (See the appendix to this note for one commentary on the reasons.)

FIGURE 19

Year-End Review of Markets and Finance

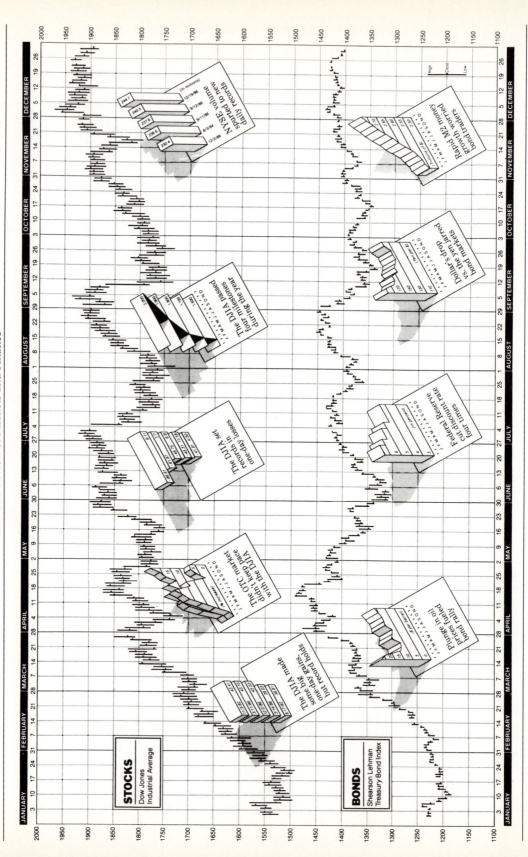

Source: Karl Hartig, "Year-End Review of Markets and Finance," *The Wall Street Journal*, January 2, 1987, p. 1B. Reprinted by permission of *The Wall Street Journal*. © Dow Jones & Company,

FIGURE 20
■
Spending Is Growing Faster Than Income

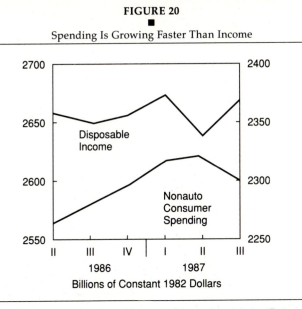

Source: Reprinted from November 9, 1987 issue of *Business Week* by special permission "Business Outlook," p. 26. Copyright © 1987 by McGraw-Hill, Inc.

The impact of the shock was felt on all the major markets (Figure 22), and eventually in the political arena, as well. While growth in the money supply had declined throughout 1986 and early 1987, the Federal Reserve Board had injected considerable cash into the struggling financial system. Parallels to 1929 imme-

FIGURE 21
■
Imports Are Jumping Again

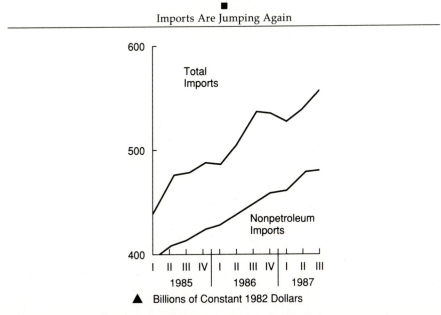

Source: Reprinted from November 9, 1987 issue of *Business Week* by special permission "Business Outlook," p. 27. Copyright © 1987 by McGraw-Hill, Inc.

■

Stock Market Averages, September–October 23, 1987

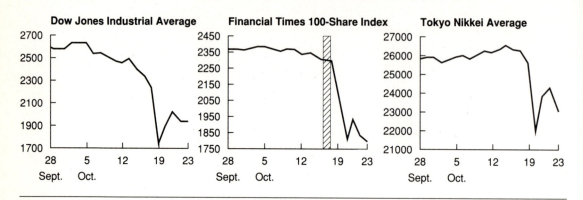

Source: "Big Bang Deregulation Helps London Survive the Burst of Market Turbulence," *The Wall Street Journal*, October 26, 1987, p. 36. Reprinted by permission of *The Wall Street Journal*, © Dow Jones & Company, Inc., 1987. All Rights Reserved.

diately leaped to the minds of the press (Figure 23), and numerous pleas for political action, or at least support, were heard. In particular, the U.S. budget deficit was cited as the initial cause for Black Monday, and Congress and the

FIGURE 23

■

The Crash: How Close an Economic Parallel?

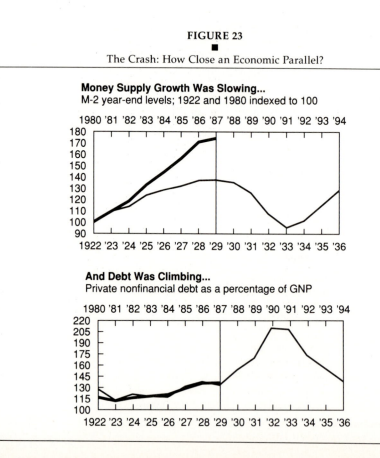

FIGURE 23 *continued*

But Trade Showed a Surplus...
Balance on goods and services as a percentage of GNP

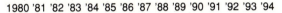
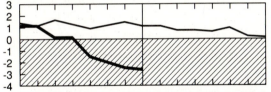
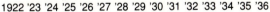

And the Federal Budget Was Balanced
Federal government surplus or deficit
as a percentage of GNP

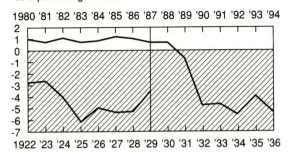

Weekly close of the Dow Jones Industrial Average,
indexed so that Dec. 31, 1928 and Dec. 31, 1986
are equal to 100

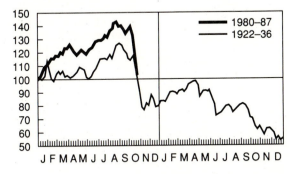

Source: "Avoiding the Economic Debacle: Comparing 1929 and 1987," *The Wall Street Journal*, October 26, 1987, p. 29. Reprinted by permission of *The Wall Street Journal*, © Dow Jones & Company, Inc., 1987. All Rights Reserved.

president were urged to take immediate action. Interest rates were cut, and the dollar, which had been supported throughout early 1987 by the United States' trading partners, went into free fall (Figure 24).

By the end of 1987, some of the fear produced by the October 19 market decline seemed to have receded. The U.S. Congress and the president seemed to be making some progress discussing the budget deficit, the country's major trading partners were cutting interest rates in order to stimulate their economies,

FIGURE 24

U.S. Dollar

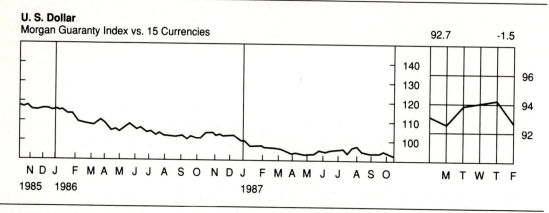

U. S. Dollar
Morgan Guaranty Index vs. 15 Currencies

92.7   -1.5

140
130
120   96
110   94
100
            92

N D J   F M A M J J A S O N D J   F M A M J J A S O   M T W T F
1985 1986   1987

Source: "Markets and Money," *The Wall Street Journal*, October 26, 1987, p. 60. Reprinted by permission of *The Wall Street Journal*, © Dow Jones & Company, Inc., 1987. All Rights Reserved.

and U.S. exporters were hopeful that the exchange-rate-driven export surge would continue and would support economic growth. Once again opportunities appeared to exist, but danger also seemed to be closer to hand than it had been since the late 1920s.

The Business Environment: A Retrospective, 1929–1987

EXHIBIT 1

Industrial Production Total
(seasonally adjusted, quarterly)

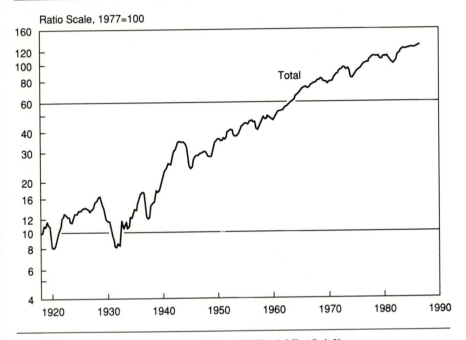

Source: Board of Governors of the Federal Reserve System, *1987 Historical Chart Book*, 28.

The Business Environment: A Retrospective, 1929–1987

EXHIBIT 2

Average Manufacturing Work Week

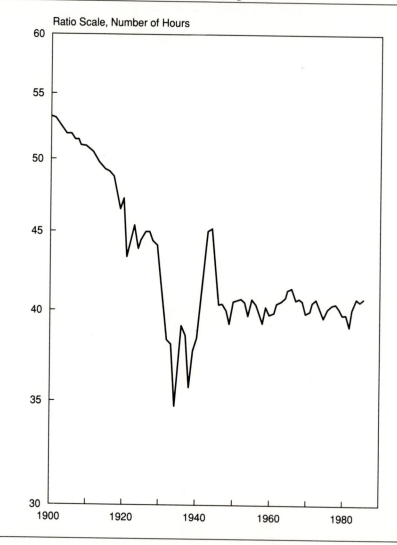

Source: Board of Governors of the Federal Reserve System, *1987 Historical Chart Book*, 11.

The Business Environment: A Retrospective, 1929–1987

EXHIBIT 3A
■
Gross National Product (GNP)[a] 1929–1983

Year or Quarter	GNP (billions of dollars)	Percent of Change from Prior Period	GNP (in 1982 dollars)	Percent of Change from Prior Period	GNP Implicit Price Deflator (Index Numbers 1982 = 100)	Percent Change from Prior Period
1929	$ 103.9	6.6%	$ 709.6	6.6%	14.6	0
1930	90.7	− 12.3	285.2	− 9.4	31.81	− 3.2%
1931	76.1	− 16.1	263.3	− 7.7	28.89	− 9.2
1932	58.3	− 23.4	226.8	− 13.8	25.69	− 11.1
1933	56.0	− 4.2	498.5	− 2.1	11.02	− 2.2
1934	65.3	17.0	239.4	7.8	27.27	8.5
1935	72.5	11.0	260.8	8.9	27.80	1.9
1936	82.7	14.1	296.1	13.5	27.94	0.5
1937	90.7	9.7	309.8	4.6	29.29	4.8
1938	85.0	− 6.4	297.1	− 4.1	28.59	− 2.4
1939	91.3	7.0	716.6	7.9	12.07	− 0.8
1940	100.4	10.0	772.9	7.8	13.0	2.0
1941	125.0	25.0	909.4	17.7	13.8	6.2
1942	159.0	26.6	1,080.3	18.8	14.7	6.6
1943	192.7	21.2	1,276.2	18.1	15.1	2.6
1944	211.4	9.7	1,380.6	8.2	15.3	1.4
1945	213.4	0.9	1,354.8	− 1.9	15.7	2.9
1946	212.4	− 0.5	1,096.9	− 19.0	19.4	22.9
1947	235.2	10.8	1,066.7	− 2.8	22.1	13.9
1948	261.6	11.2	1,108.7	3.9	23.6	7.0
1949	260.4	− 0.5	1,109.0	0.0	23.5	0.5
1950	288.3	10.7	1,203.7	8.5	23.9	2.0
1951	333.4	15.7	1,328.2	10.3	25.1	4.8
1952	351.6	5.5	1,380.0	3.9	25.5	1.5
1953	371.6	5.7	1,435.3	4.0	25.9	1.6
1954	372.5	0.2	1,416.2	− 1.3	26.3	1.6
1955	405.9	9.0	1,494.9	5.6	27.2	3.2
1956	428.2	5.5	1,525.6	2.1	28.1	3.4
1957	451.0	5.3	1,551.1	1.8	29.1	3.6
1958	456.8	1.3	1,539.2	− 0.8	29.7	2.1
1959	495.8	8.5	1,629.1	5.8	30.4	2.4

continued

EXHIBIT 3A continued

Year or Quarter	GNP (billions of dollars)	Percent of Change from Prior Period	GNP (in 1982 dollars)	Percent of Change from Prior Period	GNP Implicit Price Deflator (Index Numbers 1982 = 100)	Percent Change from Prior Period
1960	515.3	3.9	1,665.3	2.2	30.9	1.6
1961	533.8	3.6	1,708.7	2.6	31.2	1.0
1962	574.6	7.6	1,799.4	5.3	31.9	2.2
1963	606.9	5.6	1,873.3	4.1	32.4	1.6
1964	649.8	7.1	1,973.3	5.3	32.9	1.5
1965	705.1	8.5	2,087.6	5.8	33.8	2.7
1966	772.0	9.5	2,208.3	5.8	35.0	3.6
1967	816.4	5.8	2,271.4	2.9	35.9	2.6
1968	892.7	9.3	2,365.6	4.1	37.7	5.0
1969	963.9	8.0	2,423.3	2.4	39.8	5.6
1970	1,015.5	5.4	2,416.2	−0.3	42.0	5.5
1971	1,102.7	8.6	2,484.8	2.8	44.4	5.7
1972	1,212.8	10.0	2,608.5	5.0	46.5	4.7
1973	1,359.3	12.1	2,744.1	5.2	49.5	6.5
1974	1,472.8	8.3	2,729.3	−0.5	54.0	9.1
1975	1,598.4	8.5	2,695.0	−1.3	59.3	9.8
1976	1,782.8	11.5	2,826.7	4.9	63.1	6.4
1977	1,990.5	11.7	2,958.6	4.7	67.3	6.7
1978	2,249.7	13.0	3,115.2	5.3	72.2	7.3
1979	2,508.2	11.5	3,192.4	2.5	78.6	8.9
1980	2,732.0	8.9	3,187.1	−0.2	85.7	9.0
1981	3,052.6	11.7	3,248.8	1.6	94.0	9.7
1982	3,166.0	3.7	3,166.0	−2.5	100.0	6.4
1983	3,405.7	7.6	3,279.1	3.6	103.9	3.9
1984	3,765.0	10.5	3,489.9	6.4	107.9	3.8
1985	3,998.1	6.2	3,585.2	2.7	111.5	3.3
1986[b]	$4,208.5	5.3	3,676.5	2.5	114.5	2.7

[a]Quarterly data at seasonally adjusted rates.
[b]Projected.
Sources: *Economic Report of the President*, February 1983, pp. 220–225. *Survey of Current Business,* U.S. Bureau of Economic Analysis, August 1977, p. 25.

The Business Environment: A Retrospective, 1929–1987

EXHIBIT 3B
■

Gross National Product
(seasonally adjusted annual rates, quarterly)

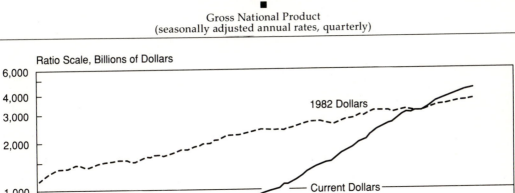

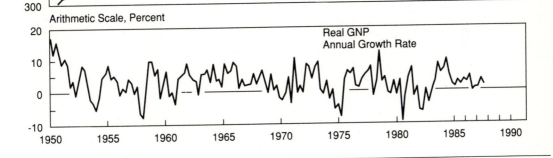

Source: Board of Governors of the Federal Reserve System, *1987 Historical Chart Book*, 12.

EXHIBIT 4

■

Net Federal Debt, Amount Outstanding (end of year,
1929–1950; seasonally adjusted, end of quarter, 1950–1987)

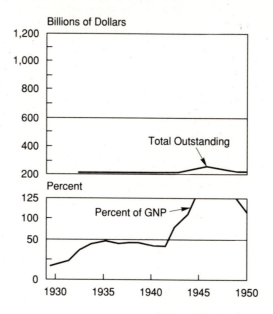

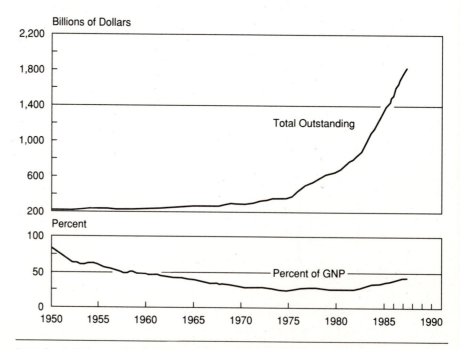

Source: Board of Governors of the Federal Reserve System, *1983* and *1987 Historical Chart Book,* 49.

EXHIBIT 5A

■

Federal Receipts, Outlays, Surplus or Deficit, and Debt Selected Fiscal Years 1929–1989

Fiscal year or period	Total			On-budget			Off-budget			Gross Federal debt (end of period)		Addendum: Gross national product
	Receipts	Outlays	Surplus or deficit (−)	Receipts	Outlays	Surplus or deficit (−)	Receipts	Outlays	Surplus or deficit (−)	Total	Held by the public	
1929.........	3.9	3.1	0.7	....	....	....	....	....	....	[1] 16.9	....	....
1933.........	2.0	4.6	−2.6	....	....	....	....	....	....	[1] 22.5	....	....
1939.........	6.3	9.1	−2.8	5.8	9.2	−3.4	0.5	0.0	0.5	48.2	41.4	....
1940.........	6.5	9.5	−2.9	6.0	9.5	−3.5	.6	.0	.6	50.7	42.8	95.8
1941.........	8.7	13.7	−4.9	8.0	13.6	−5.6	.7	.0	.7	57.5	48.2	113.0
1942.........	14.6	35.1	−20.5	13.7	35.1	−21.3	.9	.1	.8	79.2	67.8	142 2
1943.........	24.0	78.6	−54.6	22.9	78.5	−55.6	1.1	.1	1.0	142.6	127.8	175.8
1944.........	43.7	91.3	−47.6	42.5	91.2	−48.7	1.3	.1	1.2	204.1	184.8	202.0
1945.........	45.2	92.7	−47.6	43.8	92.6	−48.7	1.3	.1	1.2	260.1	235.2	212.4
1946.........	39.3	55.2	−15.9	38.1	55.0	−17.0	1.2	.2	1.0	271.0	241.9	212.9
1947.........	38.5	34.5	4.0	37.1	34.2	2.9	1.5	.3	1.2	257.1	224.3	223.6
1948.........	41.6	29.8	11.8	39.9	29.4	10.5	1.6	.4	1.2	252.0	216.3	247.8
1949.........	39.4	38.8	.6	37.7	38.4	−.7	1.7	.4	1.3	252.6	214.3	263.9
1950.........	39.4	42.6	−3.1	37.3	42.0	−4.7	2.1	.5	1.6	256.9	219.0	266.8
1951.........	51.6	45.5	6.1	48.5	44.2	4.3	3.1	1.3	1.8	255.3	214.3	315.0
1952.........	66.2	67.7	−1.5	62.6	66.0	−3.4	3.6	1.7	1.9	259.1	214.8	342.4
1953.........	69.6	76.1	−6.5	65.5	73.8	−8.3	4.1	2.3	1.8	266.0	218.4	365.6
1954.........	69.7	70.9	−1.2	65.1	67.9	−2.8	4.6	2.9	1.7	270.8	224.5	369.5
1955.........	65.5	68.4	−3.0	60.4	64.5	−4.1	5.1	4.0	1.1	274.4	226.6	386.4
1956.........	74.6	70.6	3.9	68.2	65.7	2.5	6.4	5.0	1.5	272.8	222.2	418.1
1957.........	80.0	76.6	3.4	73.2	70.6	2.6	6.8	6.0	.8	272.4	219.4	440.5
1958.........	79.6	82.4	−2.8	71.6	74.9	−3.3	8.0	7.5	.5	279.7	226.4	450.2
1959.........	79.2	92.1	−12.8	71.0	83.1	−12.1	8.3	9.0	−.7	287.8	235.0	481.5
1960.........	92.5	92.2	.3	81.9	81.3	.5	10.6	10.9	−.2	290.9	237.2	506.7
1961.........	94.4	97.7	−3.3	82.3	86.0	−3.8	12.1	11.7	.4	292.9	238.6	518.2
1962.........	99.7	106.8	−7.1	87.4	93.3	−5.9	12.3	13.5	−1.3	303.3	248.4	557.7
1963.........	106.6	111.3	−4.8	92.4	96.4	−4.0	14.2	15.0	−.8	310.8	254.5	587.8
1964.........	112.6	118.5	−5.9	96.2	102.8	−6.5	16.4	15.7	.6	316.8	257.6	629.2
1965.........	116.8	118.2	−1.4	100.1	101.7	−1.6	16.7	16.5	.2	323.2	261.6	672.6
1966.........	130.8	134.5	−3.7	111.7	114.8	−3.1	19.1	19.7	−.6	329.5	264.7	739.0
1967.........	148.8	157.5	−8.6	124.4	137.0	−12.6	24.4	20.4	4.0	341.3	267.5	794.6
1968.........	153.0	178.1	−25.2	128.1	155.8	−27.7	24.9	22.3	2.6	369.8	290.6	849.4
1969.........	186.9	183.6	3.2	157.9	158.4	−.5	29.0	25.2	3.7	367.1	279.5	929.5
1970.........	192.8	195.6	−2.8	159.3	168.0	−8.7	33.5	27.6	5.9	382.6	284.9	990.2
1971.........	187.1	210.2	−23.0	151.3	177.3	−26.1	35.8	32.8	3.0	409.5	304.3	1,055.9
1972.........	207.3	230.7	−23.4	167.4	193.8	−26.4	39.9	36.9	3.1	437.3	323.8	1,153.1
1973.........	230.8	245.7	−14.9	184.7	200.1	−15.4	46.1	45.6	.5	468.4	343.0	1,281.4
1974.........	263.2	269.4	−6.1	209.3	217.3	−8.0	53.9	52.1	1.8	486.2	346.1	1,416.5
1975.........	279.1	332.3	−53.2	216.6	271.9	−55.3	62.5	60.4	2.0	544.1	396.9	1,522.5
1976.........	298.1	371.8	−73.7	231.7	302.2	−70.5	66.4	69.6	−3.2	631.9	480.3	1,698.2
Transition quarter ...	81.2	96.0	−14.7	63.2	76.6	−13.3	18.0	19.4	−1.4	646.4	498.3	[2] 1,794.7
1977.........	355.6	409.2	−53.6	278.7	328.5	−49.7	76.8	80.7	−3.9	709.1	551.8	1,933.0
1978.........	399.6	458.7	−59.2	314.2	369.1	−54.9	85.4	89.7	−4.3	780.4	610.9	2,171.8
1979.........	463.3	503.5	−40.2	365.3	403.5	−38.2	98.0	100.0	−2.0	833.8	644.6	2,447.8
1980.........	517.1	590.9	−73.8	403.9	476.6	−72.7	113.2	114.3	−1.1	914.3	715.1	2,670.6
1981.........	599.3	678.2	−78.9	469.1	543.0	−73.9	130.2	135.2	−5.0	1,003.9	794.4	2,986.4
1982.........	617.8	745.7	−127.9	474.3	594.3	−120.0	143.5	151.4	−7.9	1,147.0	929.4	3,139.1
1983.........	600.6	808.3	−207.8	453.2	661.2	−208.0	147.3	147.1	.2	1,381.9	1,141.8	3,321.9
1984.........	666.5	851.8	−185.3	500.4	686.0	−185.6	166.1	165.8	.3	1,576.7	1,312.6	3,687.6
1985.........	734.1	946.3	−212.3	547.9	769.5	−221.6	186.2	176.8	9.4	1,827.5	1,509.9	3,943.4
1986.........	769.1	990.3	−221.2	568.9	806.8	−237.9	200.2	183.5	16.7	2,130.0	1,746.1	4,192.5
1987.........	854.1	1,004.6	−150.4	640.7	810.8	−170.0	213.4	193.8	19.6	2,355.3	1,897.8	4,408.7
1988 [3]...	909.2	1,055.9	−146.7	669.3	852.8	−183.5	239.9	203.1	36.8	2,581.6	2,025.1	4,705.8
1989 [3]...	964.7	1,094.2	−129.5	706.2	880.9	−174.7	258.5	213.3	45.1	2,825.3	2,152.1	5,023.3

[1] Not strictly comparable with later data.
[2] Annual rate.
[3] Estimates.

Note.—Through fiscal year 1976, the fiscal year was on a July 1–June 30 basis; beginning October 1976 (fiscal year 1977), the fiscal year is on an October 1–September 30 basis. The 3-month period from July 1, 1976 through September 30, 1976 is a separate fiscal period known as the transition quarter.
Refunds of receipts are excluded from receipts and outlays.
See "Budget of the United States Government, Fiscal Year 1989" for additional information.

Sources: Department of the Treasury, Office of Management and Budget, and Department of Commerce (Bureau of Economic Analysis).

The Business Environment: A Retrospective, 1929–1987

EXHIBIT 5B

■

Federal Budget, Fiscal Year Totals
(seasonally adjusted annual rates, quarterly)

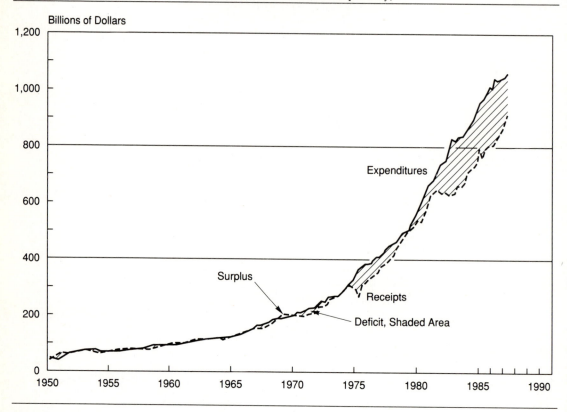

Source: Board of Governors of the Federal Reserve System, *1987 Historical Chart Book*, 51.

The Business Environment: A Retrospective, 1929–1987

EXHIBIT 6A

■

Debt in the United States
(amount outstanding; debt, end of year; GNP, annually)

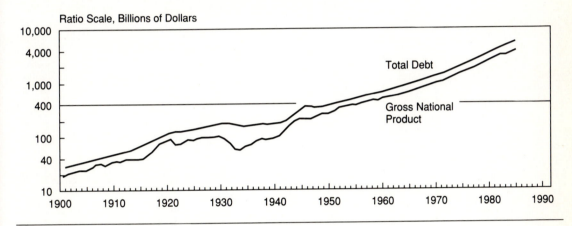

Source: Board of Governors of the Federal Reserve System, *1987 Historical Chart Book*, 42.

The Business Environment: A Retrospective, 1929-1987

EXHIBIT 6B

∎

Net Federal Debt as Percentage of GNP; Net Public and Private Debt by Major Sectors, 1916 to 1970
(in billions of dollars, as of end of year)

		Public				Private											
							Corporate			Individual and Noncorporate						Other Nonfarm		
											Farm[d]		Nonfarm Mortgage				
	Total	Total	Federal[a]	Federal Financial Agencies[b]	State and Local	Total	Total	Long-Term[c]	Short-Term[c]	Total	Production	Mortgage	1- to 4-family	Multifamily Residential and Commercial	Commercial	Financial[e]	Consumer
1970	$1,854.1	$484.7	301.1	$38.8	$144.8	$1,369.4	$793.5	$360.2	433.4	$575.9	$27.5	$31.2	$274.6	$46.3	$35.8	$33.3	$127.2
1969	1,735.0	452.4	289.3	30.6	132.6	1,282.6	734.2	323.5	410.7	548.4	26.0	29.5	261.5	42.4	35.6	32.3	121.1
1968	1,582.5	437.1	291.9	21.4	123.9	1,145.4	631.5	283.6	347.9	513.9	24.3	27.5	246.5	38.4	33.4	33.0	110.8
1967	1,438.7	408.8	286.5	9.0	113.4	1,029.9	553.7	255.6	298.1	476.2	22.8	25.5	232.0	34.9	31.1	29.1	100.8
1966	1,338.7	387.9	271.8	11.2	104.8	950.8	506.6	231.3	275.3	444.2	19.1	23.3	219.6	32.0	29.4	24.5	96.2
1965	1,234.6	373.7	266.4	8.9	98.3	870.0	454.3	209.4	244.9	415.7	18.1	21.2	208.7	28.1	27.0	22.7	89.9
1964	1,151.6	301.9	264.0	7.5	90.4	789.7	409.6	192.5	217.1	380.1	17.1	18.9	193.3	25.6	23.5	21.5	80.3
1963	1,070.9	348.5	257.5	7.2	83.9	722.3	376.4	174.8	201.7	345.8	16.4	16.8	177.1	21.5	21.5	20.8	71.7
1962	996.0	335.9	253.6	5.3	77.0	660.1	348.2	161.2	187.0	311.9	15.0	15.2	161.9	18.4	19.3	18.3	63.8
1961	930.3	321.2	246.7	4.0	70.5	609.1	324.3	149.3	174.9	284.8	13.6	13.9	148.9	15.6	17.9	16.9	58.0
1960	874.2	308.1	239.8	3.5	64.9	566.1	302.8	139.1	163.7	263.3	12.3	12.8	137.4	13.9	16.6	14.2	56.1

Year																	
1959	833.0	304.7	241.4	3.7	59.6	528.3	283.3	129.3	154.0	245.0	11.7	12.1	127.3	13.7	15.8	13.4	51.5
1958	769.6	287.2	231.0	2.5	53.7	482.4	259.5	121.2	138.4	222.9	12.1	11.1	114.5	13.6	13.7	12.8	45.1
1957	728.3	274.0	223.0	2.4	48.6	454.3	246.7	112.1	134.6	207.6	9.8	10.4	105.2	12.9	13.2	11.1	45.0
1956	698.4	271.2	224.3	2.4	44.5	427.2	231.7	100.1	131.7	195.5	9.6	9.8	96.8	12.6	13.3	11.1	42.3
1955	665.8	273.6	229.6	2.9	41.1	392.2	212.1	90.0	122.2	180.1	9.7	9.0	86.3	12.4	12.4	11.6	38.8
1954	605.9	265.9	229.1	1.3	35.5	340.0	182.8	82.9	100.0	157.2	9.3	8.2	74.1	12.3	10.4	10.4	32.5
1953	581.6	258.9	226.8	1.4	30.7	322.7	179.5	78.3	101.2	143.2	9.1	7.7	64.7	12.0	9.9	8.5	31.4
1952	550.2	249.8	221.5	1.3	27.0	300.4	171.0	73.3	97.7	129.4	8.0	7.2	57.1	11.8	10.3	7.5	27.5
1951	519.2	242.4	216.9	1.3	24.2	276.8	162.5	66.6	95.9	114.3	7.0	6.7	50.4	11.3	9.5	6.7	22.7
1950	486.2	239.8	217.4	0.7	21.7	246.4	142.1	60.1	81.9	104.3	6.2	6.1	43.9	10.9	8.9	6.9	21.5
1949	445.8	237.4	217.6	0.7	19.1	208.4	118.0	56.5	61.4	90.4	6.4	5.6	36.4	10.7	7.9	6.0	17.4
1948	431.3	232.9	215.3	0.6	17.0	198.4	117.8	52.5	65.3	80.6	5.5	5.3	32.0	10.4	7.8	5.1	14.4
1947	415.7	237.4	221.7	$ 0.7	15.0	178.3	108.9	46.1	62.8	69.4	3.5	5.1	27.1	10.1	7.1	4.8	11.6
1946	396.6	243.2	229.5	—	13.7	153.4	93.5	41.3	52.2	59.9	2.7	4.9	22.1	9.7	6.2	5.9	8.4
1945	405.9	265.9	252.5	—	13.4	140.0	85.3	38.3	47.0	54.7	2.5	4.8	17.7	9.3	4.4	10.3	5.7
1944	370.6	225.8	211.9	—	13.9	144.8	94.1	39.8	54.3	50.7	2.8	4.9	17.0	9.0	3.7	8.1	5.1
1943	313.2	168.9	154.4	—	14.5	144.3	95.5	41.0	54.5	48.8	2.8	5.4	16.9	9.2	3.8	5.7	4.9
1942	258.6	117.1	101.7	—	15.4	141.5	91.6	42.7	49.0	49.9	3.0	6.0	17.3	9.5	4.1	4.0	6.0
1941	211.4	72.4	56.3	—	16.1	139.0	83.4	43.6	39.8	55.6	2.9	6.4	17.4	9.7	5.0	5.0	9.2
1940	189.8	61.2	44.8	—	16.4	128.6	75.6	43.7	31.9	53.0	2.6	6.5	16.5	9.6	4.3	5.2	8.3
1939	183.3	59.0	42.6	—	16.4	124.3	73.5	44.4	29.2	50.8	2.2	6.6	15.5	9.5	3.8	6.0	7.2
1938	179.9	56.6	40.5	—	16.1	123.3	73.3	44.8	28.5	50.0	2.2	6.8	15.0	9.5	10.1		6.4
1937	182.2	55.3	39.2	—	16.1	126.9	75.8	43.5	32.3	51.1	1.6	7.0	14.7	9.6	11.3		6.9
1936	180.6	53.9	37.7	—	16.2	126.7	76.1	42.5	33.5	50.6	1.4	7.2	14.6	9.8	11.2		6.4
1935	175.0	50.5	34.4	—	16.1	124.5	74.8	43.6	31.2	49.7	1.5	7.4	14.7	10.1	10.8	5.2	5.2
1934	171.0	46.3	30.4	—	15.9	125.3	75.5	44.6	30.9	49.8	1.3	7.6	14.8	10.7	11.2	6.0	4.2
1933	168.5	40.6	24.3	—	16.3	127.9	76.9	47.9	29.0	51.0	1.4	7.7	14.6	11.7	11.7		3.9
1932	175.0	37.9	21.3	—	16.6	137.1	80.0	49.2	30.8	57.1	1.6	8.5	15.8	13.2	14.0		4.0
1931	182.9	34.5	18.5	—	16.0	148.4	83.5	50.3	33.2	64.9	2.0	9.1	17.2	13.7	17.6		5.3

continued

EXHIBIT 6B continued

		Public				Private											
							Corporate			Individual and Noncorporate							
				Federal Financial Agencies[b]							Farm[d]		Nonfarm Mortgage		Other Nonfarm		
	Total	Total	Federal[a]		State and Local	Total	Total	Long-Term[c]	Short-Term[c]	Total	Production	Mortgage	1- to 4-family	Multifamily Residential and Commercial	Commercial	Financial[e]	Consumer
1930	192.3	31.2	16.5	—	14.7	161.1	89.3	51.1	38.2	71.8	2.4	9.4	17.9	14.1	21.6		6.4
1929	191.9	30.1	16.5	—	13.6	161.8	88.9	47.3	41.6	72.9	2.6	9.6	18.0	13.2	22.4		7.1
1928	186.3	30.2	17.5	—	12.7	156.1	86.1	—	—	70.0	2.7	9.8	29.6		21.6		6.3
1927	177.9	30.3	18.2	—	12.1	147.6	81.2	—	—	66.4	2.6	9.8	26.9		21.8		5.3
1926	169.2	30.3	19.2	—	11.1	138.9	76.2	—	—	62.7	2.6	9.7	24.0		21.2		5.2
1925	162.9	30.6	20.3	—	10.3	132.3	72.7	—	—	59.6	2.8	9.7	21.3		21.1		4.7
1924	153.4	30.4	21.0	—	9.4	123.0	67.2	—	—	55.8	2.7	9.9	18.6		20.6		4.0
1923	146.7	30.4	21.8	—	8.6	116.3	62.6	—	—	53.7	3.0	10.7	16.3		20.0		3.7
1922	140.2	30.7	22.8	—	7.9	109.5	58.6	—	—	50.9	3.1	10.8	14.1		19.7		3.2
1921	136.3	30.1	23.1	—	7.0	106.2	57.0	—	—	49.2	3.3	10.7	12.8		19.4		3.0
1920	135.7	29.9	23.7	—	6.2	105.8	57.7	—	—	48.1	3.9	10.2	11.7		19.3		3.0
1919	128.3	31.1	25.6	—	5.5	97.2	53.3	—	—	43.9	3.5	8.4	10.1		19.3		2.6
1918	117.5	26.0	20.9	—	5.1	91.5	47.0	—	—	44.5	2.7	7.1	9.6			25.1	
1917	94.5	12.1	7.3	—	4.8	82.4	43.7	—	—	38.7	2.5	6.5	9.3			20.4	
1916	82.2	5.7	1.2	—	4.5	76.5	40.2	—	—	36.3	2.0	5.8	8.4			20.1	

[a]Net federal debt (public and agency) is the outstanding debt held by the public as shown in *The Budget of the United States Government, Fiscal Year 1974*.

[b]Comprised the debt of federally sponsored agencies, in which there is no longer any federal proprietary interest. Includes obligations of the Federal Land Banks, beginning 1947; debt of the Federal Home Loan Banks, beginning 1951; and debts of the Federal National Mortgage Association, Federal Intermediate Credit Banks, and Banks for Cooperatives, beginning 1963.

[c]Long-term debt has a maturity of one year or more; short-term debt, less than one year.

[d]Farm production loans and farm mortgages. Farmers' financial and consumer debt is included in the nonfarm categories.

[e]Financial debt is owed to banks for purchasing or carrying securities, customers' debt to brokers, and debt owed to life insurance companies by policyholders.

Source: U.S. Bureau of Economic Analysis, *Survey of Current Business*.

EXHIBIT 7

■

Debt in the United States (amount outstanding; debt, end of year; nonfederal and federal)

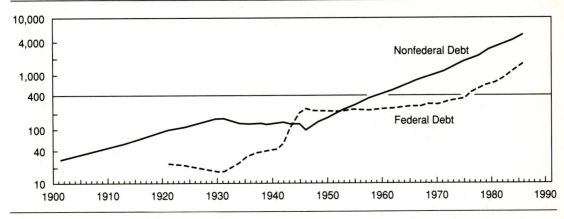

Source: Board of Governors of the Federal Reserve System, *1987 Historical Chart Book*, 42.

EXHIBIT 8

■

Short-Term Interest Rates, Money Market (discount rate, effective date of change; all others, quarterly averages)

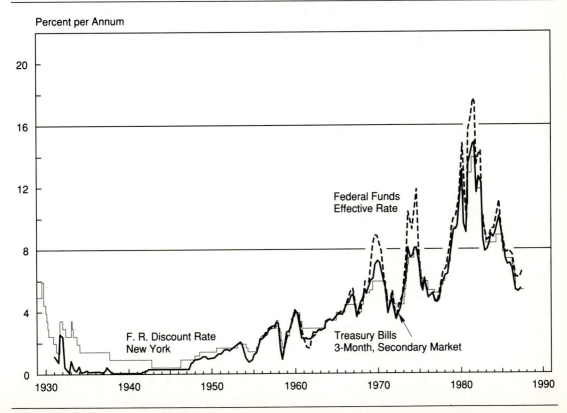

Source: Board of Governors of the Federal Reserve System, *1987 Historical Chart Book*, 98.

The Business Environment: A Retrospective, 1929–1987

EXHIBIT 9

Short-Term Interest Rates, Business Borrowing
(prime rate, effective date of change; commercial paper, quarterly averages)

Percent per Annum

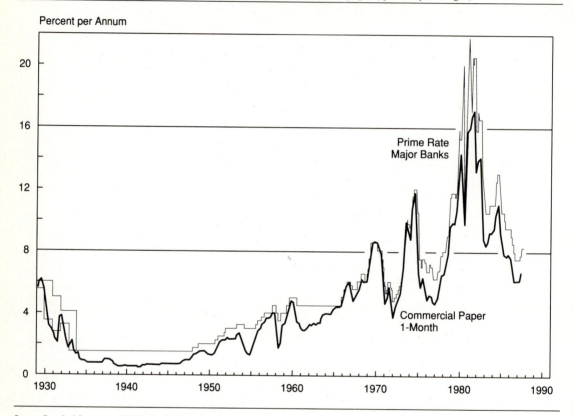

Source: Board of Governors of the Federal Reserve System, *1987 Historical Chart Book*, 99.

The Business Environment: A Retrospective, 1929–1987

EXHIBIT 10A

Long-Term Bond Yields (quarterly averages)

Source: Board of Governors of the Federal Reserve System, *1987 Historical Chart Book*, 97.

EXHIBIT 10B

■

Bond Yields and Interest Rates, 1929–1987

Year and month	U.S. Treasury securities				Corporate bonds (Moody's)		High-grade munici-pal bonds (Stand-ard & Poor's)[4]	New-home mortgage yields (FHLBB)[4]	Com-mercial paper, 6 months[5]	Prime rate charged by banks[6]	Discount rate, Federal Reserve Bank of New York[6]	Federal funds rate[7]
	Bills (new issues)[1]		Constant maturities[2]		Aaa[3]	Baa						
	3-month	6-month	3-year	10-year								
1929					4.73	5.90	4.27		5.85	5.50–6.00	5.16	
1933	0.515				4.49	7.76	4.71		1.73	1.50–4.00	2.56	
1939	.023				3.01	4.96	2.76		.59	1.50	1.00	
1940	.014				2.84	4.75	2.50		.56	1.50	1.00	
1941	.103				2.77	4.33	2.10		.53	1.50	1.00	
1942	.326				2.83	4.28	2.36		.66	1.50	[8]1.00	
1943	.373				2.73	3.91	2.06		.69	1.50	[8]1.00	
1944	.375				2.72	3.61	1.86		.73	1.50	[8]1.00	
1945	.375				2.62	3.29	1.67		.75	1.50	[8]1.00	
1946	.375				2.53	3.05	1.64		.81	1.50	[8]1.00	
1947	.594				2.61	3.24	2.01		1.03	1.50–1.75	1.00	
1948	1.040				2.82	3.47	2.40		1.44	1.75–2.00	1.34	
1949	1.102				2.66	3.42	2.21		1.49	2.00	1.50	
1950	1.218				2.62	3.24	1.98		1.45	2.07	1.59	
1951	1.552				2.86	3.41	2.00		2.16	2.56	1.75	
1952	1.766				2.96	3.52	2.19		2.33	3.00	1.75	
1953	1.931		2.47	2.85	3.20	3.74	2.72		2.52	3.17	1.99	
1954	.953		1.63	2.40	2.90	3.51	2.37		1.58	3.05	1.60	
1955	1.753		2.47	2.82	3.06	3.53	2.53		2.18	3.16	1.89	1.78
1956	2.658		3.19	3.18	3.36	3.88	2.93		3.31	3.77	2.77	2.73
1957	3.267		3.98	3.65	3.89	4.71	3.60		3.81	4.20	3.12	3.11
1958	1.839		2.84	3.32	3.79	4.73	3.56		2.46	3.83	2.15	1.57
1959	3.405	3.832	4.46	4.33	4.38	5.05	3.95		3.97	4.48	3.36	3.30
1960	2.928	3.247	3.98	4.12	4.41	5.19	3.73		3.85	4.82	3.53	3.22
1961	2.378	2.605	3.54	3.88	4.35	5.08	3.46		2.97	4.50	3.00	1.96
1962	2.778	2.908	3.47	3.95	4.33	5.02	3.18		3.26	4.50	3.00	2.68
1963	3.157	3.253	3.67	4.00	4.26	4.86	3.23	5.89	3.55	4.50	3.23	3.18
1964	3.549	3.686	4.03	4.19	4.40	4.83	3.22	5.82	3.97	4.50	3.55	3.50
1965	3.954	4.055	4.22	4.28	4.49	4.87	3.27	5.81	4.38	4.54	4.04	4.07
1966	4.881	5.082	5.23	4.92	5.13	5.67	3.82	6.25	5.55	5.63	4.50	5.11
1967	4.321	4.630	5.03	5.07	5.51	6.23	3.98	6.46	5.10	5.61	4.19	4.22
1968	5.339	5.470	5.68	5.65	6.18	6.94	4.51	6.97	5.90	6.30	5.16	5.66
1969	6.677	6.853	7.02	6.67	7.03	7.81	5.81	7.80	7.83	7.96	5.87	8.20
1970	6.458	6.562	7.29	7.35	8.04	9.11	6.51	8.45	7.71	7.91	5.95	7.18
1971	4.348	4.511	5.65	6.16	7.39	8.56	5.70	7.74	5.11	5.72	4.88	4.66
1972	4.071	4.466	5.72	6.21	7.21	8.16	5.27	7.60	4.73	5.25	4.50	4.43
1973	7.041	7.178	6.95	6.84	7.44	8.24	5.18	7.96	8.15	8.03	6.44	8.73
1974	7.886	7.926	7.82	7.56	8.57	9.50	6.09	8.92	9.84	10.81	7.83	10.50
1975	5.838	6.122	7.49	7.99	8.83	10.61	6.89	9.00	6.32	7.86	6.25	5.82
1976	4.989	5.266	6.77	7.61	8.43	9.75	6.49	9.00	5.34	6.84	5.50	5.04
1977	5.265	5.510	6.69	7.42	8.02	8.97	5.56	9.02	5.61	6.83	5.46	5.54
1978	7.221	7.572	8.29	8.41	8.73	9.49	5.90	9.56	7.99	9.06	7.46	7.93
1979	10.041	10.017	9.71	9.44	9.63	10.69	6.39	10.78	10.91	12.67	10.28	11.19
1980	11.506	11.374	11.55	11.46	11.94	13.67	8.51	12.66	12.29	15.27	11.77	13.36
1981	14.029	13.776	14.44	13.91	14.17	16.04	11.23	14.70	14.76	18.87	13.42	16.38
1982	10.686	11.084	12.92	13.00	13.79	16.11	11.57	15.14	11.89	14.86	11.02	12.26
1983	8.63	8.75	10.45	11.10	12.04	13.55	9.47	12.57	8.89	10.79	8.50	9.09
1984	9.58	9.80	11.89	12.44	12.71	14.19	10.15	12.38	10.16	12.04	8.80	10.23
1985	7.48	7.66	9.64	10.62	11.37	12.72	9.18	11.55	8.01	9.93	7.69	8.10
1986	5.98	6.03	7.06	7.68	9.02	10.39	7.38	10.17	6.39	8.33	6.33	6.81
1987	5.82	6.05	7.68	8.39	9.38	10.58	7.73	9.31	6.85	8.22	5.66	6.66
										High-low	High-low	
1982:												
Jan	12.412	12.930	14.64	14.59	15.18	17.10	13.16	15.25	13.35	15.75–15.75	12.00–12.00	13.22
Feb	13.780	13.709	14.73	14.43	15.27	17.18	12.81	15.12	14.27	17.00–15.75	12.00–12.00	14.78
Mar	12.493	12.621	14.13	13.86	14.58	16.82	12.72	15.67	13.47	16.50–16.50	12.00–12.00	14.68
Apr	12.821	12.861	14.18	13.87	14.46	16.78	12.45	15.84	13.64	16.50–16.50	12.00–12.00	14.94
May	12.148	12.220	13.77	13.62	14.26	16.64	11.99	15.89	13.02	16.50–16.50	12.00–12.00	14.45
June	12.108	12.310	14.48	14.30	14.81	16.92	12.42	15.40	13.79	16.50–16.50	12.00–12.00	14.15
July	11.914	12.236	14.00	13.95	14.61	16.80	12.11	15.70	13.00	16.50–15.50	12.00–11.50	12.59
Aug	9.006	10.105	12.62	13.06	13.71	16.32	11.12	15.68	10.80	15.50–13.50	11.50–10.00	10.12
Sept	8.196	9.539	12.03	12.34	12.94	15.63	10.61	14.98	10.86	13.50–13.50	10.00–10.00	10.31
Oct	7.750	8.299	10.62	10.91	12.12	14.73	9.59	14.41	9.21	13.50–12.00	10.00– 9.50	9.71
Nov	8.042	8.319	9.98	10.55	11.68	14.30	9.97	13.81	8.72	12.00–11.50	9.50– 9.00	9.20
Dec	8.013	8.225	9.88	10.54	11.83	14.14	9.91	13.69	8.50	11.50–11.50	9.00– 8.50	8.95

[1] Rate on new issues within period; bank-discount basis.
[2] Yields on the more actively traded issues adjusted to constant maturities by the Treasury Department.
[3] Series excludes public utility issues for January 17, 1984 through October 11, 1984 due to lack of appropriate issues.
[4] Effective rate (in the primary market) on conventional mortgages, reflecting fees and charges as well as contract rate and assuming, on the average, repayment at end of 10 years. Rates beginning January 1973 not strictly comparable with prior rates. See next page for continuation of table.

EXHIBIT 10B *continued*

Year and month	U.S. Treasury securities				Corporate bonds (Moody's)		High-grade munici-pal bonds (Stand-ard & Poor's)	New-home mortgage yields (FHLBB) [4]	Com-mercial paper, 6 months [5]	Prime rate charged by banks [6]	Discount rate, Federal Reserve Bank of New York [6]	Federal funds rate [7]
	Bills (new issues) [1]		Constant maturities [2]		Aaa [3]	Baa						
	3-month	6-month	3-year	10-year								
1983:												
Jan......	7.810	7.898	9.64	10.46	11.79	13.94	9.45	13.49	8.15	11.50–11.00	8.50– 8.50	8.68
Feb......	8.130	8.233	9.91	10.72	12.01	13.95	9.48	13.16	8.39	11.00–10.50	8.50– 8.50	8.51
Mar......	8.304	8.325	9.84	10.51	11.73	13.61	9.16	13.41	8.48	10.50–10.50	8.50– 8.50	8.77
Apr......	8.252	8.343	9.76	10.40	11.51	13.29	8.96	12.42	8.48	10.50–10.50	8.50– 8.50	8.80
May......	8.19	8.20	9.66	10.38	11.46	13 09	9 03	12.67	8.31	10.50–10.50	8.50– 8.50	8.63
June.....	8.82	8.89	10.32	10.85	11.74	13.37	9.51	12.36	9.03	10.50–10.50	8.50– 8.50	8.98
July	9.12	9.29	10.90	11.38	12.15	13.39	9.46	12.50	9.36	10.50–10.50	8.50– 8.50	9.37
Aug......	9.39	9.53	11.30	11.85	12.51	13.64	9.72	12.38	9.68	11.00–10.50	8.50– 8.50	9.56
Sept	9.05	9.19	11.07	11.65	12.37	13.55	9.57	12.54	9.28	11.00–11.00	8.50– 8.50	9.45
Oct......	8.71	8.90	10.87	11.54	12.25	13.46	9.64	12.25	8.98	11.00–11.00	8.50– 8.50	9.48
Nov......	8.71	8.89	10.96	11.69	12.41	13.61	9.79	12.34	9.09	11.00–11.00	8.50– 8.50	9.34
Dec......	8.96	9.14	11.13	11.83	12.57	13.75	9.90	12.42	9.50	11.00–11.00	8.50– 8.50	9.47
1984:												
Jan......	8.93	9.06	10.93	11.67	12.20	13.65	9.61	12.29	9.18	11.00–11.00	8.50– 8.50	9.56
Feb......	9.03	9.13	11.05	11.84	12.08	13.59	9.63	12.23	9.31	11.00–11.00	8.50– 8.50	9.59
Mar......	9.44	9.58	11.59	12.32	12.57	13.99	9.92	12.02	9.86	11.50–11.00	8.50– 8.50	9.91
Apr......	9.69	9.83	11.98	12.63	12.81	14.31	9.98	12.04	10.22	12.00–11.50	9.00– 8.50	10.29
May......	9.90	10.31	12.75	13.41	13.28	14.74	10.55	12.18	10.87	12.50–12.00	9.00– 9.00	10.32
June.....	9.94	10.55	13.18	13.56	13.55	15.05	10.71	12.10	11.23	13.00–12.50	9.00– 9.00	11.06
July	10.13	10.58	13.08	13.36	13.44	15.15	10.50	12.50	11.34	13.00–13.00	9.00– 9.00	11.23
Aug......	10.49	10.65	12.50	12.72	12.87	14.63	10.03	12.43	11.16	13.00–13.00	9.00– 9.00	· 11.64
Sept	10.41	10.51	12.34	12.52	12.66	14.35	10.17	12.53	10.94	13.00–12.75	9.00– 9.00	11.30
Oct......	9.97	10.05	11.85	12.16	12.63	13.94	10.34	12.77	10.16	12.75–12.00	9.00– 9.00	9.99
Nov......	8.79	8.99	10.90	11.57	12.29	13.48	10.27	12.75	9.06	12.00–11.25	9.00– 8.50	9.43
Dec......	8.16	8.36	10.56	11.50	12.13	13.40	10.04	12.55	8.55	11.25–10.75	8.50– 8.00	8.38
1985:												
Jan......	7.76	8.03	10.43	11.38	12.08	13.26	9.55	12.27	8.15	10.75–10.50	8.00– 8.00	8.35
Feb......	8.22	8.34	10.55	11.51	12.13	13.23	9.66	12.21	8.69	10.50–10.50	8.00– 8.00	8.50
Mar......	8.57	8.92	11.05	11.86	12.56	13.69	9.79	11.92	9.23	10.50–10.50	8.00– 8.00	8.58
Apr......	8.00	8.31	10.49	11.43	12.23	13.51	9.48	12.05	8.47	10.50–10.50	8.00– 8.00	8.27
May......	7.56	7.75	9.75	10.85	11.72	13.15	9.08	12.01	7.88	10.50–10.00	8.00– 7.50	7.97
June.....	7.01	7.16	9.05	10.16	10.94	12.40	8.78	11.75	7.38	10.00– 9.50	7.50– 7.50	7.53
July	7.05	7.16	9.18	10.31	10.97	12.43	8.90	11.34	7.57	9.50– 9.50	7.50– 7.50	7.88
Aug......	7.18	7.35	9.31	10.33	11.05	12.50	9.18	11.24	7.74	9.50– 9.50	7.50– 7.50	7.90
Sept	7.08	7.27	9.37	10.37	11.07	12.48	9.37	11.17	7.86	9.50– 9.50	7.50– 7.50	7.92
Oct......	7.17	7.32	9.25	10.24	11.02	12.36	9.24	11.09	7.79	9.50– 9.50	7.50– 7.50	7.99
Nov......	7.20	7.26	8.88	9.78	10.55	11.99	8.64	11.01	7.69	9.50– 9.50	7.50– 7.50	8.05
Dec......	7.07	7.09	8.40	9.26	10.16	11.58	8.51	10.94	7.62	9.50– 9.50	7.50– 7.50	8.27
1986:												
Jan......	7.04	7.13	8.41	9.19	10.05	11.44	8.06	10.89	7.62	9.50– 9.50	7.50– 7.50	8.14
Feb......	7.03	7.08	8.10	8.70	9.67	11.11	7.44	10.68	7.54	9.50– 9.00	7.50– 7.00	7.86
Mar......	6.59	6.60	7.30	7.78	9.00	10.49	7.07	10.50	7.08	9.00– 8.50	7.00– 6.50	7.48
Apr......	6.06	6.07	6.86	7.30	8.79	10.19	7.32	10.27	6.47	8.50– 8.50	6.50– 6.50	6.99
May......	6.12	6.16	7.27	7.71	9.09	10.29	7.67	10.22	6.53	8.50– 8.50	6.50– 6.50	6.85
June.....	6.21	6.28	7.41	7.80	9.13	10.34	7.98	10.15	6.63	8.50– 8.50	6.50– 6.50	6.92
July	5.84	5.85	6.86	7.30	8.88	10.16	7.62	10.30	6.24	8.50– 8.00	6.50– 6.00	6.56
Aug......	5.57	5.58	6.49	7.17	8.72	10.18	7.31	10.26	5.83	8.00– 7.50	6.00– 5.50	6.17
Sept	5.19	5.31	6.62	7.45	8.89	10.21	7.14	10.17	5.61	7.50– 7.50	5.50– 5.50	5.89
Oct......	5.18	5.26	6.56	7.43	8.86	10.24	7.12	10.02	5.61	7.50– 7.50	5.50– 5.50	5.85
Nov......	5.35	5.42	6.46	7.25	8.68	10.07	6.86	9.91	5.69	7.50– 7.50	5.50– 5.50	6.04
Dec......	5.49	5.53	6.43	7.11	8.49	9.97	6.93	9.69	5.88	7.50– 7.50	5.50– 5.50	6.91
1987:												
Jan......	5.45	5.47	6.41	7.08	8.36	9.72	6.63	9.51	5.76	7.50–7.50	5.50–5.50	6.43
Feb......	5.59	5.60	6.56	7.25	8.38	9.65	6.66	9.23	5.99	7.50–7.50	5.50–5.50	6.10
Mar......	5.56	5.56	6.58	7.25	8.36	9.61	6.71	9.14	6.10	7.50–7.50	5.50–5.50	6.13
Apr......	5.76	5.93	7.32	8.02	8.85	10.04	7.62	9.21	6.50	7.75–7.75	5.50–5.50	6.37
May......	5.75	6.11	8.02	8.61	9.33	10.51	8.10	9.37	7.04	8.25–8.00	5.50–5.50	6.85
June.....	5.69	5.99	7.82	8.40	9.32	10.52	7.89	9.45	7.00	8.25–8.25	5.50–5.50	6.73
July	5.78	5.86	7.74	8.45	9.42	10.61	7.83	9.41	6.72	8.25–8.25	5.50–5.50	6.58
Aug......	6.00	6.14	8.03	8.76	9.67	10.80	7.90	9.38	6.81	8.75–8.25	6.00–5.50	6.73
Sept	6.32	6.57	8.67	9.42	10.18	11.31	8.36	9.37	7.55	8.75–8.75	6.00–6.00	7.22
Oct......	6.40	6.86	8.75	9.52	10.52	11.62	8.84	9.25	7.96	9.25–8.75	6.00–6.00	7.29
Nov......	5.81	6.23	7.99	8.86	10.01	11.23	8.09	9.30	7.17	9.00–8.75	6.00–6.00	6.69
Dec......	5.80	6.36	8.13	8.99	10.11	11.29	8.07	9.15	7.49	8.75–8.75	6.00–6.00	6.77

[5] Bank-discount basis; prior to November 1979, data are for 4–6 months paper.

[6] For monthly data, high and low for the period. Prime rate for 1929–33 and 1947–48 are ranges of the rate in effect during the period.

[7] Since July 19, 1975, the daily effective rate is an average of the rates on a given day weighted by the volume of transactions at these rates. Prior to that date, the daily effective rate was the rate considered most representative of the day's transactions, usually the one at which most transactions occurred.

[8] From October 30, 1942, to April 24, 1946, a preferential rate of 0.50 percent was in effect for advances secured by Government securities maturing in 1 year or less.

Sources: Department of the Treasury, Board of Governors of the Federal Reserve System, Federal Home Loan Bank Board (FHLBB), Moody's Investors Service, and Standard & Poor's Corporation.

Source: *Economic Report of the President, February 1988*, 330–331.

The Business Environment: A Retrospective, 1929–1987

EXHIBIT 11
■
Real Interest Rates, 1931–1987
(Average 90-Day T-Bill − Change in CPI)

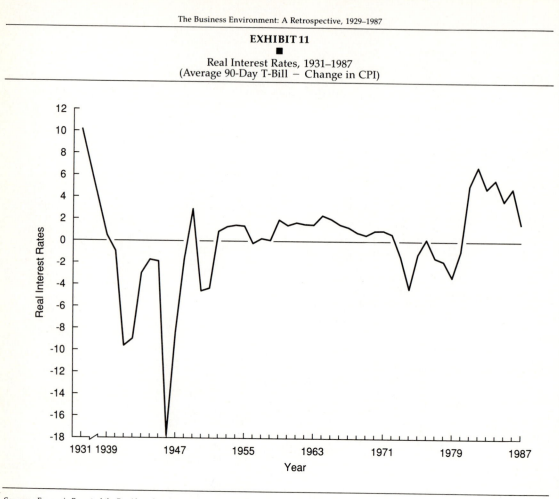

Sources: *Economic Report of the President,* January 1986; and *Stocks, Bonds, Bills, and Inflation* (Chicago: Ibbotson Assoc., 1987).

The Business Environment: A Retrospective, 1929–1987

EXHIBIT 12A

Stock Market Trading Volume
and Prices (quarterly averages)

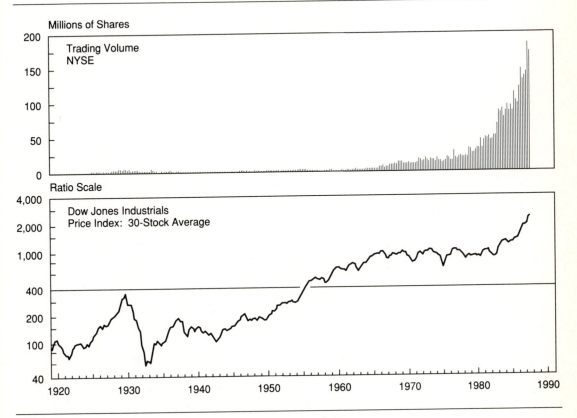

Source: Board of Governors of the Federal Reserve System, *1987 Historical Chart Book*, 94.

EXHIBIT 12B

■

Common Stock Prices and Yields, 1949–1987

Year or month	Common stock prices [1]							Common stock yields (percent) [5]	
	New York Stock Exchange indexes (Dec. 31, 1965=50) [2]					Dow Jones industrial average [3]	Standard & Poor's composite index (1941–43=10) [4]	Dividend-price ratio [6]	Earnings-price ratio [7]
	Composite	Industrial	Transportation	Utility	Finance				
1949	9.02					179.48	15.23	6.59	15.48
1950	10.87					216.31	18.40	6.57	13.99
1951	13.08					257.64	22.34	6.13	11.82
1952	13.81					270.76	24.50	5.80	9.47
1953	13.67					275.97	24.73	5.80	10.26
1954	16.19					333.94	29.69	4.95	8.57
1955	21.54					442.72	40.49	4.08	7.95
1956	24.40					493.01	46.62	4.09	7.55
1957	23.67					475.71	44.38	4.35	7.89
1958	24.56					491.66	46.24	3.97	6.23
1959	30.73					632.12	57.38	3.23	5.78
1960	30.01					618.04	55.85	3.47	5.90
1961	35.37					691.55	66.27	2.98	4.62
1962	33.49					639.76	62.38	3.37	5.82
1963	37.51					714.81	69.87	3.17	5.50
1964	43.76					834.05	81.37	3.01	5.32
1965	47.39					910.88	88.17	3.00	5.59
1966	46.15	46.18	50.26	45.41	44.45	873.60	85.26	3.40	6.63
1967	50.77	51.97	53.51	45.43	49.82	879.12	91.93	3.20	5.73
1968	55.37	58.00	50.58	44.19	65.85	906.00	98.70	3.07	5.67
1969	54.67	57.44	46.96	42.80	70.49	876.72	97.84	3.24	6.08
1970	45.72	48.03	32.14	37.24	60.00	753.19	83.22	3.83	6.45
1971	54.22	57.92	44.35	39.53	70.38	884.76	98.29	3.14	5.41
1972	60.29	65.73	50.17	38.48	78.35	950.71	109.20	2.84	5.50
1973	57.42	63.08	37.74	37.69	70.12	923.88	107.43	3.06	7.12
1974	43.84	48.08	31.89	29.79	49.67	759.37	82.85	4.47	11.59
1975	45.73	50.52	31.10	31.50	47.14	802.49	86.16	4.31	9.15
1976	54.46	60.44	39.57	36.97	52.94	974.92	102.01	3.77	8.90
1977	53.69	57.86	41.09	40.92	55.25	894.63	98.20	4.62	10.79
1978	53.70	58.23	43.50	39.22	56.65	820.23	96.02	5.28	12.03
1979	58.32	64.76	47.34	38.20	61.42	844.40	103.01	5.47	13.46
1980	68.10	78.70	60.61	37.35	64.25	891.41	118.78	5.26	12.66
1981	74.02	85.44	72.61	38.91	73.52	932.92	128.05	5.20	11.96
1982	68.93	78.18	60.41	39.75	71.99	884.36	119.71	5.81	11.60
1983	92.63	107.45	89.36	47.00	95.34	1,190.34	160.41	4.40	8.03
1984	92.46	108.01	85.63	46.44	89.28	1,178.48	160.46	4.64	10.02
1985	108.09	123.79	104.11	56.75	114.21	1,328.23	186.84	4.25	8.12
1986	136.00	155.85	119.87	71.36	147.20	1,792.76	236.34	3.49	6.09
1987	161.70	195.31	140.39	74.30	146.48	2,275.99	286.83	3.08	
1986: Jan	120.16	137.13	115.72	62.46	132.36	1,534.86	208.19	3.90	
Feb	126.43	144.03	124.18	65.18	142.13	1,652.73	219.37	3.72	
Mar	133.97	152.75	128.66	68.06	153.94	1,757.35	232.33	3.50	608
Apr	137.27	157.30	126.17	69.46	155.07	1,807.05	237.97	3.43	
May	137.37	158.59	122.21	68.65	151.28	1,801.80	238.46	3.42	
June	140.82	163.15	120.65	70.69	151.73	1,867.70	245.30	3.36	5.86
July	138.32	158.06	112.03	74.20	150.23	1,809.92	240.18	3.43	
Aug	140.91	160.10	111.24	77.84	152.90	1,843.45	245.00	3.36	
Sept	137.06	156.52	114.06	74.56	145.56	1,813.47	238.27	3.43	6.42
Oct	136.74	156.56	120.04	73.38	143.89	1,817.04	237.36	3.49	
Nov	140.84	162.10	122.27	75.77	142.97	1,883.65	245.09	3.40	
Dec	142.12	163.85	121.26	76.07	144.29	1,924.07	248.61	3.38	5.98
1987: Jan	151.17	175.60	126.61	78.54	153.32	2,065.13	264.51	3.17	
Feb	160.23	189.17	135.49	78.19	158.41	2,202.34	280.93	3.02	
Mar	166.43	198.95	138.55	77.15	162.41	2,292.61	292.47	2.93	5.18
Apr	163.88	199.03	137.91	72.74	150.52	2,302.64	289.32	2.99	
May	163.00	198.78	141.30	71.64	145.97	2,291.11	289.12	3.02	
June	169.58	206.61	150.39	74.25	152.73	2,384.02	301.38	2.92	4.75
July	174.28	214.12	157.48	74.18	152.25	2,481.72	310.09	2.83	
Aug	184.18	226.49	164.02	78.20	160.94	2,655.01	329.36	2.69	
Sept	178.39	219.52	158.58	76.13	154.08	2,570.80	318.66	2.78	4.92
Oct	157.13	189.86	140.95	73.27	137.35	2,224.59	280.16	3.25	
Nov	137.21	163.42	117.57	69.86	118.30	1,931.86	245.01	3.66	
Dec	134.88	162.19	115.85	67.39	111.47	1,910.07	240.96	3.71	

[1] Averages of daily closing prices, except New York Stock Exchange data through May 1964 are averages of weekly closing prices.
[2] Includes all the stocks (more than 1,500) listed on the New York Stock Exchange.
[3] Includes 30 stocks.
[4] Includes 500 stocks.
[5] Standard & Poor's series, based on 500 stocks in the composite index.
[6] Aggregate cash dividends (based on latest known annual rate) divided by aggregate market value based on Wednesday closing prices. Monthly data are averages of weekly figures; annual data are averages of monthly figures.
[7] Quarterly data are ratio of earnings (after taxes) for 4 quarters ending with particular quarter to price index for last day of that quarter. Annual ratios are averages of quarterly ratios.

Note.—All data relate to stocks listed on the New York Stock Exchange.

Sources: New York Stock Exchange, Dow Jones & Co., Inc., and Standard & Poor's Corporation.

Source: *Economic Report of the President*, February 1988, 356.

EXHIBIT 13
■
Year-by-Year Total Returns on Common Stocks, 1926–1987

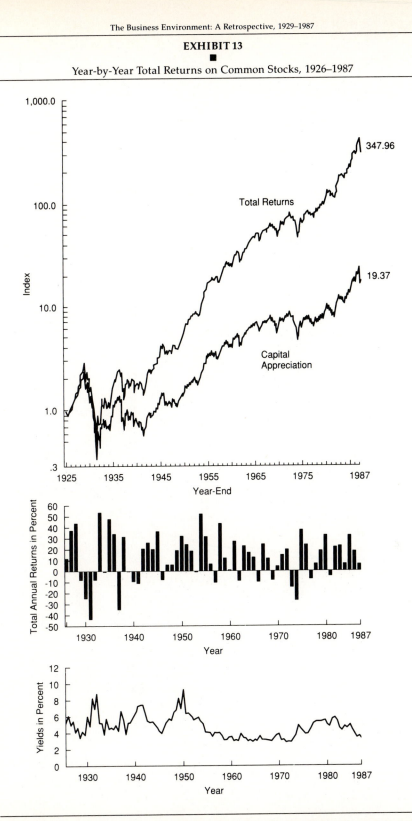

Source: Ibbotson, Roger G., and Rex A. Sinquefield, *Stocks, Bonds, Bills, and Inflation* (SBBI), 1982, updated in *SBBI 1988 Yearbook*, p. 29, (and in the Spring, 1988 update), Ibbotson Associates, Chicago. Reprinted with permission.

The Business Environment: A Retrospective, 1929–1987

EXHIBIT 14
■

Wealth Indexes of Investments
in the U.S. Capital Markets, 1926–1987

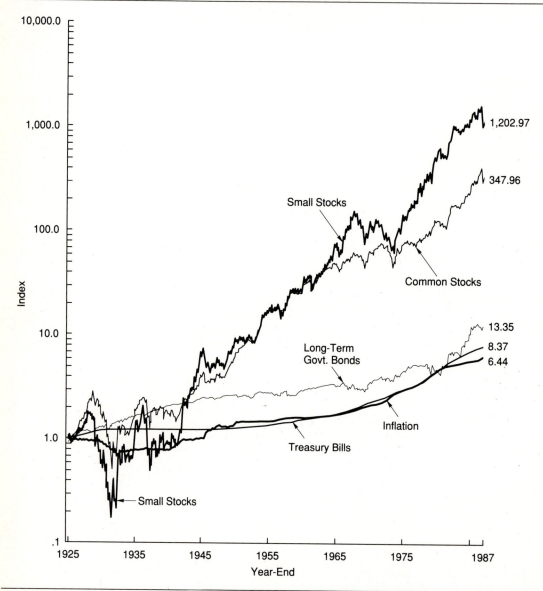

Source: Ibbotson, Roger G., and Rex A. Sinquefield, *Stocks, Bonds, Bills, and Inflation* (SBBI), 1982, updated in *SBBI 1988 Yearbook*, p. 21, (and in the Spring, 1988 update), Ibbotson Associates, Chicago. Reprinted with permission.

The Business Environment: A Retrospective, 1929–1987

EXHIBIT 15

■

Three Measures of Inflation

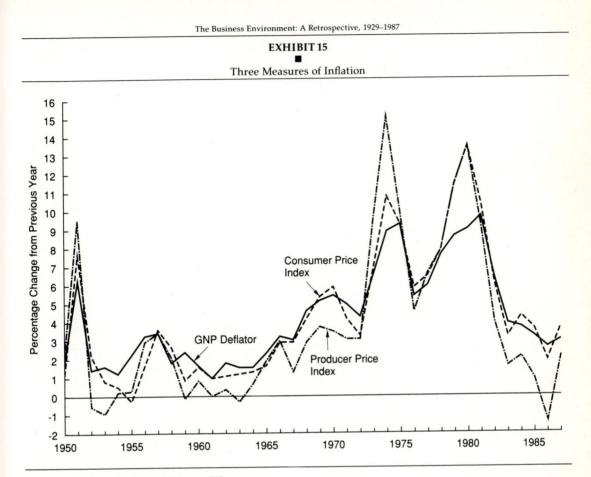

Source: *Economic Report of the President*, February 1987.

EXHIBIT 16

■

Federal Outlays as Percent of GNP

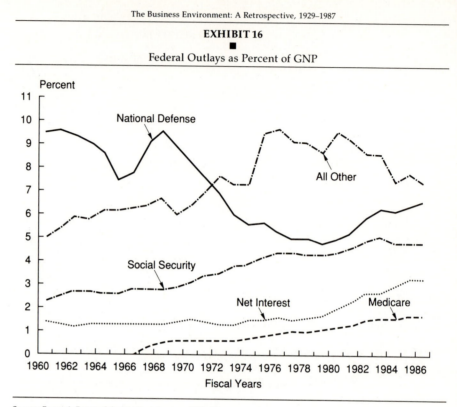

Source: *Economic Report of the President,* January 1988, 70.

The Business Environment: A Retrospective, 1929–1987

EXHIBIT 17
■

Stock and Bond Yields (earnings/price ratio: annually,
1926–1935; end of quarter, 1936; all others, quarterly)

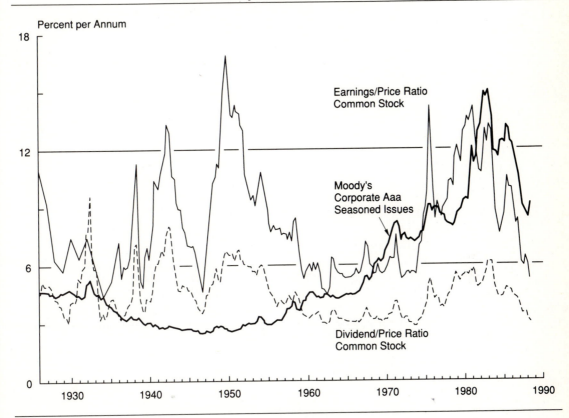

Source: Board of Governors of the Federal Reserve System, *1987 Historical Chart Book*, 95.

The Business Environment: A Retrospective, 1929–1987

EXHIBIT 18
■
Real Stock Returns, 1926–1986

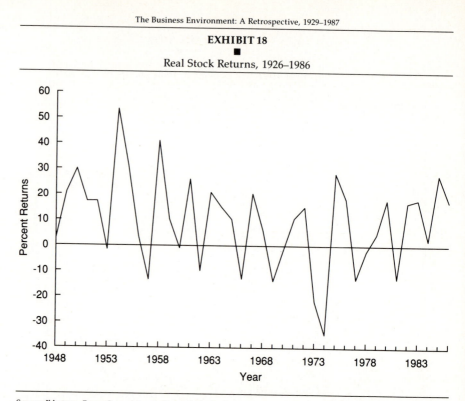

Source: Ibbotson, Roger G., and Rex A. Sinquefield, *Stocks, Bonds, Bills, and Inflation* (SBBI), 1982, updated in *SBBI 1986 Yearbook*, p. 46, (and in the Spring, 1986 update), Ibbotson Associates, Chicago. Reprinted with permission.

The Business Environment: A Retrospective, 1929–1987

EXHIBIT 19
■
Corporate Profits
(seasonally adjusted annual rates, quarterly)

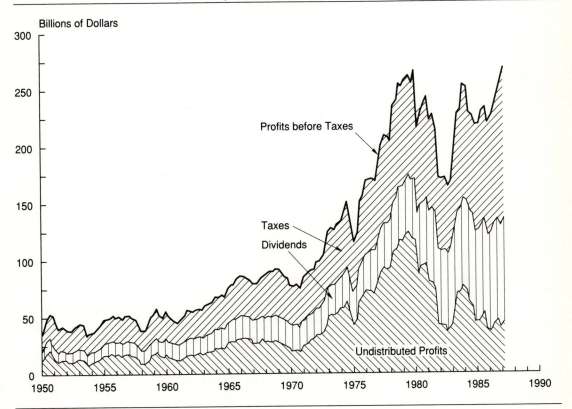

Source: Board of Governors of the Federal Reserve System, *1987 Historical Chart Book*, 60.

The Business Environment: A Retrospective, 1929–1987

EXHIBIT 20
■
Return on S&P 500 Companies' Assets and Equity

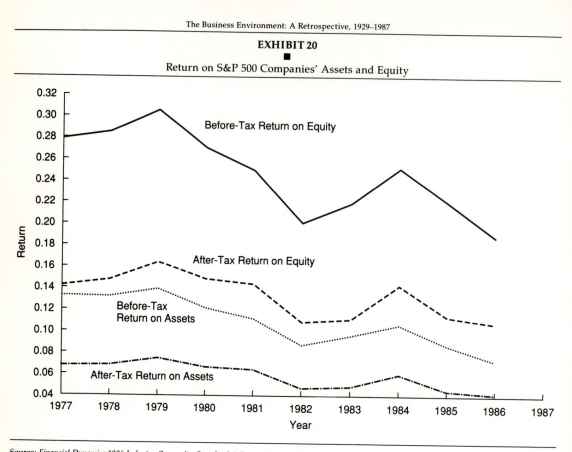

Source: *Financial Dynamics 1986 Industry Composite,* Standard & Poor's Compustat Services, Inc.

The Business Environment: A Retrospective, 1929–1987

EXHIBIT 21

■

Capital Expenditures, External Funds Raised,
Undistributed Profits (nonfinancial corporations; annually,
1950–1951; seasonally adjusted annual rates, quarterly 1952 onward)

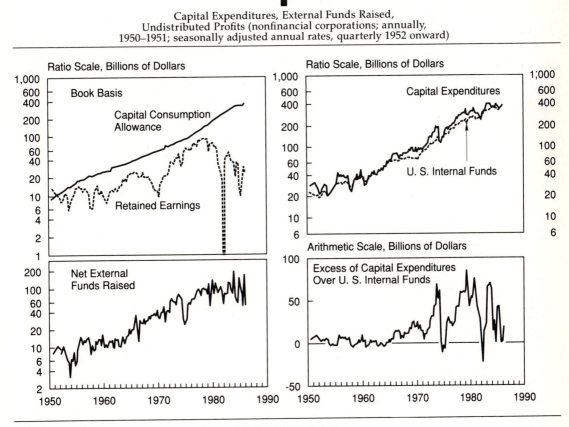

Source: Board of Governors of the Federal Reserve System, *1987 Historical Chart Book*, 61.

The Business Environment: A Retrospective, 1929–1987

EXHIBIT 22
■

Total Corporate Debt and Its Composition
(ratios for nonfinancial corporations; end of year,
1950–1951; seasonally adjusted, end of quarter, 1952-1986)

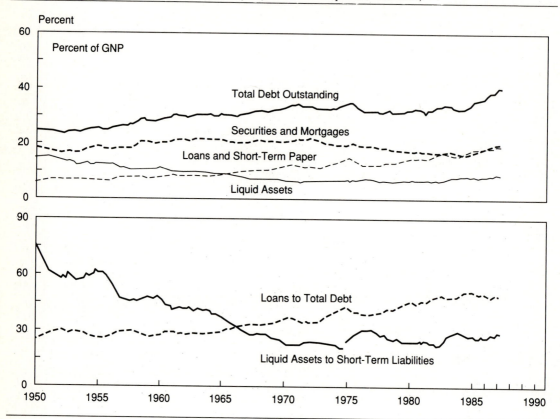

Source: Board of Governors of the Federal Reserve System, *1987 Historical Chart Book*, 64.

The Business Environment: A Retrospective, 1929–1987

EXHIBIT 23

U.S. International Transactions (current account, 1950–1986)

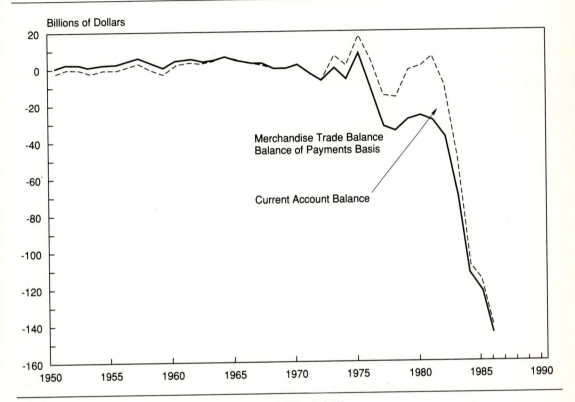

Billions of Dollars

Merchandise Trade Balance
Balance of Payments Basis

Current Account Balance

Source: Board of Governors of the Federal Reserve System, *1987 Historical Chart Book*, 100.

The Business Environment: A Retrospective, 1929–1987

EXHIBIT 24

Corporate Security Issues: Gross Proceeds, Annual Totals

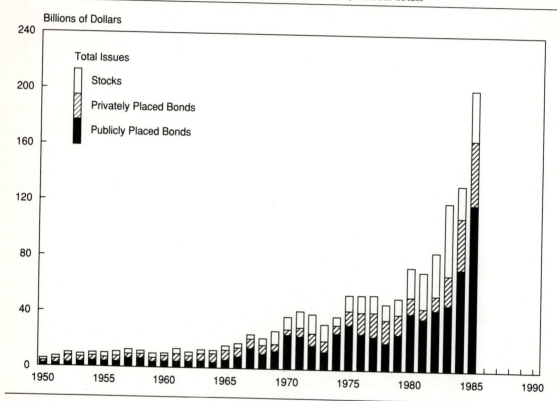

Source: Board of Governors of the Federal Reserve System, *1986 Historical Chart Book*, 59.

The Business Environment: A Retrospective, 1929–1987

EXHIBIT 25

■

Labor Force, Employment, and
Unemployment (seasonally adjusted, quarterly)

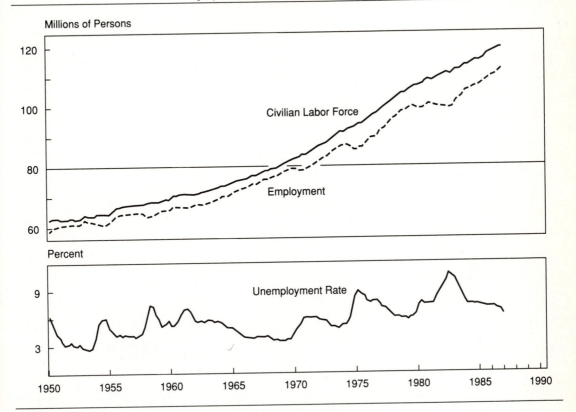

Millions of Persons

Civilian Labor Force

Employment

Percent

Unemployment Rate

Source: Board of Governors of the Federal Reserve System, *1987 Historical Chart Book*, 20.

The Business Environment: A Retrospective, 1929–1987

EXHIBIT 26

■

Determinants of Business Fixed Investments 1955–1982 (percent, except as noted)

| Year | Real investment as percent of real GNP | Capacity utilization rate in manufacturing [1] | Cash flow as percent of GNP [2] | Nonfinancial corporations | | | | Ratio of market value to replacement cost of net assets [5] |
| | | | | Rate of return on depreciable assets [3] | | Rate of return on stockholders' equity [4] | | |
				Before tax	After tax	Before tax	After tax	
1955	9.3	87.1	9.3	19.8	9.8	13.1	6.2	1.112
1956	9.7	86.4	8.9	16.8	7.9	11.6	5.4	1.104
1957	9.7	83.7	8.9	15.2	7.4	10.5	5.0	1.018
1958	8.7	75.2	8.6	12.8	6.5	8.4	3.9	1.041
1959	8.8	81.9	9.3	16.4	8.5	10.5	5.1	1.252
1960	9.1	80.2	8.9	15.0	8.0	9.9	5.0	1.222
1961	8.8	77.4	8.8	15.1	8.2	9.5	4.6	1.350
1962	9.0	81.6	9.4	17.4	10.3	11.2	6.1	1.282
1963	9.0	83.5	9.7	18.8	11.2	12.1	6.7	1.419
1964	9.4	85.6	10.1	20.2	12.5	13.3	7.8	1.521
1965	10.5	89.6	10.6	22.1	14.0	15.5	9.6	1.621
1966	11.0	91.1	10.3	21.8	13.7	15.2	9.2	1.466
1967	10.4	86.9	10.0	19.3	12.4	13.4	8.2	1.480
1968	10.3	87.1	9.4	18.9	11.3	13.8	8.0	1.523
1969	10.7	86.2	8.6	16.5	9.7	12.5	7.1	1.353
1970	10.5	79.3	7.8	12.8	7.9	8.8	4.7	1.091
1971	10.0	78.4	8.3	13.5	8.5	9.9	5.7	1.176
1972	10.2	83.5	8.6	14.3	9.1	10.5	6.2	1.258
1973	11.0	87.6	8.0	14.3	8.7	12.8	8.3	1.157
1974	10.9	83.8	7.0	11.0	6.1	11.2	7.3	.827
1975	9.7	72.9	9.0	11.9	7.7	8.5	5.2	.811
1976	9.7	79.5	9.3	12.9	7.9	8.6	4.8	.911
1977	10.2	81.9	9.7	13.9	8.7	10.2	6.3	.797
1978	11.0	84.4	9.5	13.7	8.6	10.7	6.8	.761
1979	11.5	85.7	8.9	12.1	7.4	10.2	6.6	.709
1980	11.3	79.1	8.7	10.5	6.6	8.4	5.5	.666
1981	11.4	78.5	11.0	11.0	7.7	7.7	5.1	.694
1982 [p]	11.2	69.8	9.6	9.5	7.5	([6])	([6])	.690

[1] Federal Reserve Board index.
[2] Cash flow calculated as after-tax profits plus capital consumption allowance plus inventory valuation adjustment.
[3] Profits plus capital consumption adjustment and inventory valuation adjustment plus net interest paid divided by the stock of depreciable assets valued at current replacement cost.
[4] Profits corrected for inflation effects divided by net worth (physical capital component valued at current replacement cost).
[5] Equity plus interest-bearing debt divided by current replacement cost of net assets.
[6] Not available.

Sources: Department of Commerce (Bureau of Economic Analysis), Board of Governors of the Federal Reserve System, and Council of Economic Advisers.

Source: *Economic Report of the President*, February 1983, p. 263.

The Business Environment: A Retrospective, 1929–1987

EXHIBIT 27

∎

Basic Series: Summary Statistics of Annual Returns, 1926–1987

Series	Geometric Mean	Arithmetic Mean	Standard Deviation	Distribution
Common Stocks	9.9%	12.0%	21.1%	
Small Company Stocks	12.1	17.7	35.9	
Long-Term Corporate Bonds	4.9	5.2	8.5	
Long-Term Government Bonds	4.3	4.6	8.5	
Intermediate-Term Government Bonds	4.8	4.9	5.5	
U.S. Treasury Bills	3.5	3.5	3.4	
Inflation Rates	3.0	3.2	4.8	

-90%　　　　　　　　0%　　　　　　　　90%

Source: Ibbotson, Roger G., and Rex A. Sinquefield, *Stocks, Bonds, Bills, and Inflation* (SBBI), 1982, updated in *SBBI 1988 Yearbook*, p. 25 (and in the Spring, 1988 update), Ibbotson Associates, Chicago. Reprinted with permission.

The Business Environment: A Retrospective, 1929–1987

EXHIBIT 28

■

400 Industrials[a] Per Share Data—Adjusted to
Stock Price Index Level; Average of Stock Price Indexes, 1941–1943 = 10

	Sales	Oper. Profit	Profit Margin (%)	Depr.	Income Taxes	Earnings		Dividends	
						Per Share	% of Sales	Per Share	% of Earn.
1956	54.73	8.36	15.27	2.04	2.96	3.50	6.40	1.84	52.57
1957	55.81	8.79	15.75	2.41	2.87	3.53	6.33	1.94	54.96
1958	53.48	7.70	14.40	2.38	2.40	2.95	5.52	1.86	63.05
1959	57.83	8.84	15.29	2.47	2.99	3.47	6.00	1.95	56.20
1960	59.47	8.73	14.68	2.56	2.87	3.40	5.72	2.00	58.82
1961	59.51	8.75	14.70	2.66	2.80	3.37	5.66	2.07	61.42
1962	64.63	9.81	15.18	2.89	3.16	3.83	5.93	2.20	57.44
1963	68.50	10.73	15.66	3.04	3.51	4.24	6.19	2.36	55.66
1964	73.19	11.67	15.94	3.24	3.70	4.85	6.63	2.58	53.20
1965	80.69	13.11	16.25	3.52	4.14	5.50	6.82	2.82	51.27
1966	88.46	14.48	16.37	3.87	4.35	5.87	6.64	2.95	50.26
1967	91.86	14.28	15.55	4.25	4.11	5.62	6.12	2.97	52.85
1968	101.49	16.08	15.84	4.56	5.14	6.16	6.07	3.16	51.30
1969	108.53	16.63	15.32	4.87	5.14	6.13	5.65	3.25	53.02
1970	109.85	15.54	14.15	5.17	4.23	5.41	4.92	3.20	59.15
1971	118.23	17.22	14.56	5.45	4.98	5.97	5.04	3.16	52.93
1972	128.79	19.39	15.06	5.76	5.90	6.83	5.30	3.22	47.14
1973	149.22	23.64	15.84	6.25	7.59	8.89	5.96	3.46	38.92
1974	182.10	27.97	15.36	6.86	10.22	9.61	5.28	3.71	38.61
1975	185.16	26.63	14.38	7.36	9.40	8.58	4.63	3.72	43.36
1976	202.66	29.23	14.42	7.58	10.21	10.69	5.27	4.22	39.48
1977	224.24	32.20	14.36	8.53	11.14	11.45	5.11	4.95	43.23
1978	251.32	36.19	14.40	9.64	12.14	13.04	5.19	5.37	41.18
1979	292.38	42.01	14.37	10.82	14.02	16.29	5.57	5.92	36.34
1980	327.36	43.08	13.16	12.37	13.67	16.12	4.92	6.49	40.26
1981	344.31	44.50	12.92	13.82	12.95	16.74	4.86	7.01	41.88
1982	333.86	42.67	12.78	15.30	10.95	13.20	3.95	7.13	54.02
1983	334.07	45.57	13.64	15.67	12.12	14.77	4.42	7.32	49.56
1984	379.70	51.50	13.56	16.31	14.15	18.11	4.77	7.51	41.47
R1985	398.42	53.23	13.36	18.19	13.68	15.28	3.84	7.87	51.51
P1986	388.44	52.36	13.48	19.44	10.95	14.57	3.75	8.15	55.94

NOTE: 1983 data include results of 'old' A.T.&T.; excls. $5.5 bil. charge; 1984 data reflect A.T.&T. divestiture.
[a]Based on 70 individual groups.
Stock Price Indexes for this group extend back to 1918.
Source: Standard & Poor's *1987 Analysts' Handbook*, 181.

Price 1941-1943 = 10		Price/Earn. Ratio		Div. Yields %		Book Value		Work-ing Capital	Capital Expend-itures
High	Low	High	Low	High	Low	Per Share	% Return		
53.28	45.71	15.22	13.06	4.03	3.45	26.35	13.28	13.91	4.14
53.25	41.98	15.08	11.89	4.62	3.64	29.44	11.99	13.50	4.84
58.97	43.20	19.99	14.64	4.31	3.15	30.66	9.62	14.27	3.58
65.32	57.02	18.82	16.43	3.42	2.99	32.26	10.76	14.93	3.65
65.02	55.34	19.12	16.28	3.61	3.08	33.74	10.08	15.29	4.23
76.69	60.87	22.76	18.06	3.40	2.70	34.85	9.67	15.84	3.97
75.22	54.80	19.64	14.31	4.01	2.92	36.37	10.53	16.85	4.41
79.25	65.48	18.69	15.44	3.60	2.98	38.17	11.11	17.64	4.41
91.29	79.74	18.82	16.44	3.24	2.83	40.23	12.06	18.07	5.71
98.55	86.43	17.92	15.71	3.26	2.86	43.50	12.64	18.80	6.87
100.60	77.89	17.14	13.27	3.79	2.93	45.59	12.88	19.48	8.26
106.15	85.31	18.89	15.18	3.48	2.80	47.78	11.76	20.74	8.35
118.03	95.05	19.16	15.43	3.32	2.68	50.21	12.27	21.08	8.65
116.24	97.75	18.96	15.95	3.32	2.80	51.70	11.86	21.05	9.70
102.87	75.58	19.01	13.97	4.23	3.11	52.65	10.28	20.70	10.25
115.84	99.36	19.40	16.64	3.18	2.73	55.28	10.80	22.61	9.96
132.95	112.19	19.47	16.43	2.87	2.42	58.34	11.71	24.41	10.08
134.54	103.37	15.13	11.63	3.35	2.57	62.84	14.15	26.49	11.65
111.65	69.53	11.62	7.24	5.34	3.32	67.81	14.17	28.47	14.65
107.40	77.71	12.52	9.06	4.79	3.46	70.84	12.11	30.47	14.43
120.89	101.64	11.31	9.51	4.15	3.49	76.26	14.02	31.89	14.92
118.92	99.88	10.39	8.72	4.96	4.16	82.21	13.93	33.28	17.02
118.71	95.52	9.10	7.33	5.63	4.53	89.34	14.60	34.88	19.70
124.49	107.08	7.64	6.57	5.53	4.76	98.71	16.50	36.32	26.44
160.96	111.09	9.99	6.89	5.84	4.03	108.33	14.88	36.52	29.86
157.02	125.93	9.38	7.52	5.57	4.46	116.06	14.42	35.98	33.03
159.66	114.08	12.10	8.64	6.25	4.47	118.60	11.13	34.41	31.30
194.84	154.95	13.19	10.49	4.72	3.76	122.32	12.07	36.55	25.24
191.48	167.75	10.57	9.26	4.48	3.92	123.99	14.61	38.94	30.08
235.75	182.24	15.43	11.93	4.32	3.34	125.89	12.14	39.32	31.42
282.77	324.88	19.41	15.43	3.62	2.88	124.53	11.70	40.61	29.24

The Business Environment: A Retrospective, 1929–1987

EXHIBIT 29
■

Standard & Poor's 400 Per Share Data—Adjusted to Stock Price Index Level
Average of Stock Price Indexes, 1941–1943 = 10 (millions of dollars except as noted)

Income Account	1986	1985	1984	1983	1979	1978	1977
Sales	379.81	398.42	379.70	334.00	292.38	251.32	224.24
Costs and expenses	329.74	345.19	328.31	288.44	250.37	215.13	192.05
Operating income	50.07	53.22	51.50	45.56	42.01	36.19	32.30
Other income	4.09	3.64	6.13	5.12	4.14	2.84	2.48
Total income	54.15	56.87	57.63	50.69	46.15	39.02	34.67
Depreciation	19.17	18.19	16.31	15.67	10.82	9.64	8.53
Interest	9.59	9.24	8.54	7.62	4.58	3.84	3.25
Minority interest	0.17	0.16	0.18	0.21	0.29	0.23	0.20
Income taxes	10.74	13.68	14.15	12.12	14.02	12.14	11.14
Net income	14.48	15.60	18.45	15.07	16.45	13.17	11.56
Preferred dividends	0.27	0.35	0.36	0.34	0.19	0.16	0.14
Savings from common stock equivalents	0.02	0.03	0.03	0.03	0.03	0.03	0.03
Common earnings	14.23	15.28	18.11	14.76	16.29	13.04	11.45
Common dividends	8.94	7.87	7.51	7.32	5.92	5.37	4.95
Balance after dividends	5.29	7.41	10.60	7.45	10.38	7.67	6.50

Financial Ratios =	1986	1985	1984	1983	1979	1978	1977
Current ratio	NA	NA	NA	NA	1.6	1.7	1.8
Quick ratio	NA	NA	NA	NA	0.9	1.0	1.0
Debt to total assets (percent)	27	26	25	23	22	22	22
Times interest earned	3.6	4.2	4.8	4.6	7.7	7.6	8.0
Inventory turnover	7.0	6.9	7.3	8.0	7.2	7.2	6.9
Total assets turnover	1.1	1.2	1.2	1.2	1.3	1.3	1.3
Profit margin (percent)	13.18	13.36	13.56	13.64	14.37	14.40	14.36
Return on total assets (percent)	3.97	4.41	5.80	5.10	7.24	6.58	6.49

continued

Balance Sheet							
Assets	*1986*	*1985*	*1984*	*1983*	*1979*	*1978*	*1977*
Cash and equivalent	26.61	22.76	21.01	20.52	15.27	15.34	14.10
Receivables	47.58	47.78	47.39	45.36	38.80	33.39	28.71
Income tax refund	0.40	0.22	0.14	0.29	0.07	0.04	0.08
Inventories	54.51	57.85	51.68	41.89	40.42	35.09	32.35
Other current assets	8.27	7.95	6.18	4.99	3.19	2.68	2.36
Total current assets	NA	NA	NA	NA	97.65	86.44	77.53
Net property, plant, and equipment	152.26	150.20	138.79	142.26	106.89	94.15	83.64
Inventory and advertising to unconsolidated subsidiaries	17.13	16.44	16.62	13.13	10.03	8.89	7.96
Intangibles	14.56	9.63	5.94	3.98	2.69	2.22	1.68
Other assets	36.98	33.86	24.30	16.94	7.65	6.43	5.54
Total assets	358.28	346.68	312.04	289.35	225.00	198.24	176.44

Note: Data presented in the above format reflect results for only those companies which have reported; no estimates are used. This holds true for all industry groups.
Source: Standard & Poor's *1987 Analyst Handbook*, 182.

Liabilities	*1986*	*1985*	*1984*	*1983*	*1979*	*1978*	*1977*
Notes payable	25.56	27.53	19.90	13.40	8.01	5.89	5.63
Current portion of long-term debt	4.68	3.64	3.79	2.52	1.79	1.85	1.33
Accounts payable	32.62	34.47	30.07	27.41	23.75	19.88	17.14
Income tax payable	8.20	8.25	7.82	6.84	7.26	5.87	5.13
Accrued expenses	22.66	22.28	18.31	15.68	12.61	11.11	9.40
Other current liabilities	12.45	11.07	10.27	9.09	7.91	6.96	5.62
Total current liabilities	NA	NA	NA	NA	61.33	51.56	44.25
Long-term debt	65.83	59.22	53.25	50.08	39.22	36.23	32.09
Deferred income tax	21.00	19.99	17.85	18.49	10.83	8.93	7.41
Minority interest	1.71	1.56	1.47	1.84	2.06	1.83	1.54
Other liabilities	22.16	18.90	15.11	13.93	6.90	5.45	4.68
Preferred stock	2.89	3.51	3.56	3.21	2.19	1.82	1.49
Common stock	10.44	9.85	10.29	9.53	10.37	10.34	10.05
Capital surplus	20.49	20.30	17.30	20.71	11.90	11.29	10.75
Retained earnings	107.61	106.13	103.07	96.64	80.20	70.78	64.19
Total liabilities	358.28	346.68	312.04	289.35	225.00	198.24	176.44

■

APPENDIX
Coming Full Circle: One View

1929 AND ALL THAT

By Robert L. Bartley

Back in 1985, moved by a sense that the world economy was sailing troubled waters, I spent the summer reading a stack of books about the Great Depression. Though inflation had been conquered and economic recovery was well under way, the outlook was marred by such portents as the Third World debt problem, curiously high interest rates, complaints about an overvalued dollar, and especially a rebirth of protectionism. Were we skirting the edge of some huge crackup?

Two years ago, it developed, the 1920s exhibited many parallels with the 1980s: a booming stock market, a strong economy sparked by tax cuts, a countercurrent in agricultural distress, exchange-rate disruptions, an international debt crisis—the "war debts." The history of the Great Depression may reveal mistakes that can be avoided a second time—see "Toying with Depression" in this space Sept. 5, 1985. After the stock market crash of '87, of course, the parallels, and the need for understanding, seem all the more pressing.

Understanding begins with the obvious: The Great Depression was an international event. Anyone perusing a wide sample of the literature is likely to be drawn away from the competing domestic explanations, finding more satisfaction in the writers who focus on the international accounts. Their explanation of the depth and severity of the Depression is this: The U.S. blocked the world economy by closing down its international accounts. The capital account closed in 1928, with an abrupt end to the U.S. lending that had sustained Germany and South America. The trade account closed in 1930, with the Smoot-Hawley tariff.

Source: Robert L. Bartley, "1929 and All That," *The Wall Street Journal*, November 24, 1987, p. 28. Reprinted by permission of *The Wall Street Journal*, © Dow Jones & Company, Inc., 1987. All Rights Reserved.

FIGURE A–1
■
The World in Depression:
The Contracting Spiral of World Trade

Total imports of 75 countries, monthly values in terms of the old U.S. gold dollars (millions).

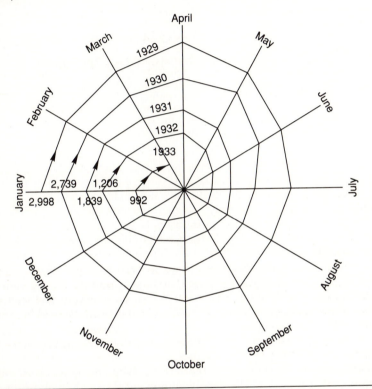

Source: Charles P. Kindleberger, "Ther World in Depression, 1929–1939." © 1973 The Regents of the University of California. Reprinted with permission from the University of California Press.

Unable either to borrow or sell in the U.S., other nations could not buy in the U.S. Many nations of course passed retaliatory tariffs. Many also engaged in competitive devaluations, hoping to improve exports through a cheaper currency; these became known as "beggar-thy-neighbor" policies. World trade imploded, as Charles Kindleberger's nearby chart shows so graphically. Each nation found that without the interdependent links with international trade and capital, prosperity could no longer continue. The Great Depression, in short, was caused by massive interruptions of international flows of trade and capital.

It follows that the Great Depression was *not* caused by the 1929 stock market crash. Popular mythology holds that the market boomed until Black Thursday and then collapsed to nothing, sending brokers jumping out of windows and unemployment leaping to 20% the next day. It did not happen that way at all. What the stock market did was trace economic and political events as they unfolded.

Kindleberger's Causalities
_____

From Charles P. Kindleberger's "The World in Depression, 1929–1939":

The explanation of this book is that the 1929 depression was so wide, so deep, and so long because the international economic system was rendered unstable by British inability and United States unwillingness to assume responsibility for stabilizing it in three particulars: (a) maintaining a relatively open market for distress goods; (b) providing counter-cyclical long-term lending; and (c) discounting in crisis. The shocks to the system from the overproduction of certain primary products such as wheat; from the 1927 reduction of interest rates in the United States (if it was one); from the halt of lending to Germany in 1928; or from the stock-market crash of 1929 were not so great. Shocks of similar magnitude had been handled in the stock-market break in the spring of 1920 and the 1927 recession in the United States. The world economic system was unstable unless some country stabilized it, as Britain had done in the nineteenth century and up to 1913. In 1929, the British couldn't and the United States wouldn't. When every country turned to protect its national private interest, the world public interest went down the drain, and with it the private interests of all.

On Sept. 3, 1929, the Dow Jones Industrials reached 381, a high not seen again for a quarter-century. On that day Congress returned from its summer recess to its task of debating the tariff. The market started to slide, unexceptionally until Oct. 24, Black Thursday. On that morning the market collapsed. At their low for the day, the Dow Jones Industrials were off 33 points, but for many stocks there seemed no buyers. The stock tape fell hopelessly behind, and exchanges outside of New York closed. Eleven prominent speculators indeed committed suicide. But in the afternoon, heads of large New York banks organized market support and quelled the plunge. The Dow finished Black Thursday down six. The papers that morning, Jude Wanniski has observed, had announced the breakup of the coalition against the tariff—making clear it would be extended beyond agricultural products.

The Great Crash came the next Monday and Tuesday. Over the two days the Dow fell from 298 to 230. The average zigzagged down further to hit the 1929 low of 198 on Nov. 13. Then came "the suckers' rally," which by April 1930 had carried the average back to 294, nearly wiping out the crash. Opposition to the tariff had been rising, but started to ebb. On June 14, 1930, just before President Hoover finally announced he would sign the bill, the Dow stood at 244. When the 30-stock average was first drawn up on Oct. 1, 1928, it had stood at 240. All that had happened was the loss of the big bull market in 1929; stocks remained at levels previously considered not only healthy but high, until the tariff went into effect.

Over the next two years, the average fell from 244 to 41.

The reasons for the real collapse are evident in Prof. Kindleberger's chart; trade closed and prosperity set. The stock market did not cause, it reflected. In an important sense, it anticipated. The individual decisions of myriad investors added up to a collective warning that errors were in the process of being made. The Great Crash gave timely warning, when there was still time to change course and avert the brink. If President Hoover had heeded the advice offered in a petition by 1,028 economists, had vetoed Smoot-Hawley, the Great Depression would in all likelihood have been an ordinary business correction despite the stock market crash.

Since World War II, indeed, only about half of sharp stock market declines have been followed by recessions. In the other half, policy makers got the message. The most notable example is 1962, the nearest thing to a crash between

1929 and 1987. The Dow Jones Industrials fell 26% in three months, compared with 48% in 2½ months in 1929. So 1962 was about half of a Great Crash, but nothing happened in the real economy. All that happened was that the Kennedy administration was smart enough to stop picking fights with steel companies. The generalized antibusiness atmosphere the markets had started to anticipate did not materialize. Stocks started to recover, and the real economy marched on unhindered. Indeed, with the 1964 tax cuts, it entered one of its best periods of the century.

Which, of course, brings us to 1987. From the high of 2722 on Aug. 25 to the low of 1738 on Oct. 19, stocks fell 36%. We have just experienced a market crash halfway between 1929, which ushered in a depression, and 1962, which did nothing. The question is not, is depression inevitable? The question is, what is the market trying to tell us?

There are two general theories of the stock market. One is called "efficient markets," which holds that the collective action of individuals neatly incorporates information about future prospects, so that a rise in the markets means something good has happened, and a fall something bad. The other is called "popular delusions and the madness of crowds," which holds that the market is an untamed beast. Those of us who hold with efficient markets have to recognize that the crowd-psychology folks often make a lot of money playing the market; their view should not be too lightly dismissed. We can pretty safely dismiss, though, the folks who believe in crowd psychology when the market contradicts their analysis, and efficient markets when it confirms their analysis.

This includes the whole twin-deficits crowd, who have been screaming that the market was wrong all during its ascent, and are now breaking arms patting themselves on the back because the money has proved them right. It would of course be nice to balance the federal deficit at some stable level of taxing and spending, but in recent months the news has been that the deficit is shrinking, not growing. The U.S. trade deficit is scarcely a sign of health for the world economy, but do we really want to close it with another Smoot-Hawley? We have already closed the capital account, with a precipitous drop in bank lending to the Third World; the trade deficit means we are at least keeping one account open.

In any event, the popular twin-deficits explanation of the crash suffers two embarrassments. It is unable to explain how the Dow ever got to 2700 to begin with. More tellingly, it cannot in itself explain why stocks collapsed in countries with trade surpluses and insignificant internal deficits. As of last week stocks were off from their highs by 29% in the U.S., 40% in West Germany and 31% in Switzerland. Like the 1929 Depression, the 1987 market crash was an international event.

What, then, was starting to happen in mid-October? The real economy was picking up. Interest rates were rising somewhat, with higher demand for funds and renewed fears of inflation. The U.S. trade deficit came in higher than expected, but it too had been around all through the market boom. The Reagan administration was increasingly beleaguered, as the Iran-Contra hearings were followed by the Bork defeat and various congressional efforts to take over foreign policy; the administration clearly had less power to battle protectionism or hold its own in tax and budget confrontations.

These trends developed during October, but the one clearly new thing was a set of proposals in Rep. Dan Rostenkowski's Ways and Means Committee. Without much advance warning, it concocted a bill that in general was anti-business and antiwealth, and in particular calculated to stop the company takeovers that had boosted the stock market. The provision to disallow interest deductions for any significant takeover borrowing was stuck in the bill with 15 minutes of discussion and made retroactive to Oct. 13. The risk arbitrage community collapsed overnight, and the decline in takeover stocks was followed by the general market debacle on the 19th.

Even given the importance of the U.S. in the world economy, though, the quickly disavowed tax proposals fail to explain the international character of the market crash. In terms of the international economy, the big new event in mid-October was the argument between the Bundesbank and Treasury Secretary James Baker. The Germans insisted on tightening monetary policy though the mark was strong, and Secretary Baker's criticism was increasingly strident. On the day before the Monday crash, he denied reports that the U.S. was seeking a lower dollar but warned, "We will not sit back in this country and watch surplus countries jack up their interest rates and squeeze growth worldwide on the expectation that the United States somehow will follow by raising its interest rates."

In mid-October, the Louvre agreement on exchange-rate stability was, if not broken, clearly foundering. Exchange-rate stability must be maintained through monetary policy. If two currencies diverge too much, the central banks must create more of the strong currency or less of the weak one. Which bank is to make the adjustment depends on some judgment about whether the world system needs more liquidity to promote growth or less liquidity to fight inflation. In the lack of some outside guidepost, the Bundesbank and the Treasury had come to different conclusions; each wanted the other to adjust.

In his criticism of the Bundesbank, Secretary Baker was clearly right. The currency markets were demanding more marks, and this demand should have been satisfied. Stifling it would hamper growth in Germany and break up the Louvre accord. The problem for the Treasury, and for that matter Germany's partners in the European Monetary System, was how to persuade the Bundesbank without a fixed guidepost to invoke.

Imaginative options might have been to try to fix the dollar-franc rate, to announce a policy of defending the dollar against gold, or to flesh out Secretary Baker's recent remarks about a commodity index. These approaches might not have saved the initial Louvre rates, but at least they would have made clear that the problem is an appreciating mark. But it's dangerous to suggest trying to punish the Germans by threatening to let the dollar fall. If U.S. officials actively want a lower dollar, the markets will start to anticipate them. In precisely this scenario, it seems to me, lies the most likely son-of-Smoot-Hawley, the most likely way international trade and capital flows can again be disrupted.

Outright protectionism still remains a threat, especially with Reagan administration officials beating up on Japan, Brazil, Singapore, Taiwan, South Korea, and even Hong Kong. But at least the Gephardt trade bill is widely seen as intellectually discredited and politically unlikely. Beggar-thy-neighbor, though, is flourishing. Eminent economists, Treasury officials and even the Federal Reserve chairman talk about a lower dollar, either advocating it or predicting it on the assumption the dollar will decline until it makes trade flows balance. In short, devaluation for competitive purposes.

These eminences, to be sure, always attach one qualification: The decline of the dollar must be "gradual." Now, a gradual devaluation will not be catastrophic; inflation rates in the two nations will offset the change in currencies, and the real economy will be unaffected. By the same token, of course, it will not help the much-discussed trade balance, any more than it did in the last two years (see lower chart). Nor has competitive devaluation ever worked for any of

FIGURE A–2
■
The Dollar and the Deficit

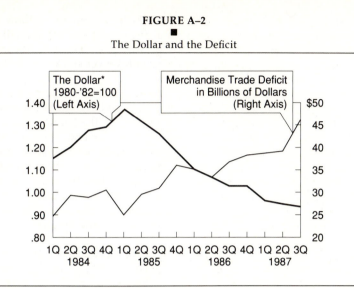

*The dollar's value against 15 industrial-country currencies weighted by trade.
Source: Morgan Guaranty Trust Co., Commerce Department.

the myriad nations that have tried it throughout the world. The usual outcome of gradual devaluation is sudden devaluation.

What if the dollar has its own Black Monday? What if it falls 25% in a day, as the Mexican peso did last week? Mexico had followed a policy of daily devaluations of the peso, until its central bank suddenly stopped supporting the free market rate. A 25% overnight drop in the dollar would be remarkably equivalent to a 25% tariff. Imports would stop. Recession would dawn immediately in Japan and other exporting countries. The immediate effect in the U.S. would be highly inflationary, and bond markets would collapse. Other nations would also hasten to devalue, spreading the effect. U.S. manufacturers would find that they are too dependent on both imported intermediates and export markets. The result would be a quick fall in production and standards of living—not only in the U.S., but at least as much in Germany and Switzerland, whose stock markets have fallen even more.

Count one guess that the market has just told us that a nightmare dollar collapse has suddenly become much more likely, as a market-closing tariff became more likely in October of 1929.

It hasn't happened yet, of course, and need not. Since the appointment of Paul Volcker by Jimmy Carter in 1979, the U.S. has been remarkably deft in dancing along the precipice. The Volcker monetary policy succeeded in stemming a worldwide inflation far more quickly than the conventional wisdom thought possible. And thanks to the Reagan tax cuts offsetting tight money, this was done without serious damage to the real economy (despite the 1982 recession, which might have been shallower had the tax cuts not been phased in so slowly). Expansion has been under way for 59 months. There has been no explosion in debt-ridden Third World nations, indeed a spread of entrepreneurialism and democracy. There of course remain problems in undisciplined federal spending, exchange-rate instability, and remaining debts and other damage lingering from the inflation. But much has been accomplished. And much would be given away if our policy makers, like President Hoover, were so shaken by the market crash they rushed to embrace the errors the market was warning them against.